# INTRODUCTION TO MANAGEMENT

Principles, Practices, and Processes

## SECOND EDITION

# INTRODUCTION TO MANAGEMENT

## Principles, Practices, and Processes

### SECOND EDITION

**DAVID SCHWARTZ**

*Georgia State University*

Business Books from
**HBJ MEDIA SYSTEMS CORPORATION**
*A Subsidiary of Harcourt Brace Jovanovich, Inc.*

ISBN: 0-15-543426-8

Library of Congress Catalog Card Number: 83-81038

Printed in the United States of America

05-434261 / 10 9 8 7 6 5 4 3 2 1

PHOTO CREDITS

Part One: Reproduced with permission of AT&T
Parts Two to Four: Courtesy of HBJ Picture Research Library
Part Five: United Energy Resources, Inc.
Part Six: Courtesy of Knight-Ridder Newspapers, Inc.

# CONTENTS

# 2

## AN OVERVIEW OF THE MANAGEMENT PROCESS, 28

# 3

## THE ENVIRONMENT IN WHICH MANAGEMENT IS PRACTICED, 49

# PART TWO    PLANNING, 77

# 4

## INTRODUCTION TO PLANNING AND MANAGEMENT BY OBJECTIVES, 79

# 5

## STRATEGIES AND OTHER PLANS, 104

# 6

## FORECASTING: GUIDE TO PLANNING, 132

# 7

## THE DECISION-MAKING PROCESS, 155

# PART THREE     ORGANIZING, 181

## 8

## INTRODUCTION TO ORGANIZING: SPECIALIZATION AND COORDINATION, 183

## 9

## DEPARTMENTALIZATION AND SPAN OF CONTROL, 204

# 10

## LINE AND STAFF AUTHORITY, 238

# 11

## DELEGATION OF AUTHORITY, 260

# 12

## GROUP DYNAMICS AND COMMITTEES, 281

## PART FOUR    STAFFING, 311

# 13

## MANAGER SELECTION, 313

# 14

## MANAGER DEVELOPMENT AND REWARDS, 341

# 15

## EVALUATION OF MANAGER PERFORMANCE, 371

# PART FIVE    DIRECTING, 401

# 16

## MOTIVATION, 403

# 17

## LEADERSHIP, 428

## 18

### THE COMMUNICATIONS PROCESS, 454

## PART SIX     CONTROLLING, 485

## 19

### AN OVERVIEW OF CONTROLLING, 487

# 20

## SPECIAL CONTROL TECHNIQUES, 517

# 21

## MANAGING IN THE FUTURE, 543

# PREFACE

*Introduction to Management: Principles, Practices, and Processes*, Second Edition, is written for the basic course in the discipline. The text is comprehensive, since for many students it will be their only exposure to the formal study of management. Many references are made to management problems and practices found in nonbusiness organizations. It is important for students to understand that all enterprises—profit-seeking and nonprofit-seeking—require effective management to achieve desired goals.

The text content is built around the five traditional functions of management: planning, organizing, staffing, directing, and controlling. This organization results in a well-rounded, yet balanced, approach to the study of a many-faceted discipline. It is hoped that students will come to visualize management as an integrated performance of activities, each of which contributes to overall performance of an enterprise.

Because of the favorable response to the organization, content, and readability of the first edition, no radical changes have been made in the revision. However, the content has been improved and updated where necessary, a new chapter and appendix are included, special features have been strengthened, and many new, realistic, and sometimes controversial examples, studies, and issues have been added throughout each chapter to illustrate basic principles. Students of management will be challenged to think critically, to evaluate, and to learn how to manage and make decisions.

## TEXT STRUCTURE

*Introduction to Management: Principles, Practices, and Processes,* Second Edition, is organized into six parts. Part One, "Introduction," (3 chapters) introduces the subject of management. This part defines management, provides an historical perspective of the discipline, gives an overview of the management process, and relates management to the environment in which it is practiced. Each of the remaining five parts considers one of the basic functions of managing: planning, organizing, staffing, directing, and controlling.

Part Two, "Planning," (4 chapters) deals with an introduction to planning and includes an explanation of management by objectives, strategies, forecasting, and the decision-making process.

Part Three, "Organizing," (5 chapters) discusses specialization and coordination, departmentalization and span of control, line and staff authority, delegation of authority, and group dynamics and the use of committees in the management process.

Part Four, "Staffing," (3 chapters) examines manager selection, explains approaches to manager development and rewards, and gives methods for evaluating manager performance.

Part Five, "Directing," (3 chapters) involves a discussion of three vital elements of the management process—motivation, leadership, and communications.

Part Six, "Controlling," (3 chapters) discusses why control is essential and explains some of the techniques used to make sure objectives are achieved as planned. A new chapter on management in the future has been added to this part.

## CHAPTER STRUCTURE

To facilitate learning, to stress the practicality of management, and to maintain interest, each chapter contains the following special features:

- *Performance Goals*  At the beginning of each chapter, learning objectives are stated to help students understand what they should know after they have studied the material.
- *Issue for Debate*  A contemporary, controversial subject is included in each chapter. These Issues help the student understand that there is more than one side to consider in making a decision and that decision making, while the very heart of managing, is never easy or clear-cut. For each subject, a brief explanation of the issue is set forth, followed by arguments for and against the proposition. Several thought-provoking questions follow each Issue to facilitate classroom discussion.

  Some of the topics included in the Issue for Debate are: "Should Senior Executives Be Personally Liable for Acts of Their Organizations That Hurt the Public?" "Is Participative Management More Effective Than Autocratic Management?" "Is the Leader More Important Than the Followers As the Key to an Organization's Success?" and "Will High-Level Unemployment (Above 8 Percent) Be a Continuing Problem in the Foreseeable Future?"
- *Managers in Action*  These provocative selections are new in the second edition and describe an actual event or situation that managers have encountered. The student is then asked to propose a solution to the problem or to evaluate the decision made. Examples of the Managers in Action feature include: "What Role Does Trust Play in Delegation, Span of

Control, and Product Cost?" "Does American Business Overemphasize Staff Management?" "Should Managers Encourage Study Circles?" and "Where Will Modern-Day Specialization Lead?"

- *Summary*   A concise review of key points and concepts is presented at the end of each chapter. The summaries should help reinforce in the student's mind what should be remembered from the chapter discussion.
- *Learn the Language of Management*   Like all major disciplines, management is developing its own specialized vocabulary. The text, therefore, defines terms used in management. At the end of each chapter, new terms introduced are listed to remind the student what new language he or she should understand.
- *Making Management Decisions*   Each chapter includes three brief exercises that require students to make decisions about specific management problems. There are no pat answers to the decision exercises. Their intent is to stimulate thought and to help the student understand that there are usually a number of ways to deal with a management situation.
- In addition to these features, each chapter also contains a group of questions for review and discussion, and a list of suggested readings.

## OTHER NOTEWORTHY FEATURES

- *Case Study*   At the end of each part, there is a Case Study. Based on hypothetical management situations, the Case Studies explore such topics as: "Management in the Public Sector — Can It Be Improved?" and "Should Middle-Level Managers Be Encouraged to Get an M.B.A.?" These case studies should provide a basis for lively class discussion.
- *Glossary*   A key goal of the first course in management is learning the terminology of the discipline. Concise definitions of more than 275 key terms are presented in a combined glossary/index at the end of the text.

## NEW TEXT MATERIALS

This second edition of *Introduction to Management: Principles, Practices, and Processes* includes a new chapter (21), "Managing in the Future." This chapter presents trends and contemporary thinking about how the practice of management may be modified in the decades ahead as we seek two basic goals: increased productivity and greater human satisfaction from work. Some observers feel that new technology, advances in the social sciences, changes in demographics, internationalism, and other factors will have a greater impact on management than the industrial revolution. The new chapter tries to bridge the gap between managing today and managing tomorrow.

Another new text feature is the Appendix, "Careers in Management." This Appendix contains four sections designed to help the student plan a career. It attempts to project the most promising managerial careers for the next two decades, based on the most current data available. It recommends and explains the use of a targeted résumé, as well as offering suggestions for finding employment and for winning favorable consideration in job interviews. Finally, the Appendix provides detailed information and discusses career opportunities for a number of specific management positions.

## SUPPLEMENTARY AIDS

To supplement *Introduction to Management*, a comprehensive Study Guide is available. Each chapter contains a matching exercise of key terms and their definitions; a decision-making exercise; and multiple-choice, completion, and true-false questions. The Study Guide should prove useful in helping students to reinforce the text material and to prepare for examinations.

In addition, an Instructor's Manual—essentially a resource book—is available. It includes chapter outlines and answers to text questions, a comprehensive test bank, and professional and trade information.

A cassette tape that includes six additional case studies dealing with real-life situations is also available to adopters of the text.

## ACKNOWLEDGMENTS

Many colleagues from many colleges and universities contributed to the ideas found in this text. James Bowman of North Harris County College, Robert Lewellen of Peru State College, and Myron (Guy) Sessions of Spokane Falls Community College were particularly helpful in preparing in-depth analyses of the first edition of *Introduction to Management* and also in reviewing new materials for the revision. Many of their suggestions and insights were incorporated into this second edition.

Appreciation is also extended to the staff of HBJ Media Systems Corporation who worked on this project: Patricia Clarke, Editorial Assistant; JoAnn Fisher, Editorial Coordinator, William Gurvitch, Production Manager, James Moulton, Director of Publishing, Business Books; and Harry Rinehart, Design Coordinator.

To you who teach management, I hope you find this text useful in explaining a challenging subject to your students.

*David Schwartz*

# WHY STUDY MANAGEMENT?

"Why should I spend several hundred hours in and out of the classroom studying this subject?" "How will I benefit?" "Will the course improve my chances in the job market?" "Is it worth the effort?" "Will I enjoy the subject?" Questions such as these come to mind as you consider studying a new academic discipline.

## BENEFITS OF STUDYING MANAGEMENT

The study of management is valuable for four reasons: it relates directly to your personal life; it is interesting and stimulating; it expands your career opportunities and income potential; and it gives you the opportunity to bring about positive change.

Each of us is managed—in school, at work, and in all the other organizations to which we belong. We cannot escape being given instructions, counsel, and assignments. Nor can we avoid being evaluated by those to whom we report.

**Management Relates Directly to Your Personal Life**

How much you enjoy being part of any organized activity, whether it be an economic or a social enterprise, generally depends more on the quality of the enterprise's management than on any other factor. You know that you are happier working under some managers than under other managers. Basic knowledge of managerial principles, practices, and processes should help you decide what kind of organization you want to join. "How does the company treat its employees?" is always a key question you should consider before accepting a job.

Even if you elect not to be a professional manager, you will still have daily opportunities to use management knowledge and techniques. You will study many topics that have application to your personal life. Knowledge of such subjects as setting goals, communicating with others, making plans, reaching decisions, and motivating others can be used, for instance, in the "management" of personal affairs. A basic course in management should help you manage your life more efficiently.

## Management Is Interesting and Stimulating

Although management is as old as civilization, the formal study of it is young. As you will see, management has both artistic and scientific elements. Furthermore, since there are few absolutely right or wrong answers to management questions, the subject becomes even more interesting. The intellectual challenge of management becomes clearer when we examine some situations that managers face and the resulting questions:

- Three people are under consideration for promotion to a management job. What criteria should be used to make the promotion decision?
- A company wants to move its corporate headquarters. What factors should be evaluated in selecting another location?
- An employee has a problem with alcohol that interferes with work. What should the manager do?
- The operating budget of a university is decreased 15 percent. What should the administration cut—faculty, staff, or supplies?
- A church committee decides that a new building is needed. How can the congregation be organized and motivated to provide enough money to go ahead?
- A downtown department store discovers it does 70 percent of its business between 11:00 A.M. and 2:00 P.M. How can it best arrange to have an appropriate number of salespersons available to meet the peak demands?
- The office work load increases significantly. Should additional people be hired, or should they be supplied by a temporary employment agency?
- Two companies merge. As a result, 20 percent of the managers of the merged companies can be released. Who goes and who stays?

Each of these questions gives rise to many others. In the last question, for example, if 20 percent of the merged organizations' managers are to be released, should terminations be based on ability? If so, how should ability be measured? Or should the guide be experience? Years of service? Age? Or should the terminations be made only in the smaller of the two companies?

Individuals who like mental exercise will enjoy studying management because it is a dynamic, changing field. Virtually every day managers face problems for which there are no clear precedents.

## Management Provides Career Opportunities

You will probably work between 70,000 and 90,000 hours in your career. You will likely spend more time working than doing anything else—except sleeping. To spend from thirty to fifty years doing what you really like is intelligent and rewarding. You owe it to yourself then to take a look at managing as a possible career. Managing is not for everyone, but it may be what you want to do.

People who can manage well or who demonstrate the potential to manage well are always in demand. And as the trend toward increased complexity in all activities continues, the need for more and better-prepared managers grows.

### Business Management Jobs

Roughly one business job in ten involves managing other people. Interestingly, most people have had no formal preparation for managing when appointed to their first management position. Having studied a basic course in management will give you a decided edge over others competing for the same job. And having knowledge of how the management process works in theory and practice should help you advance more rapidly.

### Nonbusiness Management Jobs

Keep in mind that employment opportunities for managers are not limited to business. Nonbusiness institutions, such as government, education, medicine, the military, or religion, require managers. The titles given managers vary greatly depending on the kind of organization, but the job managers perform—getting results through the efforts of other people—remains highly similar.

### Probability of Greater Reward

When you think of employment, you consider two kinds of reward—monetary and psychological. Not all managers earn large incomes, but in general they are paid substantially more than nonmanagers. Fringe benefits, too, are ordinarily more attractive and more varied for managers.

On the psychological side, some people find great satisfaction in managing. For them, being a manager provides more freedom, greater opportunity for creativity, less routine, and greater chance for self-expression than being an employee without supervisory responsibility.

**Management
Brings About
Change**

When we see problems in political, social, religious, or business organizations, we see *management problems.* As the course unfolds you will begin to understand that power in society is concentrated in people who manage organizations and that management is held fully responsible for the results of enterprises. When you see successes, such as a high level of profits, an increase in productivity, and an effective reorganization of a government agency, you have witnessed successful management. And when you see failures, such as a severe drop in sales, low worker productivity, and high employee turnover, you are observing unsuccessful management. Since management is responsible for an organization's degree of success or failure, then an excellent way to make any enterprise better is to participate in its management.

The higher you move in management, the greater your power to bring about constructive change in the organization. But by the same token, the higher you move, the greater your power to cause negative results. All of us have seen organizations either improve or become less effective by a change in senior management. Individuals who want to right what is wrong will find the study of management especially useful, since the job of managing gives an individual an opportunity to turn negative conditions—unfairness, low profits, bad service, low morale, and low productivity—into positive results.

## SUPPLEMENT YOUR STUDY IN YOUR MANAGEMENT LABORATORY

Four reasons have been given for studying management. After deciding that such study is worth the time, effort, and money, you need to answer the next logical question: "How can I learn the most possible about a complex subject?"

Classroom lectures, discussions, projects, and assignments are the most essential elements in learning about management. But you can do much more than attend classes and prepare homework to expand your knowledge. You can benefit greatly by observing the practice of management in the "laboratory," or the environment in which you live.

You are in contact with the practice of management every day. Your contacts with organized activity, whether they be with a church, a military unit, a hospital, a business, a university, or a political party, present management situations. Even certain aspects of family life, such as allocating work, developing a budget, and setting family routines and schedules, involve managing.

Certainly, all of us are touched by the management process. For example, academic life presents a variety of management situations. A college class is, in a sense, an organization. Your professor, in organizing the class, setting objectives, and motivating students, is managing. The football coach performs management activities, such as recruiting personnel, training team members, devising game plans, and dealing with players who break rules. College organizations, such as the school paper, the band, and the debating society, also illustrate management in action.

You can learn much about the management process by supplementing your academic study with careful observation of what is going on about you. As you observe you will gradually be able to differentiate between "good" and "bad" management. Even if you don't meet managers themselves, you can see the *results* of management in many forms. For example, while shopping, you may not meet the manager of the store, but you can see how well the store is being managed by observing employee motivation, customer service, and business efficiency. And, as you observe, you will also see more clearly that management is a universal function in society, inherent in each organization.

You can also discover more about the management process by "trading minds" with managers at every opportunity. Ask yourself such questions as "If I were the manager of this activity, would I conduct the affairs differently?" and "What managerial mistakes do I see being committed?" As you expand your knowledge, you will be able to consider more sophisticated questions, such as "Are five people really required to do this job, or could the organization achieve its objectives just as satisfactorily with only four people?" "What examples of waste in the use of people do I see?" "What causes inefficiency?" "How are resources being wasted?"

To those of you already working as managers, this course should be particularly relevant. In many situations you will be able to use the insights gained in class and from the textbook to help you improve your own performance. And those of you working as nonmanagers will be better able to evaluate the way you are being managed.

Few courses provide as much opportunity for interesting supplementary study as management. And trained observation can be a lot of fun, too!

# PART ONE

# INTRODUCTION

Part One of this book consists of three chapters that are intended to lay the groundwork for the study of management. Chapter 1, "The Field of Management," defines management, distinguishes between scientific and artistic management, and explains the importance of management in modern society. The subject of authority is introduced early to show that power in an enterprise is vested in managers, and the role of responsibility in management is discussed. Chapter 1 also briefly traces the history of management thought from ancient times to the present. The major approaches to the study of management are reviewed, and the approach followed in this book is explained.

Two important goals of Chapter 2, "An Overview of the Management Process," are to differentiate management from nonmanagement and to indicate the role that technical knowledge plays in managing. The chapter also defines and describes the five basic management functions—planning, organizing, staffing, directing, and controlling—that serve as the framework for this book. The interrelationship among management functions is explained, and some commonly accepted management principles are presented.

Chapter 3, "The Environment in Which Management Is Practiced," begins with a discussion of the environmental constraints, both external and internal, that limit managers' power. It then analyzes the key trends that affect management today. The point is made that managing is becoming more complex because of more government regulation, an increasing challenge to authority, a decline in the work ethic, the growth of internationalism, more technological change, slower population growth, and the liberalization of social mores. The chapter puts the economic, ethical, and social responsibilities of managers into focus and emphasizes that we live in a time of rapid change. It concludes with an analysis of the ways in which management can adapt to a changing environment.

The Case Study at the end of Part One deals with improving management in the public sector.

1  THE FIELD OF MANAGEMENT

2  AN OVERVIEW OF THE MANAGEMENT PROCESS

3  THE ENVIRONMENT IN WHICH MANAGEMENT IS PRACTICED

# 1 THE FIELD OF MANAGEMENT

**STUDY THIS CHAPTER SO YOU CAN:**

- Define and understand the term "management," and explain why job titles for managers vary.

- Differentiate scientific management from artistic management.

- Define the terms "authority" and "responsibility," and discuss how they relate to managing.

- Describe how organizations require people to sacrifice personal freedom.

- Trace the history of management thought.

- Distinguish the principle of delegation from the exception principle.

- Describe the contributions of the management theorists discussed to management theory.

- Discuss the five major current approaches to the study of management.

An **organization** is a group of people who work together to achieve common goals. There are hundreds of different kinds of organizations—businesses, universities, hospitals, churches, armies, theater groups, government agencies, and many more. Some organizations seek profit; some do not. But they all seek to attain goals of some kind.

Organized life is essential to our survival. In the absence of organization there would be chaos, anarchy, little productivity, and human suffering on a massive

3

scale. Organized life requires direction, or management. Without leadership an organization ceases to be a united, cooperative activity, and social goals cannot be achieved.

## WHAT IS MANAGEMENT?

**Management** is the process of achieving an organization's goals through the coordinated performance of five specific functions—planning, organizing, staffing, directing, and controlling. The organization is a group of people. The goal can be anything the organization seeks to do. Some goals are large, such as to visit the moon, to install a pipeline, to build a submarine, or to operate a 2,000-room hotel at a profit. Other goals are comparatively small, such as to win a football game, to get a report done by Friday, or to sell more than was sold last quarter. But regardless of a goal's size, the same functions must be performed by any organization to attain a goal.

The people whose job it is to perform the five functions that achieve goals are **managers**. However, job titles for managers depend on the organization. Managers in business organizations are usually given the title "manager." Often this title is prefaced by an adjective that suggests what is being managed. Thus, there are sales managers, customer-service managers, and electronic data processing managers. In nonbusiness organizations, the manager is given another title that fits more closely with the customs of the organization. Thus a religious organization may be managed by a bishop, a military organization by a general, a medical facility by an administrator, and a trade association by an executive director.

Job titles also vary with the manager's organizational level. In many organizations we find three distinct levels of management: top or senior, middle, and first or operational. Large organizations have more levels. The organizational level at which a manager functions is often indicated by his or her title. Table 1–1 shows examples of different titles of managers by organizational level.

### TABLE 1–1

**A Manager by Any Other Name Is Still a Manager—
Examples of Managerial Job Titles**

| Level of Management | Type of Enterprise | | | | |
|---|---|---|---|---|---|
| | Profit-seeking | Educational | Military | Government | Medical |
| First or operational | Supervisor | Assistant principal | Sergeant | Administrator | Supervisor |
| Middle | Middle manager | Principal | Colonel | Bureau chief | Assistant administrator |
| Top or senior | Senior executive | Superintendent | General | Agency head | Chief administrator |

**Scientific management** can be defined as the use of codified and verified knowledge in the planned management of any organized activity. Scientific management often involves such tools as **motion-and-time studies** (studies to determine whether a particular act can be performed more quickly and efficiently) and research to ensure that personnel are being used effectively.

Is Management a Science or an Art?

Scientific management is analytical, statistical, rational, and quantifiable. Examples of scientific management are (1) determining the precise number of man-hours needed for a given production operation and (2) using a demonstrated, reliable psychological test to select new employees.

**Artistic management**, in contrast, is the conscientious use of skill and creative imagination in planning and executing the goals of the organization. Artistic management is subjective, nonstatistical, emotional, commonsensical, and behavioral. Some examples are (1) deciding which employees to release when top management orders a cut in personnel and (2) handling a sensitive situation between a female manager and a jealous male subordinate.

Both artistic and scientific elements are involved in management. Progressive management uses the scientific method when possible. But in those situations in which scientific measurement cannot be used, managers must resort to the artistic approach.

## WHY IS MANAGEMENT IMPORTANT?

Management is important both to society and to individual enterprises. Society is a loosely knit "organization" of all the organizations and institutions that compose it. The success of any enterprise in any of our social institutions—business, religion, government, the military—depends on the effectiveness of its management. Therefore, management determines how successful we are in achieving our social, political, and business goals.

Management is extremely important to the individual enterprise. Organizations stand or fall on the quality of their management, whether they are profit seeking or nonprofit seeking. Managers—not operative personnel—are responsible for the success or failure of an enterprise. If managers are doing a "good" job, the organization is succeeding. By the same token, if managers are doing a "bad" job, the enterprise is failing. Perfect management, however, rarely exists.

Managers are important in all organizations because they have authority and because they are held responsible for results. Many business failures of the early 1980s were blamed on foreign competition, lack of consumer demand, unemployment, and high interest rates. Whatever the cause or causes of failure, management was held responsible.

**Authority** is the right to give commands, to make decisions, to take actions, and to enforce obedience. The authority of a society is vested in its managers. Whether we think of a labor union, a business, a church, a university, or a hospital, those in charge—the managers—have the power. Table 1–2 shows how authority varies

Managers Have Authority

**TABLE 1–2**

**Degree of Authority Relates to Management Level**

| Management Level | Examples of Authority |
|---|---|
| First or operational | • Make up work schedules for operative employees.<br>• Set day-to-day operational goals.<br>• Hire and terminate operative employees. |
| Middle | • Make contracts for the purchase of routine items needed by the organization.<br>• Set specific objectives for the various departments.<br>• Establish performance standards. |
| Top or senior | • Make contracts committing the organization for loans, stock issues, and purchase of major installations.<br>• Set overall objectives for some point in the future.<br>• Expand, contract, or otherwise modify the physical facilities of the organization. |

with level of management. Note that the scope of authority increases as we move from lower to higher echelons.

Although managers have great power, it is never absolute: It is always limited by various environmental constraints, such as laws and customs, which will be discussed in Chapter 3. Within these constraints, however, managers have authority over people, resources, and change.

**Authority over People**

Consider the vast power managers in a business organization have over people. In the first place, managers decide who will be employed. Then they decide what the employees will be paid, what their working conditions will be, what they will do, when they will work, the physical environment in which they will work, and who their associates at work will be. Managers also set policies for promotion, demotion, and termination.

Authority over people is exercised in many ways. For example, a senior executive may say to Jim, "We want to transfer you from Houston to Little Rock and have you take over our branch office there. Can you be ready in four weeks?" If Jim does not agree to the transfer, he risks losing his job or falling out of favor with the corporate power structure, with the result that promotions will be more difficult to come by.

Managers in business and the military have more power over people than managers in most other organizations. People who are unhappy with the management of their church, lodge, or political party can simply terminate the relationship, normally without any financial hardship. Or they may retain the relationship but dissociate themselves from the activities of the organization. But in business organizations people are more inclined to accept the power that controls a major part of their lives. If Jim in the example above found himself in a tight job market with several children and an unemployed wife, he would be apt to say, "Yes, I'll go to Little Rock."

### Authority over Resources

Managers have vast power over the resources of society because they make the decisions about what will be done and how much money will be spent to do it. While there are numerous legal and other constraints imposed on this power, managers decide such matters as what physical facilities will be constructed, what their design will be, and how they will be equipped. Managers—not operative employees—decide where to locate manufacturing plants, branch facilities, retail stores, and other facilities.

Managers do not *manage* machines or money or land, although they *control* their use. Managers exclusively manage people, not inanimate objects.

### Authority over Change

Since managers make the decisions in all organizations, they have great power to bring about change. When President Kennedy, as the senior manager of our government, declared it a national goal to put men on the moon within a decade, he was determining directly or indirectly the employment of 400,000 people to achieve the result.

Technological change, while coming from researchers, is still inspired and controlled by managers. The decisions on what to do with technological and scientific breakthroughs and on when to make changes are determined by managers, not by technicians, engineers, or physicists functioning as operative personnel.

**Responsibility** is the requirement imposed on an individual to answer to others for his or her performance, conduct, or obligations. In any type of enterprise, management is responsible for results. The purpose of any organization—whether a large corporation, a university, or an aid society—is to achieve results or goals. Management supplies the intellectual force necessary to attain the intended result.

*Managers Are Responsible for Results*

There are various ways of measuring results. In a business enterprise, results may be shown by statistics on profit, market share, or absenteeism. In a trade association, attendance, membership trends, or contributions may be indicators of results. In a police department, trends in crime statistics—percentages of crimes solved, per capita cost of police protection, and so on—suggest results. The measurement of results will be discussed more extensively in Chapters 2 and 4.

### Can Responsibility Be Delegated?

A new manager may say to his or her superior, "Well, I told my employees what to do, but they didn't do it right. So blame them, not me." The manager's thinking is faulty. A manager may delegate authority to workers to use methods of their choice to achieve a result. But the manager cannot delegate responsibility for the success of the effort. The manager is accountable to his or her superior for the faulty performance of the personnel.

To illustrate, say a department head in a music store, Jane Green, instructs an employee, John Hart, to deliver a piano to a customer. Green clearly has the

# ISSUE FOR DEBATE

## SHOULD SENIOR EXECUTIVES BE PERSONALLY LIABLE FOR ACTS OF THEIR ORGANIZATIONS THAT HURT THE PUBLIC?

Some people feel that corporate senior executives should be responsible for such undesirable practices as bribing foreign governments to get business and selling unsafe products. Many of these people feel that senior executives should be liable for all such acts, even ones they did not commit or were not aware of. Some people take an opposite view.

### YES

**Senior executives should be personally liable because . . .**

Senior executives are responsible for a corporation's strategies, politics, and procedures. Thus they must be held accountable when plans backfire.

Penalizing corporations with fines and cease-and-desist orders does little to improve the morality of senior executives.

Senior executives occupy positions of great trust. They set the example for lower-level personnel. A bad example should be punished.

Senior executives have the authority either to prevent harmful acts or to take corrective action to see that the damage is remedied and the act is not repeated.

When senior executives go unpunished for harmful acts, society becomes increasingly disenchanted with business. The result is more laws and regulations, which inconvenience everyone.

### NO

**Senior executives should not be personally liable because . . .**

Some corporations have become so large that it is almost impossible for senior executives to know everything that is going on.

Corporations are engaged in intense competition. In the battle for gaining business it is only natural for executives to do certain things that are not approved of socially.

Profit contribution is the way executives are measured. The temptation to make false claims about a product, for example, is strong.

One of the key reasons for incorporating a business in the first place is to escape personal liability for acts performed in the name of the corporation.

Senior executives are human and prone to make mistakes, many if not most of them honest. It is unfair to expect executives to be superhuman. Also, executives in nonprofit organizations make harmful mistakes too, but these usually go unnoticed.

### QUESTIONS

1. What other arguments, pro and con, can you advance?
2. In general, which side of this issue do you feel is strongest? Why?

authority to tell Hart to make the delivery. Now assume that Hart does not deliver the piano. Green is in no way relieved of her responsibility to make sure the delivery is made. She is accountable to her own superior, the assistant store manager, for the nondelivery. The assistant store manager, in turn, is accountable to his manager. Ultimately, the manager of the store is responsible for the piano's not being delivered.

It must be emphasized that the person at the top of the organization is held responsible for everything, both good and bad, that the organization does. The president of General Motors is ultimately responsible for defective workmanship in a new car. It is obvious that the president has many things to occupy his mind and may have little knowledge, if any, of the work that proved defective. But if the president had managed the next level below him properly and had this level managed the next level properly, and so on down to the operative-worker level, the mistake would not have occurred. Therefore, the president bears the responsibility.

Many matters involving management are debated. An Issue for Debate in this chapter concerns whether senior executives should be personally liable for acts of their corporations that hurt the public.

### Responsibility Deters Many People from Management Careers

One reason some people do not want to become managers is fear of responsibility. Mistakes are common, and managers make their share. If an individual fears the consequences of making wrong decisions, then he or she may not be cut out for management. Generally, the higher one moves in an organization, the greater the risk of job loss. "Heads roll" frequently at the tops of organizations when things go wrong.

**Sacrifice of Personal Freedom**

An organization is a group of people that work together toward a common goal. When people join an organization, they must conform to various rules, procedures, and policies imposed by it. Conformity requires people to sacrifice some personal freedom. Army recruits must modify their behavior in many ways. From the time they get up in the morning until they turn in at night, they are required to act in the militarily prescribed way. Similarly, new employees may be expected to conform to rules relating to working hours, safety, and coffee breaks. If they fail to conform, they may be dismissed.

The degree to which freedom is sacrificed in organized life varies depending on the type of institution and the individual's level within the organization. The military requires great sacrifice of individual freedom. Businesses generally require considerable conformity, while universities require significantly less. And as individuals move up in an organization they enjoy more freedom. Managers in a business have more freedom with regard to work habits than operative employees.

## HISTORY OF MANAGEMENT THOUGHT

Management is as old as civilization. Claude S. George, Jr., an authority on the history of management thought, has stated:

In many ways . . . primitive society was probably as complex as our own. It had its codes for the conduct of business, rules regarding the roles of parents, punishment for wrongdoing, rites for the worship of gods, manners prescribing proper ways to eat, and the like. But even more important was the understanding of the need for authority and the necessity for a system of management. Young men of the tribe surely grew up with a veneration and a fear of the "old man" or leader—and with just cause: He was *alive* and *old* because of his cunning and wisdom. Perhaps they, too, could learn from him; hence their veneration for him and his source of authority.

With the advent of practiced agriculture, man ceased roaming the countryside to hunt and collect, and with this cessation came a settled existence and the genesis of small villages. With these aggregations of people in communities the need arose for some crude method to manage the common affairs of the group. And, as one would

# MANAGERS IN ACTION

## HOW DOES THE EXERCISE OF MANAGERIAL AUTHORITY AFFECT EXECUTIVE STRESS?

Managers have authority (power) over people, resources, and change. The exercise of authority creates stress. As psychologist Paul Sherman notes, "All executives deal with stress. They wouldn't be executives if they didn't. Some handle it well, others handle it poorly."[1]

In the early 1980s the problem of stress increased as management decisions became more difficult. Managers had to terminate millions of workers, close thousands of plants, cut back on employee benefits, and scramble harder to make profits.

For many executives, increased stress causes both psychological and physical problems. On the psychological side, executives under severe stress may suffer anxiety, make poor decisions, lose their ability to concentrate, and even have nervous breakdowns. On the physical side, stress can lead to heart attacks, ulcers, headaches, and a host of other problems.

A new industry of consulting firms has evolved to help managers deal with undue stress by providing stress management programs. Stress management programs differ widely and can include some or all of the following: self-awareness training, leadership development seminars, biofeedback, psychotherapy, hypnosis, dietary advice, exercise, and medication.

Because stress management programs are new and varied, their effectiveness is still questioned. However, it is likely that programs to reduce managerial stress will become even more prominent in the future.

For further commentary on some available programs, see "Stress-Management Plans Abound, But Not All Programs Are Run Well," *The Wall Street Journal*, September 30, 1982, p. 33.

[1]Quoted in Michael Waldholz, "Stress Increasingly Seen as Problem, with Executives More Vulnerable," *The Wall Street Journal*, September 28, 1982, p. 37. Reprinted by permission of *The Wall Street Journal*, © Dow Jones & Company, Inc., 1982. All Rights Reserved.

### QUESTIONS

1. If you had to tell a good employee that his or her services were no longer needed, would it upset you emotionally?
2. If a manager cannot make tough decisions without suffering psychological problems, he or she should not be a manager. Do you agree or disagree with this statement?

expect, this bit of management devolved to the cunning, the alert, the wise, and the shrewd. As these small villages grew and civilization evolved, the managers, too, grew and evolved. They became the priests, the kings, and the appointed ministers holding power and wealth in their societies even before highly organized social, political, and military structures had been devised. Taxation, effective utilization of resources, division of labor, trade arrangements and agreements, and the making of war and peace were surely typical problems to these managers of the first full-scale primitive civilization.[1]

There are indications that some level of sophistication in management existed in ancient civilizations. The pyramids of Egypt, the largest of which contains 3.3 million stone blocks each weighing more than two tons, are examples of a tremendous organizational feat. The Code of Hammurabi of ancient Babylonia is also evidence from an ancient civilization of progress in management thought. The skillful and well-planned exodus of the Hebrews from Egypt was a monumental management achievement. Chapter 18 of the Book of Exodus in the Bible discusses two management principles in some detail: the principle of delegation and the exception principle.

The **principle of delegation** was suggested to Moses by his father-in-law, Jethro. Moses had become worn out passing judgment on all the problems his people faced. Jethro advised Moses to select competent people and to put them in charge of units of a thousand, units of a hundred, units of fifty, and units of ten. This was the principle of delegation in practice.

Then Jethro told Moses that his rulers (managers) should settle small issues themselves and bring only the big problems to Moses. This is the **exception principle.**

Records indicate that the ancient Chinese civilization also had knowledge about management functions. In the Constitution of China that was written about 1100 B.C., we find considerable advice about how to manage, as this quotation suggests:

> Eight methods he [the prime minister] holds to govern the country. The first is ritual and worship, so as to control its spirit. The second is statutes and regulations, so as to control its great officers. The third is removal and appointment, so as to control its petty officers. The fourth is emolument and rank, so as to control its scholars. The fifth is taxes and tributes, so as to control its resources. The sixth is ceremonies and customs, so as to control its people. The seventh is punishment and reward, so as to control its strength. The eighth is farming and other employments, so as to control its multitude.[2]

After the fall of the Roman Empire and during the period known as the Dark Ages, very little was written about management. This can be explained by the way people lived during that time. One authority described the situation as follows:

> People lived under hostile conditions: Self-preservation was a prime concern; and little or no attention was given to concepts as opposed to physical things. Those who wrote were the scribes, members of religious orders, and the well-educated of the court.

---

[1]Claude S. George, Jr., *The History of Management Thought* (Englewood Cliffs, N.J.: Prentice-Hall, 1968), pp. 2, 3. Reprinted by permission of Prentice-Hall, Inc., Englewood Cliffs, New Jersey.
[2]Kuo-Cheng Wu, *Ancient Chinese Political Theories* (Shanghai: Commercial Press, 1928), pp. 40–41; quoted in George, *History of Management Thought*, p. 12.

Books were written laboriously by hand and only the most important concepts were worth recording under these tedious and trying circumstances. The typical subjects included religion, governing a kingdom, waging war, and the laws of the land. Those who "knew their letters" and could read these books were the priests and scribes, the rulers and nobles, and the landed gentry. The art of management, though important to each of these groups, was not given a high priority. Managing or running a manor, for example, was often turned over to one of the underlings while the learned lord concerned himself with the more "important" matters of the day, such as hunting, riding, and gaming. Under these circumstances, it is not surprising that little or no writing on management was done during the medieval period.[3]

Although little was written about management during medieval times, management practices played an important role in the Roman Catholic Church and the military. The Roman Catholic Church is one of the oldest and best-run institutions in history. Military organizations, with their clear authority relationships, have served as a model for many enterprises.

## Early Management Theorists

The deliberate effort to learn more about how we manage and how we can manage better is relatively new. During the Industrial Revolution of the eighteenth and nineteenth centuries, in which hand tools were being replaced by machine and power tools, more interest was focused on management principles and practices.

### Robert Owen

Robert Owen, the manager of a textile mill in Scotland in the early nineteenth century, took what was then a startling approach to his personnel. Owen placed great importance on ensuring that his employees were happy in their work. He improved working conditions in the factory, reduced the length of the workday, provided meals for employees, and so on. In a speech in 1813 he claimed that for every expenditure he had made to improve working conditions, he had received twice that amount from employees in terms of greater productivity. Owen spoke of employees as "vital machines," as contrasted with the inanimate machines of the factory. He was one of the first management writers to emphasize human relations as an important component in productivity.

Owen viewed management as a profession and is referred to in management literature as "the pioneer of personnel management."

### Charles Babbage

Charles Babbage pioneered in seeking ways to analyze and control manufacturing costs. He advocated dividing work into mental and physical activities and determining the precise cost for all tasks to be done. He studied many factory operations and became a leading advocate of making motion-and-time studies to determine how long a manufacturing operation should take.

In addition, Babbage developed guidelines for weighing the relative values of machine processes against human resources. He is best known for the development, in 1833, of the principles that today are used in computers.

---

[3]Robert Hammond, *The Philosophy of Alfarabi* (New York: Hobson Book Press, 1947), p. 51; quoted in George, *History of Management Thought,* p. 29.

### Frederick Taylor

Regarded as "the father of scientific management," Frederick Taylor was chief engineer at the Midvale Steel Works in Philadelphia in the late nineteenth century when he became concerned with efficiency in production. He was dissatisfied with inefficient management, which was evidenced by such things as lack of standards for worker performance, unequal distribution of work loads, and decision making based on hunch and intuition as opposed to facts and logic.

To discover better ways to manage, Taylor conducted a variety of experiments. Many of these involved motion-and-time studies. Taylor wanted to determine how long it should take a worker or a machine to perform a given task; to develop uniform standards for work; to find a method for matching workers to jobs, allowing for differences in skill; and to learn better ways to supervise and motivate personnel.

Based on his practical experience, Taylor developed four management principles that he felt made up scientific management. (These principles will be discussed in Chapter 2.) Taylor's writings on scientific management have been translated into a score of languages. He even developed followers among people with extremely different political philosophies. Lenin, for example, was quoted in *Pravda* in 1918 as saying, "We should immediately introduce piece work and try it out in practice. We should try out every scientific and progressive suggestion of the Taylor system."

Taylor stressed the need for a harmonious relationship between management and employees. He advocated individual rewards for productivity. He wrote that both managers and workers "must take their eyes off the division of the surplus as the all-important matter, and together turn their attention towards increasing the size of the surplus."[4]

### Henry Gantt

One prominent follower of Taylor was his colleague Henry Gantt. Gantt was more interested than Taylor in the human-relations aspects of management. He strongly opposed autocratic management and felt the production methods should be fitted to the worker rather than vice versa.

Gantt made four main contributions to the evolution of management thought. First, he invented a chart for comparing actual with planned performance. The device is now called the Gantt Chart and is explained in Chapter 20. Second, he devised a task-bonus plan for paying workers. His plan paid a worker a guaranteed day wage for output less than standard, a bonus for meeting the standard, and an additional reward for output above the standard.

Gantt's third contribution was to advocate that management has a responsibility to train workers to become more skilled, develop better work habits, and perform more reliably. Finally, Gantt advanced the idea that business should concentrate on providing services, not just on making profit.

### Frank and Lillian Gilbreth

Frank and Lillian Gilbreth were a husband-and-wife team that further developed Taylor's ideas. Frank Gilbreth was interested in efficiency, while Lillian Gil-

---

[4]Quoted in Lyndall Urwick, ed., *The Golden Book of Management* (London: Millbrook Press, 1963), p. 74.

breth was most interested in the human aspects of work—the selection, placement, and training of personnel.

The Gilbreths were among the first to film workers in order to analyze motion sequences so that the most efficient way for performing specific tasks could be learned. On a broader level, the Gilbreths were early advocates of developing people through better training, improved work methods, and better work environments. They wrote that such incentives for workers as pride, competition, and desire for recognition are often as important as money, shorter hours, and promotion.

### Henri Fayol

While Taylor was interested in improving worker productivity, a French mining engineer and geologist, Henri Fayol, was concerned with the executive managerial role. Fayol is regarded as "the father of modern management theory." On the basis of his personal experiences, he developed fourteen principles of management, which are outlined in Chapter 2. Fayol's ideas were set forth in his classic book *General and Industrial Management*.

### Mary Parker Follett

A political philosopher and social critic, Mary Parker Follett brought a humanitarian view to the study of management. She was one of the first social scientists to apply psychology to business and industry. Follett contributed to the field of management by convincing business people that the social sciences have practical application in industry. She wrote extensively on creativity, participation, and professionalism.

Follett was interested in the management activity of coordination. She described an ideal organizational pattern in which managers achieve coordination through controlled communication with employees. According to Follett, four kinds of coordination are required in managing:

- Coordination by direct control of the people responsible for the work
- Coordination in the early or planning stages of an activity
- Coordination as a reciprocal relationship in all aspects of an activity
- Coordination as a continuous, or ongoing process

Follett believed that conflict can be made constructive by using an integration process in which the people involved look for ways to resolve their differences together. Effective leaders, Follett thought, do not dominate situations but motivate others to achieve results.

### Hugu Münsterberg

Hugo Münsterberg, writing at about the same time as Follett and Fayol, also took a psychological approach to management. In his pioneering book *Psychology and Industrial Efficiency*, he treated staffing (specifically, how to find employees who are psychologically suited to the work) and ways to increase productivity by varying psychological conditions in the workplace. He developed a variety of psychological tests for aptitude and screening. In fact, his ideas were so powerful that during World War I nearly every nation involved used psychological testing to select and assign newly recruited military personnel.

Münsterberg is considered "the father of industrial psychology," and for a number of years he directed the experimental psychology laboratory at Harvard University. According to Münsterberg, the role of psychology in industry is to find the best people for work to be performed, to determine what environmental conditions would result in the greatest productivity, and to improve worker morale.

### Max Weber

Max Weber, a German social scientist and philosopher, took a sociological rather than a psychological view of management. He analyzed the most prominent social institutions—the church, government, business, and the military—and developed a theory of organizational design that he called "bureaucracy." (Weber did not use the term in the negative sense we generally do today.) Writing during a time when organizations were growing rapidly in size, Weber sought to pin down the characteristics that lead to a successful institution. In his book *The Theory of Social and Economic Organization*, Weber described six guidelines for organizational design:

* The organization must function by clear and explicit rules.
* Rules and other guidelines must be in writing.
* Each individual should have a fixed set of duties.
* Each level of the organization should be under the supervision of a higher one.
* Each individual's authority should be based on competence, not an inherited right or ownership.
* Employees should not be terminated arbitrarily.

Weber's guidelines were highly influential but today are criticized for their lack of attention to the human factor in organizational design.

### G. Elton Mayo

G. Elton Mayo is termed "the father of human relations." In 1927 a team of researchers from Harvard University, led by Mayo, began a series of experiments at the Hawthorne plant of Western Electric, near Chicago. The purpose of the study was to determine the effects of lighting on productivity in the factory. Mayo and his colleagues divided workers into a control group and an experimental group. They systematically varied lighting for the experimental group while making no change for the control group. They also experimented with a number of other factors— heat, rest time, pay scales, and room temperature. As expected, improved conditions resulted in higher productivity in the experimental group. What was not expected was the rise in productivity in the control group, for which conditions had remained exactly the same. Even when Mayo's team reduced light to nearly the level of moonlight, productivity continued to improve!

These startling findings showed that special attention given to workers— even in the form of poor working conditions—has a favorable effect on productivity. Clearly, social factors were involved: Factors such as self-esteem, morale, status, and good working relationships all played a part in productivity. This discovery, referred to as the **Hawthorne Effect**, revealed the great importance of the human factor and led to increased emphasis on the behavioral sciences in theories of management.

Mayo advanced the idea that logical or economic factors are less important than emotions in managing. He noted that until recently society had changed very slowly and people had lived by a set of traditional routines and values. In modern times, however, technical change has occurred quickly and has not been accompanied by equal social change. He observed, "If our technical skills are to make sudden and radical changes in our methods of working, we must develop social skills that can balance these moves by effecting social changes of living to meet the altered situation. We cannot live and prosper with one foot in the twentieth century and the other in the eighteenth."[5]

### Chester Barnard

Another writer with a behavioral view was Chester Barnard, president of the New Jersey Bell Telephone Company for many years. Barnard wrote on a variety of management subjects, his most influential book being *The Functions of the Executive.* Barnard saw organizations as cooperative efforts, or systems of goal-directed cooperative activities. He felt management's primary functions are the formulation of objectives and the acquisition of resources required to meet the objectives. Like Follett, Barnard emphasized communication as an important means for achieving group goals. He felt employee cooperation is maximized when an ideal balance is achieved between inducements (financial and nonfinancial rewards) and contributions. Barnard introduced a new "acceptance theory" of authority: Subordinates will accept orders only if they understand them and are able to comply with them.

On a systems approach to managing, Barnard observed:

The primary efforts of leaders need to be directed to the maintenance and guidance of organizations as whole systems of activities. I believe this to be the most distinctive and characteristic sector of leadership behavior, but it is the least obvious and least understood. Since most of the acts which constitute organization have a specific function which superficially is independent of the maintenance of organization—for example, the accomplishment of specific tasks of the organization—it may not be observed that such acts at the same time also constitute organization and that this, not the technical and instrumental, is the primary aspect of such acts from the viewpoint of leadership. Probably most leaders are not ordinarily conscious of this, though intuitively they are governed by it. For any act done in such a way as to disrupt cooperation destroys the capacity of organization. Thus the leader has to guide all in such a way as to preserve organization as the instrumentality of action.[6]

### Other Early Theorists

Several other writers were influential during the 1930s and 1940s.

*James D. Mooney.* Mooney studied various organizations and, in his book, *The Principles of Organization*, set forth what he felt were the natural laws, or

---

[5]G. Elton Mayo, *The Social Problems of an Industrial Civilization* (New York: Macmillan, 1933), p. 30.
[6]Chester Barnard, *Organization and Management* (Cambridge, Mass.: Harvard University Press, 1962), p. 89.

principles, of organizing. Mooney was interested in the rationale for organized activity. He concluded that coordination was the main objective of organization. Mooney also wrote extensively on the principles of authority, specialization, and leadership.

Mooney proposed the idea that all organizations are based on a superior-subordinate relationship arranged in a hierarchical fashion. He called this the scalar principle.

*Lyndall Urwick.* In his extremely influential book, *The Elements of Administration*, Urwick brought together the ideas of Taylor, Fayol, and Mooney. Urwick believed that scientific analysis should play an important role in management. Urwick's principal contribution was to consolidate and put into meaningful form the management concepts developed by others.

*Ralph C. Davis.* Another important synthesizer of management thought, Davis studied existing management literature and developed a comprehensive system for categorizing various management principles and practices. Davis is well-known for his identification of three categories of objectives (primary, collateral, and secondary) and for his theory that the primary objective of an organization is service, rather than profits.

Today, management is one of the main disciplines taught in business schools. The concept of educating managers has received great impetus, as evidenced by hundreds of management development programs.

In the last few decades, many books on management have been published. Following are some of the most influential writers and the theories for which they are best known.

*Chris Argyris.* Argyris recommends that managers participate in sensitivity training. His most influential books are *Interpersonal Competence and Organizational Effectiveness* and *Integrating the Individual and the Organization*.

*Ernest Dale.* Dale is one of the main proponents of the empirical school of management theory (see page 20). In his book *Great Organizers: Theory and Practice of Organizations*, he reviews the practices of some successful chief executives of major corporations.

*Peter Drucker.* Drucker, one of the most prominent contemporary authorities on management, holds that management is neither an art nor a science but a practice, and that the practice should focus on results. He feels that human beings are the greatest resource in an enterprise and views technology as simply a tool. One of Drucker's most widely read books is *Management: Tasks, Practices, Responsibilities*.

Drucker has done much to focus managers' attention on the control function. He notes:

Measuring requires, first and foremost, analytical ability. But it also demands that measurement be used to make self-control possible rather than abused to control people from the outside and above—that is, to dominate them. It is the common violation of this princple that largely explains why measurement is the weakest area in the work of the manager today. As long as measurements are based as a tool of control (for instance, as when measurements are used as a weapon of an internal secret police that supplies audits and critical appraisals of a manager's performance to the boss without even sending a carbon copy to the manager himself) measuring will remain the weakest area in the manager's performance.[7]

*Frederick Herzberg.*    Herzberg is identified with the need for job enrichment. He feels that work should be made more meaningful and challenging through recognition, opportunities for self-development, and responsibility.

In his *Work and the Nature of Man*, Herzberg sets forth his motivation—hygiene theory, in which he cites four major factors that motivate people: responsibility, achievement, recognition, and growth opportunities. Herzberg notes that several "hygiene factors"—fringe benefits, good working conditions, holidays, and so on—are essential but not motivating.

*Rensis Likert.*    Likert maintains that the value of people can be measured, and that people can be managed as carefully as physical assets. He advocates extensive participation by subordinates, especially in setting goals, and he believes that organizational effectiveness can be improved when there is a high degree of interaction between superiors and subordinates. Likert's best-known books are *New Patterns of Management* and *The Human Organization: Its Management and Value.*

*Abraham Maslow.*    Maslow has developed a hierarchy of needs, described in his *Motivation and Personality.* According to Maslow, there is a distinct progression of needs that motivate people, ranging from physiological needs to self-actualization. He claims that the prime motivators are growth opportunity and involvement.

Maslow advocates a logical approach to the solution of social problems. He observes:

> Means-centered scientists tend, in spite of themselves, to fit their problems to their techniques rather than the contrary. Their beginning question tends to be, which problems can I attack with techniques and equipment I now possess? Rather than what it should more often be, which are the most pressing, the most critical problems I could spend my time on?
> Ultimately, this must remind us of the famous drunk who looked for his wallet, not where he had lost it, but under the street lamp, "because the light is better there," or of the doctor who gave all his patients fits because that was the only sickness he knew how to cure.[8]

*Douglas McGregor.*    McGregor is famous for his two views of people and their relation to work: **Theory X** (employees are lazy, headstrong, and in need of constant watching) and **Theory Y** (employees like to work and seek responsibility). McGregor argues that management practices based on Theory Y are more suc-

[7]Peter F. Drucker, *Management: Tasks, Responsibilities, Practices* (New York: Harper & Row, 1974), p. 401.
[8]Abraham Maslow, *Motivation and Personality,* 2nd ed. (New York: Harper & Row, 1970), p. 13.

cessful than those designed on Theory X assumptions. He feels, however, that in practice most management tactics are based on Theory X. McGregor's best-known book is *The Human Side of Enterprise.*

*William Ouchi.*   Ouchi developed **Theory Z** to explain the philosophical basis for the Japanese system of managing. According to Theory Z, employers provide long-term employment, encourage employees to participate in decision making at all levels, evaluate and promote employees slowly, and take a holistic concern with employees' welfare. In turn, Theory Z calls for the employee to be patient, tolerant of others, and have the ability to identify personal goals with group goals. Observers claim that Theory Z is largely responsible for high-level Japanese productivity. Ouchi set forth the essentials of Theory Z in a book entitled *Theory Z: How American Business Can Meet the Japanese Challenge.*

*C. Northcote Parkinson.*   Parkinson has set forth a number of laws of administration, the most famous of which is "Work expands so as to fill the time available for its completion." In his humorous book *Parkinson's Law,* he describes the ways in which officials are led to multiply subordinates and to make work for one another, thus increasing the levels of a hierarchy while still accomplishing the same amount of work.

*Laurence Peter.*   Peter developed the **Peter Principle**, which states that in an organization most people are sooner or later promoted from a position of competence to a position of incompetence.

Peter strongly believes that many of our contemporary problems are related to an overemphasis on growth. He notes:

> Our obsession with growth has made the world a precarious place in which to live. We have depleted our natural resources, overpopulated, overpolluted, and are rapidly approaching a point where survival is critical. As a survival objective each of us must be willing to stop escalating and start establishing quality objectives rather than quantity objectives. This is the most important of all the objectives, because it is the only one that will stand the test of time.[9]

The above is only a partial list of management theorists. Many others have made an impact, and interest in management as a field of study will continue to increase in the decades ahead. As a society becomes increasingly complex, the intellectual demands on managers expand.

## WHAT ARE THE CURRENT APPROACHES TO THE STUDY OF MANAGEMENT?

Thinking about management has greatly increased over the past several decades. Many people have contributed concepts, principles, and guidelines to manage-

[9]Laurence J. Peter, *The Peter Prescription* (New York: William Morrow, 1972), p. 149.

*"Today we'll be talking about some new approaches."*

From *The Wall Street Journal,*
Permission — Cartoon Features Syndicate

ment lore. It is natural that different approaches have evolved on how best to study the subject.

Five main approaches can be identified: empirical, management-process, behavioral, management-science, and eclectic.

**The Empirical Approach**

The **empirical approach** involves the study of actual management practices that succeeded or failed. It deals with problematic cases or incidents in hopes that managers can learn from the experiences of others. The main goal of the empirical approach is to develop guidelines for handling similar management problems in the future.

Publications such as *Fortune, Forbes, Business Week*, and *The Wall Street Journal* feature articles that describe how managers in specific organizations handled a management problem. While the empirical approach is widely used by practitioners to study management, it has two major limitations. First, future events are almost always different from past events. What worked managerially in one situation may not work in another because the environment in which management is practiced is constantly changing.

Second, learning how to manage through the study of management experiences takes a long time. Much of what is learned may be wasted, since the experiences of others in dealing with management problems may be irrelevant in dealing with future problems.

**The Management-Process Approach**

A process involves progressive movement from one point to another until an act is completed. Many management theorists use the **management-process** (or functional) **approach**, although there is considerable variation in the functions cited.

Most writers divide the management process into four to six functions. Nearly all writers treat the functions of planning, organizing, and controlling. Other functions that have been proposed are staffing, directing, leading, measuring, motivating, and communicating. In this text, five functions are treated—planning, organizing, staffing, directing, and controlling.

Proponents of the management-process approach regard management as an activity that can be performed the same way regardless of the type of organization. This approach is orderly and systematic; it considers the subject as a whole rather than as a group of unrelated topics.

The **behavioral approach** to the study of management centers on the human element in organizations. Proponents of this approach study people—either individually or as members of a group—to discover how best to lead, motivate, and communicate with them. Enterprises are viewed as social organizations, and human relations are seen as the key to maximization of individual and group contributions.

The behavioral approach extracts heavily from the social sciences for its content. Behaviorists draw from **psychology** (the science dealing with mental and emotional processes) to formulate hypotheses about personal behavior and interactions of individuals in groups. They also draw from **sociology** (the systematic study of the development, structure, and functioning of groups of people) to explain and predict the actions of people in organizations.

The behavioral approach places primary emphasis on people—their motivations, their inner drives, and how they relate to one another in group situations.

The **management-science approach** to the study of management, sometimes referred to as the mathematical or operations-research approach, emphasizes the development of mathematical models to test management hypotheses. Interest in this approach has expanded greatly as the use of computers to facilitate testing of models has become more commonplace.

This approach stresses logic and rationality in making decisions, and it is of great value in helping managers solve technical problems. The main limitation of the management-science approach is that many management problems, particularly those involving human behavior, cannot be structured mathematically.

Closely related to the management-science approach is **decision theory**, which employs mathematical techniques to a great extent. Decision theory places emphasis on establishing various alternative solutions to a problem and then making the "best" choice. As the name "decision theory" suggests, choosing among alternatives is the most basic aspect of this approach.

The **eclectic approach** to the study of management draws on the best available information from the various approaches to the study of the subject. This text uses the eclectic approach because important contributions to management thought have come out of each of the approaches previously explained.

When we examine how managers solve specific management problems, we are drawing on the empirical approach. The management-process approach is

**The Behavioral Approach**

**The Management-Science Approach**

**The Eclectic Approach**

used when we discuss the five interrelated functions performed by managers. We are employing the behavioral approach when we consider the human element in organizations. And when we examine the contributions of mathematical model builders, we are using the management-science approach.

Figure 1–1 shows how the behavioral, management-process, management-science, and empirical approaches combine to contribute to the eclectic approach to the study of management. As Robert Wetzler notes, "**Management theory** is not a single simple technique or discipline. The term is used to describe a body of many interrelated concepts and methodologies that have been developed over the years by individuals with vision and perception."[10]

**SUMMARY**

- An organization is a group of people who work together to achieve common goals. Organized life is essential for our survival.
- Management is the process of achieving an organization's goals through the coordinated performance of five functions: planning, organizing, staffing, directing, and controlling.
- Management is both a science and an art. Scientific management is the use of codified and verified knowledge. Artistic management is the conscientious use of skill and creative imagination.
- Managers in all organizations are important because they have authority, or the right to make decisions over people, resources, and change.

[10]Robert T. Wetzler, "Management Theory Can Produce a Continuing Bottom Line Impact," *MSU Business Topics,* Winter 1975, p. 5.

**FIGURE 1–1**

**Contributions to the Eclectic Approach to Management Theory**

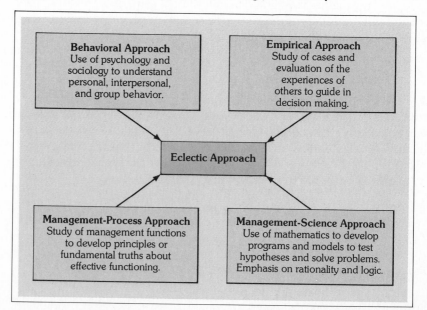

- Responsibility is the requirement imposed on an individual to answer to others for his or her performance, conduct, or obligations.
- Responsibility cannot be delegated. A manager can authorize someone to do a task, but the manager is still responsible for the performance of that task and for results.
- Because some degree of conformity to rules, procedures, and policies is required in an organization, all of its members must sacrifice some degree of personal freedom.
- Management is as old as civilization. Tribal organization is the first evidence we have of the performance of management. Management was practiced on a fairly elaborate scale in ancient Chinese, Babylonian, Egyptian, and Hebrew societies.
- Early management theorists include Robert Owen, Charles Babbage, Frederick Taylor, Henry Gantt, Frank and Lillian Gilbreth, Henri Fayol, Mary Parker Follett, Hugo Münsterberg, Max Weber, G. Elton Mayo, Chester Barnard, James D. Mooney, Lyndall Urwick, and Ralph C. Davis.
- Widely noted contemporary writers on management include Chris Argyris, Ernest Dale, Peter Drucker, Frederick Herzberg, Rensis Likert, Abraham Maslow, Douglas McGregor, C. Northcote Parkinson, and Laurence Peter.
- There are five main approaches to the study of management: empirical, management-process, behavioral, management-science, and eclectic.

## LEARN THE LANGUAGE OF MANAGEMENT

organization
management
managers
scientific management
motion-and-time studies
artistic management
authority
responsibility
principle of delegation
exception principle
Hawthorne Effect
Theory X

Theory Y
Theory Z
Peter Principle
empirical approach
management-process approach
behavioral approach
psychology
sociology
management-science approach
decision theory
eclectic approach
management theory

## QUESTIONS FOR REVIEW AND DISCUSSION

1. What do all organizations have in common? Why are organizations essential?
2. What is the central or key purpose of management?
3. What accounts for the wide variety of job titles given to managers?
4. Why is it impossible to apply the principles of scientific management in all management situations?
5. Explain why organizations stand or fall on the quality of their management.
6. Give three examples each of a manager's authority over people, resources, and change.
7. Explain why authority can be delegated, but not responsibility. Why does the fear of responsibility deter many people from careers in management?
8. Why do organizations require sacrifices of some degree of personal freedom?
9. Cite the major contribution of each management theorist discussed in the text.
10. Explain each of these approaches to the study of management: empirical, management-process, behavioral, management-science, eclectic.

## 1. Should managers always be held responsible for results?

Larry Brown is a supervisor of six computer programmers. Last week one of the programmers made a mistake in a program that caused a severe problem for a client. Larry's superior is quite irritated with him and tells him, "Look, Larry, you're responsible for all the work of your programmers. The fact that we delivered a botched-up program to the client is your responsibility."

Larry doesn't agree and explains, "Chief, that programmer who made the mistake was *assigned* to me. Basically, I don't think he's competent. I'd accept responsibility for his error if I had selected him. But I didn't, so I don't think I should be held responsible for the problem."

Who in the organization must ultimately bear responsibility for the error in the program? Why?

Is Larry's point that he did not select the programmer an adequate defense for him to disclaim responsibility? Why?

## 2. Is greater efficiency always a desirable goal?

Goodee Products makes snack foods and employs 2,000 production employees. Goodee Products is owned by World Foods, a large conglomerate. The employees are not unionized, although several elections have been held.

The president of Goodee's, Ike Miller, is under tremendous pressure from Jerome Johnson, the head of the conglomerate, to cut labor costs by replacing 400 employees with automated equipment.

Miller is opposed to the plan and tells Johnson, "Look, I've run Goodee Products for nine years, always at a profit. Labor turnover is the lowest in the industry and I've been able to keep the union out so our labor costs are also the lowest in the industry. Terminating 400 employees is certain to bring unionization, higher labor costs, and all sorts of other problems. Besides, many of the workers who would be laid off have been with us for ten years or longer. I feel a responsibility for their welfare."

Johnson replies, "You have only one basic responsibility—to operate the plant with maximum efficiency so we make more money. World Foods acquired Goodee Products because we have the capital to buy the most efficient machines available. We'll spend up to $250,000 in equipment for each worker replaced.

"Let me add this. I've had several reports from our engineers who are studying ways to put in more automated equipment that there's quite a lot of featherbedding going on. And I am aware that our leading competitors are getting ready to redesign their plants with modernized equipment."

Does Johnson have the authority to require Miller to replace workers with machines? Why or why not?

If the machines are installed, what can Miller do to prevent unionization? What can he do to lessen the emotional and financial hardships of the terminated employees?

On the basis of your study of this chapter, what is likely to happen to Miller if he refuses to implement Johnson's plan? What may happen to Johnson if his plan is not carried out?

### 3. How can managers handle a severe production cutback?

Trucks and Tractors Inc. is one of the world's oldest, largest, and most respected builders of heavy-use vehicles. At full capacity, its plants employ about 100,000 workers. Because of a deep recession, demand for products made by Trucks and Tractors Inc. is down 50 percent. One of the plants, Ajax Works, has been ordered by senior management at the international headquarters to cut its payroll by 50 percent. The plant normally employs 4,000 employees.

Discussing how best to implement this directive are the top managers of Ajax Works: president, Harry O.; production manager, Wilson G.; personnel director, Janice W.; controller, Ace V.; and legal head, Burke B. The following discussion takes place on how best to achieve a 50 percent reduction in payroll costs.

Harry: You all know why we're here. We've been directed to reduce payroll costs by 50 percent within 10 days. Now we've got to decide how best to do it, keeping in mind both short- and long-run considerations.

Wilson: I think we should turn this problem into an advantage. I feel we should ask our supervisors to rate all of our existing personnel and then terminate the 50 percent who the first line managers feel are the least desirable.

Janice: But if we follow your method, won't the union raise a fuss? The union people always advocate seniority as the criterion for dismissal.

Burke: I'm not saying I agree with Wilson's method. But there is no legal problem with the union. Our last contract gives management, under these circumstances, the right to dismiss employees we feel are least productive.

Janice: Even so, I think simply dismissing those workers the supervisors feel are least productive may not be the best solution. Granted, it is simple, and simplicity is a characteristic of any good plan. But Wilson's plan is bound to be somewhat arbitrary. Aren't the supervisors likely to dismiss the employees they like the least and not necessarily those who are below average in performance?

Harry: I think Janice has a valid point. Perhaps we should consider other alternatives.

Ace: Such as?

Harry: Well, we may want to cut the work week in half. That way, everyone could continue working—they'll just get a 50 percent check.

Ace: I'm afraid that wouldn't work. You see, an employee can draw that much from unemployment benefits. I think a lot of our people would rather be unemployed and not have to work at all than work 20 hours a week for the same amount of money.

Harry: Well, another possibility might be to furlough 1,000 workers and put the remaining 3,000 on a 30-hour work week. That way, 1,000 employees could draw unemployment and the other 3,000 would earn 75 percent of their normal income.

Wilson: If we did that, we still have to decide which 1,000 employees to let go.

Janice: I suppose we could spell out the criteria for selecting the best employees and direct our supervisors to follow our guidelines in deciding who stays and who goes.

Harry: We've got a critical decision to make and we've got to implement it within 10 days. I'm not sure the best plan has surfaced yet. Think about our problem and we'll meet again at 9 A.M. tomorrow to decide.

Which of the following alternatives makes the most sense to you?

A. Let the supervisors decide, using their own criteria, which 2,000 employees are the least desirable and furlough them.

B. Release 1,000 workers and put the remaining 3,000 on 30-hour work weeks.

What other alternatives might be considered to implement the directive "cut personnel costs by 50 percent"?

The union has no official voice in this decision. Nevertheless, would it be wise for management to consult with union leaders before reaching a decision? Why or why not?

**FOR ADDITIONAL
CONCEPTS
AND IDEAS**

Argyris, Chris. *Integrating the Individual and the Organization.* New York: John Wiley & Sons, 1964.

Argyris, Chris. *Interpersonal Competence and Organizational Effectiveness.* Homewood, Ill.: Richard D. Irwin, Dorsey Press, 1962.

Barnard, Chester. *The Functions of the Executive.* Cambridge, Mass.: Harvard University Press, 1938.

Berger, Peter L. "New Attack on the Legitimacy of Business." *Harvard Business Review*, September–October 1981, pp. 82–89.

Boettinger, Henry M. "Is Management Really an Art?" *Harvard Business Review*, January–February 1975, pp. 54–64.

Bunke, Harvey C. "Anti-Business Sentiments and the Intellectual Community." *Business Horizons,* September–October 1981, pp. 2–8.

Chang, Y. N. "Early Chinese Management Thought." *California Management Review*, Winter 1976, pp. 71–76.

Dale, Ernest. *Great Organizers: Theory and Practice of Organizations.* New York: McGraw-Hill, 1971.

Davis, Ralph C. *The Fundamentals of Top Management.* New York: Harper & Brothers, 1951.

du Toit, Derek F. "Confessions of a Successful Entrepreneur." *Harvard Business Review*, November–December 1980, pp. 44–64.

Evans, Fred J. "Academics, the New Class, and Antibusiness Ideology." *Business Horizons*, November–December 1981, pp. 40–48.

Fayol, Henri. *General and Industrial Management*, trans. Constance Storrs. London: Sir Isaac Pitman & Sons, 1949.

Follett, Mary P. *The New State.* London: Longmans, Green & Co., 1918.

Herzberg, Frederick. *Work and the Nature of Man.* New York: New American Library, Thomas Crowell, 1966.

Kantrow, Alan M. "Why Read Peter Drucker?" *Harvard Business Review*, January–February 1980, pp. 74–91.

Likert, Rensis. *The Human Organization: Its Management and Value.* New York: McGraw-Hill, 1967.

Likert, Rensis. *New Patterns of Management.* New York: McGraw-Hill, 1961.

McGregor, Douglas. *The Human Side of Enterprise.* New York: McGraw-Hill, 1960.

McGuire, Joseph W. "Management Theory: Retreat to the Academy." *Business Horizons,* July–August 1982, pp. 31–37.

Mooney, James D. *The Principles of Organization.* New York: Harper & Brothers, 1947.

Münsterberg, Hugo. *Psychology and Industrial Efficiency.* Boston: Houghton Mifflin, 1913.

Parkinson, C. Northcote. *Parkinson's Law.* Boston: Houghton Mifflin, 1957.

Ping, Charles J. "Bigger Stake for Business in Higher Education." *Harvard Business Review*, September–October 1981, pp. 122–141.

Peter, Laurence J. and Hull, Raymond. *Peter Principle: Why Things Always Go Wrong.* New York: William Morrow, 1969.

Smith, George David, and Steadman, Laurence E. "Present Value of Corporate History." *Harvard Business Review*, November–December 1981, pp. 164–173.

Taylor, Frederick W. *Principles of Scientific Management.* New York: Harper & Brothers, 1911.

Urwick, Lyndall. *The Elements of Administration.* New York: Harper & Brothers, 1944.

Weber, Max. *The Theory of Social and Economic Organization*, ed. and trans. A. M. Henderson and Talcott Parsons. London: Oxford University Press, 1947.

# 2 AN OVERVIEW OF THE MANAGEMENT PROCESS

**STUDY THIS CHAPTER SO YOU CAN:**

- Understand the differences between and give examples of managerial and nonmanagerial activities, and describe the manager's role in both.

- Explain when and to what extent managers should have technical training.

- Define and describe the five management functions.

- Explain how the management functions interrelate to form a process, and how the performance of one function affects the others.

- Distinguish between quantifiable and qualitative results in terms of manager evaluation.

- Define the term "principle," and discuss the importance of formulating management principles.

- List and explain the management principles of Taylor and Fayol.

- Discuss the generally accepted principles for each management function.

This text defines management as the process of achieving an organization's goals through the coordinated performance of five functions—planning, organizing, staffing, directing, and controlling. This chapter presents a capsule overview of the management process. Later chapters will discuss each function in greater depth.

Before considering the management functions, it is worthwhile to consider some general questions that are often posed by management students and theorists.

1. How is managing different from not managing?
2. Must managers know operational skills?
3. Are management skills transferable?
4. What are the functions of management?
5. How do the functions interrelate?
6. How is manager performance measured?
7. What are management principles?

## HOW IS MANAGING DIFFERENT FROM NOT MANAGING?

The emphasis in this book is on managers whose primary job is management. Table 2–1 shows that many people who are not considered managers in a professional and career sense nevertheless perform management functions as part of their work. For example, the dentist is managing when hiring staff person-

## TABLE 2–1

**Examples of Managerial and Nonmanagerial Activities**

| Profession | Managerial Activities | Nonmanagerial Activities |
|---|---|---|
| Airline pilot | • Preparing a flight plan<br>• Giving instructions to a copilot | • Flying a plane<br>• Making a preflight instrument check |
| Chief executive officer | • Giving projects to managers<br>• Setting company objectives | • Research<br>• Dictating routine letters |
| Trade association executive | • Deciding on a compensation program for employees<br>• Appointing committees | • Making a speech<br>• Tabulating results or a survey |
| Farmer | • Instructing employees on what to do<br>• Planning next year's activities | • Operating a machine<br>• Taking care of animals |
| Administrative assistant | • Explaining a job to a new employee<br>• Setting work schedules for secretaries | • Filing<br>• Answering the telephone |
| Foreman | • Deciding who works overtime<br>• Deciding who will be laid off | • Fixing a machine<br>• Loading a truck |
| Lawyer | • Selecting an office staff<br>• Delegating work to an assistant | • Arguing a case in court<br>• Preparing a legal brief |

nel, establishing a fringe-benefit program, or scheduling work. The dentist is not managing while working on a patient's teeth or reading a dental journal.

Most People
Manage Some of
the Time
Most people manage at least some of the time, depending upon their role in the activity they are engaged in. In her corporation, Barbara Sith is a middle manager with eight people reporting to her. In her church, she is a deacon, a position that requires some managerial activity. Sith is an officer in her civic club, and that position, too, involves some management. But in the PTA she has no title, no position, and no authority. In this case she sits in the back row and is "managed" by those who decide what project will be taken up and what her role in it will be.

Most Managers
Do Some
Nonmanagerial
Work
Few managers practice pure management in the sense that that is all they do. Nearly all managers are also involved in the performance of some nonmanagerial activities. That is, in fact, one of the main problems in organizations. It can be costly to an enterprise if highly paid managers spend time doing work that lower-paid managers and nonmanagement people can do and often do better.

When managers do nonmanagerial work, waste may result. For example, an executive with a yearly salary of $100,000 who works 2,500 hours per year is being compensated at the rate of $40 per hour. If the executive spends 15 minutes doing research in the library, the cost to the organization is $10. But if this work is delegated to a secretary, who we assume is earning $8 per hour, the cost to the organization is only $2.

It is desirable then that all work in an organization, *including the work of managing*, be performed at the lowest level capable of handling it properly. This principle is often violated. Professors may grade routine quizzes that could be reviewed by student assistants, physicians may perform work that could be handled just as well by paramedics, and business executives may dictate routine letters that could be written by a secretary.

A wise manager keeps one question in mind at all times: "Could the work I am doing be performed just as well by someone who is lower in the organization?"

## MUST MANAGERS KNOW OPERATIVE SKILLS?

Whether managers must know the skills performed by the people they manage depends on their level of management, the type of organization, and the size of the organization.

Level of
Management
As one moves up the scale, operative-skill requirements go down and managerial-skill requirements go up. At the first level of management, the supervisor may be expected to have a good knowledge of the work done by the personnel. The supervisor may need to know how to operate machines and help repair them. (Note, however, that when a manager is operating or repairing machines, the manager is *not* managing.) The account executive in an advertising agency need

not be an artist or a copywriter. The executive's job is to help plan the advertising campaign, select the proper staff, motivate the staff, and then persuade the client to accept the campaign. The account executive needs some practical expertise, but he or she needs a great deal of managerial expertise.

The closer we move to the top of the organization, the purer managing becomes. At the senior management level in most organizations, little practical knowledge is needed. Certainly an executive can supervise a secretary without knowing how to type or operate the copying machine. But the executive should know the general limits of what a secretary can do (such as the time required to type letters) so as not to create a work overload or underload.

**Type of Organization**

Although managers in many organizations do not need to know operative skills, technically oriented organizations tend to select managers with academic backgrounds and practical experience in the technical specialty involved. Managers in an architectual engineering firm, for example, with few exceptions have been educated academically as either architects or engineers and have had considerable operational experience in that specialty. Managers in a public accounting firm probably have had a rigorous academic preparation in accounting.

Technical organizations usually select managers who have been educated and trained in their specialty because technical expertise is very helpful in giving instructions, in planning work to be accomplished, and in performing other management functions, especially if the specialty's language is highly technical.

**Size of Organization**

In a small organization, a manager may need to know operative skills. The manager of a small loan office typically manages four or five people. But a good share of the manager's time may be spent in performing operative functions, such as taking loan applications and calling on accounts that are past due.

In large organizations, managers need not—in fact, cannot—know every operative skill. Say that IBM required that its president had the ability to perform every job and know every skill in the organization. Even if the applicant spent a few hundred years going to school and getting job experience, new job skills are invented more rapidly than any one individual could possibly learn them.

## ARE MANAGEMENT SKILLS TRANSFERABLE?

Operative skills are generally less important at top levels than at bottom levels. Therefore it is easier for a senior executive in one kind of organization to transfer his or her managerial skills to a different kind of organization than it is for someone at a lower organizational level.

**Chief Executive Officer** (CEO) is the position title used by some businesses to indicate the highest ranking company executive. Sometimes the CEO also holds the title of president. United Airlines hired Edward E. Carlson, who had been a hotel executive, as its chief executive officer. Eastern Airlines selected Frank Borman, the astronaut, to be its president. These airlines would probably not even consider someone who had had no experience with an airline for a first- or middle-level management job.

Frequently, a university in need of a new president will choose someone with extensive managerial experience from outside the field of education, perhaps from the military or the government. But in filling a first-level management position, such as a department head, the university would require extensive expertise in the discipline involved.

## WHAT ARE THE FUNCTIONS OF MANAGEMENT?

Chapter 1 explained that the work of managing is divided into five functions. Each function is inherent in managing and must be performed satisfactorily if the organization is to achieve its goals economically and effectively.

Figure 2–1 shows in simplified form what the five management functions involve. The descriptions in the figure are suggestive only. (Several later chapters in the text are devoted to a discussion of each of the five functions.) Note that each function interrelates with each other function. Planning obviously affects the performance of all other functions, but so do organizing, staffing, directing, and controlling. Because of the interrelationships among the various functions, management is usually viewed as a **process**, or a logical flow of activities.

**Planning:
Initiating Action**

Planning is where the management process begins. To **plan** means to set goals, or objectives, for the organization and to then develop methods for achieving them. Examples of goals are (1) to produce and market 100,000 tape recorders in the next twelve months; (2) to obtain at least 30 percent of the market within eighteen months; (3) to reduce production costs by 18 percent, supply costs by 21 percent, and utility expenses by 8 percent by January 1; and (4) to reduce absenteeism in Department A by 16 percent by December 1.

To achieve their objectives, managers must formulate four types of plans: strategies, policies, procedures, and rules. Plans should be made relative to all activities in the enterprise.

Planning involves making decisions that will be implemented later. It is important, since all other functions are performed to achieve the objectives established through the planning process.

### Levels of Planning

All managers engage in planning, but the scope of planning relates to one's level in the organization. Plans made at the top of the organization are broad and affect all departments. Top-level plans also cover a long period of time. Decisions to put a firm on a four-day work week, sell stock, or produce a new product are examples of top-level planning.

Decisions to transfer an employee to another job, purchase routine supplies, or shut down a production line are made by middle-level managers. Decisions to terminate an operative employee, rotate workers from one job to another, or assign someone to make a delivery are normally made by first-level managers.

**FIGURE 2–1**

Simplified Illustration of the Management Process

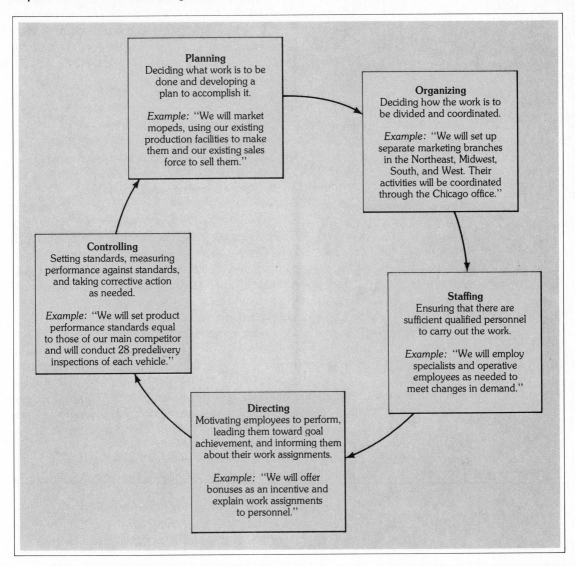

### Major and Minor Plans

To attain one major plan requires the development and execution of many minor plans. Suppose a senior manager sets a goal to sell 20 percent more units of Product A. Each divisional manager will then make plans on how to accomplish his or her share of the goal. Next, each field manager will make plans on how to achieve his or her portion of the division's share.

Keep in mind that plans designed to help achieve the grand plan must be consistent with it. Everyone must move in the same direction if the overall goal is to be achieved. For example, if the major plan is to sell 20 percent more units of Product A, lower-level managers are expected to concentrate on selling Product A, not on some activity that is inconsistent with the major plan.

## Organizing: Building a Framework to Achieve Goals

To **organize** means to put in a state of order, that is, to arrange or constitute into a coherent unity in which each part relates to each other part. Organizing involves three steps.

### Step 1: Examine What Must Be Done

Organizing begins with an examination of the work that must be done to achieve the goals of the enterprise. In studying the tasks to be performed, managers may ask, "How can we achieve our objective with the least input of human and material resources?" "What part of the production activity should we consider subcontracting?" or "What kind of engineering is required?"

### Step 2: Group Similar Tasks

Next, organizing involves the grouping of similar activities. This means establishing branches, units, work centers, or other forms of departments. Examples of questions managers ask at this point are "Do we need a personnel department to staff the organization, or should each department head perform this function?" "Should accounting and finance be separate departments or combined into one?" "How should each department relate to each other department?" and "Should we departmentalize on the basis of product, territory, function, or other factors?"

### Step 3: Assign Work

The third step in organizing is to assign required activities to managers or operative personnel. Organizing need not be complicated. When the owner of a small store tells his assistants, "John, you're in charge of the produce department; Bill, you handle the meat department; and Mary, you handle frozen foods and dry groceries," he is organizing. In large enterprises, however, organizing can be very complex. Some large corporations have specialists who work exclusively on organizational problems.

Organizing is an important function, since its performance determines operational efficiency. Probably the greatest waste in an enterprise results from the way work is organized. One frequently sees situations in which too many or too few people perform work.

## Staffing: Providing Personnel

In management, **staff** are the personnel assigned to carry out a given task. **Staffing** is the function of selecting, training, compensating, and evaluating people so that the work of an enterprise will be performed according to established standards or desired goals.

Staffing is a critically important function. People differ widely in terms of their ability to perform specific jobs. Differences in intelligence, knowledge, skill, experience, physical condition, age, and attitude all serve to complicate staffing. Various disciplines related to management, such as psychology and sociology, help managers to understand people and their potential better. Nevertheless, there is still much to learn about human behavior in order to perform the staffing function well.

Workers who cannot perform the skills expected of them—sales representatives who cannot sell and secretaries who cannot type—are proof that the staffing function sometimes is performed badly.

In performing the function of **directing**, managers try to motivate people to perform activities in the most efficient manner possible, to lead and inspire people toward goal achievement, and to communicate information about how activities should be performed.

### Motivating

To **motivate** is to stimulate active and enthusiastic interest in what is being done. **Morale**—the mental or emotional condition of an individual or group with regard to the task at hand—indicates how well managers have motivated their personnel. High morale indicates worker satisfaction and a high state of esprit de corps, while low morale suggests worker dissatisfaction and frustration.

### Leading

To **lead** is to induce people to achieve goals willingly and harmoniously. Leadership is necessary in modern-day management because people in most situations cannot be forced to perform or cooperate.

### Communicating

To **communicate** means to impart, to make known, to inform. Communicating is an art. There are great differences in the way managers express themselves and exchange ideas. Communicating involves giving instructions, issuing work orders, discussing plans, explaining results to people, and passing information through the organization.

Communicating is difficult. It is hard for people to express—whether by speaking, writing, or body language—precisely what they think and what they want done. Since communicating is an art, no one is able to reach perfection in expression. And when workers do not understand their jobs or when managers at one level receive confusing directives from a higher-level manager, trouble may result.

Additionally, many problems arise in communicating because of the tremendous competition for attention. Distractions such as noisy machines, telephones, and movement of people often make it difficult for managers to explain what they mean. Because of these distractions, the function of communicating may give some managers more problems than any other.

The **control** function involves three steps: setting standards for work performed, measuring performance against the standards, and taking corrective action as needed. In controlling the activities of an organization, managers concern themselves with the *way* in which activities are carried out.

### Control Requires Performance Standards

If the control function is to be performed, clear performance standards must be set. Unless there is a standard, a manager can only guess at how well the activity is being performed. Examples of performance standards include units produced per work hour, waste per ton of raw material used in production, percentage of goods sold that are returned, accidents per 100,000 work hours, and absenteeism per employee per month.

### The Goal of Controlling

Managers should try to do more than merely "keep things from getting out of hand." The goal of controlling is to ensure that work is performed as planned to achieve the objectives of the organization. If products are returned because of faulty workmanship, if tools or merchandise are stolen by employees, or if excessive time is required to complete a certain phase of production, then management, through controlling, must determine why. Next, management must bring about corrective action.

Corrective action can take many forms. The solution might involve retraining employees (to correct faulty workmanship), employing security guards (to stop pilferage), or reengineering a process (to reduce production time required).

## HOW DO THE FUNCTIONS INTERRELATE?

Almost all work in an organization is interrelated. How well each function is performed determines how well the other functions can be performed. It is important that individuals and departments in an organization understand how the work they do relates to the work other individuals and departments do.

The interdependency of various functions is often de-emphasized. Managers of a given function in an enterprise often become so involved in what they are doing that they fail to see how their activity relates to other activities. Table 2–2 gives examples of how functions may be performed poorly and the resulting impact on the organization.

The interrelationship of functions is important because maximum success in achieving goals requires that *each* function be performed with maximum effectiveness. While some functions, such as planning, may receive more emphasis than others, neglect of any function diminishes the final result.

Because performance of the various functions must be tied together, attention should be given to coordination if the desired results are to be achieved.

## HOW IS MANAGER PERFORMANCE MEASURED?

Since managers are responsible for the results achieved by the organization, they should be evaluated on the basis of results (as opposed to efforts expended). Discussions of other ways to evaluate managers, as well as more information on results evaluation, will be found in Chapter 15.

**TABLE 2-2**

37

The Interrelationship of the Management Functions

| Function | Example of Poor Performance | Resulting Impact |
|---|---|---|
| Planning | • Objectives are set too high or too low because of mistakes in forecasting.<br><br>• Plans are unclear.<br><br>• Plans are made without taking into full consideration the available financial, physical, and human resources. | • Too many or too few persons may be employed to reach the goal. Thus other functions such as staffing are affected.<br>• Functions such as directing and controlling are more difficult to perform.<br>• The organization cannot carry out plans properly, and organizing is hindered. |
| Organizing | • Too many departments are established.<br><br>• Work is not apportioned properly within departments.<br><br>• Too many dissimilar activities are assigned to personnel. | • Controlling becomes overcomplicated and the organization operates inefficiently.<br>• Some people are overworked and others are underworked. Performance of the directing function is complicated.<br>• Benefits of specialization are not gained and mistakes are frequent. Performance of the controlling function is affected. |
| Staffing | • An unqualified employee is assigned to a job.<br><br>• Employees are not trained properly.<br><br><br>• A trouble-making employee with a negative attitude is assigned to a job. | • The product is manufactured unsatisfactorily. This has a bearing on the controlling function.<br>• The intended production volume is not achieved. The planning function is directly affected, since plans may need to be redesigned.<br>• Other workers become dissatisfied or quit. This bears directly on the directing function. |
| Directing | • Unclear instructions are issued to personnel.<br><br>• Rules regarding safety are not communicated to personnel.<br><br>• A popular employee is dismissed for no just cause. | • Mistakes, accidents, and other problems occur. Planning, controlling, and other functions may be affected.<br>• Accidents occur. This relates to performance of other functions such as staffing and planning.<br>• Other persons become demoralized. This can bear on the performance of staffing, planning, and other functions. |
| Controlling | • Quality standards are improperly set.<br><br>• Budgetary controls are ineffective.<br><br>• Work is improperly scheduled. | • Products already sold must be recalled. Planning, staffing, and other functions are thereby affected.<br>• Financial resources are wasted. Other management functions are obviously affected.<br>• Overtime is excessive; thus the organization is unable to meet its budgetary objectives and plans must be revised. |

**Examples of Results**  Results take many forms, depending on the type of organization. In profit-seeking organizations, examples of results include profits earned, costs incurred, sales volume achieved, and share of market attained. Examples of results in nonprofit organizations may include revenues collected, membership growth, and services rendered.

Actually, results expected of managers in profit and nonprofit organizations are very similar and often identical. While we associate the word "profit" only with profit-seeking organizations, the term can also be applied in the broader meaning of "a valuable return or gain" to nonprofit organizations.

The most significant difference between profit-seeking and non-profit-seeking organizations is not the kind of results expected of managers but rather the demand imposed on managers to achieve those results. Profit-seeking enterprises tend to exercise stricter controls over managers and demand more in terms of performance. Generally, goals are more carefully set and performance is more rigidly enforced.

**Quantifiable and Qualitative Results**  **Quantifiable results** can be expressed in numbers. Profits, market share, absenteeism, cost reduction, production rates, and sales per square foot are examples of quantifiable results. Managers may also be judged on **qualitative results**— that is, results that cannot be expressed mathematically. Qualitative results include improvement of an organization's public image, development of executive capabilities, meeting of social responsibilities, and improvement of organizational morale.

Ideally, results should be measured precisely. Doing so enables a manager to determine the exact contribution that an individual or a department has made to the organization. Often, however, this cannot be done. Table 2–3 gives examples of questions related to quantifiable and qualitative results expected of managers in different types of organizations and at different levels.

**Evaluation of Results**  Results should be evaluated frequently. Generally, results are measured more frequently at the lowest levels of an organization than at the top. Daily, weekly, monthly, and quarterly production reports are commonly used for measurement. Usually, annual evaluations are made for an enterprise as a whole.

One criterion for measurement used in all types of organizations is performance within budgetary limitations. Another is efficient use of human, material, and financial resources. Trade associations and religious organizations traditionally impose fewer controls over managers than profit-seeking organizations.

## WHAT ARE MANAGEMENT PRINCIPLES?

A **principle** is a generalization that is widely accepted as true. A goal of serious thinkers in any discipline is to develop principles about the subject with which they are concerned. Henri Fayol, one of the main contributors to the evolution of management thought, strongly advocated the development of management principles.

## TABLE 2-3

**Examples of Results-Related Questions Asked of Managers**

| | BUSINESS CORPORATION | |
|---|---|---|
| **Board of Directors → Chief Executive Officer** | **Chief Executive Officer → Vice-Presidents** | **Vice-Presidents → Department Heads** |
| Questions asked of the chief executive officer:<br>• Was profit goal reached?<br>• Were projected new products developed on schedule?<br>• Were labor relations good?<br>• Were new physical facilities constructed as planned? | Questions asked of vice-presidents:<br><br>• Did the division make the expected contribution to profits?<br>• Is the inventory being kept at the desired levels?<br>• Were operating costs kept within the budget?<br>• Were specific goals achieved? | Questions asked of department heads:<br>• Was projected new equipment purchased and installed?<br>• Was absenteeism kept within workable levels?<br>• Is the department adequately staffed with lower-level managers?<br>• Were many products returned or refused by customers because of inferior quality? |
| | **UNIVERSITY** | |
| **Board of Regents → University President** | **University President → College Deans** | **College Deans → Department Chairpersons** |
| Questions asked of the university president:<br>• Was the university operated within the assigned budget?<br>• Did student enrollment reach expectations?<br>• Is the student body generally satisfied with the quality of instruction and with university policy?<br>• Is the overall public image of the university satisfactory? | Questions asked of college deans:<br><br>• Were new instructional programs implemented? Were ineffective ones modified or abolished?<br>• What were the publishing and research efforts of the college faculty?<br>• Did the college operate within its assigned budget?<br>• Was the effectiveness of department chairpersons upgraded?<br>• Was departmental prestige improved? | Questions asked of department chairpersons:<br>• What took place in the area of faculty development? What is the caliber of new faculty members? Were ineffective faculty members replaced?<br>• Did the department operate within its budget?<br>• Were courses improved in terms of content and teaching? |
| | **NATIONAL CHARITABLE ASSOCIATION** | |
| **Board of Directors → Executive Director of the Association** | **Executive Director of the Association → Directors of State Associations** | **Directors of State Associations → Directors of Local Chapters** |
| Questions asked of the executive director:<br>• Did the association achieve its revenue level?<br>• Was the level of charitable service up to expectations?<br>• Did the executive staff perform satisfactorily?<br>• Were planned new services implemented? | Questions asked of directors of state associations:<br>• Did the state association make its predetermined contribution to revenues?<br>• Were new local chapters opened as planned?<br>• Were local public relations efforts successful? | Questions asked of directors of local chapters:<br>• Did the local chapter make its predetermined contribution to the budget?<br>• Were the services provided to charitable recipients satisfactory?<br>• Were an adequate number of lay workers recruited? Did they perform as expected? |

# MANAGERS IN ACTION

## PRODUCTIVITY IMPROVEMENT HAS TO BE A PART OF THE TOTAL MANAGEMENT PROCESS

Professor Y. K. Shetty has studied productivity programs of leading companies and has developed six guidelines that managers should follow to improve productivity.

1. *Top management must support the productivity program.* Shetty notes, "Experiences suggest that top management support can be expressed in many different ways. At Beatrice Foods, for example, the emphasis in all top management major speeches was on productivity. The chairman of the board wrote a letter stating that productivity improvement should have a top priority in the company."

2. *A suitable organizational structure is needed.* Here is how Tanner Companies' productivity program is organized: "Members of the Corporate Productivity Committee are selected from different parts of the company and charged with getting the program underway. Each Divisional Committee consists of representatives from management, office workers, sales personnel, and production people, sometimes including union-working leaders. The Divisional Productivity Committee formulates a plan of action, sets goals, discusses techniques, and follows up on the progress of productivity improvement efforts."

3. *A climate conducive to productivity improvement must be created.* Shetty observes, "Managers, supervisors, and employees must *all* be aware of the productivity problems. They must realize what productivity is, what it means to their jobs and companies, and how it can be measured and improved."

4. *Productivity must be measured.* Unless performance is measured and compared against a standard, a company will not know whether productivity is improving. "The experience of companies with productivity measurement programs suggests a number of things. First, in most companies specific plans must be developed to make productivity information routinely and easily available. Second, perfect measures of productivity are difficult to devise, but useful productivity measures can be developed. Third, the measurement task will require direction and technical help from the company coordinator of the program or from an outside expert. Fourth, realistic, relatively simple, and understandable measures are the best."

5. *Plans for improvement must be developed.* "Beech Aircraft uses work simplification, methods engineering, a suggestion system, producibility engineering, and value engineering. Detroit Edison uses time study, work sampling, and management by objectives. Crompton Company uses a three-day, twelve-hour work schedule along with incentive wages. . . . Still others are using behavior modification, job enrichment, goal setting, zero-base budgeting, autonomous work groups, and so on."

6. *Productivity plans must be evaluated.* Developing a productivity program is not enough to insure greater efficiency. "Monitoring, evaluation, and feedback processes should be built into the program. A periodic review, evaluation, and analysis of the program should identify results and barriers, and may provide a basis for program redirection or revision."

Source: Y. K. Shetty, "Key Elements of Productivity Programs," *Business Horizons*, March–April 1982, pp. 16–22. Copyright © 1982 by The Foundation for the School of Business at Indiana University. Reprinted by permission.

### QUESTIONS

1. If a company wants to improve its productivity, why is it essential to consider the entire management process, not just one or two functions, such as planning and staffing?

2. Why is productivity improvement essential to a company? For the economy as a whole?

Principles are useful to managers for several reasons. First, they help managers make more accurate decisions. To the extent that managers can apply principles in any situation and eliminate guesswork, sounder decisions result.

Second, principles save time. If one learns principles of management in school, less experience is required to become an effective manager. Decisions can be made more rapidly and accurately when principles provide guidelines for action.

Third, principles enable people to pass on information from one generation to the next. Great waste occurs when a generation must relearn what a previous generation had already learned through its experience. To the extent that principles can be developed and applied, this waste can be reduced. The Issue for Debate in this chapter discusses the importance of experience versus that of formal education in moving ahead in management.

Some management principles have been discovered and more will be developed as research and contemplation about management continue. However, management principles cannot be formulated with the same precision as physical-sciences principles. There are exceptions to any rule, and there will always be more exceptions to a principle involving the behavior of people than to a principle involving physics or chemistry.

**The Management Principles of Frederick Taylor**

Frederick Taylor was concerned with scientific management, and he conducted a variety of experiments to find better ways to manage. From his practical experience, Taylor developed four management principles that he felt, in combination, constituted scientific management. These principles are:

- Develop a science for each element of a person's work, which replaces the old rule-of-thumb method.
- Scientifically select and then train, teach, and develop workers. (In the past, employees had chosen their own work and trained themselves as best they could.)
- Heartily cooperate with workers so as to ensure that all work is being done in accordance with the scientific principles that have been developed.
- Divide work and responsibility equally between managers and workers. (In the past, almost all the work and the greater part of the responsibility had been given to the workers.)

**The Management Principles of Henri Fayol**

Fayol was one of the first people to maintain that management can be taught and learned. He developed the following fourteen principles, which constituted his theory of administration. Read them. Do they make good sense?

- *Division of work:* Productivity is increased through specialization of labor.
- *Authority and responsibility:* Responsibility is the corollary of authority. Authority is derived from the status of the position and from the personal qualities of the manager (experience, intelligence, and so on).
- *Discipline:* It is essential for managers to require obedience to organizational rules and directives.

# ISSUE FOR DEBATE

## IS EXPERIENCE MORE IMPORTANT THAN FORMAL EDUCATION FOR GETTING AHEAD IN MANAGEMENT?

The relative importance of experience versus formal education for getting ahead in management is often debated. Most people agree that both are essential to success in management. But is one more important than the other? Below are some pro and con arguments.

### YES

**Experience is more important because . . .**

Experience provides a good working knowledge of practical situations. Education is often so theoretical that it does not carry over to real-life conditions.

Experience allows one to use and constantly reinforce what one is learning. Education alone often does not.

Experience is *applied* learning, whereas formal education deals with *theories* that may or may not have a practical application.

Through experience, managers meet people who may be able to help them get ahead. Professional contacts are more difficult to make in the educational environment.

Experience gives one more confidence than formal education does. When a person knows from experience that he or she can do something and do it well, self-esteem is increased.

### NO

**Formal education is more important because . . .**

Formal education provides the foundation for experience. Without formal education, what one experiences may have little meaning.

Some managerial jobs require certain minimum educational attainments. In such cases formal education is more important than experience. Promotions are sometimes denied to people who do not have a degree or a certificate.

A person with a degree is often perceived by others as being intelligent simply because he or she has a degree. Since considerable persistence is required to earn a degree, other people respect one for attaining it.

Formal education makes for a more well-rounded person. It helps equip a person to deal with individuals who have different backgrounds and experience.

Education is an organized approach to learning, whereas experience is often haphazard. Generally, one can learn more in less time through formal education than through experience.

## QUESTIONS

1. What other factors may be involved in this controversy?
2. What are the advantages of acquiring both experience *and* education?

- *Unity of command:* A subordinate should report to only one superior.
- *Unity of direction:* All closely related activities should be grouped together and headed by one individual.
- *Subordination of personal interests to those of the organization:* The goals of the organization must take precedence over the goals of individuals.
- *Remuneration:* Salaries and other rewards should be fair and should supply incentive for superior performance.
- *Centralization:* Authority should be centralized, and its location should be known to all personnel. However, the degree to which authority should be centralized depends on the situation.
- *Scalar chain:* An organization requires a hierarchy of positions or a chain of command that, under normal conditions, should be followed.
- *Order:* Materials should be arranged in a logical order and people should work in an orderly fashion to prevent waste of physical and human resources.
- *Equity:* Managers should exercise their authority fairly to obtain the loyalty of subordinates to the organization and its goals.
- *Stability of tenure:* Much waste can be avoided by reducing turnover.
- *Initiative:* People at all levels should be encouraged to think of new and better ways to perform activities.
- *Esprit de corps:* High morale results in better teamwork, which in turn leads to greater productivity.[1]

Taylor's and Fayol's work encouraged management scholars and practitioners to develop principles that have universal application. Following, arranged by functional area, are examples of generally accepted management principles.

**Examples of Other Management Principles**

### Planning Principles
*Principle of the primary objective.* "Planning should begin with a clear-cut statement of the primary goal." Without knowledge of an organization's basic *raison d'être* (reason for being), senior managers will not make full use of the organization's human, material, and financial resources.

*Principle of adequate alternatives.* "The greater the number and variety of alternatives presented to solve a problem, the greater the likelihood that the manager will make an acceptable decision." Often, however, managers do not think deeply enough about a problem to discover all logical alternatives to its solution. For example, there may be many alternatives for decreasing costs or increasing revenue.

*Principle of contingencies.* "A plan should have built into it prescribed actions to cover contingencies that may occur." In other words, managers should be prepared for unexpected yet possible events.

---

[1]Adapted from Henri Fayol, *General and Industrial Management*, trans. Constance Storrs (London: Sir Isaac Pitman & Sons, 1949).

### Organizing Principles

*Adequacy-of-authority principle.* "Sufficient authority to accomplish a task should be given to the person who is accountable for the result." People often are given a goal but are not given enough power or authority to achieve it. A supervisor, for example, may be told to increase production but may not be authorized to have employees work overtime.

*Scalar (chain-of-command) principle.* "When the line of authority from the most senior executive flows clearly to each succeeding lower-level position, fixation of responsibility and accountability is easily understood." This principle is often violated, and some people in an organization are confused about their reporting relationships.

### Staffing Principles

*Principle of developing a successor.* "Each manager should train a subordinate to take over his or her job temporarily or permanently." While often violated, this principle is basic to effective management. Often there is no back-up person able to fill a manager's position after he or she resigns, is promoted, becomes ill, or is terminated.

*Principle of manager evaluation.* "Managers are best evaluated in terms of the results they achieve." This principle is easiest to apply when results are quantifiable.

### Directing Principles

*Principle of harmony of objectives.* "A manager's personal goals should be in harmony with the organization's objectives." Obviously, a manager who is determined to perform work not in direct support of an organization's objective violates this principle.

*Principle of the manager's example.* "People are inclined to follow the example set by a manager." Implementation of this principle requires managers to ask, "Am I setting the kind of example I want followed?"

*Principle of motivation.* "Money and other financial benefits are always incomplete as a motivational force. Psychological incentives are always required to develop the highest level of motivation." Personnel want such things as challenging work and compatible workers in addition to financial benefits.

### Controlling Principles

*Principle of standards.* "A standard should be set for all activities." What is acceptable should be defined as clearly and precisely as possible for all tasks.

*Principle of measurement of performance against standards.* "Standards are useless unless actual performance is measured and compared against the standard." Measurement may take many forms, but regardless of the method, an activity should be evaluated.

*Principle of corrective action.* "When measurement of performance indicates a standard is not being met, appropriate corrective action should be taken." Failure to correct what is wrong leads to waste of human and other resources.

- Most people manage at least some of the time. And most career managers also perform nonmanagement functions.
- The knowledge of operative skills required of managers varies with a manager's level, the type of organization, and the size of the organization.
- The higher a person is in the management ladder, the more transferable his or her managerial skills are.
- The five management functions that serve as the framework for this text are:
  1. *Planning:* Deciding what work is to be done and developing a plan to accomplish it.
  2. *Organizing:* Deciding how the work is to be divided and coordinated.
  3. *Staffing:* Ensuring that there are sufficient qualified personnel to carry out the work.
  4. *Directing:* Motivating employees to perform, leading them toward goal achievement, and informing them about their work assignments.
  5. *Controlling:* Setting standards, measuring performance against standards, and taking corrective action as needed.
- Management functions interrelate. Poor performance of one function adversely affects the performance of other functions.
- Managers are evaluated in terms of either quantifiable or qualitative results they achieve. Quantifiable evaluation is in terms of numbers, such as profits or market share. Qualitative evaluation is more judgmental and subjective.
- A principle is a generalization that is widely accepted as true. Frederick Taylor and Henri Fayol were early advocates of the development of management principles.
- Management principles have been developed for each functional area. As more is learned about management more principles will likely be developed.

chief executive officer
process
plan
organize
staff
staffing
directing
motivate

morale
lead
communicate
control
quantifiable results
qualitative results
principle

1. How do managerial and nonmanagerial activities performed by individuals within organizations differ?
2. Why should all work in an organization, including the work of managing, be performed at the lowest level capable of handling it properly?
3. What role do operative skills play in managing? Why are they generally less important as one advances in management?

4. "Management functions interrelate." Explain by showing how the performance of one function affects performance of other functions.
5. Give four examples of ways to evaluate managers quantitatively and four examples of ways to evaluate them qualitatively.
6. Why is the formulation of management principles desirable?
7. What contribution did Henri Fayol make to the development of management principles? Frederick Taylor?

## MAKING MANAGEMENT DECISIONS

### 1. How can the desertion rate be reduced?

You are head of a management consulting firm that recently received a contract from the U.S. Navy to determine ways to reduce the desertion rate. You are informed that in a recent year 3.1 percent of naval enlisted personnel were absent without leave for thirty or more days.

You assemble the key people on your staff to brainstorm the assignment and try to get a handle on the problem. Their viewpoints are given below:

Jake: Well, I'd say the problem involves the planning function more than anything else. I'm guessing that the Navy isn't setting objectives that challenge the personnel, and many of their standing plans—their rules, regulations, and procedures—are probably outdated.

Jan: That may be. But I think we should focus on the organizing function. Maybe the work is so specialized that personnel become bored, or perhaps sea duty assignments are too long.

Beth: I'm sure we'll find that part of the problem is in planning and organizing. But personally I think we should take a hard look at the staffing function first. I think we'll find the Navy is selecting the wrong kind of enlistees.

Henry: I think we should begin our probe by looking at the directing function. The problem is likely to relate to the kind of leadership the personnel are receiving. You know the old saying, "If the leader leads, the troops will follow."

Walter: I think we're going to find that the key to the problem is control or discipline. The desertion rate started going up when standards for personal behavior were relaxed. The Marine Corps has much stricter discipline, and its desertion rate is lower.

Is the high desertion rate likely to be caused by poor performance in only one functional area? Explain.

Why is brainstorming a good approach to put a problem in perspective?

### 2. Is the plant manager spending too much time with the operative employees?

One year ago you—as general manager of the Wickett Company, a manufacturer of fine furniture employing 500 workers—authorized your plant manager Hugh Riley to attend a one-week management seminar. One of the instructors at the seminar stressed "visable management," maintaining that upper-level managers should communicate personally with operative employees and be seen more frequently in work areas. The instructor explained that this is what Japanese managers do.

Riley bought the idea. He returned from the seminar determined to spend at least two hours a day with the operative employees in his plant. Riley began operating machines at times, giving suggestions to employees, and passing the time of day with them.

After observing Riley's behavior for a year, you reach several conclusions. First, employee morale appears to have improved. Second, the attitudes of the first-level supervisors in the plant have deteriorated because operative employees have increasingly come to regard Riley, not their supervisor, as their boss and have gone to Riley with questions and problems. Third, because of time pressure, Riley is neglecting certain of his managerial duties and making more mistakes.

You, as a traditionalist in your approach to managing, believe that all work should be performed at the lowest competent level. You also are committed to the scalar, or chain-of-command, principle. You feel that operative employees should take their problems directly to their supervisors rather than to Riley (see the discussion of the exception principle in Chapter 1).

As general manager, what actions would you take to (1) maintain the higher morale of the employees and (2) stop the employees from bypassing their immediate supervisors?

In general, should higher-level managers communicate directly with employees several levels below them: Why or why not?

### 3. Should the We Kill Pests Company select managers from inside or outside the company?

We Kill Pests Company is a 40-year-old organization that sells pest extermination services. Since its founding, the company has selected its field managers from its most successful service personnel.

Herb German was made president of the company six months ago. He feels it might be wiser to select new managers from outside the organization. Herb calls Betsy Schlindler, training director; Dwayne Wilson, marketing manager; and Henry Price, personnel director, to his office to discuss his ideas.

German: I think we should reconsider our manager selection process. As of now, we promote into management those service personnel who seem to do the best job. Then we bring them to the home office and try to teach them how to manage. I think a better idea would be to select people from outside the company who have had management experience and then teach them what they need to know about the pest control business.

Schlindler: Are you saying it would be easier to teach the pesticide business to people who already have considerable management skills than to teach management skills to our own people who already know the business?

German: That's about the size of it. As I see it, simply because a person is a good service representative—a good operative if you will—doesn't mean that person can learn how to manage.

Wilson: I can't agree with your view. We are primarily a service company. And it takes years of experience to learn how to acquire new business and keep what we have.

Price: I agree with Wilson but for a different reason. Service managers promoted into management are known quantities. They've been under observation for years. We know their capacities before we select them for management training.

German: But I'm sure you must agree that a good service person won't necessarily be a good manager. The two activities are quite different.

Price: Assuming you go ahead with your plan, where do you expect to find candidates for our management jobs?

Schlindler: I have the same question, but I also want to know what you feel the impact on morale of our service people would be if you selected managers from outside.

German: (laughing softly) Well, I see my idea doesn't have complete acceptance. Let me ask you to think about it for a couple weeks, and we'll discuss it again.

What are the pros and cons of selecting managers from outside the organization?

Do you agree that it is easier to teach a person technical skills than management skills? Why or why not?

Based on the limited information presented above, would you endorse Herb's plan? Why or why not?

**FOR ADDITIONAL
CONCEPTS
AND IDEAS**

Bagozzi, Richard P. "Salespeople and Their Managers: An Exploratory Study of Some Similarities and Differences." *Sloan Management Review*, Winter 1980, pp. 15–26.

Culbert, Samuel A. "The Real World and the Management Classroom." *California Management Review*, Summer 1977, pp. 65–78.

Davis, Herbert J., and Rubin, Harvey W. "Professional Certification in Management." *Atlanta Economic Review*, March–April 1978, pp. 48–51.

Driscoll, James W.; Cowger, Gary L.; and Egan, Robert J. "Private Managers and Public Myths—Public Managers and Private Myths." *Sloan Management Review*, Fall 1979, pp. 53–57.

Ellis, R. Jeffery. "Improving Management Response in Turbulent Times." *Sloan Management Review*, Winter 1982, pp. 3–12.

Ferguson, Charles R., and Dickinson, Roger. "Critical Success Factors for Directors in the Eighties." *Business Horizons,* May–June 1982, pp. 14–18.

Gentry, Dwight L., and Hailey, William A. "CEO: Beginnings and Backgrounds." *Business*, September 1980, pp. 15–19.

Lio, Shu S., "The Effect of the Size of Firms on Managerial Attitudes." *California Management Review,* Winter 1975, pp. 59–64.

Maidique, Modesto A. "Entrepreneurs, Champions, and Technological Innovation." *Sloan Management Review*, Winter 1980, pp. 59–76.

Merchant, Kenneth A. "The Control Function of Management." *Sloan Management Review*, Summer 1982, pp. 43–55.

Miles, Raymond E. *Theories of Management: Implications for Organizational Behavior and Development.* New York: McGraw-Hill, 1975.

Piercy, James E., and Forbes, J. Benjamin. "Industry Differences in Chief Executive Officers." *MSU Business Topics,* Winter 1981, pp. 17–29.

Ritchie, J. R. Brent. "Roles of Research in the Management Process." *MSU Business Topics,* Summer 1976, pp. 13–22.

Vaught, Bobby C., and Hoy, Frank. "Have You Got What It Takes to Run Your Own Business?" *Business,* July 1981, pp. 2–8.

Williams, Edgar C. "Musings on Management." *Business Horizons,* March–April 1982, pp. 2–5.

# 3 THE ENVIRONMENT IN WHICH MANAGEMENT IS PRACTICED

**STUDY THIS CHAPTER SO YOU CAN:**

* Define the term "environment," differentiate between internal and external constraints, and give examples of both kinds of constraints.

* Explain the key contemporary trends that affect management.

* Discuss the main economic responsibilities of managers.

* Differentiate between ethical responsibility and social responsibility, and explain what society expects of managers in these areas.

* Define "codes of ethics," and discuss their advantages and disadvantages.

* Explain how management can adapt to a changing environment.

**Environment** is the aggregate of social, cultural, economic, and physical conditions that influence the life of an individual, organization, or community. No enterprise of any kind can operate in the absence of **environmental constraints**, or restrictions imposed by the organization's surroundings. While managers exercise power, their authority is always limited. Of necessity, all enterprises must adjust to the environment in which they exist.

**49**

# WHAT ARE INTERNAL AND EXTERNAL CONSTRAINTS?

The number of environmental constraints that managers must take into account is large. Some are **internal constraints**, or restrictions that originate from within the organization. Following are some major internal constraints that may affect management.

*Constraints imposed by organizational charters and guidelines.* Many organizations such as government agencies, religious bodies, and corporations have a written document or documents (constitutions, corporate charters, bylaws, and so forth) that spell out what the organization can and cannot do. Managers in organizations are limited by what these documents say. Restrictive documents vary greatly in the way they are written, but their intent is always the same: to define what the organization is, how it is expected to function, and what limits are set on its actions.

*Constraints imposed by limited money and personnel.* No organization, not even the U.S. government, has unlimited capital. Because of insufficient funds, managers may be unable to hire the best-qualified people, purchase the best equipment and land, and so forth. Therefore, the organization will be restricted in what actions it can take. Managers may also be limited by the personnel within the organization, who may not have the necessary skills or knowledge to carry out a planned activity. Managers of an enterprise may reject an idea for expansion in a new area because "We lack the necessary management talent at this time."

*Constraints imposed by organizational policies, procedures, and rules.* These predetermined plans place limits on what an organization can or cannot do. For example, a policy specifying that all sales will be to wholesalers tells managers that sales will not be made to ultimate consumers. A procedure specifying that employees will follow the chain of command upward in seeking redress to a grievance limits an employee's freedom to go straight to the top. And a rule stating that two members of the same family cannot work in the same department prevents such people from doing so.

*Constraints imposed by higher-level managers.* Policies, procedures, and rules such as those noted above are developed by higher-level managers. In addition, higher-level management develops the strategies—the broad-based plans—to achieve organizational objectives and thereby restricts the actions lower-level managers may take. For instance, if the general strategy calls for promoting a product primarily through television, lower-level managers are in effect prohibited from using magazines as the principal medium.

*Constraints imposed by custom.* **Custom** is defined as long-established, continual, reasonable, and constant practice considered as unwritten law and resting for authority on long consent. Customs limit what managers can do. For example, if workers have a long-established custom of taking a four-day weekend every Memorial Day, it is difficult for a new manager to change that custom without damaging employee morale.

**External constraints** are imposed from outside the organization and are generally beyond the control of the organization. Following are some major external constraints that may restrict managers in performing the five management functions.

*Constraints imposed by laws and political considerations.* Legal-political constraints include such things as laws and regulations, taxes, and political stability. Laws regulate nearly every facet of human existence. Laws come about, generally, to prevent or stop the abuse of power. When enough managers in an enterprise perform in a way counter to the best interests of society, some form of legal restraint is developed. In exercising their power over resources, managers increasingly come into conflict with those in society who question this power. Managers of petroleum companies, for instance, have experienced great difficulty in implementing their decisions regarding drilling sites. Managers may want to drill for oil in an offshore location, only to have that desire denied because of possible environmental damage. Business managers face a multitude of laws that limit their various powers. There are laws that regulate working conditions, minimum wages, the safety of workers, the sale of stock, competitive practices, pricing, product safety, business location, fair hiring practices, and so on.

Legal-political constraints have a major effect on decisions regarding the location of business. Managers of multinational companies are particularly concerned with political stability in deciding where to operate subsidiaries. Domestically, such considerations as state tax laws and **right-to-work laws** (laws providing that a person cannot be required to join a union in order to keep a job) are important factors in choosing a location.

With regard to legal-political constraints, managers can make inputs at the local, state, and national levels. Managers may testify, present evidence, or lobby to influence government decisions. In the final analysis, however, an organization usually cannot control what a government body does. For regulated public utilities, for example, rate increases must be approved by a state agency. Being under public pressure not to increase rates, the agency may rule against the utility and thereby compound the utility's problem in getting needed capital.

Businesses that operate in foreign countries have no control over the action of those countries' governments. Such businesses often are required to staff a certain percentage of their work forces with citizens of those nations. Special taxes are often placed on goods produced in foreign countries. Even nationalization of company property may occur.

*Constraints imposed by the public.* The public holds considerable power regarding what an organization can and cannot do. The consuming public, by its purchases, decides what products will succeed in the marketplace. An engineering manager may decide that three-wheel automobiles would be more efficient than four-wheel vehicles. But if too few consumers can be convinced of this, the company managers will act on this constraint imposed by the consuming public and produce the conventional four-wheel vehicle. In other cases, a company's products may be informally or formally boycotted by the public.

*Constraints imposed by competitors' actions.* A competitor, through its actions, places restrictions on what another organization can do. Pricing decisions in many firms often reflect the pricing decisions of a leading competitor. A firm may want to price its product at $10 per unit, but if this price is considerably higher than that of a competitor for a similar product, the firm will probably lower the proposed price and/or increase its advertising. Or a competing firm may hold an important patent and thus restrict other organizations' actions.

*Constraints imposed by labor unions.* Through contracts negotiated with management, labor unions restrict what management may want to do about wages, vacations, retirement plans, working conditions, and employment policies. Although most American employees are not unionized, unions have a very real influence on management practices in companies in which they do exist.

*Constraints imposed by education of potential employees.* Educational constraints—such things as the level of education of the available work force and the availability of workers with appropriate skills—have a direct effect on management. It would be extremely difficult, for example, to operate in a highly technical industry if there were few technically skilled people in the area.

*Constraints imposed by society.* Society ultimately establishes the laws and regulations under which all organizations operate. If a firm ignores social concerns regarding such matters as environmental protection, product safety, and unfair employment practices, society will react by imposing legal restrictions.

In addition, the individual members of society impose restrictions on an organization. Such sociological constraints include such matters as prevailing attitudes toward work, material gain, and change. Managing most enterprises is easier, for example, if employees have a strong work ethic than if they regard work as an unpleasant part of life.

*Constraints imposed by the economy.* Economic constraints include availability of capital, inflation, and similar factors that affect the practice of management. Business organizations are increasingly influenced by government-imposed economic policies. The Federal Reserve System has enormous power over interest rates and the supply of money. All businesses would like to borrow money at very low interest rates. But the price they must pay for the money they require is not in their control. Rather it is determined by a number of complex factors, the most important of which are initiated by the Federal Reserve Board.

## WHAT CONTEMPORARY TRENDS AFFECT MANAGEMENT?

A wise person once observed that change is the only status quo, and change seems to occur more rapidly with each succeeding generation. Certainly, the history of our nation shows that each generation experiences vastly more social, economic, and technological changes than the preceding one. Therefore, the environment in which management is practiced is constantly changing.

While all organizations are affected by change, a specific organization has little, if any, control over it. In coping with the ever-changing environment, management must follow a basic law of nature: "Adapt or die." That is, management must be flexible and adjust to change if the organization is to survive and achieve its goals.

Some of the important trends now in evidence that affect management in all organizations, not just businesses, are discussed in the following sections.

Every facet of organized human activity is regulated to some extent, a fact that complicates managing. The trend is toward more, not less, regulation. Rarely is a law repealed. Instead, the general practice is to pass more new laws and amend the old ones.

**More Government Regulation**

In the late 1970s and early 1980s, numerous government actions were taken to deregulate the transportation, petroleum, and other industries. However, on balance, regulation of business actually increased during this period.

One reason that regulation is increasing is the fact that life is growing more complex. Compare the regulations and ordinances needed in two cities, one with a population of 3,000 and the other with a population of 3 million. The individual in the small city is governed by few laws, but the individual in the large city is expected to adhere to a much greater number of regulations. The larger an enterprise, the greater the number and variety of regulations required to maintain order.

Regulation is also increasing because of society's efforts to ensure individual freedom. Most new regulation is designed to prevent one individual or firm from infringing on the freedom of another. The Federal Trade Commission exists in large part to protect one business from being unfairly taken advantage of by other businesses. It is strange but true that government regulations seem needed to maintain a free society.

Table 3–1 lists management practices of four decades ago that at the time were considered acceptable but that today, because of increased regulation, are not. In all probability today's student will find the environment in which management is practiced vastly different in the decade ahead.

People are increasingly less willing to accept authority. Indications of this trend are found in all of our social institutions. In the 1960s we saw the authority of the federal government to draft young men for military service severely challenged. "Hell no, we won't go" was loudly chanted across the land. The government's decision to create an all-volunteer army resulted in part from this challenge to authority. In more recent times, hundreds of thousands of 18 year olds have refused to register for a possible draft.

**Increasing Challenge to Authority**

The challenge to authority is very evident in the business community. At one time the top manager in an enterprise could be virtually a dictator if he or she so desired. Henry Ford I once ordered his security force to break up a protest meeting of employees in subzero weather by spraying them with water from high-pressure

**TABLE 3—1**

**What Managers Could Do in the 1940s That They Cannot Do in the 1980s**

- Deny employment to people because of race, religion, sex, or national origin.
- Discriminate in pay for no logical reason.
- Provide almost any kind of work environment without concern for worker health and safety.
- Dismiss employees without a good reason.
- Make unreported political contributions to the company's preferred candidate.
- Build machines with no concern for the pollution they may cause.
- Dump sewage and chemicals into rivers without concern for the consequences.
- Garnishee wages easily with almost no red tape.

**QUESTIONS**

1. What are some management practices that are accepted today but may be illegal three decades from now?
2. How do regulations complicate managing?

fire hoses. Imagine what would happen today if an executive used similar tactics to control employees!

Today, authority to discharge employees is being challenged. One observer who has studied legal cases in which employees sued to regain their jobs concludes, "There are intimations of a new economic order wherein the right to keep a job would be accorded protections of law akin to the right to hold property. Executives and managers must come to grips with the emerging due process rights of all employees."[1]

There are several reasons for such growing challenges to authority. First, and most important, is the abuse of power by managers. One management maxim states that if managers abuse their authority, they will meet resistance in enforcing it. When some school officials expelled male students in the 1960s for wearing long hair, they were extending their authority beyond the limits of common sense. As a result, in defiance, long hair became even more popular.

Prison riots are often caused by overzealous prison officials who impose unreasonable discipline and living conditions on inmates. Wildcat strikes and boycotts in business often stem from unreasonable work rules. Note that when a situation gets out of control in any type of organization, management must be held accountable. Management is responsible if people do not accept the authority imposed on them.

A second reason for the challenge to authority is a growing permissiveness in our society. Often, those with authority—parents, supervisors, teachers, and managers—are less inclined to use it. Suppose an instructor tells his or her class that a penalty will be imposed if a student cuts class more than three times. A number of students are absent more than three times but no penalty is levied. Soon other students will take more than three cuts because authority has not been backed with action.

[1]Tony McAdams, "Dismissal: A Decline in Employer Autonomy?" *Business Horizons*, February 1978, p. 72.

Third, there is a growing disillusionment with those in power. When managers become involved in scandals of various kinds, it is more difficult for them to exercise authority. People in organizations watch their leaders closely. They want to see those in power practice what they preach. Many managers set the wrong example and create disillusionment in those people they are managing. Consider the politician who runs for election on a platform of honesty in government and then proceeds to steal from it, the business executive who speaks out against crime and then is convicted of embezzlement, and the father who lectures his son about the evils of drugs but then has a car accident while drunk.

People tend to do as leaders do, not as leaders say. The example managers set is a critical factor in determining the acceptance of their authority.

**Decline in the
Work Ethic**

The puritan concept advanced by John Calvin that work is good, wholesome, and essential for the individual's moral well-being appears to have less appeal now than at any time in the history of our nation. Pioneers accepted the work ethic because it was needed to survive. And past generations of schoolchildren were taught that to be idle was to be bad.

Work is widely viewed as a negative, undesirable activity. Even dictionaries give as synonyms for the word "work" such terms as "labor," "toil," "travail," and "drudgery." No dictionary defines work as fun, pleasure, or joy, although for some of us those terms apply.

One frequent explanation of the decline in the work ethic is the movement toward "welfarism" in its broadest sense. When the puritan ideal of work was in vogue, there were no welfare, unemployment insurance, social security, or similar programs. Economic survival without work is now possible, as millions of people demonstrate. A second reason for the decline in the work ethic is that our advanced technology—automation, mass production, and extreme specialization—has made many jobs so routine that they bore workers, especially people who have been well educated.

The decline in the work ethic makes the job of managing more difficult. Some of the everyday management problems made harder to handle because of the decline in the work ethic include excessive absenteeism, poor workmanship, high turnover of personnel, and accidents.

Managers try to make work more desirable through such devices as **job rotation**, whereby a worker moves from one task to another, and **job enlargement**, whereby the worker performs a greater variety of tasks. (See Chapter 16 for further discussion of these approaches as well as some others.) How to motivate workers to perform effectively has become one of the greatest challenges facing management today.

**The Growth of
Internationalism**

**Internationalism**, the interrelationship among profit-seeking and nonprofit-seeking organizations from different nations, is not new. The Catholic Church, Western civilization's oldest institution, has been a multinational organization embracing many nations, languages, and cultures for centuries. But the trend toward worldwide economic organizations, called **multinationals**, has accelerated in recent decades.

There are several reasons for this trend. First, no nation can enjoy the highest possible standard of living without trading with other nations. Economic self-sufficiency becomes increasingly difficult as a nation develops its economy, since the increasing variety of products demanded cannot all be fully supplied domestically. Elementary societies may survive without a sophisticated import-export system; advanced societies cannot.

Second, internationalism results from improved communications. Through communication and travel, ideas and concepts tend to become worldwide. Third, improvement in political compatibility between Communist and non-Communist nations promotes internationalism. There is more trade and idea exchange between Communist and non-Communist nations than before.

The trend toward internationalism complicates managing, especially at senior levels. A senior manager involved in exporting must be aware of laws, politics, and customs in each of the countries sold to. Also, international trade is a two-way street. Many managers must be concerned with foreign companies that compete in our domestic markets. This is especially true for such products as automobiles, steel, and electronic goods.

## More Technological Change

While managers do not manage machines—they only manage people—technological change nevertheless has a profound effect on the management process. Managers in technological industries are concerned with developing and marketing new machines and devices. Managers in nontechnological businesses are concerned with putting the new technology to use. In doing so they must make decisions that affect people, either directly or indirectly.

To illustrate, Cliff Olt operates a medical laboratory that specializes in making blood tests and supplying the test results to physicians. Nineteen people are employed. A manufacturer of blood testing equipment demonstrates a new machine to Olt that would permit Olt Laboratories to handle the same volume of blood but with five fewer people. The machine costs $300,000.

Should Olt buy the machine? In making this decision, Olt will probably give consideration to a host of questions such as "Could we better use the money for some other purposes?" "Is it right for me to dismiss five employees?" "Would I be better off postponing the decision until the machine has been put to use by other laboratories and all the bugs have been worked out?"

In contemporary business the question "How much are we willing to invest in technology to replace a worker?" cannot be avoided.

## Slower Population Growth

Although in recent years the American population had more women of childbearing age than ever before, births in absolute numbers as well as the birthrate itself are trending down. This decline in the birthrate, with no significant change in the death rate, is changing the composition of our population. A smaller percentage of the population is in younger age groups, and a rising share of the population is in older age groups.

In 1978 the mandatory retirement age was lifted from 65 to 70. This action may greatly affect managing, since more older people are likely to be in the work force.

If the old adage "People vote their pocketbooks" is true, we can expect that as older people constitute a larger share of the total electorate, they will vote for more old-age assistance programs. It appears virtually certain that people aged twenty to thirty-five will bear a larger share of the economic burden in the future than people in that age bracket bear now.

The word **mores** refers to the fixed customs or folkways of a particular group. Mores change as time goes by. Things that were "wrong" a decade ago are becoming "right" today—or at least are being questioned. Consider the changes that have come about in public attitudes toward divorce, abortion, pornography, and the way people dress. Attitudes toward work, discipline, spending habits, law and order, religion, sexual relations, and work roles of women and men are undergoing modification. Changes in social mores affect management in many ways. Over time, work rules may have to be changed to reflect new mores.

# ECONOMIC, ETHICAL, AND SOCIAL RESPONSIBILITIES OF MANAGERS

Many people argue that the primary responsibilities of business managers are economic in nature. Their reasoning holds that the principal purpose of business is business. Society is dependent on economic activity, for without it the material side of life as we know it could not exist. Therefore, as a frame of reference, we should take note of the economic responsibilities of business managers before analyzing what their social responsibilities are and trying to resolve conflicts between the two. Three major economic responsibilities can be cited: to provide products and services, to provide employment, and to earn profits.

### To Provide Products and Services

The first economic responsibility of business is to make and distribute the products and services we, the people, want. In communist and to a considerable extent in socialist societies the work of production and distribution is conducted by governmentally supervised and controlled organizations. But in a free society private managers, not public officials, direct most of the economic activity.

People in American society have great freedom to choose what they want. We build automobiles, make electricity, manufacture chemicals, and produce countless other products because people need and want them. It is an economic responsibility of business both to discover consumer needs and wants and to do what is necessary to satisfy them.

### To Provide Employment

A second economic responsibility of business is to provide employment for people who need and want to work. If the institution of business did not provide employment, it would become a responsibility of government to do so. This in turn would require a much different social, political, and economic order. In American society, private enterprise provides approximately 85 percent of all jobs. Most of the remainder are provided by government agencies—local, state, and federal, in that order.

Clearly, the level of employment is important to the nation's economic well-being. Economists tend to agree that the maximum percentage of the work force that can be employed at any given time is 96 percent. When 96 percent of the work force is employed, we have what is called **full employment**. When only 93 or 94 percent of the people ready and able to work are employed, we experience what is called an **economic recession**. When 90 percent or less of the work force is employed, we are in an **economic depression**.

Society also expects business to make jobs interesting and challenging because jobs are important to an individual's psychological well-being. Employment that is demeaning or unrewarding in a psychological sense is undesirable. The average person has a life expectancy of about seventy-three years, or approximately 640,000 hours. A person who works 2,000 hours per year for fifty years will have worked for 100,000 hours, or about 16 percent of all waking and nonwaking moments on this earth. Time spent at work is obviously one of the central aspects of life.

### To Earn Profits

A third economic responsibility of business is to earn profits. As long as our society is committed to a capitalistic economic system, businesses *must* make profits for several reasons.

*To pay taxes.*   Businesses must earn profits to enable them to pay income and other taxes upon which other social institutions depend. In recent years, businesses have paid approximately 40 percent of federal taxes and a significant percentage of state and local taxes as well. Revenues so collected are used to help finance the extensive government programs required by society in such areas as defense, human resources, urban renewal, mass transit, and many more. If business profits were nonexistent, funding of government activities would be impossible unless, of course, society designed a different method of taxation.

Furthermore, because business provides most of the employment in society, most of the taxes paid by individuals come from income earned by working for businesses.

*To finance modernization and expansion.*   Aside from earning profits, businesses can obtain capital to modernize or expand in only two ways—through sale of capital stock or through borrowing. However, if a business does not earn a profit and shows little promise of doing so, capital stock is virtually impossible to sell. Creditors also are reluctant to lend money if profits seem unlikely to be earned. In this situation they would fear that the business would not be able to repay money advanced through loans.

Since businesses need profits in order to modernize and expand, it follows that profits are essential to create wealth. Most of the national wealth is created by businesses through economic development of privately owned resources.

*To fund research and development.*   Most of the technological research in our economy is conducted by business. A business needs profits in order to improve the quality of existing products and to invent and design new ones. It may also need profits to fund research in the fields of energy development, transportation, pollution control, and safety.

Business is sometimes criticized for engaging in the practice of **planned obsolescence**, which is the intentional changing of products so that customers will buy newer models. While there is some truth to this charge, it should be noted that business in the past has done a good job of creating new products and advancing technology. The computer, aircraft, and machine tool industries provide good examples.

Contemporary America more or less takes it for granted that business managers will meet their economic responsibilities. Today more people are concerned with the question "Is business meeting its ethical and social responsibilities?"

**Ethical
Responsibilities**

**Ethics** is the discipline that deals with what is "good" and "bad" or "right" and "wrong." Through custom the word "ethical" has come to mean "being in accord with approved standards of behavior."

Ethics has been given serious study by history's greatest philosophers. Despite the great amount of attention given to the matter of ethics, however, there is still no universal consensus as to what constitutes right and wrong. Bribery of public officials is considered highly unethical in the United States, but in some foreign countries it is a way of life and is not viewed as unethical. Each society has its own view of what constitutes a good or bad character, of what the objectives and practices of its social institutions should be, and of what things or experiences are worthwhile and desirable.

Further, ethical standards change with time. What is "right" does not always stay "right" nor does what is "wrong" stay "wrong" in the minds of people over a period of time. For example, today a much larger percentage of the American people feel it is wrong for a manufacturer to market a product that may be harmful than was the case decades ago.

Ethical standards change over time; they also change with the situation. What a person will do under one set of circumstances is not always the same as what he or she would do under another set of circumstances. An individual might consider it unethical to take advantage of poor people but think it is fine to take advantage of rich people. An employee may feel it is an acceptable practice to use the company postage meter and the WATS line for personal business but would not consider embezzling cash from the employer.

There are numerous types of organizations in society, and each tends to have its own ethical guidelines. Again, what is morally right in one situation may be morally wrong in another. For example, deception is considered unethical in many contexts. A business firm that deceives employees with regard to any aspect of their relationship to the firm (wages, hours, working conditions, chances for promotion, and so on) is considered to be acting unethically. However, there is less agreement that a firm is acting unethically when it unveils an advertising campaign designed to embarrass a competitor. And deception is one of the most admired characteristics in many sports. In football we enjoy watching the successfully executed fake handoff. In the military, the ability to deceive an enemy into making a mistake is considered highly commendable. In politics many people consider it ethical for one politician to deceive another into making an embarrassing statement in a television debate.

Stealing is generally considered to be unethical, yet there are many people who feel it was ethical to steal the Pentagon Papers and give them to the press. Stealing military secrets from a potential enemy is another practice considered both essential and ethical by many. As a former director of the CIA put it, "I think that moralists over the years have accepted some degree of clandestine work as part of the normal relationship between [nations]. In any case, is spying any less moral than developing great weapons systems, or many of the other things that nations do in their self-interest?"[2]

In some cases it is difficult for managers to function ethically because there is no universal agreement as to what "ethical" means. Even the prohibitions against lying and stealing are relaxed in some cases. While we generally feel it is desirable to tell the truth, there are situations in which it is ethical not to answer a question that has been posed. Under our system of law, attorneys are not required to reveal what clients have told them. Other conversations, as between an individual and a physician or a priest, may also be privileged. In court, one spouse cannot be forced to tell the truth about the behavior of the other.

Managers in all fields should know and understand business ethics. Aside from the question of personal morality, it should be remembered that managers are expected to set the ethical example for nonmanagers in each institution. People look to management for guidance and tend to assume that if managers do something it is ethically all right for others to do it also. The manager who advocates cheating customers is likely to inspire the same pattern of behavior in his or her personnel. Considered collectively, managers of all institutions set the ethical tone for the society.

### Codes of Ethics

**Codes of ethics,** or standards of acceptable practice, have been developed by the dental, medical, accounting, legal, and other professions. They also have been created by numerous trade associations in an attempt to encourage more responsible behavior by members. Few individual companies, however, have committed their ethical standards to writing.

*Advantages of codes of ethics.* A key advantage of a code of ethics lies in its development. For example, in creating a code for a trade association, members of an industry are in a sense forced to ask themselves "What things are we doing that are not right in the treatment of customers, suppliers, and our other 'publics' and how can we correct them?" A company developing its own code also benefits from such "soul-searching."

A second advantage of a code of ethics is that the various publics may place more confidence in enterprises that have adopted a formal ethical standard. More confidence in turn should translate into such things as more patronage and better cooperation.

Third, a carefully proposed and enforced code of ethics may be a deterrent to

[2]Interview with William E. Colby, *U.S. News & World Report*, December 1974, p. 29.

increased government regulation. Proponents of codes of ethics believe that self-regulation is preferable to control by government bureaucracies.

*Disadvantages of codes of ethics.* Few people are opposed to the idea of an ethical code, but many believe such codes have limited value in practice. Codes have been criticized as being difficult to enforce, arbitrary, excessively lofty, self-serving, and overly generalized.

**Social responsibility** is the responsibility of an organization to promote, or at least not damage, the overall welfare of the society. One observer has defined a socially irresponsible act as a "decision to accept an alternative that is thought by the decision maker to be inferior to another alternative when the effects upon all parties are considered. Generally, this involves a gain by one party at the expense of the total system."[3]

Business is often criticized for being socially irresponsible. However, it should be pointed out that other institutions also have social responsibilities that may or may not be fulfilled. The family has the responsibility to instill in a child respect for law and the rights of others. Some of the government's responsibilities are to maintain the maximum degree of freedom for the citizenry, provide equality of opportunity for all, and assist individuals in improving their living standards, both quantitatively and qualitatively.

Educational institutions seek to provide the best possible education for the people and to advance the sum of human knowledge through research in all fields of study. Organized religions set as their main objective the moral and spiritual development of people, with secondary objectives being education and charitable assistance. Labor unions have a responsibility to conduct their operations in the best long-run interests not only of their members but of society as a whole. The mass media have responsibility to inform and entertain the public in a constructive, or at least not destructive, way.

### Disagreement about Social Responsibilities of Business

Not all authorities are convinced that business has responsibilities above obeying laws and meeting its economic responsibilities. Economist Milton Friedman, for example, was asked what responsibilities he felt businesses had above and beyond maximizing profits for their shareholders. Friedman replied:

> The only entities who can have responsibilities are individuals; a business cannot have responsibilities. So the question is, do corporate executives, provided they stay within the law, have responsibilities in their business activities other than to make as much money for their stockholders as possible? My answer to that is, no, they do not. Take the corporate executive who says "I have responsibilities over and above that of making profits." If he feels he has such responsibilities, he is going to spend money in a way that is not in the interest of the shareholders. Where does he get that money? Perhaps from the company's employees. If he can pay his employees lower wages than otherwise, he'll have some extra money to spend. It may have to come from the

[3] J. Scott Armstrong, "Social Irresponsibility in Management," *Journal of Business Research,* 5 (1977), p. 185.

company's customers, if he can charge them more than they would otherwise pay. Or it may come from the company's stockholders. The crucial question is: What right does the executive have to spend his stockholders' money? Who gave him the right to decide how their money should be spent? If "socially responsive" business executives would stop and think, they would recognize that in effect they are acting irresponsibly.[4]

Our legal system traditionally has agreed with the view that corporations have a primary obligation to their shareholders. As one observer has expressed it, "The law books have always said that the board of directors owes a single-minded duty of unswerving loyalty to the stockholders, and only to the stockholders."[5]

Many people do feel managers should be responsible only to shareholders. They believe that concern for customers, suppliers, competitors, and the general public should be expressed only to the extent that their interests and behavior affect the profit-making potential of the corporation. Under this view managers should be concerned with pollution, for example, only when concerned citizens might boycott the company's products or in some other way adversely affect the profitability of the firm.

Professor Robert A. Dahl takes as strong a position as Professor Friedman but in an opposite direction:

> Today, it is absurd to regard the corporation simply as an enterprise established for the sole purpose of allowing profit-making. We, the citizens, give them special rights, powers and privileges, protection and benefits on the understanding that their activities will fulfill our purposes. Corporations exist because we allow them to do so. And we allow them to exist only as they continue to benefit us. . . . Every corporation should be thought of as a social enterprise whose existence and decisions can be justified only insofar as they serve public or social purposes.[6]

Despite the vigorous debate, the general consensus is that business now has great social responsibilities and in the future will be expected to do even more for society. As one authority sees it:

> Whatever the constraints may be, the tidal movement in our society is strongly toward a new social contract for business. The critical issues are not found in the debate about philosophy and concept. Rather, they appear in the practical management considerations of what to do and how to do it. How can a management group that is sensitive to the changing business environment decide what socially responsible policies and programs are feasible for [its] corporation to adopt? And, whatever policies and programs may be adopted, how can managers assure their effective and efficient implementation?[7]

Some more points of view about the relationship between the profit motive and the social good are discussed in the Issue for Debate in this chapter.

---

[4]Quoted in Robert A. Dahl, "A Prelude to Corporate Reform," *Business and Society Review*, Spring 1972, pp. 17–18.
[5]Eugene V. Rostow, "To Whom and for What Ends Are Corporate Managers Responsible?" in *The Corporation in Modern Society*, ed., Edward S. Mason (Cambridge, Mass.: Harvard University Press, 1959), p. 62.
[6]Dahl, "A Prelude to Corporate Reform," pp. 17–18.
[7]Melvin Anshen, ed., *Managing the Socially Responsible Corporation* (New York: Macmillan, 1974), pp. 8–9.

# ISSUE FOR DEBATE

## DOES THE INTENSE DESIRE FOR PROFIT WORK AGAINST THE PUBLIC'S WELFARE?

Some people believe that profit orientation is too strong and results in social harm. Others do not agree. Below are pros and cons about this proposition.

### YES

**The profit motive does work against the public's welfare because . . .**

Some managers are under so much pressure to earn profits that they perform illegal acts such as authorizing espionage to steal a competitor's secrets.

The pressure to earn profits causes some companies to engage in false advertising and other forms of deceptive selling.

Low-quality products can be traced to the profit motive. Manufacturers produce the quality that is most profitable, not necessarily the most desirable.

The push for profits results in waste of important natural resources. For example, in some industries there are many companies producing highly similar products. Fewer companies would mean more efficient use of resources.

### NO

**The profit motive does not work against the public's welfare because . . .**

The profit goal in a competitive economy promotes efficiency. Businesses that cannot compete effectively are forced out. This results in the survival of the fittest.

Profits earned by businesses are directly or indirectly channeled back into the economy. More, not less, emphasis should be placed on profits.

The desire for profit causes businesses to innovate, to develop new products and services. Thus all of society benefits.

Profits are an important source of taxes. By earning profits, businesses pay taxes needed to fund a wide variety of social programs.

### QUESTIONS

1. What other arguments, pro and con, can you offer?
2. In your opinion, is too much emphasis placed on profit?

### The Demand for Public Accountability

Increasingly, in all types of institutions, people are demanding more information from managers above them in the hierarchy. Trade association members are more inclined to ask their association executives, "Exactly what are you doing with the dues we pay?" Rank-and-file union members, too, are more vocal than ever before in demanding that their leaders report in detail their expenditures as well as the rationale for union activities.

The demand for public accountability affects the institution of business most. Corporate annual meetings formerly were dull affairs with only a small percentage of shareholders attending, and shareholders rarely challenged anything management reported. Now it is different. Questions such as "Why did our company do this or that?" and "How do you justify your pay, Mr. President?" are not uncommon. In response to the demand for accountability, some of our largest companies now include in their annual reports a section dealing with "human resource accounting." This section outlines what the company has done for the social good in the past year.

In addition, the general public is increasingly inclined to speak out on such issues as rate increases by public utilities; zoning of land for business, housing, and industrial uses; pollution of the environment; and product safety. People are saying ever more loudly, "Prove your position," "Explain what you are doing," and "Give us the unadulterated truth." In responding to the public, senior corporate executives now spend much time appearing before various government and citizen committees, giving interviews to the media, and making themselves generally more accessible to explain their purposes and actions.

### The Main Social Responsibilities of Business

The following are generally considered to be especially important social responsibilities of business organizations.

*To improve the safety of products and the work environment.*   Increasingly, society is calling upon business to make products safer. Business is expected to remove from the marketplace products that are defective or potentially harmful. Despite the many laws relating to product safety, the public wants business to make even more determined efforts to protect people from injury.

Many people also ask that business take greater precautions to protect workers. The Occupational Safety and Health Act (OSHA) of 1970 was intended to make the work environment safe. But some feel businesses should do even more, and on a voluntary basis, to protect workers.

On the other hand, some business leaders feel the government is making excessive regulatory demands. The chairman of the board of Procter & Gamble made this comment:

> The real problem is that excessive regulation drains away the human energy and talent that should be engaged in creative efforts. For example, today over one-fourth of P&G's research and development and product development effort is being devoted to coping with the present and anticipated environmental and human safety concerns of regulators. This is at least twice as much effort as we believe is necessary. We can stand this so long as we can increase the prices of our products to cover the cost. This is what we have had to do. There is no doubt today that consumers pay a material

price for excessive and redundant regulations every time they buy a box of detergent, a roll of paper or a tube of toothpaste. Here, therefore, is another of the important causes of inflation.[8]

*To protect and improve the physical environment.*    Our society is becoming increasingly conscious of the environment. The prevailing view is that business should do more than is required by law to eliminate water, air, solid-waste, and noise pollution. It is argued that everyone is affected by the environment and that no business or individual has the right to damage what belongs to everyone.

A term used frequently in discussions of the environment is **ecology**, the branch of science concerned with the interrelationships of organisms and their environment. Frequently cited examples of environmental abuses are failure to restore timberland that has been harvested, pouring waste chemicals into rivers and streams, reckless strip mining, and oil spills. There was little concern for the physical environment until the early 1960s. Since then, interest in environmental protection has accelerated rapidly.

The demand for a pollution-free environment has caused numerous problems for managers. Decisions about where to locate new manufacturing facilities and where and how to drill for oil can be made only after demonstrating that the environment will not be harmed. In the automotive industry, managers have been required to develop pollution-control devices for new automobiles. Industries that pour sewage and chemicals into rivers and streams are under close surveillance to make sure that steps are taken to prevent pollution. Technical and engineering people are working to develop technological innovations to bring about improvement. Pollution control, regardless of the form it takes, costs money, and management has had to develop financing plans to meet the costs involved. These costs are eventually passed on to consumers.

*To provide equal opportunities for women and minority-group members.*    An important trend affecting management is the demand for equality in employment, including opportunities to participate in management by women and minority-group members. Women accounted for approximately 47 percent of the total work force in 1982.[9] Yet only a small percentage of managerial jobs were filled by women, and most of these were at relatively low levels in the organization.

Minorities, too, are grossly underrepresented in management. They accounted for 13 percent of the work force in 1982 but of those employed only about 5 percent held managerial jobs.[10] And, as is the case with women, most members of minority groups who manage are at the lower organizational levels.

In coming years, however, we should see increasing numbers of women and minority-group members move into managerial positions. Enrollment of women and minorities in institutions of higher education and in various management-training programs has increased dramatically.

The trend toward greater equality was accelerated by the passage of the Civil

[8]Edward G. Harness, "Views on Corporate Responsibility," A talk by the chairman of the board of Procter & Gamble to its management, December 8, 1977; Procter & Gamble Company, Cincinnati, Ohio 45201.
[9]*Statistical Abstract of the United States, 1982.*
[10]Ibid.

Rights Act in 1964. Four major groups are affected by the act: employers, public and private employment agencies, labor organizations, and joint labor-management apprenticeship programs. The act states specifically:

> It shall be an unlawful employment practice for an employer
> 1. to fail or refuse to hire or to discharge any individual or otherwise discriminate against any individual with respect to his compensation, terms, conditions, or privileges of employment, because of such individual's race, color, religion, sex or national origin; or
> 2. to limit, segregate or classify his employees in any way which would deprive or tend to deprive any individual of employment opportunities or otherwise adversely affect his status as an employee, because of such individual's race, color, religion, sex or national origin.

*To obey the spirit and the letter of laws.* Increasingly, critics of business are demanding that companies obey both the spirit and the letter of the law. Currently there are many laws that companies simply do not follow. While corporations and corporate executives are sometimes cited for violation of various laws, executives are rarely imprisoned or personally fined for violations. In many cases the company will do better financially to ignore the law and then simply pay the fine. Sometimes there will not even be a fine; the conflict may be resolved through some form of voluntary agreement.

At other times businesses obey the letter of the law but do not obey its spirit. Corporations, able to employ the best legal counsel, often find a way to get around the law. Rather than doing what is morally right, a business, after the legal maneuvering is over, may end up doing only what is legally or technically right. For example, a company may succeed, through careful legal process, in avoiding most of the claims an injured worker asks for and rightfully should receive.

*To make full and truthful disclosure about products.* Society calls on business to make full and total disclosure about what it sells. In promoting products, business has traditionally "accentuated the positive and eliminated the negative." Today there is a strong social demand that business inform the public of the negative as well as the positive qualities of its products. Critics feel that makers of all products should do voluntarily what cigarette manufacturers are required to do by law: explain any dangers associated with the use of the product.

*To provide public-service programs.* Businesses often provide a wide variety of public- or community-service programs. For example, a company may recycle waste products; sponsor athletic teams for schools, little leagues, or underprivileged children; and contribute to the United Appeal or other area-wide benefit programs.

Those who favor public-service programs sponsored by business point out that such programs not only advance the social good but indirectly contribute, over the long run, to the advancement of business. Paying the tuition of employees to attend college supposedly improves their capabilities and makes them more valuable to the company. It can be argued that providing a public park may reduce tensions in the community, with the net result that employees are more effective at work. It is also argued that service to the community is good public relations and makes it easier to recruit personnel, sell the company's products, and attain other organizational objectives.

# MANAGERS IN ACTION

## HOW CONTROL DATA CORPORATION TRIES TO BENEFIT SOCIETY WITHOUT PROMISE OF IMMEDIATE FINANCIAL GAIN

The previous sections pointed out that there are disagreements about the social responsibilities of business.

Mr. William C. Norris, founder and chairman of Control Data Corporation, a giant computer company (sales in 1981 were 4.2 billion dollars), feels "Corporations, not government, increasingly will take the lead in finding new ways to solve unemployment, rehabilitate criminals, redevelop inner cities and improve schools."[1]

Examples of socially related projects Mr. Norris has championed include:

- A program to help ex-cons finance cars. (This failed when the program director, also an ex-con, stole much of the money.)
- An organization called Rural Ventures Inc. to help make small family farms more efficient.

[1]Lawrence Ingrassia, "Seeking to Aid Society, Control Data Takes On Many Novel Ventures," *The Wall Street Journal*, December 22, 1982, p. 1. Reprinted by permission of *The Wall Street Journal,* © Dow Jones & Company, Inc., 1982. All Rights Reserved.

- City Venture Corp. established to help create inner-city jobs.

Mr. Norris believes corporations, not government, should operate schools and prisons because executives are better managers than government bureaucrats. Privately managed schools and prisons would save the taxpayer money and do a better job of educating and rehabilitating people.

Critics claim that Mr. Norris has overextended Control Data in the area of social responsibility. A former vice-president of the company said, "The best thing they [Control Data] can do to be socially responsible is to make better products to increase demand so they can hire more people."[2]

But Mr. Norris is undaunted by his critics. He would prefer to be known as a business executive who helped solve the nation's social problems rather than as a person who founded a huge computer company.

[2]Ibid, p. 10.

### QUESTIONS

1. Historically, Control Data Corp. makes one of the smallest profit margins in the computer industry. One stock market analyst said the company would make more profit if it concentrated its energies on computers and didn't get involved in trying to solve social problems.

   Do you feel Control Data is right or wrong in trying to solve social problems? Why?
2. Do you feel letting private enterprise operate our prisons is a good idea? Why or why not?

## HOW MANAGEMENT CAN ADAPT TO A CHANGING ENVIRONMENT

While there are many elements in the environment that cannot be controlled, management must still prepare for change and for uncontrollable events. Specifically, managers should maintain flexibility, develop contingency plans, and use research and management information systems.

**Flexibility** in management is the ready capability for modification or change. It is the ability to adapt to new situations and new conditions. In 1974, inspired by the energy crisis, U.S. auto makers demonstrated considerable flexibility—especially for large organizations—in being able to change their product mix from heavy emphasis on big and medium-sized cars to emphasis on smaller models. To do this required the development and the execution of new production and marketing plans. These were accomplished with reasonable success and in record time considering the complexities involved.

Alert management keeps up with those changes in the environment that will affect the organization. Flexibility can be tested in a variety of ways. Suppose a competitor designs an advertising program that seriously cuts into another firm's sales. Can the affected firm adapt and counterattack quickly with a modified campaign of its own? Or suppose a key executive dies unexpectedly. Is the organization able to carry on despite the loss of the manager's intelligence and guidance? In both of these situations, organizations that have managers with an orientation toward flexibility will have the best chance of survival.

In management a **contingency** is an event that occurs without intent and that is considered possible but not probable. Accidents at work, a fire that destroys critical supplies, an illness of a key employee, an economic recession, and a loss of a key customer's business are examples of contingencies that a business organization may face.

Part of the planning function in a well-managed enterprise is to formulate contingency plans "just in case." One of the principles of sound management, originally developed in the military, is that each manager should have a back-up manager trained to do the job if for any reason the manager now in charge cannot perform. This concept, when implemented, is a contingency plan.

The airline that has standby crews available to fly if the regular crew is detained at another airport has a contingency plan. Other examples of simple contingency plans are storing repair parts so that if a machine breaks down it can be repaired quickly; keeping an adequate amount of capital in reserve to meet unexpected demands for it; maintaining reserve raw materials to cushion the effect of a problem in the supplier's organization; and having a special back-up electrical system (as in a hospital) in case there is a blackout.

A third way for management to prepare for change is through research and management information systems. Inherent in the scientific approach to management is the acquisition and use of knowledge. Much research can be generated internally. Examples are day-to-day sales data for different departments and product lines, statistics on abseenteeism, and production and quality-control reports. Such data can help management make decisions and devise new plans.

External sources of information are many and varied. Managers can read newsletters and professional journals, which often discuss the likelihood of certain events taking place and describe new problems that are beginning to develop. Trade associations, which are composed of people in the same profession or business, typically provide useful information about what is happening in the profession or industry. Numerous consulting firms exist to give advice and counsel on how to meet changing conditions.

**SUMMARY**

- No enterprise of any kind can function in the absence of environmental constraints, or restrictions. Constraints are imposed internally (by custom; organizational characters and guidelines; limited money and personnel; organizational policies, procedures, and rules; and higher-level management) and externally (by laws and political considerations, the public, competitors' actions, labor unions, education, society, and the economy).
- The environment in which management is practiced changes constantly. Some major contemporary trends that affect management are more government regulation, an increasing challenge to authority, a decline in the work ethic, the growth of internationalism, more technological change, slower population growth, and the liberalization of social mores.
- Business managers have three important economic responsibilities: to provide products and services, to provide employment, and to earn profits.
- Society is increasingly expecting managers to perform ethically, that is, to refrain from bad conduct.
- The demand for public accountability for the actions managers take is growing. People are expecting management to be more open in disclosing information.
- Society is also demanding more socially responsible behavior to promote the overall welfare of society. While people disagree over what constitutes socially responsible behavior, many believe managers should do more to improve the safety of products and the work environment, to protect and improve the physical environment, to provide equal opportunities, to obey the spirit and the letter of laws, to make full and truthful disclosure about products, and to provide more public-service programs.
- Since change is inevitable, managers must adapt to it by maintaining flexibility, developing contingency plans, and using research and management information systems.

**LEARN THE LANGUAGE OF MANAGEMENT**

environment
environmental constraints
internal constraints
custom
external constraints
right-to-work laws
job rotation
job enlargement
internationalism
multinationals
mores

full employment
economic recession
economic depression
planned obsolescence
ethics
codes of ethics
social responsibility
ecology
flexibility
contingency

**QUESTIONS FOR REVIEW AND DISCUSSION**

1. "No enterprise can function in the absence of environmental constraints." Give examples of constraints that may be imposed on each of the following: a hospital administrator, the head of a government agency, and a high-school principal.
2. Do recent signs of taxpayer rebellions suggest that the trend toward more government regulation may be reversed? Why or why not?

3. Three factors were discussed in the chapter to explain the challenge to authority. What others can you suggest to explain this trend?
4. The past two decades have seen a dramatic trend toward liberalized social mores. Is this trend likely to continue? Explain.
5. "Ethical standards change with time." What changes in ethical standards do you believe are now undergoing modification?
6. Do you believe that business executives in multinational companies should be given the right to follow the ethical practices in the host countries even though those practices are considered unethical in the United States? Why or why not?
7. What are the pros and cons of codes of ethics?
8. Business is by far the most severely criticized institution in society. What are the main reasons for this? What criticisms could be directed toward other social institutions?
9. The views of Milton Friedman and Robert Dahl toward social responsibilities differ greatly. Which view more nearly parallels your own? Why?
10. Would you favor legislation requiring producers of *all* consumer products to describe possible harm from using them? For example, would you like to see makers of alcoholic beverages describe what can happen from overindulgence? Why or why not?

## MAKING MANAGEMENT DECISIONS

### 1. What can be done if employees refuse to work with an ex-convict?

At the request of the State Board of Pardon and Parole, the personnel director of the Deft Company decides to employ J. W., an individual who was convicted ten years ago for rape and murder. The Board of Pardon and Parole is convinced that J. W. has been rehabilitated and is an excellent risk. When the employees in the department to which J. W. is assigned learn that they must work with an ex-convict, they walk off the job. The leader of the group says, "We won't work with a guy who has been convicted of rape and murder. It's not safe. And the company is required by law to provide a safe working environment. Force us to work with him and we'll sue the company."

What would you do in this situation if you were the manager in charge?

### 2. A sundry drug product is linked to six deaths. What should its maker, Health Aids Inc., do?

Health Aids Inc. manufactures and markets a variety of sundry drug items, such as aspirin, cold remedies, pain relievers, and eye drops. The company brand names are well respected by consumers.

Last week six people who consumed a cold remedy manufactured by Health Aids died. All of these people had suffered from a new flu virus and all had the same chronic kidney disease.

The Center for Disease Control has begun an investigation to determine whether the Health Aids product was a contributing factor in the deaths of the six people.

Late Saturday afternoon Tim, president of Health Aids, calls an emergency meeting of his key personnel. Present are Cline, senior staff lawyer; Madge, chief of quality control; Issac, marketing vice-president; and Karen, director of corporation communication. The following discussion takes place.

Tim: You've all heard what's happened. Six people who took our cold remedy died. These people lived in California, Arizona, and Nevada. All of them suffered from a new kind of flu virus and all had the same chronic kidney disease. The Center for Disease Control has no specific cure. Madge, was something wrong with that batch of cold remedy?

Madge: No. It met exactly the same standards established for the product four years ago when we first started marketing it. Government inspectors have already verified that fact. Now, I can't say whether our product contributed to those deaths, but I can say it's exactly the same product we've been selling for years without any problems.

What may be happening is that this new flu virus in combination with our product creates an unforeseen reaction in people with kidney disease. But there's no way of knowing until we've run a lot of tests.

Tim: I know. And that will take months. Meanwhile, we face some real problems. So far, the deaths have been confined to California, Nevada, and Arizona—the states where this new flu virus first appeared.

Now, as I see it, somehow we've got to stop any more linkage with our cold remedy and the spread of this flu.

Issac: As a first step, I suggest we recall all of the cold remedy from our distribution centers and all retail stores.

Tim: Isn't that a bit drastic? The Center for Disease Control hasn't yet proved any connection between our product and the deaths. Aren't you overreacting?

Issac: I don't think so. If there is a connection—and it seems to me there is—sales of all our products will plummet.

Cline: Not only that, we'll be flooded with lawsuits. I fully expect that the families of the six victims will bring suits against us. If there are more deaths, we can expect more legal problems.

Karen: I agree with Issac. Get all the products off the shelves immediately. And I feel we should kill all TV and radio commercials and the print promotion as fast as we can.

Tim: Well, I think we have to assume you people are right. We stand to lose hundreds of millions if we don't handle this right. But even if we recall the product immediately, how are we going to handle the press? The news about our product possibly contributing to the deaths of six people is just breaking. In a few hours we can expect the parking lots to be full of media people. How do you feel we should deal with them?

Karen: I think we should take an up-front approach. Tell them that we're cooperating fully with the investigation into the deaths and that we've recalled the product since the consumer's welfare is always first in our thinking.

Issac: I agree with Karen. The worst thing we could do would be to defend our product when we're not sure it can be defended.

Tim: What about the lawsuits that are sure to come?

Cline: Obviously, there is no way to prevent the victim's families from suing us. But I suggest we play it all low-key. We'll have to accept the suits, but I'll issue absolutely no commentary on them at this time.

Tim: Good thinking. Now here is a summary of our position. We'll recall the product, stop all promotion of it, cooperate fully with The Center for Disease Control, and make no defensive comments to the press. Okay?

And we'll meet at eight a.m. tomorrow for a reassessment of what's happening.

As a matter of overall strategy, do you think Health Aids Inc. is following the right approach?

What problems might result if Health Aids Inc. simply follows the old philosophy, "We're innocent until proven guilty?"

Do you think product recall problems will increase or decrease in the decade ahead? Why or why not?

### 3. Does the tobacco industry have a social responsibility?

The Institute for Cigarettes just received information that several senators have introduced legislation for modifying the hazardous warning on cigarette packages and advertisements from:

Warning: The Surgeon General Has Determined That Cigarette
Smoking Is Dangerous to Your Health

to a much stronger statement:

Warning: Cigarette Smoking Causes Cancer, Emphysema, Heart Disease.
May Complicate Pregnancy, and Is Addictive

The chairman of the Institute for Cigarettes, Henry Atkinson, calls Bill Abrams, chief lobbyist for the Institute, and Mary Phillips, director of public relations, to his office to discuss what should be the Institute's position on the proposed labeling change.

Henry: We've got to decide how to react to the legislation introduced in the Senate this week. As you know, cigarette consumption is dropping—from 627 billion in 1981 to 624 billion in 1982. The proposed stronger health warning on cigarette packages and in advertisements can hurt the industry even more. How do you people feel we should react to it?

Bill: I think we should defend our position—and strongly. We've already lost a lot of ground. Besides the existing warning we've got to put on all cigarette packages and in all advertisements, we are faced with no smoking areas in public buildings and on airplanes, anti-smoking campaigns by public health agencies, and the spread of anti-smoking clinics and seminars. All of these factors are causing us to lose consumers. Tobacco people are viewed as bad guys. Unless we fight this proposed regulation, our industry will continue to decline.

Mary: I disagree. If we fight the proposed new labeling information, we'll simply attract an enormous amount of media attention. This in turn will cause smokers and potential smokers to consider the possible danger and refrain from using the product. The more we try to protect our position, the less credibility we'll have with the public.

Bill: I don't think so. In my opinion the existing warning statement we're required to use helped cause the downturn in sales and threatens our future. The sales decline in cigarettes is also due to the negative publicity coming from physicians; health groups, like the Heart Association; and educators.

Mary: I won't argue your point. But let me suggest a two-part positive solution. First, go along with the proposed new labeling requirement. That way we escape months, maybe years, of anti-smoking media coverage. Second, develop a new industry-wide campaign built around the idea "Enjoy Smoking—but only in moderation."

Henry: You mean something like the distilled beverage industry uses when it tells people "drink only in moderation," and "never drive if you've consumed alcohol"?

Mary: Exactly. The liquor industry has avoided a lot of flack, in effect, by admitting their product can be dangerous. I dare say the distilled beverage industry is viewed as being more socially responsible than the tobacco industry.

Bill: I don't like your idea at all, Mary. If we don't contest the new labeling proposal all the way, we simply keep the door open for even more restrictive regulations. And who says we should be concerned with social responsibility? We have an *economic* responsibility to tobacco growers, manufacturers, wholesalers, and retailers. We're a

# PART TWO

# PLANNING

Part One explained that this text treats management as a process consisting of five interrelated steps: planning, organizing, staffing, directing, and controlling. Part Two examines planning.

Chapter 4, "Introduction to Planning and Management by Objectives," explains that all organizations must meet two inherent objectives: to survive and to produce some kind of gains. Primary and derivative objectives are discussed, followed by an analysis of the basic questions that should be asked in goal setting. The desirability of verifying objectives is emphasized. Guidelines for avoiding goal-setting errors are presented, and management by objectives (MBO) is discussed.

Chapter 5, "Strategies and Other Plans," discusses the basic plans required to achieve organizational goals. It begins with the broadest form of plan, strategies. Product, marketing, and financial strategies are examined in some depth. Strategy development in nonbusiness organizations, the need for more emphasis on strategy development, and guidelines for developing and applying strategies are considered. The remainder of the chapter concerns three other basic plans—policies, procedures, and rules. The importance and advantages of each are discussed, and the requirements for sound policies, procedures, and rules are outlined.

Chapter 6, "Forecasting: Guide to Planning," explains why forecasts are inherent in planning. Both revenue and expenditure forecasts are discussed. Much of Chapter 6 explains the types of information and techniques used in developing forecasts. However, the role of judgment in forecasting is also considered. Chapter 6 ends with an analysis of how to make forecasts more accurate.

Chapter 7, "The Decision-Making Process," discusses ways in which managers may solve generally nonrecurring problems and take advantage of opportunities that arise. The five steps in decision making are analyzed, and personality theory and its effect on decision making are considered.

The Case Study at the end of Part Two concerns a decision about whether or not to manage by objectives.

# 4 INTRODUCTION TO PLANNING AND MANAGEMENT BY OBJECTIVES

**STUDY THIS CHAPTER SO YOU CAN:**

- Explain the importance of planning.
- Discuss the two inherent objectives in all organizations.
- Define "primary objective" and "derivative objective," and describe the relationship between them.
- Identify and explain the basic considerations managers must make in setting goals.
- Explain the importance of verifying results, and differentiate between quantitative and qualitative measurement.
- Describe the guidelines that managers should follow when setting goals.
- Define "management by objectives," explain how it is applied, and discuss its advantages and disadvantages and the factors that may affect its implementation.

The management process begins with planning. More than any other function, planning determines the degree of success an organization achieves. An ill-conceived plan will not produce a good result regardless of how effectively the other management functions are carried out.

In some organizations, planning is de-emphasized in favor of status quo operations. Managers may not be encouraged to conceive new objectives, "progressive" managers may be quickly terminated, and tradition—not change—

*". . . In the short-term sense it's a tragedy . . .
although over the long run
it might not be such a bad idea . . ."*

may dictate the planning process. In such a case, the organization does not progress, and a sense of dullness begins to engulf it. Younger managers are likely to become disenchanted, and the organization is likely to fail or to be absorbed by a competitor.

One way to classify plans is by time span. Thus, we have short-run and long-run plans. A **short-run plan** covers a relatively brief period, usually not more than a year. Examples of short-run plans include a weekly production schedule, a quarterly budget, and an annual personnel forecast. Short-run plans are developed to implement long-run goals.

A **long-run plan** generally covers a period of one to three years or even longer. Such plans may involve construction of new facilities, acquisition of other companies, development of new products, and so on.

## WHY IS GOAL SETTING A KEY TO MANAGEMENT EFFECTIVENESS?

All organizations need to set goals that are carefully thought through. In practice, however, one of the most common weaknesses in management is the failure to give adequate attention to establishing objectives. Often managers permit an organization to function with hazy, almost meaningless goals, such as "to do our best to increase sales next year" or "to stay even with the competition."

Setting objectives is vital to the success of an organization. Our treatment of the planning function, therefore, begins with an analysis of this task.

## WHAT ARE INHERENT OBJECTIVES?

When most people think of objectives, they think only of specific "improvement" objectives, such as "to increase sales by 10 percent" or "to increase the membership by 5 percent." However, it should not be overlooked that each organization has certain **inherent objectives**, that is, objectives that may not be explicitly stated but that guide—or should guide—the organization's planning process. Specifically, an organization must (1) survive and (2) produce gains.

The primary goal of any organization is to survive. Obviously, an enterprise can do nothing if it ceases to exist. An analogy can be drawn between a human being and an organization. The most basic motivation of a human being is to stay alive. Most of us are not consciously concerned with survival unless we are very ill, seriously injured, physically threatened, or approaching old age. Life insurance salespeople know that it is difficult to convince healthy persons under age thirty of their need for insurance because, taking survival for granted, they believe that they will always be young and physically fit.

*Survival*

Like individuals, organizations do not give much attention to survival under normal conditions. Survival is assumed. During periods of economic stress or when an organization is struggling to gain a foothold, however, survival becomes an important consideration. During the recession of the early 1980s, thousands of small companies failed. And even great corporations such as International Harvester, Chrysler, and Pan Am fought to survive.

Failure to observe that survival is a primary goal of an organization is one of the greatest mistakes managers make. Managers who do not put survival first may take unusual risks that lead to failure, such as over-expansion, making unsound investments, or adding too many people.

### The Survival Rates of Organizations

When time is measured in decades or centuries, we find that most organizations do *not* survive. In the long run, the great majority of enterprises of all types fail outright or are absorbed by other organizations. Only a small number of business organizations that existed in the 1880s and before in the United States are still functioning a century later.

When time is measured in the short run, we find that a significant percentage of enterprises do not meet the goal of survival. In a normal year several thousand business organizations, most of them relatively young, fail or go bankrupt. Several times this number cease to exist because they "sell out" to financially stronger enterprises. Small organizations are especially prone to go out of business when the owner—manager runs out of money, dies, becomes disabled, or retires and leaves no qualified back-up manager to take over.

The inability to survive is by no means a problem restricted to small organizations. While large organizations do have a better record of staying alive, a number of prominent banks, insurance companies, and major manufacturers failed in the 1980–1983 recession. Over the long run, other types of large organizations—government bodies, churches, and universities—fail in their goal to survive.

### Survival of Component Parts of the Organization

The goal of survival is also important in another management dimension. A large organization generally is made up of many "suborganizations," such as departments, branches, chapters, clubs, or divisions. A major department store has branch stores; a bank may have many branch offices; an automobile maker has various divisions and plants in different locations. Managers of these organizational parts are also concerned with survival of their part or unit. It is common to find one segment of an enterprise failing while other units are prospering in varying degrees. A part of an organization—a branch, a department, or some other unit—may no longer contribute to the overall success of the enterprise and may need to be removed. The manager of the organizational unit may see the unit's survival as a primary objective, but this objective may conflict with larger goals of the organization (for example, to cut losses sufficiently to be able to survive or earn profits).

Top managers of all kinds of organizations must sometimes perform "organizational surgery"—eliminating, redesigning, or selling parts of the enterprises that are no longer needed, are unprofitable, or for any reason are not making a contribution to overall goals. Organizational surgery is often difficult, since the personal lives of employees may be adversely affected.

### Why Do Organizations Fail?

Numerous reasons are given to explain why organizations do not survive, such as inadequate sales, rising costs, a decline in the demand for the product, excessive competition, labor problems, changes in the environment, and even bad luck. But in most cases the fundamental reason for failure is ineffective management.

The variety of mistakes managers can make is limitless. Managers may overexpand (or underexpand), develop unacceptable products, hire people with inadequate skills, go too deeply into debt, or commit any number of other errors that jeopardize survival. As is true in the attainment of any goal, the better the management, the greater the likelihood that the objective—in this case, survival—will be attained.

The goal of survival should be considered at all times by managers. The question "How will this decision affect our chances for survival?" should be evaluated in designing all plans for an enterprise.

**Production of
Gains**

The second inherent objective of an organization is to produce gains, or benefits, that justify the organization's existence. In commercial enterprises, gains take the form of profits. Over time, businesses that do not produce profits are doomed. The

# MANAGERS IN ACTION

## HOW MANAGERS TRY TO MEET THE SURVIVAL GOAL

During the post-World War II period, 1945–1980, there were economic recessions. They were mild and short-lived. However, the recession beginning in 1980 was very severe, and the sharp economic downturn was complicated by escalating competition from foreign companies, some of whom managed their operations more efficiently than American businesses.

As a result of the recession and intense foreign competition, many businesses failed. And almost all businesses became aware that survival is not guaranteed. Here is how some firms tried to meet the survival goal.

*International Harvester* For generations, International Harvester was one of the nation's most profitable companies. By 1982, however, the company was in deep financial trouble. One survival solution the company took was to replace its chief executive officer, who in some people's eyes was a very optimistic and slow-to-act manager, with a much more conservative and decisive leader. By changing its top manager, the company hoped to gain more confidence from its creditors and renegotiate its debt.

*Bethlehem Steel Corporation* The nation's second largest steel manufacturer closed its obsolete Los Angeles plant because it was losing money.

*Huffy Corporation* This major manufacturer of bicycles closed its plant in Azusa, California, and shifted production to a more efficient existing plant in Ponca City, Oklahoma.

*General Tire and Rubber Company* Executives decided to close the company's large, 67-year-old factory in Akron, Ohio, because it was obsolete. In making the decision to close the plant, the chairman of the company, M. G. O'Neil, said "[This is] the most difficult and painful announcement I have ever made."[1]

*F. W. Woolworth Company* Because of the recession, the company closed 336 Woolco stores.

Other tactics used by companies to avoid economic disaster include: personnel layoffs, reduction in advertising budgets, postponement of new construction and modernization programs, negotiating more favorable contracts with the unions, and, in some cases, asking workers to take pay cuts.

[1]"Many Plant Closings Reflect Switch in Strategy as Well as Poor Economy," *The Wall Street Journal,* October 15, 1982, p. 37. Reprinted by permission of *The Wall Street Journal,* © Dow Jones & Company, Inc., 1982. All Rights Reserved.

### QUESTIONS

1. Many well-known companies faced difficult economic problems in the early 1980s. Yet, these are the companies which presumably could afford the most competent managers. Why do some companies with "excellent" managers get into economic trouble?
2. What can managers do to avoid getting into deep financial trouble?

reasons that profits are essential to business organizations were discussed in Chapter 3.

### Gains in Commercial Organizations

Gains in business organizations take the form of profits. Unfortunately, business managers often make the mistake of pursuing short-range profits at the expense of long-range profit goals. Alfred Rappaport has noted that many bonus and other incentive programs emphasize short-run performance to the detriment of greater profit over the long run. He observed:

> American corporation management's preoccupation with short-term financial results, particularly current-period reported earnings per share, is an important contributor to the lag in R&D [research and development] investment and capital spending. Clearly, decisions based largely on short-term results, without taking into account the expected long-term consequences, can be economically inefficient from the viewpoint of both the company and the economy.[1]

Rappaport's observation is one of the major criticisms made of American managers. It will be discussed in further detail in Chapter 14.

Over time, profits will be maximized if a business concentrates on providing the best possible product or service at the lowest possible price and on making the product easily available to consumers. Companies that make a supreme effort to satisfy their customers do better than those that are out to "make a quick buck."

The inherent objective of making a profit should be kept in perspective. Business managers should recognize that profits can be earned only through the performance of some type of service — or the provision of some type of product — that, in a competitive environment, is relatively efficient and desirable. To an automobile maker, the objective might be "to build cars of a desired quality that can be sold at a competitive price." To a restaurant owner, the goal might be "to provide food and entertainment that are sufficiently desirable in order to develop adequate patronage from the people I want to serve." Achievement of these objectives will result in gains (that is, profits) for the organization.

### Gains in Noncommercial Organizations

In nonbusiness organizations — churches, schools, charitable societies, foundations, and so on — gains are not measured in terms of profits. Gains provided by these organizations may be measured in tangible terms, such as "increased enrollment," or in less tangible terms, such as "satisfaction provided" or "good work accomplished." Table 4–1 shows examples of gains and losses for several noncommercial organizations.

### Evaluation of Organizational Gains and Losses

In profit-seeking enterprises, evaluation is comparatively simple: "Did the organization earn a profit?" and, if so, "How much?" Or, if the business did not earn profits during a given time period, "Did the organization pave the way for earning profits in the foreseeable future?"

Since most nonprofit organizations also use money, they too may be evaluated in terms of income compared with expenditures, or "bottom-line results." But sometimes a surplus is not viewed as desirable. An executive director of a powerful trade association once said: "My job is not to show a surplus every year. When I show a big balance in the treasury, in effect I'm saying to my dues-paying mem-

---

[1] Alfred Rappaport, "Executive Incentives vs. Corporate Growth," *Harvard Business Review,* July–August 1978, p. 18.

**TABLE 4–1**

85

*What Are
Primary
and Derivative
Objectives?*

Examples of Gains and Losses in Noncommercial Enterprises

| Enterprise | Examples of Gains | Examples of Losses |
|---|---|---|
| University | • Establishment of new degree programs<br>• Hiring of expert scholars<br>• Well-received public-service programs | • Resignation of key faculty members<br>• Decrease in enrollment<br>• Decline in quality of students |
| Political party | • Increase in contributions and membership<br>• Winning of elections<br>• Growth of public respect | • Decrease in contributions and membership<br>• Loss of elections<br>• Scandals |
| Research foundation | • Funding of worthwhile projects<br>• Employment of respected scientist | • Decline in funding<br>• Resignation of key employees |
| Religious organization | • Increase in contributions and membership<br>• Improvement in attendance | • Decrease in membership<br>• Decline in contributions |
| Professional business fraternity | • Well-received community projects<br>• Awards for creative effort<br>• Growth in membership | • Decline in membership<br>• Poor attendance at meetings<br>• General disinterest by members |

bers, 'I couldn't find enough creative projects to spend your dues wisely!' My job is to use every dollar I collect to help my membership."

Providing desired gains or benefits is as important to nonbusiness organizations as it is to commercial enterprises. An organization that does not adequately satisfy the needs or desires of its members sooner or later fails.

## WHAT ARE PRIMARY AND DERIVATIVE OBJECTIVES?

To this point it has been noted that all organizations have two inherent objectives that are interrelated: first, to survive, and second, to produce desired gains, or benefits. Now two kinds of goals that give more specific direction to the enterprise will be considered: primary objectives and derivative objectives.

**Primary objectives** are the broad goals that an organization establishes to give direction to its total activities. For example, a business organization may state that its primary goal is "to earn $2 million net profits in the next twelve-month period." **Derivative** (or supportive) **objectives** are goals that are set to achieve the primary objectives. In this case, some derivative objectives might be "to increase sales by 15 percent" (sales department) and "to reduce purchasing costs by 10 percent" (purchasing department).

An organization may have a number of primary objectives for a given time period, such as "to increase share of market from 19 to 24 percent," "to achieve a 15 percent return on investment," and "to construct a new manufacturing facility." Derivative objectives are often set for specific divisions, departments, or other units. Derivative objectives should always be in direct support of primary objectives. (And, as will be seen in Chapter 5, strategies should always be in direct support of primary and derivative objectives.)

## WHAT ARE FUNDAMENTAL CONSIDERATIONS IN GOAL SETTING?

Setting the objectives for an enterprise is an important part of the management process. The objectives determine how the human, material, and financial resources of the organization will be used. Mistakes in setting objectives, therefore, inevitably result in waste and inefficiency. Almost without exception, organizations that survive and produce gains have done an effective job of setting clear and attainable primary and derivative objectives. Enterprises that fail to survive or to produce gains tend to give inadequate attention to the planning function.

In establishing objectives, managers should give careful attention to eight fundamental questions (see Figure 4–1). Each question is discussed in the following sections.

**What Must We Do to Ensure Our Survival?** This fundamental question is sometimes overlooked in the planning process. Whenever a risky or highly unconventional objective is under consideration, managers should consider its potential impact on the organization's survival.

**What Must We Do to Produce Necessary Gains?** Business organizations must consider whether achievement of the objective will result in the needed profits—or whether it will pave the way for profits in later years. Nonbusiness organizations must ask whether the proposed objective will result in tangible and/or intangible gains for the enterprise.

**Why Do We Exist?** Managers who plan effectively keep in mind the *raison d'être* for the organization. "For what purposes do we exist?" is a simple but important question that should be answered. An air carrier may see its primary mission to be a passenger airline, when a more encompassing self-image would be that of a transportation company moving not only passengers but freight. Management of a hotel may think "selling a place to sleep" is its rationale for existing, when a more useful description of its purpose might be "We market rest, relaxation, meeting space, and food."

Defining the purpose of the organization helps give perspective to the goal-setting process. Unfortunately, in practice, senior managers often avoid dealing with and attempting to answer the question "What is our basic reason for existing?" If managers develop a concise, accurate description of an organization's purpose, they can generate more alternatives and select more appropriate goals from among those alternatives.

FIGURE 4–1

Basic Considerations in the Setting of Objectives

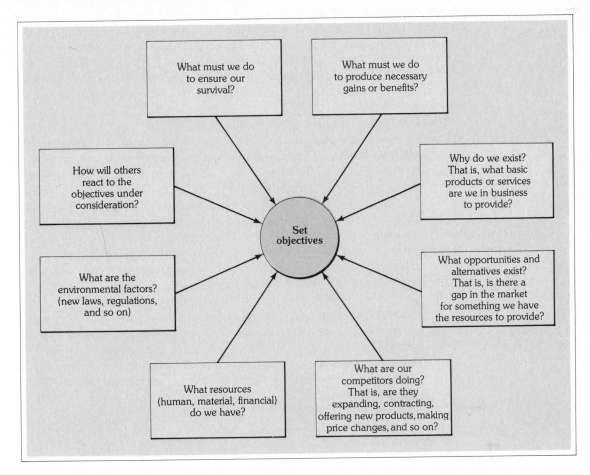

In setting objectives, managers should examine the available opportunities. Such questions as the following are aimed at discovering opportunities:

**What Opportunities and Alternatives Exist?**

- "Is there a need for a new or modified product or service? If so, should we diversify our line of products or services?"
- "What ideas that were discarded are worth reconsidering?"
- "Should we expand certain current activities because of growing customer demand?"
- "Should we expand our basic organizational purpose and enter a new, potentially more profitable field?"
- "Are there existing organizations that we should consider acquiring?"

The emphasis placed on appraisal of opportunities in the goal-setting process varies greatly. Some organizations have virtually static goals, while other organizations are more dynamic and put considerable effort into the search for opportunities.

It should not be inferred, however, that a positive reaction to opportunities is always wise. Often what appears to be an opportunity may be only a temporary condition that will soon pass. In some cases, an opportunity may be quite real, but competitive actions must be considered (see next section). When the first budget motels appeared, a number of new organizations were quickly formed to capitalize on the apparent opportunity found in marketing lower-cost accommodations. However, there was overreaction resulting in a surplus of motel rooms. Numerous organizations failed.

Consideration of the possible opportunities leads to the development of alternative courses of action. Evaluation of opportunities should be done carefully, for what appears to be an opportunity may not be or too many competitors may decide to exploit it.

## What Are Our Competitors Doing?

Most organizations have competitors. In commercial enterprises such as airlines, steel companies, banks, and food chains, competition is obvious and intense. Thus, analysis of what competitors are doing or planning to do is important in setting goals in most types of organizations. Typical questions asked by business managers relating to competitive behavior are:

- "What changes are our competitors making in their variety of products?"
- "What changes are they making in distribution facilities, advertising, and pricing?"
- "Are competitors attempting to appeal to a different market segment?"
- "What changes are they making in their production facilities and techniques?"
- "How can we best adapt to their changing strategy?"

While appraisal of competitors should be an important part of the goal-setting process, it can be carried too far. Most organizations are not highly innovative in setting goals. Instead, they can be categorized as follow-the-leader enterprises. Organizations frequently copy competitors because innovation is harder, more complicated, and riskier than copying. Innovators often fail or experience disappointing results. For example, an organization that develops a new product may market it before all the "bugs" have been worked out. Meanwhile, competitors wait, make needed refinements in the product, and then enter the market to capitalize on the demand that the innovator developed but did not adequately satisfy. The earliest automobile companies failed. Ford avoided the mistakes of his predecessors and succeeded. The Wright Brothers built the first airplane but failed to make much money later.

Product innovation and other forms of significant deviation from the practices of competitors are to be encouraged; innovation is the basis for improvement in all human activities. However, caution should be applied when setting goals that are sharply different from those of competitors. An organization must closely examine its own resources, as explained below, before implementing a distinctly new plan.

An objective evaluation of an organization's capital, physical, technical, and managerial resources should be made in the goal-setting process. Such an analysis helps managers to set goals that are both desirable and attainable.

### Capital-Resource Evaluation

All organizations require money to function, and the availability of capital sets limits on goals. When defining objectives, managers should ask and answer such basic questions as "How much will this proposed project cost?" and "What is our existing capital position? Can—and should—we borrow more money or sell more stock?"

Bear in mind that even the largest organizations, including Exxon and the U.S. government, have limited financial resources. And in most organizations much of the capital is already committed to ongoing activities: It is earmarked for rent, payment of interest, payment of wages and salaries, and other items in the budget. A new goal, therefore, may require managers either to acquire new capital or to de-emphasize or cancel another project. There are many instances of failure to attain objectives because insufficient capital was made available to achieve them.

### Physical-Resource Evaluation

In the process of goal setting, managers should also evaluate the status of production facilities, equipment, land, buildings, and other physical facilities that are or will be available. This evaluation in turn should be compared to the objectives under consideration. If a new product goal is contemplated, managers should ask such questions as "Do we have the technology to make it?" "Will producing it detract from other manufacturing operations?" "Will it involve retooling?" and "Which plant is best equipped to handle production?"

All organizations have limited physical resources, whether in the form of office space, retail stores, motor vehicles, or manufacturing facilities. Consideration of goals, then, requires that managers determine whether sufficient physical resources exist or can be acquired to reach the goals. There would be little point in an airline setting a goal of obtaining a new route if it did not have sufficient airplanes and maintenance facilities on hand or on order to handle the extra traffic.

### Technical-Resource Evaluation

When setting goals, managers should determine whether the organization has or can acquire adequate technical expertise to carry out the proposed project. An engineering firm might set a goal of obtaining a contract to design six passenger stations for a rapid-transit system. The critical question to answer before this goal is accepted is "Does our firm have the required technical knowledge to construct passenger stations, and if not, do we have adequate capital to acquire it?" No organization has unlimited legal, accounting, scientific, engineering, or other forms of technical talent. The cemeteries of dead enterprises contain many organizations that bit off more than they could chew.

### Managerial-Resource Evaluation

In contemplating goals, senior managers should evaluate the experience, maturity, and ability of management talent. "Are our managers capable of attaining the goals we are considering?" is a question that should be answered before a new project is undertaken. A related question is "If not, can we acquire the managerial talent needed to achieve the goal?" Since management must accept full responsibility for results, it is essential to make an honest appraisal of the current management's suitability for the proposed work.

**What
Environmental
Factors Should We
Consider?**

The process of setting goals should include careful consideration of economic, social, governmental, and other trends such as those discussed in Chapter 3. Expanding in the wrong phase of a business cycle, tooling up to manufacture products for which demand is decreasing, and ignoring subtle changes in consumer preferences are some mistakes that may occur when management fails to heed changes in the organization's environment. Table 4–2 shows the wide variety of events that may occur, some predictable and some completely unpredictable. Note that management may need to develop *contingency plans* to deal with future conditions that are possible but not probable.

**How Will Others
React to
the Objectives
Under
Consideration?**

Managers are not completely free to set goals since they are accountable to others. A key question that is involved in the goal-setting process is "How will those to whom we are primarily and secondarily accountable react to the goals we are considering?" A university president and his or her key advisers may consider a goal of holding classes only four days a week, giving students Wednesday off for library usage, personal pursuits, and other purposes. Before adopting such a goal, top management should consider the probable reactions of the university's primary public (its students) and its secondary public (parents, taxpayers, and others who are concerned with university operations). Students may feel cheated, or they may prefer having Friday instead of Wednesday off. Taxpayers may say, "Professors don't deserve a four-day week for what the state is paying them."

## SHOULD OBJECTIVES BE VERIFIED?

Whenever possible, an organization should set **verifiable objectives**. That is, a manager should be able to determine at the end of the planned period whether or not the goals were reached.

**Quantitative
Measurement**

**Quantitative measurement** seeks to determine information such as "Were sales goals achieved?" "Were absenteeism and turnover reduced?" and "Was the new installation completed on time?" Often, managers fail to set measurable objectives for some positions because the work is "too intangible." A public-relations manager may be told, "Joan, your job is to improve our public image." A more verifiable objective would be "Joan, your job is to visit fifty schools and explain how our organization helps the community" or "Your job is to prepare a twenty-four-page monthly publication for distribution to employees and shareholders." Or consider another example: The manager of a legal department may be advised,

**TABLE 4—2**

91

*Should
Objectives
Be Verified?*

Unforeseen Conditions Indicate the Need for Contingency Plans

| Contingencies That May Develop | Possible Impact on Achievement of Previously Set Objectives |
|---|---|
| Strikes occur in supplier organizations. | • Shortages of parts or supplies may occur. <br> • Production cutbacks may be required. <br> • New sources of supply may have to be sought. |
| Strikes occur in our organization. | • Production goals may not be met. <br> • Customers may be lost to competitors. <br> • Revenue forecast may not be achieved, forcing cutbacks on expansion plans. |
| Customers develop financial problems and cut back on orders. | • Production may need to be reduced. <br> • Key employees may be terminated because they are no longer needed. <br> • Inventories of raw materials or supplies may become excessive. |
| New or amended laws are enacted. | • Product characteristics may require modification. <br> • Methods of advertising and selling may require change. <br> • Competition may be intensified. |
| Nation becomes involved in war. | • Product line may be changed to produce war-related items. <br> • Production facilities may become too limited. <br> • Shortages may develop. |
| National economy goes into deep recession. | • Consumer income and demand go down, forcing production cutbacks. <br> • Surplus of workers may occur. <br> • New equipment orders may be canceled. |
| A major competitor changes its promotional strategy. | • A corresponding change may be required. <br> • More money may be needed for promotion. <br> • Advertising agency may no longer be adequate. |
| Climatic problems (droughts, floods, hurricanes, and so on) develop. | • Supplies of raw materials may be reduced. <br> • Physical facilities may be damaged or destroyed. <br> • Customers may be adversely affected with a resulting negative impact on demand. |

## QUESTIONS

1. For each unforeseen condition in Table 4—2, suggest one contingency plan that a firm might adopt in order to deal with it.
2. The examples of unforeseen conditions in this table are generally negative and work against precisely set goals. What are some examples of unforeseen conditions that might benefit an organization?

"Keep our legal machinery in good order. We don't want any patent infringements or other problems to complicate operations next year." A more quantitative objective would be "Settle 90 percent of threatened lawsuits against the organization out of court."

Quantitative measurement is not always possible because some goals cannot be measured numerically. Generally, the higher we go in the organization, the more difficult it is to measure success statistically. While it is fairly simple to measure downtime, product rejections, sales, and employee turnover, it is much harder to measure such things as development of improved products or setting of appropriate long-range goals.

**Qualitative measurement** is subjective in nature and attempts to evaluate whether the manager "grew" professionally, did a "good" job of developing his or her supportive managers, or "improved" morale. Qualitative measurement can be extremely difficult, especially for such highly creative fields as research, advertising, planning, engineering, design, and teaching.

The manager of a drug research laboratory may be unable to attain her objective of creating a new medicine because of totally unforeseen complications. Yet, in the discovery of an unexpected difficulty she may still have made a significant contribution. Or, a manager of industrial relations may have committed himself to working out a "favorable" contract with the union only to encounter unexpected demands that ultimately result in a work stoppage. Or, a professor may commit herself to preparing an article for a journal only to find that despite her best efforts the paper is rejected.

Even though it is more difficult to measure results of creative effort than results of routine activities, an attempt at evaluation should be made. Unless results are forthcoming over a period of time, the activity cannot be justified. If managers of a research activity do not in fact develop new products that will contribute to the organization's profits, the department may need to be eliminated or staffed with new personnel. Performance measurement is essential, then, to keep waste and inefficiency at the lowest possible level.

## GUIDELINES FOR SETTING OBJECTIVES

We need not look far to see the results of errors in planning. Merchants may buy too much, buy too little, or buy the wrong kind of merchandise for resale. Production departments may be overstaffed, understaffed, or staffed with people who aren't suited for the work. Finance departments may make faulty forecasts that result in inadequate funds to achieve goals. And the high failure rate of all kinds of enterprises suggests bad planning by managers.

Human beings cannot construct perfect plans; all plans prove faulty to some degree. The challenge to managers is to make plans as nearly perfect as possible, to reduce the degree of error. The following guidelines for setting objectives should be followed.

Often objectives are hazy and overgeneralized. Some examples are "to improve performance over last year," "to obtain a larger share of the market," and "to improve the efficiency in each department." With such objectives managers don't know exactly what is expected of them and may be confused about what constitutes satisfactory performance. Also, with vague objectives personnel are unlikely to put forth a maximum effort.

Examples of clearly stated objectives are "to reduce absenteeism to 6 percent," "to complete the construction project by September 1," and "to attain a 13 percent ROI" (return on investment).

Many department heads and other managers simply announce the objectives for the coming planning period, giving subordinates no opportunity to provide their own inputs. A flat announcement such as, "John, here's your sales quota for next year" is usually made. Since this approach does not give subordinates a chance to participate in setting goals, it can lead to lowered morale. Subordinates, if given an opportunity to participate in the goal-setting process, may suggest even larger objectives than those the superior has planned. The process of management by objectives, discussed later in this chapter, has been developed as one way of coping with these problems.

Progress made toward objectives may not be reviewed or may be reviewed too infrequently. A manager and his subordinates may meet to discuss objectives; then the manager may conclude the meeting by saying, "Betty, you know what's expected of you. In twelve months I hope you'll have a good report." There are numerous pitfalls to this approach. Performance may be lackadaisical, managers may delay taking action, goals may be only partially attained, and resources may not be fully used.

Goals must be sufficiently ambitious if they are to motivate individuals to put forth maximum effort. In effect, objectives put a limit on what the organization will accomplish. Suppose the primary objective of one firm is "to become number one in the industry," and another firm sets as its primary goal "to be one of the ten top firms in the industry." Management thinking in the first firm will differ considerably from that in the second firm. Unfortunately, managers in many enterprises do not conceive sufficiently ambitious objectives and, as a result, fail to fully harness the energies of their people.

Other mistakes may also be made: Objectives may be pointless (preparing reports that have no purpose), or they may be so overly ambitious as to constitute "dreams" that no one can be expected to achieve. Objectives should be realistic. If goals are well beyond the capabilities of an organization, apathy may become the prevailing mood.

All derivative goals in an organization should be in support of the primary goals. Too often objectives are not coordinated to achieve a basic organizational goal. If sales objectives are not coordinated with production objectives, we may find a production manager saying, "Sam, you've sold more orders than we can fill. Tell your customers we can't deliver all the products they require."

All departments, divisions, and other units should contribute to common goals. Uncoordinated objectives result in friction, interdepartmental squabbles, and much wasted effort.

## Base Objectives on the "Best Possible" Data

The best available information should be used in the goal-setting process. Plans are no better than the information on which they are based. Inaccurate, outdated, or limited information often results in bad planning. In some cases, those who could supply useful data simply aren't asked for it. Managers may ignore past experience and make decisions on the basis of their gut reactions.

## Keep Objectives Flexible

In the area of flexibility, management makes the mistake of ignoring the environmental factors discussed in Chapter 3 or of ignoring internal changes in personnel or resources. New conditions may occur, yet goals may remain unchanged. In some cases a significant shift in consumer demand or in personnel may not be taken into account. As objectives become less meaningful, managers become demoralized, and the organization fails to maximize the use of its resources.

# WHAT IS MANAGEMENT BY OBJECTIVES (MBO)?

**Management by objectives** (MBO) is a system of managing whereby managers work in conjunction with subordinates to identify goals and make plans for achieving them. Used properly, MBO helps managers avoid or minimize planning errors.

MBO as a formal management tool is relatively new, first being advocated by Professors Peter Drucker and Douglas McGregor in the 1950s. Since then, its use has become widespread; it is applied to some extent in all types of organizations. However, no two organizations using MBO will apply it in exactly the same way.

## Steps in the MBO Process

MBO involves four steps:

*Step 1:* The manager explains the rationale and methodology of MBO (the what, why, and how of the process) to subordinates. In an organization in which MBO has not been used previously, people may be quite apprehensive until they have a better understanding of the process.

*Step 2:* The superior and subordinate meet to set objectives for the coming planning period. MBO is a departure from the way objectives are usually set. Traditionally, goals are *imposed* on subordinates. "Betty, here is what is expected of you" or "Harry, your quota for next year is such and such" is still the typical way objectives are presented to people who are expected to achieve them. When MBO is used, goals are not imposed on the subordinate. Instead, the subordinate *participates* in the goal-setting process.

Let us say Harry, the superior, has an idea of what he would like to see Peter, the subordinate, accomplish. But Peter's thinking of what he feels he can achieve must also be considered. In the MBO process, the manager and the subordinate consider expectations, capabilities, and resources. Ideally, both parties have prepared for the meeting and feel free to discuss candidly what each feels can be accomplished. The result of the discussion is to arrive at mutually acceptable goals for the planning period.

*Step 3:* One or more intermediate reviews of performance are conducted to determine if the individual is making satisfactory progress toward attaining the established goals. Intermediate appraisals are essential because they can reveal unanticipated problems that have developed. In the intermediate-review process it may be learned that the goals originally established are too large (or too small) or are inappropriate because of changed conditions. Intermediate reviews thus give the manager and the subordinate an opportunity to make necessary adjustments in the objectives and the methods being used to achieve them.

In addition to their value in helping redefine goals and methods, intermediate reviews have other advantages. They help the subordinate to understand better the what, why, and how of MBO. And they can improve morale, since the manager is showing interest in what the subordinate is doing.

*Step 4:* At the conclusion of the time period set for the achievement of the objectives, a final or summary review is conducted. In this review the manager should attempt to determine "What went right?", "What went wrong?", and "How can we do better in the future?" The final review should logically lead to the setting of objectives for the next planning period. Figure 4–2 summarizes the MBO process.

### Energies Are Focused on Organizational Goals under MBO

Even in large, progressive, and well-managed organizations, much work is performed that does not relate to the principal goals of the organization. For example, sales representatives may call on prospects who never will buy; unnecessary research studies may be started; a training program may be undertaken to prepare people for a function that is being phased out; or, most commonly, people may "look busy" but not be achieving any goals set by the organization.

Implementation of an MBO program does not mean that all wastes such as these will be eliminated. However, MBO should put the main goals into more detailed focus and should help managers answer the question "Is the work being performed by subordinates helping us to get where we want to go?"

### MBO Helps to Elevate Morale

Generally speaking, motivation is improved when people have specific work targets for which to strive. Since MBO requires a reasonably precise definition of objectives, it follows that workers' attitudes should improve because workers have a better understanding of what is expected of them. MBO also permits subordinates to participate in goal setting, which further improves motivation.

### MBO Helps Correct Underemployment of Human Resources

Most people in organizations are *underemployed* (working below their maximum level of capability). Proponents of MBO claim it helps reduce underemployment.

## FIGURE 4–2

**The Management-by-Objectives Process**

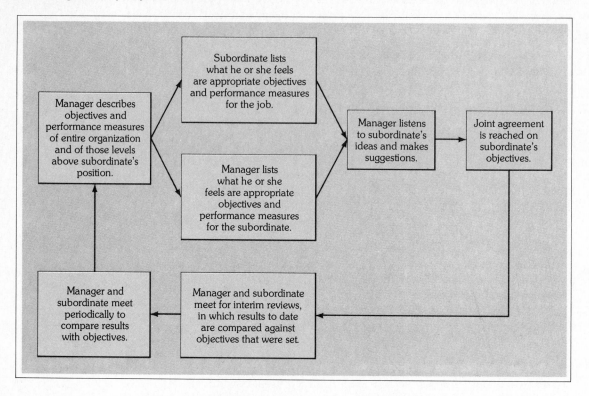

Source: Adapted from *MBO II: A System of Managerial Leadership for the 80's* by George S. Odiorne. Copyright © 1979 by Pitman Learning, Inc., Belmont, Calif. 94002.

The goals set under MBO are, to some extent, tailored to the particular abilities of the subordinates involved. In implementing MBO, managers may discover talents and skills they did not know subordinates possessed. A goal of all organizations is to obtain from each member the maximum contribution of which he or she is capable. MBO can help to achieve this, since objectives are tailored to individual capabilities.

### MBO Aids in Personnel Development

One of a manager's most important responsibilities is to develop the skills and abilities of subordinates. MBO helps to accomplish this because the manager becomes better acquainted with the personnel and therefore can develop a better understanding of their strengths and weaknesses. Further, the manager has more opportunity to coach the personnel.

### MBO Is Superior to Trait Evaluation

A common way of measuring performance is **trait evaluation**, or the assessment of a manager on the basis of such factors as cooperation, self-discipline, participation, loyalty, and conscientiousness. Many feel that MBO is superior to trait evaluation because it focuses on results, not on intangible and subjective characteristics. A manager may be loyal, cooperative, and conscientious but still may not be effective in producing work that contributes to the objectives of the organization. Or a manager may not be particularly likable but may still accomplish desired results more effectively than a highly likable person.

### MBO Takes Considerable Time

One frequent criticism of MBO is that it takes too much of a manager's time. There is no question that, if done right, MBO does require considerable time. The time needed for a manager to interview his or her subordinate is only part of the picture. Time is also required to devise the objectives and the methods needed to achieve them.

On the other hand, some argue that a manager's primary responsibility is to achieve results through his or her subordinates and that nothing, therefore, is as important as making certain these results are in fact achieved. Advocates of MBO argue that if an MBO program is properly conducted, time can be found to implement it, and the "I don't have enough time" argument is not valid.

### MBO May Be Resented by Subordinates

If MBO is not explained properly, subordinates may feel it is a device to make them work harder, devote even more time to the organization, and function in a highly prescribed manner. There are instances, especially in organizations with little experience in MBO, in which unrealistic goals are set. This obviously has a negative effect on morale.

Often people at high levels in an organization do not like MBO (at least until they fully understand it) because they consider it unprofessional. Scientists may perceive themselves as self-starters who can set their own goals and measure the degree to which the goals are achieved. They may feel it is belittling for mature, proven performers to define what they are going to accomplish and how they expect to do it. They may think, "Look at my track record. For years I've been regarded as successful. Why submit me to this?"

While this argument is understandable, it does not have validity *if* the MBO program is properly designed and implemented. The goal of MBO is not to be punitive, to put subordinates "in their place," or in any other way to adversely affect morale. Proponents argue that a well-designed MBO program is constructive and simply helps to maximize the input of each individual toward the attainment of the organization's goals.

### Conditions Change Too Frequently for MBO to Work

In our fast-paced world, conditions do not remain static. Goals set even a month or three months ago may be too large, too small, or inappropriate when examined under immediate conditions. For example, the energy problem of 1973–1974, in a very short time span, required managers in many organizations to modify previously set goals or even to scrap them entirely. Shortages, inflation, changes in consumer demand, and a host of similar factors that affect plans are not easily predicted.

A dynamic, socioeconomic environment complicates the application of

MBO. But the fact that situations change does not necessarily make the concept of MBO invalid or unreasonable. Rapid change may complicate the MBO process, but it can be compensated for, at least in part, by Step 3 in the MBO process, the intermediate review that provides for readjustment of goals and methods.

**Factors Affecting the Success of an MBO Program**

Management by objectives is more difficult to apply in practice than to grasp in theory. Despite problems in making it work, however, MBO has been successful in many organizations, and its use as a planning and evaluation tool will probably increase. Two factors that affect the success of an MBO program are the way in which the program is implemented and the management style of the organization.

### Method of Implementation

Success of an MBO program relates directly to the way in which the program is implemented. If it is not understood by those who will be involved and if it is not fully backed by senior management, then problems may occur.

In their important work on the subject of MBO, Stephen J. Carroll, Jr., and Henry L. Tosi, Jr., raise important questions relative to the implementation of MBO:

> Any organization considering MBO must be aware of the factors that influence its success or failure. Before MBO is introduced, answers to certain questions should be obtained. What should top management do to make the MBO program effective? How should the program be introduced to management? Is training needed, and if so, what kind? What should managers be asked to do under this program? Do other elements or programs have to be changed because of the introduction of MBO?
>
> Each individual manager using MBO also has certain questions to answer. Should the goals that are set be easy or difficult? Should priorities be set for goals? How many goals should be set? Who should set the goals? Me? My subordinate? Both of us?
>
> The conduct of the review process also raises questions. Should I leave my subordinate alone after the goals are set, or should I talk to him frequently about his progress? How much should I praise or criticize him in these intermediate review sessions? How much pressure should I put on him to accomplish his goals? Another very important question facing each manager is whether he should carry out the MBO process differently for each of his subordinates. Are difficult goals good for Tom but bad for Harry? Should I leave Jerry alone after goals are established or should I review his performance as much as I do Bill's?[2]

### Management Style

The effectiveness of an MBO program depends partially on the style of management practiced by top executives in the organization. Professor Heinz Weihrich has evaluated MBO under four management styles, or systems, developed by Rensis Likert. (These management styles are discussed more extensively in Chapters 16 and 17.)

- *Exploitative-authoritative:* Subordinates are not trusted and are motivated by threat of punishment.
- *Benevolent-authoritative:* Senior managers have a condescending attitude toward subordinates. Both rewards and punishments are used to motivate.

---

[2]Stephen J. Carroll, Jr., and Henry L. Tosi, Jr., *Management by Objectives: Applications and Research* (New York: Macmillan, 1973), pp. 21–22.

- *Consultative:* Managers have considerable trust in subordinates and motivate them mainly by rewards rather than punishment.
- *Participative-group:* Much trust is placed in subordinates, and managers rely almost exclusively on rewards to motivate.

Weihrich notes that "to effectively implement MBO, it must be understood that MBO is a process as well as a philosophy of managing. If this philosophy is completely incongruent with the organizational climate, problems will occur."[3] Thus, MBO cannot be expected to work well (or to work at all) if top managers are exploitative-authoritative. Because MBO requires a great deal of trust and interaction between superior and subordinate, it stands the best chance of succeeding when top managers follow a participative-group style.

The Issue for Debate in this chapter discusses the pros and cons of informality as a management style. Some managers strongly endorse informality, while others prefer adherence to a formal style.

**SUMMARY**

- Planning, more than any other function, determines the degree of success an organization will achieve.
- Two inherent objectives in all organizations are to survive and to produce desired gains or benefits to justify their existence.
- Primary objectives are broad goals an organization establishes to give direction to its activities. To achieve its primary goals, an organization must establish derivative objectives.
- In setting objectives, management should consider what the organization must do to ensure its survival and to produce gains, what the organization's basic purpose is, what opportunities and alternatives exist, what competitors are doing, what resources are available, what environmental factors may affect the organization, how others will react to the objective.
- Goals set for an organization should be verifiable. Verification can be quantitative or qualitative.
- Useful guidelines for setting objectives are to state objectives clearly, let subordinates participate, review progress toward reaching objectives frequently, make objectives challenging, coordinate objectives, base objectives on the best available data, and keep objectives flexible.
- Management by objectives is a process involving four steps: (1) The manager explains MBO's rationale to subordinates, (2) the manager and subordinates *together* set objectives, (3) intermediate performance reviews are conducted, and (4) a final review is conducted.
- Advantages claimed for MBO are that it focuses energies on goals, elevates morale, helps correct for underemployment of human resources, aids in manager development, and is superior to trait analysis. Key disadvantages are that it takes considerable time, it may be resented by subordinates, and conditions may change too frequently for it to work.
- Whether or not an MBO program will be successful depends on the way it is implemented. To succeed it must be fully understood by those involved and backed by senior management. An MBO program's effectiveness also depends on the style of management. If top managers are exploitative-authoritative, it will not

[3]Heinz Weihrich, "MBO in Four Management Systems," *MSU Business Topics,* Autumn 1976, p. 55.

# ISSUE FOR DEBATE

## IS INFORMALITY A DESIRABLE MANAGEMENT STYLE?

Some managers feel an informal atmosphere is better than a formal one. They feel both managers and subordinates should dress casually, call one another by their first names, and so on. Other managers feel formality is best. Some pros and cons of informality are mentioned below.

|  YES | NO |
|------|-----|
| **Informality is a desirable management style because...** | **Informality is not a desirable management style because...** |

**YES**

**Informality is a desirable management style because...**

Some very successful senior executives have found that the use of first names and other informal devices builds employee morale.

Informality lets managers and subordinates get to know one another better. Managers learn employees' abilities, work habits, and personal and work problems; subordinates learn managers' expectations.

In an informal atmosphere subordinates feel freer to make suggestions to superiors, and conflicts can be worked out informally. Harmony is fostered, and harder work and greater productivity result.

Human beings have an inherent need to affiliate. Informality facilitates this need, with the result that the work group is more cohesive.

Informality is morally right. *All* people in an organization are important. Artificial distinctions (separate dining areas, for example) tend to make some people feel inferior.

Action on decisions is faster and more efficient, since much communication can take place during work breaks and in other informal situations.

**NO**

**Informality is not a desirable management style because...**

Subordinates get confused when the superior is a boss one minute and a buddy the next. People need to know where they stand or they feel insecure.

Some subordinates may try to exploit informality and seek special, unwarranted favors.

If manager Mary Jones has been called Mrs. Jones for twenty years, she may resent being called Mary by her subordinates, especially much younger ones. Many people, at all levels, feel more comfortable in a formal environment.

Customers and other outsiders may consider an informal environment too unbusinesslike and may not have as much confidence in the firm.

Group cohesiveness decreases as the size of the group increases. Big organizations cannot operate informally.

Rank-and-file employees lose respect for superiors when they discover that they, too, have weaknesses. After all, familiarity breeds contempt.

## QUESTIONS

1. What other pros and cons can you mention relative to informality as a management style?
2. Would you prefer to work in an informal environment or a formal one? Why?

work well if at all. MBO stands the best chance for working when the management style is participative-group.

LEARN
THE LANGUAGE
OF
MANAGEMENT

short-run plan
long-run plan
inherent objectives
primary objectives
derivative objectives

verifiable objectives
quantitative measurement
qualitative measurement
management by objectives
trait evaluation

QUESTIONS
FOR REVIEW
AND
DISCUSSION

1. In your opinion, should managers give more attention to the goal of survival?
2. Why are gains or benefits more difficult to evaluate in non-profit-seeking organizations than in profit-seeking enterprises?
3. Show the relationship between the goal of surviving and the goal of producing benefits or gains.
4. Explain why derivative objectives should be in direct support of the primary objective.
5. Is any one of the fundamental considerations in goal setting mentioned in the text more important than the others? Explain.
6. "Most organizations don't innovate. They copy." Explain. Do your observations of business practices confirm this statement? Why or why not?
7. Why should objectives be verifiable?
8. What are the essential differences between quantitative and qualitative measurements of performance? Which is the more desirable? Explain.
9. Based on your experiences in specific situations, what guidelines for setting objectives did you observe were overlooked?
10. Would you prefer to work in an organization that uses MBO or in an enterprise in which objectives are simply dictated to subordinates? Explain your preference.

MAKING
MANAGEMENT
DECISIONS

### 1. Winning cooperation for MBO

You were recently hired from another organization to head the Business Research Department of the Chicago Metal Company. The purpose of your department is to supply nontechnical advice and information to the main divisions of the business. You have a staff of eleven, consisting of an assistant director, five research specialists (one each in marketing, management, accounting, finance, and data processing), two report writers, and three clerical reporters.

Your superior wants to develop and implement a management-by-objectives program. Several members of your staff have told you that they don't like MBO. You anticipate considerable difficulty, since eight of the eleven people have been in the department for at least five years, regard themselves as professionals, and tend to be set in their ways.

Describe what you would do to gain the cooperation of your staff. How would you proceed to replace their suspicion of MBO with enthusiasm for it?

## 2. Setting concrete objectives

Set three verifiable objectives—goals that can be measured—for each of these positions: (a) a police officer, (b) a secretary, (c) a bank teller, (d) a telephone repair person, and (e) a company president. Then describe briefly why verifiable objectives are superior to those that cannot be measured.

## 3. How can Avant Garde Airlines survive?

For 15 years Avant Garde had operated as a regional airline based in Chicago. During 1981 and 1982 it acquired two other regional airlines—one in California and one in Atlanta—which made it a national carrier. In 1983, Avant Garde found itself in deep financial trouble. Jeff Orduay, the airline's CEO, Brian Kleiman, president, and Willard Nussbaum, chief of operations, are discussing what to do.

Orduay: You've seen the second quarter results. We lost $100 million. Now, that's $50 million more than we had anticipated.

Nussbaum: I think we can trace the loss to two things. First it cost us a lot more than we anticipated to integrate our two acquisitions into what amounts to a new national airline, and second, the economic recovery hasn't yet fully impacted on the industry.

Orduay: I think you're right. But as of right now, we have one primary objective. And that's survival. Our creditors are coming down hard on us; our huge loss last quarter is making them very nervous. One way or another, we've got to cut our losses to no more than $40 million for each of the next three quarters. If we can do that, I feel certain we can begin to show a profit in 12 months.

Kleiman: In a way all of this is amusing. Last year our primary objective was to create a national airline. This year our main goal is to survive. Now to achieve our survival goal, we've already taken several steps. Let me review them. We've gotten a postponement on the delivery of all new equipment for 12 months, we've cancelled obviously unprofitable flights, and we've cut the employee force to the bone. What else can we do to achieve our primary objective?

Orduay: What I propose is this: Somehow get our employees, from flight captains to baggage handlers, to accept a 20 percent pay cut for 12 months, effective in 30 days. If we can get them to go along, we'll cut our losses enough to keep our creditors satisfied and to continue our business of building a great national carrier.

Nussbaum: That's a different objective. The economic recovery seems certain now, and our employees and their unions are not going to like the plan.

Orduay: I agree. But it's the only viable alternative I see unless we decide to sell part of Avant Garde or accept bankruptcy.

Kleiman: We're likely to lose some good people.

Orduay: Probably so. But I feel most of our employees would rather work for 80 percent of their salaries than risk unemployment.

Do you think Orduay has defined the primary objective of Avant Garde properly? Why or why not?

What actions can the management of Avant Garde Airlines take to win acceptance of the pay cut by the employees?

Bowman, Edward H. "Risk Seeking by Troubled Firms." *Sloan Management Review*, Summer 1982, pp. 33–42.

Drucker, Peter. *The Practice of Management.* New York: Harper & Row, 1954.

Fleming, John E. "Linking Public Affairs with Corporate Planning." *California Management Review*, Winter 1980, pp. 35–43.

Ford, Richard C.; McLaughlin, Frank; and Nixdorf, James. "Ten Questions About MBO." *California Management Review,* Winter 1980, pp. 88–94.

French, Wendel L., and Hollmann, Robert W. "Management by Objectives: The Team Approach." *California Management Review*, Spring 1975, pp. 13–22.

Hise, Richard T., and Gillett, Peter L. "Making MBO Work in the Sales Force." *Atlanta Economic Review*, July–August 1977, pp. 32–37.

Kudla, Ronald J., and Cesta, John R. "Planning and Financial Performance: A Discriminant Analysis." *Akron Business and Economic Review*, Spring 1982, pp. 30–36.

Leontiades, Milton. "Evaluating a Firm's Performance Potential." *Business Horizons,* August 1980, pp. 61–66.

Martin, Robert A. "The Effect of Job Consensus on MBO Goal Attainment." *MSU Business Topics*, Winter 1981, pp. 43–48.

McGregor, Douglas. "An Uneasy Look at Performance Appraisal." *Harvard Business Review*, May–June 1957, pp. 89–94.

Mescon, Timothy S.; Schauer, Michelle I.; and Lovato, Christine M. "Social-Performance Planning: Shell Sets Precedents." *Business*, March 1981, pp. 19–23.

Shuster, Fred E., and Kindall, Alva F. "Management by Objectives: Where we Stand—A Survey of the Fortune 500." *Human Resource Management*, Spring 1974, pp. 8–11.

Steiger, Thomas W. "The Dilemma of the Dirty Shirts." *Business*, March 1981, pp. 46–47.

Strickland, A. J. III. "How to Make Participative Planning Impossible." *Atlanta Economic Review*, May–June, 1978, pp. 24–27.

Wether, William B., Jr., and Weihrich, Heinz. "Refining MBO Through Negotiations." *MSU Business Topics*, Summer 1975, pp. 53–59.

Weihrich, Heinz. "MBO in Four Management Systems." *MSU Business Topics*, Autumn 1976, pp. 51–56.

Zarnowitz, Victor. "On Functions, Quality, and Timeliness of Economic Information." *The Journal of Business*, January 1982, pp. 87–120.

# 5 STRATEGIES AND OTHER PLANS

**STUDY THIS CHAPTER SO YOU CAN:**

- Define "strategy" and understand the nature and importance of strategies as a form of grand plan.

- Understand the relationship between strategy development and managerial style.

- Describe the three major kinds of strategies: product, marketing, and financial.

- Discuss the role of strategy development in nonbusiness organizations.

- Explain the need for more emphasis on strategy development and the guidelines for developing effective strategies.

- Define and differentiate among budgets, policies, procedures, and rules.

- Explain the importance of and requirements for policies, procedures, and rules.

In Chapter 4 we saw that organizations have two broad-based, interrelated goals: to survive and to produce gains, or benefits. Then we noted that, to achieve these two goals, primary objectives and their derivative objectives must be attained.

To achieve objectives, managers must design and implement a variety of plans. All managers plan because the function is inherent in the management process. The *kinds* of plans developed by managers generally relate to their level in the management hierarchy. Basic strategies—the plans that give general direction, usually covering a broad time span—are developed by managers at the top level. Middle-level managers help develop plans for the successful implementation of the strategies developed by top management. First-level managers generally are responsible for such planning activities as applying rules and regulations and making up daily and weekly work schedules.

This chapter deals with these plans—the devices an organization develops to attain basic goals.

## STRATEGIES ARE BROAD PLANS FOR GOAL ACHIEVEMENT

The term "strategy" comes from the military and in the original Greek literally means "the art of the general." The term, which is still used most extensively by military organizations, is now popular with businesses and other institutions. Today a **strategy** is a broad-based plan to achieve the objectives of an organization.

A strategy is the most generalized type of plan and is developed to achieve long-range goals. It may concern the kind of products that will be produced, how the organization will finance its activities, and what the target market will be.

Let us say a business organization's primary objective is "to earn $2 million net profits in the next twelve-month period." Strategies to achieve the objective might be (1) to open four new branches and phase out the two least profitable ones, (2) to develop new promotional programs, (3) to delete one product line and institute another, (4) to establish a research laboratory, or (5) to revise the price schedule an average of 15 percent upward.

Primary and derivative objectives, while extremely important, must be supported with strategies if the organization is to achieve its objectives. Regardless of how well considered the goals may be, if workable plans are not developed to achieve them, the result will be mediocre at best. Table 5–1 shows examples of objectives and supporting strategies.

Strategies, the "how" of goal achievement, are the responsibility of top, or senior, managers. However, inputs in strategy development may come from lower-level managers. In well-managed organizations, subordinate managers supply information and recommendations, either voluntarily or by request. A sales manager is expected to make recommendations about products, prices, and distribution facilities. Executives in the fields of production, finance, personnel, and law should contribute information and ideas to the development of strategies. For instance, in formulating a strategy on how to attain a larger share of the market, top executives should obtain the viewpoints of subordinate managers who have firsthand knowledge of market opportunities, competitive strengths and weaknesses, and other relevant information.

*Responsibility for
Strategy
Development*

Strategies are often profoundly influenced by the thinking of the organization's key executive. An interesting example concerns Revlon, the cosmetics company. Charles Revson, who headed the firm for decades, shortly before his death picked Michel Bergerac as his successor. Revson has been described as autocratic and

*The Relationship
Between Strategy
Development and
Managerial Style*

**TABLE 5-1**

**Examples of Objectives and Strategies to Support Them**

| Organization | Objective | Strategies |
|---|---|---|
| Movie theater | To increase week-night attendance by 100 percent | • Increase advertising expenditures by 50 percent<br>• Offer special week-night incentives—for example, reduced ticket rates, double features, free popcorn<br>• Choose movies that appeal to more age groups—for instance, "family type" movies |
| Social Security Administration | To maintain both benefits and payroll at present levels | • Eliminate fraudulent claims<br>• Encourage people to retire at older ages<br>• Educate public in better "self-help" medical care |
| High school | To raise mean SAT scores by 50 points | • Increase in-class attention via a behavior-modification program, emphasizing rewards for achievement rather than punishment for failure and/or misbehavior<br>• Hold special classes and assign tutors to students<br>• Expand the library. |
| Truck manufacturers | To service and return to profitability | • Close obsolete plants<br>• Encourage early retirement at least by valuable employees<br>• Renegotiate contracts with suppliers to obtain price and other concessions |
| Tire manufacturers | To introduce new low-cost radial tires and capture 10 percent of the market in first year | • Stress low price in all promotion<br>• In addition to normal outlets, retail tires through unconventional outlets, such as supermarkets |
| State police department | To reduce highway fatalities by 16 percent | • Refer people arrested for drunken driving to other agencies equipped to help with drinking problems<br>• Patrol high-accident areas more thoroughly<br>Encourage driver identification of drunken and/or reckless drivers (via telephone, CB radio) |

arbitrary. He was very prestige-conscious and developed product, promotional, and distribution strategies to create a carriage-trade image of Revlon products. Revson succeeded in building a highly successful company.

Bergerac, who heads the company today, has a vastly different style. Charged, as all senior managers are, with the charter to make the company even more successful, he has implemented strategies significantly different from those of Revson. Basically, Bergerac has put less emphasis on maintaining corporate prestige and more emphasis on increasing sales and profits. His strategies have called for selling Revlon's products in supermarkets, where they had not been sold before; introducing new products for the mass market; making major modifications in package design; and acquiring a number of health-product companies. He has also made significant changes in top management personnel to implement the new marketing approach. When Bergerac's strategies were put into effect, sales and profits doubled within three years.

There is evidence that some managers are better at strategy development than others. James R. Rawls, Donna J. Rawls, and Raymond Radosevich have postulated that two distinct types of managers can be identified: **strategic managers** and **operations managers**. According to them:

> Strategic managers are externally oriented; they must deal with financiers, suppliers, customers, and representatives of governments to develop the potential for accomplishment of the firm's objectives. Strategic management defines the "business" or mission of the firm and simultaneously determines the forms of competitive advantage that will assure success. To develop this capability, strategic management secures new resources, allocates resources among existing businesses, promotes the company image, and maintains desirable public relations. . . .
>
> In contrast, operations managers utilize the potential developed by strategic management through the efficient conversion of inputs to outputs on a day-to-day, routine basis. Operations managers allocate predetermined levels of resources among the various units and activities of the firm. Operations managers are frequently functional specialists—experts in areas such as production, marketing, finance, and research and development.[1]

The ability to formulate creative yet practical strategies is clearly a desirable quality in a candidate for senior-level management. Indications are that managers who can conceive successful strategies are in short supply compared with those who can manage operations to implement strategies.

Business managers should develop strategies for all major areas of the company. This section discusses some important aspects of strategy development in three key areas of a business: (1) the products it makes, (2) how it markets the products, and (3) how it finances operations.

**Strategy Development in Business Organizations**

### Product Strategy

Theoretically, a business organization can select from dozens, even hundreds, of different product strategies. For the sake of simplicity, however, only three broad strategies are considered here.

*Product quality.* A firm may elect to produce a low-, medium-, or high-quality product. **Product quality** refers to the degree of excellence or degree of conformity to a standard that the product possesses. Some firms, such as Mercedes-Benz (automobiles), Michelin (tires), and Hewlett Packard (electronics), traditionally have opted to produce products of a high quality compared with those of competing firms. Many other companies decide that it is in their strategic best interests to produce medium-quality or relatively low-quality products.

It is a mistake to assume that making the highest possible quality product is automatically the path to profit maximization. Often organizations that make

---

[1]James R. Rawls and Donna J. Rawls, "Identifying Strategic Managers," *Business Horizons*, Nov./Dec. 1975, pp. 74–75.

relatively low-quality products are more profitable than their competitors who concentrate on average or top quality.

Managers should consider a number of factors in deciding on a product quality strategy. Competitive considerations are very important. Planners may discover that competition for one quality level is stronger than that for another. Consumer demand, economic conditions, company experience, production equipment, quality of raw materials, and the firm's reputation are considerations that influence decisions about product quality strategy.

*Number of models, styles, or types.*   A second factor relating to product strategy is the breadth of product line. A **product line** is a group of closely related products offered by a firm. To produce every size or style or model that the public might demand would be impossible, and to produce only one type or size could be an error. In practice, the decision concerning breadth of product line is a compromise strategy.

In formulating a breadth-of-line strategy, managers should consider such questions as "Do we want to direct our efforts at a mass or a select market?"; "According to past sales records, which models sell best?"; "Have our competitors introduced a new model that suggests we follow suit?"; and "What are our financial constraints?"

*Diversity of product mix.*   A **product mix** is the total variety of products offered for sale by a business. Strategies differ greatly with regard to how diversified a company's product mix should be. Some companies elect to stay in one kind of business and concentrate their efforts on a relatively homogeneous product mix. However, during the past quarter of a century many large firms have become **conglomerates** — that is, corporations made up of previously independent companies that produce and sell totally unrelated products. Diversification through acquisition of other companies has become the key strategy for the growth of many companies.

As is the case in evaluating any kind of strategy, it is impossible to determine which is the better approach without studying in detail all factors involved. Proponents of broad product diversification argue that (1) all the eggs are not in one basket, so the business has a cushion if demand for one product slips; (2) the firm may have saturated the market for one product and may need to move into other product areas to employ fully its capital and other resources; and (3) broad diversification results in a more experienced management team, with the result that the organization is better equipped to meet new problems.

While diversification is a popular strategy for large, well-financed companies, it is not always successful. Those who argue against a widely diversified product strategy claim that it spreads management too thinly across the organization. All organizations are headed by only one chief executive officer and by a few close associates. It is unlikely that these people can give their full attention to each of a number of unrelated situations. Furthermore, broad-scale diversification may result in inadequate control of financial and other resources, and unforeseen and insurmountable problems may arise because the top management team of the parent company lacks sufficient specific experience in various product lines.

A second major strategical area involves the development of marketing plans. Again, a firm has numerous alternatives. Here we consider three aspects of marketing strategy: promotion, pricing, and channel selection.

*Promotion.* Managers work with three basic promotional tools: **advertising**, which is the impersonal presentation of information about a product; **personal selling**, which is the personal presentation of information about a product; and **sales promotion**, which is a catch-all term for devices used to attract attention to a product, such as games, contests, trading stamps, and free samples.

Three basic decisions must be made in developing a promotional strategy. First, what features of the product should be stressed most (economy, quality, attractiveness, and so on)? Second, how much should be spent to promote the product? And third, how should the product be promoted—through advertising, personal selling, sales promotion, or a combination of all three? Emphasis placed on advertising, personal selling, and sales promotion varies greatly, depending mainly on the type of product produced. Consumer products, such as soap, soup, and cereals, are promoted more aggressively through advertising than industrial products, such as cranes and earth-moving equipment. The strategy taken in advertising often can affect sales significantly.

*Pricing.* Managers have three basic strategical options with regard to pricing. They can price their product (1) above the market or competitive price, (2) at or very close to the competitive price, or (3) below the competition.

Product pricing relates closely to product quality. Although there are many exceptions, high-quality products are generally priced higher than low-quality ones.

Pricing strategy is often difficult to formulate. Managers may ask and try to answer such questions as: "Should we initially price the product relatively low to gain a foothold and then raise the price when the product is established?"; "Should we introduce the product at a higher price in an effort to give it prestige and desirability?"; and "Should we simply match our nearest competitor's price?"

Pricing strategy must also consider per-unit production costs at different levels of output. Consideration must be given to the **break-even point**, that is, the point at which income equals costs. Obviously, over time, revenue received (which is a function of price and number of units sold) must exceed costs or the firm loses money.

Many firms sell their products to other firms that resell them to ultimate consumers or industrial users. Under these circumstances, the producer must establish a price that will enable the reselling organization to make a sufficiently large profit on the item.

*Selection of distribution channels.* A **channel of distribution** is the path a product takes as it moves from producer to ultimate consumer or industrial user. The shortest channel occurs when the producer bypasses middlemen and sells directly to the consumer. A long channel occurs when the producer sells through agents who in turn sell to wholesalers who then sell to retailers. The most common distribution channels are:

Manufacturer → Consumer

Manufacturer → Retailer → Consumer

Manufacturer → Wholesaler → Retailer → Consumer

Manufacturer → Agent intermediary → Wholesaler → Retailer → Consumer

Several factors affect channel-of-distribution strategy. One is the type of product. Many industrial goods of high unit value—especially those that are custom-made—are sold directly from producers to users. At the other extreme, relatively low unit value products, such as food, hardware, and drug sundries, may pass through one or more intermediaries on their way to the ultimate user. Most companies that make food products want them retailed in thousands of stores. Since doing so would require a very large sales force, it is often more economical to distribute through wholesalers.

Another factor affecting the channel of distribution is the extent of product line. A company with a wide line of similar products is more likely to use a short channel of distribution than a company with a very narrow line because the sales cost per item sold tends to be less. In the first type of company, a sales representative can sell a number of different items while making one call. Consider a manufacturer of snack foods. If one food—say, potato chips—is produced, it would be uneconomical for the manufacturer to sell direct. But if a line of twenty foods is offered, direct sale may be best.

The degree of vertical integration also determines channel-of-distribution strategy. **Vertical integration** is the performance of businesses at different levels in an industry. The snack food company could be involved in growing, processing, and retailing. Large companies often own both production and retailing facilities. In these circumstances the channel is obviously fully controlled by the organization.

*Is a larger market share always better?* Most companies strive to increase their **share of the market**—the potential customers for the firm's goods or services. However, a larger market share does not always mean greater profitability measured by return on investment. **Return on investment** (ROI) is the ratio of net income (earnings) to invested capital (stockholders' equity).

### Financial Strategy

Developing financial strategies is important in all businesses. However, the development of sound financial strategies is often de-emphasized, especially during periods of rapid economic expansion. During such periods many organizations are inclined to spend with little caution, with the result that they are unable to meet their obligations when an economic downturn occurs. Therefore, it is important that managers determine how to acquire sufficient capital and how to use revenues resulting from business operations. In developing financial strategies, managers have the following broad alternatives to consider.

*Obtain additional capital from owners.* Typically, the financial strategy developed for a new business is the owners' putting up their own capital. Banks and other lenders are reluctant to provide venture capital unless the potential owners have assets that can be quickly converted into cash at least equal to the amount of the loan. New businesses, most of which are small, may be able to obtain some credit from suppliers of inventory and equipment, but the principal strategy owner-managers must follow is to use their own capital. Often this capital is very limited, and the business may fail because of undercapitalization.

*Sell stock to the public.* This strategy, on the surface, seems the simplest and most logical. In practice, however, it is often a difficult strategy to implement for three reasons. First, unless the business has an established record of success, investors may not be interested. Second, the popularity of common stock varies greatly with the business cycle. Generally, during boom periods shares are much easier to sell in both proven and nonproven enterprises than during periods of recession. Under normal conditions people prefer to invest their money in established organizations. But even large, old-line companies find it difficult to market new stock issues during periods of economic uncertainty.

A third limiting factor to this strategy is that existing owners may not want to see their percentage of ownership diluted, perhaps to the point where they lose control of the corporation.

*Borrow money.* Large, generally healthy business organizations often follow a strategy of selling bonds, which is a form of borrowing, to finance future operations—especially expansion programs. This method is widely used by public utilities and is also very popular with nonbusiness organizations such as municipalities and other government bodies. Small businesses, however, are seldom able to finance operations in this way. Usually a person who is seeking to launch a small business must rely on savings or borrow from friends, relatives, or the Small Business Administration. Small businesses sometimes are able to obtain capital from commercial banks.

Medium-sized and large businesses typically rely on commercial banks for a portion of their capital needs. The problem here is that the ability of banks to make loans varies considerably from time to time. How much banks can loan and the interest rate they charge are determined ultimately by the fiscal and monetary policies of the federal government. Life insurance companies, pension trusts, and other institutions may advance money, especially for certain kinds of real-estate projects.

*Obtain credit from suppliers.* Most businesses try to obtain credit from suppliers as part of their financial strategy. For the purchase of inventory, granting credit is only a short-run financing device, usually extending over a thirty- to ninety-day period. Equipment, however, can be purchased by credit-worthy organizations for longer periods, ranging up to several years.

*Decide how to use profits.* In deciding what to do with business profits, senior managers have three alternatives: (1) pay all the profits to shareholders, (2) retain all profits to expand and improve the business, or (3) declare some of the profits as dividends and retain a portion of them to help implement an expansion or improvement strategy.

The first alternative is rarely followed, since virtually all top managers want to see the business become more valuable in the future. Declaring all profits as dividends in effect limits the organization's financial capability for growth. Managers in young companies with excellent growth potential usually exercise the second alternative. They reason that plowing profits back into the business makes sense, since the money so used will generate more profits in future years.

The third alternative—allocating part of the profits to dividends and part to expansion—is a practice widely followed by large, well-established, slow-growing companies. The percentage to pay as dividends and the percentage to retain is a judgmental question. Typically the board of directors, the body that legally makes dividend decisions, will consider the special financial needs the business may have in the future, the amount of money that should be set aside for contingencies, the special expansion opportunities that may be available, and the dividend rates in recent quarters.

## Strategy Development in Nonbusiness Organizations

In terms of management in general and strategy development in particular, business and nonprofit enterprises have more in common than people sometimes think. Nonprofit organizations provide a "product," or something that gives satisfaction to people. They also perform a marketing function. Nonbusiness organizations must also deal with problems of financing. Table 5–2 shows examples of strategy alternatives that three nonbusiness organizations might encounter relative to products, marketing, and finance.

## The Need for Greater Emphasis on Strategy Development

Strategies are the most important type of plan. But, in general, too little talent, time, and other resources are devoted to the construction of strategies. Many businesses do not construct grand plans to achieve objectives, often because their primary and derivative objectives have not been clearly spelled out. Most organizations, rightly or wrongly, are oriented toward the status quo, and their managers fail to view the future as dynamic.

Whether this is proper or not is a judgmental question. On the one hand, people frequently feel more comfortable if the organization they support does not change dramatically. Most people feel at ease with a government that is stable, with social clubs that do not change requirements for membership, and with other organized behavior that places top priority on tradition.

On the other hand, some feel that managers in all organizations should be more aggressive and should develop grand strategies to guide their organizations to greater achievement.

Whether or not profit-seeking and nonprofit organizations will place more emphasis on developing strategies for goal achievement in the future remains to be seen. Regardless of one's point of view, it is apparent that human resources are often underutilized because managers fail to create comprehensive plans for the achievement of major business and social goals.

## Guidelines for Developing and Applying Strategies

Since strategies are the major plans of an organization, considerable care should be taken in their design and execution. Following are six major guidelines for strategy development.

### All Strategies Should Directly Support the Organization's Objectives

Since an organization is a group of people working toward a common end, all work should be directed toward the achievement of that end. For example, senior managers of a university may establish as a primary objective "to provide the best intellectual leadership in the region." But if strategies such as "reducing research expenditures by 20 percent" and "maintaining faculty salaries at current levels for twelve months" are established, the strategies appear to contradict the primary goal and make it harder to reach.

### All Derivative Plans Should Support the Basic Strategies

All other plans—an organization's policies, procedures, and rules—should be designed to help the organization achieve its principal goals. Put another way, the only reason for having policies, procedures, and rules is to implement strategies.

### Strategies Should Be Based on the Best Possible Forecasts

Forecasting, discussed in Chapter 6, plays an important role in the development of strategies. If revenue predictions are highly inaccurate, then strategies based on anticipated income may not work out. An organization may develop a

*"How do you want it—the crystal mumbo-jumbo
or statistical probability?"*

**TABLE 5–2**

Strategy Alternatives for Noncommercial Enterprises
Are Similar to Those for Profit-seeking Organizations

| Institution | Some Product Strategy Alternatives | Some Marketing Strategy Alternatives | Some Financial Strategy Alternatives |
|---|---|---|---|
| University | • Concentrate on certain kinds of educational programs, such as hotel administration.<br>• Limit the "product" to undergraduate education.<br>• Offer a broad-based "line" of continuing-education programs. | • Use direct-mail promotion extensively to promote enrollment.<br>• Involve community leaders in planning to add prestige to the university.<br>• Establish "chairs" to make institution more attractive to potential students. | • Raise, lower, or maintain tuition levels.<br>• Conduct fund-raising projects among alumni to pay for special activities.<br>• Develop in-depth reports to justify need for more state appropriations. |
| Private club | • Provide recreational services for all members of the family.<br>• Provide limited "live-in" accommodations.<br>• Hire name entertainers to make the club more appealing to members. | • Locate the facility in a more desirable area.<br>• Use an advertising campaign to attract new members.<br>• Prepare a regular newsletter to keep members informed. | • Increase dues to members.<br>• Increase prices to non-members who use club facilities.<br>• Conduct special "benefit programs" to raise money. |
| County government | • Develop new programs to please certain segments of the population.<br>• Revise current programs.<br>• Discontinue some programs. | • Use advertising media to sell new concepts to the people.<br>• Have government representatives explain activities to businesses and individuals.<br>• Provide incentives to people who will participate in new programs. | • Enact new taxes to pay for programs.<br>• Borrow money by selling bonds.<br>• Use existing tax revenues to fund activities. |

strategy for expansion based on its revenue forecast, but if the predicted income does not materialize, the expansion strategy is jeopardized.

### Subordinate Managers Should Participate in Strategy Development

Ideally, all managers who will help implement a strategy should participate in formulating it. Senior managers may have the right to develop a strategy and impose it on subordinate managers, but doing so is usually unwise for two reasons. First, subordinate managers normally have ideas and information that can help improve the strategy. Second, if subordinate managers help develop a strategy, they are usually more enthusiastic in carrying it out.

### Contingency Strategies Should Be Developed

An enterprise may develop what appears to be an excellent strategy to achieve its goals, but the external environment is changing constantly. A company may have a financial strategy of selling stock. What happens if a severe economic recession develops, making the sale of stock impossible? In this case a back-up plan should be available to prevent serious financial problems for the organization.

One important area in which the need for contingency planning is becoming very important is the product recall situation. Many food products, appliances, and automobiles have had to be recalled, usually because of some hazard to health or life. Organizations that have standby plans to meet such contingencies are better equipped to handle these problems than those that do not.

### Strategies Should Be Monitored Continuously

Closely related to the need for contingency plans is the need to observe how well an adopted strategy is working. Say a firm has a strategy of expanding by selling franchises. If it discovers through careful monitoring that franchising is not working as planned, it should develop another strategy. Or, if an advertising strategy isn't selling a product as planned, the strategy should be amended or a new one designed.

The monitoring of strategies is particularly important for business organizations because of a firm's inability to control competitive actions. When a company's strategies are adversely affected by changes in a competitor's product, promotion, pricing, or other strategies, some amendments may be needed in basic plans.

Various constraints are imposed on managers in performing planning and other management functions. An interesting example concerns the restrictions placed on public accounting firms in developing strategies to obtain new business. Public accounting firms are profit-seeking enterprises. While they may now advertise, they are prohibited by the American Institute of Public Accountants from making uninvited direct solicitations to acquire new clients.

**Constraints Placed on Strategy Development**

A problem, then, of CPA firms is to develop strategies for obtaining new business (called *practice development*) by inducing prospective clients to come to them. Some of the strategies commonly used are:

* Sponsoring seminars on changes in IRS regulations and various financial issues
* Hosting dinners for key people in the business community to discuss economic conditions and government trends
* Encouraging personnel to socialize with prospective clients at country clubs and civic organizations, to engage in public speaking, and to write articles for business and academic publications
* Specializing in certain kinds of industries
* Showing more interest in small prospective clients

Strategies such as these largely concern image building or public relations. But they apparently work, as evidenced by their extensive use by the "Big Eight" and other accounting firms.

Up to this point we have examined strategies, the major or grand plans designed to achieve an organization's objectives. Strategies determine to a large extent the nature of other plans—policies, budgets, procedures, and rules. In practice, a common mistake in managing is the failure to coordinate all plans needed to make strategies work. Figure 5–1 shows how plans might be coordinated in a fast-food chain in order to achieve the chain's objective.

**FIGURE 5–1**

**Coordination of Plans to Support Objectives and Strategies**

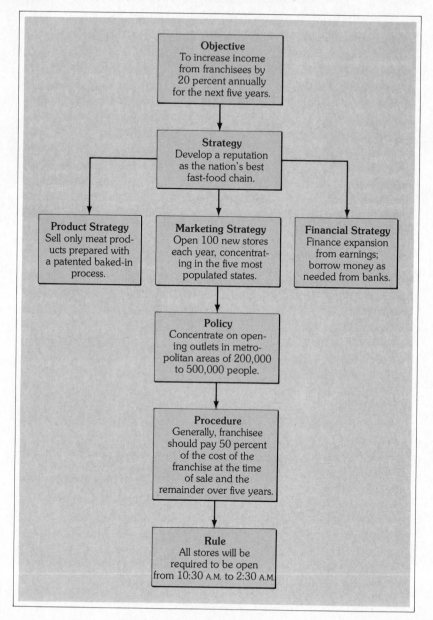

## WHAT ARE BUDGETS?

A **budget** is a plan expressed in numerical terms, whose purpose is to control operations. We normally think of budgets as control devices that indicate how financial resources are to be allocated. But budgets are also developed to allocate man-hours, equipment use, raw material use, and other resources.

Budgets are key plans, since many other plans are dependent on them. Numerous decisions a manager makes depend on how much money is allocated to perform the department's activities or how many man-hours are assigned to a task. Budgets are discussed in detail in Chapter 20.

## WHAT ARE POLICIES?

A **policy** is a broadly stated course of action to be followed as a guideline in making decisions. While a strategy is a broad, general plan that gives overall direction to an enterprise, a policy is a supporting plan that deals with a more specific aspect of ongoing operations.

A policy is a *guide*; it allows some discretion in its implementation. For instance, an example of a policy is "Preference in employment will be given to college graduates from business schools." Note that this statement is a guideline. The personnel department or other managers who hire individuals are directed to seek out college graduates who have earned a degree from a school of business. However, the policy contains the word "preference," which gives managers some latitude to hire a graduate from another professional discipline or even a non-graduate.

The amount of discretion granted a manager in applying a policy may be very narrow, as suggested by this policy: "Only fully qualified persons already working in the plant may be considered for promotion to supervisor." (Here the discretionary factor involves a determination of what is meant by "fully qualified." The manager cannot go outside the organization to select a supervisor.) Or the discretionary area may be large, as suggested by this policy: "In the case of a holdup, the manager should place the safety of customers and employees first and then use his or her best judgment in deciding how to deal with the situation." How to "place the safety of customers and employees first" allows considerable discretion, as does "use his or her best judgment in deciding how to deal with the situation."

Policies may be developed at any level of the organization; hence there may be major, minor, and operational policies. They may relate to any functional area and may cover virtually any organizational situation, ranging from the length of employee vacations to the purchase of products from customers. Policies may be written or may be implied by the behavior of managers. For example, a company may have no written policy about class of travel, but if the chief executive always flies tourist, a "fly tourist" policy is implied for all other managers to follow.

Below are specific examples of policies. In each case note that an area of discretion is permitted the manager. Note also the variety of situations that can be covered by policies.

*Examples of Policies*

*Statements to the press.* "No manager shall make any statement to the press on any matter that he or she considers possibly damaging to the best

# MANAGERS IN ACTION

## HOW MUCH INFORMATION DO SENIOR MANAGERS NEED TO MAKE WISE DECISIONS?

As the previous section suggests, strategies are key plans that, over a period of time, determine the success of an organization. Some people feel that managers receive too much detailed information, which interferes with the development of strategic planning.

Economics Professor Thomas H. Naylor observes that, "The detail required by senior management for strategic planning and budgeting is minimal."[1] Yet, in practice, executives in many companies receive vast amounts of numerical data to help them develop strategies. The result of this numerical overload is to misdirect executives' attention from truly important tasks, such as thinking about new products, elimination of unprofitable divisions, and cost control.

Professor Naylor also notes that "the tendency for senior executives to fall back on excessive accounting detail . . . does not strengthen their position. To be effective, senior management must learn to ask the right questions about strategic

plans and budgets. And the right questions do not necessarily require vast amounts of data."[2]

However, some senior managers believe they need more, not less, detailed information. To meet this need, computer-based executive information systems, also called decision support systems, are growing in popularity. These systems provide an executive with information about almost any facet of the company's activities quickly and easily.

Using an executive information system, an executive of an oil equipment supply company discovered that one product line was priced far below the competition. "His analysis showed that the company could have made a couple of million dollars more by bringing its prices closer to the competition's. His reaction was, 'If I can find this out in an afternoon, where was the manager of this division? What was he doing all year?' "[3]

[1]Quoted from the April 6, 1981 issue of *Business Week* by special permission, © 1981 by McGraw-Hill, Inc. New York, NY 10020. All rights reserved.

[2]Ibid.

[3]Mary Bralove, "Some Chief Executives Bypass, and Irk, Staffs in Getting Information," *The Wall Street Journal*, January 12, 1983, p. 20. Reprinted by permission of *The Wall Street Journal*, © Dow Jones & Company, Inc., 1983. All rights reserved.

### QUESTIONS

1. What dangers are there in an executive getting too much information for strategy development?
2. What are five critical questions that should be answered in developing a marketing strategy for a new product?

interests of the organization unless he or she has first cleared the statement with the Office of Director of Corporate Communications."

*Product recall.* "Any product manager may recall specific products from retail outlets when he or she has evidence or expert opinion that the product is or may prove to be a health hazard."

*Promotion from within.* "All promotions shall be from within the organization unless, in the judgment of the manager involved, no qualified person exists within the department to fill the position. In such an event, the manager will make the available position known to managers of other departments and ask them to recommend personnel for the position. If no individual can be found in this manner to fill the vacancy, the manager of the department involved is authorized to select an individual from outside the organization."

*Giving of gifts to customers.* "The maximum dollar limit on gifts for executives in organizations that buy from us is $100. Managers, however, are expected to spend significantly less than this amount, and the average cost of gifts should not exceed $50 per executive."

*Business ethics.* "Managers are expected to conduct themselves ethically in all situations in which they represent the company to the public. A situation that the manager feels may be a breach of ethics shall be brought to the attention of his or her superior for resolution."

*Pricing.* "Field managers shall price products at their discretion, provided that product prices are no more than 10 percent higher than those of our leading competitor and no more than 10 percent lower than those of our leading competitor."

*Inventory policy.* "Production managers will keep on hand no less than 90 days' normal requirements and no more than 120 days' normal requirements, unless the production manager feels major price increases are imminent. In such a case the manager is authorized to purchase up to 150 days' normal requirements. On the other hand, if the production manager believes a major price reduction is imminent, he or she should allow inventories to decline to 60 days' normal requirements before replenishing them."

*Improper conduct of employee.* "A manager observing an employee who appears to be experiencing the effects of a drug, including alcohol, should terminate the employee immediately unless the manager (1) feels the employee's condition will not recur or (2) believes the employee should be given a second opportunity because of past performance. Under no circumstances will the manager allow an employee to continue with the organization after he or she has been observed under the influence of drugs twice during any consecutive twelve-month period."

It is difficult to conceive of an organization's successfully achieving its goals without following policies. The main advantages of policies are discussed in the following sections.

**Advantages of Policies**

### Policies Help Save Time

Policies are designed for future situations that are likely to arise. Without policies as guidelines, employees would spend an excessive amount of time deciding each situation on its own merits. Policies save time because they provide for a way to handle similar situations. Managers do have some leeway in the manner in which they enforce policies, but most of the thinking needed to solve the problem has already been done.

### Policies Help Prevent Managerial Mistakes

Generally, policies are not developed in the heat of a situation but rather when the potential problem is being considered in depth, with attention given to both short- and long-run ramifications. If policies are created under these conditions, they are likely to be excellent guides for managers who ultimately face the situation. In contrast, if managers are required to make a large number of decisions without good guidelines, they are likely to make costly blunders.

### Policies Help Improve the Consistency of Managerial Performance

It is important that policies be developed to ensure consistency in the manner in which functions and activities are carried out. For example, policies about such matters as pregnancy leave, employment of two or more persons from the same family, and financial assistance for employees who go to school should be developed, communicated, and applied. If matters such as these are handled inconsistently, fear, distrust, and confusion result.

## Requirements for Sound Policies

A "good" policy promotes organizational effectiveness, while a "bad" policy hinders and even harms the organization. Generally, managers give too little time and attention to the construction of policies. Policy formulation is not easy, for it requires careful thought if done properly. Below are some requirements for sound policies.

### Policies Should Be Consistent with Strategies and Objectives

Policies have one key purpose—to help the organization implement its strategies effectively so that the objectives of the enterprise can be achieved. In considering a proposed policy, management should weigh its impact on *all* facets of the enterprise's activities. All managers who would implement the policy and all those who would be affected by it should be consulted before it is adopted. For example, if senior managers are considering a policy that states "We will attempt to meet competitive prices under normal conditions," they should discuss this idea with marketing managers before adopting it because the latter may have good reasons to feel that such a policy would be unfavorable in some situations.

A proposed safety policy may conflict with budgetary proposals or with engineering capabilities. A credit policy calling for more restrictive issuance of credit cards may be in conflict with the marketing manager's plan to ease up on credit requirements in an attempt to increase sales volume.

A main point in policy development, then, is to make certain that the managers of all those operations affected by the proposed policy are in general agreement. Otherwise, conflict may develop, the adopted policy may be counterproductive, and progress toward organizational goals may be retarded. "Will the proposed policy contribute positively to the attainment of organizational goals?" is a question that should be answered before a policy is adopted.

# ISSUE FOR DEBATE

## DOES AMERICAN BUSINESS PLACE TOO MUCH EMPHASIS ON NEW PRODUCT STRATEGY?

Management in American business spends a great deal of money on developing new products. Some believe the investment is justified; others do not. Below are pros and cons of giving new products a high priority in strategical planning.

| YES | NO |
|---|---|
| **Too much emphasis is placed on new product strategy because . . .** | **Too much emphasis is not placed on new product strategy because . . .** |
| By the most conservative estimates, eight out of ten new products fail in the marketplace. This represents a huge loss in talent and money. | Strong emphasis on developing new products improves productivity. |
| Money spent developing new products would be better invested perfecting existing products. | New products such as robots and word processors increase efficiency and greatly outweigh the costs of their development. |
| Many "new" products aren't really new. They are simply variations of existing products. A major reason for consumer dissatisfaction with American-made products is low quality, which results from frequent introduction of new models. | If business de-emphasized strategies for new product development, progress would slow. American firms would fall further behind in international markets. |
| Introduction of new products is often simply planned obsolescence. The net result of planned obsolescense is higher prices to consumers and lower profits to businesses. | A new product is a competitive weapon for the firm that produces it. New product development should be encouraged because it strengthens our competitive economic system. |

### QUESTIONS

1. Which side of the argument do you feel is stronger? Why?
2. What other points, pro and con can you make?

### Policies Should Be Reviewed Frequently and Amended as Needed

Management is practiced in an ever-changing environment. It follows, then, that a policy should be reviewed from time to time to see if it needs modification to help support the achievement of organizational goals. For example, a policy stating "Our supermarkets will be open from 9:00 A.M. to 9:00 P.M. Monday through Saturday unless longer or shorter hours can be justified by the store manager" may have been an expression of intelligent management intent in the past. However, the desire of some consumers to shop late at night and on Sundays has made such a policy unworkable in many areas. Or a policy of allowing employees to select their own vacation periods may need revision if too many employees elect to take their vacations at the same time — a practice that might adversely interfere with production schedules.

Henry Ford I once had an unwritten product policy expressed as follows: "We'll give the customer any color car he wants, so long as it's black." Obviously, as conditions changed and more cars in different colors were offered by competitors, Ford had to change this policy.

### Policies Should Limit the Discretion Given Managers

One of the characteristics of a policy is that it permits some discretion on the part of the managers who implement it. However, if the policy is too broad and permits *excessive* discretion by managers, it is self-defeating.

Policies are useful because they save time, help prevent managerial mistakes, and result in reasonably uniform handling of similar situations. A policy such as "The managers in charge of each department may handle all forms of employee disturbances and unrest in any manner they feel best" fails to serve the welfare of the organization. It is much too broad to have value.

If a policy is to serve as an effective guideline for handling employee disturbances, it should more clearly describe the authority of the manager in charge and spell out, within reasonable limits, the manner in which such situations are to be handled. A vague, generalized policy is almost equivalent to no policy at all.

### Policies Should Be in Writing

A policy need not be in writing to be a policy. In fact, it is probable that in most organizations, most policies are unwritten. An important exception is the government. Government agencies have policies covering almost every conceivable situation. But ideally policies should be written, for several reasons.

First, the act of writing policies tends to cause those who propose them to consider their content more carefully. Written policies have much more precision than unwritten policies.

Second, a written policy is easier to understand than an unwritten one. It can be reread and studied until its meaning and intent are clear.

Third, a written policy can be transmitted quickly to those who must implement it. A large organization may prepare policies intended for hundreds of managers. A change in policy, if it is written, can be communicated accurately and quickly to all managers involved.

Fourth, written policies are easier and less time-consuming to communicate to new managers and management trainees. An organization can have written policies placed in manuals for study, rather than have higher-level managers give long, detailed explanations.

Finally, written policies require less reliance on memory than unwritten ones. Some policies are implemented only infrequently. In such situations, having policies in written form is a great convenience to the manager.

### Policies Must Be Applied

Obviously, there is no point in having a policy if it is not applied. Therefore, a final test of the worthiness of a policy is "Are those in charge of enforcing it doing so?"

An organization that communicates policies to its personnel but does not apply them loses their respect. Employees may conclude, "Management doesn't mean what it says." Morale and discipline problems may result.

## Increasing Attention to Policy Development and Application

Policies are not new; they are as old as organized activity. However, more attention is being given to their development and fair application for the following two reasons: the trend toward larger organizations and the growing demand for equal treatment.

### Trend Toward Larger Organizations

Generally speaking, the larger the organization, the greater the need for clear policies. In a very small organization there may be no need for sick-leave or vacation policies. The manager can handle each case on its merits. However, as an organization grows larger, a more formalized set of policies needs to be developed to save the time of managers and to promote consistent application.

### Demand for Equal Treatment

Our society has long stood for equal treatment in a wide variety of situations. In practice, however, equality is not always practiced. In recent decades many groups have been demanding that they receive the same across-the-board treatment from organizations. Employees have made charges of discrimination in hiring, training, promotion, and severence. Customers have also demanded equality of treatment, especially in times of shortage, when they ask a supplier, "What is your allocation policy? We want our share." Sellers may express a demand for equality when they ask potential customers, "What is your policy on competitive bidding for contracts? We want a fair chance to sell to you." Labor union officials also demand to be informed of company policies so that they can evaluate the policies' fairness and adequacy. Thus, policies often are the subject of much communication between an organization and its employees, suppliers, customers, and other interested publics.

## WHAT ARE PROCEDURES?

Now we direct our attention to procedures, another type of plan needed to help an organization to execute its strategies and achieve its objectives.

A **procedure** is a detailed plan of action for accomplishing a given activity or handling a specific situation. A procedure indicates the specific steps to be taken in order to perform a task. In medicine there are procedures for conducting surgical operations; in the practice of law there are procedures for presenting a case in court; and in accounting there are procedures for filing tax appeals.

A great deal of the work in an organization is governed by procedures. Procedures may exist to cover such diverse activities as filling customer orders, indoctrinating new employees, distributing mail to various departments, and dealing with pickets outside the company offices. Procedures are found at all levels of an organization and in all areas.

## Examples of Procedures

A procedure is somewhat like a policy, but it specifies in more detail the kind of action required to handle a specific situation. An example of a procedure for dealing with customer complaints is:

> The salesperson will listen carefully to the complaint, ascertain the problem, and try to solve it to the satisfaction of the customer. If this cannot be done, the salesperson will introduce the customer to the assistant manager, who in turn will listen to the complaint and make whatever proposals are within his or her defined limits of authority. If this fails, the assistant manager shall escort the customer to the manager, who will make the final decision to dispose of the matter.

## The Importance and Advantages of Procedures

The importance of procedures is sometimes downplayed because procedure development seems far removed from the larger matters of goal setting, strategy development, and policy making. However, procedures are essential in most organizations and help determine the overall degree of success achieved by an enterprise. The main advantages of procedures are discussed next.

### Procedures Can Save Time and Other Resources

Well-prepared procedures contribute to more efficient job performance, reducing what otherwise might be a complicated activity to a simple routine. In the absence of procedures, managers would be required to invest excessive time in dealing with repetitive situations.

### Procedures Help in Training New Employees

Well-prepared procedures reduce the time required for people to become proficient in performing a job. Many formal and informal training programs are concerned mainly with the teaching of job procedures. With well-developed procedures, employees can be trained quickly and efficiently.

### Procedures Help in Handling Emergencies

Managers in many organizations deal frequently with emergencies or, because of potential hazards, must be prepared to deal with them. For example, managers of fire and police departments need procedures for coping with a wide variety of situations that require immediate response. When a fire breaks out or a robbery is in progress, there simply is not time to engage in elaborate planning. Rather, the manager in charge must resort to procedures established in advance for dealing with the situation at hand. In the absence of procedures, employees might behave chaotically or at cross-purposes.

By no means are all procedures effective and efficient. We still encounter inefficient handling of traffic detours, and many of us frequently wait in line because a sound procedure is not in effect for handling customer traffic. In fact, many, if not most, of the complaints people have about their interactions with organizations are really complaints relating to the organizations' procedures, not to their strategies or objectives. This is true in part because procedures—both good and bad—are most often in the public view.

If an organization wishes to maintain good relations with its customers and others, small things can make a big difference. Although procedures are comparatively minor plans, they can make a large difference in terms of results. Following are requirements for sound and effective procedures.

### Procedures Should Be Simple

Simplicity, not complexity, is a characteristic of all good plans. Procedures especially should be simple enough to be understood by both those who implement them and those who are affected by them. There is an old axiom to the effect that "Anything that can be misunderstood will be." Those responsible for developing procedures should strive to make them as easy to comprehend and implement as possible.

### Procedures Should Be in Writing

As with policies, procedures should be reduced to writing. In the process of writing out a procedure, a manager may discover flaws in it that can be corrected. Furthermore, a written procedure is easy to refer to and review.

### Procedures Should Be Tested

Because of their importance, procedures should be tested prior to full adoption. In any type of enterprise it often takes considerable time and practice to reduce an activity to smooth routine.

### Procedures Should Be Communicated Effectively

Procedures should be communicated so that they are thoroughly understood by those who are required to follow them. Often it is not enough just to publish a procedure and distribute it to the people involved. Briefing sessions may be required to explain the procedures and answer questions.

### Procedures Should Be Consistent with Objectives

A sound procedure is consistent with the objectives of the organization because its basic purpose is to help achieve these goals. In practice, there is often a serious deviation between the announced goals of an organization and the procedures used to achieve them. A department store, for example, may make public appeals such as "The customer is our first consideration in everything we do" and yet have very difficult and annoying procedures for processing applications for credit.

### Procedures Should Be Revised as Needed

Procedures, like all plans, should not be regarded as permanent. As conditions change, procedures should be revised to conform. The installation of a computer, for example, may necessitate numerous changes in procedures concerning the recording of sales transactions, the keeping of employee records, and the scheduling of overtime.

## WHAT ARE RULES?

Another form of plan is a **rule**, which is a statement that something be done or not be done in a very specific situation. Airline passengers are familiar with two simple rules required by the Federal Aviation Agency and imposed by the airlines: "No smoking is permitted while the No Smoking sign is lighted" and "All carry-on luggage must be placed beneath the seat in front of you." Rules are nonnegotiable and allow managers no discretion; they must be enforced. Table 5–3 shows examples of rules covering different situations.

While rules should be stated in simple, concrete, and objective language, it does not necessarily follow that they are arrived at quickly and without in-depth analysis. Since rules are absolute directives that managers must enforce, much consideration should be given to them before they are finalized and made operational.

**Why Are Rules Needed?**

The need for clearly defined rules is frequently overlooked or de-emphasized by managers. Yet rule setting is very important in most organizations. For one thing, rules save time. As with procedures, rules prescribe managerial conduct for recurring situations and for emergencies. The manager involved need not think through the situation. Rather, he or she simply implements the specified action.

Rules also help give employees a sense of security. Just as people prefer to play games in which the rules are specifically stated, employees feel more secure when they know what they can and cannot do.

**Requirements for Rules**

Rule setting is necessary if an organization is to achieve its goals satisfactorily. Effective rules meet four basic requirements.

### Rules Should Be Necessary

It is pointless and a waste of time to develop rules for situations that will never occur.

### Rules Should Be Expressed Positively

When rules are stated positively, they are more likely to be accepted by employees. Rules that are expressed negatively or in a threatening manner are apt to create resentment among persons required to obey them. A safety rule expressed in the following language —"You are absolutely required to wear a hard hat while in this area"—is not likely to be received as well as the same idea expressed

**TABLE 5–3**

**127**

*Summary*

**Examples of Rules for Different Situations**

| Situation | Example of Rule |
|---|---|
| Working conditions | • Employees in Department A are required to work the Saturday shift every four weeks.<br>• Employees must wear safety glasses while operating their machines.<br>• Employees who work in the bakery department must wear company-supplied hair-covering devices at all times. |
| Use of equipment | • All M11 machines are to be inspected by the maintenance department after every 200 hours of operation.<br>• No company vehicle is to be driven above posted speed limits. Any employee ticketed for speeding is required to pay all costs.<br>• No company-owned equipment may be taken from the premises without written authorization by a supervisor. |
| Customer service | • No service person is authorized to change the price of any item.<br>• Three items of identification are required when a customer wishes to cash a personal check.<br>• The store must be kept open to the public until 11:00 P.M. All customers must be out of the store not later than 11:15 P.M. |

in this language—"For your own protection against serious head and other injuries, you must wear a hard hat while in this area."

### Rules Should Be Written and Communicated

Unless they are written, rules can become very distorted over time. And unless communicated properly, rules may have no effect whatever on the behavior of persons they are designed to influence.

### Rules Should Be Dynamic

Rules need to be revised as conditions change or eliminated if the need for them no longer exists. If rules no longer cover the conditions for which they were intended yet continue to be enforced, individuals may lose confidence in other rules that are still necessary. Personnel become demoralized when unnecessary rules are imposed on them.

**SUMMARY**

• Strategies are broad plans intended to help an organization achieve its goals.
• Responsibility for strategy development rests with senior management, although lower-level managers may make some inputs.
• Strategies often reflect the management style of those who design them. A manager with a conservative approach to managing will tend to develop "safer" strategies than a manager who enjoys taking risks.
• Three broad product strategies relate to (1) product quality; (2) the number of models, styles, or types; and (3) diversity of product mix.
• Marketing strategies are needed for promotional programs, pricing, and the selection of distribution channels.

- Financial strategies must be developed to provide capital. Management may obtain additional capital from the owners, sell stock, borrow money, or obtain credit from suppliers. Financial strategies are also needed to direct the use of profits.
- Nonbusiness enterprises are also concerned with developing strategies. Like commercial organizations, nonprofit enterprises must develop product, marketing, and financial strategies.
- Generally, too little emphasis is placed on strategy development. Rightly or wrongly, most organizations are oriented toward the status quo and do not view the future as dynamic.
- Strategies should directly support the organization's objectives, be supported by derivative plans, be based on the best forecasts, have inputs from those who will implement them, include contingency plans, and be monitored continuously.
- Budgets are a form of plan needed to allocate money, equipment, raw materials, and other resources in order to achieve an enterprise's objectives.
- Policies are guides for helping to implement strategies and are needed to cover all organizational activities. Managers have some discretion in implementing policies.
- Key advantages of policies are that they save time, help prevent managerial mistakes, and improve the consistency of managerial performance.
- To be sound, a policy should be consistent with strategies and objectives, be reviewed frequently, limit managerial discretion, be written, and be applied.
- More attention is being given to policy development and application because of the trend toward larger organizations and the increasing demand for equality.
- Procedures are detailed plans of action for handling specific situations.
- Well-prepared procedures save time, help in training new employees, and help in handling emergencies.
- A sound procedure is simple, written, well tested, well communicated, consistent with objectives, and revised as needed.
- Rules are the most specific form of plan, allowing for no discretion on the part of managers. Rules save time and give employees a sense of security.
- To be effective, a rule should be necessary, expressed in a positive manner, written and communicated, and revised or eliminated as conditions change.

## LEARN THE LANGUAGE OF MANAGEMENT

| | |
|---|---|
| strategy | break-even point |
| strategic managers | channel of distribution |
| operations managers | vertical integration |
| product quality | share of the market |
| product line | return on investment |
| product mix | budget |
| conglomerates | policy |
| advertising | procedure |
| personal selling | rule |
| sales promotion | |

## QUESTIONS FOR REVIEW AND DISCUSSION

1. Why are strategies important? Can an organization be successful without effective strategies? Explain.
2. Why is it a mistake to assume that companies that sell the highest-quality products will be the most profitable?

3. What are the pros and cons of broad product diversification?
4. What basic decisions must be made in developing a promotional strategy?
5. What factors help determine a firm's channel-of-distribution strategy?
6. What are the main strategies for obtaining capital to finance operations?
7. In deciding how to use profits, what alternatives should be considered?
8. Why should more emphasis be given to strategy development?
9. How do policies differ from strategies? How do policies differ from procedures?

### 1. Policies, procedures, and rules

Assume you are the new owner of a record store. Develop three policies, three procedures, and three rules that you might use to help manage your store. Make certain you differentiate clearly among policies, procedures, and rules.

### 2. Developing a policy statement on alcoholism

You are a management consultant to a large corporation that employs approximately 800 people at the management level. The president of the company has asked you to prepare a policy statement on how the organization should deal with the problem of management personnel whose behavior suggests that they may be alcoholics. He wants you to cover all subjects relative to the problem, including discipline, dismissal, rehabilitation, furlough, and so on.

In 300 words or less, prepare the statement you would submit. Then briefly justify your viewpoints.

### 3. Should Best Cola acquire a timber company?

Best Cola is a 60-year-old soft drink company. It produces and markets soft drinks, other nonalcoholic beverages, and a line of snack foods through its worldwide system of franchises.

Best Cola has a problem: It is cash rich! How to use its cash surplus of over $4 billion is the sole purpose of the meeting called by Herbert T., chairman of the board. Those present are Herbert T., chairman; Alex F., president; Walter O., senior legal counsel; Libby R., senior investment counsel; and Bruce P., vice-president for strategic planning.

Herbert: I've called this meeting for one purpose. As you know, Best Cola has a cash surplus of over $4 billion. Currently, this money is invested in government securities and yields a fair return, but I don't think the return is large enough. For one thing, there is no appreciation in value. All we get is interest. I think it's unfair to our shareholders and to us, the management, not to use that money to get a return on our investments and capital appreciation as well. Another investment might achieve this goal.

Libby: Do you have a specific industry in mind?

Herbert: Yes. I'm attracted by the timber industry. Companies in that field have lost huge sums in recent years and at least two of them could be had for three to four billion dollars.

Alex: But Herbert, all of our expertise is in beverages and snack foods. I don't believe any of us knows much about the timber industry.

Bruce: I agree with your basic premise, Herbert. We should invest our surplus capital in an equity position or positions. But I also agree with Alex. A timber acquisition is too far out for us.

Walter: From a legal standpoint, I don't see any unusual problems in acquiring a company in a totally different industry, but I agree with Alex and Bruce. We simply have no background in timber. Best Cola is the industry leader because we have developed the best management team for the business we're in. If we don't know what we're doing, we could lose a lot of cash fast in a business we don't understand.

Herbert: (Laughing a little) Well, it seems you folks don't like my idea. But consider what we've got going for us. We know the international market. Exporting timber to Japan and other countries would be a big part of our timber business. Now, I agree we don't know the day-to-day problems a timber company faces, but we can always hire experts for that. Our main management concern would be to provide long-run strategic thinking.

Libby: There are dozens of industries that might be more attractive—motion pictures, computer software, high technology, or robots.

Herbert: I know, but those industries are already overpriced. The timber industry, on the other hand, is underpriced. The soft demand for housing in recent years makes the price of a major acquisition very attractive.

Bruce: Our shareholders view us as a food company. If we enter the timber business, we risk losing their support.

Herbert: (A little irritated) Look, our shareholders want good dividends and appreciation of their shares. They could care less about the business we're in.

Here is what I want from each of you. Think of other industries we might consider for investment and be prepared to justify your recommendations. Libby, I want you to pull together the hard facts as well as the projections for the top three timber companies. I'll call another meeting in two weeks.

And remember, any future acquisition has got to be kept confidential. We don't want speculators bidding up the stock in a company we may want to acquire.

Do you agree with Herbert's observation that shareholders are interested only in dividends and stock appreciation? Why or why not?

Herbert seems unconcerned about the lack of management experience in the timber industry. Is he correct in his view? Why or why not?

The timber industry is a slow-growth, conservative, relatively low-income business. Would it be wiser in your opinion for Best Cola to invest its surplus cash in more dynamic industries such as computers or high technology? Why or why not?

**FOR ADDITIONAL
CONCEPTS
AND IDEAS**

Bloom, Paul N., and Kotler, Philip. "Strategies for High Market-Share Companies." *Harvard Business Review*, November–December 1975, pp. 63–72.

Bowman, Edward H. "A Risk/Return Paradox for Strategic Management." *Sloan Management Review*, Spring 1980, pp. 17–31.

Cummings, William Theodore, and Daley, James M. "Strategic Management: A Marketing Segmental Approach." *Business*, November 1981, pp. 10–15.

Doz, Yves L., and Prahalda, C. K. "Headquarters Influence and Strategic Control in MNCs." *Sloan Management Review*, Fall 1981, pp. 15–29.

Foster, Richard N. "Linkage Comes to United International: A Fable for Strategists." *Business Horizons,* December 1980, pp. 66—77.

Hobbs, John M., and Heany, Donald F. "Coupling Strategy to Operating Plans." *Harvard Business Review*, May—June 1977, pp. 119—126.

McGinnis, Vern J. "The Mission Statement: A Key Step in Strategic Planning." *Business*, November 1981, pp. 39—43.

Naor, Jacob. "How to Motivate Corporate Executives to Implement Long-Range Plans." *MSU Business Topics*, Summer 1977, pp. 41—49.

Naor, Jacob. "Strategic Planning Under Resource Constraints." *Business*, September 1981, pp. 15—19.

Nielsen, Richard P. "Strategic Piggybacking—A Self-Subsidization Strategy for Non-profit Institutions." *Sloan Management Review*, Summer 1982, pp. 65—69.

Paul, R. N.; Donovan, N. F.; and Taylor, J. W. "The Reality Gap in Strategic Planning." *Harvard Business Review*, May—June 1978, pp. 124—130.

Pearce, John A. III. "The Company Mission as a Strategic Tool." *Sloan Management Review*, Summer 1982, pp. 65—69.

Quinn, James Brian. "Managing Strategic Change." *Sloan Management Review*, Summer 1980, pp. 3—20.

Rabion, Samuel, and Moskowitz, Howard R. "Optimizing the Product Development Process: Strategical Implications for New Entrants." *Sloan Management Review*, Spring 1980, pp. 45—51.

Schmaltz, Joseph H. "A Management Approach to a Strategic Financial Planning System." *Sloan Management Review*, Winter 1980, pp. 3—13.

Thomas, Dan R. E. "Strategy Is Different in Service Industries." *Harvard Business Review*, July—August 1978, pp. 158—165.

# 6 FORECASTING: GUIDE TO PLANNING

It would be much easier for managers to carry out their work if they knew the future. Most people spend considerable time contemplating the future, trying to predict the conditions that will exist at some point in time so they can plan their lives accordingly. Examples of future-related questions we may ask are "Will there be enough snow on the ski slopes for next weekend?" "What will be the demand for college graduates in my field when I graduate?" and "What investments will be the most profitable over the next five years?"

In business and other types of enterprises, the variety of future-related questions is virtually endless. Managers ask such questions for one reason: to develop plans that will succeed at a future point in time.

## WHAT IS FORECASTING?

Attempts to know the future are as old as recorded history. Most people today emphasize scientific observation, rather than divination, as the preferred method of prediction. Basically, in contemplating the future we have two broad choices: guessing and forecasting.

**Guessing** is forming a judgment or opinion without knowledge or with insufficient, uncertain, or ambiguous evidence. Synonyms for "guessing" are "conjecturing," "surmising," "assuming," and "inferring." Scientific methodology is not employed in guessing.

**Forecasting** is calculating or predicting some future event or condition as a result of rational study and analysis of pertinent data. Synonyms for "forecasting" are "predicting," "estimating," "planning," and "calculating." Scientific or quasi-scientific methodology is employed in forecasting.

Today, forecasting is widely used, and many forecasts are highly reliable. Forecasts involving scientific phenomena, such as a meteor shower or an eclipse of the sun, are so accurate that they can be termed exact. Generally, the farther a forecast extends into the future, the less accurate it will be. Short-range weather forecasting, once laughed at by many, is now reasonably accurate; long-range forecasting is still fairly inaccurate.

Forecasts involving human behavior and economic activity are particularly difficult to make. Predictions of how people will react to a new product, to changes in work procedures, or to a change in store location are often wrong. This is because no one can have absolute knowledge of all the causal factors that are responsible for some future event. A certain factor may be recognized but misunderstood, or it may be overlooked altogether. Furthermore, even if one has a good knowledge of all the relevant causal factors, it is still difficult to predict how the factors will interact and what the final result will be.

One of the most important forecasting mistakes in recent decades concerned population predictions made in the 1950s for the 1970s and 1980s. The actual population in the United States in 1982 was well below even the most conservative forecast made in 1962. Why? Were unknowledgeable or inexperienced statisticians employed? Were faulty mathematical tools used?

Neither of these explanations is correct. The errors in population forecasting occurred because the assumptions on which the forecasts were based did not consider conditions that developed later. In other words, the projections made in 1962 would have proved correct if those assumptions had held up. The new conditions that were not considered had little to do with economics. Rather they related to changes in social attitudes toward birth control, including a wider acceptance of sterilization. There were various legal changes, among them laws permitting an increased number of abortions. And since there was also a decline in the social pressures to have children, the result was that more and more couples decided to have no children or fewer children.

In recent times we have seen erroneous forecasts, relating to economic activity, inflation, and levels of unemployment, that were made by well-trained individuals using accepted statistical techniques. In most instances we can conclude that the error in forecasting is not one of mathematics; the problem is in the assumptions made. For example, many real-estate developers in the 1970s assumed that the demand for office space would continue to grow. When it did not, newly constructed office buildings in some cities went empty.

Table 6–1 shows some examples of practical questions that managers ask and try to answer through forecasting.

## Why Forecasting Is Important

Although forecasting has many limitations, progressive managers embrace it because they realize it is more reliable than either guessing or not contemplating the future at all. The more accurately a manager can predict future conditions, the better the plans he or she develops based on those predictions will be. Forecasts are the premises on which plans are built. If one major mistake is made in a forecast, an entire strategy may have to be discarded.

The need for forecasting revenues and expenses in business organizations is obvious. But other enterprises also have forecasting needs. To plan effectively, hospitals need to forecast medical service needs; government units need to project demand for public services; and schools need to forecast enrollments. All organizations need forecasting to attain maximum results. Failures of organizations can often be traced to lack of forecasting or to unsound forecasting.

## Variations in Forecasts

The variety of forecasts is endless. There are forecasts that deal with future stock market prices; with marriage, divorce, birth, and death rates; and with the success or failure of all types of plans.

Forecasts range from simple to elaborate. The manager of Smith's Hardware Store is making a simple forecast when he projects sales for the next year by averaging sales for the past five years. He may modify his forecast somewhat based on what he reads in the trade press and on what he perceives to be the local economic conditions. For him, this may be a satisfactory and even fairly reliable way of forecasting. Furthermore, chances are that it would be uneconomical for him to employ forecasting experts.

Meanwhile, organizations such as banks, industrial companies, and the U.S. government engage in very elaborate and detailed forecasting. In large enterprises such as these, many analysts work full time trying to predict events that will affect their operations.

Forecasts also vary with respect to time. A forecast may be for a very short period, such as only a day for a retailer who is planning a twenty-four-hour sale. Some organizations make quarterly and annual forecasts, while others, in addition to short-range forecasting, may make projections for a decade or more. This is especially true for enterprises that are considering large financial investments in capital equipment and installations that will not become operational for a decade or more.

**TABLE 6–1**

135

*What Are
Revenue and
Expenditure
Forecasting?*

**Some Questions That Managers Might Ask
and Try to Answer Through Forecasting**

| Area | Question |
|------|----------|
| Marketing | • How many units of each product in our line will we sell?<br>• What share of the market will we attain?<br>• Which firms will present the strongest competition? |
| Production | • When will the new production facilities be operational?<br>• What are the predicted per-unit production costs?<br>• How many workers at specific skill levels will be needed? |
| Finance | • How much money will be needed to achieve specific and overall organizational goals?<br>• What financing charges will be incurred in acquiring the needed capital?<br>• What inflation rate should we build into the budget? |

## WHAT ARE REVENUE AND EXPENDITURE FORECASTING?

In most cases, the ultimate purpose of all forecasting is to help management estimate future revenues and expenditures. As we will see later, the two are closely related.

Revenue
Forecasting

A **revenue forecast** is, roughly speaking, an estimate of the amount of money that will be brought into an organization over a period of time. (In business organizations, the term "sales forecasts" is generally used in referring to revenue forecasts.) All organizations, profit and nonprofit, employ the resource of money to achieve organizational goals. For this reason, business managers try to anticipate revenue from sales; government managers try to predict revenue from taxes and other sources; and trade association executives and union managers try to estimate how many members will pay dues. Managers in all organizations try to answer the question "How much revenue will we have to work with in the period ahead?"

### Why Is Revenue Forecasting Important?

Managers take a great interest in revenue forecasting because the amount of money brought into an organization limits the extent of the organization's activities. Revenue forecasting, then, is very important because it affects either directly or indirectly all plans made in an organization.

In the short run, an organization can spend more than it takes in in revenues (assuming it can borrow, sell shares, or postpone meeting its financial obligations). But over a period of years, it cannot continue in this way. Organizations of all kinds can fail if, over time, spending is not adjusted to income. A business that spends more money than it takes in will ultimately become bankrupt. Other organizations not subject to bankruptcy laws may simply be abandoned or discontinued if revenue does not equal or exceed expenses.

### Accuracy of Revenue Forecasting

Accuracy of revenue forecasting greatly facilitates the planning process. A correct revenue forecast makes it easier for managers to make accurate decisions about such questions as "How large an inventory of raw materials should we accumulate?," "How many people should be employed?," "Should we add new facilities?," and "How much capital is needed?" Forecasts are the assumptions underlying all planning. A serious error in revenue forecasting can lead an organization to develop plans that are worthless.

An incorrect revenue forecast means that inaccurate management decisions will be made that are costly to the organization. Too few or too many workers may be employed. Too much or too little inventory may be accumulated. Too much or too little production capacity may be provided. Consider the hundreds of thousands of businesses that failed to foresee the economic recession of 1980–83. The results of the inaccuracies in forecasting were particularly apparent in two of our largest industries, housing and automobiles. Numerous home builders found themselves with an excessive number of unsold houses "in stock," with the result that they failed. Automobile manufacturers, despite the great emphasis that they had placed on forecasting, also found themselves with excessive inventories because their forecasts of auto sales were far off the mark.

Note that a revenue forecast can be too low as well as too high. While the disadvantages of a revenue forecast that is too high are more obvious (possible layoffs, costs of carrying excessive inventories, and so on), a revenue forecast that is too low also is undesirable. For example, if a forecast is too low relative to attainable market potential, the firm stands to lose profit on unmade sales and may lose some of its share of the market. Either way, an inaccurate revenue forecast will adversely affect an organization's plans.

An **expenditure forecast** is an estimate of the amount of money an organization will spend during a specific period of time. In a well-managed organization, just as concerted an effort is made to control expenses as to increase revenues. The simple equation "Revenue − Costs = Profit" indicates the importance of holding down costs. In business, a small reduction in purchasing costs may contribute more to profits than a substantial increase in sales.

Assume that a company spends fifty cents of each dollar earned from sales for materials. If a company has an annual sales volume of $20 million, it spends $10 million for supplies. If the firm has a pretax profit of 8 percent and is able to raise its sales from $20 million to $25 million, it would increase its profits by $400,000 (8 percent × $5 million). But the firm can achieve the same improvement in profits by reducing its purchasing costs by only 4 percent (4 percent × $10 million).

### Expenditure Forecasting as a Control Technique

Expenditure forecasting is an effective tool for making managers more cost-conscious. Much waste in organizations can be traced directly to the inefficient purchasing of equipment, supplies, and services. At times managers exercise little caution with regard to spending. During periods of economic prosperity, many managers, rushing to expend operations, may be wasteful. They may hire more personnel than are needed, overbuild, purchase equipment that may not be fully used, and in other ways spend unnecessarily or excessively. During periods of economic contraction, managers are made painfully aware of their excesses in previous periods and try to remove the "deadwood," cut out waste, and reduce expenditures.

### Expenditure Forecasting and Inflation

Expenditure forecasting is especially important during periods of inflation. "How expensive will the supplies we use likely be in the period under consideration?" is a difficult but important question. If costs are expected to increase dramatically, management may need to consider raising prices on the products the firm sells. In turn, raising prices may require a revision in the revenue forecast.

For example, constructing such things as power-generating plants, pipelines, aircraft, shopping centers, rapid-transit systems, and office buildings takes a number of years. The costs of the supplies, services, and labor used in such projects may increase substantially before the projects are completed. In estimating the costs for projects that extend far into the future, management should consider the probability of inflation.

Revenue projections and expenditure plans are interdependent. Expenditure forecasts generally but not always are derived from revenue forecasts. The amount of funds to allocate for new equipment and plant improvement depends, at least in part, on anticipated income. However, in some cases expenditure forecasting influences revenue estimates. For instance, a marketing manager may argue that an additional expenditure for promotion will result in an increase in revenue that will more than compensate for the added expenditure.

**The Relationship Between Expenditure and Revenue Forecasting**

## HOW ARE FORECASTS DEVELOPED?

In making forecasts, management may turn to a wide variety of sources and apply a number of techniques. Note that a manager, if he or she wants to do an effective job of predicting results, may need to use a combination of several methods. The most common techniques and sources of information are illustrated in Figure 6–1 and are discussed in the following sections.

**Economic Data**

A tremendous variety of predictions are made each year by experts in various fields. Government agencies regularly make economic forecasts that range from the very detailed to the very general. An example of the latter is the **gross national product** (GNP), which is the total value of all goods produced and services provided in a nation annually. Predictions are made about the rate of inflation, the rate of unemployment, the supply of new workers, the retirement of old workers, housing starts, industrial and commercial construction, the cost of living, retail and wholesale prices, tax collections, imports and exports, consumer spending, business cycles, and population changes.

**FIGURE 6-1**

Methods and Tools Used in Forecasting

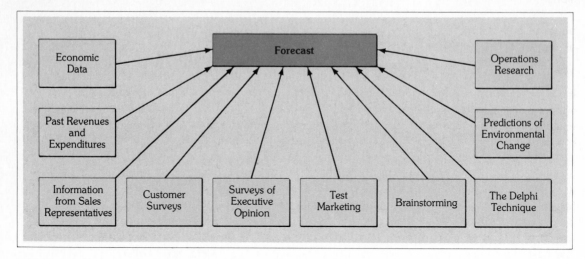

### Sources of Economic Data

Most economic data come from government agencies that collect them on a routine basis. Cost-of-living figures and wholesale price indices, for example, are developed by the U.S. Department of Commerce and released monthly. Because of the cost and complexity of collecting economic data, most organizations do not make their own projections. However, some organizations like major banks and large universities do develop and publish economic forecasts.

Other useful sources of information are periodicals, newsletters, and trade association reports. These sources may contain projections of sales for certain industries, indications of growth trends in an industry, and other useful data.

### How Valuable Are Economic Forecasts?

Most business organizations find that their future sales relate to the overall performance of the economy. If economic forecasts suggest economic growth, a business manager is more likely to develop a bullish (optimistic) forecast for the firm than if economic forecasts suggest negative conditions. However, few businesses find a perfect correlation between forecasts for the GNP and their actual sales volume. During the recession of the early 1980s, sales of new aircraft fell much below the general decline in productivity, while sales of medical equipment experienced a record-breaking high (mainly because of an aging population).

A firm that is in a declining industry may still be able to do well if it introduces a truly innovative product or is able to sell at lower prices than its competitors. Sometimes a firm with outstanding management is able to go against a general economic trend and earn large profits while its competitors are losing money. Thus, the state of the economy (or of the industry) is not always a reliable indicator of how well a firm will do.

Another problem with economic forecasts is that they frequently contradict one another. Different experts, using identical data, may draw different conclusions.

On the whole, managers feel economic forecasts are valuable but should not be relied on absolutely. As we will see later, judgment plays an important role in almost all forecasting.

## Past Revenues and Expenditures

It is often said that the best way to predict the future is to understand the past. Sales volume in the previous quarter often provides managers with a clue as to what the volume will be in the next quarter. If careful records are kept of past events, managers can often predict future events with considerable accuracy.

The record of past revenues is considered in virtually all revenue forecasts. To arrive at a forecast, some organizations simply add (or subtract) a certain percentage to or from last year's revenues. Or they may calculate the average growth rate for, say, the last three to five years. These forecasting techniques are used with the best success by relatively large organizations in industries in which demand does not fluctuate greatly from year to year. Public utilities, for example, can normally use past revenues successfully as a forecasting device. Major retailing organizations also rely heavily on past revenues as an indication of future results.

The disadvantages of using past revenues to predict the future is that no allowance is made for changes in a dynamic economy (booms, recessions, inflation, price instability, for example), for changes in competitive strategy, for internal changes (new products, new managers, and so on), or for strikes or other events that affect supply and demand.

## Consultations with Sales Representatives

In business organizations, sales representatives are often asked to forecast what they believe will be an attainable volume in their territories for the period in question. A composite of these estimates is then made to arrive at a total forecast.

Advocates of this method point out that sales representatives are closest to the buyers and should, therefore, have a good idea of the amounts that customers are likely to buy in the future. Furthermore, this method tends to elevate the morale of sales representatives, since they participate in the forecasting process.

A major limitation of this forecasting method is that sales representatives may be biased in their outlook. They may be too optimistic and project an unattainable sales volume, or they may make a deliberately low forecast in hopes that the company will assign them a low, easy-to-reach sales quota.

## Surveys of Customers

To survey customers, company representatives ask known users of the firm's products how much they plan to buy during the forecast period. Mail, telephone, or personal interviews may be used to acquire the information. Surveying customers about their purchasing plans has some important limitations, however. It can be too expensive to be practical if the firm has a large number of customers (as does, for example, a manufacturer of convenience goods). Many customers are not willing to supply such information, and even if they were, many buyers do not have a clearly formulated idea of what they intend to purchase.

Surveys of customers' intentions may be used successfully, however, when the number of customers is relatively small, as is often true in the case of firms selling to the industrial market; when customers can be approached at a reasonable cost; and when disclosing such information is in the best interests of the customer.

This method of forecasting is frequently used in situations in which products are made or modified to the specifications of the buyer. Examples of products in this category are new office buildings and other real-estate construction, machine tools, earth-moving equipment, and airplanes. And often industrial suppliers have backlogs of orders, which—assuming they are not cancelled—provide a basis for forecasting.

## Executive Opinion Method

In the **executive opinion method**, sometimes called the *jury of executive opinion*, senior-level managers ask the heads of sales, marketing research, production and other organizational units for their views about the outlook for future revenues. This forecasting method can be done quickly, represents a pool of diversified opinions, and is simple compared with some other methods. However, the method employs opinions, not facts. Furthermore, predictions are usually generalized, such as "Sales will be 5 percent above this year's sales," and are not broken down by product line, customer, and territory.

Some organizations overcome the limitations of the executive opinion method by making it the last step in the revenue forecasting process. If other methods have been used to forecast revenues, key managers will have some facts on which to base their estimates.

## Test Marketing

In some situations it is possible to set up a **test market** to predict how well a product will sell under actual conditions. Test marketing is especially useful for a new product for which no sales record exists. It is also valuable when a firm is considering marketing a product in a new territory or using a different channel of distribution. The limitations of test marketing as a forecasting device are that it is costly and time consuming.

## Brainstorming

Some years ago Alex F. Osborn, an advertising executive, developed a technique for generating ideas called **brainstorming**. The technique has been applied in solving problems not only in Osborn's own field of promotion but in many other areas, such as finding easier ways to perform a task, discovering new markets for a product, and making work more enjoyable. While not generally used as a forecasting device, brainstorming can be used to make predictions about future conditions when there is little reliable information to go on. The technique involves three steps:

1. A group of people who may or may not be highly knowledgeable about the problem under discussion is assembled.

2. Each member of the group is asked to suggest a solution. An important feature of this step is that no member of the group may criticize another person's ideas at this point. This procedure helps stimulate free thinking.
3. After a number of ideas have been presented, they are evaluated. Some ideas may be combined and others discarded. If the session is successful, one or more useful ideas result.

An interesting and workable forecasting method was developed by the Rand Corporation, a highly regarded firm that specializes in studying the future. The **Delphi Technique**, which makes use of informed judgment, consists of four steps.

First, a panel of acknowledged experts is selected. Depending on the problem under study, they may come from only one or two disciplines or from many different areas. For example, if the objective is to forecast when a comprehensive, unified theory of the so-called black holes in space will be available, experts in astronomy and astrophysics would be selected. If the objective is to predict the degree of world political stability in 1990, experts in economics, sociology, anthropology, political science, and other disciplines might be selected.

Second, the experts are given the problem and asked to make their predictions anonymously. By keeping their opinions anonymous, the panel members remain uninfluenced by what other members of the panel think.

Next, a composite report of the predictions is made. The report, which does not identify who predicted what, is submitted to the panel members. They are asked to study the composite view and amend their own opinions.

In the final step, the panel members submit their revised thinking. A final report is prepared, which becomes the forecast.

The dynamic nature of the sociopolitical environment in which management is practiced was discussed in Chapter 3. Trying to forecast what environmental changes will occur in the future is both extremely difficult and extremely important. In making forecasts of environmental change, it is particularly important to consider two related areas: political and economic changes and social changes.

### Political and Economic Changes

Many organizations are affected by changes in political leadership. Governments at the local, state, and national levels now determine how a large share of our financial resources will be spent. In turn, government expenditure patterns affect prospective sales for many industries. For example, if the party in power has a strong national defense orientation, industries that develop weapon systems can anticipate larger revenues than if that party de-emphasizes national defense. In making forecasts, managers in a host of areas—including housing, education, shipbuilding, aircraft development, and highway construction—must consider changes in fiscal policies as well as changes in government-sponsored programs.

Changes in the unemployment rate, interest rates, and general economic activity will affect demand for many products. A tractor manufacturer may forecast demand for 100,000 tractors for the next twelve months. But actual demand may exceed or fall below estimates because of changes in the economy between the time the forecast is made and the time production begins.

Changes in political leadership in other nations also affect forecasting. Leaders in foreign nations can affect domestic companies by taking various actions, such as modifying tariffs, changing tax structures, enforcing embargoes, and even nationalizing American-owned companies.

### Social Changes

Predicting changes in social attitudes is perhaps the most hazardous element of forecasting, but such changes must be considered in making plans. In style- and fashion-related industries such as the apparel business, changes can be particularly swift, and wrong predictions can be costly. Say a dress manufacturer develops an annual sales forecast for each line of dress produced. Assume further that a major change in consumer fashion preferences develops shortly after the forecast is made. If the manufacturer sticks rigidly to the forecast, it is obvious that trouble will develop.

### Futurology

Some scientists and philosophers, called **futurologists**, attempt to predict or at least to suggest what conditions will exist in the distant future (from five to fifty years or more). Futurologists raise such questions as the following:

- What will education be like in another generation or two? Will reading and writing—notoriously slow ways for acquiring knowledge—be supplemented with new techniques for transmitting information?
- Will scientists develop ways of modifying genetic material to elevate intelligence? If so, will society permit their application?
- What will our economic system be like when today's students reach age seventy?
- Will the future bring more leisure time, and if so, how will people use it?
- Will cures be found for cancer, multiple sclerosis, diabetes, and the dozens of other now-incurable diseases?
- Will orbiting space stations be used in the production of certain medicines and foods and those products for which a zero gravity is needed?

Some managers feel that forecasts made for more than a few years are essentially useless because of the many sociopolitical and economic changes that can occur over that time. The Issue for Debate in this chapter presents both sides of this argument.

### What Is Operations Research?

**Operations research** (OR) is a scientific approach to forecasting in which mathematical models are used to forecast which course of action from among the available alternatives will produce the best result. OR focuses on a system as a whole, rather than on its separate parts, and makes extensive use of logic, mathematics, and statistics.

Operations research dates back to 1937, when British scientists sought a way to make more effective use of a new discovery, radar. OR was used to forecast where and when enemy air attacks would occur. With this knowledge, British pilots were more efficiently deployed.

OR was used extensively to forecast events for many other purposes during World War II and was first taught in the United States as an academic discipline in 1948 at the Massachusetts Institute of Technology. Today OR is used in a wide variety of forecasting and decision-making situations.

### Characteristics of Operations Research

There are three essential characteristics of operations research: a systems orientation, an interdisciplinary approach, and the use of models.

*A systems orientation.* In operations research, managers examine the whole of an activity, rather than just a part, to forecast a result. The logic is that each part of an activity relates to all other parts. Sales volume, for example, affects and is affected by production, accounting, financing, pricing, and other activities that are performed in a business.

*Interdisciplinary approach.* Since operations research examines an entire system, not just one aspect of it, specialists from several disciplines are usually involved. Engineers, physicists, computer experts, and behavioral scientists may be involved in the same project. The interdisciplinary approach will probably continue to be used because of the rapid expansion of specialized knowledge.

*Use of models.* Inherent in the application of operations research to forecasting is the use of models to simulate the dimensions of a problem and to predict how results will be changed under different assumptions. In operations research, models take the form of one or more mathematical equations in which symbols are used to specify important variables (factors) and their relationship to one another.

### Steps in the Operations Research Process

*Step 1: Formulation of the problem.* In operations research, the first step is to define management's goals—for example, "to maximize sales while minimizing operating costs," "to minimize inventory carrying costs," or "to maximize market share." Management must then identify all the variables that will affect achievement of the goals. Some variables are *controllable*—that is, management is able to "set" their values. Examples of such variables are expenditures on promotion, purchasing costs, and number of sales representatives. Other variables are *uncontrollable;* managers cannot do much to influence them. Competitors' expenditures on promotion, economic factors such as the rate of inflation, and the prices of competitors' products are some uncontrollable variables.

*Step 2: Construction of the model.* In this step, management develops one or more equations that indicate the relationships among the various goals and variables. These equations may be quite complex, since the same variables often appear in several different equations.

*Step 3: Derivation of solutions.* The objective is to find the "best" values for the controllable variables. In other words, management wants to set the controllable variables at levels that will achieve the goals set forth in the model.

In some cases it is a simple matter to solve the equations and determine the best values for the controllable variables. However, as the equations become more numerous and more complex, it is increasingly impractical to proceed in this way. Therefore, management may employ a trial-and-error technique (with or without the use of a computer) in which a variety of values are inserted in the equations until the best values become evident.

*Step 4: Testing of the model.*   The model should be tested, using appropriate statistical techniques, to determine whether it may contain irrelevant or inaccurate variables and whether it may have excluded important variables. If historical data are available, management may test the model with these data to determine whether it yields the same results that were attained in real life.

*Step 5: Control and implementation of the solution.*   When implementing the solution, management must establish controls to ensure that changes in variables are taken into account and that the model is revised as necessary. Management must also develop guidelines for using the model and instruct people in how to use it.

### Examples of Operations Research Problems

*Allocation problems.*   These problems involve forecasts of distribution of resources among various alternatives, either to maximize total return or to minimize total costs. The problem is to determine how much of a resource to allocate to a specific activity. Allocation problems often involve transportation. For example, management may wish to determine the best way to distribute empty railroad cars at various locations.

*Inventory and resource problems.*   **Inventory** is usable but idle resources. Examples of inventories include machines, materials, money, products, and facilities. The need for another resource—personnel—must also be forecast. Inventory and resource problems involve forecasting how much of a resource to acquire, employ, purchase, or make and when to acquire it to minimize cost. Inventory and resource problems may involve situations such as forecasting quantities of products to purchase or make, how many people to employ, how large a new physical facility should be, and how much working capital is likely to be needed.

*Maintenance and replacement problems.*   These problems involve items that wear out through use or become obsolete with the passage of time. Items that deteriorate—such as tools, trucks, and installations—are often costly. Generally, the longer a deteriorating item is used, the more maintenance it will require, the lower the resale value it will have, and the greater the likelihood that it will be made obsolete by a new product. The problem, then, is to estimate how much maintenance is justified and to forecast when such items should be replaced. The objective is to minimize the sum of operating, maintenance, and investment costs.

# ISSUE FOR DEBATE

## IS LONG-RANGE FORECASTING A GOOD PRACTICE?

All organizations should forecast the future; the question is how far ahead should they forecast. Large businesses, various government agencies, and some other organizations attempt to forecast the future beyond five years. Some believe forecasting that far ahead is pointless. Others think it is useful.

### YES

**Long-range forecasting is a good idea because . . .**

A long-range forecast, if it is accurate, can improve an organization's chance for success, since management can plan for and adapt to the anticipated changes.

Long-range forecasting can help an enterprise to see new production and marketing techniques, changes in social values, and new government regulations. When long-range forecasts are not developed, the enterprise tends to stagnate.

Organizations caught by surprise often fail. If a firm, for example, develops a five-year forecast and updates it annually, costly surprises can be avoided.

Long-range forecasting is required for large-scale, costly construction projects such as interstate highways or shopping centers.

### NO

**Long-range forecasting is not a good idea because . . .**

Long-range forecasts for an industry are often inaccurate. If current plans are based on incorrect forecasts, then the organization will suffer bad results in the future.

National and international events are almost impossible to foresee. Since these are so important to the future, long-range forecasts are likely to be highly inaccurate.

Long-range forecasting requires highly trained specialists, making it a costly activity.

Long-range forecasts, if used as a premise for planning, may result in organizational rigidity and inflexibility.

### QUESTIONS

1. How do you feel about the value of long-range forecasting? Explain.
2. What other pro and con arguments can you advance?

*Queuing problems.* A "queue" is a waiting line. Queuing deals with items or people in sequence; management seeks to determine how many facilities to provide and how to schedule their use. The objective is to minimize the cost of providing a service while also minimizing the amount of time that users of the service must wait. Analysts may forecast the optimum number of checkout stations in a store, the number of gates and runways at an airport, the number of gasoline stations on a toll road, and so on.

### Other Applications of Operations Research

*Linear programming.* **Linear programming** is an analytical method for determining the optimum combination of resources to use in attaining a goal. It can be used when a straight-line (linear) relationship exists between variables in a problem—that is, when a change in one variable results in a proportionate change in another. For example, there often is a linear relationship between hours worked and production. If employees work 10 percent more hours, production also increases by 10 percent.

Linear programming can be used to forecast the best solution to a wide variety of problems in which the relationship among variables can be expressed mathematically. For example, it may be used to choose the best route for transporting products, to decide on the optimum number of products to produce during a given time period, to determine where to locate warehouses, or to decide on the most profitable product mix.

*Game theory.* **Game theory** involves simulating real conditions, including possible competitive responses, as closely as possible and then making decisions. To date, the main practical application of game theory has been in the military, where "war games," now called "military exercises," have long been used in training officers for combat situations. In business, game theory has been largely confined to manager-development programs.

Game theory is very complex, since dozens or even hundreds of variables may be involved. However, with the ever-increasing sophistication of computers, game theory may become more widely used in the future to aid in decision making.

## WHAT ROLE DOES JUDGMENT PLAY IN FORECASTING?

Forecasting would be relatively easy—an almost mechanical process—if all a manager had to do was consider factual information such as last year's sales, historical growth trends, and past changes in the gross national product. In most situations, however, forecasting is not that simple. Judgment is required for the great majority of events that are forecast. Managers usually make predictions partially or wholly on the basis of insight, experience, and even intuition.

A case in point concerns a manufacturer of potato chips and related products that decided to structure its advertising campaign around a series of very funny, highly entertaining television commercials. One of the senior executives fought this plan on the theory that the commercials, while entertaining to the public, would not sell the product in the desired volume. He argued that just because people like a commercial it does not follow that they will buy the product. His view was overridden by other executives, in part because market research studies had shown conclusively that people would enjoy and remember the commercials. Twenty million dollars were appropriated for the campaign. The sales forecast for the year was $120 million. Actual sales results, however, were a disappointing $60 million. The executive's intuitive feeling that cute and clever commercials entertain but don't sell proved to be right. In this case, the company would have done better if it had followed the senior manager's unscientific hunch.

Most situations involve a variety of causal factors, and many relationships are impossible to express mathematically. Thus most predictions are subjective to one degree or another. Often a forecast is a combination of quantitative predictions and a manager's rough estimate of what will happen based on his or her past experience and intuitive judgment.

Managerial judgment plays an extremely important role in forecasting changes in two areas already discussed—political and economic changes and social changes. In addition, managers must also use judgment in forecasting the effects of changes in managerial assignments, competitive strategy, and technology.

Over a period of time an organization may make a host of changes in managerial assignments. A new manager in a key position will affect the degree of success the organization will enjoy in the future, but how? This is the question that planners must try to answer, and for the most part they must do so judgmentally. An executive who has a good track record in one organization may be just as successful in a similar organization, but the precise impact of the new person cannot be forecast with great accuracy.

**Forecasting the Effects of Changes in Managerial Assignments**

Judgment also plays a part in realignments of lower-level managers. "How will the transfer of Manager A from one territory to the XYZ territory affect results?" is the type of judgmental question that should be considered in forecasting.

It is not too difficult for management to know its competitors' strategies with regard to the production of goods, promotion, customer service, and similar factors. These activities generally take place openly and have been planned. What is much more difficult to anticipate are the *future* changes that competitors are likely to make in their strategies.

**Forecasting the Effects of Changes in Competitive Strategy**

Here again judgment comes into play. Executives, thinking judgmentally about the effect of a competitor's strategy on their organization's results, may contemplate such questions as "How is this competitor likely to change its strategy in view of general economic forecasts?" and "Is this competitor likely to introduce the new product on which it has been working this year?"

Senior executives, like a player in a chess match, should have some under-standing of the personality and style of their "opponents." In World War II, senior military commanders were given in-depth profiles of their enemy counterparts. The assumption was that if military managers knew the background, habits, preferences, and behavioral patterns of the opponents, they would be better prepared to anticipate the actions the opponents would take in a given situation.

Another judgmental question managers often must answer in forecasting is "How will the new equipment, process, or technological innovation affect our costs and sales?" Often there is no experience in a company or industry to go by. In this case the predictions must be totally judgmental.

Sometimes the speed of technological change is estimated incorrectly, resulting in problems for some firms. One company in the minicomputer industry, for example, grossly misforecast the evolution of the state of the art in making pocket- and desk-size computers. It built its computers with old, costly technology, while its competitors were using new, much less expensive methods. As a result, it found itself with an unusually large inventory of minicomputers it had to dispose of at a great loss.

## HOW CAN FORECASTS BE MADE MORE ACCURATE?

Even a casual review of contemporary economic and social life suggests that many forecasts and expert predictions prove highly, even grossly, inaccurate. Mistakes made in estimating sales by geographic area, by product line, and by customer are common. So are mistakes made in predicting costs, actions by competitors, and economic activity. Following are some guidelines for making forecasting more accurate.

Have Subordinate Managers Participate in Forecasting

One of the advantages of management by objectives is that the subordinate managers who are expected to achieve the objectives help to forecast what the objectives should be. Many department heads, in seeking to develop revenue forecasts and expenditure forecasts for a future time period, also ask subordinate managers to participate by submitting forecasts of their sales and expenditures. The department head then prepares consolidated forecasts for the entire unit. Finally, the various departmental projections are combined to make a forecast for the entire organization.

There are two major advantages to such a procedure. First, consulting with subordinates may lead to the development of more accurate forecasts. Second, manager involvement raises morale. Lower-level managers tend to try harder to achieve organizational objectives if they have been involved in a part of the planning process.

Add Greater Flexibility to the Forecasting Process

Because changes now occur faster than ever before, there is even a greater danger that a forecast will become at least partially obsolete before the planning period is over. Managers should, as part of forecasting, make allowances for strikes, shortages of raw materials, adverse weather, unemployment, inflation, and a host of other

# MANAGERS IN ACTION

## SOME MANAGERS GO AGAINST FORECASTED TRENDS

All decisions involve consideration of the future. There is, therefore, a forecasting element in all plans.

Many managers in periods of economic recession cut back on plans for expansion, research, and modernization. Forecasting future bleak times, they retrench and cut back. Then, when prosperity returns, managers may become too bullish and overexpand.

Below are accounts of two managers in action who decided to expand in 1982, the worst year for the economy since the 1930s, while many of their competitors were retrenching. Were they right? Only time will tell.

Mr. Milton Porter, chairman of L.B. Foster Co., which manufactures oil well equipment and supplies, believes in the proverb "Sow in bad times, reap in good times." In 1982, when there was a glut of oil and a resulting decrease in demand for oil drilling materials, Porter forecast a major turnabout. He decided to double his company's production capacity, even though existing plants were operating at less than 70 percent capacity.

Many feel Porter made the wrong decision based on forecasts for the industry. But, according to his logic, "If we hadn't thought in 1969 that there would be a heavy increase in oil and gas drilling in the U.S., we wouldn't have grown in the oil country tubular business. You plan your activities so you have a chance at a break."[1]

Another senior manager who forecast the future differently than his competitors is Edwin Gee, chairman of International Paper Company. In 1982 when the paper industry was suffering from huge over-capacity, Mr. Gee led International Paper into a six-billion-dollar modernization-and-expansion program. Mr. Gee also stepped up research activities at International Paper. (He has a doctorate in chemical engineering.)

One observer writes, "Gee keeps pouring in the money — $675 million capital spending [in 1982] — to make things hotter for competitors in the future. With luck, the big comany will not merely survive but prevail, further proof that management does make a difference."[2]

[1]*Forbes*, July 19, 1982, p. 60, "Fond memory," by Lisa Gross and
[2]*Forbes*, July 19, 1982, p. 44, "A giant shapes up," by Kathleen K. Wiegner.

### QUESTIONS

1. Do you feel Mr. Porter's and Mr. Gee's forecasts are on target? Why or why not?
2. Generally, do you feel managers are too pessimistic during recessions and too optimistic during booms? Explain.

---

problems. A forecast should never be regarded as a sacred document that cannot be revised.

A fundamental error in management thinking is to assume that accurate predictions about the future can be made only on the basis of trends in evidence in the United States. Forecasting can be improved if more attention is given to developments outside our own boundaries.

Nations of the world are becoming increasingly interdependent. Actions

Consider Worldwide Interdependency

taken by managers in other nations frequently affect decision making by managers in this country. For example, the great emphasis placed by foreign automobile manufacturers on selling their products in the United States has had a profound influence on decision making by domestic automobile manufacturers. An increase or a decrease in world tensions affects decision making for the government, the military, and a large number of industries.

Furthermore, economic conditions in other nations affect economic conditions here. If other leading industrial nations undergo an economic decline, our economy is certain to be adversely affected.

Worldwide interdependency should become even more important as multinational companies continue to increase in number, size, and influence.

## Make Fuller Use of Internal Data

Generally, most organizations do not make full use of internal data such as sales reports in making forecasts. Management's ability to obtain and process statistical data with computers appears in many cases to exceed its knowledge of how to use such information. Some common errors are failure to recognize changes in demand for specific products until excessive inventories are accumulated, failure to recognize changes in demand by specific customers, and failure to detect future shortages or surpluses of **working capital**, that is, capital used to conduct day-to-day operations.

Properly designed and used management information systems, which will be discussed in Chapter 20, are the best way to employ internal information.

## Give Forecasting a Higher Priority

One reason forecasting is often inaccurate is because it is not given a high priority in the organization. Coming to grips with the unknown or dealing with uncertainty is psychologically uncomfortable for some managers. As a result they may downplay forecasting. Yet forecasting in order to develop plans is extremely important, since an accurate forecast can help an organization to increase its efficiency and obtain the best possible results with a minimum input of resources. Forecasting should be of primary concern to senior managers.

## SUMMARY

* A forecast is a prediction of what conditions will prevail in the future. Forecasting attempts to employ the scientific method. Guessing, the alternative to forecasting, does not.
* The more accurately future conditions can be predicted, the better the plans based on those predictions will be.
* The variety of forecasts is endless. Forecasts range from simple to elaborate and consider various time periods.
* Revenue forecasts are estimates of the amount of money that an organization will receive over a period of time. Revenue forecasts are important because spending must reflect income.
* Expenditure forecasts are estimates of the amount of money an organization will spend over a period of time. Expenditure forecasting makes managers more cost-conscious and is especially important in times of inflation.
* In forecasting future conditions, managers should consider economic data, past revenues and expenditures, opinions of sales representatives, buying plans of

customers, opinions of key executives, test market results, and predictions of environmental change.

* Brainstorming and the Delphi technique, both of which entail a group of people contributing ideas about the future, are methods sometimes used in forecasting.
* Operations research, a scientific approach that uses mathematical models to select a course of action from available alternatives, may also be used in forecasting.
* Judgment—or the use of insight, experience, and intuition—is important in forecasting the effects of changes in managerial assignments, competitive strategies, and technology.
* Forecasts can be made more accurate by having subordinates participate in the process, being flexible, considering the actions of other nations, making fuller use of internal data, and giving forecasting a higher priority.

guessing
forecasting
revenue forecast
expenditure forecast
gross national product
executive opinion method
test market
brainstorming

Delphi Technique
futurologists
operations research
inventory
linear programming
game theory
working capital

1. Why are forecasts involving human behavior, such as future birth rates, often inaccurate?
2. Forecasts sometimes prove to be inaccurate to a considerable degree. Does this suggest that forecasting is a waste of time and talent? Why or why not?
3. Why should all organizations engage in revenue forecasting?
4. How are revenue and expenditure forecasts related? How can careful expenditure forecasting contribute to profits?
5. What kinds of economic data that are collected by government agencies may be useful in making forecasts?
6. Why are past revenues and expenditures important in forecasting?
7. What are the pros and cons of consulting with sales representatives in making forecasts? Making surveys of customer expectations? Asking executives for their opinions? Conducting test marketing?
8. How do political and social changes influence forecasting?
9. What are the key characteristics of operations research? What steps are followed in its application?
10. What role does judgment play in forecasting?

## 1. Developing a forecasting system

Assume that you are assistant to the president of a thirty-unit chain of convenience food stores. Your assignment is to predict sales in units and in dollars by store and by major product category (dairy products, canned goods, frozen foods, meats, beverages, and so on) for the next four quarters.

In a brief report explain (1) what role you would require each store manager to play in the forecasting process, (2) what types of internal data you would collect regularly, (3) how much attention you would give to previous sales results, and (4) how you would evaluate the impact of inflation, competition, population changes, and the rate of unemployment on projected sales.

### 2. Should management cut the territory and increase the sales forecast?

The Zusé Company is a New York-based apparel firm specializing in making and marketing an exclusive line of women's swimsuits. For three years Sam Alison, a manufacturer's agent, has been the firm's exclusive representative in Florida. Starting from scratch, Alison developed an annual wholesale volume of $900,000. His commission is 7 percent. He also carries two other noncompeting lines.

Ann Baxter, who recently received an MBA, has made a detailed analysis of Zusé's market penetration in Florida. She forecasts that with two representatives in Florida the annual sales volume would be $1.5 million. Ann meets with the company president, Margaret Zusé, and recommends that Sam Alison's territory be cut in half, that a new Florida sales representative be hired, and that another $600,000 in sales volume be included in next year's sales forecast.

Zusé decides to fly to Orlando to ask Alison to give up half the territory. Alison is very unhappy with the plan and tells her, "I built this line. The retailers push the Zusé line because they respect me. Either I keep all of Florida or I quit."

What would you do if you were Margaret Zusé? Explain the reasoning behind your decision.

### 3. Factors to consider in making a long-term forecast

American Pulp and Timber Corporation is a 60-year-old company that produces wood and then converts it into paper products and building materials. The company owns 3,000,000 acres of woodlands in the Southeast and is considering acquiring another 1,000,000 acres.

Before deciding to go ahead with the land acquisition program, the company president, Victor Adams, wants a forecast made of the probable demand for wood in the future.

President Adams calls a meeting of several key executives to discuss the forecast. Present at the meeting are: chief economist, Jennifer Lockwood; marketing vice-president, Will Nusbaum; financial vice-president, Harriet Wooten; and marketing research director, Harry Featherbone.

Victor: Before we decide to move ahead with a major land-acquisition program, I think it is essential that we develop the best possible forecast of the future demand for wood. Even with today's genetically improved seedlings, it will be 14 to 16 years before any trees are big enough for pulp products and at least 30 years before trees are large enough for timber for building purposes. Jennifer will make the forecast with help from Harry. But I think a series of brainstorming sessions might help them in deciding what factors should be considered in making the forecast.

Harriet: I think we're all glad you want a forecast, Victor. It's going to be hard to find woodland for under $500 per acre. We're talking about a $500,000,000 program.

And there are many alternative ways to invest the company's funds. Keep in mind there will be no income for at least 14 years.

Victor: I agree with you. But historically we've made money in the forest products industry. We acquired land 50 years ago for as little as $6 per acre that is now worth $600 per acre. But let's get back to deciding what we should consider.

Harry: One of the key factors is projecting new housing—not just the number of units but the size of houses in the future and what building materials will be used. Competition from the brick industry has been severe in recent years.

Will: Another consideration is the demand for newsprint and related products. Looking down the road 15 years or so, will electronic mail and computers decrease demand? Even such things as direct deposit of payroll, pension, and social security checks could eliminate demand for millions of tons of pulp per year.

Jennifer: I think we should look very closely into packaging trends. A few decades ago the forest products industry and then the plastic industry just about destroyed the market for glass milk containers.

Harriet: Better look into the export/import side of our industry, too. We import a lot of wood from Canada and we export some, too. But how will the export/import relationship change in the decades ahead?

Victor: Good point. Now, no one has suggested finding new uses for wood-based materials.

Harry: And we should consider what wood products today are vulnerable to non-wood competitors. For example, a small company in Michigan has developed plastic pallets. Forklift people like them. They're more expensive but last longer than wood pallets.

Will: It's likely that a number of associations, universities and maybe some of the big banks and financial companies have already made forecasts of the demand for wood products. Jennifer, I suggest you do a lot of probing before you make our forecast.

Victor: It has been a productive meeting. I'll schedule another meeting in two weeks. By then, Jennifer, I hope you'll have a report expanding the idea's we've discussed so far.

Is it unrealistic to attempt to forecast demand for a product 15 to 30 years into the future? Why or why not?

What other factors may affect future demand for wood products?

In the case of wood products, what factors affecting future demand are beyond the control of a wood products company?

**FOR ADDITIONAL
CONCEPTS
AND IDEAS**

Armstrong, J. Scott. *Long-Range Forecasting: From Crystal Ball To Computer.* New York: John Wiley, 1978.

Ascher, William. *Forecasting: An Appraisal for Policy-Makers and Planners.* Baltimore: Johns Hopkins University Press, 1978.

Augenstein, Leroy G., *Come, Let Us Play God.* New York: Harper & Row, 1969.

Brennan, Timothy J. "On Not Quantifying the Nonquantifiable." *Journal of Post Keynesian Economics*, Winter 1979–1980, pp. 267–270.

Brightman, Harvey J., and Harris, Sidney E. "The Planning and Modeling Language Revolution: A Managerial Perspective." *Business*, October–November–December 1982, pp. 15–21.

Campbell, John H. "The Manager's Guide to Computer Modeling." *Business*, October–November–December 1982, pp. 10–14.

Cohen, Jacob, and Kenkel, James L. "A Credit Model Featuring External Finance and Scale Economies." *Journal of Post Keynesian Economics*, Winter 1979–1980, pp. 255–266.

Frisbie, Gilbert, and Mabert, Vincent A. "Crystal Ball vs. System: The Forecasting Dilemma." *Business Horizons,* September–October 1981, pp. 72–76.

Granger, C.W.J. *Forecasting in Business and Economics.* New York: Academic Press, 1980.

Konstans, Constantine. "Financial Analysis for Small Businesses: An Application of the Model." *Business*, April–May–June 1982, pp. 34–39.

Meadows, Donella H., et al., *The Limits to Growth.* New York: Universe Books, 1972.

Mohn, N. Carroll, and Sartorius, Lester C. "Sales Forecasting: A Manager's Primer." *Business*, May 1981, pp. 2–9.

Moyer, Reed. "Forecasting Turning Points." *Business Horizons*, July–August, 1981, pp. 57–61.

Osborn, Alex F., *Applied Imagination.* New York: Charles Scribner's Sons, 1953.

Pring, Martin J. *How to Forecast Interest Rates: A Guide to Profits for Consumers, Managers, and Investors.* New York: McGraw-Hill, 1981.

Rothermel, Terry W. "Forecasting Resurrected." *Harvard Business Review*, March–April 1982, pp. 139–147.

Sartorius, Lester C., and Mohn, N. Carroll. "Sales Forecasting Models: How to Select Them." *Business*, July 1981, pp. 34–43.

Walker-Powell, A. J. "Financial Modeling—The Quantas Way." *Business*, November 1981, pp. 23–27.

Ward, Baldwin H., ed. *The Image of the Future, 1970–2000.* New York: 1968.

Wheelwright, Steven C., and Makridakis, Spyros. *Forecasting Methods for Management.* New York: John Wiley, 1980.

# 7

# THE DECISION-MAKING PROCESS

**STUDY THIS CHAPTER SO YOU CAN:**

- Describe the nature of decisions, including the ways in which they vary.
- Explain Step 1 in the decision-making process.
- Discuss Step 2 in decision making, including the "do nothing" alternative and the need for a maximum number of alternatives.
- Describe the roles of the following in Step 3 of decision making: existing rules, procedures, and policies; available facts; research; feasibility studies; simulation; opinions of advisers; experience; public hearings; and forecasts.
- Explain Step 4 of decision making, including the parts that risk analysis, cost-benefit analysis and decision trees play.
- Discuss Step 5 in decision making, noting the roles of positive and negative impacts and human and political considerations.
- Identify and describe the four personality types of decision makers.

Every conscious choice (as opposed to instinctive behavior) is a **decision**. Non-managers and managers alike are involved in decision making. The number of decisions made by an individual in one day is impossible to calculate. Driving only a few miles on an expressway requires one to make dozens of decisions, such as to pass or not to pass, to switch lanes or to stay where one is, to speed up or to slow down, to exit or not to exit. A student may make a wide variety of decisions about what courses to take, how and when to study, how to get to classes, and so on.

Decision making is inherent in the management process; it cannot be avoided. And the quality of the decisions made is a major factor in determining the success of an organization.

## WHAT ARE DECISIONS?

In Chapter 5, we discussed four kinds of plans, strategies, policies, procedures, and rules. Each of these plans is arrived at through the decision-making process, and each may take considerable time and effort to develop. But once strategies, policies, procedures, and rules are established, they usually serve as guidelines for decision making for a considerable period of time.

In this chapter our focus is mainly on decisions that are unique and cannot be easily handled by referring to a preexisting strategy, policy, procedure, or rule. Table 7–1 shows some of the considerations that may be involved in a decision to establish a training program for employees who join a company as manager trainees. Note that someone must decide what will be done, who will do it, how it will be done, where it will be done, and when it will be done.

**Decisions Vary in Importance**

Some decisions literally involve national survival (such as deciding how to respond to a possible nuclear attack), while others involve deciding who will be asked to work overtime next weekend. Some decisions involve billions of dollars, and others involve only a small expenditure.

The importance of a decision can be measured in terms of the human, material, and financial resources that are affected by the decision. A decision made by a senior manager to terminate operations in a branch plant may affect many people. A decision by a plant manager to close down one assembly line affects fewer individuals.

What is an important decision to one person may be a relatively unimportant one to another person. Say a senior executive decides to terminate 10 percent of an organization's employees (a highly important decision). The first-level manager may then have to decide which specific individuals are to be removed. The latter is a less important decision to the organization as a whole. However, it is one that involves personal and emotional considerations and may therefore be extremely important to the first-level manager.

**Decisions Are Made at All Organizational Levels**

Managers at all levels make decisions. At the top of an organization, managers are concerned with the mapping of broad strategies and the establishment of policies. At each succeeding lower level, decisions become increasingly operational in nature. For instance, at the senior executive level the decision might be to build and sell 100,000 units in the next six months. As one descends the organizational hierarchy, decisions are more and more concerned with *how* the organization can build and sell 100,000 units in the allotted time.

**TABLE 7–1**

**157**

*What Are Decisions?*

Numerous Decisions Must Be Made to Establish a Training Program

| Type of Decision | Example |
|---|---|
| What will be done? | • Specifically, what is the training program expected to do? What are its objectives?<br>• What will the program emphasize? Management theory? Practice? A combination?<br>• How will the value of the training be measured?<br>• Will written and oral tests be required? If yes, what will be a passing score? |
| Who will do it? | • Will a professional training director need to be employed? Who will be accountable for the project?<br>• If a professional training director is to be employed, how many assistants will be assigned to the director? What should their qualifications be?<br>• Will the company executives play a role in providing the training? If so, what role?<br>• Who will decide the basic content? The company president? A committee? The department heads? |
| How will it be done? | • What instructional techniques will be used? Role playing? Lectures? Independent study?<br>• What formal instructional materials, if any, will be required? Textbooks? Films? Manuals? |
| Where will it be done? | • Where will training be given? On the job? In a formal classroom? A combination?<br>• If training is to be given on the job, will it take place at one location or at multiple locations throughout the company?<br>• Will some of the training be provided at a local college? |
| When will it be done? | • How long should the training program last? One week? A month? Six months?<br>• Will the training be provided during regular work hours, or should trainees be required to take the training on their own? |

The urgency of decisions varies greatly. In some cases managers have weeks, months, or even years to make decisions. Decisions on whether to make a major change in a product, to revamp a product line, to build a new installation in a foreign country, or to construct a rapid-transit system may take years. However, in many situations managers are forced to make immediate, or what might be termed emergency, decisions. A riot in a prison may force a warden to make an on-the-spot decision regarding the actions of guards. A fire burning out of control requires the chief of the fire department to decide immediately on a course of action. A chief surgeon in the process of conducting an operation may find

**Decisions Differ in Degree of Urgency**

something unexpected that causes him or her to issue new instructions to the surgical team.

**Decisions Are Made by Both Individuals and Groups**

Most decisions are made by individuals (although in the process of making a decision a manager may consult with other individuals). In some situations, however, groups rather than individuals make decisions. Committees, corporate boards of directors, and juries all render group-developed decisions, even though, as is often the case, members of the group may not be unanimous in their opinion.

The legislative process is another important example of the group decision-making process. A decision by Congress to enact or not to enact a proposed law is a group decision. A decision by the president or a governor to veto a bill or to sign it into law is, however, an individual decision.

In the age of computers, it is sometimes thought that machines, not people, make or can make decisions. This belief is erroneous. Even the most sophisticated computer is still programmed by human beings. Those who develop or approve computer programs are in fact the decision makers, not the machine.

**Decisions Vary in Complexity**

Some decisions, such as whether to appoint John or Sara superintendent over the night shift or whether to make Jane or Henry office manager, are simple. Other decisions have many more alternatives and are therefore more complex. If five people are qualified for a given position, the decision-making process is likely to be more complicated than if only two individuals are eligible. Just as a voter is more confused about whom to vote for as the number of candidates increases, a manager finds decision making increasingly complicated as more alternatives are presented.

## BASIC ELEMENTS IN DECISION MAKING

As shown in Figure 7–1, the decision-making process involves six basic steps. Step 1 is defining a problem or idea that must be acted upon, or "decided." Susan Merritt, assistant supervisor of a section in the claims department of an insurance company, wants a promotion to supervisor. This is an example of a problem.

Step 2 calls for the development of alternative solutions to the problem. In the case of Ms. Merritt, possible solutions are to promote her to supervisor, deny the promotion, or agree to review the request at a later date.

Step 3 is the information-gathering phase of the decision-making process. In the example of Ms. Merritt, the decision maker may want a thorough review of her performance record.

Step 4 calls for a consideration of the constraints and an evaluation of each alternative. Suppose that Ms. Merritt has only been employed in the company for six months and the company's policy is that no one can be promoted before being employed for a year. Then the alternative of promoting her would automatically be eliminated. If, however, the decision maker investigated the possibility of con-

**FIGURE 7–1**

The Anatomy of a Decision

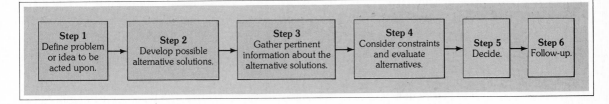

| Step 1 Define problem or idea to be acted upon. | Step 2 Develop possible alternative solutions. | Step 3 Gather pertinent information about the alternative solutions. | Step 4 Consider constraints and evaluate alternatives. | Step 5 Decide. | Step 6 Follow-up. |

straints and found that there were none, then he or she would be free to evaluate each alternative. That is, what would happen in this example if Ms. Merritt were promoted, were not promoted, or were asked to wait for a review at some future time? Management must also consider the impact of the decision on other people in the section, especially Ms. Merritt's superior. What would happen to the superior in each case?

Step 5 is to reach a decision — an action that, as we shall see, is often difficult.

The last step in the process is to follow-up or to implement the decision. If the decision is to promote Ms. Merritt, she should be given her new title, pay, statement of responsibilities, and reporting relationships.

Each of the six steps in the decision-making process is discussed further in the sections that follow.

**Step 1: Define the Problem or Idea to Be Acted Upon**

Accurate diagnosis of the problem is essential to effective decision making. Medical people know that a high fever is not the basic problem but rather a symptom of an infection of some other difficulty. Likewise, wise managers know that high employee turnover, waste, low morale, and inadequate sales usually are not fundamental problems but often symptoms of poor performance of management activities.

Managers differ considerably in their ability to perceive a problem. Early identification of a problem usually results in a better solution. For example, if a manager spots growing friction between two subordinate managers early, he or she may be able to solve the difficulty before much damage is done. If the problem goes unnoticed for too long, the result may be a major personnel problem.

Sometimes managers disagree on what the real or basic problem is. If sales decline, one manager may think the problem is overpricing of the product, another may feel competitive practices are creating the difficulty, and a third may identify the problem as weak distribution. If the problem is incorrectly diagnosed, the steps taken to solve it may only compound it.

Decisions are required to solve problems. But decisions must also be made to deal with new ideas regarding products, marketing methods, ways of financing operations, and other aspects of operating an enterprise. Creative thinking is often encouraged in organizations that are dedicated to growth and better service to their clientele.

Step 1 should result in a statement of the desired result. The desired result might be to reduce expenses, to increase sales, or to expand production. Once the desired goal of the decision process is known, Step 2 can be undertaken.

**Step 2:
Develop
Alternative
Solutions**

Once a manager knows what the problem is, the next step in the decision-making process is to develop alternative ways of solving it. **Alternatives** are the possible courses of action, only one of which may ultimately be chosen. Normally there are a number of alternatives for solving any problem. If there are no alternatives, there is no problem. For instance, Katherine Walker is general manager of twenty bookstores. Store 16 is in trouble; its revenues are well below projections. Some possible alternatives are to replace the manager, retrain the manager, relocate the store, close the store, provide more financial incentives, remodel the store, modify the inventory to better meet the interests of the clientele, or conduct a special sale.

In this example, Ms. Walker may immediately reject some of the alternatives. For example, if the manager of Store 16 has only been there a short time or if store sales were below expectations before the manager was appointed, it seems illogical to replace the manager. In practice, the number of options is ultimately reduced to two or three.

### The "Do Nothing" Alternative

One option frequently exercised by managers involved in the decision-making process is to do nothing. A manager may feel that the passage of time will solve the problem or that the problem will go away for some other reason.

Many managers who frequently elect to do nothing are sometimes described as indecisive. While doing nothing may be a wise alternative in some cases, the basic function of managers is to decide on courses of action. Most problems do not go away; they must be resolved. In the example of the bookstore, sales for Store 16 will not likely reach an acceptable level without some kind of action by the general manager.

In most organizations decisions must be made about how to achieve two broad-based goals: to increase revenues and to reduce costs. There are many possible ways to achieve these goals, and the selection is not easy. Table 7–2 shows a number of the alternatives that managers face. Note that the alternatives are broken down by functional area.

### The Need for a Maximum Number of Alternatives

A key part of a manager's job is to develop alternative courses of action. Generally, the larger the number of alternatives initially considered, the better the ultimate selection. A common weakness among managers is to review too few alternatives prior to making a decision. Increasing the number of alternatives, however, generally complicates the decision-making process. As the number of alternatives increases, the time and effort required to decide also increase.

**Step 3:
Gather
Information
Pertinent to
Alternatives**

Once the alternatives have been identified, the next step in decision making is to collect pertinent information. A manager may draw on a wide variety of information sources for guidance. The main informational inputs for decision making are existing rules, procedures, and policies; available facts; research; feasibility studies; simulation; opinions of advisers; experience; public hearings; and forecasts.

**TABLE 7–2**

**161**

*Basic Elements in Decision Making*

**The Range of Alternative Solutions Is Large**

| Examples of Revenue-increasing Alternatives | Examples of Cost-reducing Alternatives |
|---|---|
| *About products*<br>• Eliminate products that are not selling well.<br>• Add new products.<br>• Restyle old products.<br>• Upgrade product quality.<br>• Downgrade product quality. | *About production processes*<br>• Purchase automated equipment to save on labor costs.<br>• Retain engineering consultants to eliminate waste.<br>• Scale down building and modernization programs.<br>• Close down inefficient operations.<br>• Use other firms to manufacture component parts. |
| *About promotion*<br>• Increase amount of advertising.<br>• Change advertising appeals.<br>• Hire a new marketing manager.<br>• Develop new sales training programs.<br>• Add more salespeople. | *About purchasing*<br>• Defer purchase of new equipment.<br>• Perform purchasing function more efficiently.<br>• Ask for competitive bids on needed supplies.<br>• Scale down inventory reserves.<br>• Lease instead of purchase. |
| *About pricing*<br>• Raise prices on some products.<br>• Reduce prices on some products. | *About industrial relations*<br>• Negotiate better contract with union to minimize wage increases.<br>• Avoid work stoppages. |
| *About distribution*<br>• Sell through own outlets.<br>• Retain agent middlemen to reach some markets.<br>• Change channels of distribution.<br>• Sell to foreign customers.<br>• Increase number of customers. | *About personnel management*<br>• Lower absenteeism.<br>• Reduce employee turnover.<br>• Train personnel to be more efficient. |
| *About credit*<br>• Be more liberal in granting credit.<br>• Offer credit to customers who were rejected previously. | *About inventory control*<br>• Reduce inventory of supplies from ninety to sixty days.<br>• Inspect delivered items more carefully to reduce acceptance of inferior items. |
| *About asset control*<br>• Shift reserve cash assets to more profitable investments.<br>• Sell equipment and other assets. | *About quality control*<br>• Reduce product rejection rate.<br>• Conduct product inspection at each stage of the assembly process. |

## QUESTIONS

1. What other alternatives may be available to a firm both to increase revenue and reduce costs?
2. Sometimes a revenue-increasing alternative, such as granting more liberal credit, can conflict with a cost-reducing alternative, such as reducing bad debts. Explain. How should managers deal with conflicts between proposed alternatives?

### Existing Rules, Procedures, and Policies

Some decisions are relatively easy to make because they are prescribed by existing policies, procedures, or rules. Assume that in an industrial plant a rule exists stating "Any employee found in this area not wearing goggles and a hard hat will be terminated immediately." When an employee not wearing safety equipment is found in the area, the decision is simple, for it is prescribed by an existing rule: The employee must be terminated. The employee may have the right to appeal to a higher authority, but in the immediate situation the decision is mandatory for the manager because of the existing regulation.

Procedures also govern some decisions. A restaurant employee confronted by a loud and intoxicated customer may have no other alternative for handling the situation than to follow a company procedure: Politely ask the customer to leave. If that decision does not produce results, the next decision may also be dictated by procedure: Call the police.

Policies also limit the alternative courses of action that managers can take. It may be a company policy to terminate old employees last and to lay off new employees first when it is necessary to curtail operations. In this situation, managers must lay off new employees first. They may, however, have some discretion in deciding *which* of the new employees will be let go.

### Available Facts

In choosing among alternatives, managers should analyze the available facts. For instance, a manager who is trying to decide whether to close a store in a retail chain may consider such facts as the profits of the store in the past; the length of time the store has been open; the effectiveness of the manager in charge; the income, population, and other demographic changes that have occurred in recent times; and the changes in strategy in competing stores. Another example is that of the manager trying to decide whether to promote an individual. This manager may want to consider the individual's absenteeism record, educational profile, number of years of employment, previous employment history, and success on the job.

Thanks to the use of computers, managers have access to an unprecedented volume and variety of facts. Computers can be programmed to provide current information about sales by product line, labor costs, operating expenses, and many other variables. In fact, some people consider the widespread use of computers to be a factor that simplifies decision making. Others argue that computers do not make decision making easier. The Issue for Debate in this chapter presents both sides of this controversy.

### Research

While existing facts are useful to a manager, they do not always provide direct insight for making a decision. Historical information provided by a computer does not indicate how a new strategy or other plan will work in practice. For example, by studying sales at the existing price, managers cannot determine the effect of a change in price.

Research may be conducted to develop needed information. A manager facing a decision about whether to market a new product may conduct market tests to see how well the product will sell. Market research may dictate that the product be offered for sale in several test cities. A sophisticated market research

*"We must consider the health of the community, we must
consider our image and we must consider the fine of
$25,000 a day."*

project can also help determine what types of distribution outlets should carry the product, what the optimum price will be, and what forms of promotion will yield the best results.

### Feasibility Studies

An important informational input used in making certain types of decisions is the **feasibility study.** The main use of feasibility studies is to analyze the suitability of a physical location for developmental purposes. Such studies are especially useful in making decisions about major real-estate undertakings such as the development of a new shopping center or planned community.

Feasibility studies vary greatly in their level of sophistication, but a comprehensive one will involve inputs from architects, engineers, financial experts, and other professionals who can contribute expert knowledge. A feasibility study may take a number of years to complete and may be quite costly.

### Simulation

**Simulation** is the construction of a model — mathematical or nonmathematical — to represent a real condition. Simulation is not new and need not be complicated. Much training is based on simulation. When one trainee acts the role of a supervisor and another trainee plays the role of a subordinate, a simple nonmathematical simulation exists. War games have been used for centuries to determine how personnel and equipment will function under circumstances approaching actual combat conditions.

Paralleling the development of the computer has been an increased use of mathematical models to simulate reality. Models are being increasingly used to test cash-flow problems, inventory-control systems, production-line design, and other areas in which many mathematical variables exist.

The future of simulation looks bright, since it normally costs only a small fraction of the expense of developing an actual project and since the needed computer technology now exists.

### Opinions of Advisers

Generally, the higher a manager is in an organizational hierarchy, the greater the degree to which he or she relies on the opinions of advisers.

Advisers vary in ability, experience, and viewpoint. Imagine yourself in the chair of a senior executive who is making a decision about whether the company should market a new product. The legal adviser may have strong reservations because of possible infringement on a competitor's patent. The accounting and financial people may say that resources are inadequate to launch the kind of program requested by the marketing people. Labor union representatives may believe that it is a good idea because it should result in more jobs. Clearly, there can be wide differences in opinion.

Contradictory advice is not always bad. If an executive has three staff counselors who give the same advice in every decision situation, logic suggests that two of them are not needed.

An executive who is making a decision should keep in mind that advisers can rarely see the whole picture. A manager's responsibility is to evaluate each opinion and to try to resolve the matter in a way that best serves the organization's goals.

### Experience

**Experience** is knowledge or skill derived from direct observation or participation in previous events. It is the most widely employed informational input in the decision-making process. While a manager never meets exactly the same problem twice, a situation requiring a decision is often very similar to some event that the manager has previously experienced.

In higher echelons of an organization, such varied decisions as when to buy new machinery, how to acquire new capital, and where to open new retail outlets are all likely to be based, at least in part, on experience. At lower levels of management, experience is also an important factor in making decisions. For example, a manager who has learned from experience that absenteeism is generally high on Mondays will make arrangements for substitute personnel to be available on that day. And a bank manager who has learned from experience that customer traffic is unusually heavy on the first and fifteenth of each month will arrange to have extra tellers on duty at those times of the month.

# ISSUE FOR DEBATE

## DO COMPUTERS SIMPLIFY DECISION MAKING?

Some people feel that computers simplify decision making. However, others contend that computers *change* the decision-making process but do not make it simpler.

### YES

**Computers simplify decision making because . . .**

Computers make information about sales, inventory, current financial status, and other subjects available to managers very quickly. Thus decision making is faster.

Computers free managers from tedious tasks. Less time involved in routine tasks gives managers more time for analytical thinking.

Information compiled and analyzed by computers is highly accurate. Therefore the data that serve as the basis for decisions are more reliable, and better decisions result.

The use of computers facilitates a systems approach to managing (that is, an approach that deals with problems as a whole, not just their separate parts).

### NO

**Computers do not simplify decision making because . . .**

The main problems in managing involve the human element. Computers are of no help in making decisions concerning human behavior.

Much information made available by computers is irrelevant to a decision being made. Managers spend much time trying to decide what is and what is not useful information.

Information provided by computers is no better than the computer program on which it is based. Since human beings design programs, mistakes are common.

Many managers do not have a good understanding of how computers work. As a result, they may depend too much or too little on them.

### QUESTIONS

1. What other pro and con arguments can you think of?
2. What would probably happen to our society if all computers were shut down for a month?
3. In your opinion, will computers be of assistance in solving problems relating to the human element in the future? Explain.

### Public Hearings

In some situations public hearings are held to obtain information that will help decision makers make a choice among alternatives. Most such hearings are held by government agencies. Managers in state public-service commissions hold hearings when utilities request a rate change or some modification in service. Congressional committees hold hearings that give individuals who want to make a point an opportunity to do so. And zoning commissions make extensive use of public hearings in reaching decisions. (Typically, an individual wanting property rezoned makes application to the zoning board, which in turn holds hearings to which the public is invited to present information.)

### Forecasts

Forecasts are a very important source of information for making decisions. Forecasting as a planning device was discussed in Chapter 6.

**Step 4:
Consider
Constraints and
Evaluate
Alternatives**

Having gathered all the pertinent information, the manager should now be in a position to eliminate some alternatives because of constraints. Constraints may be imposed by the following internal and external factors: custom; organizational charters and guidelines; limited money and personnel; organizational policies, procedures, and rules; higher-level managers; laws and political considerations; the public; competitors' actions; labor unions; the education of potential employees; society; and the economy. Some alternatives may have to be immediately eliminated due to the internal constraint of organizational rules, procedures, or policies.

Additional alternatives may have to be excluded from consideration because other constraints have become apparent due to the information gathered about the alternatives. A proposed alternative may be illegal or contrary to government regulations. Or an alternative may be highly controversial; a manager may fear adverse public reactions if the firm decides to build a new plant in a certain location, stay open on Sundays, and so on. It may also be necessary to forgo the "best" alternative because adequate funds or personnel are not available.

Now that the manager has discarded some alternatives due to constraints, the remaining alternatives can be assessed. The most common methods of evaluation are discussed in the sections that follow.

### Risk Analysis

A **risk** is the possibility of loss, injury, disadvantage, or defeat. Risk is inherent in all decision making, since decisions always involve the future and no one ever knows precisely what future conditions will be.

Usually a number of key elements or critical variables affect the soundness of a basic decision. In deciding whether or not to introduce a new product, it is not enough to know only that people need it. Other critical elements in the decision include whether the projected market share can be attained, whether the planned selling price is feasible, and whether anticipated production and marketing costs can be maintained. **Risk analysis** means making an appraisal or evaluation of the likelihood of success of a given alternative.

To analyze the degree of risk in introducing a new product, various specialists may be asked to estimate the degree of probability that the projections will be attained. The marketing manager may be asked to estimate the probability that the projected market share and the planned selling price can be obtained, the production manager may be asked to estimate the probability that projected production costs will be attained, and so on. Each probability will affect the decision that is finally made. If a marketing manager's estimate that the probability of attaining the projected market share is 50 percent, a no-production decision is more likely than if his or her estimate is 80 percent.

If managers make projections for each variable affecting the decision, a better decision should result.

### Cost-Benefit Analysis

Basic to choosing among alternatives is **cost-benefit analysis**. With this technique, managers estimate the cost of each alternative (in terms of human, capital, and material resources) and then compare the cost to the expected benefits. For example, before a manager decides to hire another employee, he or she should estimate (1) what the individual will cost in terms of wages, fringe benefits, office space, machines, and so on and (2) how much the new employee will benefit the organization in terms of production and greater efficiency.

Some cost-benefit analyses are qualitative rather than quantitative. In an ideal world, managers would be able to quantitatively measure all the costs and benefits of a decision. But many benefits resulting from a decision cannot be measured in dollars and cents. Each year NASA receives a certain appropriation for space research, but the benefits resulting from these expenditures are not quantifiable. When a city government decides to build a new park, it is unable to quantify the benefits to be derived from the park.

Business firms often make decisions in which economic considerations are secondary to social values. A decision to go beyond government requirements for pollution control or product safety may be in accordance with the values of senior management and may also be good public relations. The decision may be appropriate even if it is not justifiable on a purely economic basis.

Society is increasingly expecting business organizations to do more for the social good, even if doing so results in less profit. Therefore, decision making may tend to be based less on economics ("How much dollar benefit will we reap from our dollar input?") and more on consideration of social benefits ("How will the decision benefit the public?").

### Decision Trees

A **decision tree** is a planning tool that shows graphically what may happen in the future if certain courses of action are taken. Consider how a decision tree might be used in the following situation.

A fairly common decision made by business executives is (A) "Should we purchase capital equipment and make the new product ourselves?" or (B) "Should we license, franchise, or otherwise empower another organization (sometimes a competitor) to make it for us?" When Alternative A is exercised, the firm has a chance of making profits on both the production and marketing of the product. But when Alternative B is followed, the firm only has an opportunity to profit from the marketing of the product.

**FIGURE 7–2**

A Sample Decision Tree

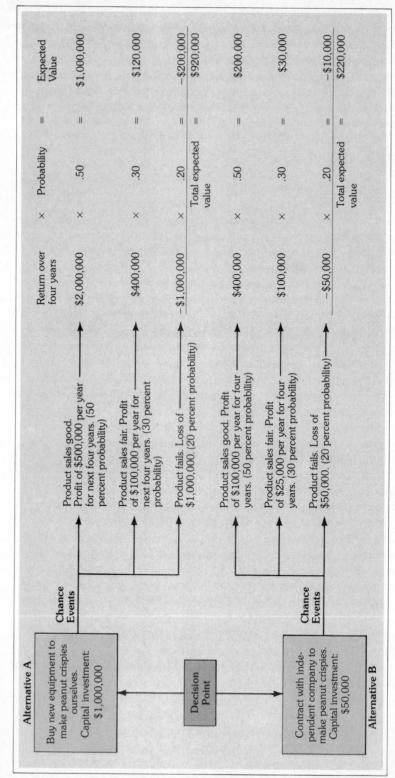

Figure 7–2 shows a simple decision tree that might be used by a maker of crackers, potato chips, and other snack foods that plans to introduce a new product, peanut crispies. Senior management is trying to decide between these alternatives: (A) "to invest $1 million in new equipment and make the peanut crispies ourselves" or (B) "to contract with another snack-food maker to produce the peanut crispies and make no additional capital investment for equipment."

As Figure 7–2 shows, decision trees deal with chance events—that is, events that may or may not happen. To make a decision tree useful, it is helpful to assign a mathematical probability to the likelihood that each event will occur so that results can be quantified. In this example, assume that there is a 50 percent probability that the product sales will be good, that there is a 30 percent probability that product sales will be only fair, and that there is a 20 percent probability that the product will fail.

Under these conditions, assuming the 50 percent estimate is on target, the firm stands to make $500,000 per year for four years, or $2,000,000 if it buys the equipment to make peanut crispies. If the same volume is achieved by contracting with a firm to produce peanut crispies, the $50,000 investment would produce only $100,000 per year profit for four years, or $400,000.

If the product had only fair sales, investment in new equipment would produce $400,000 over four years, while the contracting arrangement would produce $100,000. If the product totally failed, the $1,000,000 investment would all be lost with Alternative A, but only $50,000 would be lost under Alternative B.

Multiplying the return over four years by the probability of the event's occurring yields the *expected value* of each event. In this example, the total expected value of Alternative A is $920,000, whereas the total expected value of Alternative B is only $220,000. Thus, under the assumptions made in this example, it appears preferable to buy the new equipment.

Decision trees enable managers to grasp quickly all the possible results of a decision. In our hypothetical example, the results of exercising the two alternatives are easily comprehended. Decision trees also help managers to evaluate alternatives quantitatively, since probabilities are assigned and the different results are calculated. In Figure 7–2 the decision maker has quantitative information at hand as a basis for deciding.

Decision trees have a number of limitations, however. Like all decision-making tools, a decision tree still involves making assumptions. If the assumptions are faulty, the results can also be expected to be faulty. For instance, in the example in Figure 7–2 if the probabilities assigned to each event are incorrect, the decision based on them may also be incorrect.

Another drawback is that it takes considerable time and effort to construct decision trees that reflect all the possible events and probabilities. Our example is an oversimplified one. As the number of chance events increases, the decision tree becomes more complicated. Often a computer must be used to calculate the various probabilities and results.

The next step in the decision-making process is to select an alternative from those that have been proposed and not eliminated. This step is the most difficult one in **Step 5: Decide** the process. Table 7–3 gives an example of factors that may have to be considered in the case of an unforeseen slump in the sales of a profitable product.

In weighing the alternatives, managers should take into account positive and negative impacts of the decision, human considerations, and political consequences.

### Positive and Negative Impacts of the Decision

Few decisions are well received by everyone. Typically, some people react positively while others react negatively. Consider a decision to give a bonus of $500 to all employees. While most will appreciate this act, some may react negatively because they feel that their performance was better than average and that they should receive more than other employees. If the directors of a corporation decide to relocate the business, some employees may welcome the change, but many will react negatively. Virtually every decision will be unpopular to some degree. It is the manager's job to weigh all possible impacts on the organization as a whole to reach the "best" decision.

An alternative that appears expedient and a good idea in the short run may contain seeds of adverse reactions in the long run. In Table 7–3, consider the alternative of drastically reducing prices. While doing so may bring more sales volume in the short run, in the long run sales may be lowered because the firm's long-standing customers may feel the price reduction indicates a drop in quality.

**Personal
Considerations** Sometimes a decision appears best for the organization but may have some hazards for the decision maker personally. A department head may realize that her department can be merged into another department so that fewer personnel will be needed. If she tells her superior this idea, she is putting the welfare of the organization ahead of her own because the elimination of her department may put her job in jeopardy. Decision makers naturally ask themselves such questions as "How will key staff members view the decision?" "Will I jeopardize my own job?" and "Am I likely to be passed over for promotion because of this decision?"

### Human Considerations

While managers may use a number of quantitative decision-making tools, their decisions will frequently be based on emotional or human considerations. For example, it may be wise to transfer an employee to another department, but a manager may be so considerate of the person's emotional attachment to his or her present department that the employee will be kept where he or she is.

Managers are not analytical computing tools. A manager's outlook on any given situation may be influenced by personal problems involving family, friends, and so on.

### Political Considerations

In decision making there is often a trade-off. Typically one decision maker (A) may agree to support the decision of another manager (B) if B agrees to support A's decision. This phenomenon is very apparent in government. One politician will trade his or her vote on given legislation in exchange for the support of another politician on another issue. While trade-offs are most conspicuous in politics, they

**TABLE 7—3**

171

*Basic Elements in Decision Making*

## A Management Problem and Alternative Solutions

### PROBLEM

An unforeseen slump in sales has occurred for Brand X, one of the firm's most profitable products. New and stronger competition is considered responsible.

| Alternatives | Possible Positive Results | Possible Negative Results |
|---|---|---|
| Drastically reduce prices to maintain purchasing levels. | • Sales volume may increase to more than offset reduced per-unit price received.<br>• A new market segment may be attracted to the product. | • Consuming public may feel product quality has also been lowered.<br>• Revenue received may be inadequate to support marketing program. |
| Modify the advertising campaign to appeal to different types of customers. | • A new advertising campaign may take competitors off guard and win back lost consumers.<br>• A new campaign may enlarge our share of the market and win new customers. | • Potential customers may be confused by an unfamiliar message.<br>• Existing customers may lose confidence in the product, since they may think it has been changed. |
| Replace the product manager. | • A new product manager would have fresh ideas that might help sell more of the product.<br>• Replacing the product manager would set an example for other product managers: Produce results or leave. | • Existing personnel may be offended and some of them may quit. Possible damage to the morale among remaining employees might result.<br>• Customers may dislike having a new product manager appointed to work with them. |

### QUESTIONS

1. What other positive and negative results may develop from the exercise of each alternative?
2. What other alternatives might be considered?

are also found in other kinds of organizations. "I'll support you on this if you'll support me on that" is very common.

**Step 6: Follow-up**

The last step in the decision process is to follow up or to implement the decision reached in Step 5. Follow-up requires that the appropriate action be carried out. This may involve appropriating funds; assigning personnel; hiring new personnel; arranging for work space; or purchase of equipment, real estate, supplies, or inventory.

The skill with which a decision is implemented is a key to its success. If, for example, a decision is made to create a new position of Human Resource Manager but no plan is made for recruiting a person for the job, the decision made in Step 5 is not implemented.

# DECISION MAKING IN PRACTICE

**Example of Step 1: Define the Problem**

Computer Software is headquartered in New York City. For the last three years it has become increasingly evident to senior managers that personnel, supply, rent, and other costs are rising so fast that the continued profitability of the firm is in jeopardy. John Steiner, president of Computer Software, is aware that a problem exists and wants ideas for solving it. Defining the problem is Step 1 in the decision process.

**Example of Step 2: Develop Alternative Solutions**

Steiner calls a meeting of the executive committee to develop alternative solutions for solving the problem. Five alternative locations (Atlanta, Jacksonville, Denver, Houston, and San Diego) are suggested for a new corporate headquarters. In addition, two members of the committee recommend a "do nothing" alternative—that is, to stay in New York City and either absorb the increasing costs or pass them on, at least in part, to the firm's customers.

**Example of Step 3: Gather Information**

Steiner continues the meeting by discussing how the committee can make an evaluation of the cities recommended for the new corporate headquarters. He asks Arch Averson, the research director, to make a socioeconomic study of each city under consideration, giving careful attention to present and five-year market potential, probable attrition of personnel that would occur in a move, probable loss of present customers, and educational, recreational, and cultural facilities.

Steiner closes the meeting by emphasizing that the decision would not necessarily be made purely on a cost-benefit basis. "Human considerations," he says, "will be considered as much as possible."

**Example of Step 4: Consider Constraints**

At a later meeting with the committee, Steiner points out that there are no existing rules, procedures, or policies standing in the way of making a corporate move. The committee is free, then, to procede in evaluating the information gathered about the various alternatives. Steiner also makes two other points: (1) chambers of commerce in all the prospective cities would welcome Computer Software and (2) none of the localities under consideration has legislation that would adversely affect Computer Software's operations.

Steiner then asks Arch Averson to summarize his research into the desirability of each location. Averson points out that in terms of cost-of-living figures and labor costs at the current time, all cities are less expensive than New York, in the following order: San Diego, Houston, Denver, Atlanta, and Jacksonville. He explains that market potential in the various cities is uncertain because competition appears to be extremely heavy in all the locations. Loss of present customers will probably be greatest, in descending order, with moves to San Diego, Houston, Denver, Jacksonville, and Atlanta. Averson's rationale is that the farther away the

172

firm moves from New York, the more of its New York customers it will lose. Attrition of personnel would probably follow similar patterns.

Averson points out that many factors relating to the decision cannot be quantified. He says, "Recreational, educational, and cultural facilities in all the cities are good—but quite different. I feel this is too subjective for me to comment on. For example, as you know, many of our people ski in the winter. Of the alternative locations, only Denver offers that."

A lively discussion breaks out on the merits of the various alternatives. A strong case is made for staying in New York because many employees would not move and therefore recruiting and training expenses in the new location would be high. Also, the ever-increasing competitiveness of the software industry is cited as a reason for staying in New York. One manager argues forcefully, "We have a well-established market here. Why jeopardize it? We'd be up against stiff competition in many of these cities and would have a difficult time breaking in. We'd be foolish to move."

After a lengthy debate, Steiner, who owns a controlling interest in Computer Software, says he will make a decision about the proposed move within a week. He tells his executive committee, "I will do my best to consider the immediate and the long-run consequences—the effects on careers and families and other human considerations—as well as the probable economic impact."

Steiner decides to keep the company in New York. He tells the other senior managers, "Each of the alternative locations has a lot to offer. But when I evaluated the competitiveness we would run into in other cities, the great supply of skilled workers we have here in New York, and the ease with which those of us from the home office can travel to the branches, I decided it was best to stay put. I think I made the right choice."

*Example of
Step 5:
Decide*

## HOW DOES PERSONALITY THEORY AFFECT DECISION MAKING?

The psychologist Carl Jung built a model of personality theory on four psychological functions: feeling, thinking, sensation, and intuition. According to Don Hellriegel and John W. Slocum:

> Only one of the four functions is likely to dominate in each individual. But the dominant function is normally supported by one of the [other] functions. . . . For example, thinking may be backed by sensation, or sensation may be supported by thinking. These two combinations are regarded as most characteristic of modern man in Western industrialized societies. As a consequence, feeling and intuition are functions which are apparently disregarded, undeveloped, or repressed.[1]

**Feeling-type decision-makers** "[are] aware of other people and their feelings, like harmony, need occasional praise, dislike telling people unpleasant things,

[1]Don Hellriegel and John W. Slocum, Jr., "Managerial Problem-Solving Styles," *Business Horizons*, December 1975, p. 31.

# MANAGERS IN ACTION

## HOW FAULTY DECISIONS HELPED BREAK AN OLD CATALOG RETAILER

Making decisions is the core of the management process. Wise decisions translate into profits and progress. Unwise decisions cause problems, even organizational failure. The demise of Aldens, Inc., a 93-year-old Chicago-based mail-order company, illustrates this point.

Aldens, Inc., a subsidiary of Wickes Corporation, was the nation's fifth-largest general-merchandise catalog company. In 1981, Wickes executives discovered that Aldens was becoming unprofitable. To correct this problem, a decision was made to go outside the organization to select a new top executive to run Aldens.

The person selected, Robert H. Quayle, was the wrong man for the job. Mr. Quayle was an experienced and competent retailing executive, but he lacked firsthand knowledge of how to operate a mail-order company.

Mr. Quayle proceeded to make some basic decisions that proved to be wrong for Aldens. The first decision was to add many high-fashion items to the product line. This was a mistake because most of Aldens's customers were low- to middle-income people living in small towns and rural areas. Aldens's customers either did not want the new items or could not afford them. As a result, inventories of unsalable merchandise accumulated.

Another decision cut the profit margins on many items offered in order to compete with discount houses, even though most of Aldens's customers did not shop in large cut-rate stores.

Furthermore, Quayle acted quickly, which upset the old management team. In less than two years, 8 out of 11 key subordinates had quit. By mid-1982, Wickes executives decided drastic action was needed and they appointed a special task force to study the problem. In November 1982, the decision was made to close the operation.

Some alternative solutions to solving Aldens's problems that either were not considered or that were rejected were: (a) to concentrate efforts on fastest-selling merchandise, (b) to act quickly to dispose of products that were not selling, and (c) to make a market research study to determine what motivated Aldens's customers to buy by mail order.

When the top executive of Wickes announced the decision to close down the company to the 300 middle managers, he said, "It isn't easy for me to tell you that the combined forces of your management [Aldens] and ours [Wickes] couldn't do the job we set out to do."[1]

[1]Stephen J. Sansweet, "Management Mistakes Plus Old Problems Led to Collapse of Aldens," *The Wall Street Journal*, January 6, 1983, p. 12. Reprinted by permission of *The Wall Street Journal*, © Dow Jones & Company, Inc., 1983. All Rights Reserved.

### QUESTIONS

1. What was the basic mistake Wickes management made?
2. Can senior managers act too fast in trying to turn a company around? Explain.

tend to be sympathetic, and relate well to most people."[2] Feeling-type decision makers tend to be conformists. They make decisions that are likely to win the support of their peers, subordinates, and superiors. Managers with this personality type go to extremes to avoid disagreements. They also frequently reverse their decisions.

[2]I. B. Myers and K. C. Briggs, *Myers-Briggs Type Indicator* (Princeton, N.J.: Educational Testing Service, 1962), p. 80.

**Thinking-type decision makers** are the opposite extreme of the feeling types. They "[are] unemotional and uninterested in people's feelings, like analysis and putting things into logical order, are able to reprimand people or fire them when necessary, may seem hardhearted, and tend to relate well only to other thinking types."[3] Thinking-type decision makers emphasize intellectual approaches to problems. They prefer to use formulas and rational analytical tools that make up the scientific method.

**Sensation-type decision makers** "dislike new problems unless there are standard ways to solve them, like an established routine, must usually work all the way through to reach a conclusion, show patience with routine details, and tend to be good at precise work."[4] Sensation-type decision makers prefer working with structured problems and like to avoid decisions that involve considerable uncertainty or discretion.

The **intuition-type decision maker** "likes solving new problems, dislikes doing the same things over and over again, jumps to conclusions, is impatient with routine details, and dislikes taking time for precision."[5] Intuition-type decision makers also continuously refine problems, rely on hunches and unverbalized cues, consider several alternatives simultaneously, and do not follow a direct linear approach in problem solving.

Since the four psychological functions are found in everyone, no decision maker can be described as being only one type. Observation suggests, however, that most managers tend toward one type when playing the role of the decision maker.

**SUMMARY**

- Decision making is inherent in managing. Decisions vary in importance, urgency, and complexity and are made at all organizational levels by both individuals and groups.
- Step 1 in the decision-making process is to define the problem or idea to be acted upon.
- Step 2 is to develop alternative solutions for implementing the idea or solving the problem.
- Step 3 is to gather information pertinent to the various alternatives. Information may come from existing rules, procedures, and policies; available facts; research; feasibility studies; simulation; opinions of advisers; experience; public hearings; and forecasts.
- Step 4 is to consider constraints and evaluate alternatives. Managers must consider both internal and external constraints. To evaluate alternatives they may use risk analysis, cost-benefit analysis, or a decision tree.
- Step 5 is to decide. Consideration should be given to the positive and negative impacts of the decision and to its human and political ramifications.
- Step 6 is to follow up or to implement the decision.
- Decisions tend to reflect the personality of the decision maker, which is guided by feelings, thinking, sensation, or intuition.

[3]Ibid., p. 80.
[4]Ibid., p. 80a.
[5]Ibid., p. 80a.

decision
alternatives
feasibility study
simulation
experience
risk
risk analysis

cost-benefit analysis
decision tree
feeling-type decision maker
thinking-type decision maker
sensation-type decision maker
intuition-type decision maker

1. The text states that decisions vary in importance. Can a decision that the decision maker considers to be of little importance be of considerable importance to the person(s) affected by it? Explain.
2. Why is it often difficult to define a problem or an idea to be acted upon?
3. Normally there are a number of alternative solutions to a problem. Assume Territory Y is producing 20 percent less revenue than projected. Develop eight possible alternative solutions to the problem.
4. Why is it desirable for managers to develop several alternative courses of action in reaching decisions?
5. What are the basic sources of information managers may draw on for guidance in making decisions?
6. What is risk analysis? Cost-benefit analysis? A decision tree? How are they useful in the decision-making process?
7. Why is Step 5 in the decision process, making the decision, the most difficult?
8. How is the personality of the decision maker reflected in the decision-making process?

### 1. Should an unproductive employee be terminated?

Henry Jones, age sixty-two, is a middle-management employee who no longer can perform his job effectively. He has a good record but no longer meets the performance standards set for his job. Jones, who is in good health, has served the company for thirty-one years. Retirement is compulsory at age seventy. Jones has made it clear that he intends to work until age seventy or as long as his health remains good.

Because he is a manager and not covered by union rules, the company has the legal right to discharge him. But this solution is out of the question because the company president has stated very firmly, "We will never fire anyone who has served the organization for over thirty years."

Develop four alternative ways to solve this problem. Then, in one paragraph, explain which of your solutions you feel is best and why.

### 2. Is a day-care center a good idea?

Your company has sixty-seven female employees who have preschool-age children. These children are presently cared for in a variety of ways: Some are in day-care centers, and some are left with older children, relatives, or neighbors. The personnel director thinks it would be a good idea for the company to establish an on-premises day-care center. Her plan calls for charging the mothers 50 percent of the average price charged by day-care centers. The company would absorb the costs not met by the mothers' payments.

Prepare two arguments in favor of and two arguments against this idea. Then decide what you would do if you were the decision maker, and give reasons for your decision.

### 3. Is a vice-president for motivation necessary?

Wonder Life Insurance Company is a relatively young company—only five years old. The company specializes in selling a variety of life insurance coverage direct to consumers. The company does not sell group policies, which goes against a trend in the industry.

Peter, president of Wonder Life, is a great believer in the power of agent motivation in selling insurance policies. Two years ago he hired Frank as a vice-president of motivation. Frank gives pep talks, prepares motivational tapes, writes newsletters, talks to agents by phone, and, in other ways, tries to keep the sales force morale high.

But Wonder Life is losing money. A consultant hired to study the problem makes several suggestions—one being to terminate Frank's position. The following discussion takes place between Peter and Houston, the consultant.

Houston: Frank's position accounts for 16 percent of total company expenses. Most life insurance companies do spend quite a bit on motivation but nothing like you. And no other company, to my knowledge, employs a vice-president for motivation.

Peter: Well, I think that motivation is enormously important in selling insurance— especially the way we do it—direct to the consumer.

Houston: I understand. But let me ask you this: Can you verify how much new insurance is sold because of Frank's activities? In other words, how much of last year's sales volume can be attributed to his motivational activities?

Peter: I can't say. And I don't know of any way to find out. I guess we are purchasing motivational services largely on faith.

Houston: Exactly. Yet you are spending 16 percent of your budget on something for which you don't know the payoff.

Peter: Are you saying we should eliminate the position of vice-president for motivation?

Houston: Perhaps. I'm raising questions for you to consider—that's my job as a consultant. An alternative you do have is to purchase motivational materials from an outside source. This would greatly reduce your expenditures in this area.

Assume you are Peter. What action would you take? Develop your answer by using the five steps in the decision-making process.

Adler, Stanley. "Risk-Making Management." *Business Horizons*, April 1980, pp. 11–14.

Aldag, Ramon J., and Jackson, Donald W., Jr. "A Managerial Framework for Social Decision Making." *MSU Business Topics*, Spring 1975, pp. 33–40.

Berry, Leonard Eugene, and Harwood, Gordon B. "Using Accounting Information to Make Better Decisions." *Business*, March 1981, pp. 24–27.

Boehm, George A. W. "Shaping Decisions with Systems Analysis." *Harvard Business Review*, September–October 1976, pp. 91–99.

objectives for each of the ten expenditure classifications by department.

Debbie: Bill, to be very frank, I think your plan is more than we can handle.

Bill: Why?

Debbie: Several reasons. First, this is a major departure from our normal practice. MBO is bound to have bugs in it that we don't perceive at this point. Second, it'll require time—time that we just don't have this year. Third, we'd probably upset some of our people at every level. They may just see MBO as a way to make them work harder. And you know, people fear what they don't understand. MBO would require a lot of explaining, a lot of education. I think if we went all the way into MBO, we'd do more harm than good.

Bill: Your points are well taken. But I still feel MBO is a tool we should give a try. It might be exciting and good for morale—good for profits, too.

QUESTIONS

1. On balance, do you think MBO can be made to work in The Best in Sound? Why or why not?
2. Nothing was said in the discussion about store managers involving each of their four assistant managers in the MBO process. Should they be involved? Explain.
3. Would it be wise to test MBO in only a part of the organization before implementing it throughout the company? Why or why not?

# PART THREE

# ORGANIZING

For an enterprise's plans to succeed, its activities must be grouped in a meaningful way. This is the purpose of organizing, the subject of Part Three.

Chapter 8, "Introduction to Organizing: Specialization and Coordination," gives an overview of the organizing process and discusses the basic organizing principles. The advantages and disadvantages and the future of specialization are examined. Coordination as it relates to an organization's success and ways to make coordination effective are considered.

Chapter 9, "Departmentalization and Span of Control," explains the various bases for departmentalizing—primary function, geographic area, customers served, product, process, project, matrix organization, and task forces. Attention is also given to guidelines for effective departmentalization, to the concept of span of control, and to the factors that affect span-of-control decisions.

Chapter 10, "Line and Staff Authority," begins by noting the differences between line and staff authority. Functional authority, assistant-to positions, use of outside staff specialists, and unofficial staff advice are discussed. The chapter ends with an analysis of what managers can do to develop harmony between line and staff personnel.

One of the most difficult facts of organizing is considered in Chapter 11, "Delegation of Authority." The concept of delegation and its advantages and disadvantages are explained. Factors that determine delegation are examined, an example of ineffective delegation is presented, and guidelines for making delegation effective are provided.

Chapter 12, "Group Dynamics and Committees," analyzes why people form groups and discusses four areas of group dynamics— conformity, aggression, competition, and cooperation. Formal and informal groups are contrasted, guidelines for the effective leadership of groups are considered, and the pros and cons of group decision making are explained. The remainder of the chapter considers committees, boards of directors, and plural executives.

Part Three ends with a Case Study about delegating authority.

8  **INTRODUCTION TO ORGANIZING: SPECIALIZATION AND COORDINATION**

9  **DEPARTMENTALIZATION AND SPAN OF CONTROL**

10  **LINE AND STAFF AUTHORITY**

11  **DELEGATION OF AUTHORITY**

12  **GROUP DYNAMICS AND COMMITTEES**

# 8 INTRODUCTION TO ORGANIZING: SPECIALIZATION AND COORDINATION

**STUDY THIS CHAPTER SO YOU CAN:**

- Explain the steps in and the characteristics of the organizing function.
- Identify the basic principles of organizing and describe their pragmatic application.
- Discuss the importance of and the need for division of labor and specialization.
- List the advantages and disadvantages of specialization.
- Explain how specialization fosters interdependency between individuals and between groups.
- Define "coordination," and discuss why it is needed for the organization to achieve goals.
- Identify and explain the ways in which coordination can be made more effective.

To **organize** is to arrange or form into a coherent whole. In management, organizing involves dealing with various individuals and groups of individuals, each performing a function needed to achieve a result. Organizing directly affects the efficiency with which human and other resources are used and therefore is very important in managing.

In our daily environment we see much evidence of organizing—both good and bad. A well-executed football play tells us that the team knew the play, that

184

*Introduction
to Organizing:
Specialization
and
Coordination*

each player knew his specific assignment and performed it as planned, and that the activities of all players were properly coordinated. The musical group that gives a superlative performance, the fast-food store that consistently provides prompt, efficient service, and the space flight performed without a hitch are varied examples of the organizing function performed well.

We also see much evidence of bad organizing. Customers in a store may be standing in a long line waiting to be checked out while another cash register is unattended and two employees are stacking merchandise on shelves. A secretary may be saddled with too many tasks—taking dictation, answering the telephone, keeping the books, running errands, interviewing job applicants, and supervising several clerical workers. At the other extreme, work may be so simple and so repetitive that the person assigned to it becomes extremely bored and as a result makes mistakes.

## OVERVIEW OF THE ORGANIZING PROCESS

As Figure 8–1 illustrates, organizing can be viewed as a five-step process.

*Step 1:* Determine what activities must be performed to achieve the enterprise's objectives. All organizations perform three major activities: They produce a product or service; they market, sell, or distribute what they produce; and they finance their activities. In carrying out these major activities, organizations may perform a variety of supportive activities, such as engineering, advertising, and accounting.

*Step 2:* Divide the work to be done into reasonably homogenous or similar activities. For example, the production of a typewriter might be subdivided into the assembly of six different components that make up the final product.

*Step 3:* Assign the work to people who can perform it. This involves the staffing function, which is discussed in Part Four of the text.

*Step 4:* Departmentalize the work by assigning a manager to each group of people who perform similar activities. The manager is then held accountable for the successful performance of the work in the department.

*Step 5:* Coordinate the work of all individuals and departments so that the ultimate goal is achieved.

When organizing is performed effectively, each person knows the role or position he or she is expected to play, to whom he or she reports and is accountable, and how his or her work relates to the work of others in the enterprise.

Note that organizing interacts with the performance of other management functions. While organizing can be viewed as a five-step process, it can be separated from the performance of other functions only in a conceptual sense. As Claude S. George, Jr., has observed:

> In communicating, in directing, in fixing limits, and so on, a manager is involved with the organizing as well as the planning processes. Thoughts, for example, must be organized to some degree before they are communicated; directing and establishing relationships or hierarchies demand system and organization; and physical environment conducive to participation shows order or organization. Thus, a manager in generating the right environment for participation is a constant organizer. Organiza-

## FIGURE 8-1

**The Organizing Process**

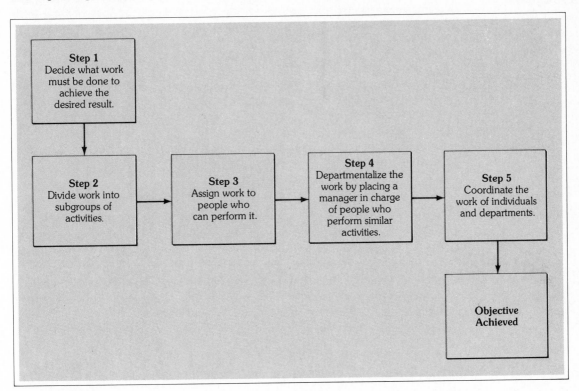

**Step 1**
Decide what work must be done to achieve the desired result.

**Step 2**
Divide work into subgroups of activities.

**Step 3**
Assign work to people who can perform it.

**Step 4**
Departmentalize the work by placing a manager in charge of people who perform similar activities.

**Step 5**
Coordinate the work of individuals and departments.

**Objective Achieved**

tion is involved in his every communication; organization is part of his every plan; and organization is a vital part of any attempt on his part to check or control activities.[1]

Organizing is essential in managing; without it there would often be chaos. Imagine what would happen in a restaurant if ten people reported for work but the work was not specialized, people were not given specific assignments, people were accountable to no one, and their efforts were not coordinated. Without organizing, only the simplest individual goals can be attained. Group goals *always* require organization.

Organizing can be relatively simple, or it can be enormously complex. John Flancher and Brenda Weinstein, both certified public accountants, decide to form an accounting firm. They agree that Flancher will specialize in personal accounts, while Weinstein will work with corporate clients. Each will have two assistants, and they will share a receptionist. Organizing here is uncomplicated.

**Organizing Can Be Simple or Complex**

[1]Claude S. George, Jr., *The History of Management Thought* (Englewood Cliffs, N.J.: Prentice-Hall, 1968), p. 165. Reprinted by permission of Prentice-Hall, Inc., Englewood Cliffs, New Jersey.

**186**

*Introduction
to Organizing:
Specialization
and
Coordination*

Now consider, at the other extreme, the complexity of arranging and coordinating the work in a large accounting firm that employs thousands of people, serves clients in many nations, and performs a wide variety of accounting and auditing services. Some organizations become so large that specialists are assigned the full-time task of defining organizational relationships.

### Organizing Is Evolutionary

Most organizations begin as small, uncomplicated enterprises. As they grow, more specialized functions are added, and the organization becomes more complex. The organizing process is evolutionary. Revisions are usually made gradually, as changes occur in volume of work done, number of employees hired, functions performed, products made, kinds of customers served, and geographical area covered.

### Organizing Should Be Dynamic

Organizing is an ongoing activity, one that is never finished. As internal objectives and environmental conditions change, an enterprise must make corresponding changes in its organizational structure. A new product line may require new departments to make and market it. Expansion or contraction in business activity may indicate that new departments be added, existing departments be dropped, or some departments be merged. Individuals may be given new job assignments under different managers or supervisors.

© Punch/Rothco

Since changes occur so rapidly in our society, there is a need for organizational flexibility. An enterprise that does not make organizational modifications as circumstances change will have a difficult time achieving its objectives and may even find its survival threatened.

All managers are involved in organizing to some extent, but the amount of time devoted to this task varies greatly. The entrepreneur who begins as a one-person business and in a period of years builds it into a 1,000-member organization will have spent a great deal of time organizing activities. In contrast, the individual who purchases a franchise will probably receive a specified organizational plan developed by the franchisor.

In most situations, a manager inherits an existing organizational structure. When Jennifer Watson is promoted to manager of the ready-to-wear department, she takes charge of a structure that is already developed. She may modify it, but she will not have to start from scratch.

## BASIC PRINCIPLES OF ORGANIZING

Over the years management theorists and practitioners have formulated a number of principles, or fundamental truths, regarding organizational structure. Brief definitions and explanations of seven organizational principles follow. While these principles are applicable in most situations, note that there are always some exceptions to the rule.

**Scalar (Chain-of-Command) Principle**

According to the **scalar principle**, authority should flow directly and clearly from the top executive in an organization to each subordinate at each succeeding level. This principle implies that best results are obtained when a clear chain of command is established and followed. If the principle is not followed in organizing, individuals will not know to whom they are responsible. Confusion, indecision, and inefficiency will thereby result.

**Unity-of-Objective Principle**

The **unity-of-objective principle** states that all individuals in the organization and the departments to which they belong should contribute to the principal objectives of the organization. An elementary example of the need to adhere to the unity-of-objective principle is rowing a boat. Unless all the people rowing the boat row together, the goal (to reach the shore) will not be achieved efficiently.

**Adequacy-of-Authority Principle**

The **adequacy-of-authority principle** means that each manager in the organization should be given sufficient authority to achieve the desired result. This principle is violated, for example, when a supervisor is instructed to produce fifty units per shift (the desired result) but is not given the authority to requisition personnel, materials, or equipment to produce the fifty units.

It is, unfortunately, common in organizations for superiors to blame bad results on their subordinates, thereby trying to avoid responsibility for what has happened. The **responsibility-for-results principle** states that even if a superior delegates adequate authority to a subordinate to achieve a goal, the superior is still responsible for the result if the goal is not attained.

For instance, the president of a business may assign a sales objective of 50,000 units to the marketing manager and give the manager sufficient authority to accomplish the goal. If the marketing manager fails in this assignment, the president is still responsible for the result. Shareholders will look to the president, not the marketing manager, for performance.

The responsibility-for-results principle does not, however, relieve subordinate managers of their responsibility to perform. The **accountability principle** holds that when managers accept a plan from their superiors, they are duty bound to carry it out. In other words, they are accountable to their superiors for results. They are expected to put forth their best efforts to achieve the stated objective.

According to the **division-of-work principle**, work should be divided and grouped in a logical manner in order to eliminate duplication of effort and other forms of waste. When two people or two departments are performing work that could just as easily be done by one person or one department, the division-of-work principle is being violated.

Ideally, states the **unity-of-command principle**, each individual in an organization should report to only one superior. However, this principle is often violated. In organizations there are many people who are responsible to two or more persons. Failure to adhere to the principle of unity of command may result in confusion ("To whom am I primarily responsible?"), fear ("If I show more allegiance to Manager A, will Manager B be offended and take punitive action?"), and inefficiency ("If I try to serve both masters, some of my work will slip").

Table 8–1 shows examples of violation of and adherence to each of the foregoing principles.

## DIVISION OF WORK AND SPECIALIZATION

An important part of the organizing function is deciding how to divide the total work of an enterprise into manageable parts. Grouping similar tasks makes **specialization**, the division of work into separate jobs, possible.

In a one-person enterprise the individual must be a jack-of-all-trades. The operator of a food store who has no assistants must buy and display merchandise, handle transactions, and even sweep out the store at night. As the enterprise grows, these and other activities can be assigned to specialists. Specialization, then, goes

**TABLE 8—1**

Examples of Violation of and Adherence to Some Principles of Organizing

| Principle | Examples of Violation | Examples of Adherence |
|---|---|---|
| Scalar (Chain-of-command) | Employee goes over superior's head to complain about a work assignment. | Employee follows the chain of command in requesting a change in an assignment. |
| Unity-of-objectives | Engineering department is designing plans for building a project that has not been approved. | Managers in the engineering department consult with senior management before beginning work on plans. |
| Adequacy-of-authority | Manager in a department store is not given authority to hire temporary salespeople for a major weekend sale. | Manager is given the authority to hire an adequate number of temporary people to handle the anticipated store traffic. |
| Responsibility-for-results | Manager writes memo to his superior emphasizing that his subordinate is responsible for a mistake that has occurred. | Manager writes memo briefly explaining what has gone wrong and indicating the corrective action that he plans to take. |
| Accountability | Subordinate manager disobeys instructions, with the result that costly mistakes occur. | Subordinate manager follows the plan outlined by the superior. |
| Division-of-work | Two nurses in medical clinic perform too many tasks; each handles billing, serves as a receptionist, performs urinalyses, and so on. Mistakes occur, confusion exists, and the clinic suffers. | Work in the clinic is assigned to two individuals. One acts as a receptionist, bills patients, and keeps records. The other performs lab work. |
| Unity-of-command | Employee in a machine shop receives orders from three superiors. Often the orders are contradictory. | Employee is accountable to only one superior. He thus should have a clear idea of the work expected of him. |

hand in hand with growth. Generally, the larger the organization, the more highly specialized the work.

Specialization permeates modern society. Professional people as well as operative employees are becoming more and more specialized in the work they perform. Some examples are accountants, who may be auditors, cost accountants, tax accountants, and so forth; lawyers, who may specialize in patents, corporate law, tax law, and other fields; engineers, who may concentrate on mechanical, civil, nuclear, or industrial engineering; and physicians, who may specialize in internal medicine, cardiology, surgery, dermatology, and so on.

The basic advantages of specialization have long been recognized. The ancient Greeks were concerned with managerial practices. In the *Republic*, a book dealing

The Positive Side
of Specialization

**190**

*Introduction
to Organizing:
Specialization
and
Coordination*

with the principles leading to the construction of an ideal state, Plato made the following observation about division of labor:

> Does a man do better if he practices many crafts, or if he restricts himself to one craft? . . . Each one of us is born somewhat different from the others, one more apt for one task, one for another. . . . Both production and quality are improved in each case, and easier, if each man does one thing which is congenial to him, does it at the right time, and is free of other pursuits. It is likely that the farmer will not make his own plough if it is to be a good one, nor his mattock, nor other agricultural implements. Neither will the builder, for he too needs many things; and the same is true of the weaver and the cobbler.[2]

Adam Smith, whose doctrine of laissez-faire contributed much to the evolution of economic thought in Western societies, also wrote on specialization. In his book *The Wealth of Nations* he gave the following example concerning the manufacture of pins:

> A workman not educated to this business (which the division of labor has rendered a distinct trade), nor acquainted with the use of the machinery employed in it (to the invention of which the same division of labor has probably given occasion), could scarce, perhaps, with his utmost industry, make one pin in a day, and certainly could not make twenty. But in the way in which this business is carried on, not only the whole work is a particular trade, but it is divided into a number of branches, of which the greater part are likewise particular trades. One man draws out the wire, another straights it, and a third cuts it, a fourth points it, a fifth grinds it at the top for receiving the head; to make the head requires two or three distinct operations; to put it on is a peculiar business, to whiten the pins is another; it is even a trade by itself to put them into the paper; and the important business of making a pin is, in this manner, divided into eighteen distinct operations, which, in some manufactories, are all performed by distinct hands, though in others the same man will sometimes perform two or three of them. I have seen a small manufactory of this kind where ten men only were employed, and where some of them consequently performed two or three distinct operations. But though they were very poor, and therefore but indifferently accommodated with the necessary machinery, they could, when they exerted themselves, make among them about twelve pounds of pins in a day.[3]

Social institutions cannot exist without specialized performance of activities. Figure 8–2 summarizes the benefits of specialization. In the following sections, these benefits are discussed in detail.

### Jobs Can Be Learned in Less Time

The more specialized a job, the more quickly it can be learned. Thus an individual learning a job becomes productive sooner and requires less training. For instance, assume two maintenance people (A and B) are to learn how to repair two types of machines. Say it takes one month to learn how to repair each machine. If A and B each learn to repair both machines, two months will be needed to train each of them. But if A learns how to repair one machine and B learns how to repair the other, the training time will be only one month apiece.

---

[2]Plato, *The Republic*, trans. G. M. A. Grube (Indianapolis: Hackett Publishing Co., 1973), pp. 40–41.
[3]Adam Smith, *An Inquiry into the Nature and Causes of the Wealth of Nations*, vol. 1 (London: A Strahan and T. Cadell, 1973), pp. 7–8. Originally published in 1776.

FIGURE 8–2

191

*Division
of Work and
Specialization*

**The Positive Side of Specialization**

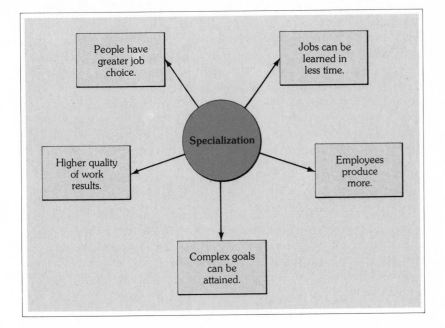

## Employees Are More Productive

Generally, the more highly specialized a job, the greater the productivity per person. Productivity in retailing, for example, when measured by sales per employee, tends to be much higher in stores in which employees perform highly specialized jobs than in stores in which employees perform numerous unrelated functions. In highly mechanized assembly-line industries, such as the automobile industry, per-worker production is much higher than in companies that do custom manufacturing.

Increased productivity has two important implications for the manager. First, employees—since they are more proficient—require less supervision. Assume that forty people are employed to do identical assembly-line work. Each person performs two separate tasks, and altogether four managers are needed to supervise the forty employees. Presumably, if the work were divided so that twenty people performed the first activity and twenty performed the second activity, all employees would become more proficient and thereby would require less supervision. Conceivably, only two managers would be needed; as a result, direct management costs would be cut in half.

The second implication is that management can get the same amount of work done with fewer people. Say there are three workers in an assembly line, each producing four units of A and four units of B per day. The total amount of work produced is twelve units of A and twelve units of B. Now suppose there are only two workers on the assembly line. One produces units of A, while the other produces

**192**

*Introduction
to Organizing:
Specialization
and
Coordination*

units of B. Through practice, they become sufficiently proficient to produce twelve units of A and twelve units of B per day. The total amount of work accomplished is the same as that achieved by the three workers who were not specialized.

### Achievement of Complex Goals Is Made Possible

The attainment of any complex objective requires the contributions of many specialists. Landing men on the moon in Project Apollo, considered by some to be the most difficult goal ever achieved, required the services of thousands of individuals who had a narrow but very deep knowledge of their specialties. In any large undertaking the number of skills required is great. Building a skyscraper, for example, requires the specialized contributions of many kinds of engineers. No one person has enough knowledge about construction to design and build a major structure, nor can any one person complete any type of complex undertaking alone.

### Higher Quality of Work Results

Normally, the greater the degree of specialization, the higher the quality of resulting work. There seems to be a correlation, for example, between the increasing specialization in the practice of medicine and the quality of medical care available. A generation ago, general practitioners were the rule. Today the great majority of physicians specialize in a small number of medical problems. Some are concerned with problems relating to only one body organ, such as the heart, eyes, kidneys, lungs, or liver. Others specialize only in surgery, others treat only children, others confine their practice to old persons, and so forth. Physicians improve through practice, and since they are concentrating on a limited number of medical problems, they are able to keep up with new developments in their field. The net effect is better treatment.

Specialization also produces better results in many other facets of organized life. Mechanics who work on only one kind of car, football players who play only one position, and instructors who teach only one discipline tend to be more effective than their counterparts who have multiple involvements.

### People Have Greater Job Choice

Because of specialization, people today have a much larger number of careers available than they did a generation ago. Forty years ago the computer industry was just beginning. Now there are a number of careers associated with it and dozens of different kinds of jobs within each career. The number of different academic disciplines has increased greatly in the last four decades, giving those who want to teach and those who want to obtain specialized knowledge a far greater choice than was previously possible.

People differ greatly in aptitudes, talents, skills, physical makeup, and interests. Specialization gives individuals a greater chance to find work that they enjoy and for which they are well suited.

## The Negative Side of Specialization

Critics of specialization claim it creates dull work because highly specialized jobs have too little challenge to hold a worker's interest. It is true that many individuals work in jobs that require only a fraction of their skill and intelligence. Because of a tight job market in recent years, many college graduates have had to accept jobs for which they are overeducated.

Whether a highly specialized job is dull depends on the amount of challenge it contains and the degree to which the individual enjoys the work. Some surgeons repeatedly perform the same types of operations yet appear to be challenged by their work. Professors normally specialize in one academic discipline and appear to be satisfied. Many actors perform the same role one hundred or more times and still enjoy each performance.

While specialization is not responsible for all job dissatisfaction, it often is a factor. Managers can minimize the negative aspects of specialization by improving the match between people and jobs, by emphasizing the importance of the activity performed, and by providing various forms of job enrichment. These approaches to raising worker satisfaction will be discussed in some detail in Chapter 16.

Specialization has also been cited as a cause of inhibited creativity and lowered morale. The Issue for Debate in this chapter considers some pro and con arguments about this allegation.

## Specialization and Interdependency

Specialization makes human beings rely more on other human beings. Individuals and groups become increasingly concerned with the actions of other individuals and groups. Consider some of the ramifications of specialization on organizations:

- Individuals within an organization become dependent on one another. If Jane does not perform her work properly, Bill may not be able to perform his work satisfactorily.
- Groups of workers (departments) within an organization become dependent on other groups. Department A must perform certain work on a product before Department B can perform additional work. If Department A misses its deadline for completion, Department B is adversely affected.
- An entire organization becomes dependent on other organizations. General Motors, for example, depends on more than 40,000 other organizations to supply it with parts, components, and materials. It depends on thousands more to sell and service what it makes.

## The Future of Specialization

It seems highly probable that there will be more, not less, work specialization in the future. As knowledge expands the number of different kinds of jobs required to use it also expands. In the decade ahead, for example, we will probably create much new knowledge about energy development and use. As that knowledge is applied, new specialized jobs will be created. There seems to be a correlation between the extent of human knowledge and the degree to which work becomes specialized. Specialization and the civilizing process go hand in hand.

Another reason that more specialization is likely in the future is the continuing increase in the number of government regulations. For instance, as tax regulations become more numerous and more complex, new job specialties will be created in the accounting field. New types of highly specialized jobs resulting from changes in laws are also likely in the legal profession and in law enforcement. Within corporations, there are likely to be more specialized positions relating to

194

*Introduction
to Organizing:
Specialization
and
Coordination*

government regulations. Consider how the implementation of the Occupational Safety and Health Act caused many firms to employ safety experts so they could take the actions needed to be in compliance with the law.

A third reason why more specialization will be required in the future is the need for more goods and services. As demand increases, there will be a corresponding need for increased efficiency. And specialization is one of the keys to obtaining a greater output per unit of labor input.

## COORDINATION

To **coordinate** means to bring together all the activities performed by an organization so that the desired result is achieved in the most efficient manner. Effective coordination is evident when individuals within a department work harmoniously and when the work produced by the various departments is synchronized carefully.

Some management authorities consider coordination to be a separate function of management. The view taken here is that coordination is inherent throughout the management process and is involved in the performance of each management function: planning, organizing, staffing, directing, and controlling.

### Why Coordination Is Essential

Coordination is necessary because of the division of labor into specialized jobs. In building a home there is considerable division of labor. Bricklayers, plasterers, carpenters, electricians, plumbers, heating and air conditioning workers, and other specialists are required. The work of each group of workers must be tied together, or coordinated, with the activities performed by each other group, if the desired result—a home built according to specifications—is to be achieved.

The larger and more complex an organization, the more difficult it is to coordinate activities. Consider the wide variety of activities that must be harmonized by an automobile manufacturer. The functions of design, assembly of hundreds of parts into components, and assembly of components into finished products must be coordinated. So must shipping of autos to dealers, arranging for financing, and many other activities.

### How Does Coordination Relate to Success of the Organization?

The successful attainment of an organizational goal in an efficient manner is evidence of effective coordination. If you visit a restaurant and are well pleased with the food and service, you have witnessed effective coordination. The result indicates that the work of various specialists—such as the maître d', the waiter, the chef, and the busboys—was synchronized to make the experience pleasurable. Had the individual contribution of any of these employees not been harmonized, the result would have been less than satisfactory.

A college band is also organized into departments, each specializing in playing certain kinds of instruments. Each member of each department in the band may be very skilled. But if the efforts of the various musicians are not coordinated properly, the result may be noise rather than music.

## MANAGERS IN ACTION

### WHERE WILL MODERN-DAY SPECIALIZATION LEAD?

Work specialization seems to be a key element in advancing efficiency and its offspring, productivity. Consider what has happened to agriculture in this century. Seventy-five years ago there were no tractors, 6.4 million farms and 26 million workhorses. Today there are about 5 million tractors, only 2.3 million farms and only a few workhorses. The workhorse is no longer a primary energy source on the farm. The 5 million tractors do three times the work of 26 million horses.[1] And agricultural production now is three times what it was 75 years ago.

Huge efficiency gains resulted with the switch from horses to tractors. For example, a horse requires 25 pounds of feed per day, whether working or not. A tractor requires fuel only when operated.

[1]Robert Shrank, "Horse-Collar Blue-Collar Blues," *Harvard Business Review*, May–June 1981, pp. 135–136.

Several changes increased specialization in agriculture. Farmers learned to specialize in growing certain grains, such as wheat, corn, or soybeans; or they specialized in raising certain animals, such as dairy cattle, beef cattle, pigs, sheep, or chickens.

Gains in agricultural efficiency caused a massive migration of people from farms to urban centers. Because of the long-term trend toward industrialization (expansion in auto sales, equipment, steel, etc.), farm workers were absorbed into the industrial work force.

Now a major labor modification is taking place in our drive for greater efficiency through specialization—utilization of the robot to perform jobs previously handled by human workers. On one hand we welcome the robot. It won't join unions, pilfer or embezzle, report to work drunk or drugged, call in sick, talk back to superiors, or demand fringe benefits. But the robot also creates concern among many people.

### QUESTIONS

1. What would you do if a robot was going to take over the performance of your job? What could you do before and after it happened?
2. What affects will robots have on the American labor market?

Or consider a more complex example: the operation of an airline. Assume that Flight 100 is at O'Hare International Airport in Chicago, preparing to depart for San Francisco in one hour. Some of the passengers who will take Flight 100 are en route to O'Hare on a number of other flights. It is important that these planes arrive on schedule so that transferring passengers can make Flight 100 on time. This requires careful coordination by air traffic controllers and the pilots involved.

Meanwhile, a number of other key activities must be coordinated if Flight 100 is to depart on time:

• Baggage of both originating and transferring passengers must be placed aboard Flight 100. The baggage may come from a dozen or more locations within the airport.

196

*Introduction
to Organizing:
Specialization
and
Coordination*

- Food and beverages provided by an independent company must arrive on time and be placed on the aircraft.
- Ground personnel must fuel the aircraft and inspect its various mechanical systems.
- Ticket counter personnel must sell tickets, check baggage, and direct passengers to the appropriate gate.
- Personnel at the gate must collect the tickets and assign seats.
- Before boarding the aircraft, the pilot must check flight plans and analyze weather reports.

When the pilot decides that the plane is ready to go, he or she talks to the air traffic controller, who will coordinate Flight 100's taxi down the runway and actual takeoff with those of other aircraft in the vicinity in order to avoid collisions. Thus, the departure of a plane on schedule reflects the successful coordination of a wide variety of tasks.

On the other hand, we see many examples of less-than-effective coordination. The receipt of only part of an order from a catalog retailer, the tardy delivery of materials to a building site, and an excessive delay in the execution of an order to purchase securities may all indicate ineffective coordination. Failure to achieve an organizational objective always indicates that there has been lack of coordination to some degree.

## Guidelines for Effective Coordination

As has been noted, coordination is exceptionally important for two reasons: It is inherent in the management process (if you don't have it, you have chaos), and it directly affects the degree of success of an organization. Coordination can be made more effective if management follows these guidelines.

### Keep Organizational Objectives in Mind

It is common for a department manager to conclude that his or her activity is the most important facet of the organization. But in truth, all departments are important, since each exists to make a specific contribution to the organization's goal. Many of us have seen an athletic contest lost because one player viewed the game as an opportunity to prove that he or she was a star rather than a member of a team.

In practice, managers often lose sight of the main purpose of the organization. A marketing manager may be so committed to her specialty that she develops the attitude "The purpose of this company is to sell more merchandise, *period*." She may then proceed to take various steps to gain more sales, such as accepting orders from customers for products for which the production division does not have production capability; authorizing an advertising campaign that significantly changes the image of the company; promising product delivery to customers at a date the shipping department cannot meet; reducing prices to unrealistic levels; and employing additional sales representatives to open up new territories for which product demand has not been determined through research studies.

In this example, the marketing manager thinks that sales, not profits, are the main objective of the company. She should check with production before accepting orders, with other senior executives before authorizing the advertising cam-

# ISSUE FOR DEBATE

## DOES SPECIALIZATION DISCOURAGE CREATIVITY AND LOWER MORALE?

Some feel that the trend toward specialization inhibits creativity and at the same time reduces the level of morale. Others believe that specialization actually encourages creativity and improves employee attitudes. Some pro and con arguments follow.

### YES

**Specialization does discourage creativity and lower morale because . . .**

The high turnover of workers in routine specialized jobs, such as cleaning-service personnel and hospital orderlies, indicates that specialization bores people and thus lowers their morale.

Society is becoming increasingly specialized. Many people now perform tasks that are so small in the total scheme of things that they become dissatisfied. Also, people are afraid that decreasing job responsibilities may lead to loss of jobs.

Specialization encourages people to think traditionally, not creatively. Traditional thinking never results in new processes, techniques, products, inventions, or other forms of progress.

People inherently dislike specialization because they interpret it to mean discipline, rules, and conformity. These negative reactions to specialization discourage people from seeking better ways to perform.

### NO

**Specialization does not discourage creativity and lower morale because . . .**

The act of developing specialized activities is in itself a creative activity. It requires creative intelligence to simplify work.

Specialization frees managers from performing routine activities, and so they need deal only with exceptions. Therefore managers have more time to think of ways to improve performance.

Automation and computerization are increasingly eliminating routine jobs. Over time, machines will eventually perform most of the boring tasks. Therefore, workers will be reassigned to more challenging work.

Much specialized work in our society is becoming very demanding of the intellectual and technical abilities of people. Energy research, emerging medical technology, and the increasing complexities of accounting are only three examples.

### QUESTIONS

1. What additional arguments, both pro and con, can you advance?
2. Which side of the issue do you think is most valid? Explain.
3. If the trend toward specialization continues, what long-range effects do you think it will have?

198

*Introduction
to Organizing:
Specialization
and
Coordination*

paign, with the shipping department before promising a delivery date, with the controller before making major price changes, and with the market research manager before opening up new territories.

An analogy can be drawn between a watch and coordination. There are many pieces in a watch, and some are much more expensive than others. But are the more costly pieces more important in helping the watch function properly and achieve its goal of telling time correctly? In large organizations there are many departments, and some have bigger budgets and more highly paid executives than others. But are the departments with the most money and the higher-paid personnel more essential to the attainment of goals?

In complex organizations, production shutdowns may occur because, through lack of coordination, an assembly line runs out of a simple "insignificant" part. Traffic tie-ups may occur because one police officer is absent and his supervisor failed to provide a replacement during rush hour. Or a flight may be delayed because the work of the baggage crew (which accounts for a very small share of the costs of operating an airline) was not coordinated properly.

### Coordination Should Begin in the Planning Phase

Coordination is always more effective if it begins when plans are first developed. If each manager who will be involved in the plan can ask and answer questions before a final go-ahead plan is designed, then coordination will be smoother.

Generally, those who will be involved in the execution of a plan should also participate in its design. Helping to develop a plan is in itself an educational process, during which many questions will be answered and each manager will gain a greater understanding of the roles other managers are to play in achieving organizational objectives.

### A Cooperative Attitude Should Be Stressed

**Cooperation**, defined here as a sincere willingness of people in an organization to help one another perform related activities, is vital to effective coordination and, in turn, to organizing and managing. G. Elton Mayo observed that successful management depends on the presence of three factors:

* The application of science and technical skill to some material good or product
* The systematic ordering of operations
* The organization of teamwork—that is, of sustained cooperation

According to Mayo:

> The third . . . is almost wholly neglected. Yet it remains true that if these three are out of balance, the organization as a whole will not be successful. . . . For the larger and more complex the institution, the more dependent it is upon the whole-hearted cooperation of every member of the group. . . . The organization of any group must secure for its members, first, the satisfaction of their material needs, and second, the active cooperation of others in the fulfillment of many and diverse social functions.

These are not ranked here as first and second in order of importance; both are important and must be simultaneously effected.[4]

Henry Gantt also emphasized the interdependency of cooperation and organizing when he noted:

A system of management may be defined as a means of causing men to cooperate with one another for a common end. If this cooperation is maintained by force, the system is in a state of unstable equilibrium. It will go to pieces if the strong hand is removed. Cooperation in which the bond is mutual interest in the success of work done by intelligent and honest methods produces a state of equilibrium which is stable and needs no outside support.[5]

Gantt's observations suggest that sound organization is needed to develop and maintain equilibrium. Good human relations certainly cannot be practiced if people do not clearly understand what is expected of them. Good organization provides a structure for attaining the mutual interests of the group. And cooperation goes hand in hand with organizing. People cannot cooperate effectively unless they understand how the roles they play and the tasks they perform in an enterprise relate to those of others.

Unfortunately, in all organizations there are examples — some very obvious — of individuals who do not project a cooperative attitude. Jealousy, pettiness, bickering, and other examples of psychological sabotage within organizations are very common. For instance:

- *Secretary:* "She didn't help me when we had that big project last month, so why should I help her?"
- *Production foreman:* "I'm not going to hurry up production. That customer can wait another ten days."
- *Senior executive:* "Clark [another senior executive] embarrassed me pretty badly last week at the meeting. I'll figure out a way to put a hold on his budget request."

Obviously, such attitudes will hamper coordination and will interfere with the attainment of organizational goals.

Obtaining cooperation is a motivational challenge. Erwin Schell has made this observation about the value of praise:

The giving of praise or commendation gratifies the instinctive desire for approval. Some executives do not favor its use. They adopt the policy of taking exceptional work for granted. They argue that the employee will then infer that what he considered unusually good was no more than what was expected. He will then set higher standards of achievement for himself. The error in this logic is found in the last conclusion. Only the rare employee finds incentive in passive acceptance of good

[4]G. Elton Mayo, *The Social Problems of an Industrial Civilization* (London: Routledge & Kegan Paul Ltd., 1962), pp. 61, 62.
[5]Henry Laurence Gantt, *Gantt on Management*, ed. Alex W. Rathe (New York: American Management Association, 1961), p. 61.

200

*Introduction
to Organizing:
Specialization
and
Coordination*

work by his chief. The usual result of this policy is to bring discouragement or the feeling that the boss is unappreciative.[6]

When an individual learns that good performance will be commended, he or she is likely to cooperate effectively with others because their performance affects his or her performance. A manager can foster cooperation in a number of other ways, particularly by fairly treating all subordinates, by carefully selecting people whose work is closely related, and by using a team approach.

### Communicate Clearly

On a number of occasions during the Vietnam War, U.S. personnel were fired upon in error by U.S. aircraft. The reason was ineffective coordination caused by a communications problem. In some cases the pilots received incorrect information about what the target was, and in other cases the pilots misunderstood their instructions. While examples as dramatic as this are rare, many of the mistakes, accidents, and problems encountered in organizations can be traced directly to a lack of synchronized effort due to faulty dissemination of information. Obviously, if people do not understand the work they are asked to do and how it relates to the work others do, harmony cannot result.

Communication may be horizontal, with personnel communicating directly with persons on the same organizational level. Or it may be vertical, taking place between individuals at different organizational levels. In either event, clear communication can aid in the coordination of activities.

SUMMARY

- Organizing is an essential management function and consists of five steps: (1) deciding what work must be done, (2) dividing the work into similar or related activities, (3) assigning people who can perform the work, (4) placing a manager in charge of people who perform the related activities, and (5) coordinating the work of individual departments.
- Organizing can differ widely in complexity, is evolutionary, and should be dynamic. The amount of time a manager devotes to organizing can vary.
- Key principles of organizing are the scalar (chain-of-command) principle, the unity-of-objective principle, the adequacy-of-authority principle, the responsibility-for-results principle, the accountability principle, the division-of-work principle, and the unity-of-command principle.
- The division of work into separate jobs is called specialization.
- Benefits claimed for specialization are that (1) jobs can be learned in less time, (2) employees are more productive, (3) achievement of complex goals is made possible, (4) higher quality of work results, and (5) people have greater job choice. The major negative aspect of specialization is that dull work often results.
- Specialization leads to interdependency of people and groups. As knowledge expands we will probably see more, not less, specialization.
- Coordination is needed to bring together all activities performed so that the desired goal is achieved. Coordination is essential because of the division of labor into specialized tasks.

[6]Erwin Haskell Schell, *The Technique of Executive Control*, 7th ed. (New York: McGraw-Hill, 1950), p. 115.

Guidelines for effective coordination are (1) keep organizational objectives in mind, (2) begin coordination in the planning phase, (3) stress a cooperative attitude, and (4) communicate clearly.

organize
scalar principle
unity-of-objective principle
adequacy-of-authority principle
responsibility-for-results principle
accountability principle

division-of-work principle
unity-of-command principle
specialization
coordinate
cooperation

**LEARN
THE LANGUAGE
OF
MANAGEMENT**

1. Cite three examples of ineffective organizing you have personally observed. For each, explain what you feel was wrong and what possible corrective action might have been taken.
2. What is meant by each of these statements: "Organization can differ widely in complexity." "Organizing is evolutionary." "Organizing should be dynamic."
3. Give an example of violations of the scalar principle, the unity-of-objective principle, the adequacy-of-authority principle, the responsibility-for-results principle, the accountability principle, the division-of-work principle, and the unity-of-command principle.
4. How does specialization relate to organizational size? Why?
5. Why is specialization necessary to achieve complex goals? What would be the likely result if a basketball team was not specialized? A large accounting firm? A hospital?
6. On balance, do you think that the benefits of specialization outweigh its negative aspects? Why? Can you foresee a time when further specialization will be impossible? Explain.
7. How does coordination relate to specialization? To organizational size?
8. Why is cooperation essential for effective coordination? What can be done to foster cooperation?

**QUESTIONS
FOR REVIEW
AND
DISCUSSION**

**1. How to reduce payroll costs by rescheduling hours of employment**

You are the manager of a fast-food franchise. The owner of the franchise, Mr. Jingles, has delegated operations to you but looks very carefully at the end-of-the-month operating statements.

In analyzing last month's statements, Jingles observes, "You know, I think our payroll costs are excessive — at least they are when compared with industry averages. We have sixteen full-time workers. Eight work from 6:30 A.M. until 2:30 P.M., and the other eight work from 2:30 P.M. until we close at 10:30 P.M., with a one-half hour break in each shift.

"I visited the store several times last month and I found the employees fairly idle after the breakfast rush between 9:00 A.M. and 11:30 A.M. Also, they weren't fully active after lunch between 2:30 P.M. and 5:30 P.M.

"I think we may be able to solve this problem through part-time employment. What I want you to do is devise a plan to reduce the number of employee hours per day by

**MAKING
MANAGEMENT
DECISIONS**

202

*Introduction
to Organizing:
Specialization
and
Coordination*

20 percent. My only guideline is that no employee works less than three or more than five hours per day."

Devise a plan to accomplish Jingles' objective.

### 2. Specialization in action

Sketch the worker specialization you have observed at (1) a supermarket, (2) a hospital or doctor's office, and (3) a state agency (such as the Department of Motor Vehicles, where drivers' licenses are issued). How might further specialization make each of these operations more efficient?

### 3. Identifying the need for organization, specialization, and coordination

Jim Brown is 32, married, has two children, and two years of college. Jim owns a home remodeling company that he started five years ago. Jim has 10 full-time employees — one clerical worker and nine skilled and semi-skilled carpenters, painters, and electricians.

Business is good, but Jim has a problem. He works 80 to 90 hours a week, which leaves him almost no time for his family. Jim performs a variety of functions for his business. He makes all the sales, writing weekly newspaper advertisements; and he handles all of the billing and the accounting.

Additionally, he personally supervises and inspects each job several times during its progress and again when it is finished. He does not have a job foreman. Jim feels he must handle the supervision because of his knowledge of home remodeling and because of his concern about good customer service.

Jim would like to expand and increase profits, but he cannot find the time to make any plans toward these goals.

What advice would you give to Jim about organization, specialization, and coordination? Specifically, what could Jim do to (a) work fewer hours and (b) find time and energy to expand?

Would a course in basic management help Jim? Why or why not?

**FOR ADDITIONAL
CONCEPTS
AND IDEAS**

Andrews, Kenneth R. "Directors' Responsibility for Corporate Strategy." *Harvard Business Review*, November–December 1980, pp. 30–42.

Biscoe, Dennis R. "Organizational Design: Dealing with the Human Constraint." *California Management Review*, Fall 1980, pp. 71–80.

Chase, Richard B. "Some Tried and True Approaches to Improve Manufacturing Productivity." *Journal of Contemporary Business*, August 1981, pp. 33–44.

Davidson, William H. "Small Group Activity at Musashi Semiconductor Works." *Sloan Management Review*, Spring 1982, pp. 3–14.

Devanna, Mary Anne. "Strategic Human Resource Management." *Sloan Management Review*, Winter 1982, pp. 47–61.

Frost, Carl F. "The Scanlon Plan: Anyone for Free Enterprise?" *MSU Business Topics,* Winter 1978, pp. 25–33.

Greenberg, Herbert M., and Greenberg, Jeanne. "Job Matching for Better Sales Performance." *Harvard Business Review*, September–October 1980, pp. 128–133.

Handy, Charles. "Through the Organizational Looking Glass." *Harvard Business Review*, January–February 1980, pp. 115–121.

Locander, William B., and Scamell, Richard W. "A Team Approach to Managing the Market Research Process." *MSU Business Topics*, Winter 1977, pp. 15–26.

Miller, Jeffrey G. "Fit Production Systems to the Task." *Harvard Business Review*, January–February 1981, pp. 145–154.

Miner, John B., and Smith, Norman R. "Can Organizational Design Make Up for Motivational Decline?" *The Wharton Magazine*, Summer 1981, pp. 36–41.

Mintzberg, Henry. "Organizational Design: Fashion or Fit?" *Harvard Business Review*, January–February 1981, pp. 103–116.

Peters, Thomas J., and Phillips, Julien R. "Structure is Not Organization." *Business Horizons*, June 1980, pp. 14–26.

Randolph, W. Alan. "Matching Technology and the Design of Organization Units." *California Management Review*, Summer 1981, pp. 39–48.

Shirley, Robert. "A Model for Analysis of Organizational Change." *MSU Business Topics*, Spring 1974, pp. 60–68.

Vandervelde, Maryanne. "Increasing People-Productivity." *Journal of Contemporary Business*, August 1981, pp. 19–32.

# 9 DEPARTMENTAL- IZATION AND SPAN OF CONTROL

**STUDY THIS CHAPTER SO YOU CAN:**

- Define "departmentalization," and identify the three steps in the departmentalization process.

- Explain the major bases for departmentalization—function, geographic area, customer, and product—noting the rationale for and considerations involved in each method.

- Discuss the other ways of departmentalizing—by process, by project, by matrix organization, and by task force—including the use of multiple bases.

- Identify the guidelines for effective departmentalization.

- Define "span of control" and the "exception principle," and explain their relationship to effective organizing.

- Describe the factors that affect span-of-control decisions.

- Explain the controversy regarding the "ideal" span of control.

Just as the parts of a machine must fit together properly if the machine is to function, the human components of an organization must mesh if the enterprise is to attain its intended results. The structure of an organization is an important determinant of the organization's success in achieving objectives. In this chapter two key interrelated elements in the organizing process are examined: departmentalization and the span of control.

## WHAT IS DEPARTMENTALIZATION?

**Departmentalization,** or arrangement of the work of an enterprise into manageable parts, is an important part of organizing. We have many words in our vocabulary that are, in some context, synonymous with the word "department." They include "division," "branch," "bureau," "board," "subdepartment," "squadron," "agency," "fleet," "group," and "diocese." Regardless of the terminology used, departmentalization involves three steps:

*Step 1:* Reasonably like or similar tasks are grouped together. For example, similar activities such as selling and advertising may be put in one department, production and engineering in another, and finance and accounting in a third department.

*Step 2:* Authority to perform these activities is assigned to a department head, who may be given one of many titles, such as chief, vice-president, chairperson, manager, commander, or administrator.

*Step 3:* The department head accepts responsibility for achieving organizational goals and is held accountable to a superior for performance.

The goal of departmentalization is to perform the work of an enterprise in the most efficient manner—that is, to obtain the best possible use of human, material, and financial resources.

## WHAT ARE THE BASES FOR DEPARTMENTALIZATION?

The following sections explain and illustrate the four primary bases for departmentalization: function, territory or geographic area, customer, and product. To help understand the organizing process, each basis for structuring an enterprise is considered separately. In practice, however, an enterprise may incorporate all four bases as foundations for its organizational structure.

**Functional departmentalization** is the process of grouping an organization's activities into logical units on the basis of the essential functions that must be performed to attain the enterprise's goals. It is the primary way in which organizations are departmentalized.

### The Three Basic Functions: Production, Marketing, and Finance

All organizations, profit-seeking or nonprofit-seeking, large or small, perform three key functions: production, marketing, and finance. An understanding of the inherent nature of these functions helps us to comprehend the what, why, and how of departmentalization by function.

What Is
Departmentalization
by Function?

**205**

*The production function.*  All organizations produce something. This activity is called the **production function**. The product may be tangible, such as a dress, or intangible, such as knowledge or entertainment. Names given to the production function vary with the kind of enterprise. In airlines it is called "operations"; in hospitals, "patient care"; and in insurance companies, "underwriting." Producing something, regardless of the product's form or name, is the central purpose of organizations.

How well the production function is performed determines the success of the organization to a large extent. A motorcycle company that produces bikes that don't operate as advertised, a school that produces low-quality education, and a hospital that provides inadequate patient service will not enjoy extensive patronage under normal conditions.

*The marketing function.*  All organizations try to market the product they create—an activity known as the **marketing function**. Obviously there is no point in producing something without making it available to its intended users. In the case of many manufacturing firms, such as those that produce blue jeans or toothpaste, the marketing function is dramatically highlighted through advertising and personal selling programs. But what is less apparent (and often less effectively conducted) is the performance of the marketing function by nonbusiness organizations.

While the term "marketing" is generally not used outside of business organizations, the function, under one name or another, is performed in nearly all enterprises. Religious organizations may mount crusades, conduct membership campaigns, and advertise modestly to attract people. In hospitals, the term "delivery of health services," suggests marketing. Educational institutions perform the marketing function in a variety of ways, such as inviting potential students to visit the campus, conducting career days, developing an active alumni association, and obtaining favorable publicity in the media.

An organization may produce a good or even an excellent product or utility, but usually if it is not "sold," success as measured by sales or public acceptance will at best be limited. Some organizations—such as those in the medical or accounting fields—may be restricted by law, professional codes, or both, in the way they promote their services, if they are permitted to promote them at all. Nevertheless, attracting patronage, if by no other means than word of mouth, is important.

*The finance function.*  The **finance function** is essential; all organizations require money to produce and market the product they offer. The methods for obtaining capital vary. Corporations may sell stock or borrow money, municipalities tax their residents and may sell bonds, religious and charitable institutions may solicit contributions, and a lodge or fraternity may collect dues.

Unless there is adequate funding for production and marketing, an organization cannot achieve its goals. In most businesses the finance department depends on marketing to generate most of the operating capital. However, when additional working or short-term capital is needed, the finance function is generally responsible for providing the financial base to operate the enterprise, usually through borrowing money or selling stock. The finance function is important in funding nonprofit organizations as well, including government agencies.

**FIGURE 9-1**

**Departmentalization by Function: Primary Departments**

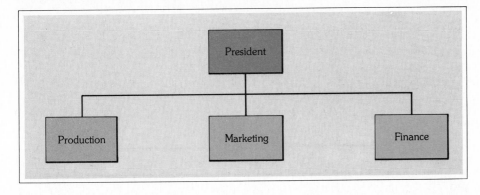

Figure 9-1 shows a simplified version of departmentalization by the three basic functional areas, which are also the primary departments. Note that this figure provides an example of an **organization chart**, which is a visual device that shows reporting relationships among people and departments.

### Derivative Functional Departmentalization

Each primary function, even in the simplest organization, consists of various subfunctions. For example, the production department in a manufacturing enterprise may perform engineering, assembly, and quality-control activities; the marketing department may handle advertising, manage salespeople, and arrange to transport the finished product; and the finance department may do all the general accounting, cost accounting, and data processing that are required.

As an organization grows and becomes more complex, it becomes necessary to further departmentalize the basic functions. Figure 9-2 shows a breakdown of the primary functions of a hypothetical manufacturing company into specialized derivative departments.

As an organization becomes even more complex, a third level of functional departments may be required. The data-processing department in Figure 9-2 may become so complex that new departments subordinate to it may need to be created—one to handle financial data and another to process marketing information.

### Advantages of Functional Departmentalization

Setting up departments on the basis of the three key functions—production, marketing, and finance—has two major advantages. First, it is logical because it groups like or similar activities together. This arrangement facilitates specialization. Production people specialize in producing the utility, marketing people specialize in selling it, and finance personnel specialize in funding all activities. Specialization may increase organizational productivity, since work is performed by specialists in each functional area who can develop an intensive understanding of their jobs.

Second, coordination is improved, since work is not duplicated in different

**FIGURE 9—2**

**Departmentalization by Function: Primary and Derivative Departments**

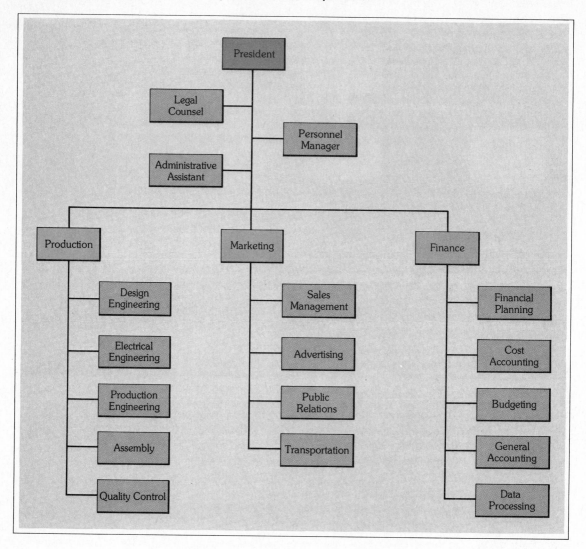

departments and since the heads of each functional department report directly to the chief executive officer. This arrangement also contributes to organizational simplicity—something all good managers seek.

### Disadvantages of Functional Departmentalization

Functional departmentalization based on primary activities is ideal for small organizations. It is logical and simple. Some weaknesses of functional departmentalization, however, become apparent as an organization grows and becomes more complex.

One disadvantage is that the **chain of command** (that is, the number of levels of management from the highest to the lowest) becomes excessively long as new levels are added. This arrangement may slow communication. Second, functional departmentalization does not enable managers of the key departments to develop much understanding of the activities in other departments. The head of marketing may learn little about how the production department works. This weakness makes it difficult to develop well-rounded executives who can serve at the top level. Some degree of narrow-mindedness may result.

### Addition of Staff Departments

Figure 9–2 shows three staff assistants reporting to the president (legal counsel, personnel manager, and administrative assistant). As an organization grows the organizational structure becomes more complex, and services of highly trained specialists become necessary. Staff departments and staff personnel are discussed in Chapter 10. It should be observed here, however, that staff specialists and departments, while important, exist only to support the performance of the primary functions of an enterprise.

**Geographic departmentalization** is the process of grouping activities by area or territory and assigning them to a given manager. A bank with branches located in various parts of a metropolitan area is departmentalized on a geographic basis, as is an automobile manufacturer that has production facilities located in different areas.

As an organization grows larger, geographic departmentalization often becomes necessary. It is virtually inescapable for growing government, business, communications, and military organizations. Table 9–1 gives examples of geographic departmentalization for different kinds of organizations. Figure 9–3 shows a simplified example of an organization that is departmentalized by function *and* geographic area.

With geographic departmentalization, ultimate authority for performing the three basic organizational functions—production, marketing, and finance—is still retained by headquarters. But some authority for their performance is delegated to departments organized on a geographic basis.

### Considerations Involved in Geographic Departmentalization

Four factors are especially important in deciding whether to departmentalize on a geographic basis. They are noted briefly below.

*Economic factors.* Economic considerations are a major reason that some organizations decide to departmentalize on a geogrphic basis. It may be possible, for example, to save taxes, reduce transportation costs, employ better-qualified people, and give better service to customers by establishing branch departments in selected geographic areas. Production and sales functions, in particular, are often departmentalized for economic reasons.

*Climatic factors.* Climate plays a large role in people's consumption patterns. Contrast the climatic differences—and their effect on spending patterns for

**TABLE 9–1**

**Examples of Geographic Departmentalization for Different Types of Organizations**

| Type of Organization | Example of Geographic Departmentalization |
|---|---|
| Police department | Divided into precincts. |
| Government | Many offices assigned to each state or each Federal Reserve district. |
| Automobile manufacturer | Assembly plants located in major population centers in the United States and around the world. Dealerships geographically arranged, located on the basis of population size or market demand. |
| Crude-oil producer | Departments located where drilling operations are promising. |
| Commercial bank | Branches located in various places near large numbers of people. |
| Medical center | Outpatient clinics and emergency treatment facilities strategically located where needed. |

**FIGURE 9–3**

**Departmentalization by Function and Geography**

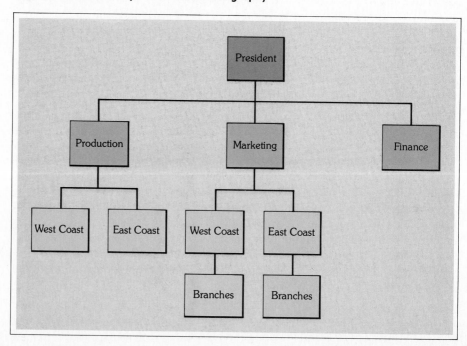

many products—between Cleveland and Los Angeles or Miami and Minneapolis. When climate is a major factor affecting consumption, geographic departmentalization is often necessary to adapt to local conditions.

*Legal and political considerations.* Laws and regulations still differ considerably among different municipalities, states, and nations, and therefore may be a factor in geographic departmentalization. Some forms of territorial departmentalization are required by federal and state laws. Federal laws require that the Federal Reserve System have twelve branches. And political factors often influence a firm's decision to establish branches in foreign countries. Zoning regulations, taxes, building codes, and the attitude of local political leaders toward economic development are examples of legal-political considerations that affect geographic location decisions.

*Convenience to "customers."* Much geographic departmentalization is undertaken to be close to the "customers" served by the organization. Department stores establish branches in outlying suburban areas, as do banks, chain restaurants, and a host of other business organizations. Public schools and government agencies also departmentalize geographically to cater to their patrons.

### Questions Involved in Geographic Departmentalization Decisions

Generally, the decision faced by managers in medium-sized and large organizations is not whether to departmentalize geographically but rather how. Questions such as these may be involved in decisions relating to geographic departmentalization: "How many branches, districts, or divisions should we establish?" "Where should we locate them?" "Should we combine certain branches with others or eliminate them?" "How much authority in each functional area—production, marketing, and finance—should be assigned to the branch manager?"

**Customer departmentalization** is the process of grouping activities in order to serve the needs of specific market segments. Figure 9–4 illustrates a simplified type of functional and customer departmentalization.

In the present context, **customer** refers to anyone who patronizes an organization. Synonyms for "customers" include, depending on the type of enterprise, "clientele," "patients," "students," "enrollees," and similar terms.

Customer departmentalization is common when an organization serves people or businesses that have significantly different needs. This form of departmentalization is undertaken when managers conclude that (1) service to customers would be improved and customer loyalty to the organization would be strengthened or (2) greater efficiency would be achieved in the use of personnel, money, and other resources.

### Examples of Customer Departmentalization

Customer departmentalization is used extensively by a wide variety of organizations. Schools organize classes on the basis of age of attendees; thus we find elementary schools, middle schools, and high schools. Major department stores, such as Sears Roebuck, have separate divisions that sell to ultimate consumers

**FIGURE 9–4**

**Departmentalization by Function and Customer**

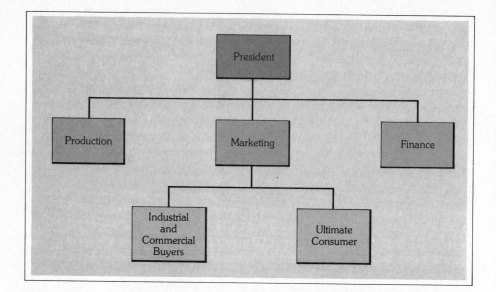

(who purchase items for personal or home consumption) and industrial buyers (who purchase products such as carpeting and furniture to use in offices) or commercial buyers (who purchase products for stores, banks, hotels, and so on).

Hospitals departmentalize to a considerable extent on the basis of patient (customer) needs. Departments may be maintained for outpatients, maternity patients, and intensive-care patients. Accounting firms are often departmentalized to serve two types of clients: corporations and individuals. Many banks, insurance companies, and brokerage houses make extensive use of this form of departmentalization.

Table 9–2 shows other ways in which customers may serve as the basis for departmental organization.

### Questions Involved in Customer Departmentalization Decisions

Generally, the broader the spectrum of the clientele served, the more likely it is that an organization will departmentalize on the basis of customers. In making decisions concerning this form of departmentalization, managers should consider three interrelated questions:

- "Is customer departmentalization really necessary to help hold existing customers and attract new ones?" Departmentalization for no valid reason is foolish and costly.
- "If customer departmentalization is necessary, how extensive should it be?" Many organizations are either overdepartmentalized or underdepartmentalized on the basis of customers served.
- "What will be the effect of customer departmentalization on organizational

**TABLE 9–2**

213

*What Are
the Bases for
Departmental-
ization?*

**Examples of Customer Departmentalization for Different Types of Organizations**

| Type of Organization | Example of Customer Departmentalization |
|---|---|
| Apparel manufacturer | Separate departments for special accounts served directly by company executives and for those served by sales representatives. |
| Church | Special departments for "customers" based on age, sex, marital status, needs. |
| Automobile manufacturer | Separate departments for fleet sales and dealer sales. |
| Publishing company | Separate departments for direct mail, retail store, and book club accounts. |
| Retail store | Separate departments for selling to industrial-buyer and ultimate-consumer accounts. |
| Multinational company | Separate departments for customers in different nations. |

efficiency?" Obviously, more managers are required as additional departments are added. Furthermore, coordination is made more complicated, and record-keeping and accounting problems may intensify.

As is true in the case of all decisions, the benefits to be derived from departmentalization must be weighed against anticipated costs.

With **product departmentalization**, activities are grouped according to products or product lines. Figure 9–5 shows a simplified example of departmentalization by function and product.

Product departmentalization is extensively used in many forms of retailing, such as in department, drug, food, and clothing stores. It is also widely used in production enterprises, one of the best known being General Motors, which is departmentalized into the Buick, Cadillac, Oldsmobile, Chevrolet, and Pontiac divisions. Table 9–3 shows other ways in which products may be used as a basis for grouping activities.

**Departmentalization by Product**

### What Are the Advantages of Product Departmentalization?

There are three major advantages of departmentalizing by product. Each is discussed briefly below.

*Specialized management is provided.* **Specialized management** is required when the products or product lines offered by an enterprise are so diverse that managers with highly specialized skills and experience are needed. In a department store, for example, the operation of a housewares department differs considerably from the operation of a men's wear department in terms of sales tactics, inventory control, sources of merchandise, advertising strategy, and pricing. In manufacturing, banking, and other types of enterprises, the products produced and marketed

**FIGURE 9–5**

Departmentalization by Function and Product

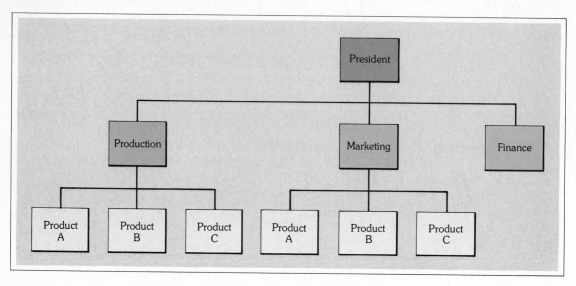

by an organization may differ so substantially that specialized persons should be placed in charge of each.

*Internal competition is promoted.*    Another advantage of departmentalizing by product is that one product line competes with another. Under this arrangement, the performance of the manager of Product A is measured, in part, by

**TABLE 9–3**

Examples of Product Departmentalization for Different Types of Organizations

| Type of Organization | Example of Product Departmentalization |
|---|---|
| Toothpaste manufacturer | Departments for each major brand. |
| Army | Units organized according to type of service (product) rendered (infantry, artillery, and so on). |
| University | Colleges, schools, programs, and so forth established on basis of type of education (product) offered. |
| Court system | Courts (departments) based on service provided (juvenile, criminal, and so on). |
| Medical center | Separate departments based on each major "product" offered, such as maternity care, nuclear medicine, and surgery. |
| Retail store | Specialized departments established for similar product lines. |
| City government | Departments based on type of service rendered. |

comparing his or her results against those of the manager of Product B. Internal competition is very real, for example, in detergent companies in which each major brand is under a "brand manager." Internal competition has long been fostered by General Motors. The manager of the Buick Division is encouraged to outsell the manager of the Pontiac Division.

Internal competition is considered healthy unless it is carried to extremes. The welfare of the total organization should take precedence over the welfare of any part or division.

*Profitability of various products is more easily evaluated.*   When an organization is departmentalized by product or product line, it is easier for top management to answer such pragmatic questions as "Where are we making (losing) money and how much?"; "Which product departments are doing an effective (ineffective) job?"; and "Should some product lines be revamped?"

### Disadvantages of Product Departmentalization

Despite its advantages, product departmentalization has a number of potential limitations. The most significant ones are discussed below.

*Additional management personnel may be required.*   Obviously, when two or more product lines are each placed under separate management, more management personnel are needed than if one management team handled all lines.

*Some duplication of effort may result.*   In some situations each product department may require its own engineering, accounting, marketing, advertising, and production staffs. As a result, personnel costs may outweigh the advantages of product departmentalization.

*Coordination may be difficult.*   Excessive departmentalization on the basis of product lines can create difficult problems in coordinating the work of the whole organization. It is difficult, for example, for the senior management of a large organization with a number of product departments to keep organizational harmony and a spirit of cooperation among all involved. Product managers may place too much emphasis on competition for money, personnel, and other organizational resources.

# OTHER BASES FOR DEPARTMENTALIZATION

There is no one best way to departmentalize activities or divide the work of an organization. The four bases for departmentalization that have been discussed are the most common, but an organization may find it more efficient to organize some or all of its activities on still other design plans. Activities may be organized on the basis of process, project, matrix, and task force.

Some organizations, particularly production enterprises, group similar manufacturing or production processes into departments. This is called **process departmen-**

Process Departmentalization

**talization.** Various processing activities in a bakery, such as mixing ingredients, baking, and packaging the finished products, become operating units. Each unit performs a specialized function, and materials, equipment, and personnel are assigned to carry it out.

## Project Organization

**Project organization** is a method of structuring an enterprise in order to carry out a specific mission. The project may be temporary, such as building a new manufacturing plant or a new weapons system. Or it may be relatively ongoing, such as servicing the needs of a specific client.

Many advertising agencies use a form of project organization. Typically, an account executive is assigned to head up the promotion of a client's product and is given authority over various departments that perform the creative and specialized services needed to produce the advertisements and place them in the media. Unless the account being serviced is very large, the full-time efforts of various departments are not needed. Therefore, the departments are also assigned to several other account executives, as is shown in Figure 9–6. In this example, each account executive reports directly to a senior account executive and is accountable to him or her for developing an advertising program for the client. Each account executive has line authority over four department heads or managers. And each department head or manager reports to four account executives. At the same time, the various department heads communicate with one another. In Figure 9–6, the directors of art, copy, TV and radio, and print media will function very much as a team in preparing the advertising for each of the account executives to whom they are responsible.

Project organization is also often used in professional accounting firms, in which an accounting specialist may work on a number of different accounts that are under the management of different executives. The project form also has wide application in legal, engineering, consulting, and other enterprises that require the services of highly skilled and specialized personnel.

## Matrix Organization

An increasingly popular form of structure is the **matrix organization**. A number of large organizations such as General Electric, Citibank, Dow Chemical, Texas Instruments, and Shell Oil have turned to the matrix form of organization.

Stanley M. Davis and Paul R. Lawrence explain the matrix as follows:

> The identifying feature of a matrix organization is that some managers report to two bosses rather than to the traditional single boss; there is a dual rather than a single chain of command.
>
> Every matrix contains three unique and critical roles: the top manager who heads up and balances the dual chains of command, the matrix bosses (functional, product, or area) who share subordinates, and the managers who report to two different matrix bosses. Each of these roles has its special requirements.[1]

Figure 9–7 shows a sample matrix organization. In this figure, some matrix managers are functional managers (in charge of production and marketing), while

[1]Stanley M. Davis and Paul R. Lawrence, "Problems of Matrix Organizations," *Harvard Business Review*, May–June 1978, p. 134.

**FIGURE 9–6**

**Example of Project Organization in an Advertising Agency**

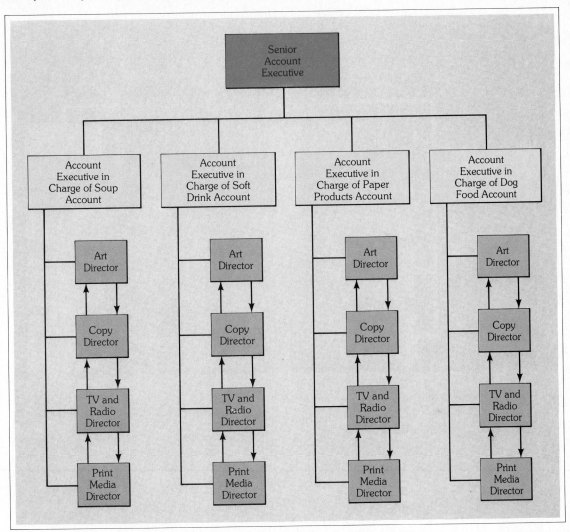

others are project managers (in charge of Projects A, B, and C). These managers share subordinates. That is, each project manager needs the services of employees in each functional area, and each functional manager is in charge of groups of subordinates within that functional area. For example, the production manager is in charge of three groups of subordinates, each of which is also assigned to either Project A, B, or C. Therefore, the groups of subordinates report to both their functional manager and to their project managers. In turn, the functional manager and the project manager report to the top manager, who oversees the organization.

**FIGURE 9–7**

**Matrix Organization**

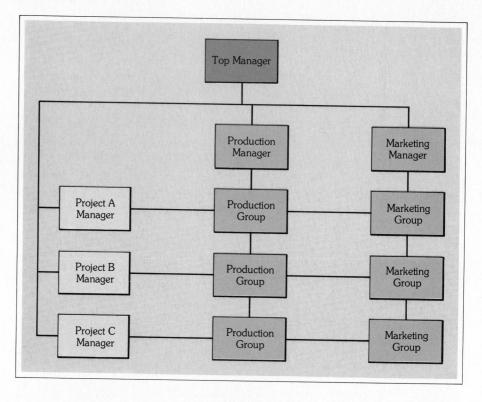

Davis and Lawrence give three situations in which organizations tend to turn toward the matrix:

- When it is absolutely essential that they be highly responsive to two sectors simultaneously, such as markets and technology
- When they face uncertainties that generate very high information processing requirements
- When they must deal with strong constraints on financial and/or human resources.[2]

The matrix organization differs considerably from the traditional functional organization. In functional organizations there is a one-to-one relationship between each superior and subordinate, job assignments are individualized, decision making is centralized, and data are kept in a central department. Functional organizations tend to be relatively inflexible, and conflicts are resolved by the superior. In a matrix organization, on the other hand, interpersonal relationships are more complex, tasks are assigned to groups, decisions are made by those closest to the activity, and data are readily shared by all persons and departments. Matrix organi-

[2]Ibid., p. 134.

zations tend to be highly flexible, and conflicts are resolved through negotiation.

A major problem in using the matrix form of organization is that the unity-of-command principle is violated because subordinates do not have a single manager to whom they are accountable. This can result in frustration, since subordinates may wonder which manager is more important. Furthermore, when an employee reports to two managers, neither manager has full authority to transfer, dismiss, or otherwise deal with him or her.

Another limitation of the matrix form is that it may lead to power struggles. One manager may compete with another manager for services of a joint subordinate. This weakness can be minimized if senior managers stress that harmony and cooperation are absolutely essential.

**Task Force
Departmentalization**

A **task force** is a temporary kind of organization that is formed to study and solve or prepare a recommendation for a unique problem that is not likely to recur. It typically represents an interdisciplinary approach to goal achievement. A task force is used when no one manager has the expertise to solve a problem. Members of a task force function as a team. They are selected for their particular expertise as it relates to the problem at hand. For example, senior management in an organization that has a plant that is not operating efficiently may appoint an interdisciplinary team of experts representing quality control, engineering, production layout, and so on to visit the facility and solve the problem. Usually the force works against a timetable for completion of its mission. When its goal is achieved, it is disbanded and its members return to their regular assignments.

Task forces may be used to perform a wide variety of activities. For instance, senior management of a conglomerate may appoint a task force to determine whether it would be wise to acquire another company; a task force may be appointed to design a new product; or a task force may be used to design a new promotion program.

Task forces may be used effectively when there is sufficient expertise within an organization to accomplish the desired result, when quick action is needed, and when personnel are available who can be spared from their normal duties.

**Multiple Bases for
Departmentalization**

Most small organizations are departmentalized only on a functional basis. Medium-sized and large organizations may also be departmentalized on the other bases that have been discussed. It is common for an enterprise to maintain separate production departments for various product lines, to operate marketing departments on a geographic basis, and to maintain special departments based on different categories of customers. A department store chain that operates several branches is departmentalized on the basis of both product line and geography. The chain may also departmentalize on a customer basis, if it opens a division to sell to commercial and industrial buyers.

Figure 9–8 shows a hypothetical situation illustrating four bases for departmentalization. Departmentalization at the top is by function, at the second level by geographic area, at the third level by customer, and at the fourth level by product. (An organization chart for an actual company would include a variety of staff departments, which will be discussed in Chapter 10.)

**FIGURE 9—8**

Hypothetical Organizational Chart Showing Four Bases for Departmentalization

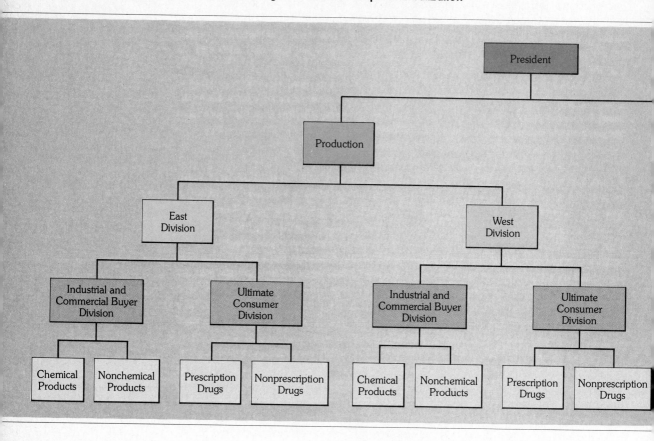

## GUIDELINES FOR EFFECTIVE DEPARTMENTALIZATION

Deciding how an enterprise should be organized into departments is always important and never easy to do properly. The following guidelines suggest ways to departmentalize effectively.

Strive for Simplicity

Grouping activities into departments is a means to an end, not an end in itself. The rationale for departmentalizing work is to help an organization achieve its objectives efficiently. Having too many departments overly complicates managing and results in too long a chain of command. An organizational structure should be as simple as possible. Creating more departments than are necessary adds to the cost of managing and leads to unnecessary bureaucracy.

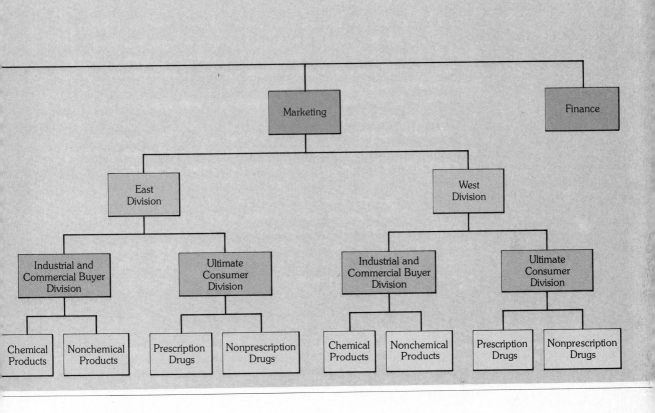

Many organizations, even some large ones, do not have a formal organizational chart. But all enterprises should. An organizational chart clarifies relationships among departments, shows lines of authority and accountability, and indicates the chain of command. It thus shows individuals where they stand in an organization's hierarchy and helps eliminate indecision and duplication of effort.

Commit
Organizational
Relationships
to Writing

The work of departmentalizing should never be regarded as finished. The environment in which management is practiced is dynamic. In any large organization, for example, new departments may be created, other departments combined, and still others eliminated. Departmentalization, as is true of all facets of the organizing function, should be under constant study.

Review the
Structure
Frequently

# WHAT IS SPAN OF CONTROL?

Up to this point we have discussed departmentalization, a key aspect of organizing. Now we turn our attention to span of control, another basic aspect of organizing. **Span of control**—sometimes called "span of supervision," "span of management," or "span of responsibility"—refers to the number of persons one manager can supervise effectively.

Figure 9–9 shows examples of narrow and wide spans of control. In Figure 9–9 (A), the vice-president supervises nine managers. In Figure 9–9 (B), the vice-president supervises only three directors, who in turn supervise nine managers. Note that as the span is narrowed the number of levels of management increases and the number of managers required also increases.

Span of control is an important consideration, since it directly affects the efficiency of the organization. For example, if the span is too wide (that is, an excessive number of people report to one manager), subordinates will receive less supervision than they need and various forms of waste will occur. If the span is too narrow (that is, an excessive number of managers are employed), the cost of managing will be unnecessarily high. Table 9–4 shows some other possible negative results of either too wide or too narrow a span of control.

Span of Control and the Exception Principle

As noted in Chapter 1, one of the earliest references to management principles is recorded in Exodus 18 in the Bible. Moses had problems because he tried to manage a whole enterprise (the migration of the Israelites to the promised land) by himself. His father-in-law, Jethro, noticed this and gave Moses some advice on organizing:

> [13]The next day Moses sat as usual to hear the people's complaints against each other, from morning to evening.
>
> [14]When Moses' father-in-law saw how much time this was taking, he said, "Why are you trying to do all this alone, with people standing here all day long to get your help?"
>
> [15,16]"Well, because the people come to me with their disputes, to ask for God's decisions," Moses told him. "I am their judge, deciding who is right and who is wrong, and instructing them in God's ways. I apply the laws of God to their particular disputes."
>
> [17]"It's not right!" his father-in-law exclaimed. [18]"You're going to wear yourself out—and if you do, what will happen to the people? Moses, this job is too heavy a burden for you to try to handle all by yourself.
>
> [19,20]"Now listen, and let me give you a word of advice, and God will bless you: Be these people's lawyer—their representative before God—bringing him their questions to decide; you will tell them his decisions, teaching them God's laws, and showing them the principles of godly living.
>
> [21]"Find some capable, godly, honest men who hate bribes, and appoint them as judges, one judge for each 1,000 people; he in turn will have ten judges under him, each in charge of a hundred; and under each of them will be two judges, each responsible for the affairs of fifty people; and each of these will have five judges beneath him, each counseling ten persons. [22]Let these men be responsible to serve the people with justice at all times. Anything that is too important or complicated can

**FIGURE 9-9**

Comparison of Wide and Narrow Spans of Control

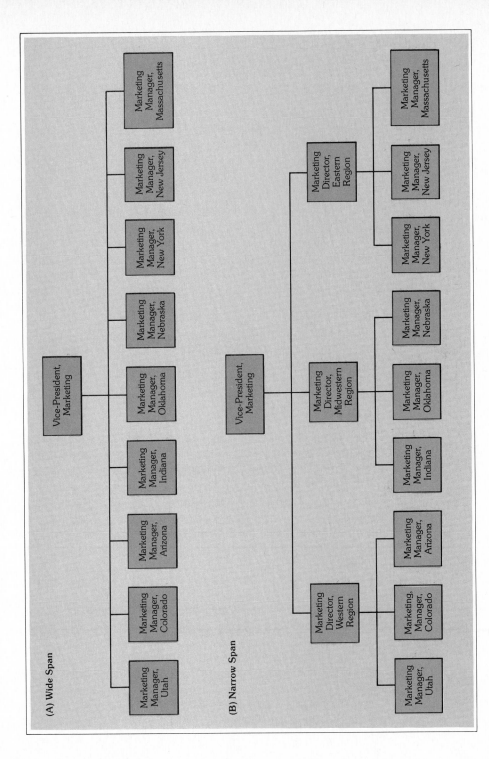

(A) Wide Span

(B) Narrow Span

**TABLE 9–4**

**Either Too Wide or Too Narrow a Span Produces Negative Results**

| Type of Span | Possible Negative Result |
|---|---|
| Too wide | • Personnel are kept waiting to see the manager and time is wasted.<br>• Supervision is inadequate, with the result that machines may be damaged, production is below standard quality, and more mistakes are made.<br>• Employees feel ignored, with the result that absenteeism and turnover may increase.<br>• The manager has too little time to spend with personnel, resulting in neglect of training and counseling.<br>• The manager's day is overly occupied with supervision, leaving too little time for effective planning. |
| Too narrow | • More levels of managing have been created, increasing red tape and slowing down communication up and down the organizational hierarchy.<br>• Managers may "oversupervise," creating employee dissatisfaction.<br>• An excessive number of managers is employed, resulting in excessive management overhead.<br>• Managers have too little to do and become bored.<br>• The chain of command is too long and employees feel lost. |

be brought to you. But the smaller matters they can take care of themselves. That way it will be easier for you because you will share the burden with them. [23]If you follow this advice, and if the Lord agrees, you will be able to endure the pressures, and there will be peace and harmony in the camp."

[24]Moses listened to his father-in-law's advice, and followed this suggestion. [25]He chose able men from all over Israel and made them judges over the people—thousands, hundreds, fifties and tens. [26]They were constantly available to administer justice. They brought the hard cases to Moses but judged the smaller matters themselves.[3]

Part of what Jethro told Moses to do is now called the **exception principle,** mentioned briefly on page 11. According to this principle, a manager should handle only exceptions to previously stated rules, procedures, and policies; routine decisions should be handled by subordinates. In other words, all work in an organization should be performed at the lowest competent level.

For example, under an existing rule, employees at an airline ticket counter can accept all credit cards that are current and not on the list of delinquent customers. A supervisor becomes involved only when an exception occurs—that is, when the card is not current or is listed as delinquent.

If the exception principle is applied properly, managers need not become involved in routine decisions and thus have more time available to plan, train

[3]Exodus 18:13–26, *The Living Bible Paraphrased*, (Wheaton, Ill.: Tyndale House, 1971), pp. 64–65. Verses marked TLB taken from *The Living Bible*, copyright 1971 by Tyndale House Publishers, Wheaton, Ill. Used by permission.

employees, and so on. The net result is that a manager can supervise more people. The span of supervision is wider, and management costs are reduced.

Unfortunately, the exception principle is often overlooked, and managers often do work that lower-paid subordinates could do just as well — perhaps even better. A highly paid executive may dictate a routine letter that a secretary can compose. A department manager may handle customer complaints that are made frequently rather than develop procedures for dealing with such problems and communicate them to subordinates. A senior manager may make arrangements with a hotel for a meeting, whereas an administrative assistant can handle this work just as well.

Violation of the exception principle can lead to several negative consequences. More managers may have to be employed, and as a result, operating costs may be unnecessarily high. Overall operational performance may be reduced because senior-level people neglect more important duties. Lower-level people, since they are not assigned the work, may miss an opportunity to grow and enlarge their job skills. And in many cases a manager is less efficient than his or her subordinate in performing a given task.

It should not be inferred that the exception principle must *always* be followed. Many managers occasionally like to perform work that can be handled by a subordinate. A manager may type a letter, answer the telephones, clear up a work area, help a subordinate prepare a routine report, and so on. Such actions may give managers some relief from stressful situations. The Issue for Debate in this chapter discusses the pros and cons of having managers perform menial tasks.

**Are There Exceptions to the Exception Principle?**

In the mid-1930s, A. V. Graicunas, a management consultant, devised a formula for determining the potential interactions that can occur when a manager has a given number of subordinates.[4] Graicunas considered three types of relationships: direct, group, and cross relationships.

**The Theoretical Limit of Spans: Graicunas's Formula**

Suppose that Joe is Bill and Bob's supervisor. Joe may have a meeting with Bill, or he may have a meeting with Bob. Joe's meeting with either Bob or Bill alone constitutes a **direct relationship**. In this case, then, two direct relationships are possible.

But Joe may talk to Bill with Bob present, or to Bob with Bill present. Both of these relationships are **group relationships.**

Furthermore, Bill may have something to tell Bob without Joe's being present, or Bob may have a meeting with Bill, again with Joe absent. These interactions are called **cross relationships**. In this case there are two.

Thus, according to Graicunas, one supervisor and two subordinates may enter into six different relationships. One way of representing the formula that Graicunas used to determine the potential number of interactions is:

[4]See A. V. Graicunas, "Relationships in Organizations," in *Papers of Administration,* ed. L. Gulick and L. Urwick (New York: Columbia University, 1947).

# ISSUE FOR DEBATE

## SHOULD MANAGERS OCCASIONALLY DO NONMANAGERIAL WORK?

An important management principle is that "All work in the organization should be performed at the lowest competent level." Most managers accept this as a concept, but many feel it is a good idea to do ordinary tasks occasionally. Below we look at some of the pros and cons of managers performing nonmanagerial tasks.

| YES | NO |
|---|---|
| Managers should occasionally do nonmanagerial work because . . . | Managers should not occasionally do nonmanagerial work because . . . |
| In doing nonmanagerial work, managers help bridge the psychological gulf between them and lower-level employees. Thus a sense that everyone is working toward a common goal is created. | Managers are hired to manage, not to perform routine tasks. Generally, they are less efficient than operative employees in performing operative functions. |
| By performing tasks such as answering the phone, typing a letter, or helping clear up a work area, the manager adds a sense of dignity and importance to these tasks. | Employees may lose respect for a manager when they see him or her doing "ordinary" work. Familiarity breeds contempt. And when employees see a manager performing below his or her level, they may perceive it as a cheap device to "humanize" management. |
| Doing the work of an operative employee gives the manager firsthand knowledge of what workers actually do. This is helpful in assessing what is involved in a process, procedure, or job function. | Managers are generally much better paid than operative employees. Therefore, when managers do nonmanagerial tasks, they raise the cost of performing the work. |
| When a crisis arises, it is important that all people pitch in to help. It isn't fair or conducive to high morale for the boss to sip coffee while everyone else tries to get a project completed on time. | Employees may feel uncomfortable when their managers work alongside them. They may feel managers are observing and judging them. |
| Managers should be able to perform nonmanagerial tasks so that activities can go on during emergencies. Managers in telephone companies, for example, fill in when the union strikes. | Union rules may prevent managers from performing operative tasks. In some union shops, managers are expressly prohibited from performing any tasks assigned to union members. |

## QUESTIONS

1. On balance, which side of this issue do you agree with most? Explain.
2. What other points, pro and con, can you make?

$$R = n + n(n - 1) + n(2^{n-1} - 1)$$

$R$ represents the total number of possible interactions; $n$ is the number of subordinates (and also the number of direct relationships); $n(n - 1)$ is the number of group relationships; and $n(2^{n-1} - 1)$ is the number of cross relationships. According to this formula, one supervisor and three subordinates may have eighteen relationships, a single supervisor and four subordinates may have forty-four relationships, and so on (see Table 9–5).

Of course, Graicunas's Formula is not intended to indicate the relative importance of different types of relationships, the amount of time a given meeting is likely to consume, or a host of other variables. The formula is a conceptual aid indicating that while one type of relationship, the direct relationship, increases in direct proportion to the number of subordinates added, the other types of relationships (group and cross) increase exponentially as the number of subordinates increases. Thus, a manager who considers adding one more subordinate may be doubling or tripling the number of potential interactions. Graicunas's theory indicates how complex the management task can become once a manager has more than a few subordinates.

We have seen that the span of control directly affects the number of managers needed. Widen the span and the number of managers decreases; narrow it and the number increases. Since managing costs money, attention should be given to selecting the "ideal" or "best possible" span.

The Economics of Finding the "Right" Span

Consider this example: Assume that a manager has six subordinates. Typically, the manager makes three contacts each day with each person. Each contact averages fifteen minutes. The total time required is calculated as follows:

3 contacts per person × 6 people = 18 contacts
18 contacts × 15 minutes per contact = 270 minutes

**TABLE 9–5**

Graicunas's Formula: Possible Interactions
with Different Numbers of Subordinates

| Number of Subordinates | Potential Number of Interactions |
|---|---|
| 1 | 1 |
| 2 | 6 |
| 3 | 18 |
| 4 | 44 |
| 5 | 100 |
| 6 | 222 |
| 7 | 490 |
| 8 | 1,080 |
| 9 | 2,376 |
| 10 | 5,210 |
| 12 | 24,708 |
| 18 | 2,359,602 |

Assume further that, through improvements in communication, better training of subordinates, and improved work procedures, the manager is able to reduce the number of contacts per day to only two and the time per contact to ten minutes. The total time now required for interactions with subordinates is:

$$2 \text{ contacts per person} \times 6 \text{ people} = 12 \text{ contacts}$$
$$12 \text{ contacts} \times 10 \text{ minutes per contact} = 120 \text{ minutes}$$

In this process 150 minutes have been saved (270 − 120 = 150). If this result can be achieved *with no offsetting deterioration in people's performances*, the manager can now supervise more than twice as many individuals and still have the same amount of time available for other activities.

The amount of savings that is possible by widening the span of control can be considerable. Assume that an organization has six managers on one level, each of whom manages four persons. Each manager receives $30,000 per year in salary and costs the organization another $30,000 for secretarial help, office space, fringe benefits, and other expenses. Total cost of the six managers is $360,000 (6 × $60,000 = $360,000). If the span can be widened from four to six with no negative effect on productivity, two managers will no longer be needed in that department, and the organization will save $120,000.

## WHAT FACTORS AFFECT SPAN-OF-CONTROL DECISIONS?

A wide variety of considerations are involved in managers' decisions regarding span. Following are the factors that most commonly enter into the span decision.

### Nonmanagerial Duties Required of a Manager

Most managers do more than direct the activities of others; they perform nonmanagerial work as well. A sales manager may manage a number of salespeople and also make sales; an academic chairperson may manage a department and also teach; an office manager may manage a clerical staff and also serve as an administrative assistant to a department head; and a manager of research personnel may also be extensively involved in conducting a research project of his or her own. In addition, managers must usually attend meetings and conferences, which are also nonmanagerial duties.

Time spent performing nonmanagerial activities detracts from the time available to manage people. Other things being equal, the more time spent on nonmanagerial work, the narrower the span can be. Conversely, the less time spent doing nonmanagerial work, the wider the span can be.

### Time Spent in Direct Interactions with Subordinates

The time that a manager must spend interacting with subordinates depends on the frequency and the length of contacts that are made.

#### Frequency of Contacts with Supportive Personnel

Generally, the more frequently a manager must confer with the people supervised, the narrower the span can be. The less frequently he or she makes

# MANAGERS IN ACTION

## WHAT ROLE DOES TRUST PLAY IN DELEGATION, SPAN OF CONTROL, AND PRODUCT COST?

Labor costs, whether at the operative, managerial, or professional levels, are one of the main ingredients in the price of a product. When an excessive number of managers are employed, the price of the products a firm makes goes up.

Managerial costs in Japan are much lower than in the United States because Japanese firms have a wider span of control. Costs of professional employees are also lower because fewer are used. Compared with the Japanese, the United States, for example, has twenty times as many lawyers and seven times as many accountants. Why?

Typically, more trust exists between Japanese workers and managers than exists between their American counterparts. Japanese companies assume that all workers at all levels are competent and trustworthy enough to put the company's interests in the forefront. Therefore, Japanese companies do not need to employ highly paid executives whose only job is to inspect and pass judgment on the work of subordinates.

Excessive cost caused by too many managers can be found in many American businesses. At Ford Motor Company, there are 11 layers of management between the production worker and the chairman. Toyota has only six layers, indicating a much wider (and lower cost) span of management.

Japanese business's trust in what their employees are doing reduces overall costs, promotes quicker action, and results in greater efficiency.

Donald E. Petersen, president of Ford Motor Company, "attributes the growth of corporate staff in America to top management's distrust of middle managers." From his study of Toyota's management, he concludes that "Japan's top executives trust their workers and assume they will do the best job they can. In the U.S., on the other hand, top executives assume they cannot trust their subordinates, so they add layers of staff to check on line operators. The result is confrontation, delay in decision making, exploding costs, and a deterioration of the business. In their struggle for power, the staff people too often ignore the problems of the business, seeking what is best for themselves instead of what is best for the company."[1]

[1]Quoted from the December 21, 1981 issue of *Business Week* by special permission, © 1981 by McGraw-Hill, Inc. New York, NY 10020. All rights reserved.

### QUESTIONS

1. How does the span of control differ between American and Japanese companies?
2. What other benefits can trust have on an organization besides reducing executive overhead?

---

such contacts, the wider the span can be. Say a major executive needs to talk with her key subordinates often, perhaps several times in a day. This frequency contributes to a narrow span. If an assembly-line foreman makes contact with his subordinates only when they cannot handle a problem, a wide span is promoted.

### Time Required per Contact

Another element that affects span of control is the time required per contact. This varies greatly. Some contacts with subordinates, such as approving the request of a retail salesperson to go to lunch at noon instead of 1:00 P.M., can be handled in only a few seconds or minutes. Other contacts with subordinates may require an hour or more, depending on the complexity and importance of the matter that needs to be resolved. Generally, time per contact decreases as one descends from the top of the organization to the bottom. Senior people find it necessary to spend more time per contact than first-level managers do.

### Manager Qualifications

Some managers are better qualified than others in terms of education, experience, training, and motivation to direct more persons. Improving the effectiveness of the manager is often the key to widening the span of control and thereby reducing the cost of management.

One approach is to select managers at each level more carefully. Another is to provide better management training. Many managers have received no formal training in the "how" of management; they have acquired their knowledge through trial and error, with the result that their effectiveness may be limited. Many managers could profit from training in such matters as delegation of work, effective communication, ability to explain job assignments, and organization. Generally, the more able the manager, the more persons he or she can supervise. The converse is also true.

### Qualifications of Subordinates

A wider span of control is possible when personnel are well trained and experienced than when they are unfamiliar with the activities they perform, since each individual should require fewer and briefer instructions. Sales managers in some apparel firms, for example, retain only manufacturers' agents who are thoroughly experienced in selling and who are well accepted by their retail customers. In such cases the span may be thirty or more, since there is seldom a need for face-to-face contacts, and instructions by telephone or letter can be brief.

Inexperienced persons with limited education generally require more of a manager's time than their experienced and better-educated counterparts. This situation points up the need for careful selection so that the right people are matched with the jobs to be performed. A carefully conducted job analysis—resulting in an accurate job specification—is a good procedure to follow (see Chapter 13).

### Complexity of Work Performed

Generally, highly standardized and routine work permits a wider span than activities that are nonstandardized and complex. For example, we find wide spans in many assembly-line operations because the work is highly standardized. At the senior level of an organization, on the other hand, the chief executive officer often has only three or four direct subordinates.

In military organizations a wide span is used to train new recruits, since the training is routine and standardized. In contrast, student pilots require a narrow span, since very close supervision is needed during flight training.

Complex work situations, in which subordinates must check frequently for advice and new instructions, require much supervisory time, and the span tends to be narrow.

The degree and effectiveness of both technical and nontechnical planning help determine how many persons one manager can supervise. On the technical planning side, if engineers have set up the simplest possible production processes, the span can be wider than if the work is unnecessarily complex. Work simplification experts are particularly valuable in production, accounting, and data-processing operations. They are often able to reduce complexity and eliminate bottlenecks, thereby improving the flow of work and reducing the amount of time that managers must spend with their subordinates. Extent of Planning

Nontechnical planning can also materially affect the span. When rules, procedures, policies, and strategies are clearly stated and understood by those who do the work, there will be fewer questions such as "What do I do in this situation?" from personnel. As a result, a manager can spend less time with each employee and therefore can supervise more individuals.

Organizations that develop and communicate their plans are able to have wider spans than those enterprises that downplay the importance of teaching plans to personnel. For example, if a retail store has clear procedures regarding such matters as returning goods, granting credit, and cashing checks, there will be relatively few exceptions for the manager to handle, and as a result, he or she can manage more people.

The more effectively work instructions are communicated, the wider the span of control can be. Conversely, the less effective managers are in communicating, the narrower the span is likely to be. Effectiveness of Communication

A manager has a two-way communications responsibility. First, he or she should *explain* the what, why, how, who, and when of the work to be done. How detailed the explanation should be depends on factors such as the employee's experience and training. However, in all cases the instructions should be accurate, clear, and simple. When instructions given in person or by telephone or mail are not clear, the individual receiving the message is likely to either make mistakes that may require the manager's time to help correct or ask more questions about what to do, answering which also requires extra time.

**Control devices** are methods used to determine if work is being performed according to plan. Sometimes a manager can develop control devices to reduce the amount of time spent with subordinates and thereby increase the number of persons he or she can supervise. One common control device is the sales report required of many sales representatives. Consider this example: Prior to developing a reporting system, one sales manager routinely spent eight hours per month with each of ten salespeople for a total of eighty hours, spending the remainder of the time performing other management duties. The new system required sales representatives to report only essential information, such as calls made, results, and new prospects. It did not require them to report on a variety of nonessential matters, such as the exact number of hours worked. The reporting system worked so well that the manager discovered one visit every other month was enough for four of the sales representatives. This resulted in an average savings of sixteen hours per Use of Control Devices month, enough to enable the manager to increase the span from ten to twelve people.

In many production situations, mechanical controls can be installed on machines so that employee mistakes are immediately indicated and the employee can normally take corrective action without assistance from his or her supervisor. The control function is discussed in Part Six of this book.

### Personal Preference of Managers

The span of control is often prescribed for lower-level managers, but executives at the upper levels of an organization are usually able to determine how many individuals will report directly to them. There are pros and cons for both a narrow span and a wide span at the top of an organization. Which is better depends primarily on the personal style of the executive involved. Some people seem to function best with only two or three people reporting to them. Other top managers prefer to supervise directly as much of an activity as possible; these managers may prefer a wider span with perhaps seven or eight direct subordinates.

### Manager's Level in the Organization

At high levels in an organization, problems are more complex than at lower levels. The more complex the issue, the more time required to resolve it. Therefore a senior executive will need to spend more time with each subordinate manager than a first-level manager needs to spend with each of his or her subordinates. Typically, these needs result in a much narrower span at the top than at the bottom of an organization. At the top of an organization the span is often only from three to five people. At the lowest or first level the span may be twenty or more people.

### Similarity of Jobs Supervised

Generally, as one ascends the organizational hierarchy, the more dissimilar the jobs one supervises become. A chief executive officer, for instance, supervises work in such dissimilar activities as production, marketing, and finance. Meanwhile, at the lowest level of management, most, if not all, activities managed are very similar; a first-level manager usually supervises only one activity, such as assembly of components or customer billing. Management of dissimilar functions contributes to a narrow span; management of similar activities contributes to a wide span.

### Physical Dispersal of Jobs

Regardless of the organizational level, close proximity of the people managed tends to contribute to a wide span, while physical distance contributes to a narrow span. For example, a manager who supervises subordinates in several cities and finds it necessary to counsel with them frequently is limited because of travel time in the number of people he or she can manage. A manager who supervises people in one location or one metropolitan area has less time lost in traveling and can manage a larger group of subordinates.

During the recession of the early 1980s, many companies widened the span of supervision to reduce cost of managing. "New office technology, including information systems, increases the productivity of executives and their staffs, making it feasible to reduce the size of management. Secretaries usually become more productive when they progress to word processors."[5]

## IS THERE A BEST SPAN?

Span of control is important because it directly affects the effectiveness of an organization and is also a major factor in determining the cost of managing. However, students of management have long contemplated whether there is an ideal span. The noted authority Colonel Lyndall Urwick observed:

> No superior can supervise directly the work of more than five or, at the most, six subordinates whose work interlocks. The reason for this is simple. What is supervised is not only the individuals, but the permutations and combinations of the relationships between them. And while the former increase in arithmetical progression with the addition of each fresh subordinate, the latter increase by geometrical progression. If a superior adds a sixth to five immediate subordinates, he increases his opportunity of delegation by 20 percent but he adds over 100 percent to the number of relationships he has to take into account. Because ultimately it is based on the limitations imposed by the human span of attention, this principle is called The Span of Control.[6]

A major study of 100 large companies conducted by the American Management Association showed that the median number of managers reporting to the chief executive was eight.[7] But the study also showed these interesting breakdowns:

| Number of Managers Reporting to the Chief Executive | Number of Companies |
|:---:|:---:|
| 1–3 | 7 |
| 4–6 | 19 |
| 7–9 | 27 |
| 10–12 | 23 |
| 13–15 | 13 |
| 16–18 | 6 |
| 19–21 | 2 |
| 22–24 | 3 |

And consider a contemporary example: Before John Ricker became chairman of Continental Corporation, the company had forty-six subsidiary companies and twenty-six affiliates in seventy-five companies. At that time, twenty-five department and division heads reported directly to the chairman. Mr. Ricker believes in a much smaller span of control and reduced the number of people

[5]Jeremy Main, "Hard Times Catch Up with Executives," *Fortune,* September 20, 1982, p. 53.
[6]Lyndall Urwick, *The Elements of Administration* (New York: Harper & Brothers, 1944), pp. 52–53.
[7]See Ernest Dale, *Planning and Developing the Company Organization Structure* (New York: American Management Association, 1952), p. 57.

reporting to him to only seven. Ricker says, "About seven is the right number to hear from you [a top manager]. Any more you might hear too much."[8]

The wide variation in both opinions and in the spans actually used suggests that there is no one best span for all organizations. This is not to say that there is not one best span for various levels in a given organization or for an organization as a whole if it is small. Although the "ideal" span is difficult to determine, managers should continually try to ascertain the span that is most efficient for them, for, as we have seen, either too wide or too narrow a span has negative effects on an enterprise.

SUMMARY

- Departmentalization is a key part of organizing and involves three steps: (1) group similar tasks, (2) assign a department head to the grouped activities, and (3) hold the department head accountable for performance of the activities.
- Four main bases for departmentalization are function, geographic area, customer, and product.
- Functional departmentalization occurs when an organization groups its activities on the basis of its essential functions. It has the advantages of being logical and facilitating coordination of activities. Its key weaknesses are that it may result in an excessively long chain of command and that managers of one function may not learn much about other functions.
- Geographic departmentalization usually occurs as an organization's size grows. Economic, climatic, and legal and political considerations as well as convenience to customers are the main reasons for geographic departmentalization.
- Customer departmentalization occurs when an organization serves customers who have significantly different needs.
- Product departmentalization is used when an enterprise wants to provide specialized management to a product or class of products, to promote internal competition, and to evaluate more easily the profitability of various products.
- Medium-sized and large organizations often departmentalize on all four bases — function, geographic area, customer, and product.
- Other bases for departmentalization include process, project, matrix, and task force.
- In departmentalizing, managers should strive for simplicity, commit organizational relationships to writing, and review the structure frequently.
- Span of control is an important consideration in organizing. If the span is too wide, an excessive number of people report to one manager. If it is too narrow, an excessive number of managers are being employed. Both errors in span determination lead to inefficiency and waste.
- According to the exception principle, a manager should handle only exceptions to previously stated rules, procedures, and policies.
- Graicunas's Formula demonstrates that as more subordinates are assigned to a manager, the number of possible reporting relationships increases dramatically.
- Factors that affect span-of-control decisions are the nonmanagerial duties required of a manager, the time a manager spends in direct interactions with subordinates, the qualifications of both managers and subordinates, the complexity of the work performed, the extent of planning, the effectiveness of communication, the use of

---

[8]Quoted in Sterling G. Slappey, "How John Ricker Cuts Big Problems Down to Size," *Nation's Business*, February 1978, p. 55.

control devices, the personal preferences of managers, the manager's level in the organization, the similarity of the jobs supervised, and the physical dispersal of jobs.
- Whether there is an "ideal" span has long been debated.

departmentalization
functional departmentalization
production function
marketing function
finance function
organization chart
chain of command
geographic departmentalization
customer departmentalization
customer
product departmentalization
specialized management

process departmentalization
project organization
matrix organization
task force
span of control
exception principle
Graicunas's Formula
direct relationship
group relationship
cross relationship
control devices

1. What is departmentalization? What is its main goal?
2. What basic functions are performed by all organizations? Why is each essential?
3. Why is organization on the basis of primary functions performed so widely used?
4. Are we likely to see more or less emphasis on organizing on the basis of geography in the future? Why or why not?
5. What are some examples of customer departmentalization?
6. At what point in the evaluation of an enterprise should top management consider organizing on the basis of products? What specific factors should be considered in making a decision to organize or not to organize on the basis of products?
7. Under what circumstances might a firm use a matrix as an organizational design?
8. What is span of control?
9. Give at least three examples in which you have observed the exception principle violated. How would you proceed to implement the concept of the exception principle if you were a top manager?
10. Why is it difficult to select the right span of control?
11. Why would the senior manager of one large organization prefer a span of only three people, while the top executive of another large enterprise might feel that a span of six or seven is preferable?

### 1. Why are changes in government reorganization slow and superficial?

Politicians often talk about the need for "reorganizing government," "streamlining government," "eliminating bureaucracy," and "eliminating duplication of services." Despite the apparent need for better organization in government, few substantive changes are made and changes that are made are made slowly.

Based on your observations of government and your understanding of departmentalization, explain in a brief report why few substantial and fast changes are made in government reorganization.

## 2. How would you departmentalize an organization?

You are president of a medium-sized manufacturing company. One of your key assistants has proposed that two separate departments—accounting and data processing—be merged into one department called the "Data Department."

Develop four questions that you would want to consider in analyzing the recommendation.

## 3. Is a transportation department a good idea?

The Comfortable Living Furniture Company is based in North Carolina and markets its products to 3200 retail stores in the 48 contiguous states.

The company is very solid financially and is looking for ways to use its surplus capital profitably. One idea suggested at a recent management meeting was to set up a transportation department to deliver the furniture products to retailers. Comfortable Living historically has used the services of trucking firms for this purpose.

Henry Jackson, president; Brenda Abernathy, customer service manager; Tom Jenkins, marketing manager; and Fred Herman, finance manager, meet to discuss whether the company should set up a transportation department.

Henry: I hope you've given the idea some thought.

Fred: I did some research on what it would cost and whether or not the new department would make money. We could afford it. But whether we could perform the transportation function as efficiently as the contract carriers we're using now is another matter. It might cost us more than what we pay the trucking firm.

Brenda: An analysis I made of retailer complaints last year showed that 257 stores found deliveries were late or merchandise was damaged in transit. If our own transportation department could do the job more efficiently and to our customers' satisfaction, I'm all for it.

Tom: I agree with Brenda. How it would affect customer service is the critical issue. But some of the late deliveries were probably our fault, maybe in the shipping department. Now, as you know, I've been wanting us to set up a retailing division for some time. We could at least experiment with a few of our own stores.

Henry: Tom, that's a different issue. In time we'll explore that possibility. Right now, we're focusing on whether or not we should enter the transportation business.

The discussion goes on for another hour with Fred concentrating on financial issues, Brenda on customer service and Tom on marketing matters. Finally, Henry decides to end the discussion.

Henry: I've listened to what each of you thinks about adding a transportation department. I'm against it for these reasons. First, we know almost nothing about the transportation field. Second, it would mean more management problems. For one thing, there would be more people to manage. Third, we are in the furniture manufacturing business. We know it inside and out. It took us 50 years to learn it and I don't think we should get into something none of us understands.

Based on the information available, did Henry make the right decision? Why or why not?

How would an affirmative decision have changed the company's bases of departmentalization?

Arbose, J. R. "Giving Absenteeism the Stamp of Approval." *International Management*, January 1981, pp. 29–31.

Cleland, D. I. "Cultural Ambience of the Matrix Organization." *Management Review*, November 1981, pp. 24–28.

Cleland, David, and King, William. *Systems Analysis and Project Management*. New York: McGraw-Hill, 1975.

Fuller, Stephen H. "Becoming the Organization of the Future." *Journal of Business Ethics*, May 1982, pp. 115–118.

Greiner, L. E., and Schein, V. E. "Paradox of Managing a Project-Oriented Matrix: Establishing Coherence Within Chaos." *Sloan Management Review*, Winter 1981, pp. 17–22.

Katz, R. "Effects of Group Longevity on Project Communication and Performance." *Administrative Science Quarterly,* March 1982, pp. 81–104.

Kerzner, H. "Project Management in the Year 2000." *Journal of Systems Management*, October 1981, pp. 26–31.

Kolodny, Harvey F. "Managing in A Matrix." *Business Horizons*, March–April 1981, pp. 17–24.

Kolodny, Harvey F. "Matrix Organization and New Product Success." *Restaurant Management*, September 1980, pp. 29–33.

Mercer, James L. "Organizing for the '80's—What About Matrix Management?" *Business*, July 1981, pp. 25–33.

Miller, W. B. "Fundamentals of Project Management."*Journal of Systems Management*, November 1978, pp. 22–29.

Potts, P. "Project Management: Getting Started." *Journal of Systems Management*, February 1982, pp. 18–19.

VanFleet, David D., and Bedeian, Arthur G. "A History of the Span of Management." *Academy of Management Review*, July 1977, pp. 356–372.

Weglarz, J. "Project Scheduling with Continuously-Divisible, Doubly Constrained Resources." *Management Science,* September 1981, pp. 1040–1053.

**FOR ADDITIONAL CONCEPTS AND IDEAS**

# 10 LINE AND STAFF AUTHORITY

**STUDY THIS CHAPTER SO YOU CAN:**

* Define "line authority" and "staff authority," and describe the differences between line organizations and line-and-staff organizations.

* Explain how the designation of an activity as line or staff depends on the kind of organization.

* Give examples of situations in which staff managers have line authority, and identify the limitations of the use of staff.

* Explain why functional authority is essential in certain situations.

* Discuss "assistant to" staff positions, including duties performed and ways to make them effective.

* Explain why and how outside specialists are used.

* Describe unofficial staffs, noting their advantages and disadvantages.

* Explain how harmony can be developed between line and staff.

**Authority** is the right or power of one person to give commands, require performance or obedience, take actions, or make final decisions. Most of the time we think of authority as giving orders to other people. However, order givers are generally also required to be order takers. When we are elected, commissioned, or appointed to manage others, we also agree, in accepting the assignment, to follow the instructions of our superiors.

Authority is always limited. In no situation does a manager have unrestricted authority. For instance, the president of the United States, who functions as commander-in-chief of the military, does not have the authority to declare war. The president of a corporation, regardless of its size, does not have authority to sell a new issue of stock to the public. This authority is vested in the board of directors, who in turn are accountable to the shareholders. Ticket personnel at airports may have authority to give a passenger who has missed a plane a free meal voucher but may not have authority to give the individual a free night's lodging.

If an an enterprise is to function effectively, it is essential that authority relationships be clearly defined and understood by all members of the organization. Confusion regarding such relationships often leads to interdepartmental friction and poor coordination of the organization's activities.

**FIGURE 10–1**

**The Relation of Line and Line-and-Staff Organization**

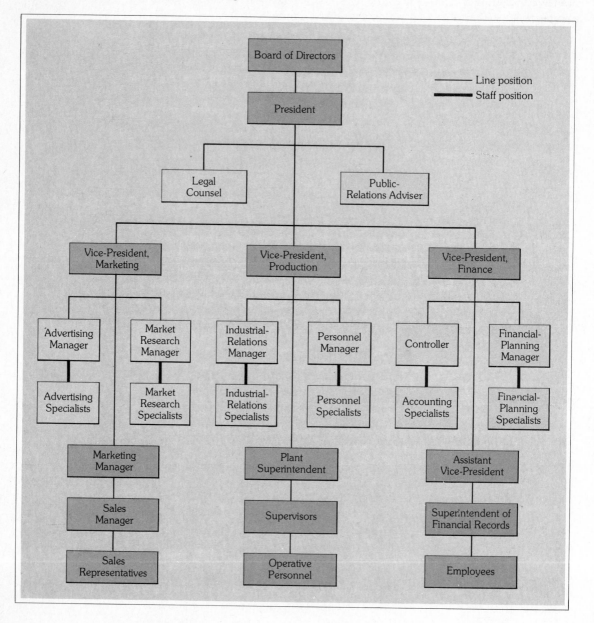

## THE LINE-AND-STAFF ORGANIZATION

The practice of management would be relatively easy if a pure line form of organization would always suffice. But early in the growth of an enterprise, work soon becomes too complex for line managers to handle it directly. Staff managers become more essential to an enterprise as it increases in size and complexity. A small machine shop needs few staff specialists. But as it grows into a large, diversified organization staff personnel will increase both in absolute numbers and as a percentage of total number of people employed.

As staff personnel are hired the character of the organization shifts from being line to being **line *and* staff**. A pure line form of organization has no staff or advisory personnel. Meanwhile, a line and staff organization has staff advisers to advise line managers on how best to perform their work. Figure 10–1 illustrates a line-and-staff organizational structure. In this example, as the organization expanded the vice-president in charge of production found that he lacked the skills to staff the department with the right kind and quality of people and to handle labor problems. The solution was to employ two new staff executives: a personnel manager and an industrial-relations expert. Similarly, the vice-president of marketing hired staff people who specialized in advertising and market research.

Note that staff personnel cannot command or issue orders to line managers unless, as will be explained later, they are given special authority to do so. In most cases staff managers act in a strictly advisory capacity. For example, in Figure 10–1 the industrial-relations manager can advise the president of the organization on labor relations but cannot issue orders to the plant superintendent on how to deal with operative employees unless he or she is expressly given the authority to do so. The president can use the advice of the industrial-relations manager to help formulate a directive that will be issued to the line managers. But the directive will come from the president, not the staff manager. Staff advises; line decides.

Staff would be unnecessary if line managers had sufficient technical and professional skills in such areas as accounting, law, data processing, engineering, and advertising. The complexity of modern organizations, however, requires highly specialized knowledge. Staff members are necessary in all but the smallest and simplest enterprises.

## An Example of Work Performed by Staff

Staff managers' roles can be more fully appreciated by examining representative functions the managers perform. Consider the type of work performed by a product research department, which is a typical staff unit.

First, acting upon the direction of line managers, the staff managers *conduct research* to create new products or modify existing ones. Second, the product research department manager may *provide advice* on the practicality of the proposed products. Because of their in-depth knowledge, product research personnel can often give an expert opinion about the feasibility of a proposed product or product change before an experimental model is designed. The advice of product research personnel may also be sought on production techniques and costs. Line managers may ask such questions as: "How much will per-unit costs be?" "How much time will be required?" "What kinds of facilities will be needed?" "What types of production control must be provided?"

Third, the research department may *provide services*. In this case, product research personnel may be asked to design or help design the production techniques required to make the product.

Fourth, the research department may *initiate new, basic research* if line management grants the authority. While research managers often are given wide latitude to engage in research they feel will pay off, they still must function within the boundaries established by line managers.

Note that in this example the staff exists to help the line achieve its primary objectives. A staff manager is not free to go in any direction; staff people are generally allowed to engage only in those activities that line management feels are in the best interests of the organization.

## Activity Designation and the Organization

Note that an activity may be a line activity in one organization and a staff activity in another. For example, accounting is typically a staff activity. However, in a professional accounting firm it is a line activity, since it involves "production" of the firm's main service — accounting advice. Similarly, provision of medical services in a manufacturing firm is a staff activity, since it is auxiliary to the firm's main line of business. However, provision of medical services in a hospital is a line activity, since such services are the hospital's main "product."

Table 10–1 shows some more staff activities that may, in certain organizations, be line activities. Staff activities are frequently identifiable by their specialized nature. However, note that line activities — for example, credit investigation or engineering services — may also be highly technical. The distinction between line and staff lies not in the nature of the activity but in the authority relationships in the organizational chart. Line managers have direct authority and make the major decisions; staff managers are in most cases advisory.

## Line Authority Within Staff Departments

A staff manager exercises line authority over the individuals within his or her own department. For example, consider a situation in which a line manager, the director of marketing, asks the director of marketing research (a staff manager) to conduct research regarding a certain product that is being developed. The line manager may dictate the kinds of information that he or she requires and how soon the data are needed. But *how* the research is to be carried out is up to the director of research. This individual will make decisions (subject, of course, to company policy) about hiring, termination, assignment of employees, compensation, promotion, and similar matters regarding the project. Thus the research director has line authority over personnel within the department to define how the work will be done.

## The Line Manager as Generalist

Significantly, the higher a line manager rises in an organization, the less important specialized knowledge becomes to him or her. High-level line managers are generalists, while staff managers are specialists. The staff managers who advise the senior executive need detailed knowledge of specialized areas, whereas senior line executives are expected to have broad knowledge of all facets of the organization.

Thus it is common in large organizations for line managers to supervise activities they themselves cannot perform. Consider, for example, the General Motors Corporation. Acquiring expertise in all technical and nontechnical areas of GM would require many lifetimes, since the number of different jobs is huge and since new types of technical work are added at frequent intervals. As a result, line managers often must supervise activities they themselves cannot perform or

**TABLE 10–1**

**What Is Designated a Line Activity Depends More on the Organization
Than on the Activity's Technical Nature**

| Some Activities Are Usually Staff Functions . . . | . . . But in These Organizations, They Are Line Functions |
|---|---|
| Technical education | Vocational schools |
| Personnel selection | Personnel placement agencies |
| Engineering | Engineering consulting firms |
| Research and development | Research and development companies |
| Marketing research | Marketing research firms |
| Credit investigation | Credit bureaus |
| Maintenance | Professional maintenance companies |

**QUESTIONS**

1. What are some other examples of activities that are generally staff but can be line under certain circumstances?
2. Why is it important in any organization to differentiate between line and staff?

cannot perform well. In the case of GM, high-level line managers must be able to exercise authority and issue orders and directives to designers, marketing researchers, economists, engineers of various kinds, data processors, accountants, and many other specialists whose jobs they do not comprehend fully.

Some top executives, it is true, may have an intensive background in one or perhaps two technical areas, but in no case would one person understand the intimate details of all key activities. Therefore many line managers must operate with a limited knowledge of the work performed at lower levels.

In large organizations it is extremely important that senior managers select competent lower-level managers who have an in-depth understanding of the work to be done. Consider an analogy: An individual does not need to know much about medicine to receive good medical advice, or to have an intimate knowledge of insurance to develop a good insurance program. To achieve these goals a person does need to know how to select a top-notch physician and a good insurance broker.[1]

**Limitations of the Use of Staff**

There are two key limitations in the use of staff: the danger of staff usurping line authority—at least in the eyes of line employees—and the placement of exaggerated confidence in the ability of staff specialists.

[1]Henry Ford I illustrated this point well when in a trial he was asked a series of questions he could not answer. Exasperated, Ford is reported to have said, "I don't know the answers to those questions, but give me five minutes and I'll find some people who do."

## Danger of Staff Usurping Line Authority

Frequently, in practice, a staff executive either takes over—or attempts to take over—authority that belongs to a line manager. For instance, due to the increase in federal regulations relating to treatment of personnel, the personnel department has risen in importance. The president of a company employing 1,000 workers hired a new personnel director to "make sure our employees are happy and don't cause us problems such as lawsuits and that sort of thing."

The new personnel director, who reported directly to the president, soon instituted an open-door policy by which employees could visit him and his staff and discuss any problems they had. In short order, employees were visiting the personnel office not to discuss usual matters relating to pensions, insurance claims, and similar problems that are the prerogative of the personnel department, but rather to complain about work schedules, work loads, the reprimand system, discipline, and other issues that are the concern of line superiors. The personnel director eagerly listened to the worker complaints and then prepared recommendations for solving them and presented the recommendations to the president.

The practice irritated the line managers because the personnel director, who was not intimately aware of conditions in the plant, was in effect going over their heads and presenting solutions. It also resulted in lowered morale and productivity because the employees no longer recognized their managers as the *real* source of authority. The real power, as they perceived it, rested with the personnel department.

Conditions deteriorated so badly that the president, after finally becoming aware of the problem, dismissed the personnel director and returned authority over line activities to the line managers.

*"That's OK Wexler. Feel free to interrupt me
anytime you consider job security irrelevant."*

From *The Wall Street Journal,*
Permission—Cartoon Features Syndicate

A second limitation in using staff specialists is that line managers place too much confidence in staff specialists' expertise. Most senior managers are generalists, not specialists. Yet, many critical management problems involve law, taxes, engineering, and other highly specialized fields. It is not uncommon for a senior executive to reason, "I'd better follow the recommendations of the staff advisers—they are the experts in their fields; I'm not."

The difficulty here is that staff advisers typically see only a part of a problem, not all sides of it. For example, a tax adviser often sees only the financial aspects of whether to acquire a subsidiary. The tax expert may not see the effect of a proposed acquisition on production or marketing activities. Or a legal adviser may not recommend a proposed acquisition because it might invite trouble with a government regulatory agency. The line managers to whom staff specialists report should ideally retain objectivity in evaluating staff recommendations, weigh the pros and cons carefully, and then decide.

## WHAT IS FUNCTIONAL AUTHORITY?

**Functional authority** is the right delegated to a manager to make decisions and issue orders to persons in a department or a division other than his or her own. Functional authority can be viewed as "situational power," since it is extended in cases in which a manager in charge of a situation does not have the skills, expertise, or knowledge to handle a problem with the desired degree of competency. Under these conditions a person with specialized skill is given the authority to issue commands.

**Examples of Functional Authority in Practice**

Consider this example: Production is a line activity, while quality control is a staff or advisory function. Normally, all decisions regarding production are made by the production manager or by his or her supportive line managers. However, if product quality does not meet required standards, the quality-control manager may be given functional authority to bring about corrective action. The chief executive officer may tell the quality-control department, "Take over production until whatever is holding things up gets straightened out."

Another example concerns the chief executive officer, who is fully responsible for the organization's performance and normally has authority over all staff departments. However, when the corporation is sued by a customer, a competitor, the government, or any other party, the board of directors may grant functional authority to handle the litigation to the firm's legal counsel.

An airline captain is fully responsible for the operation and safety of the aircraft. However, in the process of landing the airplane, the captain relinquishes certain authority to air traffic controllers (staff personnel), who make key decisions about vectoring the plane into position for the landing.

Figure 10–2 shows a simplified example of staff departments that may at times be given functional authority over line managers. Note that the president exercises line authority over two staff executives (the legal counsel and the industrial-relations manager) and over three line vice-presidents (those in charge

**FIGURE 10–2**

**Functional Authority Illustrated**

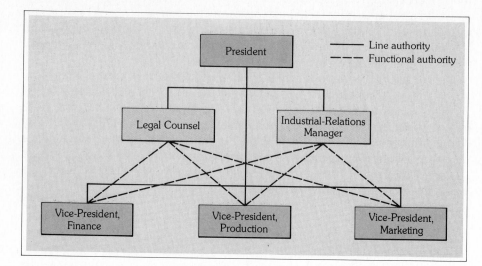

of finance, production, and marketing). The two staff executives may at times exercise functional authority over any of the three line vice-presidents. For example, all personnel in the production department are accountable to the vice-president for production, and he or she is responsible for their performance. But in the event of a strike, the industrial-relations manager may be assigned functional authority over some of the vice-president's normal activities, such as work rule enforcement. The assumption made in transferring certain powers of the line manager to the staff manager is that the latter is better qualified to handle the situation.

**Permanent Fixation
of Functional
Authority
Through Staff
Departmentalization**

Generally, the larger and more complex an organization becomes, the more essential it is that some staff managers be assigned permanent functional authority over certain key activities. Increased size and greater complexity of work require knowledge and expertise that line managers cannot be expected to have in sufficient depth to perform effectively.

Consider the case of an individual who has been made manager of a branch store that is part of a sixteen-unit city-wide chain. As a branch manager, he or she is a line executive and is responsible to a superior for sales, customer satisfaction, and profits. However, as noted below, the manager's authority may be limited in a number of areas, since much of it is granted to various staff specialists and departments:

- *Accounting services:* Authority is likely to be assigned to a company-wide or store-wide accounting department.

- *Personnel selection:* Authority may be assigned to a centralized personnel department, and the store manager may or may not be empowered to accept or reject applicants.
- *Credit approval:* Authority may be assigned to a credit department that serves the entire chain.
- *Advertising:* Authority is likely to be assigned to a central advertising department.
- *Architectural or major remodeling decisions:* Authority may be assigned to a headquarters committee or to a specialized department.
- *Selection of new types of merchandise for resale:* Authority may be assigned to a centralized merchandise committee.
- *Contracting for cleaning and maintenance services:* Authority may be retained by a committee of senior store executives.

The store manager in this case may or may not be satisfied with the way certain staff functions are imposed. But the manager must accept them or make recommendations for changing them, not to the staff specialists who perform them but rather to the senior line executive to whom he or she reports. Decisions regarding what staff activities are to be centralized and how they are to be centralized are made by senior line executives at company headquarters.

It is clear, then, that even a relatively high-level line manager must accept considerable restrictions with regard to the exercise of authority. In many cases the unity-of-command principle is violated because a line manager reports both to a line manager and to one or more staff managers who have been granted functional authority over certain activities. While unity of command is theoretically the best principle in establishing an organization's authority structure, in practice it is not always possible to employ it. In large organizations particularly, **multiple command**—the practice of requiring an individual to report to two or more managers—may be better for the organization. In assigning line, staff, and functional authority, the central question senior management should ask and answer is "What authority relationships will achieve our goal most effectively?"

## WHAT IS THE "ASSISTANT TO" STAFF SPECIALIST?

In addition to a secretarial staff, some executives employ assistants who serve as their "second head" or "third arm." The title **assistant to** is used most often for such individuals. "Aide," "administrative assistant," and sometimes "aide-de-camp" are generally synonyms for "assistant to."

Assistants are used extensively and are found in all types of organizations. Each member of Congress, for example, is authorized by law to have a certain number of "administrative assistants."

Responsibilities assigned to assistants vary, but often they are highly important. **Duties Performed**
Duties may include writing speeches, preparing meeting agenda, making recom-

mendations on a variety of matters, acting as a liaison between the executive and lower-level managers, making discreet contacts with influential individuals, and coordinating various projects.

"Assistants to" are often criticized on the grounds that they shelter key executives from the real facts of organizational life, since, to a large extent, they determine what information the executives will receive. President Nixon was often criticized even before the Watergate affair because his two key aides, H. R. Haldeman and John Erlichman (derogatorily called "the palace guards"), made him inaccessible to key persons in government who had the official right to communicate directly.

Another misuse of the assistant is the case in which the line manager in effect gives the assistant power over the line organization. Such power may take a subtle form. For example, the assistant may tell key line personnel how the chief executive officer feels about various projects and policies, what the executive's intentions are for new programs and personnel, and what course of action the executive wants followed on various matters.

Assistants should be carefully selected. They frequently become familiar with confidential and sensitive information, and so a high degree of personal integrity is extremely important. Diplomacy is also important. Often, the assistant transmits messages from the superior to line managers, and key executives may dislike taking what may seem like orders from an assistant. Lowered morale and disinterest in the organization may result if they feel that they are being told what to do by an assistant.

Executives should carefully define the relationship between the "assistant to" and the line and staff managers. Key executive personnel, for example, need to know the kind and amount of authority that is invested in the assistant. For example, they need to know whether the assistant is relaying an order from the senior executive or is just passing on information.

## USE OF OUTSIDE STAFF SPECIALISTS

A frequently cited disadvantage of the small organization is that it cannot afford to employ staff specialists to provide the sophisticated advice necessary to meet competition and changing legal, tax, and government regulations.

It is impossible to state exactly when an organization is large enough to employ staff specialists. The small organization can acquire specialized staff advice from a number of sources and pay for it as needed on a fee, retainer, or other basis at a relatively low cost compared to the cost of maintaining in-house personnel. Furthermore, when outside specialists are used and the chief executive of a small organization is not satisfied with their performance, it is usually easy to break off the relationship—much simpler than it would be to terminate an employee. Examples of staff specialists that can be used by small enterprises and the functions they can perform at modest or, in some cases, no cost are shown in Table 10−2.

Even as they grow larger, many organizations continue to rely heavily on staff

**TABLE 10-2**

**249**

*What Is "Unofficial Staff Advice"?*

Some Outside Staff Specialists and the Functions They Perform

| Outside Staff Specialists | Examples of Functions They Perform |
|---|---|
| Computer experts | • Develop computer programs<br>• Process data on a time-sharing basis |
| Certified public accountants | • Perform audit, tax, and related services |
| Pension plan consultants | • Design and service pension plans for employees |
| Law firms | • Peform legal services ranging from defending the firm against legal action to collecting delinquent accounts |
| Real-estate brokers | • Help select office, factory, or other desired locations |
| Market research firm or consultants | • Conduct market studies<br>• Advise on marketing plans |
| Bankers | • Advise on debt-financing program and overall capital structure |
| Insurance brokers | • Develop comprehensive insurance programs to protect assets |
| Industrial-relations consultants | • Help negotiate union contracts |
| Product design firm | • Design new and redesign old products |
| Personnel consultants | • Search for and screen job applicants |
| Business professors | • Provide advice on management, finance, marketing, and other key activities |

specialists from outside the company. The cost of using outside specialists is often lower, since they are usually paid only for work done and do not necessitate heavy overhead expenses for office space, fringe benefits, and so on. Furthermore, retained specialists may be more knowledgeable and effective than personnel the organization could afford to employ on a full-time basis. For example, an organization may employ one or more lawyers full time. But when a highly specific legal matter comes up—perhaps a patent infringement suit or a matter involving international law—senior management may seek highly specialized outside counsel.

## WHAT IS "UNOFFICIAL STAFF ADVICE"?

Ideas and advice do not always come to a manager through formal line or staff channels or, for that matter, from retained consultants or other experts. In day-to-day practice, managers, especially those at senior levels, are likely to be influenced to some degree by persons who are not officially authorized to make recommendations.

The term **kitchen cabinet** has come to mean unofficial and informal advisers to the head of a government who often have more influence than some members of the official cabinet. Probably all presidents of the United States have relied to some extent on advice from friends and previous associates who have no official status in the administration. Typically, these individuals stay in the background and remain unknown to most citizens and even to many members of the official administration.

Soliciting unofficial staff advice is a very widespread custom, practiced by managers in all types of institutions. Much of the rationale for executive lunches and social affairs is to obtain ideas from friends about how to solve problems or handle difficult situations.

While most managers would probably not admit it, some seek the advice of their husbands or wives in making decisions regarding such matters as employment of key personnel and modification of the product line. Or a manager's secretary, who has no official authority, may be asked for his or her recommendation on specific matters.

## Advantages of Unofficial Staff Advice

The use of unofficial staff advice is seldom discussed and has not been the subject of much academic research. Nevertheless, reliance on unofficial opinion is a fact of organizational life and therefore deserves more study in the future. Much of the input for decision making in government, business corporations, and other enterprises comes from individuals who have no formal authority to make suggestions.

A manager may seek unofficial staff advice for a number of reasons. First, it gives a manager additional sources of information. There may be only one or two people in the organization who have knowledge that is helpful in solving a problem. In such a situation an outsider's viewpoint may expand the manager's knowledge and perhaps lead to a better decision.

Second, someone not formally attached to the organization may be more objective than members of the manager's official staff. The outsider will not be affected positively or negatively by the decision based on his or her advice.

Third, unofficial advice is suited to situations that are highly sensitive and should be kept confidential. Acquisition of another company, employment of a key executive from another organization, and disposal of certain corporate assets are examples of matters that a manager may not want to risk discussing with his or her formal staff because of fears that rumors will get started. And finally, unofficial advice usually is free.

## Limitations of Unofficial Staff Advice

There are two main limitations to the use of unofficial advice. First, unofficial advisers may not be as thoroughly briefed as formal advisers about the dimensions of a problem. Formal advisers may have spent months researching a problem, while informal advisers may know relatively little about it. Second, the use of unofficial advisers, to the extent that the practice is known, can have a negative impact on the morale of members of the official staff. Resentment is a natural result, especially if the recommendations of the executive's friends are accepted and those of the official staff are rejected.

**251**

*How to Develop*
*Harmony Between*
*Line and Staff*

## HOW TO DEVELOP HARMONY BETWEEN LINE AND STAFF

It is common for misunderstandings, confusion, and distrust to develop between line managers and their staff advisers. To the extent that line and staff personnel are not acting harmoniously, the work of the organization suffers, inefficiency results, and goals may not be attained.

An ever-present question in managing is to decide which is better — participative management or autocratic management. The Issue for Debate in this chapter presents some of the pros and cons of letting lower-level managers — both line and staff — participate in the decision-making process.

It is important that staff personnel understand clearly that their primary purpose is to help line managers achieve the goals of the organization. While this relationship should be obvious, in practice it often is not. A staff manager sometimes becomes carried away with the function he or she performs and feels that it constitutes the organization's purpose. For example, line managers frequently use staff departments when they wish to have data processed. A manager in the statistical section may develop an exaggerated sense of the importance of numerical data and may request more statistical information from the line departments than is needed by the line to carry out its work effectively. Or an accounting department manager may request from and supply to line managers more accounting data than line managers need.

Staff managers should be helped to understand that while their activities are important — even crucial to the overall success of the organization — their functions are still only supportive to the main purpose of the enterprise. Staff managers should also know that their requests are always subject to line manager approval unless appropriate functional authority has been delegated to them. For example, finance is a line function. Staff managers must realize that expenditure budgets for staff departments are always subject to modification by the appropriate line managers.

Staff managers should understand that they work within a framework established by line managers and that their essential purpose is to help the line executives attain the primary objectives of the organization.

*Ensure That Staff Understands Its Advisory Role*

Just as it is important for staff personnel to understand their advisory role, it is equally important that line personnel understand how best to avail themselves of the services of staff.

There are several ways to accomplish this. First, line executives should clearly communicate their requirements to staff managers. For example, production managers (line) should work closely with personnel managers (staff) and define for them how many persons are needed and what qualifications each individual

*Ensure That Line Makes Proper Use of Staff*

# MANAGERS IN ACTION

## DOES AMERICAN BUSINESS OVEREMPHASIZE STAFF MANAGEMENT?

In recent years American business has been criticized for overemphasizing staff jobs and de-emphasizing line positions. Some argue that this is a subtle reason why Japan, which holds line jobs in higher esteem than the United States, has become more productive. Consider the following observations:

1. "In 1945 the 25 largest U.S. industrial companies had an average of six vice-presidents each [almost all line executives] ... In 1981 companies in this group had an average of 30 vice-presidents each [most of whom were staff]."[1]
2. Staff jobs increasingly are viewed as "thinking" positions, while line jobs are considered "doing" positions. Staff work has become more prestigious than line work.
3. More than 80 percent of newly graduated

[1]Arch Patton, "Industry's Misguided Shift to Staff Jobs," *Business Week*, April 5, 1982, p. 12.

MBA's go into staff work for the following reasons:
(a) The beginning pay is usually far superior to that offered line managers.
(b) Staff jobs are not as risky as line jobs. Staff jobs are more difficult to assess than line jobs. (How does a senior executive really determine how well a computer expert or a researcher or an accountant is performing?)
(c) Promotions into senior management for staff managers are often much faster than for line managers.
4. Despite the belief by many managers that business is overstaffed, the need for staff managers appears to be growing because of government intrusion into corporate activity in such matters as civil rights, tax reporting, pollution control, minority and women's rights, and various state and local requirements. The rapid growth in computerization is also a factor leading to the growing importance of staff managers.

### QUESTIONS

1. Which would you prefer, a job as a line manager or a job as a staff manager? Why?
2. Assume that staff jobs are in fact better paid and more prestigious. What could be done to make line management jobs more attractive?

should have. In this way, the personnel department is better equipped to supply the right number and kind of job applicants to the production departments.

Second, top management should make sure that line executives clearly understand the limits of staff managers' authority. Line is not required to accept staff advice and suggestions unless, of course, appropriate functional authority over the line has been delegated to staff. In practice, one sometimes encounters a forceful staff manager who assumes the right of command and proceeds to issue orders to line managers even though he or she lacks the authority to do so. In such a situation it is important that line managers, who are entrusted with the primary mission of the organization, know the extent of authority given to staff managers.

Third, line managers should know the exact circumstances under which staff managers are directed (by organizational policies and procedures or by special orders from top management) to assume functional authority. For example, a marketing manager should know the situations in which the public-relations

# ISSUE FOR DEBATE

## IS PARTICIPATIVE MANAGEMENT MORE EFFECTIVE THAN AUTOCRATIC MANAGEMENT?

At the extreme, two management styles exist: participative and autocratic. The participative style lets those affected by a decision help make it. The autocratic style is dictatorial; decisions are imposed and no input from those affected is sought. Many managers today endorse the participative style to some degree. But enough managers still endorse autocratic management to make the question "Which is better?" controversial.

### YES

**Participative management is more effective because . . .**

People tend to set higher goals—and try harder to reach them—when they participate in setting them. Participative management thus leads to greater productivity.

Many people have knowledge, experience, and ideas that can be tapped when participative management is used. Thus the quality of decisions tends to improve.

Participative management is good for morale. People like to feel they are a part of the decision-making process, not just its victim.

A spirit of cooperation results from participative management. It helps to eliminate "us versus them" conflicts.

Participative management enlarges feelings of self-worth. People tend to become more creative and feel more responsible. Since work is more challenging, fewer absenteeism and other people problems result.

### NO

**Autocratic management is more effective because . . .**

Nonmanagers often lack the experience and knowledge to make useful inputs into decisions. Managers, since they have the most knowledge of resources and needs, are better prepared to make decisions.

Autocratic management requires less time. Reaching a decision through some form of committee process is notoriously slow.

The manager is employed to manage, which includes making decisions. Subordinates are expected to carry out decisions, not make them.

Some people prefer having decisions imposed on them or may resent having to help do management's work. Assembly-line workers, for example, may argue that they are not being paid to help manage.

Nonmanagers may lose respect for a manager who requests their help in making decisions. They may regard participative management as a sign of weakness or fear on the part of the manager.

## QUESTIONS

1. What other arguments, pro and con, can you offer?
2. Is it possible for a manager to employ elements of both participative and autocratic management and be effective? Why or why not? Is it wise? Explain.

253

manager (a staff executive) has functional authority to make decisions that affect the promotional program. Hardly anything frustrates a line manager more than seeing his authority withdrawn—even temporarily—for reasons not fully understood.

Fourth, line managers should work cooperatively with staff support people and should avoid conveying the impression that line is more important than staff. In modern organizations *both* line and staff managers are essential to the achievement of goals. The problem simply is one of defining the roles that will be played by each.

## Commit Line and Staff Relationships to Writing

So important is the close liaison of line and staff to the welfare of the organization that it is a useful practice to spell out in writing how the two relate. This is the practice in military organizations, in which it is imperative that there be no question about the location of authority. Questions such as the following are answered in military policy and procedure manuals: "When does the medical officer (a staff official) have authority to ground a flight crew?" "What is the authority of a meteorologist (staff officer) to cancel naval maneuvers?" and "What limits are imposed on the authority of military police (staff personnel) to detain and confine military personnel?"

Well-managed business organizations commit to writing in policy and procedure manuals the location and the extent of authority pertaining to such matters as these: "When does a product-control manager have authority to modify product quality standards?" "Under what circumstances must a public-relations release prepared by the public-relations department (a staff department) be approved by the legal department (another staff department) or by the president or other senior line managers?" and "When does the data-processing manager (a staff person) have authority to modify computer programs that affect performance of line activities such as production scheduling?"

## Recognize the Contributions of Staff Members

As Neil B. Holbert has observed:

The life of staff is pretty much unknown to top management. . . . The staffer wants to do meaningful work and is prepared to work very hard to get it and to do it. He is also prepared to work very hard to prevent his training from being used in foolishness, idle imaginings spiced only by idle errands. His thirst for meaningful work is enormous. But since the bigger picture is often denied him, he is frustrated by his lack of knowledge that what he is doing matters.[2]

Holbert goes on to point out that staff personnel generally feel unappreciated by line management. Some of his suggestions for correcting this problem are:

- Give staff personnel more feedback on how their activities contribute or fail to contribute to the organization's overall goals. For example, a market research manager wants to know if his or her market studies helped in reaching a sales goal.

[2]Neil B. Holbert, "The Life of Staff," *Business Horizons,* June 1978, p. 80.

- Let staff personnel play a larger role in policy making. Staff members are most productive when they are asked to do more and to expand their horizons.

Holbert also points out that the knowledge required by staff personnel must be constantly updated and that "time spent for research, for committees, for reading, is part of their job, and not an afterthought. No line manager wants to be advised by advisers who have not kept in touch with the state of the art, or indeed have not helped move that state forward."[3]

Deciding whether a budgetary request for a staff activity is truly warranted is generally more difficult than making a similar decision for a line request. It is comparatively easy, for instance, to measure the contribution of additional sales-people or additional production workers and compare it against their cost. What is more difficult to determine is the contribution of additional personnel in the research or legal department.

Typically, as an organization grows, staff managers and employees are added more rapidly than line managers and employees. One university found, for example, when its enrollment grew from 12,000 to 24,000 in a period of five years, that the number of line managers (mainly deans and department heads) had doubled while the number of staff managers (security, maintenance, data process-ing, and so on) had increased fourfold. The usual reason for the disproportionate increase in staff is that growth creates complexity, and complexity in turn increases the demand for specialists.

Staff budgets are always under the ultimate control of line executives, a fact that staff managers should understand. While impossible to demonstrate mathe-matically, many management observers believe there is relatively more waste of human and other resources in the performance of staff activities than in that of line activities. One reason for this is that most staff personnel are salaried, while most production people are paid on an hourly basis. During a period of slow economic activity, production employees are usually the first to be laid off, whereas staff persons are not normally terminated until conditions worsen badly.

Furthermore, the line manager may have a less than adequate understand-ing of the need for expenditures that the staff manager wants to make. For example, the manager of data processing may say it is "absolutely essential" to hire three additional people and purchase some new equipment if the data-processing function is to be performed with maximum efficiency. Typically, line managers who evaluate such requests do not have sufficient background in the field to make such a decision. What the line manager is really evaluating is the logic that supports the staff manager's requests and the way in which these requests relate to the overall goals of the organization. The line manager may receive budget requests from several staff managers. These requests must be evaluated jointly, as well as individually, to achieve the best results.

There are two other reasons why more waste of resources may occur in staff departments than in line ones. First, results are often difficult to justify in the short

[3]Ibid., p. 82.

run. For example, how does one measure the progress—and ultimate contribution to profit—of a technical research program? Second, in large organizations staff groups tend to become highly bureaucratic. Bureaucracies, it is often argued, result in the employment of unneeded personnel.

**SUMMARY**

- Authority relationships should be clearly defined and communicated to members of the organization. There are two kinds of authority: line and staff.
- In a pure line form of organization, all authority flows in a direct line from the board of directors to the president to managers of key functions to subordinate managers and ultimately to operative employees.
- As organizations grow they become more complex, and staff departments and personnel are added. Staff personnel advise, assist, and support line operations. When staff departments are added, the organizational structure is called "line and staff."
- The designation of an activity as line or staff depends more on the organization than on the nature of the activity itself.
- Staff managers normally have no direct authority over line managers, but they have line authority over personnel within their departments.
- Line managers tend to be generalists, while staff managers tend to be specialists.
- The use of staff has limitations in that staff may usurp line authority and too much confidence may be placed in staff specialists.
- Functional authority is the right delegated to a manager to issue orders to persons in a department other than his or her own. It may become fixed through staff departmentalization.
- "Assistants to" are staff specialists that are often used by managers to prepare reports, develop agendas, coordinate activities, and perform other tasks.
- Small enterprises that cannot afford to employ staff specialists may seek specialized advice from outside consultants and experts in such fields as accounting, law, and data processing.
- Many senior executives obtain "unofficial staff advice" from friends and associates in other organizations and from other walks of life.
- It is important that harmony exist between line and staff managers. To ensure cooperation, staff should understand its advisory role, line managers should make the best use of staff personnel, line and staff relationships should be committed to writing, greater appreciation should be shown for the contributions made by staff, and staff budgets should be justified.

**LEARN
THE LANGUAGE
OF
MANAGEMENT**

authority
line authority
line managers
staff authority
staff managers

line and staff
functional authority
multiple command
"assistant to"
kitchen cabinet

1. What are the basic distinctions in the roles played by line managers and staff managers?
2. As organizations grow larger, why is it inevitable that staff departments be added? What are examples of activities that are typically staff?
3. Explain how a staff manager exercises line authority over the individuals within his or her department.
4. "The higher a line manager rises in the organization, the less important specialized knowledge becomes." Why? What are some examples of highly specialized knowledge needed to operate an airline that the president of the airline need not possess? A bank? A motion picture company?
5. Give several examples of functional authority in practice. What problems may the delegation of functional authority create?
6. What problems may result from using "assistants to" and how can the problems be avoided?
7. What are the advantages of using outside staff specialists for both small and large organizations?
8. Discuss the pros and cons of a senior manager using "unofficial staff advice."
9. In what ways can line personnel best avail themselves of the services of staff personnel?

### 1. Which do you prefer and why: line or staff?

Many people who are planning their careers never seriously evaluate whether they would like to work primarily in a line or in a staff capacity. As a result, there are many frustrated line managers who would find more satisfaction doing staff activities and many staff people who would rather be performing line activities.

In a report, explain which type of activity, line or staff, you would prefer for your career. Consider all relevant factors in your explanation.

### 2. A staff specialist is believed to be upsetting your plans. What do you do?

You were recently appointed manager in charge of marketing for a medium-sized manufacturing company. Your proposed budget and your plans for adding new sales representatives have all been modified extensively and in a manner that you think is wrong by your superior, the company president. From your own observations and from office conversations you feel that the company president is being unduly influenced by his assistant, an individual who has served in that capacity for fifteen years. You feel your plans are being thwarted by a staff specialist who does not have any formal authority to make decisions affecting your department.

What courses of action are available to you to correct this situation?

What specifically would you do and why?

### 3. An administrative assistant to the CEO causes problems for senior executives

For 12 years, Freida Baxter has been administrative assistant to Peter Rush, CEO for one of the nation's largest banks. Peter spends considerable time in Europe and

Asia. While he's away, all communications from him to senior executives are transmitted through Freida. And communications from the senior executives to Peter go through Freida. As the following conversation shows, the key managers don't like this procedure.

Bob: I sometimes wonder who really runs the bank. Last week a 10 million dollar loan I'd been working on would have been approved if I could have explained the deal directly to Peter. I feel sure that Freida decided it wasn't a good loan and told Peter to turn it down.

Sara: What I resent most about Freida is that she in effect gives me orders. She doesn't say, "Peter said do this or do that." Instead, she says, "I want you to do such and such."

Harry: Even when Peter's here, I have to beg Freida to get to see him. Every time I go to her office, she makes me feel like I'm in the second grade having to report to the principal.

Bob: The problem is even broader than just communications. I have good reason to believe that she makes most of the key decisions on salaries, promotions, and transfers.

Sara: I feel Freida has Peter wrapped around her finger. Nothing happens around here without her approval. She functions like the assistant CEO, not as the assistant to the CEO.

What advantages are there in having an administrative assistant be the communications coordinator?

If the executives are right in their assumption that Freida is in effect making key decisions, what can they do about it?

**FOR ADDITIONAL
CONCEPTS
AND IDEAS**

Carter, Forrest S. "Decision Structuring to Reduce Management—Research Conflicts." *MSU Business Topics*, Spring 1981, pp. 40–46.

Dubinsky, Alan J., and Ingram, Thomas N. "Top-Level Selling: Executive Viewpoints." *Akron Business and Economic Review*, Summer 1982, pp. 7–10.

Fisher, J. E. "Dealing with Office Politics in Authoritarian-Dominated Staff Organizations." *Publishers Personal Management*, January 1979, pp. 56–63.

Halal, William E., and Brown, Bob S. "Participative Management: Myth and Reality." *California Management Review*, Summer 1981, pp. 20–32.

Jain, S. Kumar. "Look to Outsiders to Strengthen Small Business Boards." *Harvard Business Review*, July–August 1980, pp. 162–170.

Kelly, Joe, and Khozan, Kamran. "Participative Management: Can It Work?" *Business Horizons*, August 1980, pp. 74–79.

Labovitz, George H. "Managing Conflict." *Business Horizons,* June 1980, pp. 30–37.

McConkey, Dale D. "Participative Management: What It Really Means in Practice." *Business Horizons*, October 1980, pp. 66–73.

Marx, Thomas G. "The Corporate Economics Staff: Challenges and Opportunities for the '80s." *Business Horizons*, April 1980, pp. 15–21.

Miller, Edwin L., and Burack, Elmer. "The Emerging Personnel Function." *MSU Business Topics,* Autumn 1977, pp. 27–32.

Miners, Howard. "How Staff Jobs Weaken Line Management." *Management Today,* June 1982, pp. 33–41.

Odiorne, George S. "Strategic Planning: Challenging New Role for Corporate Staff." *Business*, May 1981, pp. 10–14.

Patton, Arch. "Industry's Misguided Shift to Staff Jobs." *Business Week*, April 5, 1982, pp. 12–15.

Sharwell, W. G. "Idea Managers: A New Look at Staff vs. Line Jobs." *Management Review*, August 1978, pp. 24–25.

Turner, Arthur N. "Consulting is More Than Giving Advice." *Harvard Business Review*, September–October 1982, pp. 120–129.

Vagts, Detlev F. "CEOs and Their Lawyers: Tension Strains the Link." *Harvard Business Review*, March–April 1981, pp. 6–14.

Weinshall, Theodore D. "Help for Chief Executives: The Outside Consultant." *California Management Review*, Summer 1982, pp. 47–67.

# 11 DELEGATION OF AUTHORITY

- Define "delegation," and explain why it is essential to organizing.
- Identify and describe the advantages and disadvantages of delegation.
- Discuss the factors that determine the delegation of authority.
- Identify the ways in which managers can use power effectively.
- List and explain the guidelines for effective delegation.

In a one-person operation, all decisions and all work are vested in a single individual. However, as the owner-manager hires one or more employees, he or she must empower others to perform activities and make decisions. That is, the manager must *delegate authority* in order for the organization to achieve its objectives.

**Delegation of authority**, or granting the power to act, is inherent in the organizing process. Failure to delegate can create many problems. Overworked managers, lack of time to handle important matters, mistakes, and other forms of inefficiency can result when work is not delegated skillfully. Lyndall Urwick has underscored the importance of delegation: "Without delegation no organization can function effectively. Yet, lack of the courage to delegate properly and of knowledge how to do it, is one of the most general causes of failure in organizations."[1]

In general, the more authority delegated to lower-level employees, the more **decentralized** the organization is said to be. Conversely, the more authority retained by higher-level managers, the more **centralized** the organization is said to be.

Note that the terms "centralization" and "decentralization" are often used in other ways as well. Most commonly, they are used to denote certain characteristics of a firm's organizational chart. For example, an organization may be said to be "decentralized" if there are many branch offices, "centralized" if there is only one central office. However, in this text the terms are used to denote *the way in which authority is delegated*, not any characteristics of a firm's organizational structure.

Decentralization occurs whenever a lower-level employee is given authority to take action or make a decision.[2] Thus, nearly all organizations are decentralized to some degree. A discussion of whether authority is centralized or decentralized must necessarily deal with relative questions, not absolutes.

In management, a continuing controversy surrounds the relative importance of the person who delegates authority and the people who carry out the orders. Some aspects of this question are discussed in the Issue for Debate in this chapter.

Often delegation becomes necessary simply because there is too much work for one person (or a few people) to handle. There are several other advantages of delegation as well.

**Advantages of Delegation**

### Delegation Is Essential to Obtain Prompt Action

Most of us have been annoyed on occasion, when cashing a check or trying to obtain credit, to be told that approval by someone higher up the organizational scale is required. We are often frustrated because the person we are talking to lacks the authority to act. This wastes our time as well as the time of the person serving us. An important reason for delegation is to satisfy the patrons served by the organization. Delays resulting from "sending the matter upstairs" or getting

[1]Lyndall Urwick, *Elements of Administration* (New York: Harper & Brothers, 1944), p. 51.
[2]Note that an individual can delegate authority to act but cannot delegate responsibility for performance. Each individual is accountable to his or her superior for performance, but the superior in no way can avoid responsibility for what the staff does. This point was discussed in Chapter 1.

# ISSUE FOR DEBATE

## IS THE LEADER MORE IMPORTANT THAN THE FOLLOWERS AS THE KEY TO AN ORGANIZATION'S SUCCESS?

An enduring controversy in management concerns the relative importance of the top manager versus that of subordinates. According to Napoleon: "In war men are nothing; it is the man who is everything. The general is the head [top manager], the whole of any army. It was not the Roman army that conquered Gaul, but Caesar; it was not the Carthaginian army that made Rome tremble in her gates, but Hannibal; . . . it was not the Prussian army which, for seven years, defended Prussia against the three greatest Powers of Europe, but Frederick the Great" (quoted from Henry L. Gantt, *Industrial Leadership* [Easton, Penn.: Hive Publishing Co., 1973], pp. 11–12).

Below are some pro and con arguments about this issue.

| YES | NO |
|---|---|
| **The leader is more important because . . .** | **The leader is not more important because . . .** |
| The chief executive is ultimately responsible for the general direction of an enterprise. Thus subordinate managers' decisions do not shape final results. | No leader, however great, can achieve first-rate results with ineffective followers. Therefore, followers are just as important as the leader. |
| In times of crises, the chief executive is often forced out by the board of directors, indicating that they know who must be held accountable. Meanwhile, lower-level managers keep their jobs. | Many ideas that produce successful results come from followers. Often these contributions go unnoticed and unrewarded by the chief executive, yet they are important. |
| In all the games people play, the chief executive makes the difference. The head football coach is the big hero after a successful season. If the team fares badly, the coach may be asked to leave. | Chief executives, when honored for an achievement, often say in effect, "I don't deserve the credit. It was a team effort." They recognize the critical contributions of subordinate employees. |
| In the last analysis, ultimate power in an organization is vested in the top executive. Therefore, the top executive is the key. | The view of Napoleon, once shared by many leaders, is applicable only in totally autocratic organizations. It is outmoded today. |

## QUESTIONS

1. Which side of this issue do you feel is correct? Why?
2. What would probably have happened to the morale of Napoleon's armies (which was normally very high) if they had read this statement? Explain.

home-office approval can cost a business customers. Time is saved to the extent that authority is decentralized.

### Delegation Enables Managers to Perform Higher-Level Work

One of the principles of management is that all work, including decision making, should be performed at the lowest competent level. Executives should not be required to make minor decisions that can be made just as well, or perhaps even better, by individuals at lower levels in the organization. For example, a branch manager should generally have authority to purchase routine office supplies, thereby conserving executive time. Saving executive time means saving money. Obviously, when $30-per-hour executives are doing work that can be performed competently by $10-per-hour employees, financial waste occurs.

### Delegation Can Be a Training Experience for Supportive Staff

A good argument can be made that the main way we learn is by doing. Giving authority to new managers provides a training experience for them. Then, as the manager proves he or she can handle authority, it is natural to extend more authority. Or, if the manager fails in the assignment, the authority can be reduced.

Thomas W. Zimmerer makes the following comments on the value of delegation as a training device:

> If managers at the lower levels of an organization are not given the opportunity to exercise control over the problems they face and the people they manage, how can they be prepared to make decisions when they reach a higher level? It seems more logical to have managers begin their training by making decisions early on smaller problems. In such cases, an error in decision making can be more easily corrected, and the cost of an error is substantially less.[3]

### Delegation Can Result in Better Decisions

It does not follow that managers at a high level in an organization are best equipped by experience and knowledge to make all decisions at lower levels. Many positions within an organization are technical in nature. In these situations better decisions can often be made by lower-level personnel. Those close to a problem may be better equipped to solve it. For example, an office manager who has a detailed knowledge of office machines may be able to make a better decision about what equipment to purchase than a senior executive who is not involved with the day-to-day operation of machines.

### Delegation Can Improve Morale

One cause of low morale in many organizations is the limited authority of managers to make decisions. Many people welcome authority, for it enables them to take more pride in their work. Managers may resent not being empowered to act or to make decisions in areas in which they feel competent.

Zimmerer explains the relationship of delegation to motivation as follows:

> Delegation gives employees a greater sense of control over their own destinies. This opportunity for control is in itself a source of motivation and a source of job

---

[3]Thomas W. Zimmerer, "How to Reduce Dependence on the Boss," *Nation's Business*, February 1977, p. 55.

enrichment. An enriched job is one which emphasizes a greater involvement of each employee.

With enough delegation, the emphasis in work goals for employees shifts from doing more to doing better. Employees now believe that their role is critical to the success of the group's objectives. There is an opportunity for each employee to grow in the job. Achievement and recognition — both key motivators — become an integral part of the job.[4]

**Disadvantages of Delegation**

Despite its advantages, delegation has two potential limitations. First, control at the top may be more difficult. The farther decisions are removed from the highest level, the more difficult it is to pinpoint problem areas and effectuate corrective action. Second, in delegating, a manager may over time lose touch with what is really happening in the organization. There are many instances in which managers have delegated so extensively that they no longer know whether policies and procedures are in fact being carried out as planned. These limitations of delegation, however, can be largely overcome if the guidelines for effective delegation discussed later are followed.

Figure 11−1 summarizes the advantages and disadvantages of delegation.

## WHAT FACTORS DETERMINE DELEGATION OF AUTHORITY?

A recurring question that managers face is "Which decisions and work should we delegate, and which should we control ourselves?" The decisions of whether to delegate authority and, if so, what and how much must be made at all levels of management. Even at operating levels managers must decide whether to delegate authority for relatively routine matters or whether to keep the authority vested in themselves. Table 11−1 gives examples of questions that may have to be considered.

In determining the degree of authority to delegate, the factors discussed in the following sections should be considered.

**Importance of the Decision**

The more significant the decision, the more likely it is that it will be made at the top of the organizational structure. Managers at the top retain authority for basic decisions affecting the overall organization. Decisions relating to the budget, development of new products, refinancing of the organization, selection of new locations for expansion, and acquisition of competing companies are examples of matters that are generally not delegated to lower levels. The importance of a decision can be measured in various ways, the most significant one being cost. Generally, major expenditures can be authorized only by top executives in an organization. Stated another way, the less costly the decision, the more likely it is that it will be made at lower levels.

The importance of a decision also depends on the nature of the work performed by the organization. For a beer or soft-drink producer, the decision to

[4]Ibid.

FIGURE 11-1

Advantages and Disadvantages of Delegation

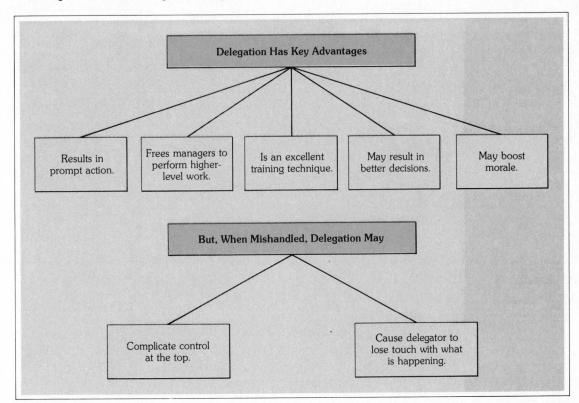

change the design of a bottle or a can is made at the highest level because packaging has a great effect on sales. On the other hand, for products sold to the industrial market, such as chemicals, packaging decisions are generally less important. The decision to modify prices can be highly important, relatively important, or relatively unimportant, depending on the situation.

In a small organization, top management may make all key decisions (regarding finance, production, and marketing) as well as decisions of secondary importance (for example, hiring of operative employees, purchase of routine items, and preparation of work schedules). Decentralization becomes increasingly necessary as an organization increases in size. It is physically and mentally impossible in large organizations to invest all authority in a top level of managers. Therefore, authority is transferred from one level of management to another level down the organization until some authority is vested in the lowest echelon. Each level of management should retain authority to make those decisions for which it has experience and qualifications and should pass down any decisions that can be made at lower levels.

Size of the Organization

**TABLE 11-1**

## Some Questions That May Have to Be Answered in Delegating Authority

| Area to Which Question Relates | Example of Questions |
|---|---|
| Expenditures | • How much money should the subordinate be authorized to spend without seeking approval?<br>• Specifically, how much can be spent for travel, contributions, research, consultations, remodeling, and other items? (Note that it is *always* important for a subordinate to know his or her full authority with regard to expenditures.)<br>• What limits, if any, should be placed on expense accounts? |
| Personnel | • Should the manager be empowered to hire hourly personnel? Salaried personnel?<br>• Should the manager be given authority to grant relocation expenses for new personnel?<br>• Should the manager be authorized to transfer, promote, and demote personnel? |
| Capital expenditures | • What authority should we invest in the manager to purchase and sell capital assets?<br>• Should the individual be empowered to purchase a new building or dispose of an existing building? |
| Physical resources | • What authority should the individual be given to purchase, repair, or dispose of machines or desks or other equipment?<br>• Should the manager have authority to contract for maintenance services? |
| Public relations | • What authority should the manager have to make statements to the press about the organization's activities?<br>• Does the manager have authority to initiate public-relations activities, such as plant tours and community projects? |
| Task performance | • Should the manager be authorized to cash checks? Grant loans?<br>• Should the individual be able to authorize advertising? |
| Emergencies | • Should the individual be given authority to deal with cases of fire, robbery, accidents, and other emergencies?<br>• What authority does the individual have to initiate programs to prevent emergencies from arising? |

## QUESTIONS

1. What other types of questions should the delegator ask and answer before granting authority?
2. What are the advantages of raising questions such as the above prior to the delegation of authority?

Managers differ greatly in their willingness to "let go" and permit lower-echelon personnel to make decisions. Often the founder of an organization is particularly reluctant to delegate authority. Sometimes the individual who started a business and watched it grow large still wants to act in a totalitarian fashion, even when greater efficiency would result from delegation. Such individuals typically are afraid to trust others to make decisions, even those of a relatively minor nature.

Professional managers too sometimes want to be involved in relatively small decisions. According to an article in *Fortune,* Charles Pilliod, former chief executive of Goodyear Tire & Rubber, commonly violated the chain of command and concerned himself with matters that most top managers would delegate. One of his subordinates was quoted as saying, "He's more dictatorial than previous people I've observed in that office. He gives me responsibility but he steps in with strong suggestions."[5]

However, many managers place great importance on delegation. Louis B. Lundborg, former chairman of the board of the Bank of America, favored a management style of extensive delegation. He observed that "for any executive to reach great effectiveness he must delegate and involve a lot of other people in doing the things he might want to do, and delegate as far down the line as he can in order to give rising younger people opportunities to try their wings. In doing this he is multiplying himself."[6]

Some managers may overdelegate and give their subordinates more authority than they can handle well. Such managers may not like the pressure of making decisions or they overestimate the ability of their subordinates.

Managers who delegate excessively run the risk of losing control over activities. Giving a subordinate manager more authority than he or she is qualified to handle can lead to excessive spending, employment of poorly qualified people, production mistakes, and a host of other problems that are difficult to correct.

Decentralization is possible only if persons are available who are sufficiently trained and experienced to accept and implement authority. Often this is not the case, and decentralization will be delayed until "we have someone ready to take over." A major reason for manager-development programs, discussed in Part Four, is to train managers who can handle increased authority successfully.

Organizations consist exclusively of people, and they naturally reflect human characteristics. Some organizations tend to be highly dynamic and place great emphasis on growth. Other organizations grow at a fairly even rate, while still others appear to stagnate. In dynamic situations, authority is decentralized at a fairly rapid pace. The dynamics of growth requires adding more managers and more levels of management, two conditions that lead to decentralization. In non-dynamic or stagnant organizations, authority tends to remain highly centralized, for senior managers see little reason to decentralize.

*Management Style and Philosophy*

*Availability of Capable Managers*

*Dynamics of the Enterprise*

[5]Quoted in Arthur M. Louis, "Charles Pilliod Was the Odd Man In at Goodyear," *Fortune,* May 1977, p. 291.
[6]Louis B. Lundborg, "A Gratifying Career That Just Won't Quit," *Nation's Business,* June 1972, p. 50.

# MANAGERS IN ACTION

## A NEW TREND: REDUCE STAFF AND LEVELS OF MANAGEMENT

During the 1960s and 1970s, American businesses added staff whenever a need was perceived for people with specialized knowledge. Thus, corporations eagerly sought staff members with expertise in such areas as financial analysis, market research, law, and accounting.

By the early 1980s, senior executives in many companies concluded that their organizations were overstaffed. For example, when B. Charles Ames became chief executive of Acme-Cleveland Corporation in 1981, he discovered that corporate earnings were way below earnings of previous years, but corporate overhead was remaining constant. According to Ames, "I reached the conclusion early that there were too many people—the bulk in middle management and corporate structure. We need to operate with fewer people who are given broader responsibilities."[1] In short order, Ames reduced the corporate staff from 120 to 50.

Robert A. Pritzker, head of the Marmon Group,

a large conglomerate, said, "One of the reasons American businesses are having a tough time competing at home and abroad is that they are over-staffed."[2]

According to Pritzker, "We don't have a staff of business analysts in our headquarters, the way most companies do to analyze capital programs. Those financial people can only crunch numbers. They can't add any original thinking. They don't know about whether a new piece of equipment would work or whether there is a market for a product. We make these decisions by talking to the operating people and finding out the thought process that the man who knows went through to rationalize an expenditure."[3]

It appears that senior mangement in the 1980s is as eager to cut back on staff personnel as it was to add them in the 1960s and 1970s.

[1]Quoted from the December 21, 1981 issue of *Business Week* by special permission, © 1981 by McGraw-Hill, Inc. New York, NY 10020. All rights reserved.

[2]Quoted from the March 7, 1983 issue of *Business Week* by special permission, © 1983 by McGraw-Hill, Inc. New York, NY 10020. All rights reserved.
[3]Ibid.

### QUESTIONS

1. Based on your observations, do you feel that there are too many staff managers in business?
2. How can senior management determine when a staff person is truly needed?

---

**Type of Organization**
For several decades there has been a trend toward the development of conglomerates, which are large enterprises that bring together into one organization a wide variety of different types of businesses. Generally, authority tends to be highly decentralized in such organizations. In evaluating the performance of a division or a subsidiary, senior-level managers in a conglomerate are primarily interested in two things: profitability and share of the market. Top managers in the various units of a conglomerate are given broad authority, and as long as results meet expectations, they act with considerable autonomy. The main reason for this is that the companies that comprise the conglomerate are often highly specialized and already have a staff of managers experienced in the particular area.

Another trend in recent decades is the growth in the number of **multinational** businesses. While definitions differ, a company is generally considered a multinational if it operates in five or more countries. A multinational company may also be a conglomerate and own subsidiaries in unrelated industries. Nestlé, a Switzerland-based multinational, is probably best known for its chocolate. But Nestlé also owns or controls companies that are engaged in a variety of fields such as hotels, restaurants, frozen foods, wine, and cosmetics.

Typically, multinational companies are highly decentralized, and senior managers in the subsidiaries have considerable freedom. The one area in which senior management of the conglomerate typically exercises closest control is finance. The key question in making decentralization decisions is to decide what activities to keep centralized and what activities to assign downward. The greatest danger in decentralization is loss of control. If decentralization were total, all control would be lost and chaos would result. Activities that should be kept centralized in a conglomerate or a multinational organization include financing, new product research, profit goals, capital expenditures, budgeting, major product policies, broad promotional plans, and manager compensation.

Figure 11–2 summarizes the factors that determine what and how much authority should be delegated.

## DELEGATION, DEPENDENCY, AND THE USE OF POWER

In a perfectly structured organization, the superior has the authority or power to hold the subordinates accountable for performance or, if performance does not result, to remove the subordinate.[7] But in the process of delegating authority, the superior becomes dependent on subordinates. This dependency can be very real. As John Kotter has noted, "As a person gains more formal authority in an organization, the areas in which he or she is vulnerable increase and become more complex rather than the reverse. It is not at all unusual for the president of an organization to be in a highly dependent position, a fact often not apparent to either the outsider or to the lower-level manager who covets the president's job."

He goes on to observe, "In other words, it is primarily because of the dependence inherent in managerial jobs that the dynamics of power necessarily form an important part of a manager's processes."

Managers are dependent not only on subordinates but on people in other parts of the organization, suppliers, customers, unions, and government agencies. But ultimately, the survival and success of a superior depend on how well he or she exercises authority. Suggestions on how to use authority effectively follow:

* *Be sensitive to what others consider legitimate behaviors in exercising power.* Managers who let subordinates down, make promises that aren't kept, and practice deception and unfairness in the administration of orga-

[7]Much of the discussion in this section is based on John P. Kotter, "Power, Dependence and Effective Management," *Harvard Business Review,* July–August 1977, pp. 125–36.

**FIGURE 11–2**

**How Much and What Authority Should Be Delegated?**

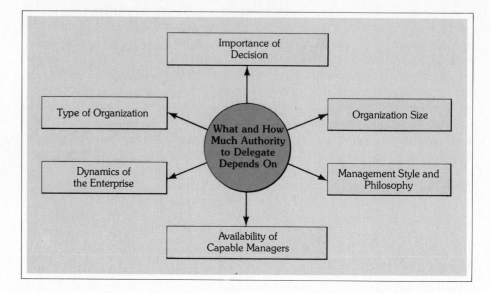

nizational rules will likely not have their dependency needs based on subordinates' behavior fulfilled for long.

- *Understand that different people respond to different methods of influence.* Some subordinates are influenced by the perceived expertise of the manager, others by a feeling of obligation to the manager for past favors, and still others by persuasion or one of many other devices.
- *Establish career goals and work toward them.* Individuals who want to exercise the use of power effectively seek out managerial positions that allow them to use power. They volunteer to handle difficult assignments in which their use of power will be highly visible.
- *Behave in a mature and self-controlled manner.* Effective managers tend not to use power for self-aggrandizement. Instead they are team oriented and give subordinates credit for goal achievement.
- *Embrace the exercise of authority and don't be afraid to use it.* In our society the general attitude toward power is negative. We tend to distrust it. But on reflection, we find that most use of authority results in good accomplishments. Effective managers feel comfortable in the exercise of power.

## AN ILLUSTRATION OF INEFFECTIVE DELEGATION

In many organizations there are problems surrounding the delegation of authority. Sometimes too much authority is delegated to a manager; at other times too little is provided. And very often the limits of authority are not communicated. Consider the following account (based on actual occurrences) of what transpired between an individual who had been granted authority to operate a branch "in the best manner possible" and his superior, the individual who granted the authority.

Clark Brown has worked for the National Bank for two years. On January 1, he is named manager of a branch in a suburb of Chicago. His boss, Ron Weatherstone, tells him, "Clark, I'm putting you in charge and I expect you to pretty much handle things on your own. Come to me, of course, if you have any major problems." The following incidents occur over the next three months.

On January 31, Brown hires an administrative assistant. He feels much of his work can be delegated to someone with experience in administrative work but does not feel his secretary has the capabilities to handle the job. He feels the employment of the administrative assistant will give him more time to visit with businesses in his area and solicit their accounts. On Febraury 4, the following dialogue ensues:

Weatherstone: Say, Clark, I just learned this morning that you hired an administrative assistant. Now, I know you probably need one out there, but the pay scale you established for the person you hired requires that the appointment be approved here at the main office. You simply didn't have the authority to finalize the apointment. I guess somebody should have informed you of that before you stepped into this problem.
Brown: But I thought I had authority to hire and fire.
Weatherstone: You do, but you only have authority to hire people who will make up to $1,500 a month. Beyond that you have to come to us and present your case to the Professional Employee Committee here at the main office for approval.

On February 13, Brown calls two office decorating companies to discuss the possibility of redecorating the branch office. He feels the office looks shabby and presents a poor image to the public. One company quotes $9,000 for the job, and the other submits a bid for $11,200. Brown chooses the company that made the $11,200 bid. He feels the proposal is worth the extra money and tells the firm to go ahead. On February 26, the work is completed and Brown submits the firm's statement to the bank's main office for payment. On March 1, his boss calls:

Weatherstone: Brown, we have a problem. Accounting just called about a bill from the Atlas Redecorating Company that you authorized. Clark, I'm sorry, but you can't authorize redecorating expenses of this magnitude. Anything over $2,000 has to be approved by the finance committee here at the main office. You see, Clark, we already have arrangements with a leading decorating firm in the city that does all our redecorating except in exceptional situations. That's why we don't give our branch managers permission to handle major redecorating problems.

On February 17, a customer of the home office comes into Brown's branch and requests a loan for $50,000. He has a good credit rating and is a long-time customer of the bank, but Brown tells him he cannot make a loan of that size and suggests that the customer visit the main office. Later that day Brown receives a call from Weatherstone, who is quite upset:

Weatherstone: Look, Clark, why in heaven's name did you turn down Jones? He's one of our prime customers—we've been dealing with him for thirty years. His record is A-OK—never a problem. He came here *very* upset—even threatened to take his account away. I, of course, apologized and approved his loan immediately. But he's still upset. You should handle loans like that at the branch level. We don't like to spend time on things like that at the main office when a good customer wants to borrow money at the branch level.
Brown: But I thought that was too big a loan for me to make.

On February 20, a solicitor for the United Appeal stops by the bank and requests a contribution on behalf of the bank. Brown tells her, "I'm sorry, but I can't make a contribution for the bank. You'll have to go to the main office and make the request." The next day Brown receives another call from his superior, Weatherstone:

Weatherstone: Look, Clark, all contributions to public agencies are handled at the branch level. Will you please not send situations like that back here? We're involved with some important policy matters right now, and frankly, we don't have the time.

On March 10, the normal low level of chatter in the bank is suddenly upset by a loud, firm voice: "This is a holdup. Everybody keep quiet." The robber approaches the tellers and says, "Put all the money in this paper bag." Brown, who is seated at an angle behind the robber, swiftly gets behind him, knocks the gun from his hand, and pins him to the floor. The robber has been stopped cold, and the customers and employees cheer. The police arrive soon, and everything gets back to normal. Thirty minutes later, Brown receives a call from Weatherstone:

Weatherstone: Say, Clark, what did you try to do today? We don't want our branch managers doing that sort of thing. I know you were an all-conference tackle at Tech, but you have no authority to try and stop bank robbers. That's a job for the police. Our standing policy is to cooperate fully with any robber to protect the safety of our customers and our employees.
Brown: But no one explained that policy to me.
Weatherstone: Everybody in the bank know's that's our policy. Look, Clark, we're a team here at Old National. I hope you'll soon learn how to play.

Several days later, after a long talk with his wife, who works in another bank, Brown calls Weatherstone: "I quit. I'm confused about how much money I'm allowed to loan out and to whom I can loan it. I can't hire the people I need. Apparently I can hire and fire some and can't hire and fire others. I can't authorize people to repair the office as I think it should be. I can't even stop bank robbers! I really don't know what I can and cannot do. You leave me no intelligent choice but to quit."

The central mistake running through these incidents is that the authority delegated to Brown, the branch manager, was not spelled out. Specifically, Brown did not know the extent of his authority to authorize redecorating, make loans, set salaries or to act on any other matters.

Examples of ineffective delegation are all about us. Anyone who has ever tried to get information from a government agency has probably experienced some form of "buck passing," with each employee saying that he or she does not have the authority to provide the information and sending the questioner to still another individual in the organizational hierarchy. Or a customer who is trying to exchange a low-cost item that was bought in a store may experience something similar, with the salesperson saying that he or she can't handle the matter and referring the person to the assistant manager and then to the manager. There are often long delays in the payment of small insurance claims because the claims adjuster must first get "home office approval."

Ineffective delegation is costly. If managers do not know the extent of their authority, they may exercise too much or too little, as in the case of Brown the banker. Generally, the more precise the definition of one's authority in a management situation, the more effective the result.

Theodore J. Krein developed an interesting test managers can use to evaluate their delegation habits. (See Figure 11–3.)

## GUIDELINES FOR EFFECTIVE DELEGATION

The guidelines presented in the following sections can help ensure that authority is delegated properly.

Managers frequently grant insufficient authority over expenditures, personnel, physical resources, and so on. Subordinates often complain, "Senior management expects more from me than I can produce because my hands are tied. I simply don't have enough authority to achieve the goals they've set." Note that a manager cannot delegate authority he or she does not have. A supervisor in a department store, for example, cannot delegate authority to a subordinate if the supervisor does not already have the authority.

A long-standing concept in management is the **principle of parity of authority and responsibility**. It means that responsibility for results cannot be greater than the authority delegated. Conversely, responsibility should not be less than the authority delegated. Enough authority should always be delegated to achieve the desired result. Suppose a supervisor is assigned responsibility to produce 1,000 units of a product in an eight-hour shift. If the individual is not authorized to hire an adequate number of workers, it is clear that insufficient authority has been granted. Lyndall Urwick noted that "to hold a group or individual accountable for activities of any kind without assigning to him or them the necessary authority to discharge that responsibility is manifestly both unsatisfactory and inequitable. It is of great

**Grant Proper
Amount of
Authority**

# FIGURE 11–3

## Evaluating Delegation Habits

| | Strongly Agree | | | | Strongly Disagree |
|---|---|---|---|---|---|
| 1. I'd delegate more, but the jobs I delegate never seem to get done the way I want them to be done. | 5 | 4 | 3 | 2 | 1 |
| 2. I don't feel I have the time to delegate properly. | 5 | 4 | 3 | 2 | 1 |
| 3. I carefully check on subordinates' work without letting them know I'm doing it, so I can correct their mistakes if necessary before they cause too many problems. | 5 | 4 | 3 | 2 | 1 |
| 4. I delegate the whole job—giving the opportunity for the subordinate to complete it without any of my involvement. Then I review the end-result. | 5 | 4 | 3 | 2 | 1 |
| 5. When I have given clear instructions and the job isn't done right, I get upset. | 5 | 4 | 3 | 2 | 1 |
| 6. I feel the staff lacks the commitment that I have. So any job I delegate won't get done as well as I'd do it. | 5 | 4 | 3 | 2 | 1 |
| 7. I'd delegate more. But I feel I can do the task better than the person I might delegate it to. | 5 | 4 | 3 | 2 | 1 |
| 8. I'd delegate more. But if the individual I delegate the task to does an incompetent job, I'll be severely criticized. | 5 | 4 | 3 | 2 | 1 |
| 9. If I were to delegate the task, my job wouldn't be nearly as much fun. | 5 | 4 | 3 | 2 | 1 |
| 10. When I delegate a job, I often find that the outcome is such that I end up doing the job over again myself. | 5 | 4 | 3 | 2 | 1 |
| 11. I have not really found that delegation saves any time. | 5 | 4 | 3 | 2 | 1 |
| 12. I delegate a task clearly and concisely, explaining exactly how it should be accomplished. | 5 | 4 | 3 | 2 | 1 |
| 13. I can't delegate as much as I'd like to because my subordinates lack the necessary experience. | 5 | 4 | 3 | 2 | 1 |
| 14. I feel that when I delegate I lose control. | 5 | 4 | 3 | 2 | 1 |
| 15. I would delegate more but I'm pretty much a perfectionist. | 5 | 4 | 3 | 2 | 1 |
| 16. I work longer hours than I should. | 5 | 4 | 3 | 2 | 1 |
| 17. I can give subordinates the routine tasks, but I feel I must keep nonroutine tasks myself. | 5 | 4 | 3 | 2 | 1 |
| 18. My own boss expects me to keep very close to all details of the work. | 5 | 4 | 3 | 2 | 1 |

Total Score

Score Key:

| | |
|---|---|
| Ineffective delegation | 72– 90 |
| Delegation habits need much improvement | 54– 71 |
| Manager still has room to improve | 36– 53 |
| Superior delegation | 18– 35 |

Source: Reprinted, by permission of the publisher, from "How to Improve Delegation Habits" by Theodore J. Krein, p. 59, *Management Review*, May 1982. © 1982 by AMACOM, a division of American Management Associations, New York. All rights reserved.

importance to smooth working that at all levels authority and responsibility should be coterminous and coequal."[8]

At the other extreme too much authority is granted. This mistake can result in a manager's "running away" with the situation, to the detriment of the organization.

[8]Urwick, *Elements of Administration*, p. 46.

There are numerous cases in which managers are given too much authority over money and make improper investments and other expenditures.

Another helpful approach is for the delegator to make sure he or she has clearly defined the results expected. For example, suppose a manager tells a subordinate to "Straighten out that problem in the AA Department." This is a vague statement of the results expected; the manager will probably have difficulty determining how much authority to give the subordinate. If, on the other hand, the manager tells the subordinate to "Get the machines put in working order and add enough workers to reach an output of six units per hour," it is simpler to determine what authority the subordinate will need. If a manager defines precisely what is to be done, he or she is in a much better position to decide how much authority to delegate.

**Define the Results Expected**

Individuals differ greatly in their ability to handle problems, initiate action, attain objectives, and perform other management tasks. In delegating, it is important that the manager consider the experience, background, and intelligence of the person to whom authority is be assigned. Generally, the more able the individual, the more authority the person will be able to handle.

**Consider the Capabilities of the Subordinate**

The following are examples of questions that the delegator should ask formally or informally before granting authority to an individual: "To what degree is the individual qualified by experience, training, education, background, and psychological orientation to handle the work to be delegated?" "Do we have control procedures to ensure that the individual will not exceed the authority granted?" and "Do we have procedures for retracting authority if the manager does not perform as expected?"

However, allowances for mistakes should be made. Robert A. Beck, president of the Prudential Insurance Company of America, has observed, "We must assume, if we delegate properly, that people will make mistakes, that they will do things differently than we would, but they will also grow in their jobs and be better performers."[9]

If authority is not clearly explained, problems can develop. A branch manager of a bank, for example, needs to know the answers to such questions as "Do I have full authority over the hiring, termination, and transfer of personnel?"; "What limits are set on the amount of money I can spend without approval from my superior?"; and "Can I deviate from other branches in terms of advertising, sales promotion, and pricing?" The results of a failure to clearly delegate authority were seen in the section on ineffective delegation.

**Make Sure the Authority Is Clearly Stated**

Note that authority relationships should be clear not only to the subordinate in question but to all others concerned as well. "Who is in charge around here?" should be known to everyone involved in an activity. Frequently, few people in an organization know precisely who has the power to fulfill a request or deal with a

[9]Robert A. Beck, "Bob Beck Speaks Out on Company Goals, Objectives, Challenges," *The Courier*, November 1978, p. 5.

situation that has arisen. Sales representatives who visit a company are often "given the runaround" in their efforts to locate individuals within the organization who have authority to purchase. College students may have a difficult time finding out who has the authority to purchase. College students may have a difficult time finding out who has the authority to make a grade change, grant a special parking permit, approve an absence from class, permit the student to take an examination late, and so on. For delegation to be most effective, it is essential that all those concerned know where authority resides.

## Modify the Authority Whenever Necessary

Managers should maintain a flexible attitude about what kind of and how much authority to delegate. Because of changes in the external environment (new laws, competitive pressures, changes in demand, economic conditions, and so forth), authority relationships may need to be altered. An organization is composed of people, and people and the circumstances surrounding them change frequently.

Some managers may require more authority than was originally delegated, either because they need it to achieve their goals or because they have proved that they can handle it. In other cases it may be wise to reduce a manager's authority because he or she is not using it properly. Authority is always revocable or subject to modification: It can always be taken back, increased, decreased, or otherwise changed by the person who granted it in the first place.

## Follow Unity of Command and Chain of Command

The unity-of-command principle should be followed in delegation. Ideally, authority should be delegated so that each individual reports to only one superior. Doing so often is not possible because of the need for staff specialists, who frequently are given functional authority. Nevertheless, a continuing goal of managers is to keep the number of persons an individual reports to as low as is practical. Simplicity of relationships is a characteristic of good organization.

Also important to follow in delegating authority is the chain-of-command, or the chain of authority from the highest manager to all subordinates at all levels. It is important for each person in an organization to know the source of authority delegated to him or her. Each manager at all levels should know what decisions should be made by him or her and what decisions must be passed upward to a superior. Therefore managers should understand the chain of command and follow it upwards and downwards. When it is violated, the working authority of a manager is endangered. For example, assume there are three managers in the chain; A, the top manager; B, the middle manager; and C, the first-level manager. If A bypasses B and delegates authority directly to C, the future authority of B to delegate authority to C may be questioned by C.

## Develop a Willingness to Delegate

Without delegation no organization can function well, and some of the largest obstacles to effective delegation are psychological. Lack of the courage to delegate properly and of the knowledge of how to do it is one of the most general causes of failure in organizations.

Many managers are afraid to delegate authority because they fear the subordinate in question will not perform satisfactorily and thus will make them look bad.

Such managers reason that the person being considered is too old, is too young, lacks experience, will not be accepted by the group supervised, or for some other reason will not perform as needed. Thomas W. Zimmerer has expressed the problem this way.

> Delegation involves taking risk; but to some degree, all management means taking risks. The executive who believes that by acting alone he can eliminate error is simply not working in the world of reality. The key to successful delegation is minimizing risk by delegating to the right persons.
>
> Failure to delegate is a trait often found in a manager who can't trust other employees to do their jobs. This manager frequently feels very insecure in his relationship with subordinates. He manifests this insecurity by attempting to do everyone's job to ensure that it is "done right."[10]

Consider also Mooney and Reiley's analysis of the failure to delegate:

> One of the tragedies of business experience is the frequency with which men, always efficient in anything they personally can do, will finally be crushed and fail under the weight of accumulated duties that they do not know and cannot learn how to delegate. Whether this condition is due to egotism which manifests itself in a distrust of the relative capacity of others, or to a training which has always been confined to a narrow horizon, and has thus destroyed the capacity to envisage great undertakings, the effect is always the same. Under such conditions growth through delegation is absolutely prevented by the character of the leadership.[11]

Certainly, authority should not be granted to those obviously unfit to carry it out. But managers must recognize that subordinates can learn from mistakes if properly coached. And much of a manager's role, even at the highest levels, is coaching. Also, if controls are placed on the authority delegated, the mistakes made by the person who is given the authority will not be critical.

A second kind of psychological problem that interferes with delegation is fear of being outshone. One can only guess at the number of promising subordinates who are denied more power because managers are afraid the subordinates will outperform them. A manager may think, "Sara is strong, competent, and aggressive. If I give her more authority, she may look *too* good, and my boss will replace me with her."

Two observations are in order in dealing with fear of subordinates. First, an effective organization is never built by holding good people back. Typically, managers make points for themselves by granting appropriate authority to able people. Second, an old maxim in management states, "Managers are judged not by what they do but by what they cause others to do." Since managers are evaluated on overall results, wise managers want their people to perform well because that reflects favorably on them.

**SUMMARY**

- Delegation of authority is inherent in the organizing process. The greater the authority delegated, the more decentralized the organization becomes. Conversely,

[10]Zimmerer, "How to Reduce Dependence on the Boss," p. 55.
[11]Mooney and Reiley, *Onward Industry*, (New York: Harper & Brothers, 1931), p. 39.

the more authority retained by higher-level managers, the more centralized the organization is said to be.

* Delegation is essential to obtain prompt action, enables managers to perform higher-level work, provides training for new and lower-level managers, can result in better decisions, and improves morale.
* The degree of authority delegated to lower-level managers depends on the importance of the decision, the organization's size, the management style and philosophy, the availability of capable managers, the dynamics of the enterprise, and the type of organization.
* Although, in delegating authority, a manager may become dependent on his or her subordinates, the manager can use authority effectively if certain guidelines are followed.
* The main guidelines for effective delegation are to grant the proper amount of authority, define the results expected, consider the capabilities of the subordinate, make sure the authority is clearly stated, modify the authority when necessary, follow unity of command and chain of command, and develop a willingness to delegate.

**LEARN
THE LANGUAGE
OF
MANAGEMENT**

delegation of authority
decentralized organization
centralized organization

multinational
principle of parity of authority
  and responsibility

**QUESTIONS
FOR REVIEW
AND
DISCUSSION**

1. What is delegation? Why is it essential in the organizing process?
2. How does effective delegation help to obtain prompt action? Enable managers to perform higher-level work? Help in training lower-level managers?
3. Explain why the highest-level manager may not always be the best-qualified person to make decisions.
4. How can proper delegation improve morale?
5. Cite an example of ineffective delegation you observed recently, explain why it was ineffective, and describe how you would correct the problem.
6. How is the degree of authority that should be delegated affected by the importance of the decision? The size of the organization? The manager's style and philosophy? The availability of capable managers? The dynamics of the organization? The type of organization?
7. Explain each of the major guidelines that should be followed to ensure effective delegation.

**MAKING
MANAGEMENT
DECISIONS**

**1. Personal experiences with ineffective delegation**

Recall a situation in which you were delegated authority for some activity—perhaps at work, in the military, or in a social organization.

In report form describe the situation and then evaluate how effectively the authority was delegated. (Refer to the guidelines for effective delegation discussed in this chapter in making your analysis.) What did the person delegating the authority do right and do wrong? How could the delegation have been improved?

### 2. How can Elaine be convinced she's qualified?

Robert Johnson is a middle manager in a computer software company. John Troboff, one of his first-level supervisors, has announced his resignation, effective in two weeks. Robert, in following company policy of promotion from within, examines the records of nine people who had reported to Troboff and concludes that Elaine Wilson, age twenty-five, is the best-qualified person to be promoted to replace Troboff.

Robert meets with Elaine and tells her what he feels is good news—that's she's the new manager. He is surprised when she declines the job.

"I really appreciate the opportunity," she says, "but I'm afraid it's not for me."

"Why?" asks Robert. "You know the job well, you're very intelligent, and the other people in the department seem to respect you."

"Thanks again, Robert, but I don't think I'm right for the supervisor's job. You see," Elaine continues, "I've never worked in management before. I don't think I could exercise authority over other people. And I wouldn't feel comfortable making work assignments, checking the programs before they're released to the client, handling disagreements, and doing the other things I've watched John do. I've been with the group for two years—those people are my friends, and I don't see how I could give orders to people I like."

Robert still feels Elaine is the best-qualified person for the promotion. What would you recommend that he do to convince her that she can handle the additional authority and should accept the promotion?

Often a person in a peer group who accepts a promotion to manage the peers is considered a "traitor." If Elaine does accept the job of supervising her former peers, can she perform the supervisory tasks and still retain their friendship? Why or why not?

### 3. Why John Wilkes quit as head coach of an NFL franchise

Two years ago John Wilkes was named head coach of the Blockbusters, an NFL franchise. Considered one of the best coaches in the league, John won seventy percent of his games during his two seasons coaching the Blockbusters. Despite a good win-loss record, John decides to quit at the end of the second season.

When a close personal friend and coach of another NFL team asks John why he resigned, John replies: "I quit because I couldn't call all the shots. Big Red Thompson [the franchise owner] required me to let him make the final decision on all new players we recruited. Every game plan had to be approved by him. Big Red even insisted on calling some key plays. And on several occasions he even decided which quarterback I'd use. Frankly, if I can't call the shots, I don't want to coach the Blockbusters. Had Big Red stayed in the front office, I think I'd have won two, maybe three, more games last season."

Does Big Red have the right to make decisions on how a game should be played?

What delegation mistakes do you see in Big Red's approach to managing?

**FOR ADDITIONAL CONCEPTS AND IDEAS**

Aharoni, Yair. "Toward an Age of Humility." *California Management Review*, Winter 1981, pp. 49–59.

Barnes, Louis B. "Managing the Paradox of Organizational Trust." *Harvard Business Review*, March–April, 1981, pp. 107–116.

Bartolome, Fernando, and Evans, Paul A. Lee. "Must Success Cost So Much?" *Harvard Business Review*, March–April 1980, pp. 137–148.

Brown, Arnold. "The Eroding Power of the CEO." *Business Horizons*, April 1980, pp. 7–10.

Gabarro, John J., and Kotter, John P. "Managing Your Boss." *Harvard Business Review*, January–February 1980, pp. 92–100.

Gordon, Scott. "Equality." *Business Horizons*, July–August 1982, pp. 73–77.

Hatano, Daryl F. "Employee Rights and Corporate Restrictions: A Balancing of Liberties." *California Management Review*, Winter 1981, pp. 5–13.

Litzinger, William, and Schaefer, Thomas. "Leadership Through Followership." *Business Horizons*, September–October 1982, pp. 78–81.

Pearce, John A. II. "An Assessment of Supervisors' Organizational Loyalty." *MSU Business Topics*, Summer 1977, pp. 50–56.

Sasser, W. Earl, Jr., and Leonard, Frank S. "Let First-Level Supervisors Do Their Job." *Harvard Business Review*, March–April 1980, pp. 113–121.

Schleh, E. C. "Handing Off to Subordinates: Delegation for Gain." *Management Review*, May 1978, pp. 143–147.

Shin, Bon Gon, and Zashin, Elliot. "Management and the New Egalitarianism: McGuire Revisited." *California Management Review*, Summer 1982, pp. 5–13.

Zaphiropoulos, Renn. "It's Not Lonely Upstairs." *Harvard Business Review*, November–December 1980, pp. 111–132.

# 12 GROUP DYNAMICS AND COMMITTEES

**STUDY THIS CHAPTER SO YOU CAN:**

- Explain why people form groups.
- Discuss the four elements of group dynamics described in the text—conformity, aggression, competition, and cooperation—and describe management's interest in each of them.
- Distinguish formal from informal groups, and state the reasons that informal groups exist.
- Discuss the relationship between management and groups.
- Describe the nature of committees, their advantages and disadvantages, and their use in government.
- Explain the characteristics and responsibilities of boards of directors.
- Discuss the reasons that some organizations use plural executives.
- Describe the guidelines for maximizing the effectiveness of committees.

As explained earlier, an organization can be defined as a group of people working toward common goals. Within organizations, there are two subgroups. **Formal groups** are created by management and make up the organization as a whole. Examples of formal groups are divisions, departments, units, work teams, and committees. On the other hand are **informal groups**, which are created by the members themselves. Examples of informal groups are people who regularly bowl together, hold gripe sessions, and meet to share ideas.

Formal and informal groups and their relationship to managing will be discussed in detail later in this chapter. First, however, it is important to understand why people form groups, the interactions among them once they are in groups, and the effects of these interactions on managing.

## WHY DO PEOPLE FORM GROUPS?

**Social psychologists**, people who study human beings in a group context, have explained that there are several reasons that people form groups. First, people live and work together because of an *inborn propensity to do so*. It is impossible to determine precisely the role that inborn drive plays in group formation, since children cannot be raised in total isolation in order to study their behavior later. However, most social psychologists believe that humans are born with a tendency to seek out and congregate with other humans.

Second, *people gather together to survive.* Babies, for example, are virtually helpless for several years. If they were not part of a group, they would die. A mature, healthy human can conceivably survive physically without contact with other humans. Perhaps the most universal characteristic of humans is the tendency to be gregarious. Most of us find being alone for extended periods of time detrimental to our emotional survival. In fact, solitary confinement is a severe form of punishment.

A third reason people join together is that *they have learned to become interdependent.* Even if we could survive alone, we have been taught to depend on others for help. For instance, we increasingly engage in work specialization because we have learned that we can satisfy our wants and desires more easily by performing only a few tasks and depending on others for the remainder.

## WHAT IS GROUP DYNAMICS?

Since managers give direction to groups of people, it is important that they understand **group dynamics**, or the interactions of people in a group setting. Social psychology has given us much understanding of this field. In the following sections some areas of social psychology—conformity, aggression, competition, and cooperation—and their relationship to managing are discussed.

Conformity    Human beings and their behavior are amazingly diverse. From culture to culture, religions, languages, political philosophies, sexual habits, business practices, communication techniques, ways of making friends, and many other behaviors vary. But within any given culture (and to an even greater extent within a subculture), there is considerable agreement. Most people in the United States, for example, eat hamburgers, endorse a capitalistic economic philosophy, drive cars, watch television, and use telephones.

Compliance with existing rules or customs is called **conformity**. Reporting to work on time, wearing "acceptable" clothing, and saying "thank you" in return for a favor are examples of conformity.

### Group-Imposed Expectations

All kinds of groups make three demands on their members: to obey the norms established for individual behavior, to accept group-created sanctions, and to give up certain rights.

*To obey the norms of the group.* Over time, all groups develop **norms**, or behavioral standards, that members are expected to meet. A work group norm might be to produce no more than a certain number of units per shift, and a norm of a lodge might be to keep information about the organization secret from nonmembers.

*To accept sanctions.* Over time, groups also develop **sanctions**, or forms of punishment, to deal with members who do not obey the norms. Some sanctions are physical; however, most group sanctions are psychological. A work crew member who produces more than the group feels he or she should may be ignored at break periods and given a cold shoulder after work. Or an employee who sides with the manager when the rest of the group is opposed may be sanctioned by being publicly embarrassed by the group or by being dismissed from the group.

*To give up rights.* All groups require that members forfeit certain rights. A group expects its members to subordinate personal desires in support of group objectives. A striking employee may not want to walk a picket line, but if the union group requires it, the employee is expected to comply. Or a member of a group may not want to make a contribution for a certain cause but will to avoid some form of sanction.

### Why Do People Conform?

Social psychologists do not agree that the need to conform is inborn. But they do agree that people can be—and obviously are—taught to conform. Three reasons that people conform are fear, insecurity, and good judgment.

*Fear.* Groups sanction members who do not conform to norms. Since most of us fear punishment in any of its many forms, we generally conform and obey the rules and customs imposed on us by organizations. We try to pay our taxes on time because we want to avoid a penalty. We generally obey work rules because we know that if we don't, we will be disciplined, perhaps even fired. Because of fear, we often conform when we don't want to.

*Insecurity.* Through sanctions, a group can exert much pressure to conform. The more insecure an individual is, the more he or she will succumb to this pressure and conform. For example, if Sally feels inferior to her group, she is not likely to dress differently or have habits or attitudes divergent from those of the group because the group may laugh at or make unkind remarks about her. Followers in any situation conform to instructions from their group leader to the degree that they feel the instructions are reasonable. Even if the leader's instructions seem unreasonable, followers may conform to the instructions because they feel inadequate to withstand the group's pressure to conform.

*Good judgment.* Sometimes people conform because they have learned that doing so produces the best results in certain situations. Typically, we will conform and accept our superior's suggestion about handling a difficult situation because we assume that he or she knows more about the problem than we do. Learning about company procedures when first employed by a company is also an example of conformity based on good judgment. Most of the time we conform and speak the common language because, in that way, people will understand us.

### Management's Interest in Conformity

To have organizations, some conformity to group-dictated behavior is needed so that activities are performed in a manner to achieve organizational goals. However, if there were total conformity, innovation would cease and the organization would suffer from total rigidity. Therefore, managers of formal groups must decide how much conformity should be required to best achieve organizational goals.

*How much conformity is desirable?* The extent to which conformity is necessary depends on several factors. One is the type of organization. Different organizations require different degrees of conformity. Because of a tradition that calls for the exercise of less authority, universities intentionally require relatively little conformity compared with other major institutions, such as military and industrial organizations.

Another factor that determines how much conformity is required is the person's level in the organization. Generally, the higher one rises in any type of organization, the less one is required to conform. Workers at the operative level in a factory are expected to conform to more rigid rules governing working hours than senior executives are.

Two reasons explain why less conformity is required as one progresses upward in an organization. First, freedom is generally granted in organizations in proportion to one's demonstrated intelligence and ability to act responsibly. A senior executive, promoted from the lower levels of an organization, has demonstrated both intelligence and responsibility; therefore, he or she is required to conform less.

Second, while conformity is necessary to the organization's everyday operations, it does not, as noted, result in the creativity, innovations, and new ideas needed to improve an organization. These qualities are needed at the top of an organization. Here lies a common organizational problem: Most people have been strongly indoctrinated with the need to conform in the family, schools, religious organizations, the military, and lower levels in the organizational world. As a result, relatively few individuals are able to think original thoughts, develop new concepts, and create plans.

In an activity involving cooperation, the contributions made by each individual are often difficult to identify. If ten people assemble a television set, it is impossible to determine the exact value added by each person. But when people compete, as in a sales contest or in an auto race, individual interests dominate.

In organized activities cooperation and competition are simultaneously involved. Production employees are expected to cooperate fully so that the end product can compete successfully with goods made by another company. Departments within an organization must cooperate so that the organization itself can compete with other organizations.

### Management's Interest in Cooperation

Managers must concern themselves with cooperation both among organizations and within one organization. **External cooperation** occurs when different organizations work together for mutual benefit. Surprisingly, managers of organizations that directly compete with one another also must cooperate in some situations. Consider these examples: College athletic directors cooperate in making rules that govern competitive sports and then compete for victories playing under the rules adopted; nations cooperate in making treaties and other agreements; competitive businesses cooperate with one another to encourage the passage or defeat of certain legislation that would affect them all.

Some forms of external cooperation are illegal. For example, cooperation among businesses in setting prices, dividing up the market, or trying to prevent entry of a new business into the market is called **collusion** and is unlawful.

All managers seek enthusiastic and willing **internal cooperation**—that is, cooperation between individuals and groups of individuals within an organization—because it is essential for an organization's survival. If individuals in an organization refused to cooperate with others, there would be no organization and no group goals would be achieved.

Because internal cooperation often requires an individual to do something that he or she would rather not do, it is seldom easy to achieve. Therefore managers must communicate an important management concept: "The interests of an organization as a whole take precedence over the interests of the individual." For example, a manager may ask an employee to work overtime, a midnight shift, or on weekends; to do extra work because another employee is absent; to accept an undesirable transfer; or to give up a personal view and accept the authority of higher-level management. The employee may not like the change but, for the welfare of the organization, will accept it. If not, he or she may exercise an option to terminate or be terminated. It is very common in organized life to hear managers make such comments as "We had to let him go—he just couldn't get along with his co-workers," "She insisted on doing everything her way, so it just didn't work out," and "He had plenty of ability and energy, but he was constantly trying to undermine the efforts of others—he just wasn't supportive."

## FORMAL AND INFORMAL GROUPS

Structured organizations consist of two kinds of groups. One is the formal group, which is created by management. A formal group has several prescribed charac-

# MANAGERS IN ACTION

## SHOULD MANAGERS ENCOURAGE STUDY CIRCLES?

Study circles are widely used in North European countries and now are found in some United States firms. Study circles are sometimes confused with quality circles. **Quality circles** are groups of employees who meet frequently with management to seek solutions to production, quality, and performance problems. Whereas, **study circles** are groups of employees that concentrate on employees' social, psychological, and educational needs, as well as what is expected of them by their employer.

Typically, a study circle:

- Is organized democratically with all participants deciding what will be discussed.
- Concentrates on the needs and interests of its members.
- Is unstructured and lacks an authority figure.
- Has no instructors.
- Shares the experience and the knowledge of the group's members.

De Ridder, an American company that employs 1,200 people, is one of the first firms to experiment extensively with study circles. De Ridder has assigned a member of its personnel department to work full-time to coordinate the activities of the study circles. Some of the results of study circles at De Ridder include:

- Discovery of new ways to evaluate jobs
- Modification in the employee-evaluation system
- Development of an incentive program to reward employees for cost-saving ideas and/or increases in productivity

In Sweden, study circles are used extensively and successfully. Some of the Swedish accomplishments with study circles include:

- Development of greater cooperation between managers and secretaries
- Improvement in delegation and team spirit
- Breakdown of traditional authoritative management styles
- Encouragement of greater initiative
- Simplification of organizational structure

Source: Reprinted, by permission of the publisher, from "Should Managers Encourage Study Circles?" by Karen Quallo Osborne and Renee Scialdo Shevat, pp. 37–42, *Management Review*, June 1982 © 1982 by AMA Membership Publications Division, American Management Associations, New York. All rights reserved.

### QUESTIONS

1. If a firm adopts the study circle concept, should employees be allowed to meet on company time? Why or why not?
2. Should management retain authority to accept or reject recommendations of study circles? Why or why not?
3. "Some critics of study circles argue the concept cannot work in the United States because American companies lack the understanding and trust that exists between management and labor in Scandinavia, Japan, and other countries where employee participation groups flourish."[1] Do you agree? Why or why not?

[1]Ibid.

teristics: It has a designated or appointed leader, a specific mission or assignment, imposed rules, specified performance standards, and known rewards and punishments. A committee is an example of a formal group. It has a chairperson, a reason or purpose for existing, rules to follow in performing its mission, certain standards to follow, and some kind of incentive. Specific formal groups—the committee, the board of directors, and the plural executive—will be discussed later in this chapter.

Within all structured organizations there also exist informal, nonstructured groups. An informal group is created by the members of the group. It consists of two or more people who usually work together, often in close proximity. In contrast to a formal group, an informal group selects its own leader, develops its own rules, sets its own performance or behavioral standards, and establishes peer sanctions and rewards.

Among people in an informal group there typically exist two elements: mutual trust and mutual interests. Members of an informal group have confidence in other members' ability to keep information to themselves and not pass it along to outsiders, who may not keep the information secret. The second element, mutual interests, results because members of an informal group belong to the same organization.

Three reasons explain why informal groups exist: transmission of information, fear, and amusement.

### Transmission of Information

Managers differ with respect to what information they feel should be disseminated through official channels and how quickly it should be sent. At one extreme, some managers tend to be highly secretive—the "don't mention this to anyone" type—and are discriminating and slow in passing along information. At the other extreme, some managers don't try to keep many matters confidential and release news quickly. In either case, few decisions can be kept from the informal group in most organizations for very long. Information about changes in personnel, production schedules, policies, work assignments, and so on is communicated quickly.

The term **grapevine** has come to mean the communications channel used by informal groups. The grapevine is informal and unstructured. Information is moved through the informal organization via conversation at coffee breaks, during rest periods, after hours, or at any other time it is convenient for one member to tell another, "Let me tell you the latest."

The most important aspect of grapevine communication is that the information being passed is not followed up with documentation. Grapevine information is based on hearsay, and there is always the strong possibility that it has been subjected to subtle changes due to misunderstandings or poor judgment during the communication process. Consequently, grapevine communication often results in the transmission of inaccurate information.

### Fear

The informal group also exists because people generally fear what they don't know. Members of an informal group are eager to learn information, factual or nonfactual, about decisions that may affect their status, security, compensation, or working conditions. By having this information, they may be able to protect themselves from some action that they think would adversely affect the group. For example, news of a speedup in production or a decision to lay off personnel may be perceived as a possible threat to personal security. Members of the informal group may be able to thwart management's decisions by taking such informal actions as, respectively, calling in sick or performing better so they won't be released.

### Amusement

An informal group is the way most gossip is transmitted. And many people find pleasure in knowing about the personal affairs of managers, the blunders other people make in their jobs, the jockeying some people engage in to win promotions or acquire more power, and the generally petty things that make up much of life. People also find amusement in informal groups through mutual interests. They may bowl together, enjoy talking together about books they have read, or share recipes.

Management
and Groups

Although informal groups are not created by management and therefore their leaders may or may not be known to management, managers should be aware that they exist. Furthermore, managers should try to use them to advantage and not try to stifle them for this reason: Informal groups cannot be eliminated. They will exist despite the efforts that managers in the formal organization may take to eliminate them. Experienced managers reason, "Informal groups exist. Let's help them pass along information that benefits the organization and effectively work with them so that organizational goals can be reached."

# COMMITTEES

A **committee** is a group of persons asked to consider, investigate, or act on some matter. Usually the committee also reports on the matter. Committees may be known by a variety of other names, such as "task force," "council," "board," "agency," or "commission."

The use of committees as a formal group is as old as the ancient tribal council. A large part of the work of managing is delegated to committees. Usually, service on a committee is only part of an individual's responsibility, and a person may serve on several committees simultaneously.

Characteristics of
Committees

The size of committees varies, ranging from two persons to many. On occasion, the Congress of the United States functions as a "committee of the whole," with all members organized as one committee. Most committees, however, have from five to twenty-five members.

Committees are found at all levels in the organization. Senior executives often form committees to decide such matters as plant expansion or new product development. Operative employees frequently form committees to make decisions about union matters.

Some committees, called **standing committees**, are permanent, such as the Ways and Means Committee in the House of Representatives. Others, called **ad** hoc committees, are formed for a specific purpose and are temporary. An advisory committee established to deal with a specific disciplinary problem is an ad hoc committee. Normally an ad hoc committee is dissolved after its recommendations have been submitted.

Most committees are created because managers feel they are needed to perform some useful purpose. However, some committees—such as corporate boards of directors—are required by law. The courts use juries, an ad hoc form of legally required committee, to decide certain issues. Many committees at various levels of government are also required by law.

Service on committees is often resisted. Many people view committee work as excessively time-consuming and question whether committees are a good way to develop recommendations for solving problems. Why, then, are they used so extensively?

### Committees Provide More Information for Decision Making

An individual rarely has full knowledge about a given subject. Therefore, at least in theory, two or more heads are better than one. The committee system is an excellent way to bring together individuals with different experiences and view-points. It is a means for pooling the talents of experts.

Chain supermarkets usually have new-product committees that decide whether or not a proposed product will be marketed through the chain. The rationale for such a committee is that a variety of viewpoints from individuals with expertise in marketing, distribution, advertising, packaging, and pricing are helpful in reaching the "best" decision.

### Committees Distribute Authority

Some committees are formed because the individuals involved do not wish to concentrate a large amount of authority in a single person. A prominent example is the military. While all military authority in our nation ultimately rests with one person, the president, most of the recommendations on how that authority is to be exercised are made by committees such as the National Security Council, not individuals. The rationale for such committees is the belief that security matters are too important to involve recommendations from only one individual.

### Committees Facilitate Coordination

An organization's various activities and functions can be better harmonized through the use of committees. For example, supervisors in a manufacturing plant may meet at regular intervals to coordinate activities and develop a production schedule. Or a chamber of commerce may hold a meeting of all committee chairpersons (thus forming a new committee) to coordinate the various programs and projects.

### Committees Foster Support for Decisions

Frequently, decisions are criticized or disliked by individuals who had no part in making them. But committees give employees an opportunity to participate in the decision-making process and therefore help develop support for the decisions that result. A manager is much more likely to support a decision if given an opportunity to present viewpoints about it than if the decision is simply imposed. Participation in the decision-making process through committees is especially important in situations in which the individuals involved will be directly affected by the decision. For instance, a research director in a manufacturing firm may not understand why the company cannot spend more money on certain projects. If this person is appointed to the budget committee, where full financial facts are available, he or she may come to understand why some new projects must wait.

### Committees Can Broaden the Knowledge of the People Who Participate

Committees can be used to inform individuals about the organization's problems, policies, and needs. Younger managers are often placed on committees not because they are expected to make significant contributions, but rather because they will be exposed to the thinking of more experienced persons. "Put Brenda on a committee and she'll gain a better understanding of how things function around here" is often a wise management decision.

Committees have certain limitations: They are expensive, often act slowly, may result in compromise solutions, and do not fix responsibility.

### Committees Are Expensive

Several people working together on one problem will cost the organization more money than if one person was working on it. A commmittee composed of nine individuals with an average income of \$50,000 per year (equivalent to \$20 per hour) would cost \$180 per hour to operate (9 × \$20). If a single executive took one hour to make the decision, only \$20 in executive time would be required. Meanwhile, the other eight executives could devote their time to other activities.

The actual time spent in a committee meeting is usually only part of the total cost. Committee members must often spend considerable time preparing for the meeting and may be required to travel extensively to attend it. If the work of the committee is considered highly important, staff persons such as researchers or typists may be required, thereby adding further to the total cost. Publication of committee reports and rental of meeting facilities are examples of still other costs that may be associated with the use of committees.

### Committees Often Act Slowly

Generally, an individual can make a decision much more quickly than a group of people. Unless guided properly, a committee organized to select a new store location may discuss extraneous issues (who is being promoted and transferred in other departments), bring up irrelevant personal matters (vacation plans), and in other ways get off the main track. And, under the usual committee procedure, all members are given the right to speak and comment on any issue. This can be very time-consuming. In many instances one or two committee members so greatly enjoy hearing themselves talk that they monopolize committee time.

### Committees May Result in Compromise Solutions

A **compromise** is an adjustment or settlement of a difference by mutual relinquishment of preferences or position. Assume that four persons (A, B, C, and D) are appointed to select a person for a key job. Assume further that three people are being considered—Smith, Brown, and Jones. Committee members A and B are solidly behind Smith, while C and D strongly endorse Brown. In this situation the committee may end up compromising and select Jones, who may not be as well qualified as either Smith or Brown.

### Committees Do Not Fix Responsibility

With the committee system, the responsibility for a decision or a recommendation that is made by the committee cannot be fixed on one individual. Individuals acting as a committee may reach decisions that they would not reach independently. For example, Tim Johnson, a timid, sympathetic person by nature, may be unable to recommend personally an unpleasant action, such as dismissing an employee, disciplining an individual, or canceling a project. But as a member of a committee, Tim may have less reluctance to help make a decision that will have negative results. Similarly, members of a jury may be hesitant individually to send some person to prison for life, but the same members collectively may reach that decision.

It is popular to downplay the importance of committees. Remarks such as "If you want to make certain nothing is done, assign it to a committee" are common. For reasons already noted, committees may be ineffective. Nevertheless, some of the most important decisions affecting our lives are made by groups of people organized as formal committees in the three branches of the federal government. State and local governments also use the committee method to develop, pass, and enforce legislation. Of all institutions in society, committees find their widest and most important use in government.

### Use of Committees in Congress

The U.S. Senate and House of Representatives make extensive use of committees. The House has twenty-two standing committees, and there are more than thirty joint Senate and House committees. Many of these committees have broad responsibilities. The Senate Foreign Relations Committee has jurisdiction over relations with foreign nations generally, treaties, boundary lines between the United States and foreign nations, protection of American citizens abroad and expatriation, neutrality, international conferences and congresses, the American National Red Cross, interventions and declarations of war, diplomatic service, land and buildings for embassies and legations in foreign countries, commercial intercourse to safeguard American business interests abroad, U.S. and international financial and monetary organizations, and foreign loans.

Congress is also empowered to establish ad hoc committees to study special issues or problems. Possibly the most famous ad hoc committee in our history was the committee that carried out the Watergate investigations.

### Use of Committees in the Executive Branch

The executive branch of the federal government also makes wide use of the committee system, with more than ten committees reporting to the president. These include the Domestic Council, the Office of Telecommunications Policy, and the Federal Property Council. These committees are only advisory to the president and are not empowered to set policies, although many of their recommendations are adopted.

### Use of Committees in the Judicial Branch

The judicial branch of government is organized by the court system, and courts are a special form of committee. The Supreme Court of the United States consists of nine justices and is the leading federal court. In addition, there are Judicial Circuit Courts of Appeals, District Courts, and special courts, such as the United States Tax Court and the United States Customs Court.

A **jury** is a body of people selected according to law and sworn to give a decision upon some matter submitted to it. Thus, juries are legally required committees.

## BOARDS OF DIRECTORS

A corporation is considered an "artificial person" under the law. Since artificial people cannot perform human functions, real people (that is, corporate directors) are held accountable for the activities of the corporation. Corporations are required by the state laws under which they are organized to establish and maintain boards of directors. A **board of directors** is the supreme governing body of a corporation. The highest ranking officer of a corporation is directly responsible to and serves at the pleasure of the board of directors. A corporate board of directors is a legally required committee.

*Characteristics
and Composition of
Boards of Directors*

The size of boards of directors varies. Small corporations may have boards with only three to five members, while large corporations may have boards with twenty-five or more members. But in all corporations, regardless of size, the directors are elected by the **shareholders**, who are the owners of the company.

In most profit-seeking corporations, owners of substantial portions of the company stock serve on the board. These owners, quite understandably, want to influence company policy because their personal interests relate to the success of the organization. Control of corporations is sometimes achieved by individuals who purchase enough stock—and thereby gain enough votes—to elect a majority of the directors to the board.

In many small corporations, the largest shareholder usually serves as the chairperson, and other shareholders, friends of the owner, and members of the owner's family are elected to serve on the board. All that is looked for in making such appointments is convenience. Typically, no advice or other service is sought. Only legally required duties are performed by these people. (Specific legal duties of boards are discussed later in this chapter.)

"Outsiders" outnumber "insiders" on the boards of large companies. *Fortune* magazine studied the 5,995 directors of the 500 largest corporations and found that 57.3 percent were not employed by the companies they directed (see Figure 12–1).[1] This is a new trend in board composition and has occurred largely because of the growing recognition that outside viewpoints are helpful in corporate management.

In theory, the board of directors is expected to hold managers accountable for the results of the enterprise. In practice, however, the composition of the board of directors may in effect protect existing managers from criticism. Certainly, if the board is staffed only with "friendly" people such as key employees of the enterprise, the firm's banker, and perhaps a supplier or key customer, then objectivity may be lacking. One idea for correcting this problem is to allow only one company employee, the *chief executive officer*, to serve on the board and to select the remainder from outside the organization. Another idea for developing a more balanced board of directors, discussed in the Issue for Debate in this chapter, is to permit nonmanagement employees to serve on it.

Corporate boards meet more often than is generally supposed. According to the *Fortune* study, 70 percent of the boards studied meet at least five times per year, and many meet from ten to twelve times per year. Compensation paid directors varies, but a number of the directors in the study are paid $1,000 per day.

Regardless of the size and composition of a board of directors, the board must always meet certain legal responsibilities. The principle ones are noted in the following sections.

**Legal Responsibilities of Boards of Directors**

### Obey the Provisions of the Corporate Charter

A corporation must obtain a charter from the secretary of state of the state in which it is incorporated. The charter prescribes what the corporation's board of directors can and cannot do. The board is prohibited from certain actions, such as dissolving the corporation, merging it with another corporation, and selling it. These decisions must be made by shareholders. This is an academic matter, of course, when the directors are also the shareholders. But if the corporation engages in activities that are not authorized by its charter or engages in illegal activities, the directors are held responsible.

### Avoid Conflicts of Interest

In 1914 the Clayton Act, a law intended to combat the growth of monopolies and their negative effects on the economy, was enacted. Prior to the passage of this act it was common for individuals to serve on the boards of directly competing companies for the apparent purposes of fixing prices at an artificially high level, fixing wages at an unreasonably low level, or keeping potential new competitors out of the market. The Federal Trade Commission continues to watch for these **interlocking directorships**, as they are called, and has held that an individual cannot serve simultaneously on the boards of companies that are even in partial competition with each other.

[1]See Lee Smith, "The Boardroom Is Becoming a Different Scene," *Fortune*, May 8, 1978, p. 150.

**FIGURE 12-1**

**Composition of Boards of Directors of 500 Large Companies**

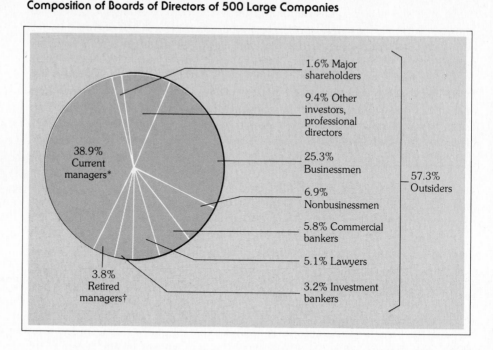

1.6% Major shareholders

9.4% Other investors, professional directors

38.9% Current managers*

25.3% Businessmen

6.9% Nonbusinessmen

5.8% Commercial bankers

5.1% Lawyers

3.2% Investment bankers

3.8% Retired managers†

57.3% Outsiders

Directors of corporations whose shares are registered for trading on a stock exchange also must conform to a number of federal laws. Directors are required to report, for example, any important change in the company that may significantly affect the value of the stock. Directors are also prohibited from manipulating stock prices by distributing false or misleading information to the stock-buying public.

### Exercise Reasonably Good Judgment

"Reasonably good judgment" is a qualitative term that is not subject to precise definition. Generally, however, directors are required to manage the affairs of the corporation prudently. They are expected to be fully informed about the affairs of the corporation and can be held responsible to shareholders for costly mistakes made through extreme carelessness.

**Other Responsibilities of Boards of Directors**

The corporate charter and **bylaws** (regulations governing an enterprise) spell out the specific responsibilities of the directors. Generally, these are the following.

### Elect Corporate Officers

The board of directors has authority to appoint all officers of the corporation. In practice, the board generally appoints only the president or chief executive officer and delegates to him or her the authority to appoint the other officers. Election of the president or CEO is an extremely important duty, for this individual will act as operating head of the enterprise and will have an enormous influence on

# ISSUE FOR DEBATE

## SHOULD NONMANAGERS BE REPRESENTED ON BOARDS OF DIRECTORS?

*Mitbestimmung*, which roughly means "codetermination" or "comanagement," is the practice of having nonmanagers on a board of directors. In many European nations, laws have been passed requiring large employers to let nonmanagers serve on the boards. In West Germany at least one-third of a board's members must be nonmanagers. The Netherlands, Austria, Denmark, Norway, and Sweden have also passed comanagement laws, but the United States has not. Below some pros and cons of *mitbestimmung* are examined.

### YES

**Nonmanagers should be represented on boards of directors because . . .**

Nonmanagers deserve a voice in management because it is their work, to a large degree, that determines how successful the company will be.

Nonmanagers, being intimately involved with day-to-day operations, may be able to make valuable observations about how to make improvements and increase efficiency.

Codetermination leads to better cooperation between labor and management. They cease to see each other as adversaries.

When nonmanagers are represented on a board, they gain a better understanding of a company's financial situation and are thus more likely to respect the occasional need for layoffs and cutbacks.

Codetermination helps preserve industrial peace. Giving workers a voice at the highest level proves to employees that their interests are represented. This leads to greater loyalty.

### NO

**Nonmanagers should not be represented on boards of directors because . . .**

Nonmanagers are not qualified to make high-level decisions, and therefore decision making by the board might be poor.

When nonmanagers are on a board, many issues can be resolved directly between workers and top management. This weakens a union's ability to bargain with management.

Decision-making power should be held by those who own the enterprise. Nonmanagers should sit on the board only if elected by the shareholders.

Codetermination complicates management because it gives workers a voice at the top. Too many worker-related issues, such as demands for higher wages and fringe benefits, may be introduced.

Codetermination can negatively affect investment abroad. German workers on the board of Volkswagen, afraid of losing jobs, for years blocked Volkswagen's plan to build a plant in the United States.

### QUESTIONS

1. Do you feel that a codetermination law is needed in the United States? Why or why not?
2. How would American workers react to a codetermination policy? Explain.

the enterprise's success. Over a period of time, virtually every aspect of the organization will bear the imprint of the top executive.

### Decide on Key Financial Matters

The board of directors must make decisions about financial matters, such as whether to procure capital through the sale of additional shares or through borrowing. Directors also must decide whether profits should be distributed as dividends to shareholders, used to retire (repay) debt, retained as working capital, or used to expand the business. Obviously, decisions such as these affect the interests of shareholders, for they directly affect the profit-making ability of the company over a period of time.

### Give Broad Direction to the Enterpise

A well-functioning board takes an active role in formulating the broad strategy of the organization with regard to such matters as expansion programs, new ventures, and modification of organizational structure.

### Maintain Corporate Continuity

The board of directors is obligated to ensure that the corporation continues to exist. The board must fill vacancies caused by the resignation or death of board members.

## THE PLURAL EXECUTIVE

The term **plural executive** refers to a committee that has been assigned authority to make decisions and to perform management functions. In this sense, a corporate board of directors is a plural executive. It has the power to plan, organize, staff, direct, and control—and does not merely advise.

Plural executives are sometimes found in government agencies in which members of a port authority or public-service commission are so constituted. Some business organizations establish "executive," "management," "policy," or "finance" committees that serve as plural executives. Action-oriented committees such as these may formulate basic strategy, decide on key policies, allocate money and other resources to various projects, settle disputes between divisions of the enterprise, or make other high-level decisions.

Manufacturers Hanover Trust, one of the world's largest banks, operates without a chief executive officer. Its plural executive consists of a chairman and a president who make key decisions together. When asked how this "joint command" works out, Gabriel Hauge, who was then chairman, commented:

> When the present administration of the bank took charge in February 1971, the retiring chairman referred to me in the press announcement as "leader of the team." I have always liked that designation. While John McGillicuddy supervises credit and liability matters, I oversee the investment side, that is, our portfolio and trust departments. We divide up other areas for [review], but all major decisions we make jointly. We have as intimate an administrative partnership as any I know. It works well.[2]

[2]Gabriel Hauge, "Choosing Strategies for Business Success," *Nation's Business*, June 1977, p. 33.

Japanese corporations make almost universal use of management committees. Professor Kono notes:

> Eighty-six percent of large corporations have management committees. The average number of members of these bodies is approximately ten. They meet once a week, making decisions as a group. The members are usually the chairman, president (managing director), and four to six executive directors. Each member has broad responsibility for corporate decisions covering several departments, receiving reports from these departments and giving advice to them. They are not identical to department heads. They are in charge of general management and strategic decisions.
>
> In the United States, there is a growing tendency to have a group at the top, but the number of members is smaller than in the Japanese case. In the U.K., management committees are not frequently used, but rather the individual managing director or chairman makes the final decisions. If there is a group at the top, the number of members is usually three to five, and it is often an informal meeting.[3]

## GUIDELINES FOR MAKING COMMITTEES EFFECTIVE

Collectively, committees account for enormous expenditures of time and money. It is common for some persons in the business world, in the government, and in the academic community to spend one-fourth or more of their time either attending committee meetings or preparing for them. It is important, then, for those in charge of committees to make them as effective as possible. Committee effectiveness can be achieved if the following principles for successful committee operations are observed.

When asked "How long should a man's legs be?" Abraham Lincoln replied, "Long enough to reach the ground." The same type of answer applies to "How large should a committee be?" The answer: "Large enough to do the most efficient job." Deciding how large a committee should be is always judgmental. Relatively large committees are desired when:

Establish the Right Size of the Committee

- A principal purpose of the committee is to inform the members who comprise it.
- Widely differing talents and experience are needed to make the recommendation or decision.
- The scope of the committee's activities is very broad. In these cases, however, it may be wise to divide the work into subcommittees.

Relatively small committees are desired when:

- Speedy action is needed.
- The matter assigned to the committee must be kept confidential. Obviously, the more persons serving on a committee, the greater the chance of information leaks.

[3]Reprinted with permission from *Long Range Planning*, Vol. 15, Toyohiro Kono, "Japanese Management Philosophy: Can it be Exported?," Copyright 1982, Pergamon Press, Ltd.

If a committee is too small, there may be insufficient informational input to develop the best possible decision or recommendation. Some ideas may never be developed, and members may not think of all possible alternatives.

On the other hand, if a committee is too large it may become unwieldy, irrelevant information may be presented, time may be wasted, and the costs may be greater than the benefits expected from the committee's deliberations. Also, some individuals may feel uncomfortable in a large committee and may be reluctant to express their viewpoints. Feeling insecure, these people, who may have useful ideas, do not contribute.

## Select the Right Members

The results achieved by a committee depend to a great extent on the capabilities of the members it comprises. Individuals who have had considerable experience serving on committees agree that a common mistake is the assignment of ineffective or otherwise unsuited persons to serve on the committee. Sometimes this happens when people are assigned for purely political reasons. At the other extreme, people are sometimes assigned to a committee as a form of punishment, which represents a gross misuse of the committee system.

When unqualified people are assigned to committees, success is certain to be limited. Therefore, the following factors should be evaluated when selecting people for committee membership.

### Interest in the Committee's Purpose

Potential committee members should have a committed interest in the committee's purpose. Those who are selecting the committee should ask themselves, "Will the individual under consideration help the committee achieve its goals?" The more interest a member has in the committee's purpose, the more the person will contribute and the more willing he or she will be to do necessary homework in preparation for committee meetings.

### Knowledge and Experience Related to the Committee's Purpose

The person under consideration for committee membership should have the ability or potential ability to make a contribution. This is a broad requirement for committee membership. "What is the individual's knowledge and experience with regard to this committee?" is a question that people who select committees must ask.

### Psychological Compatability

People who are being considered for committee membership should have the ability to compromise; they should be able to modify their viewpoints so that group consensus can ultimately be reached. They should also be balanced—that is, not too dominant or too submissive and willing to both listen and talk. If the individual's ideas and attitudes are too far from those of the rest of the committee, the committee will not be able to function effectively.

## Select the Right Chairperson

A committee **chairperson** is the individual held accountable for the performance of the committee. The chairperson may be appointed by the person(s) who established the committee or may be elected by members of the committee. Committee chairpersons are selected in four basic ways. First, a chairperson may be appointed by the individual or group of individuals who established the committee. This is a widespread practice in business organizations. Or a chairperson may be elected by members of the committee. This is a common practice in many nonprofit organizations. Third, a chairperson may be nominated by a **committee on committees** (a committee that in turn elects the members of other committees). This procedure is common in universities, trade associations, and political parties. Finally, a chairperson may be established by legislation or by previously developed rules. Individuals holding certain positions in the executive branch of government are automatically designated as chairpersons of specific committees. Both houses of Congress have rules that determine who will serve (or at least who probably will serve) as chairpersons of particular committees.

While it is not always easy to determine who is right for the job, there is general agreement that an effective chairperson should possess the following qualities: planning ability, objectivity, diplomacy, experience, and efficiency.

**Define Instructions Clearly**

To make effective use of committees it is important to prepare and communicate a clear set of instructions. The instructions should spell out (1) the committee's purpose; (2) the committee's authority; (3) a deadline for completion of the committee's work; (4) money, staff, and other resources assigned to the committee; (5) the name of the chairperson or instructions on how the chairperson is to be selected; (6) whether the report will be oral or written; and (7) to whom the final report will be made. Figure 12–2 illustrates how these seven instructional objectives may be accomplished. In the figure, the organization in question is a government agency.

**Define Operating Procedures Clearly**

Often committees are given considerable latitude in the way they function. In other cases, those who establish the committee may impose close operating procedures on it. Sometimes there is a compromise, with those who established the committee setting broad operational guidelines and the committee itself establishing specific operating procedures. In any event, if the committee is to be effective, clear procedures should be established indicating (1) when, where, and for how long the meetings will be held; (2) what voting procedures will be followed; (3) whether noncommittee members will be eligible to attend; and (4) plans for reimbursement. Figure 12–3 illustrates how operating procedures can be communicated simply.

**Provide Needed Information and Staff Assistance**

Those who establish committees should supply the committee members with whatever information they will need to make an intelligent decision or recommendation. A committee established to recommend a new financial policy should have access to a variety of financial reports and forecasts. In similar fashion, a committee established to study ways to reduce absenteeism should be given information about such matters as causes of absenteeism in that and other organizations, solutions developed elsewhere, and types of workers most frequently absent.

**FIGURE 12-2**

**Sample Memo Giving General Committee Instructions**

```
TO:       Members of the Contract Review Committee
FROM:     Alex Watkins
SUBJECT:  General Instructions
DATE:     February 29, 1980
```

The purpose of the Contract Review Committee is to study methods for the effective handling of disputes between prime contractors and our agency [item 1--statement of purpose].  The committee is asked to make recommendations for dealing with such disputes [item 2--definition of authority] and to submit them to me by June 2 [item 3--deadline for completion of work].

The committee is authorized to spend $20,000 for travel and other expenses incurred while interviewing prime contractors.  Two law students working part time for the agency have been assigned to the project [item 4--resources that will be available].

Because of her extensive experience in dealing with prime contractors, I'm asking Connie Pearson to serve as chairperson [item 5--appointment of chairperson].

I'm asking that the committee's report be in written form and be presented to the State Board of Highway Accounts after I have reviewed it [items 6 and 7--in what form and to whom the final report will be made].

Assistance in the form of staff personnel may also be required to make a committee work well. Such help may be fairly routine, as when clerical personnel are appointed to handle note taking and report preparation, or it may involve a more complicated matter, like the provision of funds to retain experts on the problem at hand. The key point is that committees should be given all the tools they need to accomplish their objective.

**Expedite the
Committee's Work**

Those who established the committee should set reasonable and realistic deadlines for the completion of its assignment. There is no point in assigning work to a

FIGURE 12–3

**Sample Memo Giving Committee Operating Procedures**

```
TO:       Members of the Contract Review Committee
FROM:     Connie Pearson, Chairperson
SUBJECT:  Operating Procedures for the Contract Review
          Committee
DATE:     March 7, 1980



On the basis of informal discussions with each of you
and with Alex Watkins, who established the committee, I
have set the following procedures for operation of the
Contract Review Committee.

We will meet on the last Fridays in March, April, and
May between 9 A.M. and 12 P.M. in my office.  No meet-
ing will extend beyond three hours [item 1--when,
where, how long].

I expect that numerous matters will come up for a vote.
A simple majority will carry.  And Robert's Rules of
Order will apply [item 2--voting procedures].

Some of the information we will discuss is considered
sensitive.  Therefore, public meetings will not be held
[item 3--whether nonmembers will be able to attend].

Some of you will be traveling to acquire information
for our deliberations.  Please submit travel plans to
me for authorization.  Reimbursement will be made upon
receipt of a voucher [item 4--reimbursement].
```

committee if it is not given adequate time to study the matter. The general practice is to allow more time than is needed for a full and adequate consideration of the matter at hand. Therefore, it is a wise procedure for those responsible for the committee to confer with the chairperson and make sure the time allotted is not excessive.

It is also a good idea to check frequently on the committee's progress to ensure that the deadline will be met. Such reviews may reveal that the committee needs more information or staff support to achieve its purpose within the time allotted. In many cases interim progress reports are prepared.

## Require a Final Report

A final report should always be required of a committee. It is best that the report be in writing, since a written report can state precisely what the committee has decided or recommends and can go into greater detail than is normally possible only when an oral presentation is made.

It is wise to require committee members to read and sign the final report. This practice prevents future disagreement over what the report actually contained. If some committee members strongly disagree with the final conclusions reached by a majority of the committee, a minority report showing the views of the dissenters may be in order. This procedure is standard practice in the operations of congressional committees, whose members often reach conclusions along party lines.

## Take Action on the Committee's Report

Some action should always be taken on the final report. If nothing else, the report should at least be acknowledged. However, simple acknowledgment does not go far enough. If those who authorized the report feel the proposals it contains are inappropriate or otherwise unsatisfactory, they should explain why to the committee.

An important reason for some form of action on a committee report is to maintain respect for the concept of a committee system. In the absence of action, either positive or negative, a committee member might think, "I spent over 100 hours on research and committee attendance and no action at all was forthcoming. Next time I'm asked to serve on a committee, I'll find a good excuse to get out of it."

## SUMMARY

- People form groups for a variety of reasons: an inborn propensity to do so, the interdependency necessitated by work specialization, and in order to survive.
- Group dynamics deals with the interactions of people in a group setting and is concerned specifically with conformity, aggression, competition, and cooperation.
- Conformity is compliance with existing rules or customs. Groups require members to conform by obeying group norms, accepting group sanctions, and giving up certain rights. People conform because of fear, insecurity, and good judgment. How much conformity is desirable depends on the type of organization, the person's level within the organization, and the kind of task being performed.
- Aggression is offensive action that is caused by frustration, annoyance, or attack. Aggression may be either socially acceptable or unacceptable.
- Competition is a struggle between two or more individuals or groups to obtain the same object. People compete because of limited resources and cultural encouragement. Competition may be either internal or external.
- Cooperation is a joint effort by two or more people to attain a common goal, and requires an individual to subordinate his or her self-interests.
- Formal groups are created by management and are task oriented. Informal groups are created by group members. They exist to transmit information, overcome fear, and amuse.
- A committee is a group assigned authority to consider, investigate, or act on some matter. Committees vary in size, are found at all organizational levels, and may be permanent (standing) or temporary (ad hoc).

- Committees are used to provide information for decision making, distribute authority, facilitate coordination, foster support for decisions, and broaden the knowledge of people who participate. However, committees also are expensive, often act slowly, may result in compromise, and do not fix responsibility.
- Boards of directors are required by law for corporations. Legal responsibilities of boards of directors are to obey provisions of the corporate charter, avoid conflicts of interest, and exercise reasonably good judgment. Other responsibilities include electing corporate officers, deciding key financial matters, giving broad direction to the enterprise, and maintaining corporate continuity.
- A plural executive is a committee that has been assigned authority to make decisions and perform management functions.
- Guidelines for maximizing the effectiveness of committees are: to establish the right size of the committee, select the right committee members, select the right chairperson, define instructions clearly, define operating procedures clearly, provide needed information and staff assistance, expedite the committee's work, require a final report, and take action on the committee's report.

## LEARN THE LANGUAGE OF MANAGEMENT

formal groups
informal groups
social psychologists
group dynamics
conformity
norms
sanctions
aggression
frustration
annoyance
attack
competition
external competition
internal competition
social facilitation
external cooperation

collusion
internal cooperation
quality circles
study circles
grapevine
committee
standing committee
ad hoc committee
compromise
jury
board of directors
shareholders
interlocking directorships
bylaws
plural executive
chairperson
committee on committees

## QUESTIONS FOR REVIEW AND DISCUSSION

1. Why is some degree of conformity required in an organization? Will there likely be more or less conformity in organizations in the future? Why or why not?
2. Give several examples of conformity you have experienced that you feel were unnecessary.
3. Can aggressive behavior in group situations be eliminated? Explain.
4. Competition is fostered by limited resources and cultural encouragement. In your opinion, which is more important? Why?
5. Generally, do you feel you are more productive working alone or in a group? Why?
6. Explain why cooperation and competition are simultaneously involved in organized activities.
7. How can managers make effective use of informal groups?
8. The committee form of organization is a controversial one. Why?

9. How do you account for the extensive use of committees in government?
10. Do you feel that in the future boards of directors will include more people from outside the organization? Why or why not?
11. What are the advantages and disadvantages of a plural executive?

## MAKING MANAGEMENT DECISIONS

### 1. The tennis court is a mistake.

John Appleton is a personnel director for the Ajax Foundry, a company employing 120 production workers. The workers are earthy types who like the outdoors. Each spring, with only the direction of informal leaders, the employees plant a garden on a quarter acre of land adjacent to the parking lot. During lunch breaks, some of the workers care for the garden, and they regard it as an enjoyable way to relax from the heavy work they do.

In March, Appleton attends a university-sponsored seminar entitled "The Role of Sports in Building Employee Morale." He is excited by what he hears. He returns home on Friday and immediately calls a paving company to concrete the garden area into a tennis court.

When the workers arrive on Monday morning, they find a well-laid-out court and a number of tennis racquets and balls.

A month later no one has used the court. Many of the workers have complained that they miss the garden, and their dissatisfaction has had a negative effect on morale and productivity.

What basic mistake did Appleton make? Explain.

### 2. A new employee is too ambitious

Sam Bracton joined the Acme Insulation Company as an installer. Sam, who had owned his own business until it failed during an economic downturn, is a hard worker. Soon he is resented by other employees on the job because he demonstrates in his day-to-day work that production standards are too low. By example, Sam is, unknown to him, showing that more work should be required of all employees.

One afternoon a long-time employee and informal leader of the group tells Sam to slow down. He says, "If you don't, there won't be enough work and one or two of the boys will be laid off."

You are Sam's supervisor and learn about this incident. You know that if everyone worked as hard as Sam, there would, in fact, be one surplus employee.

What action would you take? Why?

### 3. Does group decision making work?

In many companies, decisions are made autocratically with little if any input from other managers. J.C. Penney Company is an exception. The company relies heavily on group decision making.

Does it work? In 1981, most large retailers had declines in profits. Penney's earnings rose 44 percent. Management observers credit Penney's success to group decision making.

A management committee consisting of 14 top officers debates and decides issues ranging from personnel policies to public affairs and merchandising. Numerous subcommittees make decisions on lower-level matters.

Penney's also uses the plural executive idea. Four top executives make up what the company calls "office of the chairman."

If group decision making works so well for Penney's, why don't more companies use it?

Will there likely be more group decision making in the future? Explain.

FOR ADDITIONAL
CONCEPTS
AND IDEAS

Andrews, Kenneth R. "Corporate Strategy as a Vital Function of the Board." *Harvard Business Review*, November–December 1981, pp. 174–184.

Behling, Orlando, and Holcombe, F. Douglas. "Dealing with Employee Stress." *MSU Business Topics*, Spring 1981, pp. 53–61.

Buchan, P. Bruce. "Boards of Directors: Adversaries or Advisors?" *California Management Review*, Winter 1981, pp. 31–39.

Carroll, Daniel T. "Boards and Managements: Ten Challenges and Responses." *Harvard Business Review*, September–October 1981, pp. 62–66.

Dubinsky, Alan J., and Hansen, Richard W. "Managing Sales Force Composition." *MSU Business Topics*, Spring 1981, pp. 14–20.

Elrod, J. Mitchell, Jr. "Improving Employee Relations with Focus Groups." *Business*, November 1981, pp. 36–38.

Fox, Harold W. "Advisory Board: Resource for Closely Held Companies." *MSU Business Topics*, Summer 1979, pp. 25–30.

Lagges, James G. "The Board of Directors: Boon or Ban to Stockholders and Management?" *Business Horizons*, March–April 1982, pp. 43–50.

McAlmon, George. "Corporate Boards: The Black Boxes." *Business Horizons*, March–April 1981, pp. 25–29.

Mace, Myles L. *Directors: Myth and Reality*. Boston, Mass.: Division of Research, Graduate School of Business Administration, Harvard University, 1971.

McSweeney, Edward. *Managing the Managers*. New York: Harper & Row, 1978.

Mueller, Kirk. *Board Compass: What It Means to Be A Director in a Changing World*. Lexington, Mass.: D.C. Heath, 1979.

Schwartz, Felice N. "'Invisible' Resource: Women for Boards." *Harvard Business Review*, November–December 1980, pp. 6–19.

Shanklin, William L., and Ryan, John K., Jr. "Should the Board Consider this Agenda Item?" *MSU Business Topics*, Winter 1981, pp. 35–42.

Shaw, Marvin E. *Group Dynamics: The Psychology of Small Group Behavior*, 2nd ed. New York: McGraw-Hill, 1976.

Stokes, Judy Ford. "Involving New Directors in Small Company Management." *Harvard Business Review*, July–August 1980, pp. 170–175.

*The Touche Ross Survey on the Changing Nature of the Corporate Board*. New York: Research & Forecasts, Inc., 1978.

# CASE STUDY

## SHOULD AGENTS BE GIVEN MORE AUTHORITY?

Jayne Garment Company markets a line of medium-priced women's apparel throughout the United States. It uses a sales force of thirty-five manufacturers agents who are paid a straight commission on sales and receive no expense allowance.

Each year a meeting of all agents is held in Chicago to review the previous year's results and to plan the following year's activities.

At this year's meeting the agent sales force seems very upset about a Jayne policy that gives them no authority to negotiate price and no authority to promise a specific delivery date for merchandise shipments.

The president of Jayne decides to bring the problem into the open for discussion.

President: We've been in business twenty-nine years. Some of you have been with us since the beginning. Now, all of you know it has always been our policy to control prices and delivery dates in the home office in New York. Why is there so much clamor for changing our policy?

Agent A: Let me put it to you straight. In my territory alone, I'd say I lost $50,000 volume last year because I couldn't make a modest adjustment in price. Had I been authorized to cut prices only 5 or 10 percent in some situations, I'd have gotten the orders.

Agent B: And I lost a lot of orders because I couldn't guarantee a specific delivery date. Our retail customers, when they plan sales, want to be sure the merchandise will be there when the sale is on.

President: I understand what you're saying. But we've always been a one-price house. If you agents start negotiating, conceivably every retailer will pay a different price for the same product. Pretty soon we'll have no credibility among our customers. And who knows, we may even have the Federal Trade Commission on our back.

Agent C: Let's go back to the delivery date issue. Why can't we have authority to guarantee a delivery on or before a specific date?

President: Well, you understand enough of the manufacturing side of the business to know we have tremendous coordination problems. What we try to do is manufacture one basic garment at a time. Since we have upwards of fifty different garments, we simply can't fill each order as it comes in. We've got to fill orders from stock, and we obviously can't ship till the ordered garments are in stock.

Agent D: Well, I think I speak for most of us when I suggest you find a solution to these problems. All of us are losing commissions, and you're losing a lot of volume.

Agent E: I've been with Jayne since you started it twenty-nine years ago. What has happened in recent years is simply this: A lot of our competitors have decided to give their agents more of the authority we're requesting. There's a lot more wheeling and dealing out there. I strongly recommend you give us the power to do some wheeling and dealing too.

### QUESTIONS

1. What organizational problems are apparent in this case?
2. If you were the president, what corrective action might you take to solve the problems? Explain.
3. What are the pros and cons of giving agents authority to set prices within limits?
4. What are some possible ways the manufacturing side of the business could be reorganized to help eliminate the delivery problem?

# PART FOUR

# STAFFING

Part Four treats three main aspects of staffing, or the "people" function: selecting, developing and rewarding, and evaluating managers. All enterprises involve people who are expected to perform certain activities to achieve goals. People have always been the key resource in organizations, and recognition of their importance continues to grow. Increased competition for the services of managers, easy mobility from one enterprise to another, and an ever-expanding legislative recognition of the rights of individuals are three of the reasons for contemporary interest in the staffing function.

Chapter 13, "Manager Selection," discusses the general job requirements for all managers and some of the main tools used to match managers with specific jobs—job analyses, descriptions, and specifications. Other areas treated include the pros and cons of promoting managers from within the organization and recruiting managers from outside, sources of information about potential managers, forecasting the need for managers, and the future use of women and minority-group members in managing.

"Manager Development and Rewards," Chapter 14, focuses on ways to help managers attain their fullest potential and the role of financial and nonfinancial compensation as rewards. Specific treatment is given to both internal and external approaches to developing manager capability. Guidelines are provided for designing and implementing both manager-development programs and manager-reward systems.

A difficult aspect of staffing concerns determining the effectiveness of a manager's performance. Chapter 15, "Evaluation of Manager Performance," deals directly with this problem. It begins with a discussion of judgmental and developmental evaluation. Specific evaluation techniques—results, trait, behavior, functional performance, and informal evaluation—are treated. Manager evaluation as it relates to career planning is discussed, and suggested guidelines for effective evaluation are presented.

Part Four ends with a Case Study entitled "Should Middle Managers Be Encouraged to Get an M.B.A. Degree?"


13   **MANAGER SELECTION**

14   **MANAGER DEVELOPMENT AND REWARDS**

15   **EVALUATION OF MANAGER PERFORMANCE**

# 13 MANAGER SELECTION

Selecting managers is an exceptionally important part of the staffing function. To a large degree, the abilities of managers determine how successful an organization will be.

No individual in any organization reaches perfection in the art and science of managing. Nevertheless, some managers are much more effective than others at the same organizational level. Some football coaches have a much better win-loss record than others; some corporate executives consistently show better profit results than other top managers; and some university deans develop much stronger academic and public-service programs than their colleagues in other educational institutions.

All organizations want to select the best possible managerial candidate for each position. But doing so is never easy. People differ in basic abilities, intelligence, experience, education, and motivation.

## BASIC JOB REQUIREMENTS FOR MANAGERS

In the following sections, nine requirements that are commonly regarded as necessary if a manager is to perform effectively are discussed.

Note, however, that each of these qualities is subject to interpretation. Two people reviewing the qualifications of an applicant may differ considerably in their opinions of how well the candidate meets the requirements. Nevertheless, it is useful in the selection process to keep these characteristics in mind.

Also note that the requirements discussed are considered universal for all managers regardless of level. Emphasis upon them, however, is not. One requirement, such as the desire to manage, may be more important in selecting a senior executive than a first-level supervisor.

**Desire to Manage**  The desire or will to manage differs among individuals. Some people relish the power that is associated with managing and the opportunity it provides to make things happen. Other people prefer not to manage, for several reasons. First, an individual may be happy in his or her present position and may simply have no desire to take on managerial duties. Second, a person may not want to accept responsibility for the performance of others because he or she lacks confidence and is afraid of failure in the new position. Third, in a situation in which promotion to a first-level management position is made from among operative employees, an individual may not want to be in charge of former peers. An otherwise qualified person under these circumstances may feel he or she is a "traitor" to old friends and may feel uncomfortable in giving them orders. Finally, a person may dislike the idea of being a manager because the position requires making some decisions that may be unpleasant, such as terminating an employee or denying someone a promotion.

Generally, the more an individual *wants* to manage (or do anything else for that matter), the more successful the person will be. Unfortunately, it is never easy to measure an individual's desire. For persons who are already managing and are being considered for a promotion, the desire to manage can be judged by observing whether the individual likes managing in his or her present job. For individuals being considered for their first management position, desire may be indicated by how eagerly the individual seeks the job. "Has he expressed interest in the job at least once?" "Does she appear to be highly motivated to move upward in the organization?" "Has he done anything on his own, such as take a course in basic management, to indicate he wants to be a manager?" These are some questions that can help one to evaluate the untried candidate's desire to manage.

The problem of determining the desire to manage is more difficult when considering a person from outside the organization. In such a case, observation of the individual as a manager is not usually possible, and so more attention may be given to other factors.

A second general qualification that all managers should have is a working knowledge of the management process. Ideally, a managerial candidate should have a solid understanding of the management functions, the interrelationships among departments, the necessity for effective coordination, and the imperative need that the organization achieve results. In practice, however, surprisingly few managers and prospective managers have a good knowledge of what the work of managing entails. For many jobs in our society—such as those in law, medicine, dentistry, accounting, and engineering—formalized preparation and the passing of appropriate examinations are required. However, most candidates for managerial jobs have had no formal training or education in management. An increasing number of managers have had some exposure to managing, but most practicing managers learned what they know about managing largely through trial and error and through observation.

Knowledge of the Management Process

Assessment is particularly difficult in the case of an operative employee who is being considered for promotion to the level of supervisor. Since such employees lack experience in managing, it is hard to predict performance. Often, as is discovered every day by middle managers, good workers may not make good managers.

A candidate for a managerial position should have the necessary degree of intelligence and the ability to think analytically. While intellectual abilities may not be important for, say, a job of first-level supervisor, they become increasingly important at higher levels in an enterprise. As one ascends the organizational ladder, there is more need to conceptualize broad-based plans, evaluate complex proposals, and make judgments about highly abstract matters.

Intellectual Capabilities to Handle the Job

Managers should have the ability to win respect from their subordinates, peers, and supervisors within an organization. Situations in which subordinates will not follow instructions because they lack respect for the manager are common. Often peer-level managers in other departments will not cooperate with a manager because the manager is incompetent, unfair, selfish, petty, dishonest, or negative on most matters. But, very importantly, individuals cannot be forced to respect someone else. Even in the military, where discipline is rigid compared with that in other types of organizations, respect must be earned; it cannot be achieved solely on the basis of rank.

Ability to Earn Respect

The amount of respect an applicant appears to have for himself or herself is often the best clue in determining the ability to earn the respect of others. Individuals with a negative self-image lack the confidence needed to win the voluntary support of others.

A manager at any level must report upward to his or her superior, communicate with managers on the same level, and issue instructions to subordinates. Skill in passing on information accurately, comprehensively, and concisely—whether in writing or orally—is an important quality needed by all managers (see Chapter 18). The inability to communicate effectively leads directly to mistakes, accidents, confusion, repetition, and other negative results.

The inability of many business-school graduates to write simple, clear English often hinders their career progress. Following are three examples of poor writing by business-school graduates, cited in an article in *Nation's Business:*

- A graduate student writing a critique of a restaurant operation had this to say: "The customers flow into the restaurant at a rate of arrival, which is influenced by the size of the door. Then they flow to the tables at the rate of being seated."
- An honor student wrote about his undergraduate days as follows: "At times my grades reflected average work spending more of my time in related interest. My last year I decided to concentrate most of my time in course study achieving the grades which I was capable of maintaining. Placing me on the dean's list both semesters."
- Another graduate student wrote the following as part of a report: "Working in the area of funeral service you become exposed to many problems and recipients of health care programs. Acquiring some insight to the workings of the hospital and their role in the community. Realizing these institutions have a great affect and influence the lives of people in our public health communities."[1]

In commenting on the problem of poor writing, *Nation's Business* reports: "Examples of atrocious writing by business-school graduates are constantly being sent to the schools by business executives. These executives are dismayed at finding that employees who were ticketed for eventual high-level jobs can write no better than tenth graders."[2]

Selectors of individuals to fill management positions typically pay close attention to grammatical mistakes made in application letters. They also take note of applicants' ability to express themselves clearly and correctly in verbal communication.

The nature of organized life requires that each manager interrelate with other managers to help attain organizational goals. Thus, in assessing a prospective manager, it is important to consider such questions as "Will he work well with other people?" "Will she subordinate her personal interests to the welfare of the entire organization?" and "Will he make personal sacrifices to help other individuals?" Persons who insist on always doing things their own way do not usually make successful managers.

[1]Quoted from "The Mystery of the Business Graduate Who Can't Write," *Nation's Business*, February 1977, pp. 60–62.
[2]Ibid., p. 62.

*"2:30! I must get back to the office.*
*My people have been loafing for over an hour already!"*

From *The Wall Street Journal.*
Permission—Cartoon Features Syndicate.

**Integrity**

Since managers occupy positions of trust within organizations, high-level integrity is an important quality. Managers have control over the human, financial, and material resources of an enterprise, and they have many opportunities to cheat in one way or another if they are so inclined. Embezzlement, theft of company property, deceptive trade practices, falsification of work records, and favoritism are just some of the many unethical practices that managers may engage in. White-collar crime accounts for more losses to all types of organizations than employee pilferage and customer shoplifting combined."[3]

Integrity on the part of managers is also important because they set the example for nonmanagers. A manager who is strongly deficient in integrity is, by example, likely to weaken the moral fabric of those reporting to him or her.

Integrity can be measured only subjectively, for each individual has a different concept of right and wrong. Nevertheless, careful attention should be paid to this quality, since lack of integrity is a common problem in all types of organizations. Managerial candidates who have records of being underhanded or who have been involved in situations in which unethical behavior was apparent should not be considered for positions of trust.

**Loyalty to the Organization**

A manager is expected to be loyal to the organization and to its underlying philosophy. In effect, a disloyal manager is a psychological saboteur who works against, not for, organizational goals.

Loyalty is an intangible quality and is difficult to measure, but it is indicated in a number of ways. For example, in the case of a manager being considered for a

[3]See Norman Jaspan, *White-Collar Fraud,* (Atlanta: Equifax, Inc., Summer 1978), pp. 8–11. Jaspan claims that the greatest amount of dishonesty occurs at the supervisory and executive levels.

promotion, does the manager interpret policies developed by senior management to his or her subordinates favorably, or does he or she speak negatively about them? A manager may not approve fully of certain directives that are expected to be enforced. But in explaining them to subordinates, the manager has an obligation to interpret them as essential to the organization's welfare. Managers who speak negatively about the organization while off the job are also displaying disloyalty.

John A. Pearce, in a noteworthy study of supervisors' organizational loyalty, identified the following fourteen types of behavior as indicators of loyalty:

* To refrain from any actions off the job which could harm the reputation of the organization.
* To work for only one employer at a time.
* To study information related to the job on my own time.
* To purchase my organization's products or services rather than those of competitors.
* To ensure that my family's conduct reflects favorably on the organization.
* To vote for issues and individuals which support the interests of the business community.
* To get enough rest and sleep necessary for effective performance on the job.
* Not to drink alcoholic beverages immediately before or any time during the working day.
* To return to work promptly after all established work breaks.
* To tell management whenever I observe another employee breaking a rule.
* To depart work no earlier than the established time.
* To be active in groups and clubs which promote the general interests of business.
* To hold the goals of the organization above personal nonwork goals which affect the job.
* To work at home on my own time if necessary to finish a job.[4]

In some organizations, first-level supervisors are appointed from the ranks of unionized employees. In such a situation, management must try to assess whether the new manager would focus his or her loyalty on the company or would continue to give it to the union. The old saying to the effect that one cannot serve two masters and do them both justice holds true.

Some clues to the loyalty of candidates new to the organization can be observed by the skilled interviewer. For example, individuals who speak well of their previous employers are more likely to have the required degree of loyalty than persons who are extremely negative about them.

**Personal Stability**  There are three problems that often adversely affect a manager's ability to perform effectively: addiction to alcohol or other drugs, severe financial problems, and

---

[4]John A. Pearce, II, "An Assessment of Supervisors' Organizational Loyalty," *MSU Business Topics*, Summer 1977, p. 53.

domestic difficulties. These problems are very common and cost organizations billions of dollars each year.

Applicants who have personal problems that are likely to interfere with managing are poor risks. Unfortunately, such difficulties may be easy to conceal until a person is well into his or her managerial career, when they begin to have a damaging effect on the person's work. The general consensus today is that an individual's private life is his or her own business and that the way an employee lives should not be prescribed by an organization. However, if elements of an individual's personal life are interfering significantly with his or her ability to work effectively, there is a legitimate reason not to promote the individual (and in some cases to terminate him or her).

319

*How to Match
Managerial
Candidates
with
Specific Jobs*

## HOW TO MATCH MANAGERIAL CANDIDATES WITH SPECIFIC JOBS

The foregoing requirements are only broad guidelines for the selection of managers. In practice, the work of managing is extremely varied and depends on the kind of organization, the person's level in the organization, and the specific results expected.

Most job titles are too general to be of much use as indicators of the qualities, skills, and experience a person should possess for appointment to a management position. For example, a plant manager in a furniture factory faces significantly different problems than a plant manager in a fertilizer company. The job of supervisor in a garment manufacturing company differs greatly from the job of supervisor in a steel mill. The position of vice-president in an advertising agency is very dissimilar from a job with the same title in a bank. Therefore, more detailed descriptions are needed to define the qualifications a prospective manager should have and the duties he or she will perform.

**Job Analyses**

In some cases a job is adapted to an individual's qualifications. However, it is much more common for a manager to be fitted to the job to be done. A systematic, detailed study of a management position is called a **job analysis**. It examines what specific activities are to be performed. Table 13–1 shows a sample job analysis.

To be of greatest use a job analysis should evaluate in depth the work to be performed. The more detailed the analysis, the easier it is to select the best-qualified person to fill the position.

**Job Descriptions**

A job analysis tells us what a job involves, while a **job description** is a written statement explaining the specific tasks to be performed, the reporting relationships of the job holder, and the results expected. Table 13–2 shows a sample job description for a department head in a peanut company.

A job description is helpful to the person accepting a management position because it clarifies the what, why, and how of the assignment. Unfortunately, formal job descriptions often are not prepared, leading to unnecessary manager frustration. In the absence of formal job descriptions, managers may be in doubt about

**TABLE 13–1**

**Examples of Information a Manager Job Analysis Should Supply**

| Aspect of Job | Duties |
|---|---|
| Planning | • Planning work to be done<br>• Scheduling work<br>• Setting budgets<br>• Requisitioning supplies |
| Organizing | • Dividing work among personnel<br>• Coordinating work with other managers<br>• Deciding reporting relationships of subordinates |
| Staffing | • Approving new job applicants<br>• Training new employees<br>• Promoting employees<br>• Transferring and terminating workers |
| Directing | • Communicating instructions to employees<br>• Motivating personnel |
| Controlling | • Controlling costs<br>• Measuring work output against standards<br>• Taking corrective action as needed |
| Reporting relationships | • Manager should report to next higher manager |

the answers to such questions as "What are the limits of my authority?" "To whom do I report on specific problems?" and "How does my work relate to that of other managers in the organization?"

**Job Specifications**    A **job specification** details what qualifications an individual must have to perform the work involved. It may specify such factors as required educational attainment, needed previous experience, and health status. The well-prepared job specification is an excellent aid in recruiting and selecting managers.

**TABLE 13–2**

**A Sample Job Description for a Department Head**

| POSITION TITLE: Peanut Production Superintendent<br>INCUMBENT: _____ | |
|---|---|
| LOCATION: | REPORTS TO: Production Superintendent |
| ACTIVITY: Production | DEPARTMENT: Peanut |
| DATE OF DESCRIPTION: | WRITTEN BY: |

**TABLE 13-2** *(Continued)*

| REVISED DESCRIPTION: | APPROVED BY: |
|---|---|
| POSITION NUMBER: | |

I. Purpose

    To provide overall supervision and coordination of all production activities and the handling of raw materials to the finished product.

II. Accountabilities

1. Assure proper scheduling and operation of peanut production.
2. Ensure the production of high-quality products at lowest cost by coordinating production activities.
3. Hire, train, and supervise the employees in his or her department to assure continuing competence in all production areas.
4. Maintain and control all areas of production cost through proper supervision.
5. Improve production process by the innovation and implementation of new ideas.
6. Motivate and insure high degree of morale.
7. Ensure a sanitary and safe production operation by executing certain control programs in compliance with company policies and practices.
8. Ensure all company policies adhered to and implement any disiplinary action required.

III. Relationships

    This position reports to the production superintendent regarding all aspects of production.

    Four general foremen, supervising ninety-nine employees, report to him or her. The department superintendent and general foremen review daily orders for production purposes. The incumbent coordinates with the maintenance supervisor daily for maintenance work. The personnel manager and incumbent review qualifications of prospective employees. The incumbent is in contact with the warehouse supervisor to schedule raw materials and packaging supplies as well as quality control to insure proper quality standards.

IV. Scope of Job

    This position directs, coordinates, and integrates department production and scheduling. The incumbent is responsible for achieving maximum output with efficient, low-cost operation. He or she is also responsible for departmental safety, sanitation, and human relations.

    The incumbent must exercise sound judgment to assure effective coordination and integration of production and scheduling.

V. Production

    Production is scheduled on a daily basis. The incumbent coordinates with the production superintendent on daily production schedules; with the department foremen in scheduling according to department and shipping priorities.

    He or she is responsible for the production of all products made in the department, and is concerned with yields, processes, etc., to insure an efficient operation. Exacting quality standards must be met on the products. The products are sensitive to many factors that may result in substandard conditions. Correction may involve machine or ingredient adjustments. On all quality problems the incumbent refers to the production deficiencies. Waste control, housekeeping, sanitation, safety, and production costs require constant effort to assure satisfactory performance.

    He or she is aware of any capital project installation and maintenance work that may affect production. He or she studies, develops, and initiates process changes for increased efficiency. Considerable ingenuity and planning is required to achieve reduction of production cost while maintaining quality products.

VI. General

    The people who direct these activities bring major functional problems to the incumbent for guidance, direction, establishment of priorities, and resolution of differences. The incumbent coordinates with all positions required for the smooth operation of the production system. He or she assists in the selection of employees within the department and trains them to assure current and future high level performance.

    The peanut department superintendent keeps the plant production superintendent informed of production performance and problems through weekly production goals and priorities and through approval for capital investment that he may suggest.

Source: Tom's Foods, Columbus, Georgia. Reprinted by permission.

Most small organizations do not conduct formal job analyses or prepare formal job descriptions and job specifications. However, as organizations grow in size and complexity—and therefore formality—the need for them increases.

Job analyses, descriptions, and specifications are usually most precise at the first level, less precise at the middle level, and far less exact at the top level of management. This is true for two reasons. First, precisely what the manager is expected to do is more easily determined at the lowest level of managing than at higher levels. First-level management jobs are more contained and easier to describe than higher-level management jobs. Second, at the higher levels managers are given wider latitude in the way they execute their assignments. A senior manager may simply be told, "Improve our profit position. How you do it is up to you so long as you operate within the budget and follow company policy."

## PROS AND CONS OF PROMOTING MANAGERS FROM WITHIN

A policy of **promotion from within** means that management positions are filled by persons who are already part of the organization. Promotion from within is a common policy. Some large organizations, such as Sears Roebuck, IBM, and General Motors, rarely go outside the company to recruit managers. The military services also rely on promotions from within to fill management vacancies.

One important advantage of promotion from within is that it generates internal competition for higher-level positions. When people know that higher-level jobs will be filled with individuals who are already part of the organization, they are inclined to perform more effectively in hopes of earning a promotion.

A second advantage is that promotion from within generally improves morale. Employees appreciate that the organization is controlled by persons who came up through the ranks rather than by "outsiders." This advantage is not universal, however. As we will see, in some circumstances internal promotion may adversely affect morale.

Third, when promotions are made from within, managers are dealing with known qualities. The individual being considered for promotion has been under observation for months, probably years, and his or her strengths and limitations should be well known. On the other hand, when individuals are hired for management-level positions from outside the organization, it is difficult to obtain full, accurate, and objective information about their qualifications. References, personal interviews, and credit investigations can reveal much information, but they still may not answer such questions as "How effective is the individual?" "Why does this person want to change organizations?" and "Does the individual have personal problems that may detract from performance?"

A fourth advantage of promotion from within is economy in money and time. No fees need be paid to outside recruitment organizations, and no travel expenses need be paid to applicants. And since all prospective candidates for the promotion are within the organization, the promotion decision can be made more quickly than when an outside search is conducted.

The most serious weakness of a promotion-from-within policy is that the best-possible person for the vacancy may not be part of the organization. Internal candidates may lack sufficient experience, knowledge, management ability, intelligence, or skill in dealing with people. For this reason, most organizations have a flexible policy toward promotion. Promotions are normally made from within, but when a properly qualified individual is not available, an outside search is made.

Disadvantages of Promotion from Within

Second, promotion from within may lead to a problem called **inbreeding**. An enterprise may tend to stagnate if all managers share the same organizational experience. Bringing in managers with different backgrounds can result in new ideas and new approaches to the attainment of organizational goals.

A third disadvantage of internal promotion is that it may create internal disharmony. Each of five managers may feel best equipped for the job of plant superintendent. If one of the five is given the promotion, the other four may be reluctant to cooperate.

A fourth potential limitation of promotion from within concerns the Peter Principle, which holds that most managers are promoted until they ultimately reach their level of incompetence. If a manager proves successful in one level, he or she keeps being promoted to higher levels, until he or she cannot perform well. The Peter Principle is controversial. Some of its pros and cons are discussed in the Issue for Debate in this chapter.

## PROS AND CONS OF OUTSIDE RECRUITMENT OF MANAGERS

While most organizations make the majority of their management promotions from within, outside recruitment of managers is nevertheless a widespread practice. Outside recruitment is used extensively for highly specialized positions for which no personnel within the organization are qualified. A firm may decide to establish a consumer-affairs department but find that no one in the organization is qualified. Under these conditions, the only alternative is to make an outside search.

In other cases an organization may be expanding too rapidly to develop an adequate supply of managerial talent. Under such circumstances, outside selection of managers is essential to keep up the momentum.

Another reason for recruiting managers from outside the organization is to give the enterprise a new, vigorous orientation. Existing managerial candidates may be overly conservative in viewpoint and be handicapped by years of traditional thinking—thinking that may have produced a stagnant organization. The Chrysler Corporation, rather than promoting from within, hired Lee Iacocca as its chief executive after he was terminated at the Ford Motor Company.

Often, organizations that are looking outside for managers use the services of **executive search firms** (also called *manager placement firms*). These are businesses that solicit résumés from individuals looking for positions and then try to place each job hunter with an appropriate organization. Usually, for higher-level

Use of Executive Search Firms

positions the hiring organization pays the required fee, which averages 30 percent of the annual compensation of the manager placed.

Three advantages of using an executive search firm are (1) professional placement firms often can do a more efficient job of finding the "right" manager, (2) the company may not have the time to do its own search, and (3) confidentiality is preserved.[5]

Executive search firms are growing in popularity. Between 1977 and 1981, search firms belonging to the association of Executive Recruiting Consultants reported a 74 percent increase in business.[6] Much of this increase is due to what executive search people refer to as the "decline of cronyism," or the hiring of a friend of a member of the board of directors.

Despite the growing popularity of executive search firms, conventional methods are more widely used in outside recruitment of managers, particularly at lower levels. Advertising in trade and other business publications is one method. *The Wall Street Journal* is used extensively for this purpose. Through advertising, a management position is given wide exposure, and the company may remain anonymous if it wants to.

Other sources for outside recruitment include trade associations, many of which maintain placement bureaus; friends and acquaintances of existing managers; college placement offices, especially for management trainees; and unsolicited résumés from individuals seeking a career with the organization.

## Advantages of Outside Recruitment

The major advantage of recruiting managers from outside the organization is that a selection can be made from a much greater number of individuals. There may be only a few persons within the organization who warrant consideration, but when an outside search is made, a large number of applicants can be evaluated. It is not uncommon for an advertisement for a manager in *The Wall Street Journal* to draw several hundred responses. The efforts of an executive search firm may also turn up dozens, even hundreds, of potentially qualified persons.

Another advantage is that it brings individuals into the organization who have different backgrounds and who can, perhaps, help the enterprise maintain vitality. In the advertising field, outside recruitment of account executives is relied on extensively to help stimulate new thinking. Academic organizations, research institutions, and foundations also do much outside recruitment for managers in an effort to obtain fresh, nontraditional thinking.

Sometimes, outside recruitment is used to give an organization a totally new direction. For instance, it is fairly common for a board of directors that is dissatisfied with the performance of an enterprise to select a new chief executive officer from outside the firm who they feel may be able to "turn the organization around."

## Disadvantages of Outside Recruitment

An important limitation of outside recruitment is that the individual selected will lack specific experience in how the organization functions and how the various departments interrelate. A certain amount of time normally elapses before a

---

[5]Donald F. Dvorak, "Executive Search: Management Headache or Opportunity for Creative Change?," *Management Review*, April 1982, pp. 27–39.
[6]Herbert E. Meyer, "Headhunters Cast a Wider Net," *Fortune*, September 7, 1981, pp. 65–67.

manager recruited from the outside understands the system well enough to function effectively.

A second disadvantage is cost in money and time. If executive search firms are used, substantial fees must be paid. And normally several weeks or months are required to find a manager who has the proper qualifications.

A third limitation is that some adverse quality of a person recruited from the outside may go undetected despite a thorough investigation. Promotion from within, in contrast, provides ample opportunity for observation of the prospective manager's decision-making abilities and other skills needed for effective managing.

## SOURCES OF INFORMATION FOR MANAGER-APPOINTMENT DECISIONS

Manager-appointment decisions are extremely important because, over time, the quality of management personnel determines the degree of success achieved by an organization. The more extensive and reliable the information that management has about a candidate, the better the selection decision should be. Key sources of information about manager applicants are past performance, personal interviews, in-depth investigations, tests, and assessment centers.

**Personal Interviews**

A personal interview or, for key positions, a series of interviews is an important source of information about applicants for managerial positions. The personal interview is the oldest and most widely used procedure for evaluating managerial candidates. An interview provides indications of the applicant's poise, intelligence, communication skills, interests, and attitudes. A problem with the personal interview is that it may be deceptive. The interviewee may be able to make a very good first impression but not a good lasting impression.

**Past Performance**

Unquestionably, the best predictive guide about an individual's future performance is his or her past behavior. If a candidate is presently working in the organization, it is relatively easy to assess past performance. Many organizations keep a dossier or employment file on all managers. If such a record is well kept, it will contain a thorough documentation of the person's employment history, revealing both strengths and weaknesses in past performance, special training received, types of positions held, and skills acquired. A good record in lower-level jobs is not, of course, a guarantee that the individual will perform well in a higher-level position. But it is the best guide available.

Past performance is obviously more difficult to assess for an individual who is not presently employed by the organization. In such cases references can be requested from various sources, such as current and previous employers, educators, and others who know the individual well. References are often a poor source of information, however, since many people who write them are reluctant to supply negative but pertinent information. They may withhold subtle observations that suggest the individual has character deficiencies, personal problems that

# ISSUE FOR DEBATE

## IS THE PETER PRINCIPLE VALID?

The Peter Principle says in effect that every manager tends to rise to his or her level of incompetence. Many believe this statement is true, since they have worked for superiors who could not perform their tasks effectively. But others disagree and feel the Peter Principle is not an accurate statement. Below are some pro and con views.

### YES

**The Peter Principle is valid because . . .**

Many people are promoted for reasons other than ability and good performance. Promotions may be based on a person's relation to the business by blood or marriage; seniority; politics; or a person's appearance, speech, personality, or ability to fit the corporate image. Thus, many managers function at a level at which they are not competent.

The many organizations that fail or at best earn little profit indicate that their managers, at least in some cases, were incompetent.

Frequently managers are promoted on the idea that they will grow in the new assignment and perform it satisfactorily. But often they don't, meaning they have reached their level of incompetence.

The high turnover in some organizations due to frustration and dissatisfaction caused by weak, ineffective leadership means that many managers have been promoted to their level of incompetence.

### NO

**The Peter Principle is not valid because . . .**

If the Peter Principle were true, ultimately all managers at all levels would be incompetent. Observation suggests this simply is not true. There are many highly successful organizations.

No one benefits if a manager is promoted to a level at which he or she cannot perform effectively. Great care is used in organizations to select the best-possible individuals to fill management jobs. Mistakes are made, but they may be less frequent than is perceived.

No one is perfect. What is described as level of incompetence really means managers at any level make mistakes.

Many organizations have extensive manager-development programs. These prevent managers from being promoted to levels at which they cannot function well.

## QUESTIONS

1. In your opinion, how valid is the Peter Principle? Explain.
2. Of what general value to effective managing is the Peter Principle?

interfere with job performance, or an inability to motivate others. Countless manager-appointment decisions prove incorrect because too much emphasis was placed on favorable reference reports.

To partially overcome the limitations of references, many organizations make use In-Depth Investigations of companies that specialize in assembling information about individuals' personal habits, financial stability, involvement in lawsuits, and other sensitive data. Some companies, the model being Equifax, are able to assemble a great deal of information, positive and negative, about a person. One problem in using such information is that the applicant, if turned down for the position because of the information, has the legal right to inspect the report. If it can then be proved that the information is incorrect, the organization that rejected the applicant may become involved in a lawsuit. Nevertheless, in-depth investigations are used extensively. In general, the more important the position is, the more comprehensive the requested report will be.

Often job candidates are given tests that seek to measure their personal charac- Tests teristics, potentialities, or special abilities. Generally, an individual's responses on a test are compared with those of others who have been tested, and a percentage score is assigned.

A number of types of tests are used. The most common ones are

- *Intelligence tests* — Seek to measure mental abilities such as verbal comprehension, word fluency, memory, inductive reasoning, facility with numbers, speed of perception, and spatial visualization.
- *Achievement tests* — Seek to measure an individual's ability to perform specific tasks.
- *Aptitude tests* — Try to identify underdeveloped as well as developed personal talents or capabilities (for example, mechanical aptitude).
- *Interest tests* — Seek to pinpoint an individual's major interests.
- *Personality tests* — Attempt to measure such personal characteristics as maturity and temperament.

Dozens, even hundreds, of different tests are available for the various types of tests noted. Tests, when used, are administered late in the selection process and then only to individuals who appear basically qualified for the position to be filled.

The testing of candidates for managerial positions — and particularly the use of personality tests — is controversial. Some authorities completely refute testing on the grounds that it is not an accurate predictor of managerial success. Those opposed to testing can cite many examples of individuals who did poorly on various tests intended to predict management success but who nevertheless performed exceptionally well as managers. Examples of the converse can also be readily identified.

Many observers take a middle position on psychological testing. They feel it may be useful in the selection process but should be considered only one input among many; they do not advocate rejection of a managerial candidate solely on the basis of test results. Past performance and personal desire to succeed as a manager are believed to be more important in the total selection process.

### Advantages of Testing in Manager Selection

Proponents of testing claim several advantages for it. First, when properly designed and administered, tests are relatively objective. Intelligence, for example, can be measured more objectively through testing than through conversations with or observation of an individual.

Second, a test is normally administered to thousands of people, and test scores are later correlated with job performance. Tests thus help an organization to find managers who fit the mold the organization wants. Once an organization has developed a profile of what it considers to be a successful manager, it can test people to determine whether they fit the profile.

Third, tests can yield information about an individual's psychological makeup that is not obtainable from interviews or résumés. Results of a personality test may reveal things about an individual that even he or she does not know.

Fourth, tests sometimes are more acceptable to the individual being considered than any other evaluation device. A candidate may prefer to be denied a management position or a promotion because he or she scored too low on a battery of tests rather than because "the interviewer didn't think I could handle the job" or some other subjective reason.

### Disadvantages of Testing in Manager Selection

Critics of testing cite several disadvantages inherent in the practice. First, tests do not take an individual's previous job performance and other qualifications into account. This limitation is important, since previous performance is generally agreed to be the best indicator of an individual's future on-the-job behavior. And tests cannot accurately measure some of the most important characteristics of success, such as an individual's motivation or how hard he or she will work to succeed.

Second, tests—even if they do accurately measure an individual's abilities and psychological makeup—can only measure these qualities *today*. They cannot measure them, say, five years from now. People, including their capabilities and psychological structure, change over time. An individual who is denied a management position now because he or she scored too low may, through work experience and changes in the environment, be able to make a satisfactory score at some point in the future. Excessive reliance on test scores may result in the elimination of some highly promising candidates.

Third, some feel that tests discriminate against minorities. This criticism is frequently leveled at intelligence tests, many of which evaluate vocabulary development. It is claimed that different cultures have somewhat different vocabularies, and therefore members of minority groups are placed at a disadvantage.

Finally, the most fundamental criticism of testing is the claim that the work of managing is too varied and intangible for anyone to be able to construct a test that will predict an individual's future success. Most critics who hold this view will admit freely that tests can be designed to determine whether an individual can be a successful computer programmer, accountant, or even physician. But the job of managing remains too undefinable for employers to rely very heavily on tests.

Some organizations have established **assessment centers** (also called *evaluation centers*) to appraise candidates for management positions. Typically, in an assessment center managerial candidates are given tests, are interviewed intensively, make oral presentations on how to diagnose and solve specific problems, and participate in group discussions. A key technique in an assessment center is to ask the applicant to play various roles. A leading department store chain's assessment center asks applicants to play the roles of an employee handling an irate customer, holding a meeting of departmental personnel, dealing with a problem that is causing friction between two employees, and so on.

One advantage of an assessment center is that managers can observe how an applicant would probably behave in a real situation. And since a number of people observe the applicant, several opinions about his or her fitness are available.

A problem with evaluating managerial candidates through assessment centers is the high cost. A typical evaluation lasts from three to five days and is quite expensive. A second limitation is the training of the people who make the assessments. It is difficult to pin down what, specifically, they should look for in making the evaluation. Assessment is always partially subjective, and managers frequently disagree about whether an applicant has performed well or poorly.

## HOW TO FORECAST THE NEED FOR MANAGERS

Assume an organization is fully staffed with 100 managers covering all levels. Over time, this supply of managers will diminish as some managers leave the firm, some retire, and so on. Unless an organization forecasts its need for managers, it may become understaffed or staffed with less-than-desirable managers. Forecasting the need for managers is therefore an important consideration in managing.

Managing forecasting can be seen as a four-step process, as described below.

### Step 1: Take Inventory of Existing Managers

If an organization has an up-to-date organizational chart, this step is simple. One need only count the obvious management positions that exist. The count should be made by organizational level, since the qualifications for managers obviously change as the organizational ladder is ascended.

### Step 2: Estimate Attrition

Five forces are at work to reduce the supply of existing managers: Some managers may die, others may become physically or mentally unable to work, some may quit and join other organizations, a few may be terminated or demoted, and a few may retire.

If an organization has existed for a number of years and has grown at a fairly even rate, past history of attrition should provide a good guide in estimating the number of existing managers who will need to be replaced during the planning period. However, for younger, more dynamic organizations it is difficult to make attrition estimates.

### Step 3: Evaluate the Quality of Existing Managers

Since attrition will occur at each level in the managerial hierarchy, evaluations should be made at all levels to determine which managers are promotable and which are not. This step should answer such questions as "How many first-line supervisors will be qualified for middle-management positions by the end of the planning period?" and "How many people at middle levels will be ready to move up?" Normally, as managers are promoted, their previous positions must be filled.

In considering the supply of potential managers, attention should be given to the standards set for management positions. As standards are lowered the supply of potential managers increases; conversely, as requirements for management jobs are elevated the supply of prospective managers declines. For example, if an organization requires a Master of Business Administration degree for promotion to a certain level, the supply of potential managers is much smaller than if only a Bachelor's degree is stipulated. And if no specific educational requirements are imposed, the supply of prospective managers becomes still larger.

Requirements for management positions will probably be raised in the decades ahead, for several reasons. First, since the number of laws and regulations imposed on organizations is almost certain to increase, a wider and deeper knowledge of the environment in which management is practiced will be needed. Second, the technology directly and indirectly affecting management positions will become increasingly complex. Thus, managers will need more advanced training if they are to function effectively. Finally, as worker expectations rise, more effort will be required to make jobs interesting and meaningful.

### Step 4: Consider Future Expansion or Contraction

Most organizations are growth-oriented and plan to be larger in the future than they are today. Planned growth generally means that more managers at all levels will be required.

Sales estimates are an obvious guide for business enterprises in assessing manager needs. They are particularly valuable in service industries that have heavy labor inputs and do not lend themselves to technology. In such industries, the number of additional managers required may be in direct proportion to sales increases.

While most organizations prefer to grow, in short-run situations some enterprises find it necessary to terminate managers. Managers generally have more job security than operative employees, but during periods of severe economic recession management personnel may also be released.

Some organizations terminate managers on the basis of the amount of time they have been with the organization, with the last hired being the first to go. In situations in which several managers have performed approximately equally, seniority is a fair basis for a termination decision. However, in many cases seniority is no indication of productivity, and a decision to reduce the number of managers can be viewed as an opportunity to improve the quality of management. Periods of retrenchment may provide an opportunity to prune ineffective managers from the management structure—although in some cases humanitarian considerations will prevail, and an individual whose performance has been declining will be kept on and given another chance.

Organizations exist in an exceptionally dynamic environment—a fact that greatly complicates the process of forecasting future management needs. A painstakingly developed manager forecast may be upset by any number of unforeseen occurrences—a division may be closed or a new one added, one department may be split into two or two departments may be combined into one, a product line may be phased out or another added, the company may be acquired by another organization or it may buy out a competitor, and so on.

Such contingencies affect the validity of all forecasts. Nevertheless, an effort should be made to predict manager requirements in a systematic fashion. If nothing else, forecasting keeps an organization focused on the future, and better overall managerial planning should result.

## USE OF WOMEN AND MINORITY-GROUP MEMBERS IN MANAGER STAFFING

Until the 1960s the overwhelming majority of managers in business, the military, government, and other social institutions were male and white. Over the past two decades the proponents of equal employment rights for women and minority-group members have become very outspoken. Finally, they succeeded in inducing action on the part of Congress, the executive branch, and the courts to end discriminatory personnel practices. Title VII of the Civil Rights Act of 1964 prohibits discrimination in employment based on race, religion, national origin, or sex by any employer with fifteen or more employees who engage in interstate commerce.

Discrimination in promotional policy is now clearly illegal. Even so, efforts on the part of senior management to use women and minority-group members more fully in management vary greatly. Some organizations have done nothing substantial to encourage, train, or otherwise prepare women and minority-group members to assume management positions. Other organizations have appointed "affirmative-action directors," whose jobs are to seek out qualified women and minority-group members for management jobs.

Women and minority-group members still account for much less than their proportionate share of managers. However, there are definite trends toward greater use of both women and minority-group members in management. It will probably be many decades, however, before these groups are proportionately represented in the ranks of management.

While women are increasingly represented at the first and middle levels of management, only a few have reached the highest levels. According to Boone and Johnson, "Although the backgrounds of the corporate elite are widely varied, they do share one characteristic: they are almost unanimously male. Although a search for names of female corporate leaders will produce such well-known executives as Olive Beech, Mary Wells Lawrence, Lynn Salvage, Patricia Carbine, Mary Hudson, and others, only one woman—Katherine Graham of *The Washington Post*—heads an organization that ranks in the top 800 business firms."[7]

Nevertheless, we can expect to see increased advancement of women to the highest echelons in business. When Herman Kahn, the futurist, was asked to predict how long it would take for women to account for 25 percent of the chief executives of the 500 largest corporations in the United States, he replied, "About two thousand years. But make it 10 percent and I'll say within twenty years."[8]

**As Managers, Are Women Different from Men?**

Stereotypes about women indicating that they have limited qualifications to manage have long existed. Examples are

- Women prefer working for a "nice" manager rather than a competent one.
- Women insist on short hours and a pleasant working environment.
- Women are too complacent to want to get ahead on the job.
- Women lack the ability to conceptualize and make abstract plans.
- Women expect special treatment because they are women.

In a significant study, William Reif, John Newstrom, and Robert Monczka discovered that stereotypes such as those above have no basis in reality. They conclude:

> There is considerable research evidence to support the fact that women managers psychologically are not significantly different from their male counterparts and that they may possess even superior attributes and skills in some areas related to managerial effectiveness. From a social psychological standpoint—that is, how they view themselves as a part of the environment within which they operate—this study has shown that women managers have much in common with men. Differences do exist, but mostly in ways that would serve to increase the probability of women functioning well as managers. It is recommended, therefore, that organizations begin treating women as equals, not because of moral obligations or pressures from outside interest groups to improve female-male ratios, but because they would more effectively utilize valuable human resources."[9]

Despite the fact that women appear at least equal to men in their potential abilities to manage, there are still two main obstacles in their way. First is the still strong attitude on the part of some male executives that for one reason or another women do not "fit" the model of a manager. Second, some women lack the self-confidence to seek out management positions and to try to move up in the hierarchy.

Two observers note that the movement of large numbers of women into management will not be easy, expressing their view as follows:

> The movement of qualified women into management is of mutual interest to organizations and to women. But the problems that stand in the way of this movement are many and complicated. These problems will not be solved by simple prescriptions.

[7]Louis E. Boone and James C. Johnson, "Profiles of the 801 Men and 1 Woman at the Top," *Business Horizons,* February 1980, p. 48.
[8]Wyndham Robertson, "The Top Women in Big Business," *Fortune,* July 17, 1978, p. 59.
[9]© 1975 by the Regents of the University of California. Reprinted from *California Management Review,* volume XVII, no. 4, pp. 72–79 by permission of the Regents.

The realities of the situation must be revealed and confronted so that realistic action can be taken.

It would be unfortunate if in the years to come women fail to make a dent in the corporate hierarchy despite the fact that more and more educated and competent women are being turned out. Yet we cannot help but feel this will be the case unless greater commitment and greater creative effort [are] forthcoming from aspiring women, schools of business and public administration, and men and women already working in organizations.[10]

## MANAGERS AT THE TOP: WHO ARE THEY?

Several years ago *Fortune* magazine conducted a study of the chief executive officers of the 500 largest industrial corporations and the 300 largest life insurance companies, diversified financial enterprises, retailers, transportation companies, and utilities in the United States.[11] Collectively, these 800 organizations employ one out of four Americans and are responsible for producing over one third of our gross national product.

Only a fraction of 1 percent of present and future managers will ever be selected to serve at the uppermost level of management in American businesses. Nevertheless, because these people represent the pacesetters in management and because their thinking tends to shape the thinking of hundreds of thousands of other managers, it is useful to examine some of the results of the *Fortune* study.

Figure 13–1 shows some of the findings of the study. Please note that a similar study conducted today might reveal some differences in the backgrounds of top executives, particularly with regard to education, career emphasis, and family background. As part A of Figure 13–1 indicates, only a small share of the top managers (about one in ten) came from poor families, and even a smaller share (about one in twenty) came from wealthy families. The great majority of senior executives came from the lower-middle class or the upper-middle class. Thus the widely held notion that top executives come mainly from the wealthy class is not true.

Part B of Figure 13–1 shows that over 95 percent of the chief executives attended college, with the great majority receiving degrees. Part C indicates that business was the most popular field of study, for both undergraduate and graduate work. In terms of career emphasis (see Part D), marketing was the major field, followed closely by finance. But according to *Fortune*:

Scientific and technical schooling, nuts and bolts business experience seems to have become less important. The proportion of executives with their primary experience in production, operations, engineering, design, and R & D [research and development] has fallen from a third of the total to just over a quarter. And the number of top officers with legal and financial background has increased more than enough to make up the difference. Lawyers and financial men now head two out of five corporations.[12]

[10]Ronald J. Burke and Tamara Weir, "Readying the Sexes for Women in Management," *Business Horizons,* June 1977, p. 35.
[11]See Charles G. Burck, "A Group Profile of the *Fortune* 500 Chief Executive," *Fortune*, May 1976, pp. 173–76.
[12]Ibid., p. 176.

**FIGURE 13–1**

A Profile of 800 Top CEOs in the United States

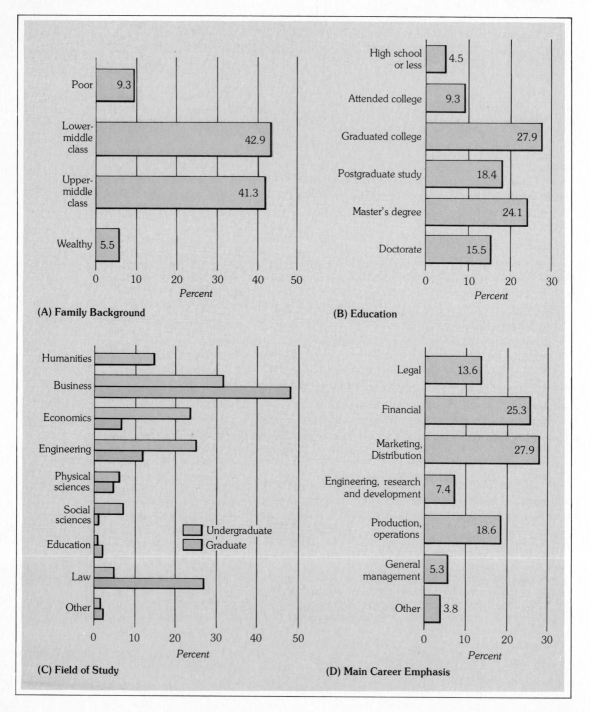

(A) Family Background

(B) Education

(C) Field of Study

(D) Main Career Emphasis

Source: Charles G. Burck, "A Group Profile of the *Fortune* 500 Chief Executives," *Fortune*, May 1976, pp. 173–76. Courtesy of Joe Argenziano for *Fortune* Magazine; © 1976, Time Inc.

# MANAGERS IN ACTION

## HOW CAN WOMEN ACHIEVE SUCCESS IN MANAGEMENT?

Professor Corine T. Norgaard surveyed 124 women managers to gain a perspective on the problems and progress women are experiencing in the business world today. She discovered that a woman's progress depends largely on the company she works for and her own personal makeup.

The variety of responses indicates that it was easier to characterize the degree of women's success in business when there were *no* women managers. The problem was clear: with very few exceptions, women were simply excluded from the ranks of management. Now women managers are becoming more prominent in the corporate landscape. However, the variety of routes and roadblocks that women with similar backgrounds have encountered as they've advanced their careers indicates a disparity of experience that makes it difficult to generalize.

Employer discrimination was the one problem that 50 percent or more of the managers in Professor Norgaard's survey agreed upon as being a major problem for women today. The majority of the women surveyed agreed that it is no longer difficult for women to be hired, but once hired they continue to encounter differences in pay for equal work, as well as unequal consideration for promotion. Yet they differed in opinion as to whether this was personal employer bias or continued societal conditioning. Most of the women who were earning higher salaries and who had higher level jobs had changed companies to advance their careers. Additionally, as indicated by the former secretary quoted below, switching companies often made it easier to shake off associations with secretarial roles.

I was a secretary for five years and I knew my boss's job. When he got promoted, I felt capable of performing it, but there was no way I could get my qualifications evaluated. In addition, he wanted me to move up with him and wasn't enthusiastic about helping me move out of the secretarial role. I had to move to another company to get away from the image of the secretary."

On the other hand, changing companies isn't always necessary. Another manager who also advanced to management from the secretarial field said:

My company is making a real effort to help interested women move out of secretarial and clerical jobs. I'm the success story which is held up to these women and they are told, "See, you can do it, too."

Ninety-one percent of the women managers reported that their companies offer some form of support for people interested in advancement. Most of this support is in the form of financial assistance with job-related training and educational programs, in-house training, and posting of job opportunities. To a lesser degree, some of the companies offered flexible working hours and child-care facilities that more overtly assisted the working mother.

Women's ability to advance their careers also seems to be affected by their own willingness to accept the pressures of multiple demands, and their ability to deal with any concerns they may have about their quality of life or any conflicts with spouses. Given that an employer is not discriminatory and/or is supportive, a successful woman would seem from this survey to be one who is not ambivalent about the demands of her career and one who is able to pursue that career fully, whether or not she has to make adjustments.

Of the women surveyed, slightly less than half were single, and two thirds of those had never married. Of those who were or who had been married, only half had children.

Source: "Problems and Perspectives of Female Managers" by Corine T. Norgaard, *MSU Business Topics*, Winter 1980, pp. 23–28.

## QUESTION

1. Approximately one half of all business school graduates in recent years were females. And about 80 percent of honor graduates were women. Will these facts affect the acceptance of women in management in the decade ahead? Why or why not?

Here are some other findings of the *Fortune* study:

- Approximately 25 percent of the fathers of the senior managers were clerical workers, skilled laborers, unskilled laborers, and farmers. Thus many who reach the top come from ordinary backgrounds.
- Slightly more than one fourth (26.3 percent) of the top managers were born in the West and the South, although these regions have almost half the U.S. population (49.7 percent). The Midwest and Northeast, with 50.3 percent of the population, produced 69.9 percent of the senior executives.
- Most top executives are not frequent job changers. Over 85 percent have worked for only one to three companies. Only one chief executive officer in twenty-five has worked for five or more companies.
- Most senior managers (82 percent, or about four out of five) are between the ages of fifty and sixty-four. Only 3.4 percent are over sixty-five, and only 14.3 percent are forty-nine or younger.

**SUMMARY**

- Selection of managers is important because the abilities of managers to a large degree determine the success of an organization.
- To manage effectively, individuals should have a desire to manage, knowledge of the management process, the intellectual capabilities to handle the job, the ability to earn respect, skill in communicating, a cooperative attitude, integrity, loyalty to the organization, and personal stability.
- Job analyses are useful in matching managerial candidates to jobs because they serve as a basis for the preparation of job descriptions and job specifications, which detail, respectively, what the job involves and what qualifications a person must have for the job.
- Managers may either be promoted from within or are sought outside the organization. Both methods of selection have advantages and disadvantages.
- There are several sources of information about managerial candidates. Past performance is the best predictive guide of an individual's future performance as a manager. A company may also use personal interviews, in-depth investigations (which assemble information about an individual's habits, financial stability, and so on), a variety of tests, and assessment centers.
- Steps in forecasting the need for managers are (1) take inventory of existing managers, (2) estimate attrition, (3) evaluate the quality of existing managers, (4) consider future expansion or contraction.
- Women and minority-group members are grossly underrepresented in managing. However, indications are that their representation will improve in the future.
- Most managers who reach the highest levels in business came from middle-class backgrounds, attended college and attained degrees, studied business, and have career emphases in the areas of finance and marketing.

**LEARN THE LANGUAGE OF MANAGEMENT**

job analysis
job description
job specification
promotion from within

inbreeding
executive search firms
assessment centers

1. Why is the desire to manage so important as a requirement for a manager? Do you know of an individual without a strong desire to manage who has succeeded as a manager? Explain.
2. Suppose an individual lacks skill in communicating effectively through the written word. What can he or she do to remedy this problem?
3. Suppose you are asked to rate the integrity of another person. Explain how you would proceed.
4. How would you measure an individual's loyalty to an organization?
5. You have been asked to make a job analysis of an office manager. Explain how you would go about it.
6. Under what conditions is it likely that an organization will go outside to find a manager?
7. Would you object to having an in-depth investigation done about you that revealed court records, financial transactions, and similar information? In your opinion, are such investigations really necessary?
8. Suppose you are denied a management job or a promotion because you scored too low on one of the tests mentioned in the text. How would you react? In general, how do you feel about testing as a basis for manager selection?
9. Evaluate assessment centers as a device for evaluating candidates for managerial positions.
10. In your opinion, will a larger share of the working population probably be classified as managers a decade from now? Explain.
11. Women and minority-group members are proportionately underrepresented in managing. Do you feel organizations should give them a break by lowering requirements for selection as managers?
12. What conclusion can you draw on what it takes to become a senior executive?

### 1. Winning acceptance of a female manager

The Smith, Hardley, & Yager Company, an engineering firm, has never had a female manager before. Smith, the chief executive of the company, recently met a woman, Ms. Ralston, who he believes would make an ideal manager of a department of seven drafting engineers. She is a graduate engineer and has had five years of experience as a manager with the Army Corps of Engineers. Her record there is excellent.

Before appointing Ms. Ralston manager of the department, Smith decides to speak to the engineers she will supervise. Without exception, they seem cool, even hostile, about the idea.

In a brief report, outline several things you think the chief executive could do to prepare the drafting department to accept and cooperate with the female manager.

### 2. Which management candidate would you select?

Assume that you are a middle manager in the customer-service department of a large insurance company. There is presently an opening for supervisor, and you have narrowed your choice to three persons. Assume further that each of these people is twenty-seven years old, has been with the company for three years, and performs duties similar to the others. The supervisor you select will *not* manage former coworkers. Each person's abilities are summarized in the following chart.

| Requirement | Henry Gruber | Barbara Hensel | Joe Simpson |
|---|---|---|---|
| Desire to manage | • Has asked for several raises, but not for additional responsibility. | • Has asked for a promotion to supervisor twice. | • Has intense desire to get ahead.<br>• Is studying management subjects after hours. |
| Knowledge of the management process | • Was a petty officer in the Navy for two years. | • Seems to have an instinct for organizing and processing work. | • Takes short cuts and avoids excessive red tape in doing his job. |
| Intellectual capabilities | • Reads no fiction. | • Reads much fiction. | • Seldom reads fiction. |
| Ability to earn respect | • Other employees seem to trust him yet rarely confide in him. | • Seems to be a leader in the informal organization. | • Socializes with several other employees after work. |
| Skill in communicating | • Is very quiet and speaks in short sentences. | • Listens more than she talks. | • Talks a great deal with other employees. |
| Cooperative attitude | • Helps others when asked but rarely volunteers to assist.<br>• Is regarded by fellow workers as a loner. | • Is very cooperative.<br>• Is eager to help new employees learn routines. | • Works overtime willingly when necessary.<br>• Volunteers to help other employees when they are overloaded with work. |
| Integrity | • Withheld information that he was released from naval service with a less than honorable separation. | • Misstated her academic attainments on original employment application. | • Was involved in a cheating incident in sophomore year in college. Was suspended for two weeks. |
| Loyalty to the organization | • Seems neutral. There is no reason to suspect any disloyalty or any genuine loyalty. | • Won an award three months ago for bringing in the most new customers. | • After an illness, came back to work before he was fully recovered. |
| Personal stability | • Is married, has two children, owns own home. | • Has been divorced twice; now lives alone with one child. | • Is single and has involvements with several different women. |

On the basis of the limited information in the chart, which person would you choose to be supervisor? Why?

What other information about each candidate would you like to have before making the decision?

### 3. Should résumés be checked? How?

John Adams, President of Financial USA #One, was shocked by an article he read in *Time* called *"Embellishment Yes, Lying No."* The article stated:

> On the basis of fake résumés, a man with a high school diploma was hired as a safety engineer of a nuclear power plant, a woman without a medical degree worked as a doctor at four New York City hospitals, and a man who had never passed the bar was taken on as a lawyer by the brokerage firm of Paine Webber. The saga of Paul Arthur Crafton, 59, showed how creative job résumés can be. A professor at George Washington University, Crafton allegedly used false identities to join six other college faculties in the past four years. Crafton, who is trained as an engineer, has billed himself as an expert in computers, mathematics, finance and business administration. Now out on bail, he faces 27 counts of forgery, theft by deception, false swearing and tampering with official documents.[13]

The article went on to say that there are outright lies on 22 percent of all résumés. After finishing the article, Mr. Adams calls his Human Resource Manager Barbara Long.

Adams: Barbara we must get 2000 résumés a year from people wanting management jobs. How do you verify the information the job applicants give us?
Long: Well, if we think an applicant has qualified for a slot we have, we do a few checks. But mostly we take job résumés at face value. We assume they are honest.
Adams: Stop assuming anything. I want all résumés from people we give serious consideration to be checked carefully.

Cost/benefit analysis should enter into all decision making. If benefits don't outweigh costs, a "do it" decision is wrong. What are the possible benefits of Adam's directions to Long that all résumés of job candidates under serious consideration are to be checked? The limitations?

Companies that provide résumé checking services exist. What are the pros and cons of using a résumé checking service?

Baron, Alma S. "What Men Are Saying About Women in Business." *Business Horizons*, January–February 1982, pp. 10–14.
Baron, Alma S., and Witte, Robert L. "The New Work Dynamic: Men and Women in the Work Force." *Business Horizons*, August 1980, pp. 56–60.
Josefowitz, Natasha. "Management Men and Women: Closed vs. Open Doors." *Harvard Business Review*, September–October 1980, pp. 56–65.
Kaufman, Lois, and Wolf, John B. "Hotel Room Interviewing—Anxiety and Suspicion." *Sloan Management Review*, Spring 1982, pp. 57–61.

**FOR ADDITIONAL
CONCEPTS
AND IDEAS**

[13]John Leo, "Embellishment Yes, Lying No," *Time*, May 9, 1983, p. 82. Copyright 1983 Time Inc. All rights reserved. Reprinted by permission from *Time*.

Kerin, Roger A. "Where They Come From: CEOs in 1952 and 1980." *Business Horizons*, November–December 1981, pp. 66–69.

Kovach, Kenneth A. "Subconscious Stereotyping in Personnel Decisions." *Business Horizons*, September–October 1982, pp. 60–66.

Laurence, Thomas. "Sexism, Racism, and the Business World." *Business Horizons*, July–August 1981, pp. 62–68.

Levinson, Harry. "Criteria for Choosing Chief Executives." *Harvard Business Review*, July–August 1980, pp. 113–120.

McLane, Helen J. *Selecting, Developing and Retaining Women Executives: A Corporate Strategy for the Eighties.* New York: Van Nostrand Reinhold, 1980.

Mines, Herbert T. "Finding and Using Executive Talent." *Business Horizons*, June 1980, pp. 45–48.

Neff, Thomas J. "How to Interview Candidates for Top Management Positions." *Business Horizons*, October 1980, pp. 47–52.

Norgaard, Corine T. "Problems and Perspectives of Female Managers." *MSU Business Topics*, Winter 1980, pp. 23–28.

Peter, Laurence, and Hull, Raymond. *The Peter Principle: Why Things Go Wrong.* New York: William Morrow, 1969.

Rosen, Benson; Templeton, Mary Ellen; and Kichline, Karen. "The First Few Years on the Job: Women in Management." *Business Horizons*, November–December 1981, pp. 26–29.

Stybel, Laurence J. "Executive Placement vs. Outplacement: Knowing the Difference." *Business*, September 1981, pp. 41–43.

Tyler, J. Larry. "Ten Good Reasons for Engaging a Retained Search Firm." *Business*, September 1981, pp. 44–45.

Veiga, John, F. "Women in Management: An Endangered Species?" *MSU Business Topics*, Summer 1977, pp. 31–35.

Welch, Mary Scott. *Networking: The Great New Way for Women to Get Ahead.* New York: Harcourt Brace Jovanovich, 1980.

# 14

# MANAGER DEVELOPMENT AND REWARDS

**STUDY THIS CHAPTER SO YOU CAN:**

- Define "manager development," and describe its goals.
- Identify and discuss the internal and external approaches to manager development.
- State and explain the guidelines for manager-development programs.
- Describe the manager's personal role in manager development.
- Define and explain the application of each of the following types of financial compensation: salaries, bonuses, profit-sharing plans, pension plans, and employee stock ownership plans.
- Explain the factors that affect financial compensation.
- Discuss the nonfinancial rewards for managers.
- State and explain the guidelines for the design and implementation of a manager-reward system.

The two aspects of the staffing function are (1) to develop the abilities of managers so they *can* perform their activities with maximum effectiveness and (2) to reward them so that they *will* put forth their best efforts.

The passage of time does not guarantee that an individual will acquire more wisdom, skill, proficiency, or effectiveness. Over a given period some individuals "grow" more than others in terms of abilities, job success, and leadership. In part, this growth is a reflection of one's inherent talents and drives. However, to a large degree such growth is influenced by the organizational environment in which one finds oneself. Designing appropriate systems to develop and reward managers is a key part of the staffing function.

## WHAT IS MANAGER DEVELOPMENT?

**Manager development** is the process of establishing programs and an organizational climate that will help individual managers better their skills, expand their knowledge of their particular jobs, and improve their attitudes toward the organization and its goals. A well-designed development program should emphasize all aspects of the manager's job.

Manager development includes any activities that are designed to directly or indirectly improve a manager's abilities, ranging from highly formal training programs (such as classroom instruction) to highly informal interactions (such as on-the-job counseling). There is a need for such programs in all organizations — business firms as well as government agencies, the military, educational institutions, and other nonprofit organizations. Even a small, one-person business needs some form of manager development if it is to grow and prosper.

Not all organizations have formal programs of manager development, but most recognize the need for such activities, even if informal. The overall rationale for manager growth and development can be summed up in two words: better results. Managers are the key to the success of any organization. Over time, organizations that downplay manager development are likely to experience difficulty in achieving results.

Any number of occurrences may indicate that there is a need to improve the capabilities of managers: for example, inability to obtain a satisfactory share of the market, ineffective use of financial resources, problems with quality control, and in some cases difficulty in surviving. While perfection in managing is impossible, a properly designed program for manager growth and development should result in greater productivity with the same input of human and financial resources.

**The Goals of Manager Development**

The overall goals of manager development are to strengthen managers' skills, expand their knowledge, and improve their attitudes (see Table 14-1). But there are some more specific reasons for the establishment of development programs, which are discussed in the following sections.

### To Compensate for Managers' Lack of Previous Training or Experience

The rationale for a manager-development program is that many first-level supervisors have had no preparation for management. Often, in lower-level management, an individual with no background in supervision is simply told, "There's a vacancy for a supervisor on the first shift. You have a good employment record, so we're giving you a chance at the job." Since managing is not the same as doing work that is supervised, the individual may or may not work out. His or her chances of success, however, are enhanced when an appropriate manager-development program is in effect.

## TABLE 14–4

### Motivating and Nonmotivating Climates for Developing First-Level Managers

| Area of Manager Growth | Progessive Climate | Regressive Climate |
|---|---|---|
| Accessibility of senior managers for consultation about organization philosophy | • Accessibility is considerable.<br>• There are informal discussions at meetings, luncheons, sporting events.<br>• There is candid exploration of what the enterprise is trying to do.<br>• Senior managers are highly visible. | • There is little, if any, accessibility.<br>• Lower-level managers are told only what they must know to handle immediate problems.<br>• There is no exploration of the "why" of major policies and decisions.<br>• Senior managers keep their distance. |
| Encouragement of junior managers to take courses on their own time at local universities | • Managers are strongly encouraged.<br>• Organization pays part or all of costs involved, assuming that managers do satisfactory work. | • Managers are not encouraged; if managers want more education, that's their business.<br>• Organization does not bear educational costs for its managers. |
| Encouragement of managers to join and participate in trade and professional associations | • Managers are strongly encouraged to participate when evidence is submitted that the professional or trade group shows promise of adding to their management skills and knowledge. | • View is taken that such activities are purely incidental to the manager's job of managing and should not be encouraged. |
| Provision of library services and subscriptions to publications that relate to the organization's purpose | • Information from external sources is put freely at the disposal of managers. Managers are encouraged to read extensively. | • View is taken that managers get all the information they need to manage internally.<br>• Reading of information other than internal reports is considered time-consuming and therefore expensive. |
| Encouragement of managers to attend management seminars and training programs sponsored by other organizations | • Managers are encouraged to attend if (1) the training experience appears to have significant potential advantages and (2) the managers' work will not be neglected in their absence. | • Managers not permitted to participate because (1) they might be exposed to concepts that are different from those espoused by the organization and (2) the money involved could be better spent on other activities. |
| Encouragement of managers from different departments to meet frequently in an informal way to exchange ideas | • There is strong encouragement.<br>• Efforts to develop a cooperative spirit and a more informal management team are fostered. | • Exchange of ideas is discouraged. View is taken that managers in each department should specialize and learn more about their activity, not more about the activities of other managers. |
| *Results* | • A strong attempt is made to enlarge the scope and vision of managers and provide for their growth. | • The outlook of managers is likely to be narrow.<br>• Growth is not provided for. |

Source: Slightly adapted from *American Business: An Introduction,* 5th ed. by Ferdinand F. Mauser and David J. Schwartz, © 1982 by Harcourt Brace Jovanovich, Inc. Reprinted by permission of the publisher.

tion, it is reflective of the philosophy of senior management. While there are certainly exceptions, a progressive attitude toward manager development generally pays off in better results.

While manager-development programs should be sanctioned by senior-level management, the individual manager is not relieved of his or her personal responsibility for growth. Managers who adopt the attitude "I'll try to learn what they want me to but no more" really should not be managers, for they lack the important qualities of personal initiative and motivation for self-betterment.

Individually, managers can do much to increase their knowledge and improve their skills. By reading management literature, attending university classes, and having informal discussions with other managers, they can learn more about management theory and about the inner workings of the organization. The desire to learn and to increase one's capabilities is a valuable quality in a manager regardless of his or her level.

## FINANCIAL REWARDS FOR MANAGERS

While managers are expected to be dedicated and loyal to their organizations whatever their compensation may be, they tend to work harder for — and gravitate more toward — enterprises that will pay them the most handsomely. Careful attention, therefore, should be given to the planning of an organization's financial-reward program.

The main financial methods for rewarding people are salaries, bonuses, profit-sharing plans, pension plans, and employee stock ownership plans. While these methods are common for managers and nonmanagers alike, they will be discussed in the following sections in terms of managers only.

Salaries
A **salary** is a fixed payment that is typically calculated on a monthly or annual basis. It is usually amended annually, although it may be adjusted more frequently to coincide with a manager appraisal review. A salary is the main financial incentive for a manager.

One advantage of a salary as a form of financial reward is its simplicity in administration; it is an exact amount and does not have to be recalculated at each pay period. A salary also provides security for the manager, since it is a fixed sum and therefore he or she need not worry about the amount of compensation.

On the negative side, a salary, because it is a fixed amount, may lead to complacency, since incentive is lacking to put forth extra effort. And a salary does not closely relate pay to performance.

Because of the limitations of salary as a reward, many organizations supplement it with other types of compensation programs. The most important of these are discussed in the following sections.

Bonuses
Many senior executives believe that **incentive compensation**, or some form of financial reward that is directly related to results achieved, is more important as a motivator than salary. For example, when George Mueller became chief executive officer of System Development Corporation, a 4,000-employee enterprise, profits

had dropped from $1 million a month to almost zero. Mueller expressed the problem and his solution as follows:

> The company was likely to go broke. Managers were not really profit-motivated. You have to be, if you are going to have a successful company.
>
> The quickest way I could think of to cause management to worry about profits was to cut the salaries of about fifty top executives but then extend incentives which would allow the executives to more than make up for the cuts.
>
> The move turned out to be quite constructive, I think. We were able to do some profitable things in the next year. By and large, everyone ended up making more than he had made before.[3]

The most common form of incentive compensation for managers is the **bonus**, which is a sum of money given to an individual in addition to salary. Many profit-seeking organizations use bonuses as an incentive to bring about superior performance. Nonprofit organizations make less use of bonuses, partly because of tradition and partly because results in nonprofit organizations tend to be more difficult to measure.

### Bases for Bonuses

The ideal basis for bonuses should be contribution to profits. However, it is often difficult to measure precisely how much one individual or one department has contributed to profits. Therefore, some other bases for bonuses are waste reduction, increase in sales, reduction in absenteeism, and improvement in employee productivity.

A bonus may be given to either an individual or a group. An **individual bonus**, as the term suggests, is given only to certain people who have performed in an outstanding manner. A **group bonus**, if declared, is given to all people within the organization — or all people in a department. The people will not necessarily share equally in the bonus. Usually, the more common practice is to give larger individual bonuses to higher-ranking managers. It is interesting to note, however, that members of the team that wins the annual Super Bowl, while not management personnel, do share the bonus equally even though all players do not make exactly the same contribution.

### Advantages of Bonuses

When properly designed, bonuses have several advantages. First, they should encourage greater effort and thus should benefit both the organization and the individual. The promise of a possible bonus adds some excitement to managing and can be a morale booster. Second, in the case of group bonuses, each manager in a sense is "his brother's keeper." A bonus system may encourage managers to work together more harmoniously, since poor performance by one manager adversely affects the performances of others. Third, bonuses can be used indirectly to solve specific organizational problems. For example, waste of materials might be a serious problem in a manufacturing firm. If senior management bases company bonuses on degree of waste reduction, significant improvement may result.

[3]George E. Mueller, "Profiting from the Revolution in Technology," *Nation's Business*, August 1977, p. 46.

### Disadvantages of Bonuses

The principal limitation of bonuses as incentives is the difficulty in measuring the contribution to results of the managers who are involved. Assume that marketing managers in an organization are offered a graduated bonus based on an increase in sales volume over a twelve-month period. Conceivably, a major increase—and hence a major bonus—could occur because of unusually weak performance by competitors, an especially well-designed product (here some of the credit should go to the designers), or an unforeseen increase in economic activity. Alternatively, managers may do an excellent job yet not achieve the sales goal—and not receive a bonus—because of conditions beyond their control, such as a strike or an economic recession.

A second limitation of bonuses is that they add to the complexity of managing. It takes considerable skill to develop an effective bonus system and considerable time to administer it.

Edward Meadows has noted a third weakness of bonuses and other forms of incentive compensation.

> Are American executives rewarded for being bad managers? A number of experts on executive compensation think so. They believe that the kinds of bonuses and incentive compensation routinely paid out to top corporate officers tend to bias their behavior toward the short term, at the expense of the long-term health of their companies—and ultimately of the U.S. economy.
>
> Even in a good year the annual bonus can twist management priorities. An executive who wants to hype earnings per share might skimp on capital spending, research-and-development outlays, or maintenance. Merger deals can be bad marriages and still pump up reported EPS [earnings per share].[4]

Finally, in the case of group bonus plans, morale may be adversely affected. There is always a risk that some managers will feel they are not being adequately rewarded for their contribution in comparison with other managers. Any time a group reward is made, there is a danger that Mr. Brown will think he performed better than Ms. Green and should receive more. This problem is roughly analogous to the effect on student morale when a professor gives A's to all students. The stronger students are likely to feel that they were treated unfairly.

### Profit-Sharing Plans

**Profit sharing** is a method by which a predetermined share of profits is paid to qualified personnel. The percentage of profits set aside for profit sharing varies greatly but rarely exceeds 10 percent. Generally, profit-sharing plans require shareholders' approval and are modified only infrequently. Typically, all persons participating in a profit-sharing plan receive a certain percentage of their salaries as profit distribution.

Profit-sharing plans can be divided into two categories: cash and deferred. Under a **cash profit-sharing** plan, each manager's share of profits is distributed at regular intervals, usually annually. In **deferred profit-sharing** plans, a manager's share of profits is invested in a fund that will be available when he or she reaches a certain age or ceases to be employed by the firm.

[4]Edward Meadows, "New Targeting for Executive Pay," *Fortune*, May 4, 1981, pp. 176, 177.

### Advantages of Profit Sharing

Proponents of profit sharing for managers claim several advantages for it. First, a profit-sharing plan serves as a group incentive to manage more effectively. Such a plan should result in greater individual effort, better cooperation, greater receptiveness to changes in methods and policies, more initiative in making suggestions, and more attention to waste reduction.

Second, profit-sharing plans — since they give managers an opportunity to earn more than their stated salaries — may reduce turnover and may help attract better managers to the organization. Third, profit-sharing plans do not represent a fixed commitment on the part of an organization. If profits are not earned in a certain year, no cash outlays for profit sharing need be made.

### Disadvantages of Profit Sharing

One disadvantage of profit sharing is that those most responsible for making the profits may not receive any more rewards than those who contributed little. Those who contribute most may prefer bonuses or some other form of incentive. Second, unless the profit-sharing plan increases profits more than it costs over a period of time, it works to the disadvantage of the shareholders. The shareholders, who are the owners of the business, have a right to expect their dividends and the value of their stock to increase because of the plan. If profit sharing for managers has the net effect of subtracting from owners' dividends and from growth of their equity, it is extremely doubtful whether the plan should be continued.

**Pension plans** are a common form of financial reward for managers. Their use is becoming increasingly popular because of favorable tax treatment. Money invested by an organization in pension plans approved by the Internal Revenue Service is not taxed because it is considered a legitimate business expense. And if the recipient of the pension contributes to the plan, he or she pays no tax on the money invested until retirement, when benefits are received. At that point the manager will normally be in a lower tax bracket.

From the organization's standpoint, the main benefit of a pension plan is that it encourages managers to stay with the organization. If a manager leaves before a certain number of years, he or she may not receive any of the money put aside or may receive only a portion. Also, the longer a manager participates in a pension plan, the larger the retirement income will be. Therefore, by helping to reduce manager turnover, pension plans may make the organization more stable.

For the individual manager, a pension plan is presumed to have a positive effect on morale, since it helps meet the individual's need for security. Often, however, managers take a pension plan for granted and do not perform more effectively because it exists. Age is also a consideration. Younger managers may not be motivated because a pension plan has been established for them and may prefer to earn a larger salary even if they have to pay income taxes on it.

In 1974 Congress enacted the Employee Retirement Income Security Act, which has greatly increased the popularity of **employee stock ownership plans** (ESOPs). Under the act a company is permitted to invest up to 15 percent of its payroll in a stock ownership plan whose beneficiaries are employees (managers as well as operatives).

An ESOP works in the following manner:

1. The company contributes cash or stock or both to an employee stock ownership trust, which is typically run by a three-member committee.
2. The amount contributed is a certain percentage of the employee's earned salary or wages.
3. The trust may also purchase company stock from individuals or in the open market with the dividends it earns.
4. Shares in the trust are distrubuted pro rata to employees at certain times, either at regular intervals or when an employee terminates, retires, or dies (in the latter case the shares become part of the person's estate).

Many companies favor ESOPs because company contributions to such funds are tax deductible and because employees tend to be more enthusiastic about achieving production, sales, and other goals if they have a personal stake in seeing the company do well. Many senior executives feel ownership of stock by managers and employees is a strong incentive. Richard Jacob, chairman of the Dayco Corporation, commented as follows: "Employees own about 40 percent of our stock. Executives, former executives and their families own another 15 percent. . . . [Stock ownership by employees] gives us a lot more push. [The personnel] have an attitude of come on, let's really do it. Stock ownership is an important factor with the salaried employees."[5]

However, ESOPs also have some important limitations. An ESOP is more complicated than a pension plan and therefore more costly to implement. Furthermore, if a company has poor results, the value of its stock may drop, and employees may be dissatisfied with the plan.

## Factors That Affect Financial Compensation

Manager compensation differs greatly, depending mainly on the type of organization, the size of the organization, the type of industry, the importance of the manager's job, competitors' practices, and supply and demand. Note that all these factors are interrelated. Table 14–5 shows salaries and bonuses paid to key executives as reported in a study by Sibson and Company, a firm that specializes in advising businesses on manager compensation programs.

### Type of Organization

At lower and middle levels of management, compensation is fairly similar from organizaton to organization. For example, a middle manager in a profit-seeking enterprise may receive approximately the same compensation as a middle manager in a government agency. However, the picture changes considerably as we move to higher levels of management. Senior managers in profit-seeking organizations generally receive much greater compensation than their counterparts in educational institutions, the military, and the government. Thus the *range* of compensation is much greater in profit as opposed to nonprofit organizations.

---

[5]Quoted from Henry Altman, "Turning Ideas into Profits," *Nation's Business*, April 1978, p. 68.

# MANAGERS IN ACTION

## GOLDEN PARACHUTE PLANS: A NEW EXECUTIVE PERK

A "Golden Parachute" is a provision in an executive's employment contract that guarantees the executive a cash settlement—usually equal to several years' pay—if the employing company is acquired by another company. The settlement is paid by the acquired company.

Golden Parachute clauses were unheard of a decade ago, but now about 15 percent of the nation's largest companies include them in their contracts. Typically, a Golden Parachute plan covers one to six executives in a company and provides the covered executives with two to three years' salary if their employer is taken over.

Two reasons why stockholders in a company will approve Golden Parachutes for key executives are (1) so that top executives won't arbitrarily oppose takeovers (by other companies) that would benefit the shareholders and (2) because the existence of such plans may make the company a less desirable takeover candidate.

Adapted from Frederick C. Klein, "A Golden Parachute Protects Executives, But Does It Hinder or Foster Takeovers?" *The Wall Street Journal*, December 8, 1982, p. 56. Reprinted by permission of *The Wall Street Journal*, © Dow Jones & Company, Inc., 1982. All rights reserved.

### QUESTIONS

1. Does a Golden Parachute plan provide an incentive to key managers to manage more effectively?
2. Is it fair for a small number of key executives to have a Golden Parachute plan while most managers in a firm do not? Explain.
3. Might the existence of a Golden Parachute plan actually encourage executives to let their firm be taken over by another?

## TABLE 14–5

### Average Pay Levels of Key Executives (In Thousands of Dollars)

| Revenues | Chief Executive Officer | | Top Financial Executive | | Top Manufacturing Executive | | *Top Division Executive | |
|---|---|---|---|---|---|---|---|---|
| | Salary | Bonus | Salary | Bonus | Salary | Bonus | Salary | Bonus |
| $10 million to $25 million | $ 95 | $ 21 | $ 55 | $ 9 | $ 56 | $ 9 | $72 | $15 |
| $25 million to $50 million | 118 | 31 | 65 | 12 | 63 | 10 | 82 | 20 |
| $50 million to $100 million | 141 | 44 | 75 | 17 | 69 | 12 | 93 | 25 |
| $100 million to $500 million | 209 | 77 | 101 | 28 | 83 | 17 | 117 | 38 |
| $500 million to $750 million | 258 | 101 | 118 | 37 | 92 | 20 | 134 | 44 |
| $750 million to $1 billion | 277 | 119 | 128 | 42 | 95 | 22 | 141 | 50 |
| $1 billion to $5 billion | 386 | 189 | 168 | 62 | 112 | 29 | N.A. | N.A. |

*Revenues are for division only.      N.A.: Data not available      Source: Sibson & Company

Source: Adapted from W. Donald Gough, "Recession in Executive Pay Hikes," *Nation's Business*, December 1982, p. 69.

### Size of Organization

Generally, for profit-seeking enterprises, the larger the organization, the higher the salaries and bonuses paid to senior managers. The apparent rationale for larger companies paying top executives more than smaller organizations is that the job requirements for a top executive tend to be more demanding in a large company. There is also more competition for top-level posts as organizations increase in size.

### Type of Industry

Salaries paid managers in business organizations vary greatly depending on the industry. Banks and retailing organizations, for example, typically pay their top managers significantly less than manufacturing companies. The apparent justification for paying senior executives more in some industries than in others seems to be based on custom and job intangibles. In some industries it has been the practice to pay relatively "high" or "low" for so long that now it is traditional. Also, it is often possible to pay a lower salary if a job has many intangible "pluses," such as a pleasant working environment and little job pressure.

### Importance of the Manager's Job

The most logical salary determinant is the importance of the manager's job. Measuring job importance is difficult, but some of the more common criteria include the following:

*Level in the organization.* Obviously, the top executive in an organization occupies the most important position, for he or she is ultimately responsible for all activities performed by the enterprise. Generally, as the organizational ladder is descended, each succeeding level of managers receives less compensation.

*Contribution to profit.* In business organizations an effort may be made to determine how much a manager contributed to the firm's profit as a basis for his or her compensation. In the marketing department this is sometimes possible, but generally it is very difficult to assess specific contributions. For example, a jump in sales volume may be due to the efforts and intelligence of the marketing manager, or it may be traceable to an exceptionally well-designed product. It is particularly difficult to determine the contributions of staff personnel. How, for instance, does one measure the effect on profits of a house physician, a personnel manager, or a plant maintenance engineer? Thus, while contribution to profits is theoretically an ideal basis for compensation, in practice it is very difficult to determine.

*Number of persons reporting to a manager.* While this basis is used occasionally, it is not a particularly good measure of job importance. First-level supervisors may have the largest number of persons directly responsible to them, but the decisions they make are relatively minor compared with those of higher-ranking managers. Furthermore, at higher levels a real danger exists when a person managing eight persons is paid more than, say, a person supervising six individuals. The latter manager will be encouraged to add two or more subordinates whether they are needed or not. Organizations tend to become bureaucratic when rewards are based on the number of people who are managed.

*Size of the manager's budget.*  A better justification can be made for assessing job importance partly on the basis of the budget a manager controls. A good case can be made that the importance of a manager's decisions relates to the amount of money controlled.

### The Manager's Education and Experience

Education and experience may be valid factors in helping to determine a manager's salary. The assumption is often made, for example, that, other things being equal, a person with an M.B.A. degree is better qualified, and therefore worth more money, than a person with only a B.S. degree. The assumption is also often made that an individual with, say, ten years' experience is more capable of performing a certain management job than a person with only five years' experience.

But note that a manager's effectiveness can best be measured by the results achieved, not by apparent qualifications for the job. Although a small percentage of the chief executive officers in the nation's 500 largest companies have earned Ph.D. degrees, some executives in this group have no degrees, and the value of experience varies widely.

The length of time a manager has spent with one organization may also affect compensation. Whether or not seniority should be a basis for rewards is discussed in the Issue for Debate in this chapter.

### Competitors' Practices

To a large extent, manager compensation depends on what managers holding like positions in similar organizations are paid. If other things such as chances for promotion, working conditions, fringe benefits, and geographic location are about the same, managers will gravitate to organizations that offer the highest compensation. A firm must be willing to meet the competitive salary schedule or risk losing its more capable managers.

### Supply and Demand

The price of managerial talent, like the price of other resources, is based to some extent on supply and demand. When computers first became popular, comparatively few persons were experts in data processing and exceptionally high salaries were offered to managers who were skilled in this area. During periods of economic recession, the supply of some types of managers may exceed demand, with the result that salaries for these managers are kept relatively low.

*Manager Rewards During Economic Downturns.*  Managers are not immune to cuts in financial benefits during recessions. One observer notes, "Having grown accustomed in the last decade or so to hearty annual pay increases and an ever richer banquet of benefits, the American executive now suddenly finds himself sitting at a much less lavish table. In past recessions, the burden fell mostly on blue collar workers, who could be laid off and called back on demand. But as the blue collar force shrank, the old way of coping with hard times became inadequate as well as one-sided."[6]

---

[6]Jeremy Main, "Hard Times Catch Up with Executives," *Fortune*, September 20, 1982, p. 50.

In 1982, during a deep recession, some of the actions taken by companies were as follows:

- Ford Motor Company reduced the size of its white collar staff from 72,400 to 53,400.
- Caterpillar demoted 1,000 managers and cut the pay of all its managers.
- Pan American World Airways cut the pay of all employees by 10 percent, eliminated 15 percent of its managers (including 15 vice-presidents), and reduced vacation time for managers.
- Polaroid encouraged employees with 10 or more years service to take early retirement.[7]

## NONFINANCIAL REWARDS FOR MANAGERS

Researchers and practitioners in management agree that most managers want much more than money from their jobs. Psychological factors such as "challenge," "interesting work," "opportunity to realize my potential," "a feeling that I am appreciated," and "good people to work with" are often more sought after than unusually high salaries, bonuses, and other forms of financial compensation. Such factors may provide great incentive for a manager to put forth his or her best effort.

Executives earning hundreds of thousands of dollars per year may accept government jobs paying only a fraction of that amount. W. Michael Blumenthal, for example, took a $335,000 pay cut—from $401,000 received as chairman of the Bendix Corporation to $66,000—when he decided to serve as Secretary of the Treasury in the Carter administration. He also was required to place his estimated $3 million worth of stocks and bonds in a **blind trust** (a trust over which he had no control).[8]

It is not uncommon to see a manager with only moderate enthusiasm for developing his department exhibit great energy in some nonprofit activity such as building a Little League athletic team or running the management association of a condominium. Often managers use more money as an excuse for a job change when other factors are the true reason for the switch. For example, a manager may say, "The XYZ Company made me an offer so attractive I just couldn't resist," but the true reason may be that he feels he will be more appreciated at XYZ. At times managers do not really need more money but they desire it because, among other things, it may improve their self-image.

Some of the most important nonmonetary rewards are discussed in the following sections.

**Power**    Many managers seek the power to make decisions regarding human, financial, and material resources. A manager may enjoy exercising power over people in the form of hiring, assigning duties, compensating, and even terminating. The promise

---

[7]Ibid, pp. 50–52.
[8]"The Too High Price of Public Service," *Fortune,* December 1977, p. 160.

# ISSUE FOR DEBATE

## SHOULD SENIORITY BE A BASIS FOR REWARDS?

Seniority is an increasingly important consideration in managing. Managers in nonprofit organizations, especially in educational and government institutions, are often rewarded with pay and job security on the basis of seniority. Some people feel seniority is an appropriate basis for rewards; others do not.

### YES

**Seniority should be a basis for rewards because . . .**

The longer a manager is with an organization, the more valuable he or she is to the organization. People who remain with the same firm for a long time become familiar with the problems that are likely to arise and learn, through experience, the best ways to handle them.

Loyalty to the organization should be rewarded.

Basing rewards on seniority is fair. If two people are well qualified for advancement, it is only right to promote the one who has been there longer.

Most people seek security in work situations. Basing rewards on seniority helps provide security. Thus people are likely to be more productive.

Morale and job stability are related. When an older manager is terminated because of below-standard performance, the morale of all managers is adversely affected.

### NO

**Seniority should not be a basis for rewards because . . .**

Time served on a job is not a valid basis for rewards. Productivity should be rewarded, not time spent with the organization.

Rewarding seniority tends to protect unproductive employees.

New managers may dislike the seniority system. They may reason, "I'd have to stay here for years before I rose to the salary level I desire."

The security of seniority may result in lower productivity. Managers who have been with a firm for a long time may relax because they "have it made."

A little insecurity is good, for it keeps managers on their toes. They will be more concerned about doing their best because if layoffs are made, they will have a better chance of keeping their jobs.

### QUESTIONS

1. What additional arguments, both pro and con, can you advance?
2. Do you think seniority will become a more important factor as a basis for rewards in the future? Why or why not?

of even greater power if performance improves may be a great stimulus to some managers.

Status symbols are sometimes used instead of more money as a reward. A career military officer may be more motivated by an important medal or prestigious assignment than by the prospect of more money.

Generally, the higher one rises in management, the more status one is afforded. Examples of symbols that suggest high status and presumably elevate a manager's self-concept are use of the executive dining room; a good job title; a uniform with special styling, as in the military; an office that is large and has carpeting, a good location, a window, good furniture, and a big desk; use of the corporate jet or limousine; a private as opposed to shared secretary; a key to the executive washroom; and membership in prestigious business or country clubs.

Note that status symbols do not remain status symbols if they are too easily attained. The position title of "vice-president," for example, has lost some of its original status because many organizations, such as banks, confer the title on a significant number of managers. The title "vice-president" may still have considerable public-relations value, however, since many of a bank's customers will be impressed by it. On balance, status-related rewards are important and can be used to improve manager performance. However, they should not be easy to acquire or they will cease to convey superior performance and will become the object of cynicism instead of admiration.

Challenge Some managers feel rewarded by assignments that are new, difficult, or otherwise challenging. A manager may feel highly rewarded if given the opportunity to open a new territory or to manage the introduction of a new product. Assignments such as these are often welcomed because they give an individual an opportunity to demonstrate his or her capabilities.

## GUIDELINES FOR AN EFFECTIVE MANAGER-REWARD SYSTEM

The objective of a manager-reward system is to attract and hold the best possible managers and to encourage them individually and collectively to put forth the best possible effort to achieve goals. In designing and implementing a reward system, the following guidelines should be observed.

Consider the
System
in Its Entirety Both financial compensation and nonfinancial rewards should be considered in developing a reward system because both are essential to effective motivation. Money alone is not enough to stimulate maximum manager productivity. Managers also require good leadership, appreciation, respect, and status to perform at their best.

Generally, the better the manager's performance, the more attractive the financial and nonfinancial rewards should be. Failure to base rewards on performance is a "disincentive," for it encourages managers to perform below their level of capability. A reward system that fails to relate compensation (both financial and psychological) to performance may result in the loss of the organization's best managers.

Nothing in organized life should be viewed as static, since the environment in which management is practiced is dynamic. Adjustments in the manager-reward system may be warranted due to improvements in performance, increased responsibilities, a rise in the cost of living, the attainment of additional education and experience, or relocation to another geographic area. Failure to keep a reward system up to date is one of the main reasons for manager turnover.

In practice, bonuses, pension plans, and other forms of incentive compensation often become so complex that many managers do not understand them. A simple, straightforward explanation that states "Here is how the plan works and here is how you stand to benefit" helps improve the effectiveness of any reward system.

Of all the guidelines for preparing an effective manager-reward system, fairness is usually the most difficult to apply. Different managers have differing concepts of fairness. Further, as noted earlier, it is hard to determine the contributions that some managers make to organizational success. Even when a management-by-objectives plan is in operation, it still is usually more difficult to evaluate the contribution of a staff manager than the contribution of a line manager.

In seeking to make a reward system as fair as possible, managers should try to establish objectives for the position that can be measured or verified, determine the compensation for a comparable job in other organizations, and be as objective as possible in performance evaluation. Objectivity is enhanced when two or more people must approve the rewards given to a manager.

* Manager development is the process of establishing programs and an organizational climate to help managers improve their skills, knowledge, and attitudes.
* Manager development may be needed to compensate for lack of previous training or experience, to prepare managers to replace those who leave, to attract superior entry-level managers, and to prevent manager obsolescence.
* Internal approaches to manager development include formal and informal orientation, level-to-level progression, job rotation on the basis of department or geography, coaching, organizational development, temporary or acting management assignments, service on committees, and assistant-to positions.
* External approaches to manager development include university-sponsored programs, services offered by trade and professional associations, services offered by consulting firms, and informal activities such as management clubs.

**SUMMARY**

- For manager development to be effective, it is essential to pursue manager development at all levels, evaluate the development program regularly, and provide top-management support of the program.
- In spite of the existence of manager-development programs, managers still have a personal responsibility for growth.
- The main types of financial rewards are salaries, bonuses, profit-sharing plans, pension plans, and employee stock ownership plans.
- The main factors that affect financial compensation are the type of organization, the size of the organization, the type of industry, the importance of the job, the manager's education and experience, competitors' practices, and supply and demand.
- Most managers want more than monetary rewards. They are also rewarded by nonfinancial or psychological benefits, including power, status, and challenge.

## LEARN THE LANGUAGE OF MANAGEMENT

| | |
|---|---|
| manager development | bonus |
| orientation | individual bonus |
| formal orientation | group bonus |
| informal orientation | profit sharing |
| coaching | cash profit sharing |
| organization development | deferred profit sharing |
| in-house training | pension plans |
| invitational training programs | employee stock ownership plans |
| salary | blind trust |
| incentive compensation | |

## QUESTIONS FOR REVIEW AND DISCUSSION

1. "The passage of time does not guarantee that an individual will acquire more wisdom, skill, proficiency, or effectiveness." Explain. How does this truism relate to manager development?

2. Are the basic goals of manager development the same for all types of organizations? Explain.

3. What are the advantages and limitations of these forms of manager development: level-to-level progression, job rotation on the basis of department, job rotation on the basis of geography, coaching, and organization development?

4. Do you think that colleges and universities will play a larger role in providing manager development programs in the future? Why or why not?

5. Why is it desirable to provide manager development programs at all organizational levels?

6. Which one of the following financial compensation plans would you prefer and why: (a) a relatively large salary but no bonus or profit sharing; (b) a relatively small salary but an opportunity to earn a large bonus; or (c) a modest salary, no bonus, but participation in a profit-sharing plan?

7. Evaluate the motivational power of each of the following: salary, bonuses, profit-sharing plans, pension plans, and employee stock ownership plans.

8. How do you account for the fact that bonuses as a percentage of total compensation paid to top managers are larger in very big companies than in small companies?

9. Why are nonfinancial rewards important? Can they be more important than monetary rewards? Explain.

10. Most organizations pay far more attention to developing formalized financial reward systems than to preparing formalized nonfinancial reward programs. Should they, in your view? Explain.

### 1. Should operative employees be better rewarded than managers?

Generally, managers are paid more both in money and psychological rewards than the operative employees they manage. But there are exceptions. Managers of professional athletic teams may receive less than the superstars they manage, movie directors may be paid less than the actors they supervise, and some marketing managers receive lower incomes than outstanding sales representatives.

In report form explain the rationale for paying operative employees more than managers in situations such as those mentioned above.

Do you feel that this is a good management practice? Why or why not?

### 2. How does one convince top managers that they need training?

Assume that you are a management consultant specializing in management training and development. The president of a medium-sized company with thirty first-level managers asks you to submit a proposal for a training program for them. The president is a tough, dictatorial, egotistical, "old school" type manager. As you discuss the matter with him, it becomes apparent to you that training the first-level managers would do little if any good. The president and his corps of upper-level managers are not setting the right kind of example for the first-level managers. Your diagnosis of the situation is that the president and key managers should take your Senior Manager Development Seminar before you do any first-level training.

Explain how you would proceed to convince the president that top-level managers need training.

### 3. How to choose a mentor

In a 1982 *Advanced Management Journal* study of 1,200 people who were promoted to high-level management jobs, two thirds stated that they had a mentor or guide during most of their careers. Clearly, a person who wants to win promotions in management stands a better chance if he or she has a mentor to serve as a coach. Some mentors are better than others. The selection of the right mentor is an important decision.

What criteria should one use in choosing a mentor?

What should a person do to win the full cooperation of a mentor?

Bronstein, Richard J. "The Equity Component of the Executive Compensation Package." *California Management Review*, Fall 1980, pp. 64–70.
Dalrymple, Douglas J.; Stephenson, P. Ronald; and Cron, William. "Wage Levels and Sales Productivity." *Business Horizons*, December 1980, pp. 57–60.

**369**

Derr, C., Brooklyn C., and Turner, Claire Jacob. "Careers in Collision? The Changing Role of the Executive Wife." *Business,* April–May–June 1982, pp. 18–22.

de Vries, Manfred F. R. Kets. "Organizational Stress: A Call for Management Action." *Sloan Management Review*, Fall 1979, pp. 3–14.

Foster, Kenneth E. "Does Executive Pay Make Sense?" *Business Horizons*, September–October 1981, pp. 47–51.

Fox, Sanford L. "The Best Executive Team Money Can Buy." *Business*, July 1981, pp. 44–46.

Gray, Bonnie J., and Landru, Robert K. "What Price Allegiance? A Case of Managerial Ethics." *Business*, January 1981, pp. 23–28.

Kelsey, Harry, Jr. "Practicing What They Preach: Successful Management Development Programs." *Business Horizons*, December 1980, pp. 3–6.

Kraus, David. "Executive Pay: Ripe for Reform?" *Harvard Business Review*, September–October 1980, pp. 30–51.

Pyle, Richard L. "Trimming the Corporate Waist with Fitness Programs." *Business Horizons*, April 1980, pp. 70–72.

Runzheimer, Rufus E. "How Corporations Are Handling Cost-of-Living Differentials." *Business Horizons*, August 1980, pp. 38–40.

Staples, William A., and Coppett, John I. "An Exploratory Study of Training Programs for New First-Level Sales Managers." *Akron Business and Economic Review*, Fall 1980, pp. 36–41.

Stern, Allen D. R. "Retaining Good Managers Without Golden Handcuffs." *Business Horizons*, November–December 1981, pp. 77–81.

Suojanen, Waino W., and Hudson, Donald R. "Coping with Stress and Addictive Work Behavior." *Business*, January 1981, pp. 7–13.

# 15 EVALUATION OF MANAGER PERFORMANCE

**STUDY THIS CHAPTER SO YOU CAN:**

- Differentiate between judgmental evaluation and developmental evaluation, and explain how these methods relate to effective managing.

- Explain the role of evaluation in promotions and terminations.

- Describe how results evaluation works and explain its strengths and limitations.

- Discuss the extent of use of trait evaluation and the advantages and disadvantages of evaluating managers on this basis.

- Explain how behavior-evaluation rating systems are developed and their advantages and disadvantages.

- Describe how managers can be evaluated on the basis of their ability to perform management functions and the advantages and disadvantages of this method.

- Understand the role of informal evaluation of managers and the strengths and limitations of this approach.

- Explain the relationship of manager evaluation and career planning.

- Identify and explain the guidelines for effective manager evaluation.

An important part of the staffing function is the evaluation of the performance of managers. Since managers are the key to an organization's success, it follows that their individual positive contributions and weaknesses should be discovered and used as a basis for building a stronger, more effective organization.

Furthermore, evaluation serves as a basis for corrective action. If a manager does not achieve assigned objectives, then corrective action of some kind is indicated. The unsuccessful manager may need guidance, retraining, more financial support, or additional employees. In some cases he or she may need to be dismissed or transferred.

Performance appraisal is receiving increasing attention because of its importance to the entire management process, as this observation suggests.

> Although few experts say that appraisal systems should ignore whether specific job goals are achieved, most are wrestling with ways to assure that performance appraisal does more than simply determine salaries. They want a system that will pinpoint specific managerial behavior that should be reinforced or discontinued, serve as a personnel development tool, provide realistic assessment of an employee's potential for advancement, and—a particularly hot issue in the 1980s—stand up in court as a valid defense in discrimination suits.[1]

Evaluation of the performance of individuals is inherent in organized life. It begins in the family unit, where children are appraised by parents. It continues in school and in the various organizations we become a part of throughout life. We are being judged or evaluated all of our lives.

## JUDGMENTAL AND DEVELOPMENTAL EVALUATIONS: RATIONALE FOR APPRAISAL

Manager evaluation can be characterized as either judgmental or developmental. **Judgmental evaluation** is the assessment of manager performance in order to make decisions regarding promotion, transfer, compensation adjustments, or termination. It helps a manager answer questions such as these:

* *Promotability:* "Is the person promotable?" "Can he or she handle larger responsibilities?" "If so, in what area and at what level?"
* *Transfer:* "Does the individual's performance suggest that he or she be transferred to another position or geographic area?"
* *Compensation:* "On the basis of the evaluation, should the individual receive a raise?" "Should additional fringe benefits be provided?"
* *"Termination:* "On the basis of performance and other factors, would the best interests of the organization be served if the individual were terminated?"

Judgmental evaluation, then, is used to help decide on the use and reward of human resources. Since an organization's monetary resources are always limited, this type of evaluation is extremely important. Unless conducted accurately and objectively, it can lead to serious problems—particularly in the areas of compensation and promotion.

Judgmental evaluation may be carried out in one of two ways: The performance of one manager may be compared with the peformance of other managers, or a manager's performance may be compared against some absolute standard.

[1]Quoted from the May 19, 1980 issue of *Business Week* by special permission, © 1980 by McGraw-Hill, Inc., New York, NY 10020. All rights reserved.

373

*Judgmental and
Developmental
Evaluations:
Rationale
for Appraisal*

**Developmental evaluation** is used to help a manager determine what action should be taken to help the person being evaluated improve his or her performance. The evaluator attempts to answer such questions as "What recommendations should be made relative to specialized training, professional growth, and development of management skills?" "What is the likely prognosis of the person's career?" and "What should the individual be told to help improve his or her performance?"

A promotion is usually accompanied by more pay, status, and power. Many managers are strongly motivated by the prospect of being promoted, for it is the most tangible form of reward and tells the person moving up, "You've done a good job, and we have confidence that you can take on a larger assignment."

Promotions, however, should be based on very careful evaluation of the candidate's ability to manage, leadership skills, and other factors that affect results. An individual's performing well at one level certainly does not guarantee superior performance at a higher level. As the Peter Principle suggests, some people are promoted to a level at which they prove to be incompetent. Thus, care should be taken to promote the most promising people because managers are, after all, responsible for results.

Another reason why promotions should be based on sound, thorough evaluations is the possible negative impact on morale if a less-than-best candidate is chosen. There is probably always some resentment among candidates who want the promotion but don't receive it. But if the person who is promoted later proves ineffective in the higher-level job, the resentment of the turned-down candidates may turn to hostility, and real problems may result.

Termination may be voluntary, required because of age (see the Issue for Debate in this chapter), or demanded by a superior. Voluntary termination can result from a number of factors, such as another organization promising the person more immediate and long-range financial and other rewards; the individual's feeling that his or her days are numbered and that forced termination is likely; the person's simply not liking the organization, its policies, and the environment it provides; or the employee's spouse being transferred.

Management is interested in voluntary termination because it seeks to retain the most promising individuals for future, more responsible positions. If careful and objective evaluations are made of managers, it may be possible, by using the appraisals, to convince managers who contemplate leaving to stay. On the other hand, if the evaluations reveal that an individual is performing poorly and has little hope, if any, of moving upward, voluntary termination may be welcome, for it may help management avoid demanding termination.

Since managers are not protected by union contracts, demanding their resignations is not particularly difficult. It has been said that while operative employees may be on probation for ninety days, managers are on probation for life, indicating that nonmanagers acquire built-in job security, while managers do not. An important exception to this observation concerns managers who work in the public sector. Forced termination of managers in government bureaucracies is

# ISSUE FOR DEBATE

## IS MANDATORY RETIREMENT OF MANAGERS BASED ON AGE A GOOD IDEA?

In 1978 Congress extended the mandatory age for retirement from sixty-five to seventy for nonmanagers. Many corporations, however, require that managers retire by age sixty-five or earlier. Some feel that managers should not be required to retire before age seventy; others believe that they should. Some pro and con arguments are presented below.

| YES | NO |
|---|---|
| Mandatory retirement based on age is a good idea because . . . | Mandatory retirement based on age is not a good idea because . . . |
| If older managers remain in the work force, there will be less opportunity for younger managers. | Many people are just "getting started" as they approach old age. Winston Churchill became prime minister of England at age sixty-six. |
| After years of imposed routines, schedules, and activities, it should be a basic human right *not* to work. | Allowing managers to work as long as they are physically and mentally able would relieve some of the strain on our social security system. |
| IBM, one of the nation's best-managed organizations, requires its chief executive officer to step down at age sixty. | There is little, if any, correlation between managerial effectiveness and age. |
| Older managers tend to become too conservative. Organizations need managers who enjoy taking risks. | Older managers presumably have more experience than younger managers. Organizations need the wisdom that comes with age. |
| Managers older than sixty-five are two generations removed from people entering the work force. They can't understand the needs of younger employees. | A basic tenet of effective managing is to judge managers on results achieved. As long as managers are effective they should continue managing. |

## QUESTIONS

1. Which of the above pro and con arguments do you feel are largely valid? Invalid?
2. Do you think that attitudes toward older people working will be significantly different when you retire? Why or why not?

exceedingly complex and may involve such a long process that some managers who should be terminated are not.

If termination is to be demanded, it should be based on a clear evaluation of the individual's performance. The superior making the demand should have the most objective information possible indicating that the person being told to leave is not performing satisfactorily and, in all likelihood, never will. Demanding that people terminate is never easy. Yet it is necessary in some situations if an organization is to perform at its best.

## METHODS FOR EVALUATING MANAGERS

There are five main types of evaluation systems, each of which is explained briefly below and described in detail later in this chapter.

**Results evaluation** (also called *performance evaluation*) assesses a manager in terms of what he or she actually accomplished over a period of time. It deals with quantifiable achievements, such as units produced, volume sold, waste reduced, and turnover of the manager's employees.

**Trait evaluation** (also called *attribute evaluation*) judges a manager's performance in terms of personal characteristics. An evaluator may seek to assess the degree to which the manager is loyal, cooperative, or dependable.

**Behavior evaluation** appraises a manager in terms of how he or she went about achieving the results. It focuses on what the manager did—the process or techniques he or she used to achieve goals—rather than on whether desired objectives were actually achieved. Behavior evaluation is receiving increasing attention by scholars who are especially interested in the developmental goal of manager evaluation. For evaluation to bring about improvement in manager performance, they argue, it must pinpoint what the manager is doing right and what he or she is doing wrong.

**Functional performance evaluation** assesses a manager's ability to perform managerial functions. It trys to determine how well the manager performs as a manager.

**Informal evaluation**, unlike the approaches already discussed, employs no structure or design. It is the most subjective evaluation method and is based solely on observation of a manager's performance.

As will become apparent, the various methods used for appraising managers vary in complexity. Trait evaluation and behavior evaluation may require the employment of professors, management consultants, and psychologists to help design and implement the rating instruments. For this reason, most small and many medium-sized organizations do not use these evaluation systems. However, outside experts have the advantage of having been exposed to managers in many organizations and therefore may be more objective in making appraisals than evaluators within the organization.

The other methods of appraisal can also be complex. Results evaluation is conceptually simple but measuring results in many management positions can be very difficult. Evaluation based on functional performance can also be more complex than the term suggests. Informal evaluation, while simple in concept, is complicated because of its subjectivity.

## Results Evaluation

All goals should be verifiable. In other words, at the end of a planning period it should be possible for a superior to evaluate a subordinate in terms of "Did he or she actually attain the goals that were set?"

All jobs in organizations have one purpose: to produce work of some kind that is needed by the organization to help it achieve its goals. Managers should make every effort to define as precisely as possible exactly what an individual is expected to do. The ideal results-evaluation system will then measure as objectively as possible how well the person performed the job. Ideally, verifiable objectives should be statistically measurable—for instance, units produced or sold, percentage of increase in sales, or output per worker.

Even when specific goals or quotas are set, results are not always used as a basis for evaluation. The manager making the evaluation may be "too busy" to evaluate performance against goals or may decide that an individual's performance is "too intangible" to appraise. But evaluation on the basis of results is automatic if a management-by-objectives program is in effect, since the process requires it.

### How Often Should Results Be Evaluated?

Evaluation of manager results can be continuous (made on a day-to-day basis) or periodic (made at certain intervals, such as weekly, monthly, or annually). Thanks to modern management information systems, ongoing appraisal of results attained by managers is possible in many situations. Continuous evaluation is particularly well suited for line managers in food stores, small loan companies, drugstores, motels, and other companies organized as chains. Computer printouts can be used to determine whether the managers are meeting sales, cost, inventory, and profit goals. In these types of organizations, manager promotions, transfers, demotions, and terminations are constantly taking place, indicating that performance is being monitored continuously. Managerial realignments do not follow a nice, easily defined time schedule. Whenever a manager's performance does not satisfy the superior, corrective action is likely to be taken.

Continuous evaluation is much more difficult in the case of staff managers. How does one measure on a short-term basis the results achieved by managers in charge of accounting, computer operations, legal affairs, or public relations? For managers such as these, periodic evaluations are generally made.

Periodic evaluation of results is also used when objectives require considerable time to attain. Senior-level executives generally receive a quarterly or annual evaluation, based on overall results for the period in question.

### Advantages of Results Evaluation

Evaluating managers on the basis of how well they succeeded in meeting predetermined objectives has two main advantages. First, it gets to the heart of managing. The real purpose of managing is to achieve objectives. It follows, then, that the best way to evaluate managers is to ask "Did they in fact achieve the goals that were set for them or set in part by them?"

Results are a far better indication of manager performance than effort put in. Hard work is certainly an admirable quality in a manager, and most successful managers do work very hard. But in the final analysis it is results that count, not effort expended. Professors frequently hear students who have received a low mark on a term project complain, "I spent three entire weekends on this report. I *deserve* a higher grade." But grades, like all types of performance ratings, should be based on the quantity and quality of work produced, not effort invested.

Evaluating a manager in terms of results produced is also better than appraising his or her performance in terms of managerial behavior because it is more objective. A manager may "behave properly" and still not achieve goals. Furthermore, results evaluation is superior to functional performance evaluation. A manager may appear to know how to manage but still not deliver what the organization requires—results.

### Are Results Always Applauded?

Many management theorists take the view that results are all that really count in manager evaluation and that personality or likableness should be of little, if any, consequence. In practice, however, compatibility of a manager with his or her superior is often of major importance.

An interesting example was the dismissal in 1978 of Lee Iacocca as president of Ford Motor Company by Henry Ford II, former chief executive officer of the company. Iacocca had had a long and highly successful career as a Ford executive, having come up the ranks to the number two position. In the year prior to his dismissal, sales had increased from $29 billion to $38 billion, and profits had almost doubled.

Yet Iacocca was dismissed. According to a report in *Time*, a Ford director said "The body chemistry wasn't right." The report went on to say:

> Both Ford and Iacocca can be at times charming, abrasive, cordial and arch. A clash of their personalities was all but inevitable from the moment that Ford, the celebrated heir who liked to remind subordinates that "my name is on the building," elevated Iacocca, the ambitious hired manager, to president in 1970. Early rumored to have the inside track on the job of chief executive upon Ford's retirement at the age of sixty-five in 1982, Iacocca made the mistake of encouraging subordinates to regard him as the dauphin.[2]

Besides the ability to generate results, the ability to work with others, especially one's immediate superior, is a consideration in management appraisal. The body chemistry between superiors and subordinates should be right, as the above example indicates. For this and other reasons, trait evaluation, discussed next, has a place in manager-appraisal systems.

### Disadvantages of Results Evaluation

Despite its strong advantages, results evaluation has several important shortcomings. First, external conditions beyond the control of the manager may make goal attainment either impossible or too easy.

[2]"Upheaval in the House of Ford," *Time*, July 24, 1978, p. 60.

In many cases a manager will perform well but still will not succeed in attaining preset objectives. For example, a marketing manager in a company doing business with the government may not be able to meet her preset sales goals because contracts are canceled through no fault of the manager. Or a manufacturing manager may have set, in conjunction with his superior, a production goal of 100,000 units only to see that objective unattained because a strike occurred in the plant of a parts supplier.

For some types of organizations, especially business enterprises, external conditions are often very volatile. Unforeseen weather conditions, strikes, changes in government policies, or a decrease in the supply of money with a corresponding increase in its cost are just a few of many events beyond the control of individual managers. When such events occur, goal attainment may be impossible. Certainly a manager should not be rated negatively when conditions beyond his or her control adversely affect results.

On the other hand, external conditions may change in a way to make goal attainment much too easy. A marketing manager doing business with the government may obtain an unexpected large contract because of a change in government spending and procurement policy, not because of personal efforts. Should the marketing manager then receive very laudatory appraisal because sales exceeded the preset goal even though he or she was not responsible? Or a production manager may be able to make products below projected costs because of a substantial decline in the price of raw materials. Does this event, which obviously is not related to the manager's skill, qualify the manager for commendation?

A second limitation of evaluating managers against verifiable objectives is that internal conditions beyond the manager's control may change. An organization is a group of interdependent departments and individuals working together to achieve a common goal. When one department falters, other departments experience difficulties too. A marketing manager may not be able to attain preset objectives if the production department, through faulty maintenance or for some other reason, does not produce enough products of the right quality. Nor can the manager of the accounting department achieve an objective of installation of a new financial-controls system if managers of other departments do not cooperate and supply needed data.

On the other hand, internal conditions may change in such a way that goal attainment becomes too easy. A production manager may find it easier to maintain production schedules because of a new incentive plan designed by the personnel department, not solely because he or she performed extraordinarily. Or an inventory manager may be able to reduce inventory shrinkage because of a new control system designed by personnel in charge of the management information system.

At least a partial solution to these two limitations is to exercise some flexibility when appraising managers. The evaluator should take into consideration factors beyond the control of the manager being rated. He or she should ask such questions as "Given the changed conditions, should the manager actually have achieved more than he did?" "Did she respond effectively to change?" and "Were the goals established realistic, or were they too high or too low?"

**Trait Evaluation**

Trait or attribute evaluation, as discussed here, is a formal method of manager appraisal because it is carried out in a planned manner. Trait evaluation involves appraising subordinates in terms of personal characteristics such as "loyalty to the company," "fairness," "initiative," "ambition," "cooperation," "dedication," "decisiveness," and "ability to handle stress." It may also include judging the individual on work-related qualities such as "knowledge of the job," "ability to plan," and "ability to follow through on work assignments."

Most trait-evaluation systems give the evaluator four or five alternative ratings for each characteristic considered important, such as "excellent," "good," "fair," and "poor." Typically, a rating scale similar to the one shown in Table 15–1 is used. While the system in Table 15–1 is not perfect, it is a good guide for trait evaluation of managers in any type of enterprise.

Trait-evaluation instruments may also ask the reviewer to answer several open-ended questions such as "What training or other action do you recommend for performance improvement?" and "Would you recommend this person for reassignment? Why or why not?" Thus, the approach offers an opportunity for informal appraisal as well.

### Extent of Use

Trait evaluation is used extensively in a variety of organizations. The military uses a rating form at least annually to appraise its approximately 300,000 commissioned officers. The Civil Service, Social Security Administration, and other federal government agencies, as well as state and local governmental institutions, use this method in evaluating their hundreds of thousands of managers. Trait appraisal is also used by some business organizations.

### Advantages of Trait Evaluation

One basic advantage of trait evaluation is simplicity. The form on which the reviewer's comments are recorded is usually short and requires little time to complete. Furthermore, trait-evaluation forms can be used to appraise management positions of different types and at different levels in an organization. Other formal methods of manager evaluation are more difficult to apply across the board.

### Disadvantages of Trait Evaluation

Trait evaluation has several important limitations. First, and very importantly, it always involves the assessment of one human being by another, which inevitably results in less-than-total objectivity. However well the rating form is designed, there is certain to be some subjectivity on the part of the rater, particularly where personality factors are concerned. In addition, some managers are inclined to rate people more highly than other managers. This is largely because no two evaluators have precisely the same understanding of terms used in the evaluation process, such as "initiative," "attitude," "cooperation," and "bearing." Nor do two raters agree completely on what is "standard," "below standard," or "far below standard."

Because objectivity is lacking, trait evaluation provides only a subjective analysis of how well a manager is performing now and will probably perform in the future. In many organizations, trait evaluation is not well respected as a rating tool either by those who do the rating or by those who are rated. Accordingly, many managers feel trait evaluation is a waste of time and do not make a serious attempt to conduct the evaluation carefully.

**TABLE 15–1**

**Trait Evaluation System Used by the U.S. Air Force**

| Performance Factors | Far Below Standard | Below Standard | Meets Standard | Above Standard | Well Above Standard |
|---|---|---|---|---|---|
| 1. Job knowledge (depth, breadth, currency) | | | | | |
| 2. Judgment and decisions (consistent, accurate, effective) | | | | | |
| 3. Plan and organize work (timely and creative) | | | | | |
| 4. Management of resources (manpower and materials) | | | | | |
| 5. Leadership (initiative, human relations, accept responsibility) | | | | | |
| 6. Adaptability to stress (stable, flexible, dependable) | | | | | |
| 7. Oral communication (clear, concise, confident) | | | | | |
| 8. Written communication (clear, concise, organized) | | | | | |
| 9. Professional qualities (attitude, cooperation, bearing) | | | | | |
| 10. Equal opportunity participation (sensitivity and treatment) | | | | | |

Source: Adapted from Department of the Air Force, AF Regulation 36–10.

A second weakness of trait evaluation is that evaluators are likely to give unwarranted high grades to most individuals they rate. The concept of "standard" generally means "in the middle." But analysis of rating forms filled out by managers shows that individuals tend to be given highly inflated appraisals such as "very good," "excellent," or "superior." The tendency to give undeserved high ratings obscures the distinction between a truly outstanding manager and a mediocre one. This, in turn, makes it difficult to promote managers on the basis of true merit.

A third disadvantage of trait evaluation is that possession of a certain attribute may not affect or relate to performance. For example, an individual may be subjectively rated as "highly intelligent" yet have changed jobs more often than any manager in the organization. There is a serious question regarding what specific traits, if any, are always common to the practice of effective management.

Fourth, there often is a "halo effect," meaning that a rater who feels a manager has one good quality (such as high intelligence) will rate the individual high on other factors as well. Or conversely, if the evaluator believes the person lacks good judgment, he or she will probably rate the person low on other traits as well.

Evaluation of managers on the basis of traits does not focus directly on what can be done to help a manager improve performance. To help remedy this deficiency, a relatively new formal method of appraisal, called behavior evaluation, has been developed.

Behavior-evaluation instruments are concerned with actual job behavior. These instruments identify the key aspects of the manager's job and describe a range of highly effective to very ineffective ways of performing various activities. Then, the evaluator can note which description of behavior is closest to the manager's actual performance.

The behavior-evaluation method emphasizes manager development; it deals directly with what is needed to help a manager improve future performance. William Kearney has noted: "Behaviorally based performance appraisal is an important supplement to MBO because it attempts to get at the *how* of performance. It identifies effective behaviors known to produce consistently superior performance leading to results against which actual behavior may be compared. Hence, it is an especially powerful developmental tool."[3]

We have seen that trait-evaluation instruments are generally used to evaluate managers who perform widely differing jobs and at various organizational levels. In contrast, behavior-evaluation instruments are designed for a specific job or jobs that are closely related. Kearney observes: "They pinpoint explicit behaviors that are critical to effective performance, thereby providing job-based information to individuals that will lead to getting results. Most appraisal instruments are designed to cover a broad category of jobs. Since they are neither derived from nor tailored to a specific job, they cannot provide the developmental help found in behavioral scales."[4]

### Steps in Constructing a Behavior-Evaluation Instrument

The development of a behavior-evaluation instrument, which is usually accomplished by a group of managers working together, consists of four identifiable steps.

*Step 1.* Managers of subordinates who perform highly similar work meet and decide what behavioral areas should be evaluated. For example, important job dimensions for managers of a fast-food company that should be evaluated may include ability to explain company policies and rules to employees, ability to keep records, and ability to handle customer complaints.

There is no set number of job dimensions that must be evaluated, but Kearney suggests that a complete behavior-evaluation instrument would contain approximately ten to twelve aspects of the manager's work.[5]

[3]William J. Kearney, "The Value of Behaviorally Based Performance Appraisals," *Business Horizons,* June 1976, p. 78.
[4]Ibid.
[5]Ibid., p. 79.

*Step 2.*   For each behavioral area the managers developing the rating instrument prepare written statements, based on observed job performance, that indicate from excellent to very poor performance. For example, statements relative to ability to handle customer complaints might range from "The manager can be expected to do everything possible to solve the complaint and keep the customer's goodwill" to "The manager can be expected to tell the customer to shut up and leave."

*Step 3.*   The various written statements are evaluated by the managers. Statements that are vague or subject to misinterpretation are eliminated.

*Step 4.*   The statements are arranged on a scale (sometimes called a **behavior-anchored rating scale** [BARS] or a *behavior expectation scale*). Usually, nine items are included. "One" on the scale indicates the worst possible behavior and "nine" indicates the best possible behavior. Figure 15–1 is an example of a behavior-evaluation instrument. It shows expectations of effectiveness of a manager who supervises sales personnel.

### Advantages of Behavior Evaluation

Objectivity is a major advantage of this evaluation method. Behavior evaluation is more objective than trait evaluation, since behavior — not personality — is being judged. Personality traits are evaluated differently by different observers. And it is much easier to relate behavior than personality to performance.

Furthermore, developing the scale is a learning process for managers. In the process of developing the rating scale, managers are forced to examine carefully the way subordinates perform their work. As a result, managers should discover ways to help subordinates perform more effectively.

A behavior-evaluation system also serves as a developmental guide. The system indicates the areas in which a manager needs specific training or guidance. In contrast, basing an evaluation only on results or traits does not indicate specifically what is needed to improve the manager's output. Kearney sees this as a clear advantage because "subordinates and managers alike can then see the difference between what behavior occurs and what should occur. Moreover, subordinates know exactly how they should behave to be more effective. Most present-day appraisal systems do not provide these all-important diagnostic data."[6]

Finally, a behavior-evaluation system concentrates on performance under the individual's control. Appraisals made strictly on the basis of verifiable results, as we have seen, may be unfair, since the manager's own performance is not the only factor involved. Sales may go up or down because of economic forces, not because of the marketing manager's effort or lack of effort. Or a production manager's performance may look bad not because he or she was ineffective but for reasons beyond his or her control. Behavior evaluation, then, "attempts to enhance the individual's control over result-producing behavior. Most other appraisal instruments do not make these crucial distinctions between behavior, performance, and effectiveness."[7]

[6]Ibid., p. 78.
[7]Ibid.

**FIGURE 15–1**

Expectations Rating Scale of Effectiveness of Department Manager
in Supervising Sales Personnel

| | | |
|---|---|---|
| | 9 | *Could be expected to conduct a full day's sales clinic with two new sales personnel and thereby develop them into top sales people in the department.* |
| *Could be expected to give his sales personnel confidence and a strong sense of responsibility by delegating many important jobs to them.* | 8 | |
| | 7 | *Could be expected never to fail to conduct training meetings with his people weekly at a scheduled hour and to convey to them exactly what he expects.* |
| *Could be expected to exhibit courtesy and respect toward his sales personnel.* | 6 | |
| | 5 | *Could be expected to remind sales personnel to wait on customers instead of conversing with each other.* |
| *Could be expected to be rather critical of store standards in front of his own people, thereby risking their developing poor attitudes.* | 4 | |
| | 3 | *Could be expected to tell an individual to come in anyway even though she/he called in to say she/he was ill.* |
| *Could be expected to go back on a promise to an individual whom he had told could transfer back into a previous department if she/he didn't like the new one.* | 2 | |
| | 1 | *Could be expected to make promises to an individual about her/his salary being based on department sales even when he knew such a practice was against company policy.* |

Source: John P. Campbell, Marvin D. Dunnette, Richard D. Arvey, and Lowell V. Hellervik, "The Development and Evaluation of Behaviorally Based Rating Scales," *Journal of Applied Psychology,* 57 (1973), 15–22. Copyright 1973 by the American Psychological Association. Reprinted by permission of the author.

### Disadvantages of Behavior Evaluation

One major disadvantage is cost. Behavior evaluations are expensive because the rating scales require considerable time to construct. Usually a number of managers must participate in the development of a rating scale. This requires time for which there are alternative uses. And, of course, time to a business represents money.

Another potential disadvantage is unfamiliarity. Practicing managers tend to fear what they do not understand. Since behavior evaluation is relatively new and requires considerable initial work, some managers may prefer a more familiar evaluation method, such as trait evaluation.

Finally, behavior-evaluation systems tend to be feasible only in relatively large organizations. Small and medium-sized organizations find it difficult, perhaps impossible, to develop behavior-evaluation systems that can yield statistically valid results. Kearney makes this observation: "There must be several managers available to develop the scales. A dozen managers would be a minimum to generate sufficient data, sort the behaviors and then scale them. There must be a large number of subordinates performing the job for which more and less effective behaviors are to be identified and scales developed."[8]

### Use of Behavior Evaluation

Behavior evaluation is relatively new and has not been widely tested in pragmatic studies. However, in a pioneering study, Millard, Luthans, and Ottemann used the technique with considerable success in evaluating the behavior of 117 interviewers and claims deputies in a state department of labor. Using a BARS approach, they were able to measure the performance of personnel with far greater accuracy than was possible with the customary trait-rating scales. They found that their behavior-evaluation method had statistically significant advantages over trait evaluation. Behavior evaluation will probably receive much more attention in the future.

Functional
Performance
Evaluation

Another approach to evaluating managers is in terms of their ability to perform the basic management functions of planning, organizing, staffing, directing, and controlling. Harold Koontz and Cyril O'Donnell, advocates of this appraisal method, make this comment: "The best approach the authors have found is to utilize the basic concepts and principles of management as standards. If they are basic, as they have been found to be in a wide variety of managerial positions and cultures, they should serve as reasonably good standards."[9]

To implement this system, a checklist of questions can be developed that helps the evaluator pinpoint strengths and weaknesses of the manager being appraised. Table 15–2 shows examples of questions dealing with each functional area that may be asked in the evaluation process.

### Advantages of Functional Performance Evaluation

The basic advantage of manager appraisal based on functional performance is that it can reveal specific strengths and weaknesses in the individual's performance as a manager. If the evaluation reveals that a manager does a poor job of delegating or communicating, corrective action, perhaps in the form of coaching, is indicated. This approach to appraisal forces the evaluator to consider the full spectrum of the manager's job—all of the functions performed.

Another advantage of evaluation based on performance of management functions is its wide applicability. Individualized rating devices such as those required for behavior evaluation are not required.

[8]Ibid., p. 82.
[9]Harold Koontz and Cyril O'Donnell, *Management: A Systems and Contingency Analysis of Managerial Functions,* 6th ed. (New York: McGraw-Hill, 1976), p. 500.

**TABLE 15-2**

385

*Methods for
Evaluating
Managers*

Sample Checklist for Functional Performance Evaluation

| Functional Area | Appraisal Questions | Above Average | Average | Below Average |
|---|---|---|---|---|
| Planning | How effective is the manager in:<br>• Scheduling work?<br>• Setting goals for subordinates?<br>• Establishing rules and procedures? | ____ <br> ____ <br> ____ | ____ <br> ____ <br> ____ | ____ <br> ____ <br> ____ |
| Organizing | How effective is the manager in:<br>• Delegating authority?<br>• Assigning work?<br>• Dividing work into specialized activities? | ____ <br> ____ <br> ____ | ____ <br> ____ <br> ____ | ____ <br> ____ <br> ____ |
| Staffing | How effective is the manager in:<br>• Matching people to job roles?<br>• Implementing training programs?<br>• Administering compensation programs? | ____ <br> ____ <br> ____ | ____ <br> ____ <br> ____ | ____ <br> ____ <br> ____ |
| Directing | How effective is the manager in:<br>• Writing reports to supervisors?<br>• Keeping turnover within acceptable limits?<br>• Inspiring personnel to put forth their best efforts? | ____ <br> ____ <br> ____ | ____ <br> ____ <br> ____ | ____ <br> ____ <br> ____ |
| Controlling | How effective is the manager in:<br>• Establishing attainable performance standards?<br>• Bringing about corrective action when needed?<br>• Following up to make sure standards are met? | ____ <br> ____ <br> ____ | ____ <br> ____ <br> ____ | ____ <br> ____ <br> ____ |

### Disadvantages of Functional Performance Evaluation

The major limitation of evaluating managers on the basis of functional performance is subjectivity. As is true with trait-evaluation systems, what is considered "above average," "average," and "below average" depends to some degree on the standards and perceptions of the evaluator.

A second limitation is that the ratings do not relate directly to performance or results. Conceivably, a manager can perform some or even all of the functions in the way a model manager should and still not attain organizational goals. Finally, as is the case with trait evaluation, there may be a tendency for the evaluator to inflate the ratings.

Four methods for evaluating managers on a formal or systematic basis have been examined. All formal systems for appraising managers attempt to measure performance, skills, or attitudes as accurately as possible. Informal evaluation, on the

*Informal
Evaluation*

other hand, does not use formal instruments such as rating scales. Informal evaluation is an ongoing, unstructured way of appraising a manager's performance.

### Uses of Informal Evaluation

Informal evaluation of managers is the rule in most small organizations. The superintendent of a construction project can usually tell by observation which managers are performing satisfactorily and which are not. The manager of a machine shop who has only five supervisors reporting to him can observe their behavior on a daily basis. The manager can note how workers relate to the supervisors and how the supervisors solve problems that develop.

In medium-sized organizations, informal evaluation is also generally the rule, especially in those with relatively unsophisticated senior managers who may not know about or appreciate appraisal tools such as results evaluation, MBO, and trait evaluation. If they do understand formal manager-appraisal systems, they may feel that such systems are not designed for medium-sized companies, that they are too expensive, or that formal appraisal is not necessary.

Interestingly, informal evaluation is also the rule in the highest echelons of most large organizations. In all probability, the president of a university is not evaluated by the board of regents or the trustees on a formal basis. The board considers such questions as "Is the faculty reasonably happy?" "Are the president's requests for money in line with the requests of other units in the system?" and "Is progress being made toward full accreditation for all programs?"

Nor does the president of a large corporation rate key executives in a formal fashion. Senior managers are observed firsthand. Day-to-day discussions with them will suggest whether their performance is satisfactory.

The military services use formal systems for officer appraisal through the ranks of colonel and captain (Navy). But appraisals of key military managers, the generals and admirals, are made informally.

*"Collins, you show the potential of someday commanding a
leadership position like mine . . . so I've decided to fire you."*

The apparent rationale for not subjecting senior managers in most institutions to formal appraisal is that success at the top echelon is related to many intangible factors. It is extremely difficult to make a formal evaluation of leadership, insight, strategical skill, and acumen, all of which are highly important at the top level of an organization. It is also likely that senior managers would resent being rated under most of the formal systems discussed in this chapter. A senior executive may feel that being rated on the basis of actual results is all that matters.

### Advantages of Informal Evaluation

One basic advantage of informal evaluation is that it is simple. No forms must be filled out and analyzed, no structured interviews are required, and no formal procedure must be designed and implemented.

A second advantage is its low cost. With informal evaluation, no skilled experts need be retained to design and implement the system.

Third, informal evaluation can lead to insights regarding day-to-day managing. While observing a subordinate performing activities, a manager can point out errors and make suggestions for improvement on the spot.

### Disadvantages of Informal Evaluation

Many organizations are too small to make effective use of a formal manager-evaluation system. For them it would be impractical. The disadvantages of informal evaluation noted below are intended to apply only to organizations that are large enough to use a formal system but have elected not to do so.

The greatest limitation of informal appraisal is that it tends to be subjective and judgmental. Evaluations may be based more on personal feelings toward the individual than on actual performance. If the manager likes the person being evaluated, the rating tends to be better than if some ill feelings exist.

Second, informal evaluations do not facilitate a planned follow-through for corrective action. The informal appraisal exists only in the evaluator's mind and is not a matter of record or in readily usable form. And a manager who evaluates his or her subordinates only on the basis of personal observation may overlook such matters as "What help is needed to improve?" and "How much tangible improvement has she or he made in performance in the past year?"

## MANAGER EVALUATION AND CAREER PLANNING

Manager evaluation provides information useful in making decisions regarding promotions, compensation levels, transfer, and termination and in deciding what action should be taken to help the manager improve his or her abilities. To the manager being evaluated, appraisal thus relates to planning his or her career in management. Laurence L. Ferguson, who has studied career patterns of managers, has raised some interesting questions relative to career planning and progression:

- Why do about one half of the carefully screened, highly promising new college graduates hired by large corporations leave during the first three to six years?

- Why do so many really high-potential individuals end up in dead-end situations?
- What job situations cause incumbents consistently to be overrated by their peers and supervisors?
- What are the characteristics of "graveyard" jobs—jobs in which no individual ever looks good and which can damage the career of a highly promising man?
- What characteristics (other than previous performance in lower-level jobs) are critical for success in top jobs of broad responsibility?
- Why do so many successful managers say, at the midpoints in their careers, that they do not know the real promotion criteria in their company?"[10]

Ferguson believes that hiring, promotion, and other personnel decisions are still largely based on intuition (which is very expensive, since it so often is inaccurate) rather than on scientific analysis. Because of computerization, he feels that it should be possible to make far more accurate decisions about who should be selected for management in the first place, what paths (types of management jobs) managers' careers should follow, and when managers can handle larger responsibilities.

To make manager career planning more scientific, Ferguson advocates the following practices:

- *Develop predictive information about the factors that lead to success in managing.* While this step is difficult, Ferguson believes predictors of a manager's career progress can be designed if companies collect detailed information about how mature, successful managers handle problems, make and implement decisions, and perform other aspects of their jobs.
- *Study on-the-job behavior of successful managers.* Using the services of social scientists, studies should be made on such topics as How do successful managers resolve conflicts? Persuade others to cooperate? Communicate? Exercise judgment? Make decisions?
- *Store and use data.* Information collected through research should be analyzed and used in manager career planning. If the research is conducted and analyzed properly, various correlations can be drawn. For example, a person's kind and amount of education can be compared with his or her success as a manager."[11]

Ferguson advocates the use of a model to aid in career management (see Figure 15–2). He explains how his model could be used as follows:

As the model is now envisioned, the manager would make his selections in a perfectly normal and independent fashion. Any properly qualified manager would have access to the appropriate bank of personnel information in the central data storage and processing system. From his desk, he could ask for and receive—in seconds—

---

[10]Laurence L. Ferguson, "Better Management of Managers' Careers," in *New Insights for Executive Achievement* (Cambridge, Mass.: *Harvard Business Review*, 1968), p. 112.
[11]Ibid.

complete information about all individuals in the storage bank who meet the specifications he designates. The manager could change the specifications, ask for special analyses, and in general get, to the extent that prior inputs have been adequate, answers to any questions he wants to ask the computer.

All he need do is be able to talk in terms of the attributes, characteristics, and limitations he wants to impose. He could, at his command, get tabular lists, frequency distributions, correlation coefficients, predictive data, and almost anything else he is ingenious enough to think of that might help him reach a decision. From an array of qualified candidates, he would finally make a choice, and a promotion would be accomplished.[12]

The Ferguson system could be adapted so that subordinates could learn what they should do to select specific career paths and prepare for promotions along the way. In addition, social scientists increasingly recognize that a person's self-perception or self-image influences his or her success. Dr. Harry Levinson of The Menninger Foundation has asked, "Will a promotion be an opportunity—or a big step toward failure?" His answer: "A promotion can be as threatening to one man as it is reassuring to another, because it raises questions that concern his emotional and psychological makeup. ... How he *feels* about himself is often more critical to his success or failure than what he *is* objectively."[13]

## GUIDELINES FOR EFFECTIVE MANAGER EVALUATION

There is no perfect way to evaluate manager performance. As we have seen, the task of appraisal is complex. Nevertheless, six guidelines can be followed to make manager appraisal more effective: Keep the system simple; avoid personal bias and subjectivity; encourage frank evaluations; advise personnel of the methods and purposes of evaluations; make evaluations at frequent, stated intervals; and use the results of evaluations constructively.

An evaluation system should be no more complicated than is absolutely necessary to achieve the objectives established for it. In practice, many evaluation systems are too complex, take too much time to implement, and are too costly for the anticipated results. Therefore, in studying any proposed evaluation system, managers should ask such questions as "What value can we expect to derive from it?" "How much time will it require?" and "Will the purpose of the evaluation system be understood?"

**Keep the System Simple**

Regardless of whether a manager-evaluation system is informal, based on trait analysis, or designed to fit into a management-by-objectives program, there is always some possibility that the personal prejudices of the evaluator will show through. For example, the person making the appraisal may be opposed to the idea of female managers and may discredit to some degree the performance of his

**Avoid Personal Bias and Subjectivity**

[12]Ibid.
[13]*Think,* January–February 1965, p. 7.

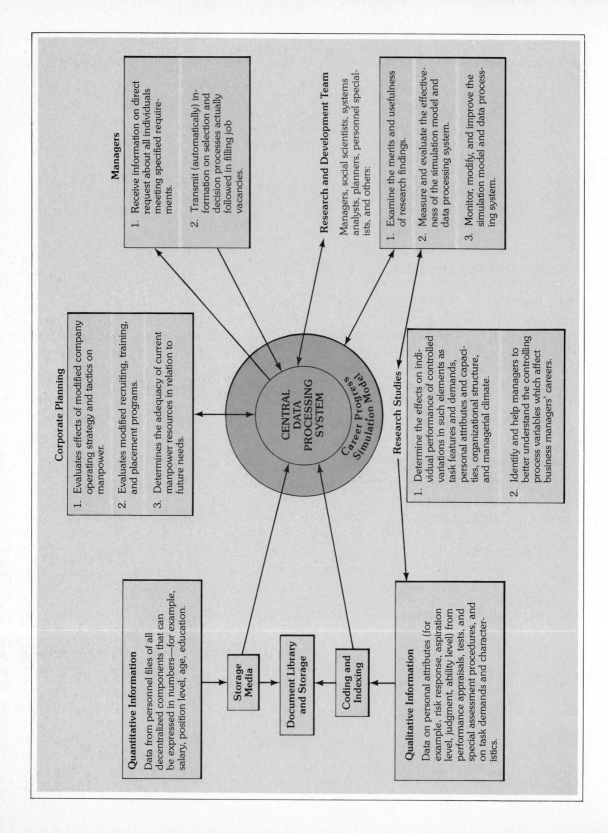

**Managers**

1. Receive information on direct request about all individuals meeting specified requirements.

2. Transmit (automatically) information on selection and decision processes actually followed in filling job vacancies.

**Corporate Planning**

1. Evaluates effects of modified company operating strategy and tactics on manpower.

2. Evaluates modified recruiting, training, and placement programs.

3. Determines the adequacy of current manpower resources in relation to future needs.

**Research and Development Team**

Managers, social scientists, systems analysts, planners, personnel specialists, and others:

1. Examine the merits and usefulness of research findings.

2. Measure and evaluate the effectiveness of the simulation model and data processing system.

3. Monitor, modify, and improve the simulation model and data processing system.

**Research Studies**

1. Determine the effects on individual performance of controlled variations in such elements as task features and demands, personal attributes and capacities, organizational structure, and managerial climate.

2. Identify and help managers to better understand the controlling process variables which affect business managers' careers.

**CENTRAL DATA PROCESSING SYSTEM**

*Career Progress Simulation Model*

**Quantitative Information**

Data from personnel files of all decentralized components that can be expressed in numbers—for example, salary, position level, age, education.

**Storage Media**

**Document Library and Storage**

**Coding and Indexing**

**Qualitative Information**

Data on personal attributes (for example, risk response, aspiration level, judgment, ability level) from performance appraisals, tests, and special assessment procedures, and on task demands and characteristics.

# FIGURE 15–2

## Simplified Managerial Manpower Selection and Career-planning Model

Source: Laurence L. Ferguson, "Better Management of Managers' Careers," in *New Insights for Executive Achievement* (Cambridge, Mass.: *Harvard Business Review*, 1968), p. 123. Reprinted by permission of the *Harvard Business Review*. Adapted exhibit from "Better Management of Managers' Careers" by Laurence L. Ferguson (March–April 1966). Copyright © 1966 by the President and Fellows of Harvard College; all rights reserved.

female subordinate. At the other extreme, the evaluator may be very much "pro women" and may therefore give a female subordinate an unwarranted high evaluation.

Avoiding bias is difficult. However, evaluators should make every effort not to let their subjective feelings about an individual affect their appraisal.

**Encourage Frank Evaluations**

Perhaps it is not possible to completely eliminate personal bias in an evaluation system. But some progress can be made if the evaluation system has the full support of senior management and if senior managers expect honest, objective reporting even if it discredits an individual. Most managers do not like to make a negative report about a subordinate, even if it is justified. But if managers are taught that the welfare of the organization must take precedence over the welfare of individuals, then greater objectivity in the evaluation process should result.

**Advise Personnel of the Methods and Purposes of Evaluations**

In many organizations, subordinates are not aware of what methods, if any, are being used to appraise them. This is a grave error. A manager should know from the first day at work that he or she is being evaluated and what methods are being used. This information should be communicated positively and related to the reward system.

It is also important that people being evaluated clearly understand the purposes of the appraisals. Unless they do, they may regard evaluation as a negative, time-wasting process. Any evaluation system should be explained to people as being to *their* advantage as well as to the advantage of the organization. If compensation, promotion, and other personnel decisions are to be based on evaluations, subordinates should be told. In addition, subordinates should know that evaluations are intended to help them, since the objective is to show the way to better performance.

Knowing the methods and purposes of evaluation can serve as an incentive for manager improvement. If managers know that promotion is based on evaluation (and assuming a promotion is desired), they will try harder to excel, since they will see personal benefits as a result of good performance.

**Make Evaluations at Frequent, Stated Intervals**

Managers should be evaluated at a frequency sufficient to show their weaknesses in managing so that any weaknesses can be corrected quickly. When evaluations are made too infrequently, problems resulting from ineffective managing, such as inefficiency, excessive absenteeism, turnover, and unsatisfactory sales volume,

# MANAGERS IN ACTION

## WHAT HAPPENS WHEN SENIOR MANAGERS DON'T GET RESULTS?

Some people think that a top executive position is very secure. This is not necessarily so. The safest job in a big company might be that of a janitor. The riskiest job is a senior management position.

Why are top executives ousted? Some typical answers given are: failure to turn the company around, failure to build a forward-looking management team, or the company (under the executive's direction) lost too much money. In other words, senior managers are fired when they fail to get the results desired by the board of directors or higher authority to whom they report.

How does it feel to get fired? "Getting fired from any job is painful. But being forced out of a highly visible top job, with headlines trumpeting the news, can be devastating."[1] Often the terminated executive is angry, emotionally hurt, and may doubt personal self-worth.

What do fired executives do? "The problem that most fired executives face is not a lack of job offers but a lack of comparable job offers."[2] Many executives go into consulting, a field sometimes referred to as "the graveyard of unwanted executives." *Business Week* observes, "Those deposed chiefs who have landed new jobs very quickly for the most part have settled either for stepped-down titles or much smaller companies."[3]

Getting fired is not all bad, however. Dismissed senior executives typically receive handsome severance benefits. Some even receive a consulting contract with the company that fired them.

[1] Quoted from the September 15, 1980 issue of *Business Week* by special permission, © 1980 by McGraw-Hill, Inc. New York, NY 10020. All rights reserved.

[2] Ibid.
[3] Ibid.

### QUESTIONS

1. What other reasons besides "failure to get results" may be responsible for executive dismissals?
2. It is sometimes said that people with strong security needs are not cut out for top management jobs. Assuming this statement is true, how does it relate to career planning?

tend to worsen. Frequent evaluations are also fair to the manager being appraised. People at any level in an organization want to know where they stand.

However, the frequency for making appraisals varies depending on such factors as the level of the job, how long the individual has held the position, and the emphasis placed on evaluation by top management.

For many nonmanagement jobs, an individual is placed on probation for a certain period, usually sixty or ninety days. At the end of the probationary period, the individual's performance is evaluated to determine whether the employee should be given permanent status or terminated.

Typically, for management positions, the higher the level in the organization, the less frequent the performance reviews. The main rationale for this is that both errors and successes in managing can be noted more easily at lower levels than at higher levels. It is easier to evaluate how well a manager of a convenience food store is performing than to appraise how good a job the director of merchandising for the chain is doing. Results at lower levels are more apparent than those at higher levels.

Generally, the longer an individual has held a job, the less frequent the appraisals are. A management trainee may be evaluated monthly or quarterly; managers with several years experience may be appraised only once a year.

Finally, the importance attached to evaluations by senior management helps determine the frequency of making appraisals. Top managers in some organizations favor infrequent appraisals because they feel evaluations are too costly to conduct.

The view taken here is that evaluations are a useful management practice and that they should be conducted at stated intervals. Furthermore, the stated interval should be communicated to the people who will be evaluated.

**Use Results of Evaluations Constructively**

A common form of waste in management is to conduct evaluations and then make only partial or even no use of them. Managers should recognize that evaluations can serve three useful purposes.

First, an appraisal of how well a manager has performed in the past should serve as a guide to helping him or her perform more effectively in the future. This is especially true when performance is measured by results. The manager and the subordinate *working together* can use the evaluation to determine what specific action is needed to bring improvement. Perhaps supervision techniques are a problem. Or the individual may need to develop better work schedules or may have made mistakes in hiring or assigning workers. Whatever the problems suggested by a review of the evaluation, some effort should be made to solve them.

Second, appraisals can and should serve as a basis for decisions about promotion, transfer, termination, reassignment, compensation, and other manager staffing issues. To make important decisions such as these without the benefit of the best possible evaluation of a manager is a disservice to the organization and an injustice to the manager.

Third, evaluations can be used by senior management to assess the overall quantity and quality of its managerial talent. A firm that is contemplating a broad expansion program might do well to hold off if evaluations of its managers, considered collectively, show inadequate managerial capabilities. The converse is true. An organization may find through a study of manager evaluation that it has underutilized available talents, and expansion should be undertaken.

**SUMMARY**

- Evaluation of the performance of individuals is inherent in organized life. Evaluation may be judgmental (affecting decisions about promotions, compensation, transfers, and termination) or developmental (revealing what is needed to help the person perform better).
- Evaluation based on results assesses a manager in terms of what has been actually achieved. It gets to the heart of managing and is objective. However, results may be beyond the control of the person being appraised.
- Trait evaluation judges a manager's performance in terms of personal characteristics and is used extensively. It is simple, can be applied to different kinds of

management jobs at different levels, and can easily be supplemented with informal comments. But such ratings tend to be subjective, are often too high, and may reflect differing standards of evaluators, may not relate to performance, and may be distorted by a halo effect.

- Behavior evaluation is a relatively new technique that appraises managers in terms of how they went about achieving results. It is more objective than trait appraisal, provides a learning experience for managers, yields ideas for improvement, and concentrates on performance under a manager's control. However, it is costly, unfamiliar to many managers, and difficult to apply in small organizations.
- Functional performance evaluation assesses managers' ability to perform managerial functions. It can reveal specific strengths and weaknesses of an individual's performance as a manager, but it is subjective and the ratings do not directly relate to performance or results.
- Informal evaluation is based solely on observation of performance. It is simple, involves little cost, and provides insight into daily managing, but it is also subjective and does not lead to planned corrective action.
- Laurence L. Ferguson advocates using evaluation systems more carefully in career planning by developing predictive factors that lead to success in managing, studying on-the-job behavior of successful managers, and storing and using the data.
- Guidelines for effective manager evaluation are to keep the system simple; avoid bias and subjectivity; encourage frank evaluations; advise personnel of the methods and purposes of evaluations; make evaluations at frequent, stated intervals; and use results constructively.

**LEARN
THE LANGUAGE
OF
MANAGEMENT**

| | |
|---|---|
| judgmental evaluation | behavior evaluation |
| developmental evaluation | functional performance evaluation |
| results evaluation | informal evaluation |
| trait evaluation | behavior-anchored rating scale |

**QUESTIONS
FOR REVIEW
AND
DISCUSSION**

1. Explain why it is impossible for a person in an organization to escape being evaluated.
2. Why should promotions and terminations be based on careful and thorough evaluations?
3. Evaluation based on results is a key appraisal method. How might you use this technique to evaluate a manager of a convenience food store, a manager of the production department in a large manufacturing company, and a manager of a hospital?
4. Results evaluation is particularly difficult for staff positions. How might you evaluate the following in terms of results: a public-relations director, a head of a legal department, and a director of advertising?
5. Why is effort put forth—or time put in—not a good basis for evaluation?
6. How can the key problems in trait evaluation be minimized? Why, do you think, is trait appraisal so widely used in government organizations?
7. Criticize the evaluation form in Table 15–1. In what ways do you feel it could be improved?
8. Following the example of the behavior-evaluation rating form in Figure 15–1, develop a nine-point scale of expectations for one of the following positions: a production department supervisor, an office manager, or an advertising account

executive. What does the experience of developing a scale suggest about this way of evaluating managers?

9. Suppose, in evaluating a manager on the basis of performance of management functions, you discovered that the manager was very effective in planning, organizing, and controlling but was weak in staffing and directing. What would you do?

10. If you were a senior manager in a large organization, would you object to being evaluated through use of a formalized appraisal system? Why or why not?

11. Career planning for managers has not traditionally been closely related to evaluations. How can this be explained?

### 1. How does one evaluate a scientist?

Dr. George Rogers heads the research department of a paint manufacturer. His main responsibility is the development of new products. His secondary responsibility is bringing about corrective action when quality falls below standards.

Dr. Rogers made a major contribution to the company four years ago when he developed a new paint that is now widely used by airlines. Since then, Dr. Rogers has not developed any new paints, although his department spends almost $500,000 each year.

The company president feels that every department head must be evaluated each year on the basis of results. He knows Dr. Rogers is a sensitive individual who feels an evaluation is demeaning and is unnecessary for professional scientific researchers.

The president asks for your advice. He tells you, "We've spent almost $2 million on research since Rogers developed Z43A [the paint used by the airlines]. Frankly, I'm concerned. Maybe Rogers developed it by accident. Tell me, how do I evaluate Rogers?"

What would your response be? Explain.

### 2. Evaluating Wanda Jones for promotion

Wanda Jones has been a supervisor for three years in the National Computer Software Company. Her work has been excellent, and now you are considering her for a position of more responsibility — one that would require extensive travel to meet with important customers.

You ask your two key associates what they think of promoting Ms. Jones. They frown on the idea. Harry Jackson tells you, "It's a bad idea. She's great from 9:00 A.M. to 5:00 P.M., but her off-duty life is a mess. Keeps company with a bunch of weirdos." Mabel Sauder agrees: "Frankly, you'd be jeopardizing the conservative image of our company if you made her a national accounts service manager. Sooner or later she'd be involved with some of our clients, and that would lead to problems."

What would you do and why?

### 3. Should subordinates evaluate superiors?

New Technology makes components for computers. It employes 2,500 people. Recently the company founder, Daniel Stanley, employed Hal Porter to head up the personnel deaprtment. Daniel told Hal when he hired him that one priority was "to improve the performance of our managers."

Hal has an idea he thinks has merit. The following discussion takes place between Hal and Daniel.

Hal: I'd like to institute a "bottoms-up appraisal system." By that I mean each manager in the company would be evaluated every six months by the people who report to him or her. This would give the manager being evaluated feedback from his or her subordinates about how good a manager he is.

Daniel: You said every manager in the company would be evaluated by his subordinates. Would this mean my direct subordinates would evaluate me?

Hal: That, of course, is your decision. I thought we'd confine the evaluations to the supervisory level at first. All operative employees would evaluate the supervisors. Later, we could let the supervisors evaluate the middle managers and the middle managers appraise the senior managers.

Daniel: A big part of your job is to help us develop managers. What specific benefits would your "bottoms-up appraisal system" provide?

Hal: I see three advantages. First, the subordinates have the most direct knowledge of how a manager manages. Second, the information obtained should help the manager improve. And third, letting subordinates appraise the manager should be good for their morale.

Daniel: I have some serious reservations about your idea. First, I don't believe subordinates—especially operative employees—are qualified to evaluate their superiors. Second, the managers being evaluated may pass out favors to get better appraisals. And third, subordinates may think they now have a means to get rid of superiors they don't like.

What do you think of Hal's idea?

What benefits in addition to those stated by Hal might result if a "bottoms-up"appraisal system was adopted.

Daniel makes a strong case against the plan. What other limitations do you foresee?

**FOR ADDITIONAL
CONCEPTS
AND IDEAS**

Brinkerhoff, Derick W., and Kanter, Rosabeth Moss. "Appraising the Performance of Performance Appraisal." *Sloan Management Review*, Spring 1980, pp. 3–16.

Gigkioni, Giovanni B.; Giglioni, Joyce B.; and Bryant, James A. "Performance Appraisal: Here Comes the Judge." *California Management Review*, Winter 1981, pp. 14–23.

Glicken, Morley D., and Janka, Katherine. "Executives Under Fire: The Burnout Syndrome." *California Management Review*, Spring 1982, pp. 67–80.

Gordon, Paul J., and Meredith, Paul H. "Creating and Using a Model to Monitor Managerial Talent." *Business Horizons*, January–February 1982, pp. 52–61.

Lawrence, Barbara S. "The Myth of the Midlife Crisis." *Sloan Management Review*, Summer 1980, pp. 35–49.

Millard, Cheedle W.; Luthans, Fred; and Ottemann, Robert L. "A New Breakthrough for Performance Appraisal." *Business Horizons*, August 1976, pp. 66–73.

Murray, Victor, and Gandz, Jeffrey. "Games Executives Play: Politics at Work." *Business Horizons*, December 1980, pp. 11–23.

Near, Janet P. "The Career Plateau: Causes and Effects." *Business Horizons*, October 1980, pp. 53–65.

Niehouse, Oliver L. "Breaking the Promotion Barrier with Flexible Leadership." *Business*, October–November–December 1982, pp. 22–26.

Schwarzkopf, Ed A., and Miller, Edwin L. "Exploring the Male Mobility Myth." *Business Horizons*, June 1980, pp. 38–44.

Sloma, Richard S. *How to Measure Managerial Performance.* New York: Macmillan, 1980.

Stybel, Laurence J.; Cooper, Robin; and Peabody, Maryanne. "Planning Executive Dismissals: How To Fire a Friend." *California Management Review*, Spring 1982, pp. 73–88.

Stybel, Laurence J. "Getting Over Getting Fired." *Business*, January 1981, pp. 48–51.

Swinyard, Alfred W., and Bond, Floyd A. "Who Gets Promoted?" *Harvard Business Review*, September–October 1980, pp. 6–21.

Winstanley, N. B. "Legal and Ethical Issues in Performance Appraisals." *Harvard Business Review*, November–December 1980, pp. 186–192.

# CASE STUDY

## SHOULD MIDDLE MANAGERS BE ENCOURAGED TO GET AN M.B.A. DEGREE?

John Glover, president of Ace Construction Company, has recently been named to the business advisory committee of a local university. While serving on the committee, Glover becomes impressed with what he learns about the graduate program in business. He comes up with the idea of requiring all nine of his middle managers to enroll in the university's M.B.A. program. Glover decides to discuss the idea with Wayne Wilson, the executive vice-president of Ace Construction. The following discussion takes place.

Glover: What do you think of my idea of requiring our middle managers to enroll in the local M.B.A. program on a part-time basis?

Wilson: You did say require, didn't you? At the outset I think it's going a bit far to require anybody in the company to go to school.

Glover: OK. I'll back off from requiring and adopt a posture of strongly suggesting that they enroll. Those who turn down the opportunity are saying in effect, "I'm not willing to pay the price of advancement."

Wilson: I agree with your concept. I wish the company I was with before I joined Ace would have made me such an offer. Maybe I'd be in your office if it had! But seriously, I see a number of potential problems.

Glover: Such as?

Wilson: First, I understand the university has some strict enrollment qualifications. I have my doubts that all nine of our middle managers could meet them. Now suppose two or three of our people were rejected. That could prove embarrassing and could adversely affect their performance. Or suppose they were accepted but flunked out. In effect, the university would be telling us that some of our managers have more ability than others.

Glover: You have a good point there, but I'm willing to take the risk. After all, we believe in competition. Do you have any other reservations about the idea?

Wilson: Yes, I do. We both know that at least two of our middle managers have gone as far as they can. Frankly, I think we'd be wasting money to enroll them in an M.B.A. program.

Glover: You have a point there.

Wilson: I perceive another problem. How many of them really want to work on an M.B.A.? It seems to me that the people who are strongly motivated in that direction would have already begun work on an advanced degree.

Glover: Any other problems?

Wilson: Well, a final point I think we should consider is our managers' expectations. An M.B.A. takes a lot of work. It's natural, I think, for those who succeed to expect some kind of reward on completion—more money or a promotion. And I don't see how we can guarantee that. But if we don't promise them something, we may end up losing some of our better people.

Glover: Well, you've certainly raised some important considerations. What do you suggest? After all, we both are strongly committed to management development.

Wilson: Two thoughts come to mind. First, offer to pay the costs of an M.B.A. to those managers who want to enroll. But don't apply pressure. Make it strictly voluntary.

A second idea would be to retain a number of professors at the university to design a manager-development program for our managers. The program could be tailored to our present and future needs.

Glover: Thanks for your analysis. Let's think more about it and decide in a couple of weeks. I definitely feel we need to do something to develop the full potential of all our people.

## QUESTIONS

1. What other problems may arise from requiring all middle managers to pursue an M.B.A.?
2. If you were a middle manager in the Ace Construction Company, how would you react to an implied command that you work toward an M.B.A.? Explain.

which they are qualified and that they participate in setting goals and methods for achieving them.

**411**

*Major Theories of Motivation*

Hall:
The Relationship
Between a
Manager's
Motivation
and Success
as a Manager

Most studies of motivation have focused on what motivates lower-level employees, not managers. An important work that employed sophisticated techniques attempted to determine how behavioral patterns of managers relate to their performance. In a five-year research project, Jay Hall, a social psychologist, studied over 16,000 managers representing many different companies in an attempt to determine the behavioral differences among high, average, and low achievers. Hall was able to verify statistically many of the concepts developed by Maslow, Herzberg, McGregor, and Likert.

He discovered that the need for self-actualization is the dominant motivational influence for high achievers, that ego-status needs are the main motivator for average achievers, and that low achievers are mainly interested in creature comforts.

Hall found that a manager's level of personal motivation directly affects his or her subordinates' desire to achieve. He notes:

> Not only does personal motivation affect a manager's achievement level, so does his perception of the motivational process and his consequent practices in the management of motives. Indeed, in what appears to be a casual fashion, a manager's achievement is directly linked to the motivational profile of his subordinates. A sobering thought is inferred: *The needs and quality of motivation characterizing a manager's subordinates may say more about the manager than about his subordinates.*[7]

Hall also observed that managers who are high achievers make extensive use of participative management:

> Low Achievers, as reported by their subordinates, make minimal use of participative practices; Average Achievers make only slightly greater use. High Achievers, according to their subordinates, not only employ far and away greater amounts of the technique, but so much so that participative methods may be said to be a major characteristic of the High Achieving approach to management.
> . . . Only subordinates of High Achievers report the kind of satisfaction, commitment and pride in work that characterizes the work force of healthy organizations. Low Achievers, and to some extent Average Achievers, employ practices which result in repressive and frustrating circumstances typically found in neurotic organizations.[8]

Hall draws the following conclusion from his study:

> The High Achiever's approach to management can result in not only sweet dreams of success, but true excellence — be it in a small firm, one of *Fortune's* 500 or the Oval Office. Each of us has the option of becoming an Achieving Manager because the manager's achievement may be traced to the behaviors he employs. If we would make one impression, let it be this: Managerial achievement does not depend upon

[7]Jay Hall, "To Achieve or Not: The Manager's Choice," *California Management Review*, Summer 1976, p. 11.
[8]Ibid., p. 13.

the existence of personal traits and extraordinary skills unique to outstanding individuals. It depends on the manner in which the manager behaves in conducting organizational affairs and on the values he holds regarding personal and interpersonal potentials. All of which can be learned. *The key to becoming an Achieving Manager is to learn to behave like one.*[9]

# BASIC FACTORS THAT MOTIVATE

Researchers and theorists in management and in behavioral psychology are not in full agreement as to what motivates people—and to what degree—to perform work in organizations. There is a general consensus, however, that the following factors are involved in motivation.

**Challenging Work**  In our language, "work" is usually thought of in nonchallenging, negative terms such as "toil," "drudgery," and "travail." Boredom may be a motivational depressant. To motivate personnel to perform at their best, managers should try to make work as challenging as possible, keeping in mind that what is challenging to one person may not excite another. Conducting an orientation session for new employees may be exciting to someone just appointed as an instructor in a training department but boring to the head of the department. Loading trucks day in and day out may be challenging to someone with limited education but may prove utterly unchallenging to a young person just out of college. Because of these individual differences, managers should consider the worker's aptitude, interest, intelligence, skills, and education in making work assignments.

People often debate whether work is more challenging and motivation higher in large bureaucracies than in smaller organizations. This topic is discussed in the Issue for Debate in this chapter.

**Participation in Planning**  Generally, as was indicated by Likert's and Hall's findings, employees are more strongly motivated if they are asked to help plan their work and shape the environment in which it is performed. Salespeople tend to perform better if management permits them to help set their quotas, plan how to cover their territories, and help develop their sales presentations.

The higher in an organization one goes, the more participation in planning is a strong motivational force. Senior-level people are, in fact, often insistent on being able to directly participate in planning their roles in the organization. Even at lower levels participation is important. A supervisor may be motivated when permitted to make decisions about scheduling work; an employee may be motivated when allowed to select the tools needed to perform the job; and a short-order cook probably likes to decide how to clean the grill.

There are, however, exceptions to participation in planning as a motivational force. Some employees are more comfortable—and therefore we assume better motivated—when the manager spells out in detail what they are expected to do

[9]Ibid., p. 17.

and how. Some students prefer a professor who gives absolutely cut-and-dried assignments to the instructor who allows considerable freedom in homework assignments. Effective motivation requires that managers recognize individual preferences among personnel. What turns one person on may turn another person off.

The desire for recognition and the improved status it brings appears universal regardless of position, age, education, and other factors. All of us seem to want approval from our peers as well as from our superiors. When Jim, a fire fighter, is singled out for the good job he did in fighting a fire, he is likely to be motivated to do even better at the next fire. Executives may be motivated by such things as a company car, titles, special dining facilities, and a club membership. Recognition, of course, must be sincere and based on above-average performance, or it will not be appreciated by the recipient and will be resented by others. Giving Joe a fancy title for no reason will probably not motivate him to perform better in the future.

Almost anything can be a status symbol if it is recognized by the group as a badge of distinction. A key to the executive washroom, a large office, a ten-year pin, a reserved parking space, and carpeting on the floor are just a few of the almost countless ways recognition—and thereby status—can be conferred.

Not everyone wants more responsibility and power. Not all soldiers want to become officers, not all sorority sisters want to be president of the group, and certainly not all employees desire the responsibility and the power that comes from being made supervisor. Nevertheless, a significant number of individuals who are part of organized groups *do* in fact want more responsibility and are motivated by the prospect of attaining it. In fact, it is probable that more people want to become bosses than the number of vacancies permit. When an executive dies or is fired, a number of people usually jockey to get the job.

In a constructive way, then, management should devise a plan for using the chances of promotion, more power, and greater responsibility as a way to motivate people to perform more effectively.

The need for **security**—that is, the desire to be free from fear of such things as job loss, demotion, and loss of income—apparently is inherent in all of us. The degree to which individuals desire security varies considerably among people. To some, security is all-important. Individuals who put security foremost will put up with almost any inconvenience and maltreatment just to hang on to their jobs. Even among management personnel there are individuals who strongly dislike their jobs but nevertheless keep them because they are afraid of losing their retirement benefits.

One of the most difficult tasks facing management is to determine how much security should be provided. Security is a strong motivator, but too little or too much can be harmful. If too little security is provided, workers will seek jobs in which there is more assurance of steady employment and job benefits. On the

# ISSUE FOR DEBATE

## DO BUREAUCRACIES STIFLE INITIATIVE AND WEAKEN MOTIVATION?

A bureaucracy has clear-cut division of labor, many regulations that control people and performance, job assignments based on technical qualifications determined by formal procedures, and a clearly structured authority hierarchy. Many people think that these factors weaken motivation. Others do not. Below are some pro and con points about bureaucracies.

### YES

**Bureaucracies do stifle initiative and weaken motivation because . . .**

Webster's Dictionary defines "bureaucracy" as "a system marked by . . . lack of initiative and flexibility . . . and by a tendency to defer decisions to superiors or to impede action with red tape." Thus by definition, bureaucracies stifle initiative and weaken motivation.

Employees in nonbureaucratic organizations typically enjoy less security than those in bureaucracies, so they must be more motivated to keep their jobs.

Entrepreneurs, the antithesis of bureaucrats, are among the most motivated persons. Bureaucratic employees, on the other hand, must follow prescribed regulations. Their motivation may be weakened because their freedom to make decisions is limited.

In bureaucracies it is easy to pass a problem upward or sideward rather than solve it. When the buck is easily passed, a person may take less interest in what is going on, boredom may increase, and lowered morale may result.

### NO

**Bureaucracies do not stifle initiative and weaken motivation because . . .**

An in-depth study over a ten-year period by a noted social scientist lead him to conclude, "All levels of bureaucratic employees, blue collar as well as white collar, enjoy richer lives than nonbureaucrats—both on and off the job." (Melvin L. Kohn, "The Benefits of Bureaucracy," *Human Nature*, August 1978, p. 60.)

Bureaucracies limit the power of managers to dismiss subordinates. Thus subordinates have more security—something that motivates many people.

Contrary to opinion, bureaucratic employees are more receptive to change than other workers. This is because, to a greater extent than the others, they come from urban backgrounds, have more education, and work in a more challenging environment (see Kohn, "Benefits of Bureaucracy," p. 64).

America is dominated by bureaucracies—big government and big business. Most of the research, innovations, and new technology comes from bureaucracies. How could that be if, in fact, they stifled initiative and weakened motivation?

### QUESTIONS

1. On balance, which side of the issue is strongest? Why?
2. Which would you prefer working for, a bureaucracy or a nonbureaucratic organization? Why?

other hand, if too much is given, workers may develop a lackadaisical attitude and produce at a low level.

Managers of Lincoln Electric are strong believers in security as a motivator. The company is one of the leaders in its field and is widely regarded for its productivity and its incentive system, which includes "job-evaluated base rates that are average for the industry and area; extensive use of individual piecework incentives; a very large quasi-profit sharing bonus; encouragement of creativity and entrepreneurship at every level; promotion almost entirely from within; merit ratings; a well-developed program of fringe benefits; and guaranteed continuous employment."[10]

Since 1958 Lincoln Electric has guaranteed continuous employment for its regular employees. The commitment calls for forty-nine workweeks per year with a minimum of thirty hours per week. Lincoln Electric does far more than guarantee employment to achieve goals, but its attention to providing security for employees is a key part of its overall motivational program.

**Independence of Action**

Probably all of us desire at least some independence of action. A cab driver may prefer to select the exact streets he or she uses to reach a destination rather than have this information dictated by the dispatcher. Little children often express exasperation when a teacher or a parent insists that they perform a task a certain way and angrily may say, "Let me do it my way."

The desire to be one's own boss is especially strong in some people who, for whatever reason, appear to have more self-reliance than others. Franchising organizations capitalize on this and appeal to the desire for independence of action by promising "Be your own boss and join us." Each year thousands of people leave organizations to set up their own businesses. Many salespeople are motivated by the promise of comparative independence of action. "I just couldn't stand being tied to a desk all day shuffling papers" is a comment often heard by individuals who elect to become outside salespeople.

Complete dictation of how a job is to be performed, however simple the job may be, lowers motivation. Part of the problem in motivating many assembly-line workers is their resentment at having to perform work that allows no deviation from prescribed procedures. As will be explained later, one of the goals of job enrichment is to overcome or at least reduce dissatisfaction resulting from extremely detailed and prescribed plans.

**Opportunity for Personal Growth**

Most people would like to grow in skill, professional capability, and experience. A strong motivational device is to promise—and then deliver—an opportunity to an individual to grow more skillful as a result of a work experience.

The desire for personal growth ties in with the fact that people are goal-oriented creatures. An employee may ask, "Will I be a better individual (like myself more) if I pursue this work?"

Organizations that offer training and educational programs, travel, job rotation, and other job-building experiences are using personal growth as a motivator.

[10]Robert Zager, "Managing Guaranteed Employment," *Harvard Business Review*, May–June 1978, p. 104.

## Opportunity for Advancement

Closely allied to personal growth as a motivator is opportunity for advancement. Not everyone wants to be promoted to higher levels in the organization, but a significant portion of the work force does.

Some of the best potential job candidates are turned off when they learn promotions are unusually slow and hard to come by. One of the greatest appeals of young, aggressive organizations is "You can get ahead fast with us."

The desire to advance varies, of course, among individuals. Some are frightened by aggressive organizations that provide opportunities for promotion; to them the desire for security is a stronger influence. They prefer a very stable organization in which they are sure of a job.

## Money and Other Financial Rewards

The role of money as a motivational factor has been controversial, especially over the past two decades. Research to date has not yielded any hard conclusions about the importance of money for individuals of different ages, social classes, cultural background, job types, or organizational levels. The research of Herzberg, as noted, suggests that money is more a dissatisfier than a motivator. But many people at least *appear* to value money highly.

Certainly for some individuals money is the strongest motivational influence. People who are very hard pressed financially may be more highly motivated by money than by any other factor. The fact that many people moonlight indicates that money is important. But in some situations money and other financial rewards are not as effective in stimulating superior performance as most people believe.

For example, suppose you supervise ten clerical employees. They are paid the prevailing wage for the type of work they do. Through your persuasive skills you are able to induce your senior management to double their pay immediately. What would probably happen to the quantity and quality of their output? No one knows, but it is most unlikely that productivity would increase in proportion to the increase in compensation. Productivity might even drop! "Now that we're making so much more money, we can take more days off and not work as hard" might be the response of some workers. In any event, most employees would soon become adjusted to the new, higher pay and take it for granted.

Consider some other indications that money may be overrated as a motivator:

* Generally, the longest and most difficult strikes to settle are in relatively high-paying industries such as steel production, the airlines, and coal mining. Lower-paid employees, even if unionized, are less likely to call for work stoppages because of money matters.
* Supervisors often find it difficult to induce employees to work overtime, even for double the normal pay. Employees may prefer to participate in leisure activities than make more money.
* People with very high incomes are often willing to accept substantial pay cuts to serve as government employees or to join university faculties.
* Some highly motivated members of various religious orders work for what amounts to room and board and security in their old age.
* Countless thousands of people, highly motivated, work for no compensation in hospitals and for charitable organizations such as the Red Cross.

The desire for recognition and status is closely related to the desire for money. The salary an individual receives is important because (since the more one earns the "better" one is) it is a status symbol. It "proves" to others that one is superior. Joe, a $100,000-per-year executive, may be pleased with his compensation until he learns that Ray, whom he regards as his inferior, also makes $100,000. Joe now wants more money not because he needs it to meet his financial needs but because his ego is damaged.

**Good Working Conditions**

Working conditions, which include both physical and psychological factors surrounding a job, vary in importance as a motivator. We often find persons working in ultra-modern job environments with the newest equipment and pleasant facilities who are not highly motivated. On the other hand, some people who work in unattractive environments are extremely motivated.

## FACTORS THAT COMPLICATE THE TASK OF MOTIVATION

Motivating people to perform in desired ways is difficult because knowledge about motivation is largely subjective. There are far fewer hard facts about how the mind works than about physics. It is not known precisely why some people work harder than others or why some people are more prone to make mistakes than others.

We begin to appreciate the complexity of motivation when we try to answer such a question as "What does it take to get Jill to do a better job, to work harder, to produce more, and to cooperate more effectively so our group goal can be achieved?" Some specific factors that complicate motivation are explained in the following sections.

**People's Wants Differ**

Not all persons are motivated to the same degree by the same motivators. Effective managers understand that people differ in cultural background, intelligence, ambition, education, ethical standards, and many other respects. We know that most people want status. But what is a status symbol to one person may not be important to another. Bill may regard the size and location of his office as a badge of his success. But Harry, a manager on the same level, may not even care whether he has an office. To him an important status symbol may be heading up the United Appeal Campaign or serving on a certain committee.

People also differ in their feelings concerning rewards. For example, Judy is motivated by the possibility of promotion. She works long hours, takes work home, and tries to improve her managerial skills. Meanwhile, Anne is content with her job and puts forth only enough effort to keep it. She would refuse a promotion if offered one.

As a result of such differences, managers must tailor their motivational efforts to individuals. The most effective manager is one who is aware of the special needs and desires of his or her staff members.

# MANAGERS IN ACTION

## UNCONVENTIONAL MANAGEMENT STYLE MOTIVATES TANDEM COMPUTER PERSONNEL

In 1982, Tandem Computers celebrated its seventh birthday by reaching a sales volume of more than $300,000,000. Its plans for the next three years call for an employee force of 11,000 (up from 3,000 in 1982) and sales of $1 billion.

What is behind the phenomenal success of Tandem? A good product line obviously. But many companies with "good product lines" do not come close to the success of Tandem.

Close observers feel the success of Tandem is tied directly to the management philosophy of the company's founder-president, James G. Treybig. Before starting Tandem, Treybig earned a B.S. in engineering and an M.B.A. from Stanford and worked for Texas Instruments and Hewlett Packard.

Treybig believes "all people are good" and advocates stock ownership for all employees, promotion from within, no time clocks or reserved parking spaces and a lot of special perks for employees at all levels.

Employees are exposed to a continuous barrage of company indoctrination urging loyalty, hard work, respect for co-workers, and self-esteem. Orientation lectures, special breakfasts, newsletters, and seminars are used to convey the company philosophy to the employees.

Treybig believes that most companies are over-managed. Often a job applicant is exposed to 20 hours of interviews. Prospective co-workers interview all job applicants with whom they would work. In this way, employees are not forced to work with people they don't respect.

The management atmosphere at Tandem can be described as open, spontaneous, nonjudgmental, brotherly, egalitarian and technically proficient.

Source: Adapted from Myron Magnet, "Managing By Mystique at Tandem Computers," *Fortune*, June 28, 1982, pp. 84–91.

### QUESTIONS

1. Jim Treybig's management philosophy seems to work very well at Tandem. Will it work as well in all companies? Explain.
2. In general, do you feel most companies should rely more on ideology in motivating employees? Why or why not?

---

**People's Wants Change Over Time**

A young employee just starting out may be intensely motivated to succeed, win promotions, make more money, and acquire power. Over the years, as his or her career settles down, he or she may gradually become more interested in security and holding on to the position already acquired. In part, changes in job expectations relate to changes in responsibilities in one's personal life. Younger employees are more likely to have strong monetary needs than middle-aged people.

Another example of how motivation may change over time concerns Winston Churchill. When young, Churchill was turned off by the discipline of attending classes, making reports, and earning his marks. But when presented with the challenge of leading Britain through its darkest hour, he was exceptionally motivated.

People are better educated than in the past, employees have more rights, people are more affluent, much work has become boring, and there is a tendency to reject authority. All these conditions complicate managing. Motivating factors that worked well a decade ago may be ineffective today.

Social Conditions Are Dynamic

Motivation is also made more complicated because numerous factors that affect it are beyond the control of managers in the work situation. All individuals have personal problems that affect their job performance but that a manager usually cannot solve (see Table 16–1). Some large companies do have special services to help employees with certain problems such as alcoholism and other forms of drug addiction. For the most part, however, management is either unaware of an individual's off-the-job problems or, if it is a matter of company policy, does not try to intervene.

Management Lacks Control Over the Nonwork Environment

## HIGH MORALE: THE RESULT OF MOTIVATION

High morale is a confident, resolute, often self-sacrificing attitude of a group that has strong faith in its leadership and believes organizational goals can be achieved. Low morale is just the opposite. It is characterized by depression, lack of confidence, and a negative ("who gives a damn") attitude toward the achievement of a goal.

Table 16–2 lists factors that often contribute to high or low morale. Research concerning the precise relationship between morale and the attainment of organizational goals is exceptionally difficult to conduct. Morale is intangible and hard to evaluate in an objective way. However, the general consensus among academic theorists and practicing managers is that there is a correlation between the level of morale and productivity *at least over the long run.* That is to say, a group with high morale will have less turnover and absenteeism, have fewer accidents, produce more, use resources more efficiently, cooperate more effectively, and in other ways be more productive than a group with low morale.

However, there are also indications that *at least in the short run*, low morale may result in high productivity. For example, during periods of recession and tight job markets, the rumor may spread that 20 percent of the work force may be furloughed. Under these circumstances worker morale is low, but employees may produce more in hopes of keeping their jobs. Or members of a department that is likely to be eliminated may perform unusually well in an effort to convince senior management not to terminate their operation. To use an extreme example, a group of sailors whose ship has sunk ten miles from shore may have very low morale but may still be very productive in rowing to shore or in trying to be spotted by other ships.

## WHAT IS JOB ENRICHMENT?

**Job enrichment**, also called *job reform*, is the process of designing jobs to make them more interesting, challenging, and meaningful. It includes planned efforts of

**TABLE 16–1**

**External Influences over Which a Manager Has Little or No Control Can Affect Worker Performance**

**PROBLEM**

For a moment, assume you are manager of an eight-member department in a public utility. Below are examples of personal problems these individuals have that may adversely affect their performance.

- Jane, twenty-seven, is extremely unhappy over a romance of three years that is now ended.
- Bill, twenty-one, is going to night school but is failing both courses he's taking. He tries to sneak time on the job to study.
- Mary, forty-seven, appears to have a serious drinking problem and frequently appears belligerent and short-tempered.
- Harry, fifty-six, is absorbed with preparing for his early retirement in four years. His mind is distracted much of the time.
- Bill, thirty-four, your assistant manager, is going through a divorce and custody battle over the children.
- Sally, thirty-one, is undergoing psychiatric care for problems relating to childhood difficulties.
- Jim, fifty-one, has a wife who is terminally ill and is a severe emotional and financial drain.
- Fred, twenty-seven, has developed diabetes and has become extremely depressed over his inability to control it.

**QUESTIONS**

1. Are problems such as the above typical or atypical in organizations today?
2. To what extent should a manager concern himself or herself with the personal problems of employees? What, if anything, can a manager do about each of the above problems?
3. Are non-job-related problems likely to increase or decrease in the years ahead? Explain.

management to make jobs more satisfying, such as giving workers greater freedom in choosing work methods and letting them help plan their work. Job enrichment thus affects morale.

Job-enrichment programs have been developed by many U.S. companies, including General Foods, Procter & Gamble, AT&T, and Texas Instruments. In the past decade, much attention has been focused on a number of Swedish companies, particularly Volvo, for their efforts to make work more meaningful and rewarding. In the Volvo organization, work teams have replaced the traditional assembly line.

**Types of Job Enrichment**

The most common forms of job enrichment are discussed below.

**Job rotation** permits workers to move at frequent intervals from one task or activity to another. In many instances, job rotation reduces boredom. It also gives employees more experience.

**Job enlargement** entails adding more tasks to a job to make it less boring. The idea behind job enlargement is to increase workers' interest. Most job-enlargement programs involve an increase in the number of tasks, duties, and

**TABLE 16–2**

**421**

*What Is
Job Enrichment?*

**Factors That Raise and Lower Morale**

| Morale Stimulants | Morale Depressants |
|---|---|
| Organizational objectives are in line with what the group wants. | Management forces an objective on personnel against their wishes. |
| Chances of success in achieving the objectives are good. | The cause appears doomed even before the effort is started. |
| Individuals take pride in being part of the organization. | The organization has a bad reputation among its employees. |
| The work is interesting and satisfies the needs of individuals. | The work is dull and highly repetitious and lends itself to a half-hearted effort. |
| Individuals are permitted to participate in at least part of the decision-making process. | Management issues orders in a dictatorial fashion. Little freedom of expression is tolerated |
| Supervision is no tighter than necessary, and pressure on individuals is minimized. | Supervision is very strict, and heavy pressure is placed on workers to conform to work rules. |

**QUESTIONS**

1. Low morale exists in many industrial, commercial, educational, military, and other types of organizations. Why?
2. Think of one organization you belong to and describe the general state of morale. Then explain why you feel this state exists.

responsibilities given to workers. A salesperson has his or her job enlarged when invited to participate in discussions about changes in products, selling methods, pricing, and packaging.

**Job redesign** is the restructuring of a job to make it more appealing to workers. A salesperson's job may be redesigned by changing the territory or by permitting the person to specialize with certain customers.

**Flextime** is another morale-building device that is finding steadily increasing use. Usually, flextime requires all employees to be at work during a core period, say from 11:00 A.M. to 3:00 P.M., but the employees decide when they will begin and end their workday. Flextime is now used in many companies, such as Exxon, John Hancock Mutual Life Insurance, Control Data Corporation, and Hewlett-Packard.[11]

J. Richard Hackman, Greg Oldham, Robert Janson, and Kenneth Purdy have developed a model for job enrichment.[12] According to them, three conditions must be met if a worker is to be challenged by a job: There must be experienced or felt meaningfulness of the job, personal responsibility for the job, and knowledge of results. If these conditions are met, the person feels good and performs well. If,

*A Model for
Job Enrichment*

[11]See Vernon Louwiese, "Raising Productivity With Flexible Work Hours," *Nation's Business*, November 1976, p. 28.
[12]© 1975 by the Regents of the University of California. Adapted from *California Management Review*, volume XVII, no. 4, pp. 57–71 by permission of the Regents.

however, one of these conditions is missing — if, for example, the person receives no feedback on results — motivation drops significantly.

Hackman and his colleagues point out that before a job is restructured to make it richer and more challenging, the job should be studied carefully to pinpoint as precisely as possible what aspects of the work should be changed. Once a careful, objective diagnosis of the job is completed, the five "implementing concepts" discussed next should be used to make job enrichment work.

*Form natural or logical work units.* Workers should be given a sense of responsibility for an identifiable body of work, not be asked to perform only fragments of many different projects.

*Combine tasks.* Workers should be given more related work to do to form a larger module of work. For example, when workers assemble a complete appliance, they are likely to have more task identification than if they had assembled only a part of the appliance. Also, since more skills are required when tasks are combined, workers should experience greater challenge.

*Establish client relationships.* According to Hackman and his associates, it is important to enable and encourage employees to establish direct relationships with the people they serve. That is, a typist should have direct contact with the person who requests the typing, and a computer programmer should have a direct relationship with the person requesting the program. This procedure can result in considerable improvement in motivation, and feedback is improved because the worker knows immediately whether the work is satisfactory or not.

*Employ vertical loading.* Vertical loading entails adding more planning, other responsibilities, and more control to workers' jobs. Some of the ways suggested to achieve vertical loading include:

* Give job holders greater responsibility for scheduling work methods and checking quality.
* Give employees more authority.
* Give people more freedom over time management — that is, let them decide when to start and stop work and take breaks.
* Delegate more control over budgets. Let personnel know more about the costs of their jobs and how money is being spent.

*Open feedback channels.* This practice enables people to know as quickly as possible how well they are performing. Besides establishing closer client relationships as discussed above, managers can improve feedback by letting workers handle quality control and giving performance records directly to those who do the work.

### Quality of Work Life Programs

**Quality of Work Life programs** (QWL) gives nonmanagement personnel a voice in decisions that affect them, such as job assignments, working hours, rest breaks, and work rules. Interest in QWL programs is increasing because, as this observation suggests, they work. "Case histories of successful QWL programs demonstrate that they can improve product quality and productivity, reduce absenteeism and turnover, and increase job satisfaction for workers. In 1972 only about 25 case studies had been accumulated; now more than 1,000 have been reported."[13]

The potential for QWL is promising. A Ford executive said, "Once you start that process, you're going to release the greatest source of energy you've ever seen in a plant."[14]

**SUMMARY**

- A key part of a manager's job is to motivate people to *want* to perform effectively.
- The environment greatly influences motivation.
- Reward versus punishment is a component of most motivation theories.
- Maslow's hierarchy-of-needs theory holds that people are motivated by five kinds of needs: physiological, safety, love, esteem, and self-actualization.
- Herzberg developed a motivational theory in which he distinguished between hygiene, or maintenance, job factors and motivational factors.
- McGregor explains motivation in terms of Theory X (people basically don't like work) and Theory Y (people like work).
- Other theorists who have made important contributions to motivation theory include McClelland, Likert, Mayo, Vroom, Skinner, and Hall.
- Basic factors that motivate include challenging work, participation in planning, recognition and status, more responsibility and power, security, independence of action, opportunity for personal growth, opportunity for advancement, money and other financial rewards, and good working conditions.
- Motivation is difficult because our knowledge of it is largely subjective, people's wants differ and change as time passes, social conditions are dynamic, and management cannot usually control the nonwork environment.
- Generally, high morale is correlated with increased productivity in the long run.
- Job enrichment, the process of making jobs more interesting and meaningful, is being increasingly used to improve worker motivation. Types of job enrichment include job rotation, job enlargement, job redesign, and flextime.

**LEARN THE LANGUAGE OF MANAGEMENT**

motive
hierarchy of needs theory
self-actualization
two-factor motivation theory
hygiene job factors
motivator factors
Theory X management
Theory Y management
Theory Z management
need-based motivation theory
participative management motivation theory

Hawthorne effect
preference-expectancy theory
motivation through positive reinforcement
security
job enrichment
job rotation
job enlargement
job redesign
flextime
Quality of Work Life programs

[13]"Quality of Work Life: Catching On," *Business Week*, September 21, 1981, p. 72.
[14]Ibid., p. 76.

1. "Managers are judged not by what they do but rather by what they cause others to do." Explain. How does this concept relate to a football coach? A sales manager? A production supervisor?
2. Develop five kinds of rewards and five kinds of punishments you might use to reduce absenteeism in an office, cause a salesperson to exceed his or her quota, and decrease the accident rate in a factory. Generally, which do you feel is the better motivator, rewards or punishments? Why?
3. In your opinion, which of the five needs in the Maslow hierarchy is the most difficult to satisfy? Why?
4. Herzberg noted, "The conditions that surround the doing of the job cannot give [the worker] basic satisfaction. . . . It is only from the performance of a task that the individual can get the rewards that will reinforce his aspiration." What does this statement tell the manager about motivation?
5. You have a choice of working for a Theory X manager or a Theory Y manager. Which would you choose and why?
6. Explain the essentials of the motivational theories advanced by McClelland, Likert, Mayo, Vroom, and Skinner.
7. What is the relationship between a manager's level of motivation and the motivation level of his or her subordinates?
8. Explain how each of the following factors affects motivation: challenging work, participation in planning, recognition and status, responsibility and power, security, independence of action, opportunity for personal growth, opportunity for advancement, monetary reward, good working conditions, and competition.
9. How does morale relate to motivation?
10. Explain what job enrichment is. What steps should be taken to make it work?

**1. Motivation through a plan for guaranteed employment.**

Ohio Steel is a foundry that makes steel castings. Under normal conditions the company employs 900 production workers and 100 management, sales, administrative, and clerical personnel.

The business is quite cyclical and is subject to economic booms and slumps. While the company is nonunion, relationships with employees have not been good. Turnover for the past decade has averaged 4 percent per month. Absenteeism is higher than average for similar companies.

George Schultz was recently named chief executive officer of Ohio Steel. Schultz, age forty-three, had served as the company president for three years. He feels that the basic problem facing the company is a turned-off, uninspired work force. As the new chief executive, he feels the time has come to bring about corrective action by instituting a guaranteed employment plan. He sends the following memo to the corporate board of directors and the department heads:

TO: Members of the Board and Department Heads

FROM: George Schultz

SUBJECT: Preparation of a Plan for Guaranteed Employment

I feel the time has come to make a major shift in our relations with the work force by offering a guarantee of forty weeks' work per year to each employee who has been with us continuously for twenty-four months (two years).

Such a plan, properly implemented, can benefit Ohio Steel in the following ways:

- Build a more loyal and cooperative work force.
- Reduce turnover and the resulting costs of recruitment and training.
- Reduce absenteeism.
- Deter employees from attempting to unionize.

As part of the proposed plan for guaranteed employment, management would assert its rights to:

- Reassign workers from one job to another when the work load goes up or down in different departments.
- Discharge a worker for any cause before two years of continuous employment have been fulfilled.
- Require up to ten hours overtime per employee per week for up to twenty weeks per year.
- Determine standards for both quantity and quality of work produced.
- Require that all new employees work twenty-four continuous months before being given guaranteed-employment status.

Please come to the next Executive Committee Meeting prepared to discuss implementation of the Guaranteed Employment Plan.

What problems may result if the Schultz plan is implemented?

Is the promise of greater job security likely to increase workers' incentive to be productive? Why or why not?

How important do you feel guaranteed employment is as a motivational factor?

## 2. The bonus program no longer motivates

In 1976 the management of the South Carolina Textile Company decided to pay a $200 cash bonus to each nonmanagement employee. The bonus appeared to have positive results. In succeeding years the practice of paying a $200 bonus to employees was continued.

Now, years later, the bonus is taken for granted and no longer seems to have a positive affect on employee performance.

The president of the company brings up the matter at a management meeting. He tells the managers, "I don't think the bonus is achieving its purpose. Everybody expects it. I want some recommendations from you people about what we should do: Continue with it because it now is considered a routine part of the pay package, discontinue it, give some other kind of award, or what have you. We simply cannot afford to pay out money without a return."

You've been with the company six months. What advice would you give the president?

Does any form of reward, monetary or nonmonetary, tend to lose its impact after repeated use? Explain.

### 3. How short-run evaluations can cost a company

Julian Thomas, chairman of the board of the All-Purpose Chemical Company, has called a special meeting of the board to announce the resignation of Bill Johnson, president of a company division, and to make plans for finding a successor. Eleven members of the board are present.

Julian: Before we discuss a replacement for Bill, I think I owe you an explanation of what has transpired since we named him president 30 months ago. Bill spent the first year settling into the job and learning our system. The second year, Bill took certain actions that made his division look very good. Profits were up 52 percent. This made Bill look great on paper. Since our bonus system is tied directly to profits, he received the largest award of any division president.

As you know, Bill's enormous success was picked up by the business press, and he is proclaimed as the jet-propelled wonder boy in our industry. Five days ago he called to tell me he was resigning to accept another job—at twice his salary with us.

The problem is Bill's success will cost the division money in the future. Basically, Bill did two things—all within his authority—that will hurt us down the road. First, he sold some highly profitable assets. This made the statement look good. Second, he cut way back on contracts for new equipment, research, plant modernization, training, and other activities that cost money in the short run but make money in the long run.

Before we talk about a successor for Bill, I recommend we develop a way to encourage managers to think of the long run, say three to five years.

Did the board grant too much authority to Bill?

Would a bonus system based on three years performance instead of one be feasible? Consider such factors as the needs of managers for income in the short run, the turnover of managers, and the possible impact on manager productivity.

**FOR ADDITIONAL CONCEPTS AND IDEAS**

Blanchard, Kenneth, and Johnson, Spencer. *The One-Minute Manager.* New York: William Morrow, 1983.

Cook, Curtis W. "Guidelines of Managing Motivation." *Business Horizons*, April 1980, pp. 61–69.

Davis, Keith. "Low Productivity? Try Improving the Social Environment." *Business Horizons*, June 1980, pp. 27–29.

Deitsch, Clarence R., and Dilts, David A. "Getting Absent Workers Back on the Job: The Case of General Motors." *Business Horizons*, September–October 1981, pp. 52–58.

Doyle, Stephen X., and Shapiro, Benson P. "What Counts Most in Motivating Your Sales Force." *Harvard Business Review*, May–June 1980, pp. 133–140.

Henderson, Richard I. "Designing a Reward System for Today's Employee." *Business*, July–August–September 1982, pp. 2–13.

Ingram, Thomas N., and Bellenger, Danny N. "Motivational Segments in the Sales Force." *California Management Review*, Spring 1982, pp. 81–88.

Jonsson, Berth. "The Quality of Work Life—The Volvo Experience." *Journal of Business Ethics*, May 1982, pp. 119–126.

Kovach, Kenneth A. "Improving Employee Motivation in Today's Business Environment." *MSU Business Topics*, Autumn 1976, pp. 5–12.

Likert, Rensis. *New Patterns of Organization*. New York: McGraw-Hill, 1961.

Lockwood, Diane L.; Luthans, Fred; and Millard, Cheedle, W. "The Impact of a Four-day Workweek on Employees." *MSU Business Topics*, Spring 1980, pp. 31–38.

Mayo, G. Elton. *The Human Problems of an Industrial Civilization*. Boston: Graduate School of Business Administration, Harvard University, 1946.

McClelland, et al. *The Achievement Motive*. New York: Appleton-Century-Crofts, 1953.

McGregor, Douglas. *The Human Side of Enterprise*. New York: McGraw-Hill, 1960.

Meyers, Kenneth A. "Why Companies Lose Their Best People—And What to Do About It." *Business Horizons*, March–April 1981, pp. 42–45.

Moberg, Dennis J. "Job Enrichment through Symbol Management." *California Management Review*, Winter 1981, pp. 24–30.

Naor, Jacob. "How to Motivate Corporate Executives to Implement Long-Range Plans." *MSU Business Topics*, Summer 1977, pp. 41–49.

Ouchi, William. *Theory Z: How American Business Can Meet the Japanese Challenge*. Reading, Mass.: Addison-Wesley, 1981.

Porter, Alan L. "Work Ethic—An Idea Whose Time Has Gone?" *Business*, January 1981, pp. 15–22.

Scanlan, Burt K. "Creating a Climate for Achievement." *Business Horizons*, March–April 1981, pp. 5–9.

Skinner, B. F. *About Behaviorism*. New York: Random House, 1976.

Skinner, Wickham. "Big Hat, No Cattle: Managing Human Resources." *Harvard Business Review*, September–October 1981, pp. 106–114.

Vandervelde, Maryanne. "Increasing People-Productivity." *Journal of Contemporary Business*, August 1981, pp. 19–32.

Vroom, Victor H. *Work and Motivation*. New York: John Wiley & Sons, 1964.

Wurf, Jerry. "Labor's View of Quality of Working Life Programs." *Journal of Business Ethics,* pp. 131–138.

# 17 LEADERSHIP

Leadership is an integral part of management. Daily we hear such comments as "She is a very effective leader" "The company failed because it lacked leadership" "He's a good man but he can't lead" "What this country needs is fresh leadership" and "Leadership makes the difference between success and failure."

**Leadership** is the art of inspiring subordinates to perform their duties willingly, competently, and enthusiastically. A **leader** is one who, by example and talent, plays a directing role and wields commanding influence over others.

One of the most interesting observations of life is that all animals that live in groups have leaders. All kinds of creatures — not just humans — have leaders. Lions, elephants, baboons, insects, dogs, fish, and birds have leaders. In nonhumans, the leader usually is a male. He makes most of the decisions and gets his choice of mates, food, and physical place. When the group is threatened, the leader plans the defense. Or if an attack is to be made on another group, the leader organizes it.

All human groups also have a leader. Such diverse organizations as street gangs, college classes, parent-teacher associations, political parties, prison inmates, and elderly people in nursing homes generally have someone who emerges as the final authority on what to do. Often the leader has no title, but who the person is nevertheless is clear.

## Chosen Versus Appointed Leaders

In many organizations, the group chooses the leader. In a street gang, a person may become the leader after demonstrating that he or she can fight harder or steal more than other members of the group. In democratic groups, such as political parties and labor unions, leaders are elected.

Most groups are informal and their leaders are usually chosen in an informal way without an actual vote of the members. The individual who speaks out, displays the most confidence, and has ideas that are compatible with those of the group ends up as the leader. Dominance in a physical or psychological way is characteristic of such leaders. When a leader dies, quits, or fails to achieve an important objective, a power vacuum develops. The new leader will be one who can dominate the thinking of the group and win the "election."

However, in most formal organizations leaders are not chosen but are appointed by someone outside the group. For example, an army lieutenant is appointed not by the company he or she is to command but by higher military commanders. Leaders in the Catholic Church are not elected by the membership but are appointed by the church establishment. A corporate president is appointed by the board of directors, not elected by the personnel who make up the organization.

Often the group being led does not readily accept an appointed leader, feeling the person may not be qualified for the post. An appointed leader, not having been elected, must frequently work hard to gain the support of the group. Student and faculty unrest sometimes develops because a state board of regents has appointed a university president who was not selected by the group. To overcome this problem, search committees composed of students and faculty often have a part in the selection process.

All managers are expected to inspire individuals to work willingly, cooperatively, and enthusiastically toward the achievement of an objective. While ability to lead is often not spelled out in the job description for a manager, it is implied.

### Are Leaders and Managers the Same Thing?

Often the words "leader" and "manager" are used interchangeably, as if they were synonymous. The terms do have somewhat different connotations, however. Abraham Zaleznik, professor of social psychology at the Harvard Business School, writes that "managers and leaders are very different kinds of people. They differ in motivation, personal history, and in how they think and act."[1]

In terms of how managers perceive themselves, Zaleznik observes, "Managers see themselves as conservators and regulators of an existing order of affairs with which they personally identify and from which they gain rewards. Perpetuating and strengthening existing institutions enhances a manager's sense of self-worth; he or she is performing in a role that harmonizes with the ideals of duty and responsibility."[2] Leaders, on the other hand, in Zaleznik's view "tend to be . . . people who feel separate from their environment, including other people. They may work in organizations, but they never belong to them. Their sense of who they are does not depend upon memberships, work roles, or other social indicators of identity.[3]

Zaleznik goes on to note that managers and leaders differ in how they conceive work and in how they relate to others. According to him, managers give subordinates limited choices, whereas leaders encourage people to seek fresh approaches to problems. Managers prefer order and routine behavior, while leaders try to create excitement in work.

In terms of interpersonal relationships, subordinates often perceive manag-

[1]Abraham Zaleznik, "Managers and Leaders: Are They Different?" *Harvard Business Review,* May–June 1977, p. 70.
[2]Ibid., pp. 74–75.
[3]Ibid., pp. 75–76.

*"Do you know what we need around here?
A take-charge guy."*

ers as "inscrutable, detached, and manipulative."[4] Leaders, on the other hand, are described with emotionally charged adjectives. According to Zaleznik, "Leaders attract strong feelings of identity and difference, or of love and hate. Human relations in leader-dominated structures often appear turbulent, intense, and at times even disorganized. Such an atmosphere intensifies individual motivation and often produces unanticipated outcomes."[5]

Despite the perceived differences in the psychological makeup of managers and leaders, leadership is expected from all who manage. An important part of management is inducing people to work with zeal, to put forth their best efforts, and to achieve difficult goals. This aspect of managing requires what is called leadership.

One subtle though useful explanation of the difference between leadership and managing is provided by Professor Keith Davis:

> Leadership is a part of management but not all of it. . . . Leadership is the ability to persuade others to seek defined objectives enthusiastically. It is the human factor which binds a group together and motivates it toward goals. Management activities such as planning, organizing, and decision making are dormant cocoons until the leader triggers the power of motivation in people and guides them toward goals.[6]

**Task Versus Social Leaders**

Some leaders are task oriented, whereas others are socially oriented. Task leaders are needed when special skills are required, and therefore they need considerable expertise in the work being managed. The foreman on the assembly line, the manager supervising loading or unloading of freight, and the office manager charged with getting a report out on time are examples of task leaders. Task leaders, who may be temporary, have a limited role. They control, direct, and organize a group to carry out a specific job. Generally, their influence is limited to the specific task being done. Task leaders are usually firm, directive, efficient, and intense about getting the job done.

On the other hand, social leaders are needed when diplomatic and persuasive skills are required to achieve an objective. They tend to be more supportive, encouraging, conciliatory, and less direct than task leaders. They concentrate on the social aspects of the situation and try to get the group to cooperate smoothly and happily.

One individual can function as both a task and a social leader simultaneously. However, these two types of leadership are often divided between two individuals. On a ship, for example, the captain generally functions as the social leader, while the executive officer acts as the task leader. The latter makes personnel assignments, handles disciplinary problems, and directs most of the task-oriented activities. The captain, meanwhile, leads on a "higher" level and performs more of a social role.

It appears that leaders are more likely to arise during crises such as war, revolutions, or depressions than when conditions are stable. When people feel threatened, they are eager to follow someone who appears able to protect them

**Emergence of
Leaders in
Crisis Situations**

[4]Ibid., p. 74.
[5]Ibid., p. 75.
[6]Keith Davis, *Human Relations at Work* (New York: McGraw-Hill, 1967), pp. 96–97.

and return conditions to normalcy. Thus crises provide opportunities for leaders to emerge.

Most of the men who are considered our greatest presidents are associated with national emergencies—Washington with the Revolutionary War, Lincoln with the War Between the States, Wilson with World War I, and Roosevelt with World War II. Generals who are considered great, such as Patton, Eisenhower, and MacArthur, also emerge during times of war. Social activists, such as Martin Luther King, Jr., tend to emerge during periods of unrest when social conditions are in need of change. One of the attendees at a conference on leadership made this comment: "In a time of crisis you will have a leader. Maybe a Hitler, a Roosevelt, or a Huey Long. Somebody will lead when a society is collapsing—not necessarily a good leader, but a leader."[7]

Historical assessments of a person's leadership abilities depend greatly on whether the person was in power during a time of crisis or a time of peace. Presidents Harding and Coolidge generally are not rated great, yet most of their terms in office were marked by good economic times and no war. How would our "great" presidents be remembered if wartime conditions had not prevailed? Would MacArthur be remembered as a great military leader had World War II not occurred? Would Martin Luther King, Jr., be regarded as an outstanding leader if he had not come to prominence during the race riots of the 1960s?

Similarly, the corporate president who manages a profitable organization is not as likely to be perceived as an effective leader as his or her counterpart who takes over a firm that is bankrupt and guides it back to profitability is.

## THEORIES OF LEADERSHIP

There are many theories of leadership. Those of Rensis Likert, Chris Argyris, Fred Fiedler, Robert Blake and Jane Mouton, and Kurt Lewin are discussed briefly in the next sections.

**Likert's Styles of Leadership**

Rensis Likert, a pioneer in studying styles of leadership, has developed four systems for classifying leaders. According to Likert, leadership is a continuum ranging from highly dictatorial to exceptionally participative. Likert's four classifications are:

- *System 1*—**Exploitative-Authoritative**: Leaders in this category are autocratic. They do not seek the opinions of subordinates but make all major decisions independently. They motivate through fear and punishment.
- *System 2*—**Benevolent-Authoritative**: Leaders in this classification have a "plantation mentality" or "big daddy" approach to leadership. In essense, they say to subordinates, "I'll treat you all right and see that your needs are met if you play along with the system and don't deviate from tradition."

[7]Statement attributed to Lester Thruow, M.I.T. economist, in "Leadership: The Biggest Issue," *Time*, November 8, 1976, p. 32.

They sometimes seek advice from subordinates, but they make key decisions themselves. They use both fear and rewards to motivate.

* *System 3* — **Consultative**:  These types of leaders have considerable confidence in their subordinates, delegate extensively, encourage subordinates
to make recommendations, and rely on rewards more than punishment to
motivate.
* *System 4* — **Participative-Group**: Leaders using this style intentionally
seek to involve members of the group in the decision-making process.
They liberally delegate authority and use rewards, not punishment, to
motivate.

Likert is an advocate of System 4, or participative-group management. Much
of his research suggests that subordinate-centered leadership is more effective in
achieving group goals than Systems 1, 2, or 3.

No two managers have exactly the same leadership style. Because personalities differ, styles differ also. According to Likert's analyses, two extreme
leadership styles can be identified: autocratic and participative. In practice, most
leaders fall in between and are neither totally autocratic nor totally participative.
Table 17–1 compares the two styles of leading.

### Autocratic Management

**Autocratic management** is characterized by leaders who make most decisions themselves, issue orders that they expect to be obeyed exactly as given, and
appear to be very much in command. Authoritative leaders like to determine all
policies and specify the procedures they want subordinates to follow. Autocratic
leaders tend to be dominant, intolerant of the way others feel, and unconcerned
about whether or not the group likes the plan. In the process of managing,
autocratic leaders may bruise some egos.

Napoleon was a classic autocratic leader. He imposed his will on subordinates, scolded his generals, tried to make all key decisions alone, demanded
complete obedience, insulted his subordinates, and generally remained aloof and
scornful.

Because autocratic leaders consult little with subordinates, they may miss out
on much good information that would help improve decision making. However,
autocratic leadership does result in faster decisions and there is never any doubt as
to who is in charge. As will be seen later, there are some situations in which
autocratic leadership is essential.

### Participative Management

**Participative management** is characterized by democratic leaders who invite
members of the group to make suggestions about who will do what as well as how
and when it will be done. Their role is more that of a coach or a guide than a
dictator. Participative leaders are more compliant, are less directive, and try to get a
group consensus before acting.

Generally, participative leadership works best with professionals and at senior
levels in an organization. When a manager is directing other managers who are
strong-willed and determined, it is essential that a participative style be used. For

## TABLE 17–1

**Autocratic and Participative Leadership Compared**

| An Autocratic-style Leader . . . | A Participative-style Leader . . . |
|---|---|
| *Threatens personnel.* "Either achieve the objective or you're fired, demoted, transferred, or disciplined." | *Encourages personnel.* "Achieve the objective and you'll be rewarded in some manner." |
| *Says and thinks "I."* "I am going to achieve the objective." | *Says and thinks "we."* "We (the group) are going to achieve the objective." |
| *Takes full credit for positive results.* "Only through my efforts were we able to solve the problem." | *Gives personnel credit for success.* "You people deserve credit for our achievement. Your efforts made it possible." |
| *Blames personnel for failures.* "You people are responsible for the problem. Had you listened to me and done what I said, we would have succeeded." | *Accepts responsibility for failures.* "I am fully responsible. Had I managed this activity properly, the results would have been positive." |
| *Makes work drudgery.* "I know this job is boring, but you're paid to do it, so do it." | *Makes work a game.* "Let's enjoy this job. It can be fun if we all pitch in." |
| *Personally decides on all goals and work methods.* "Here is what you should do. And here is how you must do it." | *Invites personnel to help decide on goals and work methods.* "What do you feel you can do best? And how would you like to do it?" |
| *Knows all the answers.* "My way is best. After all, I'm in charge so I know how to do it." | *Seeks advice from personnel.* "What are your recommendations? Is there an easier, more effective way to achieve the result?" |
| *Relies on his authority.* "The organizational chart says I'm in charge so you've got to cooperate with me." | *Depends on demonstrated ability.* "I have achieved similar goals before and with your help we'll achieve this one." |

example, a college administrator cannot be as autocratic as a plant manager in a manufacturing industry.

Dwight Eisenhower, both as a military officer and as a president, generally demonstrated a participative management style. On most issues he sought advice from subordinates, encouraged debate over ways to solve problems, and liberally delegated authority to key assistants.

### Management Style Relates to the Situation

Some situations require managers to act autocratically. A prison warden may have to make an autocratic decision regarding how to deal with demands of prisoners who have taken a guard hostage. In contrast, when the prison warden has more time for contemplation, he may use a participative management style, asking other officers how to plan for a possible riot.

**Argyris's Immaturity-Maturity Theory**

Behavioral scientist Chris Argyris has conducted extensive research on the relationship between individual needs and organizational requirements. Argyris maintains that employees tend to place their own needs ahead of the organization's welfare. He argues that to the extent that this occurs, conflict, apathy, and discord result.

Argyris's **immaturity-maturity theory** argues that for managers to lead effectively and for subordinates to develop a greater interest in the goals of the enterprise, personnel should be provided with a climate in which they can mature. Argyris argues that leaders move people from

| a state of | to | a state of |
|---|---|---|
| Passivity | | Activity |
| Dependent behavior | | Independent behavior |
| Rigid behavior | | Adaptive behavior |
| Limited interest | | Deep and committed interest |
| Short-run thinking | | Long-run thinking |
| Feeling subordinate | | Feeling on top |
| Limited self-awareness and self-respect | | Highly developed self-awareness and self-respect[8] |

Providing an organizational climate that fosters maturity may lead to less frustration and anxiety and more creativity and personal dedication to organizational goals. On the other hand, people tend to have different maturity requirements and expectations. These differences make it difficult to implement Argyris's recommendations.

Professor Fred Fiedler and his associates have conducted considerable research on leadership styles among such diverse groups as students, infantry units, and upper-level managers. Fiedler has found that the success of a leader is not based on personality traits alone. Other factors, particularly those of a situational nature (kind of organization, nature of the task, characteristics of the people being managed, and so on), also determine how effective a manager will be in leading.

In the Fiedler model three major factors that influence a leader's style are identified:

- *Position power.* Position power is derived from organizational authority — that is, the authority that is "built in" to the manager's position by directives, custom, and rank in the management hierarchy. Fiedler points out that the more position power a manager has, the easier it is for him or her to induce people to follow.
- *Task structure.* This dimension concerns the clarity with which tasks or jobs are defined. When tasks are vague or loosely defined, the manager has more difficulty in measuring performance and holding people responsible than when jobs are clearly and precisely spelled out.
- *Leader-member relations.* Fiedler considers this dimension to be the most important. It refers to the degree to which subordinates trust, have confidence in, and are loyal to the leader.

**Fiedler's Contingency Theory of Leadership**

[8]Based on Chris Argyris, *Personality and Organization* (New York: Harper & Row, 1957), pp. 50–51.

In performing his studies, Fiedler considered two styles of managing: task-oriented and people-oriented. Task-oriented managers are primarily interested in and motivated by seeing work objectives achieved satisfactorily. People-oriented managers are mainly interested in building a cooperative, harmonious working environment and in developing successful interpersonal relationships.

To develop a method for assessing a manager's orientation, Fiedler conducted research to determine how individuals perceive other people in a group. He found that people who perceive their co-workers in highly favorable terms tend to be people oriented, whereas those who view their associates in unfavorable terms tend to be task oriented.

Fiedler's research led to the development of a **contingency or situational theory of leadership.** He formulated this conclusion: "Except perhaps for the unusual case, it is simply not meaningful to speak of an effective leader or an ineffective leader; we can only speak of a leader who tends to be effective in one situation and ineffective in another."[9]

Fiedler goes on to note that in order to achieve group goals more effectively, better training of leaders and an appropriate organizational climate are needed. According to him, "If we wish to increase organizational and group effectiveness we must learn not only how to train leaders more effectively but also how to build an organizational environment in which the leader can perform well."[10]

## The Blake-Mouton Managerial Grid®

The **Managerial Grid** developed by Robert Blake and Jane Mouton (see Figure 17–1) often plays a part in organization development. The Grid is a device for assessing the orientations of managers to the work of the organization and to the people who are expected to perform the work. Five styles of leaders can be identified:

* 1, 1 — Expends a bare minimum of effort to get work done; has minimal standards.
* 9, 1 — Achieves efficiency of activity by designing work so that human beings do not interfere.
* 1, 9 — Gives careful attention to people to create meaningful relationships and a friendly atmosphere.
* 5, 5 — Obtains satisfactory or adequate performance by equating the necessity for performance with reasonable morale.
* 9, 9 — Accomplishes work with the help of thoroughly dedicated people who trust and respect one another and have a feeling of a common purpose or goal.

It is assumed that all organizations endorse and work toward the 9, 9 point on the Grid.

The Blake-Mouton Grid is a convenient way to classify leadership styles. Senior managers, if they are objective, can get a reasonably clear idea of what kind of leadership they are providing. In order to move closer to the 9, 9 point on the

---

[9]Fred E. Fiedler, *A Theory of Leadership Effectiveness* (New York: McGraw-Hill, 1967), p. 371.
[10]Ibid.

**FIGURE 17–1**

**437**

*Theories of Leadership*

**The Blake-Mouton Managerial Grid**

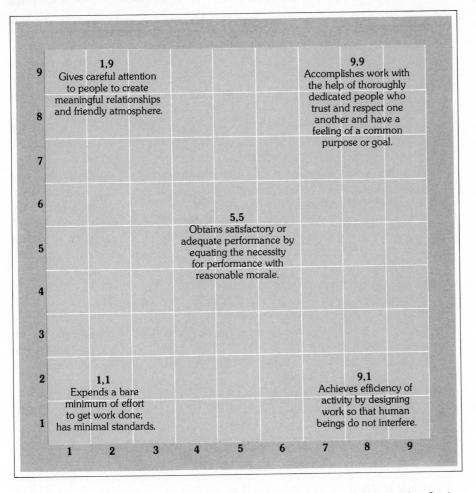

Source: The Managerial Grid figure from *The New Managerial Grid,* by Robert R. Blake and Jane Srygley Mouton. (Houston: Gulf Publishing Company, Copyright © 1978), p. 11. Reproduced by permission.

Grid, they may need to select managers more carefully, give more attention to incentives, and provide leadership training for key personnel.

Kurt Lewin was a pioneer in the study of group dynamics and behavior modification. His studies focus directly and indirectly on leadership and indicate that each group is different and has a personality of its own. His research shows that one individual may be able to lead one group but not another. Furthermore, he discovered that the personalities of the members of a group tend to form a group personality. Lewin's contributions to our understanding of group behavior and leadership of groups are many. But on balance his research helps underscore the

**Lewin and Group Dynamics**

wisdom contained in the old saying "The more we know about something, the more we know we don't know." Lewin has taught us that group dynamics and the emergence of leaders are exceptionally complex subjects.

## PERSONAL CHARACTERISTICS OF LEADERS

Some managers are able to obtain results far greater than expected through effective leadership. Great leadership ability is rare, however. Management scholars and practitioners alike agree that truly exceptional leaders are in short supply. Some managers cannot inspire their supportive personnel to achieve even minimal results. In the military services there are still minor mutinies, in production enterprises there are still walkouts and industrial sabotage, and in schools there are still student boycotts—all of which suggest that leaders are not inspiring the group to achieve organizational goals.

Leadership is an intangible quality. Since effective leadership is an art, seeing its results is much easier than describing precisely what it is. Leaders can best be judged by the behavior of their subordinates, not by what they profess. When followers perform well, cooperate effectively, and put forth extra effort to achieve group goals, the manager is described as a good leader. When people perform badly, fail to cooperate, and do a minimal amount of work, the manager is described as a weak or ineffective leader.

The personality of a manager alone does not indicate leadership ability. Some effective leaders are brash, loud, aggressive, and gregarious. (See Figure 17–2.) Other effective leaders may be quiet, soft-spoken, and mild-tempered. Nor is popularity synonymous with leadership ability. The most popular secretary in an office may not be the best person to be office manager. A leader must be more than a nice person.

The personal backgrounds of effective leaders also vary greatly. Education, family status, and similar factors are poor guides to predicting a person's chances of being an effective leader. Leaders may or may not have university educations; they may come from high-, middle-, or low-income families.

While it is difficult to pin down the precise qualities that make a superior leader, leaders do seem to share certain personal and behavior characteristics. The main ones are described in the following sections.

**Ability to Inspire Others**

Many people believe that the ability to inspire others, which is the most essential qualification for leadership, cannot be learned. Robert Fulmer notes that there is an "undefinable ingredient" in leadership:

> The individual is the undefinable ingredient that makes the vital difference. Imagine two identical twins who receive all the same training in management theory and have all the same benefits. Even if such a situation could be created in a test tube we would not be surprised to witness the management careers of the two heading off in different directions and ending up poles apart.
> Why? What makes the difference between the two? There exists somewhere the gist of the manager, his soul, his philosophy of life, his basic approach to life and other

# FIGURE 17–2

## Leadership Styles of Current and Former Top Executives

- How others see him    • How he sees himself

**Robert Abboud, Chairman and C.E.O. First Chicago Corp.**

- Known as "Idi" Abboud ... bright, abrasive, aggressive, extremely ambitious ... very tough on people ... used to dress down his peers as well as subordinates ... likes to make decisions solo.

• Declined to be interviewed.

**Alex Massad, Executive Vice President Mobil**

- Creates a lot of sparks ... thinks nothing of putting in eighteen hours, seven days a week ... always a hard driver and impatient ... He's antagonized a lot of people and they've stayed that way.

• I just work hard ... I don't know what my management style is ... Ask my superiors if they think I'm tough.

**Thomas Mellon Evans Chairman and C.E.O. Crane**

- No question he is a genius ... has his own ideas and pursues them ... doesn't listen well, so he is frustrating to work for ... most glaring trait is his lack of feeling for people.

• Declined to be interviewed.

**Andrall Pearson, President PepsiCo**

- Everyone has to be a superperformer ... presenting a marketing plan is like going through the third degree ... If you're insecure, don't work for him ...

• We flushed out a bunch of people not digging deeply enough–people should think about why they are here. That is one reason I am tough to deal with.

**Maurice Greenberg, President and C.E.O. American International Group**

- Extremely blunt ... accomplished at belittling people in front of others ... You haven't achieved any standing if you haven't experienced his wrath.

• I like running a winning ball club ... that calls for total commitment ... If you consider that a sacrifice, you are in the wrong company ... I look for discipline in people.

**Don Rumsfeld, President and C.E.O. G.D. Searle**

- Fast-paced, urgent ... when people argue with him–God it can be tough ... demolishes anyone who blows smoke at him.

• You not only let someone who has not been obeying you go, you do it publicly so everyone knows that breaking the rules brings immediate punishment ... We got rid of a bunch for the good of the rest.

**Richard Jacob, Chairman and C.E.O. Dayco**

- Do something wrong and he lands on you, all 300 pounds of him ... uses rough language ... but he's fair, cares about his people ... you either love him or hate him.

• I am very demanding ... won't tolerate laziness ... If you aren't prepared to bust your ass, you had better find another job.

**Robert Stone, Executive Vice President Columbia Pictures**

- Known as Captain Queeg when he ran Hertz ... A galley master who, hearing that the rowers would die if the beat were raised to 40, would say, "Make it 45."

• I'm a hands-on manager. At Hertz I put in a business review that was painful if you didn't know the answers. Professionals never have a problem with Bob Stone.

**David Mahoney, Chairman and C.E.O. Norton Simon**

- Presents a smooth front but more explosive than he seems ... Irish temperament with short fuse ... becomes enamored of someone but that wears off ... made Norton Simon known for executive turnover.

• I insist that, goddammit, we do our best every day ... I'm intense in everything I do and I expect that others will be too.

**William Ylvisaker, Chairman and C.E.O. Gould**

- Uses Marine Corps boot-camp approach ... creates aura of power and wealth and reminds people it all flows from him ... They won't go to the bathroom without his permission.

• Tough means unfair and unreasonable. This company is managed objectively ... I don't think you have to be tough anytime.

Source: "Oh, What They Say About the Boss," in *Fortune*, April 21, 1980, p. 65.

human beings. This weightless component cannot be bought, sold, or built into an individual. If he *has* it, it can be nurtured and cultivated. If he doesn't have it, all the leadership training courses in the world can't make him a leader.[11]

Often the word "charisma" is used in discussions of leadership. In early Christianity charisma was a special gift or talent divinely granted to a person. It exemplified the power to heal or make prophesies. Today **charisma** indicates the qualities of being extra special, attractive, and unusually interesting. According to Webster's Dictionary, it is a "personal magic of leadership arousing special popular loyalty or enthusiasm." Not all leaders have charisma. Most people agree, however, that Presidents Kennedy and Roosevelt had the "magic touch" associated with our understanding of the term, while Presidents Johnson, Nixon, Ford, and Carter lacked it.

## Ability to Understand Human Behavior

There is no limit to the number and variety of interpersonal problems that arise in managing. "How can the jealousy between Mary and Bob be resolved?" "What does the union really want?" "Will Peter be accepted by his new peers?" are examples of questions a manager, in leading, may wrestle with in a short period of time.

Keith Davis notes that successful leaders are strong in terms of their human-relations attitudes: "Successful leaders realize that they get their job done through people and therefore try to develop social understanding and appropriate skills. They develop a healthy respect for people, if for no other reason than that their success as leaders depends on cooperation of people."[12]

## Similarity to the Group

Those who emerge as leaders are generally not too different from the group. A senior executive would probably not be accepted as a production foreman by the workers because of the wide differences between his education, viewpoints, and interests and those of the group. For similar reasons, it is unlikely that a university president would be well received by the college security force as its manager.

## Verbal Assertiveness

By nature leaders seem not to be shy. They are able to present their views in a confident manner and to hold their position when attacked. A leader has the ability to speak up when others feel they should not because their ideas might be ridiculed.

There seems to be considerable merit in the idea that the various organizations in the world are indeed shaped more by speakers than by writers. Christ, a classic example, wrote nothing. Years after the crucifixion several of his disciples put his philosophy into words.

Many leaders whom we either admire or despise greatly—for instance, Castro, Gandhi, Martin Luther King, Jr., Stalin, Roosevelt, Churchill, Muhammad Ali, Hitler, de Gaulle, and Huey Long—are noted for their ability to persuade others with the spoken word. In the preface to *Mein Kampf*, Adolf Hitler makes this

[11]Robert M. Fulmer, *The New Management* (New York: Macmillan, 1974), p. 336.
[12]Davis, *Human Relations at Work*, pp. 99–100.

observation that underscores the importance of verbal assertiveness as it relates to leadership: "I know that one is able to win people far more by the spoken word than by the written word, and that every great movement on this globe owes its rise to the great speakers and not to the great writers."[13]

Some psychological studies indicate that leaders talk more than followers and lead to the following conclusion:

> The most active member in terms of communication is also usually the leader of the group. At the simplest level, the most active person is the leader because he has the most influence on the group. He determines the course of conversation (most of what is said comes from him), he initiates interactions by asking questions, he receives the most replies and he makes the most suggestions and gives the most orders. Whatever the group is doing, he plays a central role. An outside observer would consider him the group's leader—and the group concurs in this opinion. Usually the person who talks the most is perceived as the leader by the rest of the group. Thus, amount of communication is a critical determinant of leadership."[14]

Just talking, however, is not an indication of leadership. The *content* of what is said is part of a leadership personality. Leaders tend to communicate in a supportive, encouraging manner with such statements as "How can I help?" "What's your opinion, George?" "You're doing OK," and "We'll get it done on time." Other people with negative outlooks who talk a lot but do not come across as leaders are more inclined to make statements such as "Do it this way," "I don't think your plan will work," "There is too much pressure on us now," and "You'll have to work it out yourself."

**Willingness to Communicate Honestly**

To be a leader a manager should tell the truth; otherwise a credibility gap develops. Winston Churchill did this when he explained the realities of war and the "blood, sweat, and tears" that would be required to achieve a victory.

Many managers are afraid to tell the full truth. They may either exaggerate the good side of a situation or minimize the bad side of a situation. For example, when employees are to be laid off or when pay raises cannot be met, some managers try to sugarcoat the issue.

Once a manager loses credibility, it is very difficult to regain. For instance, if a sales executive conveys the impression to his or her sales staff that it is easy to sell a new product when in fact it is not, soon the staff will lose confidence in that person as a leader. Or consider the German propaganda directed at German soldiers during World War I: It conveyed the impression that British, French, and American troops were ineffective. In combat the German soldiers learned that this was just not so, and they began to lose confidence in their leaders.

A leader should be willing to discuss issues and problems that are not particularly pleasant but are important to the situation at hand. Effective organizations are built on integrity. Their leaders are straightforward and fair in their conduct and speech.

[13]Adolf Hitler, *Mein Kampf* (New York: Reynal and Hitchcock, 1940).
[14]Jonathan L. Freedman, J. Merrill Carlsmith, and David O. Sears, *Social Psychology*, 2nd ed. (Englewood Cliffs, N.J.: Prentice-Hall, 1974), p. 155.

**Dedication to the Organization's Goals**

In all types of organizations there are difficult tasks to achieve, such as increasing sales, cutting costs, obtaining new accounts, or selling stock. The effectiveness of a leader depends to a large extent on how committed he or she is to the objectives being sought. Dedication is demonstrated by hard work, self-sacrifice, and an air of complete commitment. Managers who are skeptical about the worthiness of a goal do not inspire their followers.

The coach of a basketball team twenty points behind at half time who tells the players, "Well, we've blown this one," is not demonstrating dedication to the objective (that is, to win even if the odds are great). Nor is the manager who tells his personnel, "I'm not certain that our company should introduce this new product." A leader's behavior should demonstrate that he or she believes in the cause being undertaken.

Dedication to an objective means the willingness to try again when there appears to be little hope, to accept a setback without remorse, and to keep at a project until it is completed.

Keith Davis makes this interesting observation about the motivation of leaders: "Leaders have a strong personal motivation to keep accomplishing something. As they reach one goal, their level of aspiration rises to other goals; so one success becomes a challenge for more success."[15]

**Ability to Set an Example to Be Followed**

In practice managers often display a "Do as I say, not as I do" behavioral pattern. But individuals tend to do as a manager does, not what he or she says. If a manager says, "We have to work harder" or "Let's cut out the inefficiency in this operation" and then proceeds to work less and to employ unneeded assistants, a credibility gap develops. Lower performance and standards by subordinates almost certainly will result.

If a manager wants hard work from other people, he or she must set an example of working hard. If a manager plans an economy campaign, he or she must resist spending foolishly. An effective leader knows that people observe his or her behavior and will tend to behave in similar ways.

**Willingness to Take Risks**

One observer made this comment relative to risk and leadership: "One constant [in being a leader] is the willingness to take risks, to row the boat out beyond the shore without assuming that you will be able to get back.[16]

Risk is the possibility of loss, injury, disadvantage, or defeat. Generally, maintaining the status quo is not indicative of leadership. People seem to want to follow someone who will take them to "the promised land" even if some risk is involved. Leaders cannot take too great a risk because doing so may make their followers too fearful, and panic or desertion may result. But taking risks in the right proportion makes organizational life more exciting.

Examples of willingness to take risks include introducing a new product, putting one's job on the line for something one believes in, making a key personnel appointment, and making a corporate investment. The willingness to take risks is

---

[15]Davis, *Human Relations at Work*, p. 100.

[16]Statement attributed to Lewis Engman, former head of the Federal Trade Commission, in "Leadership: The Biggest Issue," *Time*, November 8, 1976, p. 40.

also something that many people admire, and hence they tend to follow the person who takes chances. The football coach who goes for the more risky two-point conversion and a chance to win the game rather than try for the easier one-point play and a tie is demonstrating the kind of risk many people admire. Even if the gamble doesn't pay off, many people may feel the coach did the right thing and will support him in the future.

As noted before, managers cannot delegate responsibility for activities assigned to them. However, in practice, ineffective managers often attempt to dodge responsibility, especially when things go wrong. The sales manager who blames the sales force for not attaining the quota is not practicing leadership.

**Willingness to Assume Full Responsibility**

Blaming others for one's own failures or weaknesses is never admired. Taking full responsibility even when one could shift it to some other person is. After the Bay of Pigs fiasco, some of President Kennedy's advisers suggested that he put the blame on the Eisenhower Administration, since it had done much of the planning for the invasion. But President Kennedy held firm and told the public, "I take full responsibility." Criticism that had been growing quickly diminished.

People respect managers who take full responsibility when things go wrong. They also respect managers who pass credit on to them when an effort is successful. The production manager who sincerely and enthusiastically praises his or her personnel when a goal is achieved — say, improved quality or no accidents in three months — wins their support and is regarded as a leader. Conversely, people do not respect a manager who personally takes the credit and the glory.

**Willingness to Be Supportive of Personnel**

Being supportive of personnel also means working in their behalf with upper-level management to get them the financial and physical resources needed to do their jobs. People resent a manager who does not provide them with pay, fringe benefits, working conditions, and other resources that are at least equal to those received by people in other departments. Managers exercise leadership when they promote the interests or causes of their subordinates.

Other ways to show support of personnel include taking a sincere interest in their problems, providing encouragement, and passing on their suggestions to higher-level management.

The Chinese philosopher Lao-Tse wrote the following description of a leader about 2,500 years ago:

A leader is best when people barely know he exists
Not so good when people obey and acclaim him,
Worse when people despise him.
"Fail to honor people, and they fail to honor you."
But when a good leader, who talks little,
Has done his work, fulfilled his aim . . .
They will all say . . . "We did it ourselves."

To **compromise** is to settle a difference by arbitration or by consent through mutual concession. Parties who compromise agree to reduce their demands and reach an intermediate solution.

**Skill in the Art of Compromise**

Settling differences is a vital part of leadership, since disputes are bound to arise in all organizations. At budget time, for example, each department in a business or university wants more money. An effective leader is able to get warring factions to modify their positions. Many of the best decisions result from a "meeting of minds."

Most high-level decisions are compromises. We see this in government, in which virtually all laws are the result of debate. Compromises are involved in many small decisions too, such as who will work on Saturday or which department will be responsible for a given activity. Compromising is often the only way to achieve a goal. People who refuse ever to compromise are generally not effective leaders. Even when a manager is convinced that his or her way is best, he or she should listen to the ideas of associates and subordinates.

**Ability to Tolerate Criticism**

Harry Truman once said, "If you can't stand the heat, get out of the kitchen"— meaning that if you can't tolerate personal attack you shouldn't make plans that affect others or take a stand on controversial issues.

Leaders, since they often have radical or unusual ideas, are subject to far more criticism than followers. Those who develop broad plans and direct people to carry them out must be willing to accept criticism, often severe, from those affected by the plans, from the media, and from the public.

## CAN LEADERSHIP BE LEARNED?

Not all people want to lead; some prefer to follow. It is common in organizations for individuals at one level of management to turn down opportunities for promotion to higher levels. Most people, however, do enjoy a leadership role and want to improve their leadership abilities.

Certainly the inspirational element of leadership is an art, not a science. However, it is noteworthy that many people in the arts—such as painting, drama, and music—do improve their skills through education and guided experience. It follows, then, that managers can bring about some improvement in their leadership abilities through conscientious effort. Specific actions that may help are noted below.

*Read about leadership.* Hundreds of books have been written about leadership, and thousands of magazine articles that touch directly or indirectly on leadership concepts appear every year. Leadership styles of many successful and unsuccessful leaders have been documented.

*Observe those in leadership situations.* How do they handle people? What do they do in crisis situations? While the ability to inspire is very intangible and individualized, a manager can yet learn different ways of handling problem situations by observing effective leaders.

Blake, Robert R., and Mouton, Jane S. *The New Managerial Grid.* Houston: Gulf Publishing Co., 1978.

Boone, Louis E., and Johnson, James C. "Profiles of the 801 Men and 1 Woman at the Top." *Business Horizons*, February 1980, pp. 47–52.

Davidson, William L. "CEO Management Style in the Closely Held Company." *Business Horizons*, February 1980, pp. 60–63.

Drumwright, Membe. "Contingency Theories of Leadership: A Review." *Baylor Business Studies*, August–September–October 1981, pp. 29–44.

Finn, David. "Public Invisibility of Corporate Leaders." *Harvard Business Review*, November–December 1980, pp. 102–110.

Howard, Ann, and Wilson, James A. "Leadership in a Declining Work Ethic." *California Management Review*, Summer 1982, pp. 33–46.

Keys, Bernard, and Bell, Robert. "Four Faces of the Fully Functioning Middle Manager." *California Management Review*, Summer 1982, pp. 59–67.

Kirotaka Takeuchi. "Productivity: Learning from the Japanese." *California Management Review*, Summer 1981, pp. 5–19.

Kurtz, David L., and Boone, Louis E. "A Profile of Business Leadership." *Business Horizons,* September–October 1981, pp. 28–32.

Lewin, Kurt. *A Dynamic Theory of Personality.* New York: McGraw-Hill, 1945.

Litzinger, William, and Schaefer, Thomas. "Leadership through Followership." *Business Horizons*, September–October 1982, pp. 78–81.

Niehouse, Oliver L. "Breaking the Promotion Barrier with Flexible Leadership." *Business,* October–November–December 1982, p. 22–26.

Rehder, Robert R. "What American and Japanese Managers Are Learning From One Another." *Business Horizons*, March–April 1981, pp. 63–70.

Schein, Edgar H. "Does Japanese Management Style Have a Message for American Managers?" *Sloan Management Review*, Fall 1981, pp. 55–68.

Schiming, Richard C. "Two Views of the Future of the Entrepreneur." *Akron Business and Economic Review*, Summer 1982, pp. 22–25.

Schriesheim, Chester A.; Tolliver, James; and Behling, Orlando C. "Leadership Theory: Some Implications for Managers." *MSU Business Topics*, Summer 1978, pp. 34–40.

Terutomo Ozawa. "Japanese World of Work: An Interpretive Study." *MSU Business Topics,* Spring 1980, pp. 45–56.

Waters, James A. "Managerial Assertiveness." *Business Horizons*, September–October 1982, pp. 24–29.

# 18 THE COMMUNI-CATIONS PROCESS

**STUDY THIS CHAPTER SO YOU CAN:**

- Differentiate between the different kinds of internal communications, and explain the informal group as a communications channel.

- Describe the roles and characteristics of the five elements in the communications process.

- Identify and discuss the ways to make communications more effective.

- Explain the relationship between image building and communications and the factors that affect an organization's image.

- Discuss the role of public relations in communications.

To **communicate** means to make known, to impart, or to transmit information. Communication is an integral part of managing. Managers transmit and receive ideas, reports, data, and other forms of information needed to make an enterprise function.

In a business enterprise, work instructions must be communicated to employees. Prospective customers must be notified about the products available. Vendors need information about the firm's needs for raw materials, equipment, and supplies. Government agencies require information about income, expenses, and compliance with various laws.

Giving instructions, explaining problems, showing someone how to do something, attending conferences, reading, and listening occupy most of a manager's time. Communicating, then, is a costly management activity.

A plan may be excellent, but if it is not communicated effectively, its objectives probably will not be achieved. For instance, a plan may call for assigning George to increase production of product A by 10 percent. But if the production manager is not informed that production is to be increased, the plan will obviously fail. Effective communication by the legal staff can prevent lawsuits, and effective communication by accountants can minimize taxes. Effective communication can also result in better inventory control, more efficient deliveries, and better overall performance.

Generally, the success achieved by an organization reflects the effectiveness of its communications. Many negative results, such as accidents, mistakes, wasted resources, and duplicated effort, can be traced directly to poor communication.

**455**

*Kinds of
Communication:
External
and
Internal*

## KINDS OF COMMUNICATION: EXTERNAL AND INTERNAL

In organizations communications may be viewed as internal and external. **Internal communications** take place between people within an enterprise, while **external communications** occur between members of an organization and people outside it.

All organizations generate internal communication. Communication flows within an organization are multidirectional. When we think of communicating, we usually visualize messages being sent *vertically downward*, from one level to lower levels by way of the chain of command. This is the path that most orders and instructions take. But much communicating is *vertically upward*, from lower to higher levels. Managers require information from their subordinates about their problems, work in progress, and other data that relate to what the organization is doing. Figure 18–1 provides a simple illustration of vertically downward and vertically upward communication.

*Internal Communication*

**Direct horizontal communication** occurs when an individual in one department sends a message to another individual at the same organizational level in another department. A message from the sales manager to the production manager is direct horizontal communication if both individuals are at the same level.

**Indirect horizontal communication** occurs between people at different organizational levels in different departments. In most organizations there is much of this zigzagging or diagonalizing of messages. A middle manager in the transportation department may communicate directly with a first-level manager in the sales department, or the head of the accounting department may communicate directly with a middle manager in the finance department.

**FIGURE 18–1**

**Vertical Communications Within an Organization**

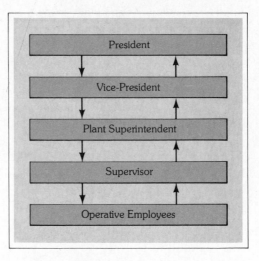

### The Informal Group as a Communications Channel

The word "grapevine" has come to mean an informal means of circulating information, news, or gossip that has been obtained secretly or from private sources.

All organizations have a grapevine, or an informal communications channel. It is very difficult to keep information secret in an organization; news will flow through the grapevine with or without the approval of management. The grapevine creates a problem in that the information that is communicated is usually only partially based on fact or may be incomplete. And as news passes through the grapevine, it generally becomes distorted.

Some managers deliberately use the grapevine to sample people's opinions on various ideas. A plant manager may test out employee reaction to a proposed change in work schedules by mentioning the idea to someone he or she knows will pass it along. Then, in a short while the workers' feelings about the new plan will get back to the manager.

Managers should keep in mind that grapevines exist not just because people like to gossip, speculate, and spread rumors. They may also exist because management has not designed a communications system that promptly supplies people with the information they feel they should have. Generally, the more fully and accurately management keeps people informed, the weaker the grapevine will be.

**External Communication**

All enterprises also initiate communication with individuals and groups outside the organization. Figure 18–2 shows some of the organizations with which a snack food company may communicate.

Generally, as an organization grows, external communications increase and may include thousands of suppliers, wholesalers, retailers, and other types of

**FIGURE 18–2**

**457**

*Elements
in the
Communications
Process*

**Example of External Communication**

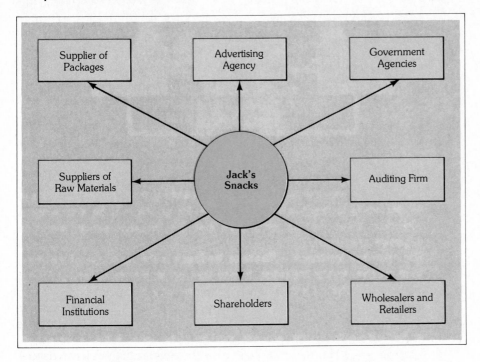

organizations. And managers often complain that far too much external communication is required by government. This matter is discussed in the Issue for Debate in this chapter.

## ELEMENTS IN THE COMMUNICATIONS PROCESS

As shown in Figure 18–3, communications can be thought of as a process involving five elements:

- *The message sender* —The **message sender** is anyone who wants to communicate something to someone else. All of us —managers and nonmanagers —are message senders.
- *The message* —The **message** is the information the message sender wants to communicate. It tells the message receiver to do something —buy a product, perform work, keep informed, and so on.
- *The message vehicle* —The **message vehicle** is the method used to transmit the message. A message may be conveyed through speech, in writing, in the form of pictures, and in other ways.

**FIGURE 18–3**

**Elements in the Communications Process**

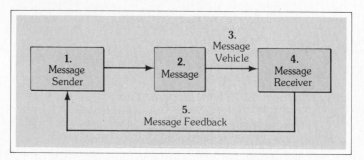

* *The message receiver* — The **message receiver** is the person the message sender wants to reach with the message. He or she may be a superior, a coworker, a subordinate, or anyone else the message sender wants to influence or inform.
* *The message feedback* — **Message feedback** is the response of the message receiver to the message. It may take on an infinite variety of forms, such as compliance with an order, purchase of a product, or provision of information.

The five elements in the process interact. Say Jane Willis, a personnel administrator (the message sender), wants to develop a training program on how to manage time for first-level supervisors. Ms. Willis puts her proposal (the message) in the form of a memo (the message vehicle) and sends it to her superior, Ms. Clonts (the message receiver). Ms. Clonts then gives her reaction (the message feedback) to Ms. Willis.

As noted, everyone is a message sender. The other four elements of the communication process are discussed in greater detail in the following sections.

**The Message**

The content of a message is any information that is being transmitted. Messages deal with all aspects of organized activity, such as plans, work to be done, methods to employ, time schedules, quality standards, personnel assignments, inventory, and financial matters.

Most messages seek to induce people to act to achieve a goal. A foreman who explains how to operate a machine wants to induce employees to maintain product quality and avoid accidents. A second key purpose of communication is to inform, rather than to cause people to take specific action. A manager may receive numerous reports, for instance, that are intended to keep him or her abreast of a situation or to help shape attitudes toward a situation.

Some messages are very simple. "Please get me a cup of coffee," "Turn on your engine," and "Where is the nearest restaurant?" are examples of the hundreds of easily understood messages most people transmit and receive daily.

At the other extreme, some messages are very complex. Some may take thousands of pages to transmit. For instance, all of the plans, instructions, designs,

# ISSUE FOR DEBATE

## DOES THE GOVERNMENT REQUIRE TOO MUCH COMMUNICATION FROM BUSINESS?

The federal government yearly requires businesses to submit voluminous information about their operations. In addition to providing a wide variety of data for income tax purposes, some businesses are also required to submit information about prices charged, wage and salary increases, minorities employed, safety precautions, environmental-damage controls, and so on. Probably most managers feel the government demand for information is excessive. But there are some who feel it is not. Below are some pro and con statements about this issue.

### YES

**The government requires too much communication from business because . . .**

Filling out government-required reports is expensive. It takes a big business thousands of hours each year to supply information to the government, and often different government agencies require the same information. This time could be used more productively to run the business.

Reporting to the government is an invasion of a company's privacy. Businesses should have the same rights as individuals not to disclose sensitive information.

Apparently, little use is made of much of the information collected by government. Much information required on census forms, for example, serves no constructive purpose.

Excessive record keeping results from government demands for information. A good rule in management is to keep no more records than are needed.

### NO

**The government does not require too much communication from business because . . .**

As our economy becomes more complex, the government needs more information to decide what programs are required to serve the public interest and what new legislation may be needed to protect the private-enterprise system.

Information is required by the government to determine whether a business is obeying various laws. For example, without extensive financial information, how could the IRS know whether a business is paying all the taxes it should?

Much of the information collected from businesses, such as census data, is later shared with them. Such information helps business to plan more effectively.

Most people apparently approve of the government demands. If voters didn't approve of what legislators did, they would replace their representatives with others who would require less reporting.

### QUESTIONS

1. What other pro and con statements can you make?
2. Which side of the issue do you feel is stronger? Why?

procedures, test results, and other information required to develop a new passenger aircraft would require a number of trucks to transport.

Often a message contains a series of orders that add to its complexity. A manager may tell a supervisor something like, "On Tuesday get 300 units out, take care of the union problem, arrange the work schedule for the rest of the month, and get someone to repair the loading dock. And if you can get to it, be thinking about how to rearrange the warehouse — it's a mess." This message carries several specific instructions.

## The Message Vehicle

Many vehicles, or media, are available to transmit messages from senders to receivers. Some examples are:

- *Face-to-face contact* — One-to-one personal discussion, several people in personal discussion, committee meeting.
- *Written statements* — Memos, status reports, reports giving recommendations, tax reports, research studies, public-relations releases (telling of promotions, hirings, broad changes in policy), letters (providing and/or requesting information, giving congratulation, selling), computer printouts (showing sales, purchases, or inventories by product line, product, or price or showing wages, salaries, or deductions).
- *Advertisements* — Radio, television, newspaper, magazine, billboard, direct mail.
- *Telephone and telegraph* — Emergency and routine information, requests for information.

Note that some message vehicles are symbolic rather than verbal. A whistle indicates it's time to start or stop an activity. A siren communicates a warning. A traffic signal says stop, go, or proceed with caution. Billboards seek to persuade people to buy. I.D. cards tell others that a person can be given access to a certain area. Because of increasing worldwide tourism and language barriers, symbols are being used more and more often to communicate traffic regulations and to identify eating facilities, rest rooms, and transportation facilities.

### Which Vehicle Is Best?

The message vehicle to use in a given situation depends on a number of factors, such as:

- *Urgency* — If a situation requires immediate action, a telephone call or personal visit, not a letter, seems indicated.
- *Importance* — A major shift in policy may best be explained to key people at a conference, not in a memo or a letter.
- *Need for documentation* — If legal proof may be needed later, a telegram should be used instead of a telephone call.
- *Delicacy of the message* — If the message is sensitive, such as notice of a promotion or a termination, a face-to-face conversation should probably be arranged rather than sending a memo or a letter.

- *Cost considerations* —When the message is intended for a large number of people, a news item or an advertisement may be used instead of telephone calls, telegrams, or personal letters.
- *Future reference to information* —Often a message may need to be referred to later. In this case, a written vehicle (letter, memo, report, and so on) or a tape recording is best.

### Body Language as a Message Vehicle

Many messages in organizations are delivered face to face, a practice that introduces another facet of communication: **body language**. To paraphrase Marshall McLuhan, the medium—a person's voice and body—may be part of the message. Two individuals can say exactly the same words, but the message receiver may react to them in quite different ways. Consider the message "Move on—you're holding things up." The message receiver would probably react differently if the sender were 6 feet 2 inches rather than 5 feet 3 inches. And a person who says, "I'd like to apply for a job" will get very different reactions if he or she looks directly into the message receiver's eyes and speaks in a steady voice than if he or she looks down and mumbles.

People "say" a great deal about themselves without speaking a word. Some of our physical characteristics that speak for us, each of which can be subdivided into numerous subcharacteristics, are: body build, height, weight, posture, hairstyle, moustache (or no moustache), beard (or no beard), eye contact, complexion, voice, mannerisms, handshake, gestures, hygiene, manner of walking, and facial expressions.

What a person wears also sends a message to others. A colonel in military uniform says one thing to people he meets; he says something else when dressed as a civilian. A salesperson dressed in sports clothes conveys one thing to an executive interested in buying a computer service; he might convey something quite different if he were dressed in a three-piece suit. In recent years there has been a growing recognition that clothing plays a large part in the way people react to an individual.

**The Message Receiver**

The message receiver is the individual or group that the message sender wants to reach. A manager may need to reach other managers within the organization, superiors, subordinates, suppliers, the general public, customers, government agencies, shareholders, contractors, or competitors.

The content of the message should be prepared with the message receiver in mind. Managers who want their messages to be understood and acted upon will try to understand the psychological makeup of their receivers and design messages that will attract and hold the receivers' attention.

### Knowledge of Message Receivers

People who prepare advertising messages have an obvious need to know a great deal about the psychological, economic, and demographic characteristics of their target customers. But so do supervisors issuing work instructions, creditors writing "Pay your bill" letters, engineers explaining a new machine, and company presidents addressing shareholders who are unhappy over last year's earnings.

If the message sender overestimates the intelligence and knowledge of the receiver, the latter will not understand the message and the sender's goal will not be achieved. On the other hand, if the sender underestimates the intellectual capabilities of the receiver, the latter may feel insulted and may not do what the message sender wants.

Income, status in the organization, responsibilities, and other socioeconomic characteristics also influence the way people perceive messages. A message directed toward union members may be worded differently than information sent to supervisors. And information directed toward senior executives may be phrased differently than a message sent to first-level managers.

Perception of a message is also influenced by how well the receiver knows the sender. Take a manager who customarily issues orders very tersely: "Hey Harry, get this done today—and get the lead out." To experienced employees this order may be perceived positively; that's the way the boss always issues commands when he feels good. But to a new employee, such a command may be viewed with fear. Because people differ in so many ways, they interpret messages differently. This places great responsibility on the message sender to tailor each message to the individual receiver.

Unfortunately, few communicators understand much about human behavior, which helps explain why so many messages are misunderstood or ignored. Later in this chapter some pointers on making messages more understandable are provided.

### Attracting and Holding the Attention of Message Receivers

Attention is difficult to capture and hold for two reasons: The competition for it is intense, and the attention span of message receivers is limited. Consider the competition for attention a manager faces in communicating with a supervisor in a busy factory. Machines are making loud noises, one or more phones may be ringing, and several workers may be standing close by waiting to ask questions. Numerous other factors, such as the temperature, a health problem, pressure to complete work under a tight deadline, or the memory of a bad argument with a spouse, may compete with the manager's message for the supervisor's attention.

Despite such pleas as "Give me your full and undivided attention for a few minutes" and "Please observe carefully what I am demonstrating," people's minds have a notorious habit of wandering. No one is able to concentrate fully on one subject for very long. At the conclusion of a particularly lively class, the author asked the students to write anonymously three or more things they had thought about during the class that were totally unrelated to the subject discussed. An almost unbelievably large and diverse list resulted.

Managers at higher levels in an organization may also have severely limited attention spans. Assume a group of five managers is meeting to decide where to hold the next company convention. One manager suggests holding it in Hawaii. This communication may break the attention of another manager who begins to relive a good or a bad experience she has had in the islands and temporarily forgets the purpose of the meeting.

Effective message senders use a variety of devices to cause receivers to refocus their attention on the matter being discussed. A change in one's voice, comments such as "Let's get back to it" or "Let's take out pencils and make some notes" and direct questioning of the message receiver on some points are common ways to recapture wandering minds in a conference.

Message feedback is the action taken by the message receiver once the message has been conveyed. In some cases, such as when people are instructed to reduce output by 10 percent, feedback can be measured quantitatively. Often, however, feedback can be judged only qualitatively. For example, a senior executive who has proposed a major policy change might receive a cool, warm, or enthusiastic response.

The Message Feedback

Feedback is important because it indicates whether the communications process has succeeded, that is, whether the desired result has been accomplished and, if so, how well. Feedback is also important because it can guide the message sender in preparing future messages. For example, if a written message fails to achieve the result of reduced absenteeism, then perhaps a stronger message should be designed.

## GUIDELINES FOR MAKING COMMUNICATION MORE EFFECTIVE

An ongoing goal of all managers should be to improve the effectiveness of their communications. Better communications result in fewer mistakes, more sales, more productive employees, fewer disagreements, and other benefits. It can be argued forcefully that if an employee does not understand a message, the man-

*"Mr. Pointman, while you were out, a Miss or a Ms. or a Mrs. Valdy or Volney or Balmey left a garbled message for you."*

©Punch/Rothco

463

ager has not communicated effectively. If an employee does not understand a warning and is injured, ultimate responsibility still rests with the manager. Similar logic tells us that if a truck driver makes a delivery to a wrong address or if a production supervisor produces more units than are needed, ultimate responsibility rests with their managers because in some way they did not communicate effectively.

Knowledge, skill, and time are vital in the creation of effective messages. A sales representative who has a thorough knowledge of the product, is well trained in selling skills, and takes time to prepare for a presentation can be expected to do well. A salesperson who lacks either knowledge, skill, or preparation time will usually do poorly.

Some ways in which managers can make communications more effective are discussed below.

## Strive for Brevity

A basic goal of those who want to communicate effectively should be to make the message as brief and simple as possible. Many respected philosophers have endorsed keeping things simple. Confucius said, "A great man never loses the simplicity of a child." Ralph Waldo Emerson observed, "Nothing is more simple than greatness, indeed to be simple is to be great."

Just as a machine should have no unnecessary parts, a message should contain no unnecessary words, paragraphs, or sections. And it should avoid complicated, ambiguous words and illustrations. Some people feel it is a mark of great ability and intelligence to appear profound, but it is not. We should banish the fear of being too simple in communicating with others.

One way to keep communications brief is to avoid trite, pompous, or verbose expressions. Such phrases weaken a message, take extra space, and tell the message receiver that the message sender is mentally lazy. Table 18-1 shows some examples of how such expressions can be simplified.

There is a negative correlation between the length of a communication and its effectiveness. The longer a memo, a letter, or any other kind of message, the less likely that it will be read and digested in its entirety. The shorter the message, the more likely that it will be understood and acted upon.

An unusually long letter, report, or oral presentation usually indicates one of three things about the message sender: He or she lacks knowledge about the subject being communicated (and uses more and larger words than are necessary to cover up this deficiency), lacks skill in communicating, or did not take enough time to prepare the message.

Interestingly, more time is often required to prepare a short message than a long one. There is much truth in the old saying, "I would have written you a letter half as long if I had had twice as much time." And contrary to popular belief, the Gettysburg Address, one of the briefest and best-written political speeches in history, went through several drafts and required many hours of Lincoln's time.

Another reason a message should be brief and simple is to prevent distortion. Ideally a message should be so well prepared that it undergoes no changes as it passes from one person in the organization to another. In practice, however, information communicated orally often becomes so twisted as it goes from level to level that its original meaning is lost.

**TABLE 18—1**                                                                    **465**

Bad Language Forms Can Be Made Better

| Bad Form | Better Form |
|---|---|
| "The undersigned" | "I" |
| "At the present time" | "Now" or "Today" |
| "At the earliest possible moment " | "Soon" |
| "Allow me to express my appreciation" | "Thank you" |
| "The writer thinks that" | "I think" |
| "At a later date" | "Later" |
| "In the neighborhood of" | "About" |
| "In view of the fact that" | "Because" |
| "Subsequent to" | "After" |
| "Without further delay" | "Immediately" |

The simpler the message, the less likely that it will become distorted as it passes from person to person in the organization. Another way to keep a message from becoming distorted is to develop an effective feedback system, as discussed later in this section.

Most people have two vocabularies: the general vocabulary of the society in which they live and the specialized vocabulary common to their occupation. Specialized vocabularies are found in all fields: Physicians, engineers, truck drivers, computer programmers, and professors all speak and write a language common to their job. When a specialist is communicating with a nonspecialist, words and examples that laypeople understand should be used. If the group to be reached is known to use and understand specialized words, then the appropriate specialized vocabulary may be employed.

**Use Vocabulary
Appropriate to the
Message Receiver**

Thousands of costly mistakes are made daily in organizations due to inaccurate messages. For example, a department store printed the following information as part of an advertisement: "We will be closed Saturday, April 7." What was intended was: "We will be closed Sunday, April 7." Most customers believed the Saturday part of the message, and customers were off 80 percent.

**Strive for
Accuracy and
Completeness**

Inaccurate information is responsible for common blunders such as delivering products to the wrong address, ordering the wrong supplies, producing too few or too many units, and repairing machines badly. Incorrect information also is one of the leading causes of accidents. Over the years, most crashes of commercial aircraft have resulted from wrong information. One tragic example was the crash on December 1, 1974, of a TWA Boeing 727 twenty-five miles northwest of Dulles International Airport in Washington, D.C. All 92 persons on board were killed in the crash. The accident occurred while the flight was descending for an approach to a runway at Dulles during poor weather conditions. The National Transportation Safety Board (NTSB) determined that the probable cause of the accident was the crew's decision to descend to 1,800 feet before the aircraft had reached the approach segment where that minimum altitude applied. In its report on the accident, the NTSB stated: "The crew's decision to descend was a result of inadequacies and *lack of clarity* in the air traffic control procedures *which led to a misunderstanding* on the part of the pilots and of the controllers regarding each other's responsibilities during operations in terminal areas under instrument meteorological conditons" [author's italics].[1]

A message should be complete as well as accurate. When communicating is done hastily under severe time pressure, key facts may be omitted and the message may fail to achieve its objective because it contains too little information. Some examples of oral messages that are incomplete and may cause confusion are "See that Mr. Smith gets this" (when there are several Mr. Smiths in the organization) and "The midnight shift should report back to work" (without specifying which day is meant). Some examples of incomplete written messages are bills that do not indicate what the charge is for, contracts that do not include key clauses, advertisements that do not tell where the product can be purchased, memos that do not provide complete instructions, and policies that do not cover frequent occurrences.

It is good practice for the message sender to ask, "Does the message contain all the information needed for the receiver to act on it?"

## Be Selective in Receiving and Sending Messages

Managers both receive and send messages. Managers can improve communication by receiving only those messages they should handle and by sending messages only to those people who should receive them and only as frequently as necessary.

### Selectivity in Receiving Messages

As one moves up the management ladder, it becomes increasingly difficult to absorb all the communication messages directed toward one. There simply is not enough time to read in detail and digest all the publications, reports, letters, and advertisements that are sent to a senior executive. Nor is there usually time to see all visitors personally and take all phone calls.

Generally the solution is to apply the exception principle, which, as noted previously, states that all problems and activities should be handled at the lowest competent level in an organization. In the ideally structured organization a manager at any level will receive only those problems that cannot be solved by someone at a lower level.

When the exception principle is followed, only a small percentage of the messages received by an organization reach the top executive. However, the exception principle should be only a guideline. Often, good public relations require a senior manager to deal with some relatively unimportant matters. If employees, customers, reporters, or representatives of citizens' groups feel the senior manager is inaccessible, ill will and "bad press" may result. Therefore, when messages directed toward a senior executive are rechanneled to someone at a lower level, care must be exercised not to offend the message sender.

[1]"National Transportation Safety Board Report," *Aviation Week and Space Technology,* February 9, 1976, pp. 64–68.

Note that people who distribute incoming mail, receive telephone calls, and act as receptionists for visitors can play a key role in directing messages. Unfortunately, these activities are often viewed as routine and no one develops clear procedures for handling incoming messages. As a result, an individual may be shuttled from one person to another in seeking a solution to a problem.

### Selectivity in Sending Messages

Most of us receive many messages that have little meaning for us. At work we may receive memos and reports that do not concern our activities; at home we may receive direct mail advertisements for products that are of no interest to us.

In deciding who should receive a message, managers should ask, "Who has a need to know?" This question is often judgmental. Should, for example, members of the sales department be informed about changes in production schedules? If the changes affect time of delivery to customers, sales personnel should be informed. But if the revision in production schedules does not affect delivery, then passing on this information to the sales department may be pointless.

Managers must also decide how frequently communications should be sent. Too much communication creates a problem, for, as a general rule, as the number of messages increases the attention given to each decreases. In some businesses, so many memos are distributed by administrators that managers begin reading them indifferently. Too much communication dulls the receiver's senses. The more memos and reports issued, the fewer read, studied, and acted upon. Many people pay little attention to direct-mail advertisements because they are overwhelmed by them.

The other extreme, too little communication, also presents problems. If communications are too infrequent, individuals may lack information needed to perform their work effectively. It is common to hear an employee complain, "I haven't gotten the word yet so I don't know what to do."

Too little communication also creates psychological problems. Most of us crave attention. When communication is too infrequent, an individual may feel unwanted and may become depressed, resentful, or angry.

There is no easy way to determine how frequently communications should take place. Determining the ideal frequency always involves trade-offs and is therefore a judgmental matter. Table 18–2 shows examples of questions to ask to determine the best frequency of communications.

**Be Empathic: Trade Minds with the People You Want to Influence**

A key purpose of many messages is to get people to act in a desired way. To succeed in attaining this goal it is helpful to ask oneself, "If I were the message receiver, how would I react to this message? Would I understand it? Act positively on it?" Table 18–3 shows examples of different communications situations and "trade minds" questions that one might ask.

In using the "trade minds" technique, a message sender should consider the other person's situation (including his or her interests, income, intelligence, and background); ask, "If I were in the other person's situation, how would I react to this?"; and then prepare the communication that would be appropriate for the other person.

**TABLE 18-2**

**Examples of Questions to Ask to Determine the Best Frequency of Communications**

| Type of Communication | Questions |
|---|---|
| Performance evaluation under an MBO program | • What are the pros and cons of performing the evaluation monthly? Quarterly? Annually?<br>• How would the frequency of the evaluation affect morale? Performance? |
| Report to stockholders, limited partners, or other investors | • Are quarterly reports necessary or would an annual report be adequate?<br>• What cost factors are involved? |
| Student grade reports | • How does the frequency of grade reports relate to student learning?<br>• Would time spent by the professor compiling grade reports be better used in preparing teaching materials? |
| Computer printout of sales, expenses, and other financial information | • How important is the information?<br>• How frequently must plans be revised to meet changing conditions? |
| Manager meetings | • How much cost would each meeting involve?<br>• What tangible and intangible benefits would result from the meetings?<br>• Is there new information managers should have? |

**Get People's Attention**

Keeping in mind the enormous competition for an individual's attention, it is to a manager's advantage to condition people to receive messages. All of us have heard such expressions as "Pay attention," "Let me have your attention," "Now

**TABLE 18-3**

**Examples of the "Trade Minds" Technique**

| Situation | For Best Results, Ask Yourself . . . |
|---|---|
| Giving someone work instructions | "Looking at this from the viewpoint of someone who is new to the job, have I made myself clear?" |
| Writing an advertisement | "If I were a typical prospective buyer, how would I react to this ad?" |
| Telephone manners | "If I were the other person, what would I think of my telephone voice and manners?" |
| Manner of giving orders | "Would I like to carry out orders if they were given to me the way I give them to others?" |
| Appearance | "What would I think of my superior if he or she were dressed like me?" |
| Preparing a speech | "Considering the background and interests of the audience, what would I think of this remark?" |

hear this," or "Listen carefully" at work, in the military, or at home. These statements try to condition receivers to give more of their attention to the message.

The failure of individuals to give their attention to a message varies greatly, and it is not just a factor of intelligence. Some highly intelligent managers may tune off and do not receive most of the messages aimed at them.

Conditioning people to pay attention to messages is not easy. Some people ignore signs that warn of danger or indicate one-way traffic or some other hazard.

Words are abstractions; unless we know the language, a word has no meaning. But as we learn a language we associate nouns such as "mountain," "money," "man," "woman," and "car," with mental images. Then our mental images of such nouns are modified and sharpened by using adjectives. Thus, our image of a car is modified by words such as "big," "small," "expensive," "old," and "red."

Pictures, charts, diagrams, and other visual devices are always much less abstract than words ("One picture is worth a thousand words"). Their use often helps to clarify a report, a sales presentation, or another message. The person designing a message does well to ask, "Can I use some kind of visual aid to explain this subject?"

**Use Visual Devices If Appropriate**

In some situations, particularly those in which people are being taught to perform an activity, several devices should be used to deliver the message. Assume that a football coach wants to teach his team a new play. He may begin by diagramming it on a chalkboard; next he may show movies of how the play was carried out by another team; and finally he may have the team practice "running" the play. In many forms of training, such as instruction on how to make a sale, drive a truck, or operate a machine, a four-element technique is used: (1) a written explanation of "how," (2) an oral explanation of "how," (3) a visual explanation of "how," and (4) a practice demonstration of "how."

In some situations the message must be delivered by an actual demonstration if it is to be understood. How can one teach someone to put on a blouse, operate a typewriter, or repair an engine without demonstrating? While some people may be able to learn solely from written or spoken instructions, an actual demonstration usually facilities the learning process.

With many messages, such as those conveyed in training programs and advertising campaigns, multimedia communications are recommended. The more senses (sight, sound, smell, touch, and taste) that become involved, the more likely that the message will be understood.

**Use a Combination of Communication Media**

It is said that Plato, one of the most widely read authors in history, rewrote the introduction to his *Republic* seven times before he was satisfied. Many managers would do well to follow Plato's self-imposed, hard-to-satisfy example.

Certainly, those who prepare messages intended for a large number of people should not release them until the communication is as simple, clear, and concise as possible. Following this practice saves the time of the message receiver and helps ensure that he or she will do what the message sender wants.

**Put More Work into Communications**

In practice, however, managers—even at high levels—often issue compli-cated, confusing, and lengthy statements to lower-level managers. The result may be misunderstandings, arguments, resignations, and other difficulties that could have been avoided if the statement had been reworked and polished. And every day, in all kinds of organizations, work instructions are not carefully prepared. The result can be disappointing employee performance.

## Develop an Effective Feedback System

One way to make sure people understand a message is to develop a system whereby they indicate to the sender that they understand. We are all familiar with the message sent by the fellow on the bus: "Tie a yellow ribbon around the old oak tree." When he sent the message, presumably by letter, he asked for feedback, or a reaction to the message.

Various methods are used in a feedback system. Aircraft pilots, for example, acknowledge orders to indicate that they understood the message. In some military units individuals are required to repeat the instructions they receive from their superior. In this way the sender knows that the subordinate understands what he or she is expected to do and that no message distortion has occurred.

International Paper Company provides a good example of effective internal communications. For many years the company had experienced difficulty in its labor relations. Finally, senior management realized that the solution was to reevaluate its system of employee communications. Management's rationale was that if employees and union leaders had realistic facts about the company prior to labor negotiations, better agreements would result.

"The first step in this evaluation process was a review of all of the company's employee communications, from regularly issued publications to bulletin boards and meetings. The analysis included the type of information provided, the sources and accuracy of the information, the content and quality of every publication, how often each one came out, and who was getting copies."[2]

The result of this survey of group publications throughout the company was the creation of a new structure for internal communications. Publications would be designed to ensure the following:

- *Editorial control*—Provision of information that was consistent, concise, and useful to its target audience
- *Distribution control*—Provision of information to the people who need it, when they need it, at the lowest cost possible
- *Coordination*—Insuring that each form of internal communication serves a well-defined, unduplicated purpose.[3]

Furthermore, improved publications were only one part of the revised com-munications system. The company also took steps to improve other forms of communication. For example, previously, top executives met to discuss key issues

[2]Gerard Tavernier, "Using Employee Communications to Support Corporate Objectives," *Management Review*, November 1980, p. 10.
[3]Adapted, by permission of the publisher, from "Using Employee Communications to Support Corpo-rate Objectives" by Gerald Tavernier, pp. 8–13, *Management Review,* November 1980 © 1980 by AMACOM, a division of American Management Associations, New York.

at two to three-day conferences. Some of these top executives shared the information they learned with their managers; others did not. Now the company makes a videotape summarizing the conferences, which is then distributed to all managers. The managers are then able to discuss key issues intelligently with their employees. All managers are under heavy pressure to keep employees informed about what the company is doing and why.

Because communicating is expensive, one of the best ways to improve its effectiveness is for managers to ask questions that may lead to better, more economical ways of transmitting information. Table 18–4 shows examples of questions managers should ask.

## IMAGE BUILDING AND COMMUNICATIONS

To this point the communications process and ways to make the transmission of information more effective have been discussed. On a broader level, an important aspect of communications involves the creation of an organizational image or corporate identity.

Over time, people develop an **image**—a mental conception or impression—of an organization. At the extremes, people may have very negative or exceptionally positive attitudes toward an enterprise. Some examples of corporate images are "That's a progessive business, on the move—they use the most up-to-date equipment and their people are first-class" "The company makes good products and I like the people who work there" and "ZYZ Oil Company gouges the public and is helping to destroy the environment."

The image an organization communicates is important for several reasons. First, it helps determine the number of customers that the organization attracts. People tend to avoid patronizing businesses that have a bad image. Second, the image an organization projects is a key factor in attracting personnel. Most people, especially the best qualified, want to work for organizations that are perceived as progressive and fair. Third, an organization's image influences its ability to acquire capital. Investors and lenders are influenced by the reputation an organization projects.

*Factors That Affect an Organization's Image*

An organization's identity is built by a large number of factors. Some of the most important ones are organization name, personnel, clientele, products or services offered, and the building and its location.

### Organization Name

Insofar as the image of an organization is concerned, a rose by any other name definitely does not smell the same. The name given to an organization has a great effect on the way the organization is viewed by the public.

A group of fifty students in no way "preconditioned" about image development were asked by the author to write their impressions of two restaurants, one named Joe's Place and the other named Joseph's Kitchen. The students were given no information about these establishments except that a friend had invited

**TABLE 18–4**

### How to Reduce Costs and Improve Effectiveness of Communications

| Communications Element | Examples of Questions to Ask |
|---|---|
| Letters | • Would telephone calls cost less or be more effective?<br>• Would form letters meet our needs or should letters be personalized?<br>• Should we give a letter-writing course to our managers? |
| Memos | • What guidelines should we follow to reduce the number, length, and complexity of memos?<br>• How can we induce people who receive memos to read them? |
| Telephones | • Should we ask the telephone company to give our receptionists training in using the telephone?<br>• Can we cut telephone costs by using different equipment and services? |
| Meetings | • How can we shorten the lengths of our meetings?<br>• What can we do to get more participation by all who attend?<br>• Can we achieve desired results with fewer meetings? |
| Subscriptions to publications and information services | • Are all the publications and reports we buy being read?<br>• Could several managers share the same information? |
| Major conferences | • Considering overall cost-effectiveness, should we hold major conferences less frequently, hold them more frequently, or make no change?<br>• What is the most economical location for major meetings?<br>• Are we inviting only the people who should attend? |
| Performance review meetings | • How frequently should they be held?<br>• What specific topics should be discussed? |
| Computer-supplied information | • Is our computer programmed to give us the information we need?<br>• Could it give us more useful data?<br>• Are the computer reports being used? |
| Word-processing equipment | • Would more modern equipment reduce the costs of preparing correspondence and reports?<br>• Should we ask an office equipment firm to analyze our operations? |
| Travel | • Are we requiring ample justification in support of travel requests?<br>• Do we audit travel expense vouchers carefully? |

them to visit each. They were asked to describe what they would *expect* to find in each place. Table 18–5 summarizes the most frequently mentioned expectations.

In another situation students were asked to give their reactions to two used-car companies, one called John Stevens's Used Cars and the other named

**TABLE 18–5**

**Comparison of "Joe's Place" and "Joseph's Kitchen"**

| Joe's Place—<br>What Students Expected To Find | Joseph's Kitchen—<br>What Students Expected To Find |
|---|---|
| Dirty, greasy-spoon type of place. | Everything suggests efficiency, cleanliness, and a high-class atmosphere. |
| Broken-down bums eat there. | Patronized by middle-income and upper-income groups. Professional and clerical employees eat there. |
| Located in an old, decaying part of town—maybe in a slum or bordering on a slum. | Located in a better part of the city—possibly next to a new suburban shopping center. |
| Coffee served in big mugs that are stained and look unclean. | Establishment looks clean, neat, and orderly. |
| Menu is dog-eared and dirty; meals are identified by number. | Menu is relatively high-priced. |
| Personnel are discourteous and their uniforms are dirty. | Waitresses are attractive and polite. |
| Long row of stools at a counter; only three or four tables, and these are old and dirty. | No counter; all tables and booths. |
| Looks like a place that is robbed frequently. | Makes one feel safe and secure. |
| Everyone there is an adult. Not a place for children. | Considerable family patronage, especially in the evenings. |
| Wouldn't go there; not really safe and would be bad for my reputation. | Would like to be seen there; sounds first-class. |

Honest John's Used Cars. Without knowing anything else about these two fictitious car dealers, students quickly differentiated between them. John Stevens's Used Cars was pictured as having an attractive location, a neat and clean appearance, courteous and well-trained salespeople, fair prices, clean cars, and honest car warranties.

The name "Honest John's Used Cars" had just the opposite effect from what the word "honest" should imply. Without exception the students felt that Honest John was less honest as a car dealer than John Stevens. The feeling was that Honest John would charge all he could get away with. Honest John's Used Cars was visualized as being headquartered in a small shack in a secondary location. Students described its appearance as second rate, with light bulbs strewn all over the area, and its salespeople as low-class, unintelligent, and lacking in integrity. The cars were probably not guaranteed, but, if they were, the guarantee was apt to be worthless. The firm's primary appeal was to suckers.

As a final example of the power of a name, consider the following study:

A recent study by S. Gray Garwood of Tulane . . . shows the impact of expectations on behavior. Garwood compared sixth-grade children with desirable names (Jonathan, James, John, Patrick, Craig, Thomas, Gregory, Richard, and Jeffery) with children with undesirable names (Bernard, Curtis, Darrell, Donald, Gerald, Horace, Maurice, Jerome, Roderick, and Samuel). He found that the children who had names that teachers liked were better adjusted, had higher expectations for academic success, and scored higher on achievement tests than children with names that teachers disliked.

Teachers probably convey their expectations by tone of voice, smiling, creating a warmer learning environment, giving students information about their performance, or actually devoting more teaching time to the students they prefer. Providing more information and teaching time can lead to the differences in academic achievement that Garwood found. The quality of the learning environment can lead students to believe in the teacher's expectations and lower or raise their own expectations for success.[4]

Managers are involved in naming many things—companies, divisions, branches, products, projects, and so on. Since names do affect acceptance, care should be taken in selecting them. Important as a name is, however, other factors are related to image building. Walter Margulies, a consultant in corporate communications, has noted:

> A new name is only a simple, though quite visible, part of a corporate identity program. In some cases, it is only a cosmetic change which could obscure rather than enhance corporate identity.
>
> A single negative example may serve to reinforce this point. When Universal Oil Products changed its name to UOP Corporation, it decided to try to register the initials on the public consciousness by running an advertising campaign that asked the question "What is a UOP?" After all the company's expensive efforts, people are still wondering what a UOP is.[5]

### Personnel

The public also forms impressions of an organization through contacts with the people who work for it or belong to it. The physical appearance of personnel, their attitudes, their abilities, and similar factors communicate a great deal to the public. Employees who are bright, alert, eager to serve, and courteous convey an impression vastly different than personnel who are lackadaisical, indifferent, and impolite.

A corporate image is designed consciously or unconsciously by senior people. But in practice, lower-level employees often do more to create an image than higher-level personnel do. While most people never meet company presidents and other senior executives, the public comes into direct contact with salespeople, bank tellers, repair personnel, delivery people, receptionists, secretaries, and telephone operators. Managers in many organizations would do well to take steps to improve the image conveyed to the public by its first-level employees.

### Clientele

The people who patronize an organization do contribute to its image, but there is not always a correlation between the "quality" of a firm's customers and its success. Possibly the best image can be defined as one that helps the business acquire the kind of clientele it wants. In the example of Joe's Place versus Joseph's Kitchen, many people would feel that Joseph's Kitchen is the better-managed establishment because it has a "better" clientele. However, not all successful businesses appeal to the upper end of the socioeconomic scale. The drugstore

---

[4]Mary G. Marcus, "The Power of a Name," *Psychology Today*, October 1976, p. 108.
[5]Walter P. Margulies, "Make the Most of Your Corporate Identity," *Harvard Business Review*, July–August 1977, p. 71.

with a "cut-rate" image conceivably can be better managed, as measured by financial returns, than a drug outlet that projects an "apothecary" image. In similar fashion, a hotel chain that appeals to lower-income travelers can be (and often is) more profitable than a hotel that seeks high-income guests. The profitability of some chain hamburger, variety, and discount stores also illustrates this point. Comparing two companies such as Joe's Place and Joseph's Kitchen is like comparing peaches with pears.

### Products or Services Offered

To a very real extent people form an image of an organization on the basis of the kinds and quality of products offered. In the case of commercial products one hears such remarks as, "I like to shop there—they have the brands I like" or "They have shoddy merchandise—I won't waste my time shopping there."

People also form impressions of the "products" offered by such varied organizations as fraternities, churches, universities, and political parties.

### The Building and Its Location

In every community more prestige is attached to certain locations than to others. Some locations are more attractive, convenient, modern, large, and clean than others. The image the public has of an organization is fashioned in part, and often subconsciously, by these physical factors.

The building in which the organization is housed also affects its image, particularly in the case of retail establishments. An old run-down building in a shabby location helps to create a depressed image; an entirely different impression is projected by an attractive new building in a "desirable" location.

The "quality" of a physical structure changes over time as the building ages and its environment changes. For decades one of the most prestigious addresses in New York City was the Empire State Building, but over time the location deteriorated substantially. It is common for some organizations to move to new locations from time to time in an effort to revitalize their image.

**Management's Responsibility for Image Development**

Management must bear full responsibility for the image communicated by the organization. In many organizations, little conscious concern is given to the image communicated. But in the well-managed organization, executives give this subject serious consideration.

Once aware of the importance of organizational image, managers frequently ask, "What is the right image for us?" This question is not easily answered because there is no one image that is best for all enterprises. Image has been likened to personality, and just as there is no one personality that is best for all individuals, no one image is best for all organizations.

Development of the right image is a three-step process:

1. Select the primary target market (most likely purchasers) for the organization's products. This may be done in terms of social, economic, or cultural factors.
2. Answer the question "What must we do to develop and communicate an image that appeals to our target market?" Consideration should be given

to the name of the organization, behavior of personnel, the kind and quality of products (or services) offered, advertising and public realtions, existing clientele, and building and/or location.

3. Review the image projected regularly, since internal and external changes occur continuously.

An image cannot be changed overnight. For an existing organization the public already has formed an image; years may be required to communicate a major modification. Very importantly, an image change must be coordinated and carried through in all facets of the organization's operations. Merely changing the organization's name without also changing the way it serves people will generally be viewed negatively.

## Image Building Through Public Relations

For our purposes, **public relations** (PR) is defined as a planned and organized effort by a business to obtain the goodwill or favorable attitudes of the public. Public-relations activities range from publicity in the media to appearances by executives before government committees to community beautification projects.

Public relations has two broad purposes. The first is to interpret company policies and performance as being in the public interest. For example, "We must increase utility rates so we can build generating plants to insure adequate power in the future." The second purpose is to counteract gossip or rumors caused by the distortion of facts. For example, "The statement in the press that we are unfair to minorities is not true. Here are the facts . . ."

Over the years the term "public relations" has become tarnished and suggests to some a mechanical, artificial, even dishonest approach to influencing public opinion. Therefore, some businesses now refer to public relations as "external affairs," "external relations," or "public affairs," hoping that terms such as these will lend greater credibility to the activity of influencing public opinion.

Many large enterprises place great emphasis on public relations. At AT&T, Exxon, Mobil Oil, and Quaker Oats, individuals who head this activity sit on the top policy-making boards.

Public relations activities have been performed in an organized manner for many years. However, new emphasis is being placed on this activity. Business is becoming increasingly associated with public issues such as energy, environmental protection, inflation, taxation, health, discrimination, and unemployment. On matters such as these, business has often been cited as working against the public interest. Louis Banks, former managing editor of *Fortune* (a probusiness publication), observed:

> There is a long-standing bias against corporate business in the general media—among general assignment reporters and editors of television, radio, daily newspapers, and many general magazines. The reasons are complicated and range from simple ignorance of corporate practice to a mindless pursuit of the kinetic or sensational. (One corporate public affairs vice-president says: "If it doesn't light up or blow up, television can't handle it.")[6]

[6]Louis Banks, "Taking on the Hostile Media," *Harvard Business Review*, March–April 1978, p. 125.

# MANAGERS IN ACTION

## HOW TYLENOL USED POSITIVE COMMUNICATION TO SOLVE A PROBLEM

*What Happened: The Event.* In 1982, seven people in the Chicago area died after taking Tylenol capsules which contained cyanide. It was soon determined that the poison had not been put into the capsules in the manufacturing process. Some person outside the company was responsible. Fear swept the nation.

Tylenol is manufactured by McNeil Consumers Products Company, a subsidiary of Johnson & Johnson. Because of the importance of the crisis, Johnson & Johnson senior executives took over management of the problem.

As news of the poisonings spread, sales of Tylenol plummeted.

*Response to the Event.* Johnson & Johnson executives reacted quickly and positively to the problem. They took the following specific steps:

1. Recalled 31 million bottles of the capsules with a retail value of $100 million.
2. Established good working relationships with the police and health authorities investigating the case.
3. Developed a tamper-resistant package. (Later the FDA required all makers of over-the-counter drugs to have tamper-proof packages.)
4. Surveyed consumers to learn their reactions to the crisis.
5. Urged Tylenol capsule users to switch to tablets.
6. Developed a new advertising campaign, "We've worked hard to gain your trust. We'll work even harder to keep it."

### QUESTIONS

1. How else might Johnson & Johnson executives have responded to the crisis?
2. What is likely to have happened if Tylenol told the public: "Don't blame us. We're not responsible for the problem. Why lose confidence in our product?"

### Does Personal Publicity About Executives Always Pay?

Many public-relations firms believe that a good way to create a positive image for a firm is to build a good image of its top executive. On the positive side, personal publicity about the top executive can show that the business is, after all, headed by a human being who is more like than unlike other people. However, personal publicity about the senior executive, like all attempts at good public relations does not necessarily work.

In a speech before a consumerist symposium, John D. deButts, as chairman of AT&T, humorously made a point to illustrate that personal publicity may not pay. His comments follow:

> My appointment as Chairman of the Board of AT&T was an event the news media treated as something short of earthshaking. By the account of some presumably sophisticated observers, the Bell System was simply plugging in another of its bland, interchangeable executives.
>
> Over the next two years I made something like 150 speeches, granted every interview requested, and generally did my best to convince whoever might care that people—not machines—ran the telephone company.

477

So what happened?

Along came a survey by the Roper organization designed to test public recognition of a variety of public figures—from Henry Kissinger to Bette Midler.

The survey showed that two percent of the American people recognized John deButts as a corporate executive. Six percent thought I was a cabinet officer. Three percent thought I was a labor leader. One percent thought I was an astronaut.

Undaunted by that blow to my self-esteem, I pressed ahead. I made 100 more speeches, appeared on *Face the Nation* and *The Today Show*, and even got sued by the Justice Department.

Then there was another Roper survey.

Now, instead of two percent recognizing me as a business leader, one percent does.[7]

He brought down the house.

**SUMMARY**

- The success achieved by an organization reflects the effectiveness of its communications.
- Within an organization, communications flow downward and upward vertically and directly and indirectly horizontally. Much information is communicated informally through the grapevine. Generally, the better informed people are, the weaker the grapevine will be.
- All enterprises initiate external communications with individuals and groups outside the organization, such as suppliers, government agencies, financial institutions, and shareholders.
- Basic elements in the communications process are the message sender, the message, the message vehicle, the message receiver, and the message feedback.
- Messages have two key objectives: to induce people to act and to inform. The complexity of messages varies greatly.
- Message vehicles may be face-to-face contacts, written statements, advertisements, and telephone and telegraph messages. The message vehicle used depends on the situation.
- The content of the message should be shaped with the message receiver in mind because competition for attention is intense and attention span is limited.
- Message feedback indicates whether the communications process has succeeded and can serve as a guide for future messages.
- To make communications more effective, managers should strive for brevity, use vocabulary appropriate to message receivers, strive for accuracy and completeness, be selective in receiving and sending messages, be empathic, get people's attention, use a combination of communications media, put more work into communications, and develop an effective feedback system.
- Factors that affect an organization's image include its name, personnel, clientele, products or services, and building and location.
- Public relations has two broad purposes: to interpret the company's policies and performance as being in the public interest and to counteract gossip or rumors caused by a distortion of facts.

[7]Quoted in John Costello, "Jests Can Do Justice to Your Speeches," *Nation's Business*, January 1978, p. 39.

communicate
internal communications
external communications
direct horizontal communication
indirect horizontal communication
message sender
message

message vehicle
message receiver
message feedback
body language
image
public relations

1. Of the five elements in the communications process, which do you feel is most important? Why?
2. What factors should be considered in deciding which communications vehicle should be used?
3. What specific types of information about the message receiver should the message sender consider?
4. Why is it so difficult to attract and hold the attention of message receivers? What can the message sender do to overcome these problems?
5. Why are many messages overly complex?
6. In your opinion, which is more important for most managers: exercising selectivity in receiving messages or exercising selectivity in sending messages? Why?
7. Why is it wise for a message sender to empathize with the message receiver?
8. How will communications change in the next decade?
9. Why is it often advantageous to use a combination of communications media in presenting a message?
10. Why is image building important to an organization? Do you feel most businesses pay adequate attention to creating an effective image? Explain.
11. Explain why there is no one image that is best for all enterprises.

**1. How to make an ambiguous communication clear**

The following is an actual memo issued to employees via the bulletin board:

TO ALL EMPLOYEES

Effective Thursday, employees who work nights will remain on for several extra hours to help unload new supplies to reach us soon. Those individuals whose names begin with A through L will work on the outside. The others will do it from the inside. There will be extra compensation for this. Your usual supervisors will be in charge. If there are questions, ask them. Failure to cooperate will be dealt with.

The General Manager

Criticize this memo in the following manner: For each sentence state at least two ambiguities that are present. Then, in one or two paragraphs write a clear memorandum.

**479**

## 2. Is a company publication needed?

You are the president of a thirty-five-year old company that manufactures chemicals and employs 260 regular employees. Two months ago you hired Jan Brillo to fill a newly created position of Director of Personnel Services. One of Ms. Brillo's first recommendations is to publish an employee newsletter. She feels this would be an excellent vehicle for communicating important information, such as company objectives, policies, customer relations, and safety rules, to the employees. She argues it could also be a morale builder because each month several employees could be singled out for such things as special work accomplishments, years of service, safety records, and new babies.

What are some of the possible disadvantages to an employee publication?

## 3. Communicating a top management decision disliked by lower-level managers

Top management of the Citizens Bank has decided that its sixteen suburban banks will be open Saturdays from 9:00 a.m. to 2:00 p.m. For years the branches have been closed on Saturdays.

Marge Wilson, one of the branch managers, dislikes the decision. And she anticipates her subordinates will detest the action by top management. Having to work until 2:00 p.m. on Saturday will interfere with employees' recreational plans, family activities, household chores, and the like. To compound the problem, employees will not receive additional compensation. Their working hours will be cut one hour per day for the regular five working days.

The branch managers were told to communicate the decision to their employees. Marge decides to send a memo to her employees and then follow it up with a meeting to answer questions.

Here is the memo Marge wrote:

> To: All Employees
> From: Marge Wilson
> Subject: New Banking Hours
>
> Effective February 12 the bank will be open on Saturdays from 9:00 a.m. to 2:00 p.m. I dislike this top management decision as much as you. In fact, I detest it. Nor is it a wise decision, for I'm sure customer service will suffer.
>
> You will not receive any extra compensation for working on Saturdays. Instead you will work one hour less each day, so the total number of hours worked will remain the same. I think this is very unfair but there's nothing I can do.

What is wrong with the tone of this memo?

Even though Marge dislikes the decision, should she support it? Why or why not?

How could Marge interpret the decision as being good for the employees?

**FOR ADDITIONAL
CONCEPTS
AND IDEAS**

Aaker, David A. "Developing Corporate Consumer Information Programs." *Business Horizons,* January–February 1982, pp. 32–39.

Aronoff, Craig E., and Baskin, Otis, W. "Public Relations—An Integral Part of Your Management Team." *Business,* November 1981, pp. 16–22.

Bellenger, Danny N.; Bernhardt, Kenneth L.; and Hendon, Donald W. "Communicating to the High-I.Q. Consumer." *Business,* May 1980, pp. 43–47.

Brooks, Jeb, and Brooks, Earl. "The Role of Top Management in Negotiations." *MSU Business Topics*, Summer 1979, pp. 16–24.

Crompton, John L. "Public Services—To Charge or Not to Charge?" *Business*, March 1980, pp. 31–40.

DiGaetani, John. "The Business of Listening." *Business Horizons,* October 1980, pp. 40–46.

Divelbiss, R. I., and Cullen, Maurice R., Jr. "Business, the Media, and the American Public." *MSU Business Topics,* Spring 1981, pp. 21–28.

Hughes, Robard Yongue. "How to Get the Truth." *Business Horizons*, August 1980, pp. 15–16.

Hunsaker, Phillip L. "Communicating Better: There's No Proxy for Proxemics." *Business*, March 1980, pp. 41–48.

La Barbera, Priscilla A., and Rosenberg, Larry J. "How Marketers can Better Understand Consumers." *MSU Business Topics*, Winter 1980, pp. 29–36.

O'Keefe, Robert D., and Chakrabarti, Alok K. "Coordination and Communication in Industrial Innovation: The R & D Marketing Interface Problem." *Baylor Business Studies*, February–March–April 1981, pp. 35–44.

Pickard, Geoffrey L. "Using One-on-One Communications for Better Recruiting Results." *Business*, November 1981, pp. 44–46.

# CASE STUDY

## SHOULD THE ANNUAL MEETING BE HELD VIA SATELLITE?

In recent years some national organizations have conducted annual manager meetings by closed-circuit television. Instead of bringing all managers to one location, managers assemble in selected regional locations in theaters or auditoriums. The meeting is then conducted on television.

Alex Hager, president of National Money Corporation, a personal finance company with 3,200 offices, is considering holding the next manager meeting via television. Hager asks Brenda Shartle, the coordinator for the national meetings, and Fred Herman, the company's executive vice-president, to discuss the idea with him.

Hager: As both of you know, I've been toying with the idea of holding our next annual manager meeting by television, and I'd like to have your thinking. This represents such a dramatic change I would want board approval before going ahead.

Herman: I've done some checking cost-wise, and it appears we'd save a lot of money. We could hold a four-hour televised meeting broadcast to ten locations for about 25 percent of what our last two-day meeting cost. On top of that, the managers would only be away one day. Now they're gone three days—two to meet and one to travel.

Hager: Another good feature of a TV meeting is that all managers could attend. Up to now we've restricted the meeting to the 400 middle- and upper-level people. But with TV the 3,200 people who manage our offices could attend.

Shartle: Yes, but the meetings are always geared to middle- and upper-level people.

Hager: No big problem there. You plan a portion of the meeting exclusively for upper-level people — say two hours just for the upper-level group.

Herman: In a strict economic sense, it would cost less and we could expose all managers at all levels to our plans for next year. But I'm concerned about the motivational impact of a TV meeting. Our people really enjoy our annual meetings. Let's face it, the annual meeting has become a tradition. It's part vacation, too. People out there look forward to it.

Shartle: I think Mr. Herman has a good point. As you know, I've been coordinating the national manager meeting for seven years, and I've always been impressed with how much those attending participate. And I know it impresses them very much to be able to talk with the president face to face.

Herman: Yes, the motivational factor concerns me. The managers in Ohio and Texas, for example, won't be turned on by a one-day meeting in Cleveland or Dallas. To them it would mean only work, not fun and work. And keep in mind, we always have an awards banquet.

Hager: But I see so much to support a TV meeting. Control for one thing. The meeting would be taped, so we could make sure there are no mistakes. Another plus is its dramatics. Five years from now a lot of companies will be doing this, but in the finance business it would be a first. I think the managers would be excited. And we'd be sure to get some good press out of it.

Herman: There's another problem as I see it. Our meeting format always encourages participation. Managers raise questions and we answer them on the spot.

Hager: Well, I'm sure we can arrange some way for two-way communication via television.

Shartle: Not if it's all taped.

Hager: OK, we tape part of it and have part live on a two-way basis.

Herman: I think we're overlooking what may be the most serious limitation to your ideas. At our traditional meetings we are in session six hours per day for two days, or twelve hours total. Now the television format calls for only four hours. It would be extremely difficult to compress what we need to communicate into four hours.

Hager: I've still got two weeks to decide whether to recommend this to the board. In the meantime, Ms. Shartle, would you get the reactions of three or four of our regional managers?

## QUESTIONS

1. Based on the information presented, would you recommend a televised meeting? Why or why not?

2. Can you think of other factors that should be considered? Explain.
3. Is closed-circuit television likely to become more important for manager meetings in the future? Why or why not?
4. Do you think that a meeting conducted on closed-circuit television would have as much motivational impact as a traditional meeting? Why or why not?

# PART SIX

# CONTROLLING

Part Six treats controlling, the fifth major function in the management process. Like the other four principal functions, controlling is inherent in managing. The three aspects of controlling—setting standards, measuring performance against standards, and taking corrective action as needed—are critical to the overall success of an enterprise.

Chapter 19, "An Overview of Controlling," consists of a detailed explanation of the three steps involved. For the first step, setting standards, the main quantitative and qualitative standards are described. For the second step, strategic control points, engineered measuring devices, ratio analysis, comparative statistical analysis, sampling, personal observation, and level of satisfaction are discussed as ways to measure performance. Taking corrective action, a key part of controlling, is explained in terms of prescribed and judgmental corrective action. Guidelines for effectively taking each step in the control function are presented.

"Special Control Techniques," Chapter 20, describes the use of revenue and expense, cash, capital-expenditure, time and material, balance-sheet, variable, and zero-base budgets as they relate to the function of control. Guidelines for making effective budgets are presented. Audits and break-even analysis are also explained as control devices. The chapter also includes discussions of the Gantt Chart, network analysis, and management information systems and the part they play in controlling.

"Managing in the Future" discusses key trends that are likely to affect the way the five management functions—planning, organizing, staffing, directing, and controlling—will be performed in the years ahead. The probable impact of the Age of Information on managing is reviewed. The best and worst job prospects for the coming years are also presented.

Part Six ends with a Case Study that concerns a successful subsidiary's losing money.

19   AN OVERVIEW OF CONTROLLING

20   SPECIAL CONTROL TECHNIQUES

21   MANAGING IN THE FUTURE

# 19 AN OVERVIEW OF CONTROLLING

STUDY THIS CHAPTER SO YOU CAN:

- Explain the importance of and steps involved in controlling.
- Discuss the leading forms of quantitative and qualitative standards.
- Describe the relationships between product standards and specific organizations.
- Explain the guidelines for effective standard setting.
- Describe how strategic control points, engineered measuring devices, ratio analysis, comparative statistical analysis, sampling, personal observation, and satisfaction level are used to measure performance.
- Discuss the guidelines for measuring performance effectively,
- Explain the role of corrective action in the control function.
- Differentiate between prescribed and judgmental corrective action.
- Describe how corrective action can be made effective.

**Control**, an inherent function in managing, is needed in all organizations to make sure that plans are carried out and desired results are achieved. In the well-managed organization, all activities—ranging from spending money to producing products and services to monitoring personnel performance—are subjected to the control process. It consists of three steps.

*Step 1 is to set standards for performance of activities.* A **standard** is the model or level of performance to be attained. It is the measure by which performance is judged as "good" or "bad," "acceptable" or "unacceptable." Standards may be expressed in such terms as product quality, profits earned, expenses incurred, sales volume, product rejection rate, number of customer complaints, and rate of absenteeism.

*Step 2 is to measure performance against standards.* The objective of measurement is to answer the question "How well are we doing in meeting the standards set for our activities?" An appraisal of performance leads to the third step in the control process: corrective action.

*Step 3 is to take corrective action as needed.* To *correct* is to amend, remedy, rectify, or in some other way make right what is wrong. The objective of **corrective action** is to "get things back on track" so that standards are met or, if they cannot be, to set new standards.

The three steps interrelate. Table 19–1 illustrates how each step is essential in the control process. Corrective action obviously cannot take place unless there is a need for it (as dictated by the measurement of performance). And, of course, measurement cannot occur unless there is a standard against which to measure.

Many people don't like the word "control." Until we understand what the word means, it may suggest confinement, reprimand, punitiveness, or limitation of rights.

But the function of control can be viewed positively. It is the activity that makes right what is wrong and is therefore one of the most challenging and exciting activities managers perform. Consider just a few situations in which managers have an opportunity to make improvements through control:

- Bill's sales are well below his quota (standard). As his manager, what action would you take?
- More products prove defective than is allowable under the production standard. What would you do?
- A police officer has been found guilty of using excessive force (more than the standard permits). What would you do?
- Senior management sets a goal of 10 percent more profit than last year. The company earns only 1 percent more. What would you do?
- A student is failing a course, meaning her grades are below a passing standard. What would you do?

Furthermore, control is necessary if an organization is to operate efficiently. Imagine for a moment what would happen in a university if no controls existed to ensure that plans were implemented as designed. First, there would be no way to determine whether deans, department heads, and other administrators were spending money as the senior officers of the university intended. Money intended for instruction might be spent on a useless activity. And if standards were not set and actual performance against them was not measured, the quality of instruction would probably go down, food service would deteriorate, more property would be stolen, and the overall quality of the educational experience would decline. In brief, in the absence of a control system, students would end up being cheated.

A system to ensure that plans are carried out is essential in managing all types of organizations. For example, if controls were not placed on the practice of medicine, many more people would die from its malpractice. Controls help all

**TABLE 19–1**

Measuring Performance Against Standards Leads to Corrective Action

| Standard | Measurement of Performance | Examples of Possible Corrective Actions |
|---|---|---|
| There should be a net profit of 6 percent on sales for the fiscal year. | Company makes no profit. | • Replace managers considered responsible.<br>• Make modifications in product line.<br>• Reprice certain products. |
| Joe Brown should produce eight units per day. | Joe produces six units per day. | • Give Joe additional training.<br>• Terminate Joe.<br>• Revise the standard downward.<br>• Transfer Joe to another job.<br>• Provide Joe with a different machine. |
| Budgeted expenses for Joan's trip to New York are $1,210. | Joan spends $1,530. | • Evaluate why expenses totaled more than the budget and, if they are not justified, reprimand Joan.<br>• Don't approve future travel requests.<br>• Consider the matter a learning experience, and explain to Joan why personnel must live within travel budgets. |
| Inventory level should be 100 units at the end of the month. | Inventory level is 165 units. | • Conduct special sale to move surplus units.<br>• Counsel manager to show him or her how to avoid the problem in the future.<br>• Reduce prices.<br>• Increase promotion.<br>• Remove manager. |
| Sales volume should be $1 million annually for each store in a chain. | Store B has sales volume of $1.4 million. | • Revise standard upward.<br>• Promote manager of Store B to position of more responsibility. |
| All employees in Area D are required to wear a hard hat. | Jim Wilson receives a head injury. He was not wearing a hard hat. | • Terminate Jim.<br>• Discipline Jim.<br>• Counsel Jim about the importance of obeying the hard-hat rule.<br>• Communicate the rule more effectively to personnel. |
| Sixty percent of a construction project is to be completed within ninety days. | Forty-six percent of the project is finished after ninety days. | • Initiate overtime to put project back on schedule.<br>• If the problem relates to suppliers, discuss problem with them.<br>• If the problem is due to labor relations, seek solution.<br>• Reconsider original standard. Is it too high?<br>• Put new manager in charge. |

managers answer a critically important question: "How well are we doing?" Controls also help managers devise ways to improve performance that is below standard.

# STEP 1 IN CONTROL: SETTING STANDARDS

Failure to set standards is a common weakness in managing. Frequently, what constitutes "an honest day's work" or "good service" or "prompt delivery" is not spelled out. In the absence of clearly defined performance standards, effective control is impossible.

Performance standards are needed for all activities performed in an enterprise. In the absence of standards we cannot answer such questions as "Is Ms. Rothwell performing competently?" "Should we discontinue Brand A?" "Is our advertising agency doing a good job?" and "Is product scrappage at a satisfactory level?" In a sense, standards are performance targets. When they are set, managers attempt to at least meet them and, perhaps, exceed them. Set standards may be either quantitative or qualitative.

Quantitative Standards

**Quantitative standards** are criteria for judging results that can be expressed in dollars, time elapsed, percentages, weights, distance, or some other numerical fashion. Quantitative standards have two basic advantages. First, they are reasonably precise. Adequate performance is indicated in terms managers understand. For example, if a revenue standard is set at $120,000 per store per month, managers know what is expected of them. They may not agree with the standard (feeling it is too high or even too low), but they understand it.

A second advantage of quantitative standards is the relative ease with which they are measured. Tens of thousands of control devices, ranging from simple thermostats to elaborate computer programs, have been developed to compare performance against standards automatically. Even when mechanical or electronic devices cannot be used to measure results, quantitative standards are easy to measure because they mean about the same thing to all managers.

Some of the most frequently used quantitative standards are discussed in the following sections.

### Time Standards

Time standards indicate how much time should be required to achieve a specific result. Examples of time standards are: average time per letter typed should be eight minutes; each employee will work 37½ hours per week; construction of a new house should take sixty working days; flight time between Atlanta and Chicago is 103 minutes; and interview time per employee is limited to thirty minutes.

### Cost Standards

Cost standards indicate how much money should be spent to perform an activity. Examples of cost standards are: material cost per unit should be $42.60; labor cost per unit should be $16.60; and cost of supplies should be $800 per month.

### Revenue Standards

Revenue standards indicate how much income should be received from specific operations or activities. Examples of revenue standards are: revenue per salesperson per month should be $78,000; sales volume should be $8 million per quarter; product X should generate $266,000 in revenue for the first year; revenue per passenger bus mile should be seven cents; and average sales per customer should be $188.

### Historical Data

Managers often use past results as a basis for estimating future satisfactory performance. A farmer may know from records kept over a five-year period that average corn production per acre on a certain plot is 100 bushels. The farmer may then use 100 bushels as the standard for future years.

Historical standards, while convenient and easily established, have a major weakness in that they do not take into consideration changes in methods and techniques that may occur in the future. The farmer in the above example may use more or less fertilizer for the next year's crop, plant a different kind of seed, plant earlier or later than normal, or in some other way change the production plan. And future weather conditions may differ significantly from those in the past.

Historical data are often a useful guide but generally should be supplemented with other inputs in setting a standard.

### Market Share

Many firms develop a performance standard that concerns the percentage of the total market they want to acquire. Thus a major automobile company may aim for a market share of 22 percent of all units sold, or a beverage company may seek to attain a market share of 36 percent of all products of its type.

A problem with using market share as a standard is that it does not, by itself, indicate profitability or "bottom-line results." For example, to acquire or maintain a certain share of the market may require that a firm cut prices unrealistically or spend an excessive amount for promotion. Or a company may spend too much money on new product development in an effort to maintain its market position. Actions such as these may greatly shrink profits.

### Productivity

Standards for productivity are needed for all activities in an enterprise. Standards for measuring sales productivity might be expressed as sales per employee per day, week, or other time period; sales per square foot in a retail outlet; or sales per distribution outlet.

Meanwhile, standards for measuring production productivity might be stated as units produced per man-hour worked, units produced per machine per shift, or scrap or waste per machine per shift.

Productivity is a key standard, since it indicates the efficiency with which operations are conducted. As is true for all standards, however, deciding what the standard should be is difficult. Variables that should be considered in setting productivity standards include past performance, degree of mechanization or automation, employee training, incentives, and standards in similar enterprises. Judgment usually plays a role in the setting of productivity standards.

### Return on Investment (Return on Stockholder Equity)

As a form of standard, **return on investment** (ROI) is the ratio of net income (or earnings) to invested capital (or stockholders' equity). For example, if the total net income is $2 million and the total invested capital is $10 million, the ROI is 20 percent.

$$\frac{\$ \ 2 \ \text{million}}{\$10 \ \text{million}} = 20 \ \text{percent}$$

The annual *Fortune* magazine study of the 500 largest industrial companies, published in May of each year, shows return on investment for all firms included. Table 19–2 shows the ten companies that had the highest ROIs in 1982 and the median ROIs for major industries surveyed in 1982 and 1981.

Companies with multiple divisions and multiple product lines often use ROI as a measuring device for different divisions and different products as well as for the company as a whole. In this way managers of divisions and products can see how well they have employed the capital assets assigned to them.

An important advantage of using ROI as a standard is that doing so causes managers to focus on a key result area—the use of capital. (A *key result area* is an aspect of a company's operations that has a direct bearing on profitabiity of operations. Examples include production costs, sales volume, interest expense, and cost of sales.) Using ROI is far superior to using only market share as a standard, since a firm can have a large share of the market and yet operate at a loss. A second benefit of ROI is that it forces managers to examine all facets of the business, such as turnover, sales, working capital, inventory levels, capital investment, production costs, sales costs, and transportation expenses. All these factors influence the profitability of an enterprise, which in turn helps to determine how much the business earned on its invested capital.

On the negative side, in calculating ROI it may be necessary to allocate general costs, such as administrative expenses, among several divisions or product lines. Unless the cost-accounting system is comprehensive and equitably designed, managers of different divisions or product lines may feel the ROI figures arrived at do not adequately represent their performance. In a large company one division may have had a very successful year in terms of profits, but another division may have performed so badly that the enterprise as a whole showed no return on investment. In cases such as these, care should be taken to ensure that the successful managers are not blamed for the overall poor corporate performance.

A second limitation of using ROI as a standard is the complexity of the calculations. Accounting theories and practices vary considerably, and two accounting managers may arrive at different ROIs depending on how depreciation and other costs are treated.

### Profitability (Return on Sales)

While ROI indicates the ratio of net profit to invested capital, **profitability** (also called "return on sales") can be expressed as a ratio of net profits to sales. For example, if a firm earns profits of $5 million on sales of $50 million, the profitability rate is 10 percent:

TABLE 19–2

493

**Return on Stockholders' Equity**

| The Ten Highest | Sales Rank* | Percent† |
|---|---|---|
| Rath Packing | 490 | 128.3% |
| United Merchants & Manufacturers | 423 | 60.2 |
| Brunswick | 274 | 52.8 |
| Lockheed | 56 | 49.5 |
| Coleco Industries | 444 | 48.5 |
| Tosco | 112 | 43.8 |
| Morton Norwich Products | 295 | 35.6 |
| Monfort of Colorado | 296 | 34.5 |
| GAF | 394 | 32.6 |
| American Home Products | 76 | 30.4 |
| **The Industry Medians** | **1982** | **1981** |
| Musical instruments, toys, sporting goods | 32.6% | 9.2% |
| Pharmaceuticals | 16.9 | 18.0 |
| Beverages | 16.7 | 19.2 |
| Soaps, cosmetics | 16.0 | 16.8 |
| Publishing, printing | 15.5 | 16.4 |
| Food | 15.3 | 14.4 |
| Measuring, scientific, photographic equipment | 12.8 | 15.6 |
| Petroleum refining | 12.5 | 16.4 |
| Office equipment (includes computers) | 12.4 | 13.3 |
| Apparel | 12.3 | 16.2 |
| Electronics, appliances | 11.7 | 14.3 |
| Metal products | 11.7 | 14.1 |
| Aerospace | 11.7 | 15.0 |
| Mining, crude-oil production | 9.0 | 17.6 |
| Chemicals | 8.6 | 13.5 |
| Shipbuilding, railroad and transportation equipment | 8.6 | 14.4 |
| Industrial and farm equipment | 8.5 | 13.9 |
| Paper, fiber, and wood products | 8.0 | 12.0 |
| Textiles, vinyl flooring | 6.3 | 7.8 |
| Motor vehicles | 5.1 | 7.6 |
| Glass, concrete, abrasives, gypsum | 4.3 | 9.6 |
| Rubber, plastic products | 1.9 | 10.4 |
| Metal manufacturing | .0 | 12.4 |
| Leather | N.A. | N.A. |
| Furniture | N.A. | N.A. |
| Tobacco | N.A. | 19.5 |
| Jewelry, silverware | N.A. | N.A. |
| All industries | 10.9 | 13.8 |

*Sales Rank indicates rank among the 500 leading industrial companies.
†Percent indicates the percent of return on stockholders equity.

Source: "The *Fortune* Directory," *Fortune*, May 2, 1983, p. 248. Reprinted by permission.

$$\frac{\$ \ 5 \ \text{million}}{\$50 \ \text{million}} = 10 \ \text{percent}$$

Profitability standards may be based on past experience, performance of other firms in the industry, and judgment. Table 19–3 shows the ten companies (among the *Fortune 500* leading industrial firms) that had the highest profitability ratios in 1982 and the median profitability ratios for major industries surveyed in 1982 and 1981.

**TABLE 19–3**

**Return on Sales**

| The Ten Highest | Sales Rank* | Percent† |
|---|---|---|
| Fort Howard Paper | 433 | 17.2% |
| Brunswick | 274 | 17.0 |
| United Merchants & Manufacturers | 423 | 17.0 |
| SmithKline Beckman | 131 | 15.3 |
| Joseph E. Seagram & Sons | 225 | 15.2 |
| Brown Forman Distillers | 415 | 15.0 |
| Capital Cities Communications | 384 | 14.5 |
| Standard Oil (Ohio) | 21 | 14.3 |
| International Flavors & Fragrances | 478 | 14.1 |
| Eli Lilly | 132 | 13.9 |

| The Industry Medians | 1982 | 1981 |
|---|---|---|
| Pharmaceuticals | 9.9% | 9.1% |
| Publishing, printing | 6.5 | 7.1 |
| Musical instruments, toys, sporting goods | 6.1 | 3.4 |
| Measuring, scientific, photographic equipment | 5.9 | 6.9 |
| Office equipment (includes computers) | 5.9 | 6.1 |
| Beverages | 5.4 | 5.5 |
| Soaps, cosmetics | 5.2 | 5.0 |
| Electronics, appliances | 4.5 | 4.4 |
| Chemicals | 4.0 | 5.4 |
| Petroleum refining | 4.0 | 4.4 |
| Metal products | 3.8 | 4.4 |
| Apparel | 3.4 | 3.4 |
| Food | 3.3 | 3.3 |
| Paper, fiber, and wood products | 3.2 | 5.0 |
| Industrial and farm equipment | 3.2 | 4.6 |
| Mining, crude-oil production | 3.0 | 11.7 |
| Shipbuilding, railroad and transportation equipment | 2.8 | 4.5 |
| Aerospace | 2.8 | 4.0 |
| Textiles, vinyl flooring | 2.1 | 2.9 |
| Motor vehicles | 1.7 | 2.6 |
| Glass, concrete, abrasives, gypsum | 1.5 | 3.1 |
| Rubber, plastic products | .9 | 3.0 |
| Metal manufacturing | .0 | 4.4 |
| Leather | N.A. | N.A. |
| Furniture | N.A. | N.A. |
| Tobacco | N.A. | 7.9 |
| Jewelry, silverware | N.A. | N.A. |
| All Industries | 3.6 | 4.6 |

*Sales Rank indicates rank among the 500 leading industrial companies.
†Percent indicates the percent of return on stockholders equity.

Source: "The *Fortune* Directory," *Fortune*, May 2, 1983, p. 249. Reprinted by permission.

Profitability ratios are useful guides in controlling operations. If a firm falls below what management considers a fair return on sales, corrective action is indicated. Basically two factors enter into profitability: sales volume and all costs of doing business. Profitability is affected by any alteration in sales or business costs. For example, profitability is negatively affected if the firm paid too much for the merchandise it resold, if production costs were excessive, or if the firm had too large a debt, requiring payment of excessive interest. In any event, failure to meet the profitability standard suggests the need for a careful review of operations.

### Quantitative Personnel Standards

While some standards relating to personnel are qualitative, many can be expressed quantitatively. Objective standards can be set for such items as employee turnover, accidents, absenteeism, grievances, and suggestions received from personnel.

Setting personnel standards may not be easy. In the case of employee turnover, what constitutes an acceptable standard? Last year's turnover? The average for the past five years? The average for the industry? What is considered a satisfactory standard may differ widely. Nevertheless, personnel factors are important in all organizations, and standards should be set for them even if such standards are based only on "good judgment." Without standards, there is no basis for measurement.

**Qualitative Standards**

A basic limitation of quantitative standards is that it is difficult to apply them to all activities. Not all standards can be expressed in time, weights, percentages, dollars, or other numerical measures. For example, a goal of an airline may be "to maintain a good relationship with the union." Does the absence of a strike, walkout, or slowdown necessarily indicate existence of a good relationship with the union? How does one set a quantitative standard to measure the performance of the research department or the personnel department? Because of the difficulty in setting quantitative standards for all activities, qualitative standards are also needed.

**Qualitative standards** are subjective standards used to evaluate circumstances that cannot be measured quantitatively. Examples include: "All employees are expected to be loyal to the organization," "Personnel are expected to regard themselves as members of a team and to cooperate effectively," "Employees are required to be neatly attired," and "In all contacts with customers, employees should have a positive attitude and not display hostility."

Because they are subjective, qualitative standards are difficult to use in evaluating performance. In the examples above, two managers making evaluations may have considerably different opinions about what constitutes loyalty, cooperation, neat attire, and positive attitudes.

**Externally Imposed Standards**

Some performance standards are not set by managers of individual enterprises. Rather, they are imposed by government agencies and, to a lesser extent, by trade and professional associations. For example, the Occupational Safety and Health Administration sets certain standards for worker safety; the Federal Trade Commission sets standards for some forms of advertising; the Food and Drug Administration sets standards for product labeling. Various government agencies also dictate standards for such diverse activities as minimum wages, employment of minorities, and sale of securities to the public. Legal, medical, dental, and accounting societies also prescribe performance standards that their members must meet.

# MANAGERS IN ACTION

## HOW TO CONTROL EXPENDITURES FOR STAFF SERVICES

Staff activities have greatly expanded in recent years due to increased complexity of business, more government regulations and greater use of computers and related technology. According to two observers, "While no management intentionally establishes unneeded staff services, it is not unusual to find the costs for these services increasing at a greater rate than that of company revenues. Still more often, total corporate staff expenses may be reasonable, but the costs of specific staff functions are excessive compared to their perceived contributions."[1]

Clearly, it is difficult to exercise control—set standards, measure performance against standards, and bring about corrective action—for staff activities such as public relations, legal services, advertising, safety, and personnel. As a result of the difficulty in controlling staff activities, unnecessary personnel may be added, staff may interfere with line functions and actual staff costs and benefits are not measured with precision.

Below is a five step approach to better control of staff activities:

1. *Select a Concept of Staff Organization.* Should staff activities be centralized in the corporate headquarters, decentralized among the operating units or should some staff activities be centralized and others decentralized?

2. *Define Mission and Roles.* A mission statement describes the broad purpose of each staff activity and the role statement describes the specific functions to be performed.

3. *Determine Staff Support Needs.* This step helps answer the question, "What staff support is really needed for the organization to achieve its objectives?" Answering this question helps to eliminate duplicated and unnecessary staff activities.

4. *Identify Opportunities to Improve Productivity.* To the extent possible, results of staff activities should be quantified and then compared with money and other resources used to achieve them. This step can reveal waste and inefficiency

5. *Establish a Course of Action.* Once areas of low staff productivity are identified, the final step is to make the indicated changes in staff activities.[2]

[1]"Assessing the Productivity of Corporate Staff Services," *Management Review,* November–December 1982, p. 22.

[2]Adapted, by the permission of the publisher, from "Assessing the Productivity of Corporate Staff Services" by John Hoffman and Orry Shackney, pp. 22, 23–27, *Management Review*, November-December 1982 © 1982 by AMA Membership Publications Division, American Management Associations, New York. All rights reserved.

### QUESTIONS

1. How can you explain the fact that staff departments tend to grow proportionately faster than corporate revenues?
2. Do you feel the five step approach to exercising better control over staff activities is practical? Why or why not?

One characteristic of imposed standards is that they are often minimal. Many, possibly most, enterprises set standards higher than those imposed on them. A second characteristic is that they often come about to meet a serious public problem. The standards governing gasoline mileage for new automobiles were occasioned by a growing dependence on imported fuel.

People are inclined to think that the organization with the highest overall standards is the most successful. In some situations this is true. But there are so many exceptions in practice that no generalization can be made about an organization's degree of excellence and its success. Questions managers in any type of organization should answer are "What general quality level of product or service are we commited to provide?" "What degree of excellence should we seek to supply—low, medium, high, or very high?"

Consider two companies that have decided to make candy bars. The first company, Goodie Bar, sees as its target market the rank-and-file, unsophisticated candy bar eaters, people who are not greatly concerned with health and nutrition and who are very price conscious. The senior management of Goodie Bar will probably decide that the degree of product excellence should be medium or even low. The second company, Bar Delight, selects as its market segment people who are discriminating in food preferences, nutrition minded, and not price conscious. The management of Bar Delight will probably decide that the quality of its product should be high or even very high.

In both companies, the overall product standard determines the guidelines for standards in such matters as product ingredients, production processes, and distribution outlets (see Table 19–4). The candy bar manufacturer aiming at the mass market would probably be foolish to set top standards for product ingredients. It quite likely would price itself out of the market. If the producer aiming at the gourmet candy market bought low-quality ingredients, it would likely fail in its objective. Discriminating buyers would recognize inferior ingredients and not buy in sufficient quantities.

Another example helps illustrate how goals set at the top of an organization help fashion the standards in performing various activities. School A and School B both have M.B.A. programs. School A's objective over the next five years is to get its program fully accredited. School B's goal is to develop the finest M.B.A. program in the region. In this case, because School B's goal is larger than School A's, B will set higher standards for its faculty, library materials, computer equipment, administration, students, and physical facilities than A will.

Deciding on the overall standard—and on subsequent standards for all activities in an organization—is difficult. In business organizations four main factors should be considered:

- *Demand factors*—Demand should be analyzed to answer such questions as "How large is the total market?" and "How much of the market would probably buy a low-, medium-, or high-quality product?"
- *Competitive factors*—Competitors should be appraised to determine their strengths and weaknesses. "Which quality level seems most vulnerable?" is a key question.
- *Resource factors*—A firm attempting to decide what general standards its product should meet should analyze its own capabilities. Some questions a firm should answer are "What level of expertise do we have?" "How much money is available?" and "What is the status of our productive facilities and our distribution network?"
- *Cost factors*—In most cases, as standards rise costs for performing activities also rise. Managers must decide whether the organization can afford

**TABLE 19-4**

**Two Companies in the Same Industry May Set Different Standards**

| Area to Which Standard Relates | Goodie Bar Company Overall Standards | Bar Delight Company Overall Standards |
|---|---|---|
| Quality of sugar, oil, and other ingredients | Medium to low | High to very high |
| Production processes | Ordinary | Sophisticated, highly technical |
| Packaging | Low standards | High standards |
| Product shelf life | Short | Long |
| Distribution outlets | Low qualifications | Selective; high quality |
| Production environment | Meet minimum health standards as required by law | Adheres to standards that are above the minimum |

the higher standards. For example, in manufacturing, a zero rejection rate of parts produced is a laudatory goal. Achieving zero or near-zero rate may be possible if more trained personnel, more sophisticated machines, and more complicated control systems are employed. But management must ask whether such a rejection rate is practical and worth the additional cost.

In practice, management in large organizations may elect to offer products meeting different standards under different brand names.

Whether product quality standards are adequate is a controversial subject and is discussed further in the Issue for Debate in this chapter.

**Guidelines for Setting Standards**

Standards *are* required in managing. The question then is not whether to establish standards for activities but rather how to choose appropriate standards and win support for them. Some guidelines are set forth below.

### Set Standards at Appropriate Levels

The word "appropriate" is a subjective term and therefore means different things to different people. It is used here to mean a reasonably attainable level under existing conditions. If work standards are set too low, human and other resources are wasted; if they are set too high, mistakes, employee frustration, and other problems may develop.

Before a standard is set, as much knowledge of the activity as possible should be accumulated and evaluated. Factual analysis as a basis for setting standards helps to win their acceptance.

Motion-and-time studies made of production activities are helpful in developing realistic standards. In the case of office operations, companies that manufacture office equipment may be a good source of information regarding standards for clerical performance. In setting standards for salespeople, useful information may be attainable from marketing consultants.

# ISSUE FOR DEBATE

## ARE PRODUCT QUALITY STANDARDS SET TOO LOW?

A frequent criticism of American business is that managers set standards that are too low for mass-produced products. Some people don't agree, feeling that the standards set are adequate. Below are some pro and con statements about this issue.

| YES | NO |
|---|---|
| **Quality standards for products are set too low because . . .** | **Quality standards for products are not set too low because . . .** |
| Many domestically produced products, such as automobiles and appliances, wear out or prove defective long before comparable foreign-made products do. | Most consumers will not make a repeat purchase of a product that does not give satisfactory service. The fact that many consumers repurchase the same brand indicates that product standards are adequate. |
| Some producers deliberately follow a policy of planned obsolescence by making products that will have a short life. By doing so consumers are forced to replace the products sooner. | In effect, consumers set product quality standards. For most mass-produced products, there are different qualities available. |
| Many accidents—some fatal—result from poorly made products. | Product quality standards are constantly improving. Automobiles, for example, are much more efficient than they were a decade ago. |
| Frequent product recalls are proof that quality standards are set too low. If producers raised quality standards, fewer products would have to be recalled, benefiting both the producer and the consumer. | If only the highest possible quality standards were set, few people could afford to buy products, and mass production could not take place. |
| Low product standards often make money for the producer at the expense of the consumer. | Business is profit oriented. If more money can be made by producing relatively low-quality products, that is what business will make. |

## QUESTIONS

1. What other pro and con arguments can you offer?
2. Some managers feel that more profit can be made by producing high-quality products than by making low-quality products. How do you feel and why?

The important point is that standards should not be developed without a clear understanding of the work to be done. For example, in setting a performance standard for machine operators at checkout stands in a retail store, consideration should be given to such matters as (1) the training provided in how to operate the machine; (2) the speed, accuracy, and dependability of the machine; and (3) other duties required of the machine operator.

It is common for people to object to standards because "Too much is expected of me." Sales representatives are often heard to say, in effect, "My quota is way too high—there's no way I can attain it. And, if by some miracle I do, they'll only raise it again next year." If management is careful to set realistic, obtainable standards, there will be fewer complaints of this nature.

### Keep Standards to a Reasonable Number

Standards are often criticized and resented because they require additional work. Managers may complain that more standards mean more reports, inspections, and red tape, all of which interfere with their "real" or important activities. In particular, there is almost universal dislike of government-imposed standards because complying with them costs time and money that could be used better in other ways.

In many cases an excessive number and variety of standards do exist, which waste managers' time and create resentment. Some jobs are "overengineered": So many standards are set that measuring performance against the standard becomes too time-consuming. The author is aware of a drug-store chain that set eighty-six standards for the performance of its store managers! Ultimately, after careful study, this list was reduced to twelve, and overall performance improved greatly.

### Have People Expected to Meet Standards Help Set Them

Many people do not like standards that are imposed on them without their having any say in the matter. Participation in setting standards goes a long way in making them acceptable.

Sales personnel may be invited to set their own quotas (performance standards). These may need to be modified as deemed appropriate by the sales manager, but at least the salespeople will be making some input into the standard-setting process. A construction manager can be invited to recommend a time standard for the completion of a project. Again, the standard may need to be amended by higher authority, but the manager will not feel that the completion time has been imposed in a dictatorial way. Whether the task is large or small, those affected by the standard should be invited to help set it.

### Communicate Standards Effectively

It is common to hear employees make such comments as "What do they expect of me?" and "I never know whether or not I'm doing a good job." Statements like these indicate that performance standards have not been communicated. In the well-managed enterprise, each person knows what standards have been set for his or her performance and the degree to which he or she is meeting them.

### Explain Why Standards Are Required

Generally, people dislike or fear standards that are not explained to them. They accept standards much more readily when they understand why the standards are needed. If a senior manager imposes higher standards of work ("Produce twelve units per hour instead of nine") or tighter cost standards ("All departments are required to operate with no budget increases") without explaining why, there is almost certain to be considerable dissatisfaction. On the other hand, if the manager explains why the new standards are necessary ("The company lost money last quarter," "Jobs will be lost unless productivity improves," and so on), acceptance will be greater.

Students will object less to showing the contents of their briefcases at library exits if they know how many books are being stolen; secretaries may not mind a considerable temporary increase in work if they know why it is required; and production workers may willingly accept ten-hour workdays if the reason for them is explained.

When basic standards affecting the entire organization are being changed, it is important that the reasons for the modifications be properly communicated to senior and middle managers. Many management meetings are held to communicate major changes in performance standards. Government officials increasingly hold seminars in major cities to explain revisions in government-imposed standards, such as changes in tax regulations and procedures.

### Condition People to Want Higher Standards

Standards for the same kinds of activities vary greatly in different organizations. Some athletic coaches set much higher standards for their teams than other coaches. Service is better (meaning higher standards are adhered to) in some restaurants, hotels, beauty salons, and government offices than in others. And all students know that a "B" for one professor would probably be an "A" from another teaching the same course.

In addition to winning acceptance for standards, an important art in managing is to motivate personnel to want even higher, though still attainable, standards. Often managers and nonmanagers alike feel that average performance is satisfactory. But exceptional managers view average as the "best of the worst and the worst of the best." To them, exceeding standard performance is a commitment.

## STEP 2 IN CONTROL: MEASURE PERFORMANCE

Step 2 in the control process is measuring performance against standards. It involves comparing what was accomplished with what was intended to be accomplished. Measuring performance is always the middle step in the control process, following the setting of a standard and preceding the taking of corrective action.

A standard serves no purpose unless the degree to which it is met is determined. It is pointless for an instructor to proclaim "We will have a surprise test each day class attendance is below 80 percent" and then not take (measure) attendance. It is useless to set a per-unit production cost of $10 and then not measure actual costs.

Measurement of performance is also needed because it tells managers when corrective action is required. Without measurement of performance, managers have no way of answering such key questions as "How well are we doing?" and "What should we do to improve performance?"

In some situations performance can be measured objectively with considerable precision. In other cases it must be evaluated subjectively. Performance can be measured by strategic control points, engineered measurement devices, ratio analysis, comparative statistical analysis, sampling, personal observation, and level of satisfaction.

## Strategic Control Points

Standards should be set for all activities. And ideally, performance of each activity should be measured against the standard set for it. In practice, however, it is seldom possible or economically justifiable to check everything that is being done. What is very important in managing is to pick **strategic control points** for measurement—those activities that can make or break the enterprise. Examples of strategic control points are noted below.

### Income

In virtually all organizations income is a key control point. Business managers keep close tabs on sales income; trade association and union executives monitor dues; managers of religious organizations and political parties keep track of contributions. A signal that income is off significantly usually indicates a need for some form of corrective action.

### Expenses

Expenses over a period of time cannot exceed income, or the organization will fail. Thus expenses are a critical control point and are of primary concern in most organizations. Key expense data are reviewed daily by some managers.

### Inventory

The level of inventory is highly significant in many organizations, especially those engaged in retailing, wholesaling, manufacturing, and processing. Inventory is not as critical in service businesses, since most services—such as those concerned with hair styling, athletic events, and weight reduction—cannot be "stored" in the literal sense. Nevertheless, managers of hotels and airlines are always concerned about the number of empty rooms and seats, for they mean lost revenue.

For a production enterprise, inventory size is a key control point because it helps determine whether production should be increased, cut back, or kept constant. For a merchant, inventory size may indicate a need to buy more, buy less, conduct special sales, or raise or lower prices.

### Product Quality

Inspection of products to determine whether they meet quality standards is a key control activity in many organizations, such as drug manufacturers, food processors, and automakers. Generally, the more health and safety considerations relate to consumption of a product, the more important quality control is.

### Absenteeism

In most organizations absenteeism is important as a control point. In some situations it is exceptionally important. For example, "How many people are absent today?" is a critical control question a construction manager asks daily, since a certain minimum number of people is usually required for a construction crew to operate. Absenteeism is also a strategic control point for airlines, since absent crew members must be replaced or flights may have to be canceled.

### Safety

In many types of organizations safety of personnel is not a critical factor. However, in construction enterprises, airlines, some forms of manufacturing, and nuclear power plants, safety is a prime concern and is subject to close inspection.

An almost unbelievably wide variety of mechanical, electronic, and chemical engineering devices are available to measure machine operations, product quality, production processes and inventory levels. Often, as in the case of a simple thermostat, the measuring device has a built-in mechanism to make the necessary corrections.

**Engineered Measurement Devices**

To an increasing extent, even human behavior is subject to measurement by engineering devices. Many stores use closed-unit television cameras to detect shoplifters. Some retailers place special tags on merchandise that activate an alarm if the item is carried past a screening device near an exit. In some states and for specific purposes, businesses administer polygraph tests to measure the honesty of personnel. And some libraries have electronic systems that detect individuals who are leaving with unchecked library books.

Many supermarkets use lasers to read the Universal Product Code printed on each grocery item. This greatly speeds up the checkout process. It also eliminates the costly manual marking of prices on each item.

When information from the scanners is transmitted to a computer inventory, adjustments can be made automatically. Items sold can be automatically subtracted from the inventory. Then inventories can be replenished automatically by the supermarket's computer sending information directly to the wholesaler or producer.

Some supermarkets have scanners that electronically transfer funds to pay for the food items from the shopper's bank account to the store's account. The two benefits to this procedure are added convenience for shoppers and lower check-processing costs for both the banks and the stores.[1]

Because of the highly technical nature of engineering devices for measuring performance, an in-depth discussion of them is beyond the scope of an introductory text. But managers who are not trained in engineering should at least be aware that technical measurement devices play an important part in an overall control program.

[1]"Supermarket Scanners Get Smarter, *Business Week,* August 17, 1981, p. 91.

**Ratio Analysis**  To make an intelligent analysis of an organization's performance, it is often necessary to examine the records of similar organizations or of the organization itself from an earlier period. It is frequently difficult to compare individual balance-sheet or income-statement items because of differences among organizations, changes in the marketing environment, differences in the volume of business handled by a single firm, and many other factors. But sometimes a great deal can be told about the performance of a firm, or an industry, by examining the relationship of one business variable to another. This method of evaluation is called **ratio analysis.** The ratios shown in Table 19–5 are widely used by business executives to measure the performance of their own and other firms.

**Comparative Statistical Analysis**  Another useful performance-measuring device is the comparison of statistical data within the organization with information covering similar activities in related enterprises. This method of evaluation is called **comparative statistical analysis.** Trade associations and government agencies are major sources of such data. Many private organizations also collect and disseminate statistical information that is useful in comparing one organization's results with those of another.

The volume and the variety of available statistical information are enormous. For example, without too much difficulty such diverse comparisons as the following can be made: Farmers can compare their per-acre crop yields with those of farmers in other locations; police departments can measure crime rates in their communities against those in other localities; school administrators can compare per-pupil appropriations with amounts spent in other districts; hospital administrators can measure their medical costs against those of other hospitals; personnel directors can compare their accident rates with those of other enterprises; and performances of athletes can be compared statistically simply by reading the daily newspaper.

Comparative statistical data are only a general guide for measuring performance, since no two organizations are the same. Nevertheless, they have a place in appraising results in all organizations.

**Sampling**  **Sampling** is a performance-measuring method that evaluates product quality by testing a few items of an entire batch. Sampling is used to measure quality in many industries, especially those that produce in bulk or batches, such as milk processing, orange-juice concentrate production, and petroleum refining. Sampling is less likely to be used for complicated mechanical products. Most mechanical products, such as appliances, are individually tested prior to shipment.

**Personal Observation**  As noted, there are many mechanical, accounting, and statistical ways to measure performance. But valuable as these may be, they are not enough to make sure that performance meets standards. Personal observation of the work being done and the people doing it is also needed. Personal observation may be either informal or formal.

TABLE 19–5

**Key Business Ratios Used to Measure Business Performance**

| Ratio | Obtained by | Purpose |
|---|---|---|
| Current assets to current debt | Dividing current assets by current debt. | To determine a firm's ability to pay its short-term debts. |
| Net profits to net sales | Dividing net profits after taxes by net sales. | To measure the short-run profitability of the business. |
| Net profits to tangible net worth | Dividing net profits after taxes by tangible net worth (the difference between tangible assets and total liabilities). | To measure profitability over a longer period. |
| Net profits to net working capital | Dividing net profits after taxes by net working capital (operating capital on hand). | To measure the ability of a business to carry inventory and accounts receivable and to finance day-to-day operations. |
| Net sales to tangible net worth | Dividing net sales by the firm's tangible net worth. | To measure the relative turnover of investment capital. |
| Net sales to net working capital | Dividing net sales by net working capital. | To measure how well a company uses its working capital to produce sales. |
| Collection period (receivables to credit sales) | First, dividing annual net sales by 365, to determine daily credit sales, and then, dividing notes and accounts receivable by average daily credit sales. | To analyze the collectability of receivables. |
| Net sales to inventory | Dividing annual net sales by the value of the firm's merchandise inventory as carried on the balance sheet. | To provide a yardstick for comparing the firm's stock-to-sales position with that of other companies or with industry averages. |
| Fixed assets to tangible net worth | Dividing fixed assets (the depreciated book value of such items as buildings, machinery, furniture, physical equipment, and land) by the firm's tangible net worth. | To show what proportion of a firm's tangible net worth consists of fixed assets. Generally, this ratio should not exceed 100 percent for a manufacturer and 75 percent for a wholesaler or retailer. |
| Current debt to tangible net worth | Dividing current debt by the firm's tangible net worth. | To measure the degree of indebtedness of the firm. Generally, a business is in financial trouble when this ratio exceeds 80 percent. |
| Total debt to tangible net worth | Dividing current plus long-term debts by tangible net worth. | To determine the financial soundness of the business. When this ratio exceeds 100 percent, the equity of the firm's creditors in the business exceeds that of the owners'. |
| Inventory to net working capital | Dividing merchandise inventory by net working capital. | To determine whether a business has too much or too little working capital tied up in inventory. Generally, this ratio should not exceed 80 percent. |
| Current debt to inventory | Dividing current debt by inventory. | To determine whether a business has too little or too much current debt in relationship to its inventory. If current debt is excessive, the firm may have to dispose of inventory quickly, at unfavorable prices, to meet its obligations. |
| Funded debt to working capital | Dividing funded debt (long-term obligations such as mortgages, bonds, serial notes, and other debts that will not mature for at least one year) by net working capital. | To determine whether the firm's long-term indebtedness is in proper proportion to its net working capital. Generally, this ratio should not exceed 100 percent. |

Source: By permission of Dun & Bradstreet Credit Services, a company of The Dun & Bradstreet Corporation.

### Informal Personal Observation

Informal observation is commonly used on a day-to-day basis. At the first level of management, it should be routine for managers to observe worker performance and solve minor problems (take corrective action) on the spot. Some activities are measured on the basis of sample personal observations of the activity performed. For example, a sales supervisor need not observe all sales presentations made by a sales representative for a month to know whether the person is meeting performance standards. Perhaps only a small sample—one or two presentations—will give the supervisor a clear indication of what corrective action may be needed. Or an executive may be able to judge the capability of a subordinate to conduct a training session by sitting in on one or two presentations, not on a total series of presentations.

Informal observation is also an important measurement method used by higher-level executives. Consider these examples: The president of a large airline frequently flies incognito on business trips to observe how well passengers are served and whether the crew makes a determined effort to follow all regulations. The president of a university spends at least four hours a week chatting informally in campus coffee shops with faculty and students selected at random in order to acquire information about what is actually happening and how effectively educational standards are being met. The top executive of a department store makes periodic inspection tours of the store, making mental notes of how customers are being served, how merchandise is being displayed, and other key factors.

Personal observation is often the best way to investigate a situation in which something is suspected of not being up to par but the factual evidence (reports, for example) suggest that everything is fine. "I think I'd better spend a couple of days with Manager X and see firsthand what is happening" is a typical comment of an executive who feels some on-the-spot observation is needed.

The main limitation of informal observation is that it tends to be casual. The manager may not be trying to observe specific performance and therefore may not perceive mistakes. On a routine trip through a department, the manager's mind may be at least partially occupied by some other problem that limits his or her ability to observe.

### Formal Personal Observation

Informal personal observation, as noted, may be casual and is not a deliberate attempt to measure performance against a standard. It may be only incidental to some other activity that a manager is performing. The main objective of formal personal observation, however, is to measure performance against standards.

Formal observation, which is planned, is a widely used method for measuring performance. It is particularly useful to help a manager determine, with a high confidence level, whether jobs are being performed with maximum efficiency. Formal observation is a purposeful activity unto itself. To perform it correctly, the manager must give his or her full attention to the person or activity being measured.

Formal observation can be used for a wide variety of situations. For example: The in-flight performance of commercial airline pilots is regularly measured by representatives of the Federal Aviation Agency; the in-class performance of teachers in many school systems is measured by school administrators who observe classroom behavior; the skill and techniques of a surgeon may be measured by a senior medical person who observes the surgeon performing an operation; and the selling effectiveness of a sales representative may be measured by a manager who travels with him or her and observes sales presentations.

The main advantage of formal observation is that it tells the manager whether or not a job is being performed in accordance with standard job procedures. A main limitation is the time required, since formal observation often is a one-on-one situation. For this reason, formal observations of all jobs in an organization is virtually impossible. Therefore, formal observation is often limited to jobs that are critically important to health and safety.

### Scheduled Versus Surprise Observation

When measuring performance a basic question is "Should the person to be observed be notified in advance of the observation or should he or she be surprised?" If people know ahead of time that they are to be observed, they may perform in a better-than-average fashion, thus making the measurement misleading to some extent.

Unscheduled observations tend to give a more normal reading of performance. Many fast-food franchisors make surprise visits on franchisees to evaluate service, cleanliness, and other performance factors under the most realistic conditions possible. Military commanders often conduct surprise inspections to measure normal readiness. Bank examiners have a habit of dropping in on banks unexpectedly so that book jugglers cannot prepare for the visit.

Much information that is useful in measuring performance against standards comes from comments made by customers, employees, students, and others affected by the activity. For example, praise of a salesperson's performance by a customer suggests that the individual is performing well. A complaint about the salesperson's behavior suggests the opposite.

**Level of
Satisfaction**

If workers complain more than normally that working conditions are unsafe, that their supervisors practice discrimination, or that co-workers do not do their share of work, then chances are that certain standards are not being met. If customers voice an unusually large number of complaints about a product's malfunctioning, indications are that product quality is below the intended standard. And when government agencies step into the picture to examine such diverse activities as accounting practices (IRS), relationships with competitors (FTC), and employee safety (OSHA), then indications are that some standards are not being met. Few investigations by government agencies are "routine." Most are prompted by complaints from customers, employees, competitors, private individuals, or citizens' groups.

Managers in all organizations should be complaint conscious. Some complaints may have no basis in fact, but most should be regarded as symptoms of some form of below-standard performance in the organization.

Performance measurement is never easy. But it can be simplified and made effective if the following guidelines are observed.

### Be Economical

Measuring results against standards always costs money and time. Although standards should be set for all activities, precise measurement of every activity may cost more than it is worth. One common waste is requiring personnel to complete lengthy reports that are not used. Another is installing sophisticated devices to detect minute deviations in performance. One way to make measurement economical and still achieve its objectives is to use sampling. Also, managers should concentrate on measuring strategic control points—those activities that have the most impact on the success of the organization.

### Be Prompt

Delays in measuring performance automatically create delays in bringing about corrective action. If a certain product is not selling as planned, the sooner the manager responsible for it knows that a problem exists, the sooner corrective action can be taken. Or if a faulty product is being manufactured or processed, the sooner the matter is brought to the attention of the manager in charge, the more quickly the problem can be rectified. Prompt measurement of performance is particularly important with regard to strategic control points.

### Be Accurate

Inaccurate measurement leads to mistakes in corrective action. Performance of some activities can be measured very accurately by machines and devices of various kinds. But when measurement is made solely by observation, errors may occur unless exceptional care is used.

### Be Systematic

As much as possible, the information used to measure performance should be collected and disseminated systematically. Ideally, no one in an organization should be required to supply the same information more than once. Senior management in a business needs a variety of information about product sales, inventory, available money, payroll costs, and similar factors that affect decision making. Through computerization, a vast amount of needed data can be obtained, analyzed, and communicated if the right management information system is designed. Management information systems are discussed in Chapter 20.

## STEP 3 IN CONTROL: TAKE CORRECTIVE ACTION

The third step in the control process, taking corrective action, is an essential part of control. More often than not, plans are not executed exactly as they were drawn. Mistakes and deviations are extremely common. Corrective action is called for when performance does not meet the standards set for it. A very large part of a manager's job is trying to correct what goes wrong.

Corrective action may involve very simple acts, such as adjusting a machine or giving an employee instructions on how to perform work properly. It may also involve highly complex acts, such as turning an unprofitable company into a profitable one or holding down costs in a period of inflation.

For many routine malfunctions, corrective action is immediate. Overcharging a customer at a checkout stand can be corrected quickly. But for more complex problems, such as reversing a decline in sales, months or even years may be required.

Correcting a problem is often more difficult than discovering it. It is relatively easy to determine that sales are below projected standards or that costs are exceeding the budget. But correcting problems such as these is often very difficult.

Ideally, plans should be developed with prescribed or built-in corrective action. **Prescribed corrective action** is a predetermined way to handle problem situations spelled out in company rules, procedures, and policies. For example, a rule, which is the simplest kind of plan, can be written to include corrective action in case it is violated: "Every lunch box, toolbox, bag, or package must be inspected by a guard as employees leave the plant. Failure to permit inspection will result in confiscation of the container for inspection and termination of the employee." In this example, failure to obey the rule includes corrective action—confiscation of the container and termination of the employee.

Policies, another form of plan, permit some discretion on the part of the manager. However, some type of corrective action can still be built into a policy. Say a policy states, "When a customer is ninety days delinquent, no additional credit will be supplied until his or her file is reviewed. The review will determine the next action." In this case some of the corrective action is prescribed (no additional credit), while part of it is judgmental (the review of the file).

Prescribed corrective action has the advantage of convenience and simplicity. However, it should never be developed arbitrarily. It should always be based on a careful study of previous experience or on simulation of possible results under assumed conditions.

### Prescribed Corrective Action for Routine Situations

Despite the best efforts of managers, some problems are certain to recur. To save time and money and reduce frustration, managers should develop plans with built-in corrective action to deal with common problems encountered in managing, such as absenteeism, machine breakdowns, and unsatisfactory employee performance. Table 19–6 shows some examples of plans for routine situations that include appropriate corrective action.

### Prescribed Corrective Action and Emergencies

Prescribed corrective action in the form of carefully prepared procedures is needed to cover emergency situations—even if these situations are highly unlikely to occur. Banks train personnel in how to deal with robbers, schools have procedures to follow in case of fire, hospitals have auxiliary generators in case of power failure, prisons have standby procedures for dealing with riots, and very elaborate procedures exist to handle the accidental launch of a nuclear missile.

**TABLE 19–6**

**Some Routine Situations That May Be Handled by Prescribed Corrective Action**

| Situation | Example of Prescribed Corrective Action |
|---|---|
| Wrong merchandise is delivered to a customer. | Store employees pick up wrong items and deliver right merchandise. |
| Employee is intoxicated at work. | Employee is immediately sent home. |
| Jane fails to report for work. | Bill fills in for Jane. |
| Product proves faulty. | Employee makes adjustment based on the warranty. |
| Machine A breaks down. | Supervisor calls the repair department for service. |

**Judgmental Corrective Action**

Much of the corrective action that is required at lower levels of management can be prescribed. Higher in an organization, however, judgment—not prescribed plans—becomes increasingly important in deciding how to correct what has gone wrong. **Judgmental corrective action** is not spelled out in predetermined rules, procedures, or policies. It is based on the experience, knowledge and wisdom of the person(s) who decide what remedial action is needed. The make-or-break forms of corrective action always involve judgment. For example, revenue may fall below the acceptable standard, production costs may exceed standards set, or employee turnover may exceed the standard. Usually there is no clear precedent for making critically important corrective-action decisions.

Where judgment is concerned, there are no manuals available to provide solutions. Instead managers must rely on experience, observations of how problems in similar enterprises were solved, opinions of other managers, and the "feel" of the situation to develop appropriate corrective action.

While prescribed corrective action leaves little, if any, room for flexibility, judgmental problem solving permits considerable latitude. There is more challenge in using judgment than in implementing prescribed plans. But there is also much greater risk.

Judgmental corrective action usually requires considerable time and an evaluation of numerous alternative solutions. Say a 400-room hotel, the Sleepwell, is losing money. Occupancy averages 50 percent, while the *break-even point* (the point at which the hotel begins to make money) is 70 percent. The three restaurants and two lounges are also unprofitable. Some of the possible corrective actions that management may consider are: persuade the unions not to demand pay increases for a certain period of time, increase advertising to attract more guests, acquire a new sales manager, reduce the number of employees, remodel the hotel, remodel the restaurants and lounges, lease the restaurants and lounges to outside interests, sell the hotel, rename the hotel, provide better service, raise prices, reduce prices, provide free services such as parking and airport pickup, seek more convention business, replace employees whose performance is below standard, convert several floors to offices for businesses, establish special weekend rates, try to attract a "better" clientele, offer weekly and monthly rates, and convert a portion of the hotel into small suites for retired people.

In trying to turn the Sleepwell into a profitable operation, management in all likelihood would consider numerous other alternatives and take a number of actions to correct the problem. Judgment plays a key role in this process.

Without corrective action, the control function would be incomplete. There is little point in setting standards and measuring performance against them if the problems that come to light are not corrected. The following guidelines are useful in making corrective action effective.

Guidelines for Taking Corrective Action

### Deal with Problems, not Symptoms

Managers should search for the fundamental problem and not base corrective action only on symptoms. For example, lack of employee motivation is one of the most frequently cited "problems" in organizations. But the absence of desired motivation is usually not the real problem. It is only a symptom of one or more underlying problems. Low motivation may be caused by ineffective supervision, unsatisfactory working conditions, or some other problem.

Another common situation many organizations face is inadequate sales of a product. Managers may conclude that the product is simply inferior to competing products. But deeper analysis may show that the product is not being accepted because of distribution in the wrong type of outlets, lack of effective sales promotion, or incorrect pricing.

Table 19–7 shows examples of apparent versus real problems. Obviously, the kind of corrective action needed relates to the actual, not perceived, difficulty.

### Be Prompt in Taking Corrective Action

A common error in managing is failure to take corrective action promptly when standards are not met. An employee's work may have been unsatisfactory for some time, but nothing has been done about it. A professor may have received poor evaluations from students for years, but no counseling has been given on how he or she could improve performance. Unused and obsolete equipment may have remained in a warehouse for years, taking up space and costing insurance, but no effort has been made to dispose of it.

One reason that problems are not solved promptly is that some managers are indecisive with regard to critical problems. A manager may have several alternatives for a corrective-action decision but have difficulty deciding which one to choose. He or she may hope the problem will go away, thinking, "Perhaps the unsatisfactory employee will quit, die, or retire" or "Perhaps the economy will improve and profits will be restored."

Second, human relations considerations often stand in the way of prompt action. For example, investigation of a problem may indicate that the best solution is to dismiss Beth. But Jill, her manager, finds it extremely difficult to terminate an employee, and so Beth stays on.

Third, and perhaps the most legitimate reason for not taking corrective action, is lack of resources. No organization has all the money or talent it would like. As a result, not all problems can be solved promptly. Lack of resources may be a constraint on corrective action. But it should not prevent managers from doing what they can to correct a problem even if the solution must be a compromise.

**511**

## TABLE 19-7

**Careful Diagnosis Is Required to Discover Real Problems**

| Problem Situation | Superficial Analysis of Problem | Careful Analysis of Problem |
|---|---|---|
| Output is below standard. | Workers are lackadaisical. | Humidity is much too high, causing workers to become easily fatigued. |
| Union is causing problems. | Union leaders aren't cooperative. | Managers are not providing a positive work environment. |
| Manager of Department A is not performing effectively. | Manager is incompetent. | Manager has not been delegated sufficient authority to perform functions effectively. |
| Betty and Bob don't work well together. | Betty and Bob are troublesome employees. | Betty's and Bob's desks are too close together. |
| Fred is not performing his job well. | Fred's intelligence is too low to do his job. | Fred has a sight problem, making it impossible for him to read instructions. |

In all types of organizations managers should be encouraged to correct problems quickly. The old saying "A stitch in time saves nine" holds true for most situations encountered in managing.

### Whenever Possible, Build Corrective Action into Existing Plans

Ideally, plans (rules, procedures, policies, and strategies) should have built into them the appropriate action to take if something goes wrong. For example, a clothing merchant may plan to sell all summer apparel before July 15. In the sales plan, however, the merchant probably will include a policy to reduce considerably the price of unsold merchandise after July 15, since it is unlikely that all items will be sold by that date. And, as part of their testing plan, most instructors include a policy on make-up exams that automatically prescribes the corrective action if a student is absent.

Prescribed correction action saves time and is efficient. However, major problems in an organization usually have no prescribed solutions and require considerable use of judgment.

### Consider Constraints

*Constraints May
Limit
Corrective Action*

In taking corrective action, managers should bear in mind that various environmental constraints limit the problem-solving actions that managers may take. As explained in Chapter 3, such constraints may be imposed by custom; organizational charters and guidelines; limited money and personnel; organizational policies, procedures, and rules; higher-level managers; laws and political considerations; the public; competitors' actions; labor unions; the education of potential employees; society; and the economy. Table 19-8 shows examples of conflicts that may develop between what managers may want to do and constraints imposed on their behavior.

**TABLE 19–8**

513

*Summary*

**Examples of Constraints on Corrective Action**

| Problem | Corrective Action Manager May Want to Take | Possible Constraints |
|---|---|---|
| Labor union threatens to strike. | Kick the union out. | Laws forbid it. |
| Students feel Professor Toot Tootle is incompetent. | Fire him. | Tenure rules say no. |
| Coal-mine operator wants to reduce operating costs. | Strip mine and not repair the environmental damage. | Desired action violates laws. |
| Machine frequently breaks down. | Buy a new machine. | Money is not available. |
| Company needs additional sales to meet revenue needs. | Add eight new stores. | There is insufficient capital. |
| Revenue is inadequate. | Raise prices. | Competitors may maintain prices, making raising prices an unwise decision. |
| Organization needs a certain new product to compete effectively. | Produce new product. | Competition has a patent on a highly similar product, making infringement a real possibility. |
| A member of a church violates membership rules. | Expel the individual. | Higher-level managers (for example, deacons) say no. |
| Sales do not meet projections. | Increase advertising. | Senior management decides available money is to be used for other purposes. |
| Apartment builder is seeking a location to build a new, low-cost complex. | Build near an exclusive residential neighborhood. | Pressure by homeowners prevents it. |
| Per-unit production costs are too high. | Speed up production to reduce overtime. | A clause in the union contract says no. |

Wise managers ask questions such as "What are the legal ramifications of what we want to do?" "Will top management go along with this plan?" and "How will our competitors react to our strategy?"

**SUMMARY**

- The control process involves three steps: setting standards for the performance of activities, measuring performance against standards, and taking corrective action as needed.
- Quantitative standards are objective criteria for measuring performance. They are reasonably precise and relatively easy to apply. Quantitative standards can involve time, cost, revenue, historical data, market share, productivity, return on investment, personnel and profitability.
- Qualitative standards are subjective criteria for measuring performance. They lack the precision of quantitative standards and are more difficult to apply.
- Externally imposed standards are performance criteria set by a government agency, a trade association, or some other outside organization.

- The highest possible standards are not always the most profitable. Factors to consider in deciding what quality standards to set for a product include demand for the product, competition, the firm's resources or capabilities, and cost.
- Standards should be set at appropriate levels and kept to a reasonable number. Managers should have people who are expected to meet standards help set them, communicate standards effectively, explain why standards are needed, and condition people to want higher standards.
- Strategic control points for ensuring performance against standards are income, expenses, inventory, product quality, absenteeism, and safety.
- Common measurement techniques and tools are engineering devices, ratio analysis, comparative statistical analysis, sampling, formal or informal personal observation, and level of satisfaction.
- To be effective, performance measurement should be economical, prompt, accurate, and systematic.
- Managers take prescribed corrective action when such action is dictated by previously developed plans and take judgmental corrective action when no clear precedent exists.
- If corrective action is to be effective, managers must deal with problems, not symptoms; take corrective action promptly; build corrective action into existing plans whenever possible; and consider constraints.

**LEARN
THE LANGUAGE
OF
MANAGEMENT**

| | |
|---|---|
| control | strategic control points |
| standard | ratio analysis |
| corrective action | comparative statistical analysis |
| quantitative standards | sampling |
| return on investment | prescribed corrective action |
| profitability | judgmental corrective action |
| qualitative standards | |

**QUESTIONS
FOR REVIEW
AND
DISCUSSION**

1. What is the purpose of control? Mention at least five possible consequences of control being ignored.
2. Explain how the three steps in the control process interrelate.
3. Give three examples each of quantitative and qualitative standards as they relate to control in manufacturing, in marketing, and in finance.
4. Are businesses likely to face more externally imposed standards in the future? Why or why not?
5. Are the highest standards always the most profitable? Explain.
6. What is the purpose of measuring performance against standards? Explain why performance measurement is inherent in the control process.
7. Why is it important that managers know what consistutes strategic control points?
8. Explain each of the following measurement techniques: engineered measuring devices, ratio analysis, comparative statistical analysis, personal observation, and level of satisfaction.
9. How do prescribed corrective action and judgmental corrective action differ? Give three examples of each.
10. Name five specific constraints that may affect corrective action.

## 1. How to prepare employees for a job study

Assume that you are employed in the personnel department of a farm equipment manufacturer. Management has decided to conduct a study of worker performance to find ways to improve efficiency. Part of the study will involve making movies of employees doing their jobs.

The goal of this study is to increase employee productivity. No employees will be released, but the amount of work they perform may be increased in order to handle the steadily increasing demand for the company's products.

The head of production is concerned that employees will resent being filmed, thinking that speeded-up performance and job terminations will result.

Your superior asks you to write a memo to the first-level supervisors telling them how to tell the employees that the motion studies are not to be feared.

Write the memo.

## 2. Pros and cons of very high standards

Standards should be set for the performance of all activities. There is often disagreement among managers regarding how high standards should be set. In report form, prepare three advantages and three disadvantages of establishing very high standards for the performance of one of the following: a clerical person, a sales representative, a computer programmer, or a hospital employee. Then explain how the nature of the activity helps determine the level of performance standards.

## 3. Is the polygraph a control solution to employee theft?

Bargains is a large discount retailer of cameras, televisions, clocks, radios, and similar merchandise. Inventory is maintained on the computer. A physical inventory—actual counting of all items in stock—at year's end revealed four percent less merchandise was in stock than the computer reported. Customers and/or employees were stealing.

The following discussion takes place between Janet Wilson, the store manager, and Bill Brown, the assistant manager.

Janet: We can rule out customer shoplifting. Our control procedures at checkout stands are excellent. The detection devices we installed two years ago are virtually foolproof.

Bill: So you're saying employees are stealing.

Janet: I don't like to say it, but I'm sure they are. I think we have no choice but to give them lie detector tests.

Bill: If we do that, we're going to scare a lot of our people and make some of them angry.

Janet: You're probably right. But I don't think we have a choice. Some of our employees are stealing and they're stealing a lot.

Bill: But some of our people have been with us for years. They won't like taking a lie detector test. They may even decide to join the retail employees union. And if we do go ahead with the polygraph, do we use it as part of the employment process? Do we give it to all employees including the supervisors? And suppose someone refuses to take the test. What do we do?

How would you react to being required by your employer to take a polygraph test?

If the decision is made to administer the lie detector test, should all employees, including Janet and Bill, be required to take it? Should people being considered for employment be tested?

**FOR ADDITIONAL
CONCEPTS
AND IDEAS**

Bender, Paul S.; Northup, William D.; and Shapiro, Jeremy F. "Practical Modeling for Resource Management." *Harvard Business Review,* March—April 1981, pp. 163—174.

Franklin, William H., Jr., and Franklin, Stephen F., Sr. "Analyzing Small Business Mistakes: A Guide for Survival." *Business*, January—March 1982, pp. 15—20.

Hayes, Robert H., and Abernathy, William J. "Managing our Way to Economic Decline." *Harvard Business Review,* July—August 1980, pp. 67—77.

Janson, Robert L. "Graphic Indicators of Operations." *Harvard Business Review,* November—December 1980, pp. 164—170.

Konstans, Constantine, and Martin, Randall P. "Financial Analysis for Small Business: A Model for Control." *Business,* January—March 1982, pp. 21—26.

Leonard, Frank S., and Sasser, W. Earl. "The Incline of Quality." *Harvard Business Review,* September—October 1982, pp. 163—171.

Mechline, George F., and Berg, Daniel. "Evaluating Research—ROI is not Enough." *Harvard Business Review,* September—October 1980, pp. 93—99.

Reddy, Jack. "Incorporating Quality in Competitive Strategies." *Sloan Management Review,* Spring 1980, pp. 53—60.

Ricchiute, David N. "Illegal Payments, Deception of Auditors, and Reports on Internal Controls." *MSU Business Topics,* Spring 1980, pp. 57—62.

Shaginaw, Donald H. "Business Forms Management: Key to Productivity . . . And Profit." *Business,* April—May—June 1982, pp. 49—50.

Smith, Martin R. *Manufacturing Controls.* New York: Van Nostrand Reinhold Co., 1981.

Tewell, Rich. "How to Keep Quality Circles in Motion." *Business,* January—March 1982, pp. 47—49.

Waters, James A., and Chant, Peter D. "Internal Control of Managerial Integrity: Beyond Accounting Systems." *California Management Review,* Spring 1982, pp. 60—72.

Wiegand, Robert E. "'Buying In' to Market Control." *Harvard Business Review,* November—December 1980, pp. 141—149.

# 20 SPECIAL CONTROL TECHNIQUES

**STUDY THIS CHAPTER SO YOU CAN:**

- Explain the nature and use of revenue and expense, cash, capital-expenditure, time and material, balance-sheet, and variable budgets.

- Define "zero-base budgeting," and describe how it is used.

- Identify and describe the guidelines for making effective budgets.

- Explain how audits are used as control devices, including internal, external, and management audits.

- Discuss how break-even analysis is used in controlling.

- Explain how a Gantt Chart works.

- Discuss the use of network analysis, including PERT and CPM, in controlling and planning activities, and note the advantages and disadvantages of this technique.

- Show how management information systems can be used to aid control, note their advantages and disadvantages, and explain how they can be effectively developed.

A variety of techniques are available to help managers set standards, measure performance against them, and take corrective action as needed. Used properly, the control devices discussed in this chapter help managers carry out plans effectively.

# KINDS OF BUDGETS MANAGERS USE

A **budget** is a plan expressed in numbers for the purpose of controlling operations. It is the most important control device. Budgets are used to control not only the use of money but also such other factors as man-hours per project, use of materials, inventory size, and supplies.

Budgets are performance standards. They represent projected results that managers believe can be attained in a future time period. Budgets are always prepared for a specific period of time. Organizations most typically establish budgets annually, although weekly, monthly, or quarterly time periods may also be used. In the case of capital budgeting, the time period may be a number of years.

The overall budget for an organization is really a composite of budgets for divisions, departments, and other organizational units. The chief value of budgets is that they force managers to account for the way resources are used and funds are spent. Deviations from a budget automatically indicate a need for corrective action.

The main types of budgets are described in the following sections.

**Revenue and Expense Budgets**

Sometimes referred to as an operating budget, a **revenue and expense budget** spells out the anticipated revenues and the predicted expenditures for the period in question.

Since most of the firm's revenues come from the sale of goods or services, it is desirable that a careful sales forecast be made. Consideration should be given to past sales, expected changes in demand for the products or services offered, changes in competition, general economic conditions, and other factors that may affect future sales.

To add greater precision to the budgeting process, the revenue budget should show anticipated sales by product, territory, division, distribution outlet, or other organizational unit. A retail store, for example, should forecast sales for each department to arrive at a composite revenue projection.

Projecting expenses is the second step in completing a revenue and expense budget. Specific expense categories vary widely, depending on the kind of business, but the more common ones include materials, rent, labor, utilities, travel, supplies, security, and maintenance. Just as revenue projections should be broken down by organizational unit, expense forecasts should also be carefully assigned so that individual managers will be directly accountable.

**Cash Budgets**

A **cash budget** is a projection of cash receipts and cash disbursements for the budget period. **Cash flow** is a company's total of incoming and outgoing cash. A cash budget is necessary because revenues from sales may not coincide with the amount of cash required to pay expenses. Most businesses are seasonal in nature, meaning that revenues are greater in some months than in others. In seasonal businesses, expenditures often exceed revenues during some periods of the year.

A properly managed cash budget helps a business take advantage of special discounts offered by some vendors to customers who pay cash. A carefully prepared cash budget also helps a firm avoid costly short-term borrowing.

**Capital-expenditure budgets** plan for long-term investments whose expense and return on investment will be covered beyond a one-year period. Typical capital items include buildings, manufacturing facilities, equipment, major installations, machinery, and other long-term investment items. Expenditures are made on capital items in the hope that there will be more profits in the future through improved or expanded operations.

Capital-Expenditure Budgets

Capital items are generally purchased infrequently and after careful study. A major problem in budgeting for capital expenditures is that money is being committed for several years in advance. In making these budgets managers must try to forecast revenues far into the future. Capital budgeting, then, is an important part of long-range planning.

In many organizations, whether or not a product can be produced at a profit depends on the number of man-hours required. A **time budget** shows a forecast of the labor input, usually translated into dollars, required to produce the item in question. Such a budget is an excellent standard for measuring the performance of production managers, for it tells whether they are meeting projected labor costs.

Time Budgets and Material Budgets

**Material budgets** are forecasts of how much material will be required to achieve a result, such as constructing a building or manufacturing a product. Like other budgets, they serve as a standard against which actual performance can be measured.

A **balance-sheet budget** is a composite of all the other financial budgets and reflects anticipated **assets** (what the enterprise will own), **liabilities** (what the organization will owe), and **owner's equity** (the excess of assets over liabilities) at some point in the future. A balance-sheet budget indicates the expected financial status of the firm at a future time if the various other budgets are met.

Balance-Sheet Budgets

**Variable** (or *flexible*) **budgets** are intended to reflect changes in expenditures that result from changes in revenues. Variable budgets try to answer the question "How will a change in revenue (more or less than projected) affect expenditures?"

Variable (Flexible) Budgets

Some expenditure items, called **fixed** (or *nonvariable*) **costs,** are not affected by changes in revenue in the short run. They include property taxes, depreciation, insurance, and administration. But other costs tend to vary with revenue; these are called **variable** (or *direct*) **costs.** Examples include costs for materials, labor, some maintenance, energy, supplies, and selling.

The goal of variable budgeting is to determine how variable costs will change with revenue resulting from sales. Once this is determined, department managers are periodically given, in effect, two budgeted amounts: one based on fixed cost items, and a second to cover variable costs based on short-run projected revenues.

The firm still uses its revenue and expense budget as a basic guide but regularly updates it on the basis of short-term changes in revenue.

Figure 20–1 shows a hypothetical chart illustrating the fixed and variable costs of a business. The chart assumes that fixed costs are the same regardless of whether no or 600 units are sold. Note that the fixed costs do not vary with sales, at least in the short run. The variable costs are shown to increase as sales volume increases.

Variable budgets, like any other kind of plan, should be flexible and should not be regarded as hard plans that must be followed exactly as designed.

Zero-Base
Budgeting

**Zero-base budgeting** (ZBB) is a budgeting method that requires every dollar of proposed expenditures to be justified for each budget period. Previous budgets are ignored under the zero-based budgeting process.

In traditional budgeting—often called **incremental budgeting**—the person preparing the budget must justify any *added* expenditures that are to be made. He or she does not justify budget expenditures that are being carried over from the preceding years; it is assumed that these past expenditures are appropriate and should be continued. Under zero-based budgeting, no such assumption is made. With each new budget that is prepared, the manager must justify every dollar of expenditure from scratch (that is, from "zero base"). For example, the manager of a research department who is preparing a budget would need to justify new requests for funds. He or she would also, however, have to justify funds being spent for ongoing research projects.

Under zero-base budgeting, senior and middle managers arrange the various programs of an organization into "decision packages," for which they evaluate the purpose, costs, benefits, and consequences of each course of action. Top management then selects the decision packages that appear best, and the plans are revised as necessary.

The main advantage of ZBB is that it requires managers to think through their activities and provide maximum justification for budget requests. By using ZBB, managers are forced to break the common budgeting habit of simply saying, "I need X percent more next year to operate my department." For ZBB to be used successfully, five requirements must be met:

- Disciplined systems and guidelines for [ZBB's] implementation are required.
- ZBB must be carefully related to the fundamental, long-range goals of the enterprise.
- Top management in the organization must give full and unqualified endorsement to the concept.
- The ZBB concept must be sold to managers as being in their—and the organization's—best interest.
- ZBB should be explained as an opportunity to innovate and create new ideas, not as a negative suppressant on spending.[1]

[1]Logan M. Cheek, "Zero-Base Budgeting in Washington," *Business Horizons,* June 1978, pp. 24–25.

**FIGURE 20–1**

**521**

*Kinds of Budgets Managers Use*

Fixed and Variable Costs

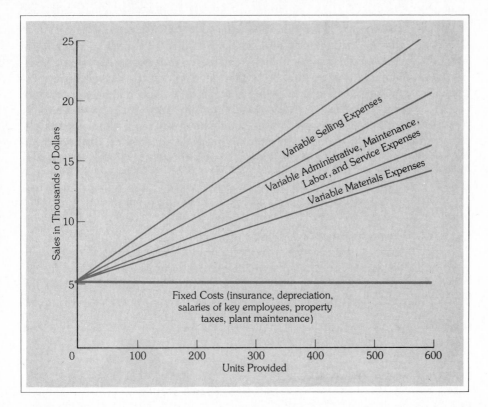

All managers must operate within the confines of budgets, and many managers develop them or at least help in their preparation. Following are guidelines for making effective budgets.

Guidelines for Making Effective Budgets

### Budgets Should Be Flexible

The most common error in making budgets is to view them as an inflexible model for the expenditure of money, time, materials, and other resources. Perhaps this mistake is made because budgets, like other plans, are expressed in dollars, time periods, or other numbers, not only in words. Numbers are specific and mean the same thing to everyone. If events indicate that it is wise to spend more or less during a given period, budgets should be modified accordingly.

### Budgets Should Not Be Viewed as Ends in Themselves

Because of their highly specific nature, budgets take on the aura of laws, not tools to help achieve organizational goals. Managers may tend to view budgets in terms of "thou shalt" and "thou shalt not." They may be afraid to take advantage of opportunities to purchase equipment, raw materials, and supplies at attractive prices; to authorize additional advertising expenditures when such action seems wise; or to take other actions that ever-changing conditions suggest are needed. If managers are to budget effectively, they must realize that a budget should never serve as a substitute for good judgment.

### Those Affected by Budgets Should Be Involved in Their Preparation

A common error in making budgets is for higher-level managers to impose them on lower-level managers, rather then let the lower-level managers participate in their preparation. Participation in budget development by those who are expected to implement them is wise for two reasons. First, managers are more willing to support and execute plans—in this case budgets—if they have a hand in their development. An imposed budget can create resentment, whereas participation in budget planning results in more enthusiastic acceptance. Second, those who are close to actual operations have firsthand knowledge of opportunities for increasing revenues and minimizing expenditures. A branch manager often has better knowledge of how much can be sold in a given period and of what the marketing costs will be than a senior executive in the home office.

### Budget Requests Should Be Justified

For budgets to be effective managers should be required to think through each budget request. Too often one year's budget serves as a precedent for the next year's. For example, if Department A spent $10,000 for supplies this year, the assumption is made that it will require at least that amount next year. Using last

*"I'm afraid, gentlemen, we shall have to add our names to the list of endangered species."*

© Punch/Rothco

year's budget as a precedent for next year's budget is not only lazy, but it stifles incentive to think creatively about ways to use resources more effectively.

### Budgets Should Serve as Incentives for the Efficient Use of Resources

Budgets always serve as incentives but not necessarily the right ones. For example, a common practice in large bureaucratic organizations is to base manager compensation and other rewards in large part on the size of the manager's budget, not necessarily on the efficiency with which it is used. While there is considerable logic in paying a manager of a $5-million budget more than a manager of a $3-million budget, this practice can lead to problems. The manager with the lower budget may reason, "The way for me to get ahead is to justify a higher budget whether or not it really is needed." To "justify" a larger budget, a manager may request more people than are really needed or authorize projects that may not advance organizational goals. Doubtlessly, many large corporate structures and "empires" within government agencies are created because rewards are equated with the size of the budget controlled by a manager.

Another common way that budgets are used as improper incentives is to reduce next year's budget unless the manager spends all of this year's budget. Under such a system it is common, as a fiscal year is about to end, for managers to determine how much money remains in the budget and then spend it for activities that often have little, if any, value to the organization. In the budgeting process, managers who end the budget period with a surplus should be rewarded, not penalized—assuming that they achieved their goals.

## WHAT ARE AUDITS?

An **audit** is an investigation of activities. The term "auditing" is usually associated with verification of financial records and practices. But the term may also refer to an examination of nonfinancial aspects of an organization. Unlike many other control devices, audits are not ongoing; they are usually conducted only periodically.

Two kinds of audits, internal and external, deal primarily with financial data. A third kind of audit, the management audit, focuses primarily on management practices.

**Internal Audits**

Some organizations use their own personnel to conduct financial audits—hence the term **internal audit**. The purpose of internal audits is to examine financial reports in order to determine if they accurately and honestly reflect the financial condition of the enterprise.

One advantage of internal audits is that the people making the evaluation already have knowledge of the inner workings of the organization. Furthermore, expenses for outside experts are not normally incurred.

A disadvantage of internal audits is that the individuals doing the auditing may lack the skills and training required to make the evaluation. They may also lack objectivity. Those conducting the audit may "overlook" certain deficiencies to protect their own interests.

**External audits** are conducted by persons outside of the company—primarily public accounting firms. The principal advantage of such audits is objectivity. Public accounting firms are independent organizations and are required by professional accounting standards to report financial conditions and practices as they actually exist. A second benefit of external audits is that professional accountants generally have much more varied experience than internal personnel. This extra experience is helpful in discovering problems that involve the financial affairs of an enterprise.

A **management audit**, sometimes called an organizational audit, involves an evaluation of the overall operation of an enterprise—its basic strategies, plans, and policies; the competency of its key personnel; its profitability; its financial resources; and its future direction. Examples of questions a management audit tries to answer are "What are our basic strengths and weaknesses?" "How effective are our key managers?" "What does the future hold for our industry?" "What share of the market should we strive for?" "Should any major changes be made in our product line or distribution channels?" "What can be done to better adjust to existing and emerging competition?" "Are we developing managers for the future?" "Are our fiscal policies sound?" "Is our research and development activity oriented in the right direction?" and "What can be done to improve our return on investment?"

Management audits may be conducted by personnel within the organization, who engage in a process of self-study, or they may be performed by public accounting firms or management consultants.

Management audits have two basic benefits. First, they require the evaluators to look at both the specific aspects of organizational activities and the organization as a whole. Second, they may reveal numerous opportunities to improve performance.

## WHAT IS BREAK-EVEN ANALYSIS?

**Break-even analysis** is a method for determining the relationship between cost and revenue at various sales levels. Its main goal is to show the point at which it is profitable to produce and sell a product.

For instance, in Table 20–1, all the prices considered are high enough to cover the average variable costs and make some contribution to total fixed costs. A per-unit price of $50 covers the average variable costs of $25 and contributes $25 to total fixed costs ($150). If we divide the total fixed costs ($150) by the contribution to fixed costs ($25), we know how many units must be sold to break even. In this case, six units at a price of $50 must be sold to recover all costs. This is the point at which costs and revenue are equal:

$$\text{Costs} = \$150 + \$25(6) = \$300$$
$$\text{Revenue} = (\$50)6 = \$300$$

Any sales above six units contribute to profit.

**TABLE 20–1**

525

*What Is
the Gantt Chart?*

Calculating Break-Even Points Arithmetically

| Price per Unit | Total Fixed Costs | Average Variable Costs | Contribution to Fixed Costs | Sales Needed To Break Even |
|---|---|---|---|---|
| $50 | $150 | $25 | $25 | 6.0 units |
| 60 | 150 | 25 | 35 | 4.3 units |
| 70 | 150 | 25 | 45 | 3.3 units |
| 80 | 150 | 25 | 55 | 2.7 units |
| 90 | 150 | 25 | 65 | 2.3 units |

Source: David J. Schwartz, *Marketing Today: A Basic Approach,* 3rd ed. (New York: Harcourt Brace Jovanovich, 1981), p. 287. © 1981 by Harcourt Brace Jovanovich, Inc. Reprinted by permission of the publisher.

Figure 20–2 graphically shows the data in Table 20–1. The points at which revenue derived from selling the product equals costs are shown. The area below the horizontal line at $150 shows total fixed costs. The area above the line shows total variable costs. The other lines show the sales (revenue) associated with each of the five suggested prices. The places at which the price lines intersect with the total-costs line are the break-even points for each price.

Although graphing break-even points gives a good visual estimate of the quantities that must be sold at each price if costs are to be recovered, it does not show the price that is most profitable. For a realistic price to be set, the number of units that can be sold at each price level must be estimated.

**Combining Demand with Break-even Analysis**

The most profitable price, and the fewest losses, can be discovered by incorporating market demand into break-even analysis. If the price is multiplied by the quantity that can be expected to be sold at that price, a schedule of the anticipated revenue can be arrived at in each case. This revenue schedule is then graphed and superimposed on the break-even chart (see Figure 20–3). Because profit equals revenue minus costs, profit is the greatest at the point at which the difference between revenue and costs (the vertical distance between the curve and the total-costs line) is greatest. In this case, the point of maximum revenue equals the point of maximum profit—six units. If costs had dropped sharply because more units were produced, the picture might have been different.

## WHAT IS THE GANTT CHART?

In the years between 1875 and 1920, giant corporations emerged as a result of the Industrial Revolution. As the size and complexity of industry increased, industrial leaders sought more effective methods for planning, scheduling, and controlling the vast quantities of physical and human resources that were required in the

# MANAGERS IN ACTION

## HOW THE NATION'S LARGEST AUDITING AGENCY OPERATES

The GAO is by far the largest auditing organization in the nation and employs approximately 6,000 people, 4,200 of whom are professional staffers. About 70 percent of the professional staff members were trained in accounting or auditing. The other 30 percent are engineers economists, mathematicians, statisticians, and computer specialists.

The General Accounting Office has the following basic purposes: to assist the Congress, its committees, and its Members in carrying out their legislative and oversight responsibilities, consistent with its role as an independent nonpolitical agency in the legislative branch, to carry out legal, accounting, auditing, and claims settlement function with respect to Federal Government programs and operations as assigned by the Congress; and to make recommendations designed to provide for more efficient and effective Government operations.

In general, the audit authority of the General Accounting Office extends to all departments and agencies of the Federal Government. Exceptions to this audit authority relate principally to funds relating to certain intelligence activities.

Where audit authority exists the General Accounting Office has the right of access to, and examination of, any books, documents, papers, or records of the departments and agencies.

The General Accounting Office has statutory authority to investigate all matters relating to the receipt, disbursement, and application of public funds. Additionally, GAO's audit authority covers wholly and partially owned Government corporations and certain nonappropriated fund activities. By law, it is authorized and directed to make expenditure analyses of executive agencies to enable the Congress to determine whether public funds are efficiently and economically administered and expended; and to review and evaluate the results of existing Government programs and activities.

The scope of the audit work of the General Accounting Office extends not only to the programs and activities which the Federal Government itself conducts but also to the activities of State and local governments, guasi-governmental bodies, and private organizations in their capacity as recipients under, or administrators for Federal aid programs financed by loans, advances, grants, and contributions.

GAO's audit activities also include examining and settling accounts of the Federal Government's certifying, disbursing, and collection officers, including determinations involving accountability for improper or illegal expenditures of public funds.

Within this audit authority is a responsibility to report significant matters to the Congress for information and use in carrying out its legislative and executive branch surveillance functions.[1]

[1]*The United States Government Manual 1982/83*, Office of the Registrar, National Archives and Records Services, Washington, D.C., 1983, pp. 41–44.

## QUESTIONS

1. The GAO is the official auditing agency of the federal government. Intentionally the agency maintains a low profile and its activities are not widely publicized. In your opinion is this good or bad? Why?
2. In virtually every political campaign the public hears charges of government inefficiency, corruption, and waste. Considering the size and power of the GAO, are these accusations likely to be valid or not? Explain.
3. To help control fraud and abuse in federal programs the GAO maintains a nationwide hotline which permits any taxpayer to call GAO auditors with information concerning misuse of federal funds. Do you think this is a good idea?

**FIGURE 20–2**

527

*What is
the Gantt Chart?*

Calculating Break-Even Points Graphically

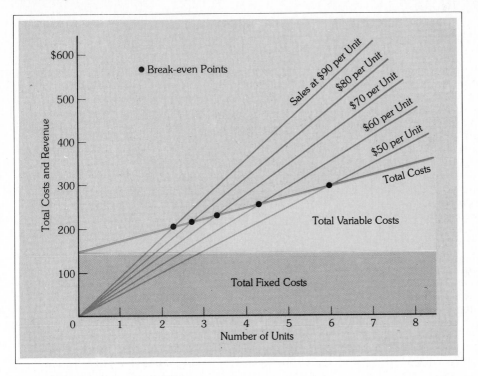

Source: Adapted from David J. Schwartz, *Marketing Today: A Basic Approach,* 3rd ed. (New York: Harcourt Brace Jovanovich, 1981), p. 288. © 1981 by Harcourt Brace Jovanovich, Inc. Reprinted by permission of the publisher.

production process. During this period, management as a distinct discipline entered the scientific management era. In the early 1900s, Henry L. Gantt, a colleague of Frederick Taylor, developed a chart that provided a major step toward the control methods that industry managers practice today.

The **Gantt Chart** is a graph on which projected and completed phases of production are plotted in relation to specific increments of time. An example of the Gantt chart is illustrated in Figure 20–4. The increments of time necessary for the desired degree of control are recorded on the horizontal axis of the chart. Various phases of activities are broken down into detailed categories and recorded on the vertical axis. Projected spans of time allotted to the performance of each phase of activity are plotted, and production is recorded as it progresses. For example, production of part #038 is scheduled to begin on January 26 and end on March 23. The shaded area indicates that completed production equals that required on March 9.

As a scheduling or planning device, the Gantt Chart allows the manager to monitor the use of resources. At a glance he or she knows when and where specific

**FIGURE 20–3**

**Calculating Profitable Output**

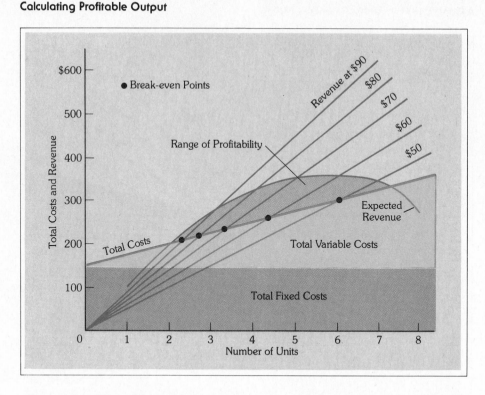

Source: Adapted from David J. Schwartz, *Marketing Today: A Basic Approach,* 2nd ed. (New York: Harcourt Brace Jovanovich, 1977), p. 554. © 1977 by Harcourt Brace Jovanovich, Inc. Reproduced by permission of the publisher.

resources will be needed. Having such information is especially important when one phase of an operation cannot start until another phase has been completed.

As a control device, the Gantt Chart allows the manager to compare both projected and completed phases of production in relation to one another and in relation to time. Consequently, he or she can evaluate the overall progress being made. At any point in time, a glance at the chart enables the manager to give a quick answer to the all-important question "Where are we now?" Moreover, this chart emphasizes any potential or actual slippages. For example, on March 16, all materials necessary for the completion of the entire project should be on hand and ready for final distribution. If this is not the case, the manager will know ahead of time and can make other arrangements, such as locating alternate suppliers, adjusting schedules, or rearranging the distribution of supplies to keep production balanced.

An important feature of the Gantt Chart is that it facilitates the assignment of control. Managers can plot progress, take care of any problems before a crisis develops, and provide top management with timely production reports.

The Gantt Chart has been criticized because using it requires considerable time to incorporate scheduling changes. However, mechanical and acetate boards

**FIGURE 20–4**

A Gantt Chart

| Elements of Production | 1984 4th Quarter | | 1985 1st Quarter | | | 1985 2nd Quarter | |
|---|---|---|---|---|---|---|---|
| | November 3 10 17 24 | December 1 8 15 22 29 | January 5 12 19 26 | February 2 9 16 23 | March 2 9 16 23 30 | April 6 13 20 27 | May 4 11 18 25 |
| Plan, organize, and schedule production process | | | | | | | |
| Acquire materials | | | | | | | |
| Production Part #038 | | | | | | | |
| #043 | | | | | | | |
| #020 | | | | | | | |
| #056 | | | | | | | |
| #091 | | | | | | | |
| #176 | | | | | | | |
| #240 | | | | | | | |
| #590 | | | | | | | |
| Sub-assembly #1 | | | | | | | |
| #2 | | | | | | | |
| #3 | | | | | | | |
| Performance testing | | | | | | | |
| Final assembly | | | | | | | |
| Shipping schedule | | | | | | | |

Source: Adapted from Elwood S. Buffa, *Modern Production Management,* 4th ed. (New York: John Wiley & Sons, 1973), p. 576. Copyright © 1973, John Wiley & Sons, Inc. Reprinted by permission of John Wiley & Sons, Inc.

with movable pegs, cards, or lights have been developed to solve this problem. If a Gantt Chart is properly planned, these adaptations facilitate rapid reorganization of projected and completed phases of the production process.

Industry has continued to grow in size and complexity. Henry Gantt's concept of identifying phases of activity and graphing them against time forms the foundation for many current control devices. One of the most important, network analysis, is discussed next.

## WHAT IS NETWORK ANALYSIS?

**Network analysis** can best be described as a technique whereby the whole of a project is broken down into specific parts so that the nature, proportion, function, and relationship of each part can be evaluated in relation to other parts and in relation to time.

Network analysis is not intended for use on routine or frequently repeated projects. It was developed for use on extremely complex projects that must be completed within a strict time frame. For example, network analysis was used to plan and control the Polaris Missile Project and Project Apollo. Other practical applications of this technique are research and development projects, installation of complicated machinery, relocation or redesign of physical plant facilities, extensive advertising campaigns, and complex construction projects.

The first step in developing a network analysis model is to separate and identify each part of the project. *Events* are instantaneous points in time that serve to mark progress in the life span of a project. Events serve as signals that preceding activities have been completed and succeeding activities can begin. For example, two major events are the beginning and the end of a project. *Activities* are the time-consuming tasks that are mandatory for the completion of the project. If beginning construction on a new factory is a major event in the network, then all tasks leading to that event are considered activities. For example, the event "begin construction" may be preceded by such activities as "select design," "locate site," "collect bids," "select contractors," and "arrange financing."

The second step in developing a network analysis model is to put the events in sequence and estimate the amount of time required for each activity. Some events can occur simultaneously, while others must be performed in a specific order; consequently, proper sequencing can reduce the total amount of time required for a project. Estimating the time required for each activity is a difficult step in the process. In some cases, there is little knowledge about the length of time required to complete an activity.

This second step in developing a network analysis model generally causes the most difficulties for managers. This is especially true when managers are asked to construct a network for which there is very little existing information. You can imagine the problems faced by the experts working on the Polaris Missile Project. The final model included over 70,000 parts, and several subnetworks were required to accurately represent the complexity of the undertaking. This step can be facilitated if managers repeatedly ask themselves these questions: "What activities must be completed before a specific event can take place?" "What activities cannot begin until a specific event is reached?" and "What activities and/or events can occur simultaneously?"

The third and final step in developing a network analysis model is to create a graphic representation of the events and activities. A simplified model is presented

**FIGURE 20-5**

531

*What Is*
*Network Analysis?*

**A Network Analysis Model**

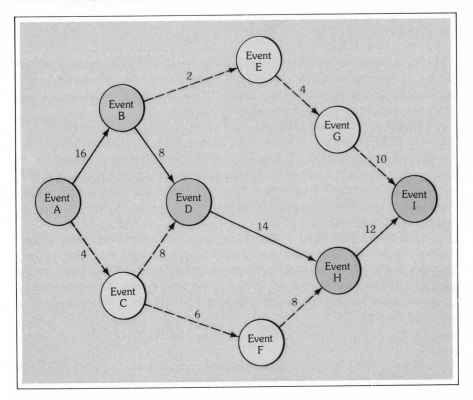

in Figure 20-5. This model portrays a set of events and activities. The related series of activities that connect one event with another are called **paths.** The direction of the activity flow is indicated by the direction of the arrows. The length of the arrows is insignificant.

The path in the network that requires the most time to complete is called the **critical path.** For example, in Figure 20-5, Events A, B, D, H, and I mark the critical path. Identifying the critical path allows a manager to spot the series of activities that are most likely to cause a delay in the completion of the project. For example, reducing the length of time between Event C and Event F would not shorten the life of the project since these events are not on the critical path. Efforts to reduce the length of the project should be concentrated on activities between Events A, B, D, H, and I.

A network analysis model provides the manager of a complex project with a valuable tool for comparing planned performance against actual performance. If completing certain activities exceeds the estimated length of time, managers can assess the probable effects of shifting resources, extending project completion dates, or compensating for performance variations. An important feature of the network analysis technique is that it shows where control efforts should be directed.

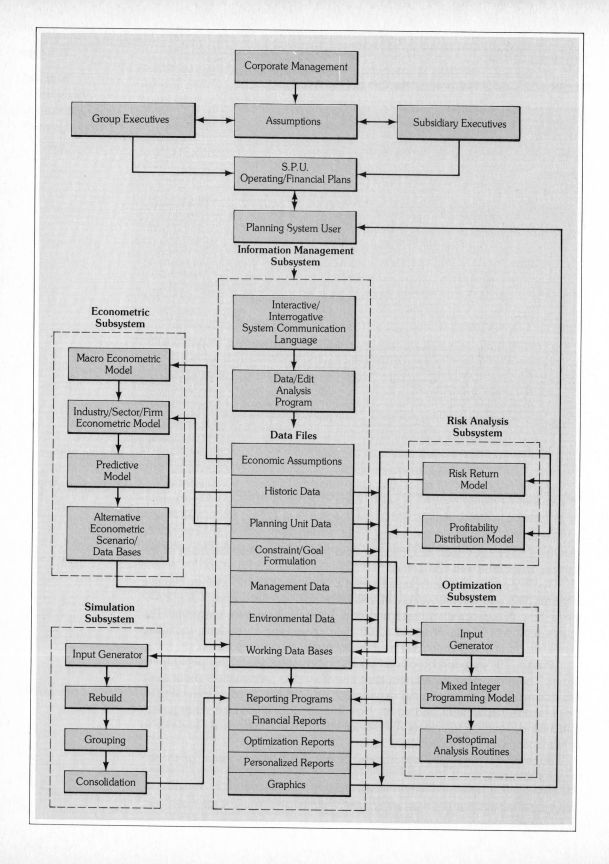

FIGURE 20–6

535

*What Are
Management
Information
Systems?*

A Computer-Based Corporate Planning System

Source: William F. Hamilton and Michael A. Moses, "A Computer-based Corporate Planning System," *Management Science,* October 1974. Reproduced by permission.

Table 20–3 shows examples of information that an effective information system can provide to executives in different kinds of organizations. While the specific information needs vary, in general an information system should answer such questions as "What was our income last week (month, year, or yesterday) by product category compared with income in a previous time period?" "What were

## TABLE 20–3

Examples of Information That a Well-Conceived MIS Should Provide

| Type of Enterprise | Examples of Information Needed |
|---|---|
| Airline | • Operational status of each aircraft<br>• Location and availability of each flight crew<br>• Number of seats sold and still available for each scheduled flight for the next twenty days<br>• Number of operating hours remaining until each aircraft must be given a major inspection<br>• Actual income and expenses compared with those budgeted |
| Department Store | • Inventory status by department and product class (size, color, and so on)<br>• Sales volume in dollars and in units by department<br>• Status of work force—absenteeism, personnel costs, and so forth<br>• Expenditures by department and by activity (advertising, store maintenance, and so on)<br>• Funds available for special activities (for example, remodeling, special promotions) |
| Bank | • Condition of loans already made (due dates, number and amount overdue, and so on)<br>• Condition of demand and time deposits (amount on deposit, withdrawal rates, and so forth)<br>• Number of customers by activity (borrowers and depositors)<br>• Expenditures by classification compared with those budgeted<br>• Income from various sources compared with anticipated receipts |
| Manufacturer | • Inventory status of finished products (number, condition, location, and so on)<br>• Income from sales compared with that in forecast<br>• Inventory of raw materials, parts, and components<br>• Expenditures by expense category compared with those in forecasts<br>• Condition of work force (number working, laid off, absent) |

our expenditures in the period under review by activity (maintenance, security, advertising, and so on) and by department, branch, or division?" "What is the status of our inventory—numbers of units by product category, condition, and location?" "What is the status of capital availability?" and "What is the status of personnel—are we overemployed in some departments (a condition suggesting layoffs may be needed) or are we underemployed in some areas (a condition suggesting new hirings may be in order)?"

## Benefits of an MIS

Several advantages can be cited for management information systems. First, activities can be better coordinated than when information is developed and maintained on a departmental basis. For example, when sales data and inventory information are in the same system, knowing when to adjust production levels can be virtually automatic.

Second, more information is available. Because of the large capacity of present-day computers, data for which there is only an occasional need can be processed and stored. Therefore, more and different types of information are available.

Third, information is more rapidly available. A computer can provide information more quickly than a phone call to another manager. Finally, the costs of collecting and analyzing data can be reduced because less clerical time is required.

## Limitations of an MIS

Management information systems are far from perfect and generally have not equaled the early expectations held for them. One of the key limitations of an MIS is that better decisions do not automatically result. Deciding always involves choosing among alternatives. Even when an MIS provides extensive information, a manager may still make a bad choice. Judgment, we must remember, always enters into decision making. It is common for two managers who receive the same data to draw different conclusions about what action to take.

Another drawback is that security of information is jeopardized, since information is made available to multiple users (that is, different individuals and departments), some of whom may not have a need to know. Confidentiality and privacy are thus more difficult to maintain.

A third disadvantage is that the people who design the MIS are often technical specialists who do not clearly understand what information managers need and in what form. At the same time, managers do not always know what information they need. Furthermore, in their zeal to inform management, information specialists often commit two errors: They develop more information than is needed, and they fail to summarize it so that it can be easily used. Deciding what information and how much of it is needed is the responsibility of the manager who will base decisions on the information. A production manager charged exclusively with operations in a Chicago plant does not require detailed information about operations in the company's plant in Los Angeles.

Finally, in many organizational structures the MIS group lacks a clear identity, resulting in confusion about lines of authority and reporting relationships. Originally, computer operations were assigned to the company accounting department. But confusion exists in many organizations about where to locate the broader-based information systems.

Some people feel that control in general and management information systems specifically put limits on creativity. This matter is discussed in the Issue for Debate in this chapter.

Problems of installing and using management information systems can be minimized when the following guidelines are observed:

- Ideally, a management information system should collect, process, store, and disseminate data for *all* departments.
- The system should be designed so that all needed information is available. At the same time, care should be taken not to collect, process, store, or disseminate data that are not needed.
- Information about a given activity, event, condition, or person should be collected only once. A manager should not be required to supply the same data twice.
- The MIS group needs a clear identity in the organizational hierarchy. Its reporting relationships as a staff unit should be understood.
- Members of the MIS group should have the ability to communicate effectively with managers who have a limited understanding of how computers work.

**SUMMARY**

- Budgets are the most important control device and can be used to control not only money but also time, materials, and other resources.
- Revenue and expense, cash, capital-expenditure, time and material, balance-sheet, and variable budgets are the kinds of budgets most frequently used.
- Zero-base budgeting requires managers to give maximum justification for all budget requests. It requires careful administration to be effective.
- Managers should make budgets flexible, visualize them as tools rather than ends in themselves, involve those affected by budgets in their preparation, make sure all requests are justified, and use budgets as incentives for the efficient use of resources.
- An audit is a control device that is primarily used to verify an organization's financial records, although it can be used to examine nonfinancial aspects of an organization as well. Audits may be conducted internally or externally.
- Break-even analysis is used to tell managers the sales level at which it is profitable to produce and market a product.
- A Gantt Chart facilitates planning activities so that different tasks can be accomplished on schedule. It helps managers know at any given time "Where are we now?"
- Network analysis is used to help plan and control complex projects. It helps managers minimize the amount of time needed to produce a result. The two most common forms of network analysis are PERT and CPM. Key advantages of network analysis as a planning and control technique are that it forces managers to think in

# ISSUE FOR DEBATE

## DOES CONTROL DISCOURAGE CREATIVITY?

Some people feel that setting standards, measuring performance against them, and taking corrective action when needed hinders creativity. Others take the opposite view—that control encourages people to seek new and better ways to achieve results. Some pro and con arguments follow.

### YES

**Control does discourage creativity because . . .**

Standards represent the acceptable norm. They do not indicate or encourage the best-possible performance.

Controls encourage mediocrity. People are usually satisfied if they meet the standard. For example, often there is no incentive for reducing expenditures and managers are not challenged to put forth their best efforts. Therefore they are satisfied if they can operate within planned expenditures.

People inherently dislike control because they interpret it to mean discipline, rules, and conformity. These negative reactions to control discourage people from seeking better ways to perform.

Corrective action is often a cop-out. For example, a manager may elect to terminate an employee who performs below standard rather than think creatively about how to help the employee improve.

Control encourages people to think traditionally, and such thinking never results in new processes, techniques, products, or other forms of creativity.

### NO

**Control does not discourage creativity because . . .**

Devising controls is in itself a creative activity. It requires intelligence to set standards, measure performance, and take corrective action.

Control does not necessarily encourage mediocrity. Managers can be given bonuses and other incentives for exceeding standards.

A well-designed control system frees managers from performing routine activities. When standards are established, managers need deal only with exceptions. Thus they have more time for thinking of ways to improve performance.

Controls provide knowledge of how well activities are performed. This knowledge encourages managers to ask two questions that require creative thinking: "How can we do better?" and "How can we do more?"

A key element of control is corrective action, much of which requires originality in devising solutions to problems that have not been experienced before.

### QUESTIONS

1. What other pro and con arguments can you suggest?
2. In your opinion, have the controls you've experienced in jobs you have held encouraged you to think creatively about ways to increase the quality and/or quantity of your output? Explain.

depth, leads to better coordination, and indicates possible deviation in a plan before it occurs. Its major drawback is complexity.

- Management information systems, facilitated by the development and widespread use of computers, are becoming increasingly popular to help managers perform routine operations, allocate resources, and control activities. Key benefits of an MIS are that coordination is better, more information is available, and information is available more rapidly. Main limitations are that better decisions do not automatically result, security of information is jeopardized, specialists who design the MIS may not understand what information is needed and in what form, and the MIS group often lacks a clear identity within the organization.

budget
revenue and expense budget
cash budget
cash flow
capital-expenditure budgets
time budget
material budgets
balance-sheet budget
assets
liabilities
owners' equity
variable budgets
fixed costs
variable costs

zero-base budgeting
incremental budgeting
audit
internal audit
external audit
management audit
break-even analysis
Gantt Chart
network analysis
paths
critical path
PERT
CPM
management information systems

1. Explain how budgets are used as performance standards.
2. Define and explain the use of revenue and expense budgets, cash budgets, capital-expenditure budgets, time and material budgets, balance-sheet budgets, and variable budgets.
3. Why are audits essential for effective control?
4. Banks are often audited by bank examiners by surprise. Why? Are surprise audits a good idea for conducting internal auditing? Explain.
5. What is the principal purpose of break-even analysis? Is break-even analysis complicated by inflation? Why or why not?
6. What factors led to the development of the Gantt Chart? How might a Gantt Chart be used to schedule and control the building of a house?
7. Explain why network analysis is not intended for use on routine or frequently repeated projects.
8. Are management information systems likely to become more important in the future? Explain.

## 1. What to do about the rotten apple

There is an old proverb that says a rotten apple will spoil the whole barrel. An analogy can be drawn with management. An employee with a negative attitude can cause other employees to become negative or even cause them to want to quit or be transferred.

Alice Gomper is a problem employee. She finds fault with everything her superior does, and her work is barely standard. Yet dismissal is out of the question, since under union rules there are no grounds for termination. She knows her rights and takes delight in knowing that she is untouchable.

Explain what you would do in an attempt to correct this problem.

## 2. What data should a management information system provide?

Assume that you are district manager of a retailing chain. Twelve stores, each with annual sales of between $1 million and $3 million, are under your direct supervision. With the aid of your technical experts, you are preparing an information system to give you data on a regular basis to help you manage more effectively.

Make a list of specific kinds of information you would want, briefly explain why you would want each kind, and indicate how frequently you would require it.

## 3. How managers react to budget cuts

Wallace Adams is president of Beautiful, a cosmetics company. Sales are down 23 percent from a year ago, and the company is now operating at a loss.

To avert a financial disaster, Wallace feels expenditures must be cut. He tells George Olt, head of marketing, and David Armstrong, head of production, that they must cut their budgets by 20 percent.

George replies, "Cutting my budget is a mistake. When sales are down we should spend more, not less, on advertising and other forms of promotion. If my budget is cut we won't be able to market the four new products David has been working on. And if my budget is cut, I'll have to eliminate several of our marketing research people."

David replies, "Cutting my budget is a mistake. It means I'll have to cancel orders for some labor-saving equipment, cut back on laboratory research, and dismiss some key employees—people we will need desperately when sales improve. Cutting my budget this year will certainly impact negatively on future profits."

Besides cutting the budget, what other options does Wallace have to avoid a financial disaster?

Do George and David's arguments seem valid?

**FOR ADDITIONAL
CONCEPTS
AND IDEAS**

Anthony, Robert N. "Making Sense of Nonbusiness Accounting." *Harvard Business Review,* May–June 1980, pp. 83–93.

Barnea, Amir; Sahah, Simcha; and Schiff, Michael. "A Format for Directors' Information Systems." *California Management Review,* Fall 1980, pp. 33–38.

Baruch, Hurd. "The Audit Committee: A Guide for Directors." *Harvard Business Review,* May–June 1980, pp. 174–176.

Boulton, William R. "The Changing Requirements for Managing Corporate Information Systems." *MSU Business Topics,* Summer 1978, pp. 4–12.

Cornwall, Deborah J., "Human Resource Programs: Blue Sky or Operating Priority?" *Business Horizons,* April 1980, pp. 49–55.

Cowen, Scott S.; Dean, Burton V.; and Lohrasbi, Ardeshir. "Zero-Base Budgeting as a Management Tool." *MSU Business Topics,* Spring 1978, pp. 29–40.

Dubinsky, Alan J., and Hansen, Richard W. "Sales Force Management Audit." *California Management Review,* Winter 1981, pp. 86–95.

Jackson, Donald W., Jr. "Grouping Segments for Profitability Analyses." *MSU Business Topics,* Spring 1980, pp. 39–44.

Keen, Peter F.W. "Decision Support Systems: Translating Analytic Techniques into Useful Tools." *Sloan Management Review,* Spring 1980, pp. 33–44.

Martin, Desmond D., and Kitnzele, Philip L. "An Approach to Integrating Management by Objectives and Human Resource Accounting Concepts in Profit Making Enterprises." *Akron Business and Economic Review,* Summer 1981, pp. 7–12.

Meldman, Jeffrey A. "Educating Toward Ethical Responsibility in MIS." *Sloan Management Review,* Winter 1982, pp. 73–75.

Michel, Allen. "The Inflation Audit." *California Management Review,* Winter 1981, pp. 68–74.

Nash, John F., and Hermanson, Roger H. "Wanted: A Code of Ethics for Internal Accountants." *Business,* November–December 1980, pp. 12–17.

Reckers, Philip M.J., and Stagliano, A.J. "Auditor Independence as Perceived by Financial Analysts." *MSU Business Topics,* Winter 1981, pp. 30–34.

Stettler, Howard F. "Two Proposals for Strengthening Auditor Independence." *MSU Business Topics,* Winter 1980, pp. 37–42.

Williams, John J. "Designing a Budgeting System with Planned Confusion." *California Management Review,* Winter 1981, pp. 75–85.

Wooton, Leland M., and Tarter, Jim L. "The Productivity Audit: A Key Tool for Executives." *MSU Business Topics,* Spring 1976, pp. 31–41.

# CASE STUDY

Four years ago Consolidated Conglomerate acquired Scientific Tools, an eighteen-year-old family-owned company headed by its founder, Isaac Davidson. Consolidated gave Davidson and his family shares in Consolidated then valued at $4 million. Under the agreement Consolidated put Davidson's shares in a trust so that he would be unable to sell them for ten years. Consolidated also gave Davidson a ten-year management contract at a $200,000 yearly salary. The contract also stipulated that Davidson would have absolute autonomy in operating Scientific Tools for the life of the contract. He would in effect continue to operate the company as if it were his own.

Scientific Tools had a remarkable earnings record. Its profits had increased every year since it was founded. Consolidated executives took note of this when they acquired the firm. That is why they decided in the negotiation process not to interfere with the management of Scientific Tools.

Since the acquisition, Consolidated Conglomerate has been undergoing bad times in a number of its key divisions—so bad that the stock is worth only 25 percent of what it was when Davidson sold. His $4 million is now worth only $1 million. And, interestingly, Scientific Tools has shown an operating loss for the first time in history, even though demand for the products it makes has been good.

The senior vice-president of Consolidated, Peter Jenkins, calls a meeting to discuss this problem with Jim Flesch, the controller, Jane Washington, legal counsel, and Herman Darby, head of corporate acquisitions.

Jenkins: I've explained the problems to you. In a nutshell, Scientific Tools is losing money—and for no obvious reason. Business is good in their line. What do you think has happened and how can we correct the problem?

Flesch: Well, the key problem is that we acquired an organization but no control over it. We have no headquarters people working inside Scientific and that's bad. Our acquisition contract was stupidly negotiated.

Washington: Hold it, Flesch. I handled the negotiations for the acquisition. But all of you made your inputs. The consensus four years ago was don't rock the boat. Scientific Tools had been making more money every year before we acquired it, and if you'll recall, during the negotiations Davidson *insisted* that he retain full control for ten years.

Jenkins: Let's not get sidetracked. We're here this morning to solve a problem. Again, what has happened and how do we correct it?

Darby: I don't like to say this, but I believe the operating loss of Scientific is related to the drop in the value of our shares.

Washington: Will you explain?

Darby: We all believe that Davidson is an honorable man. But even the most honorable people go sour. What may be happening is this: Davidson has seen the value of his stock in Consolidated drop from $4 million to $1 million. And when our shares started going down, Davidson couldn't sell because his shares are in a trust. We required him to do that to prevent him from unloading all of his stock at once. Now, he may be engaging in some hanky-panky, thinking it's justified because of the severe plunge in the value of our shares.

Jenkins: Specifically, what may he be up to?

Flesch: Oh, there are lots of ways he could be siphoning off money. Since we have no headquarters people inside Scientific, we can only guess. He may be taking kickbacks from suppliers, selling off assets, buying personal property with corporate funds, falisfying records—lots of ways. They're all illegal but often very difficult to detect.

Washington: That's a possibility. The credit investigation company we use told me that corporate mergers often lead to dishonesty.

Jenkins: What you're saying about Davidson may or may not be true. For the moment I want to give Davidson the benefit of the doubt. After all, none of us know much about the precision tool business. Let's meet again Thursday and decide what we should do.

## QUESTIONS

1. How was the control function violated in this case?
2. How would you proceed to determine whether Davidson is in fact diverting company assets to his personal use?
3. Assuming you discover Davidson is using Scientific's assets for his personal use, what would you do?

# 21 MANAGING IN THE FUTURE

**STUDY THIS CHAPTER SO YOU CAN:**

- Understand how managing in the future will differ from contemporary management.

- Discuss how the emerging Age of Information will affect the way the planning function is performed.

- Explain why organizations in the future may be smaller, rely less on middle managers, and depend more on first-level supervisors.

- Appreciate why the staffing function will be concerned with employee retraining, will place greater emphasis on manager development, and will be involved with assimilating more women into management.

- Explain why participative management will become more widespread, communication will be faster and easier, and the influence of organized labor will decline.

- Interpret the impact of the new technology on performance of the control function.

- Relate the trends of greater decentralization, increased demand for protection in international trade, more emphasis on quality of life, and an older work force to managing.

The meaning of management will not change in the future. It will always be defined as achieving an organization's goals through the coordinated performance of five functions: planning, organizing, staffing, directing, and controlling. But the manner in which these functions are performed and the problems that will arise in managing will change dramatically in the decades immediately ahead.

Delaware Governor Pierre du Pont IV noted that "The transformation of our jobs, the movement of our people, the improvements in our skills over the first 80 years of this century have been stunning. But it is entirely likely that those changes will be matched and exceeded during the final 20 years of the century."[1]

In the late 1970s, American managers began to realize an important fact. The nation no longer led the world in overall productivity—the best gauge of managerial performance. Japan, for example, was outperforming the United States in automobile and appliance production and in other areas as well.

One of the main reasons for management change is foreign competition. The United States imports approximately 28 percent of its cars, 18 percent of its steel, 55 percent of its consumer electronics products, and 27 percent of its machine tools.[2] The realization that we were falling behind foreign competitors prompted managers, government officials, professors, and futurists to ask three important questions about the future—"What trends will affect managing in the future?" "How must management be modified to deal with forecasted changes?" and "How can productivity, through better management, be improved?"

How future performance of management functions may be affected by existing and emerging trends is discussed in this chapter.

## PLANNING IN THE FUTURE

**Emergence
of the Age
of Information**

Some futurists picture tomorrow as the **Age of Information.** People will develop, process, and use ever-increasing amounts and kinds of information in both their work and private lives. The increase in the use of computers, satellites, and television will make information easier to transmit. This trend will profoundly change the way people learn, shop, manage their money, and perform other tasks. It will also significantly alter the way managers plan, organize, staff, direct, and control management activities.

The Age of Information will impact most importantly on the planning function. Forecasting future events and conditions should improve because more relevant data can be collected and analyzed. Top-level decisions, such as whether or not to introduce new products, acquire capital, build new facilities, or merge with another organization, should entail less risk because more information will be available. Revenue and expenditure forecasting will become more accurate because of the immediate availability of data.

Procedures for performing work will be computerized, thereby reducing errors and simplifying management. Work rules, the simplest form of plan, are likely to be liberalized. People will be given more freedom to manage themselves. One observer notes: "The times of 'business as usual' with its authoritarian leadership style will not come back. The new norms are in the direction of worker participation and individualization of working hours and working conditions."[3]

Survival will continue to be the number one objective of organizations. More businesses failed between 1979 and 1982 than in any period since the 1930s. Yet

[1]Charles P. Alexander, "The New Economy," *Time,* May 30, 1983, p. 62. Copyright 1983. Time Inc. All rights reserved. Reprinted by permission from *Time.*
[2]Ibid., p. 63.
[3]Reprinted with permission from *Long Range Planning,* Vol. 15, J. G. Wissema, "The Modern Prophets—How Can They Help Us?", Copyright © 1982, Pergamon Press, Ltd.

during the last recession, managers had more information on which to base decisions than ever before. This fact suggests that information alone does not guarantee business survival and success.

Managers will still have to choose among alternative courses of action. Major decisions will always by made by people and will reflect the intelligence, experiences, and education of the individuals who make them.

The Age of Information will greatly facilitate planning, but the computers that supply the information that managers need will still be programmed by people. And people will still exercise judgment to decide which course of action to pursue.

The age of information will be greatly stimulated by **high technology**. Major advances are predicted in computers, lasers, genetic engineering, robotics, instrumentation, medicine, energy development, and other technologies.

Expansion
in High Technology

## ORGANIZING IN THE FUTURE

The way activities are organized will reflect existing trends. Work will be more decentralized; employees will be closer to problems involving them.

The plural executive, discussed in Chapter 18, should become more popular as organized life becomes more complex. Wider use of committees will occur.

The impact of computers and automation will affect the organization function. "It is beyond doubt that a great deal of technology already exists for improving managerial productivity . . . computerized telephone exchange, for example, can produce a much higher level of telephone effectiveness through facilities such as conference calls."[4]

Work groups will be smaller, since mass-assembly operations will be less important, and jobs will be more specialized.

As a result of the deep recession of the early 1980s and due to the continuing technological revolution, staff managers whose main function is to supply advice will be relatively less important in the future. One report states:

Less Dependence
on Staff Managers

> The clear loser in the new organization is the staff. Relied on in the prosperous 1950s and 1960s to cope with increasing size and complexity as companies diversified, expanded geographically, and acquired other companies, they grew in geometrical proportion to profits. Government regulations in the 1970s required even more staff. Since the size of staffs was equated with power and money, senior managers pressed for ever-further enlargements. And the top manager, the CEO, required the largest staff of all to supervise the rest. Indeed, says Pearl Meyer, executive consultant at Handy Associates Inc.: "American business got to be a pretty cushy place."[5]

Many leading companies, such as Crown Zellerbach, Beneficial Corporation, General Electric, Brunswick, Chrysler, and Xerox have cut back drastically on staff

[4]David Butler, "The Office of the Future," *Management Today*, October 1980, p. 121.
[5]Quoted from the April 25, 1983 issue of *Business Week* by special permission, © 1983 by McGraw-Hill, Inc., New York, NY 10020. All rights reserved.

*"You mean one still has to?"*

© Punch/Rothco

personnel to reduce costs and to improve efficiency. In the decade ahead, senior managers will be reluctant to hire staff personnel unless they contribute more than they cost in salaries and benefits.

**The Importance of
Middle Management
Is Declining**

The role of middle management is likely to decline in importance in the decade ahead. Due mainly to the increasing use of computers, relatively few people will be employed as middle managers.

> The onrushing electronics revolution is changing the role of the middle manager and forcing a radical restructuring of the corporation's middle ranks, shrinking them drastically in the best-managed companies. Just as the industrial revolution changed hierarchies, radicalized labor, realigned political forces, and created widespread social and psychological disruption, the technological revolution is producing pain and strain. The initial impact is being felt by the middle manager, who typically earns $25,000 to $80,000. And, as in the earlier upheaval, the woes overshadow even the most glowing promises of the future.[6]

Modern computer technology impacts on middle management by making it simple for first-line supervisors to transmit key data directly to top-level managers. Middle-level managers will become less essential in the collection, analysis, and interpretation of data developed by operative-level personnel. For instance, sales data developed by a convenience food store can be transmitted directly to company headquarters, thereby making it unnecessary for a middle-level management team to interpret the data and then forward it up the ladder.

[6]Quoted from the April 25, 1983 issue of *Business Week* by special permission, © 1983 by McGraw-Hill, Inc., New York, NY 10020. All rights reserved.

There are indications that computer technology will replace the need for many middle managers and enlarge the duties of those who remain, as this observation indicates.

> Technology is also changing the very nature of and need for middle-management jobs. Sales staff in industries ranging from brokerages to pharmaceuticals are, or soon will be, consulting their computers—rather than their managers—for pricing, inventory, and market information. With less paperwork, sales managers can cover larger territories and get faster feedback on performance and problems. Similarly, computer-aided design and manufacturing allowed Chrysler Corporation to halve its engineering group to 4,000 without sacrificing its product-development programs."[7]

Middle management, it appears, will be affected directly and significantly by the new technology. Direct communications between the bottom and the top of organizational structures will become more common. And, while middle managers will become less important, first-line supervisors will become more important and will be given more responsibility. Consultant Barry A. Stein states, "The first-line supervisor will become more important rather than less in the movement toward flatter and more flexible organizational structures."[8]

## STAFFING IN THE FUTURE

The staffing function will change dramatically in the years ahead. One major challenge will be **employee retraining**—preparing workers replaced by new technology for other kinds of employment. Unless displaced workers are retrained, many will be permanently unemployed, thereby creating a burden on society. Retraining is complicated by the fact that employees requiring it have no skills and limited educations. Meanwhile, many jobs of the future will require both skills and considerable education.

When senior management determines that a lower-level manager's job is obsolete or is not making a contribution to profit, it can dismiss the individual or retrain the person for a management position that is needed. Most companies exercise the first option and simply terminate the individual. A few companies, however, such as IBM and General Electric, provide retraining for managers whose jobs are no longer needed.

It is probable that the federal government will play a larger role than private industry in retraining programs. One government official predicts that " . . . people will now be changing jobs four times during their working careers. That will make retraining a permanent part of American business and society."[9]

Table 21–1 shows a projection of the numerical increase and decrease for certain kinds of jobs. Note that some of the jobs that will have the most openings—janitors, salesclerks, cashiers, and fast-food workers—are not particularly challenging, particularly to those who are well-educated.

Changes in
Kinds of Jobs
Available

[7]Quoted from the April 25, 1983 issue of *Business Week* by special permission, © 1983 by McGraw-Hill, Inc., New York, NY 10020. All rights reserved.
[8]Quoted from the April 25, 1983 issue of *Business Week* by special permission, © 1983 by McGraw-Hill, Inc., New York, NY 10020. All rights reserved.
[9]Alexander, p. 68.

**TABLE 21–1**

**Help Wanted (Number of jobs in thousands)**

| Ten best prospects . . . | 1980 | 1990 | + or − |
|---|---|---|---|
| Secretaries | 2,469 | 3,169 | +700 |
| Nurses' aides | 1,175 | 1,682 | +507 |
| Janitors | 2,751 | 3,253 | +502 |
| Sales clerks | 2,880 | 3,359 | +479 |
| Cashiers | 1,993 | 2,445 | +452 |
| Nurses | 1,104 | 1,542 | +438 |
| Truck drivers | 1,696 | 2,111 | +415 |
| Fast-food workers | 806 | 1,206 | +400 |
| Clerks | 2,395 | 2,772 | +377 |
| Waiters | 1,711 | 2,072 | +361 |

| Ten worst prospects . . . | 1980 | 1990 | + or − |
|---|---|---|---|
| Postal clerks | 316 | 310 | −6 |
| Clergy | 296 | 287 | −9 |
| Shoe machine operators | 65 | 54 | −11 |
| Compositors and typesetters | 128 | 115 | −13 |
| Graduate assistants | 132 | 108 | −24 |
| Servants | 478 | 449 | −29 |
| College teachers | 457 | 402 | −55 |
| High school teachers | 1,237 | 1,064 | −173 |
| Farm laborers | 1,157 | 940 | −235 |
| Farm operators | 1,447 | 1,201 | −246 |

Source: Charles P. Alexander. "The New Economy." *Time*, May 30, 1983, p. 64. Copyright 1983 Time Inc. All rights reserved. Reprinted by permission from *Time*.

On the brighter side, new jobs will be created to design the robots and other machines that will replace many of the workers who now perform simple jobs. Many other new jobs will be available, such as programmers, systems analysts, word processor operators, and office-machine maintenance workers. Because many of these jobs will require more skill, unemployment may be a major social and economic problem in the near future. The Issue for Debate in this chapter discusses the possible problems of high-level unemployment in the years ahead.

**More Managers
Will Seek
Advanced Education**

Many individuals already working as managers will go back to school. Executive MBA programs designed for experienced managers are sure to flourish. So will highly specialized short seminars covering a wide variety of topics that relate to managing. Some colleges and universities will find that their main target market is not young people pursuing academic programs, but older people who need to update their knowledge and skills.

Why will more managers return to school? One possible explanation follows:

. . . Consulting firms such as Arthur D. Little both use and sell executive training extensively. The hunger for management education is most often attributed to the need-to-keep-up-with-increasingly-rapid-change-in-this-ever-more-complex-world. The middle-aged manager especially may need help. Arnold K. Weinstein, Dean of Arthur D. Little's Management Education Institute, explains 'You're 45 years old with a bachelor of arts degree and you have bright young MBAs with the latest techniques working for you. You can't understand the language. You feel obsolete and threatened. So you go to school. Subjects that weren't taught awhile back at business school, like productivity and information systems, have become important, while traditional subjects, such as strategic planning, need a new look. Younger executives may realize that all the quantitative and analytical thinking they acquired at business school left out the human side of management. So the curriculum abounds in "soft" subjects, such as the art of criticizing subordinates constructively."[10]

In the past decade the MBA became highly distinguishable. *Business Week* reported that in the decade 1972 to 1982 the number of institutions granting MBAs increased by 75 percent, and the number of MBA degrees awarded tripled.[11] The number of people making applications to MBA programs may decline in the years ahead. According to the *Business Week* report more and more companies are disenchanted with MBA programs.[12]

**The Conventional MBA Degree May Decline in Value**

As a result of a decline in the perceived value of an MBA, many colleges and universities will place more emphasis on shorter courses, seminars, and workshops.

Colleges and universities are taking other steps to bring business education in line with the "new management." The *Business Week* report goes on to state:

> . . . B-schools are frantically undertaking the most massive overhaul of their curricula in 20 years. To basic courses in operations management, they are now adding electives in manufacturing systems, robotics, and manufacturing strategy. Several are starting joint programs with engineering schools. New organizational-behavior courses now focus on such issues as managing innovation and introducing automation into the workplace. And schools are weaving "the international perspective" into the curriculum and are integrating the computer into courses ranging from corporate finance to production.[13]

Staffing will become more complex because of the switch from structured conventional working conditions to **flexlife work**—working conditions the employees prefer. For example:

**Less Stuctured Working Conditions**

> The four-day week: the 19-day month: the executive sabbatical: leave to take further education: re-employment of retired executives: voluntary early retirement—all these and many other current developments are part of a worldwide change in life cycles in general.

> Not that Shakespeare's description of the seven ages has ceased to apply today. But the bard's calendar of progress from mewling infant to doddering second childhood seems to have less relevance to modern man—and to the modern manager.[14]

Other challenges facing those who perform the staffing function are (a)

[10]Jeremy Main, "The Executive Yearn to Learn," *Fortune*, May 3, 1982, p. 240.
[11]"Who Will Retrain the Obsolete Managers?" *Business Week*, April 25, 1983, p. 76.
[12]Ibid., p. 80.
[13]Quoted from the April 25, 1983 issue of *Business Week* by special permission, © 1983 by McGraw-Hill, Inc., New York, NY 10020. All rights reserved.
[14]Norris Willatt, "The Flexlife Future," *Management Today,* June 1980, p. 81.

assimilation of more women into management positions, (b) an older work force, and (c) demand for more fringe benefits such as employee counseling about personal problems.

## DIRECTING IN THE FUTURE

Directing, the function of motivation, leadership, and communication, will be modified greatly in the future. One change will be a major shift from autocratic — we-they management to participative management. Roger Talpaert wrote an interesting article about management from the vantage point of the next century in which he observes: "... Few would now argue that the axial principle of our present society is participation. It is unthinkable today for people to contribute to any form of collective action without being able to influence goals and choices."[15]

It seems certain that de-emphasis of autocratic "do-as-I-say-management" will continue and new emphasis will be placed on participative "let's-work-this-out-together-management." Barry Stein, president of a consulting firm, says, "They [foremen] aren't going to control people anymore. They have to coach them, help do the planning, approve organizational direction, and make sure the directions are clear. It will be an enabling function rather than a control function."[16]

Closely allied to the trend toward participative management is wider use of ad hoc committees or task forces to solve problems. Groups of key executives will be assembled to develop strategies for marketing, finance, and production problems and, when their work is complete, they will be disbanded.

**Communicating Will Be Faster and Easier**

Because of office automation and more varied uses of computers, communicating will be faster and easier. According to George T. Plotzke:

> Information management systems, e.g., data communications, electronic document communications or mail systems, electronic filing, and sensor-based systems like those used for energy conservation, will continue to grow. A major link in the chain of communications evolution will be the integration of all office systems. This will allow the user to access information anywhere in the system, from any convenient point on the system.[17]

Much of the communication equipment to be used in the future is already available. But new devices are almost revolutionary, as one observer notes.

> Another key piece of equipment in the office of the future will be the text-and-graphics terminal. Evolved from the word processor, this device will permit the creation of documents which contain graphic as well as textual material. Such devices are

---

[15]Roger Talpaert, "Looking Into the Future: Management in the Twenty-First Century," *Management Review*, March 1981. (New York: AMACOM, a division of American Management Associations, 1981) p. 25.

[16]Quoted from the April 25, 1983 issue of *Business Week* by special permission, © 1983 by McGraw-Hill, Inc., New York, NY 10020. All rights reserved.

[17]George T. Plotzke, "New Technology Creates The Office of the Future," *Management Review*, February 1982. (New York: AMACOM, a division of American Management Associations, 1982) p. 15.

# ISSUE FOR DEBATE

## WILL HIGH-LEVEL UNEMPLOYMENT (ABOVE 8 PERCENT) BE A CONTINUING PROBLEM IN THE FORESEEABLE FUTURE?

### YES

High-level unemployment will be a continuing problem because . . .

Foreign competition's wage rates are much lower than American wage rates. In effect this means we will continue to export jobs to other nations.

Japan, a leading exporter to the United States, has far more robots than the United States. It will take us years to catch up. However, when we do, Nobel Laureate Wassily Leonteif foresees mass joblessness. He says, "The computer and the robot are already beginning to replace white-collar workers. Man, as a factor of production, has only two aspects: physical and mental. Both are being replaced.[1]

Many workers who are or will be displaced by technology lack the education and intelligence to be trained for technical jobs. Many others are too old to be retrained.

Manufacturing workers who are replaced by technology have been well paid. They are not likely to settle for relatively low-pay service jobs and will remain unemployed by choice.

[1]Alexander, p. 64.

### NO

High-level unemployment will not be a continuing problem because . . .

Although the number of people in the labor force grew from 80 million to 104 million between 1970 and 1980, the growth rate is now slowing rapidly because of the low birth rates in the 1960s and 1970s. Less demand for jobs will reduce unemployment. In the 1970s, the work force increased an average of 2.7 percent per year. In the 1980s, it will grow by only 1.5 percent per year.

Many new jobs will be created to design, make, operate, and service the new computers, lasers, robots, and other technological developments. During all recessions, prophets of doom forecast permanent high levels of unemployment. These forecasts are forgotten when prosperity returns.

Our educational system is being revamped to prepare young people for the new technology.

If high-level unemployment continues, the government will take action to create more public-service jobs.

## QUESTIONS

1. What other arguments can you address in support of each position?
2. Based on your reading and observations, do you believe high-level unemployment will continue to be a problem over the next decade? Why?

already in fairly widespread use in the printing industry, and improved versions will enable textual and graphic material to be sent and received by communicating with other text-and-graphics terminals, with communicating word processors, and with facsimile terminals. It is inevitable that the text-and-graphics terminal will rapidly evolve into the general-purpose work station of the office; and will appear in forms suitable for both secretarial-cum-clerical and managerial use.[18]

Leadership in the future will continue to be an art. Rogert Talpaert sees the essential qualifications for leadership in the years ahead as follows:

> The most important qualifications of today's 21st Century manager are political skill and moral credibility. Both of these qualifications will exist in an organizational setting where there is consensus on goals and choices. Although the manager may well be an expert in some of the tools and techniques used in resource optimization, this expertise is not the core of his ability. A managerial role is hardly a profession, nor is it necessarily a permanent responsibility. Rather, it seeks to facilitate common human endeavors of any size and at all levels.[19]

## Better Cooperation Between Labor and Management

The directing function has long been complicated by conflicts between organized labor and management. The trend toward fewer workers joining labor unions will continue. One reason is the projected decline in employment in mass-production industries where workers are easier to organize. Another factor supporting this trend is unions are less popular among highly skilled workers.

It seems essential that labor and management must work together more harmoniously as one observer notes:

> American managers must cultivate a closer relationship with labor to replace the often antagonistic "we-they" approach. Many U.S. companies are successfully copying the Japanese practice of using so-called quality circles, which are teams of workers that meet regularly on company time to discuss production snafus and bottlenecks. In 1979 Dover Elevator Co. formed quality circles at its Horn Lake, Miss., plant. Says Robert Scott, Dover's quality-circle coordinator: "It has done so many good things you can't even count them. I suppose if it were to be put in dollar terms, we have had a $12 to $15 payback on each dollar invested in the program."[20]

To make our economic system more productive and able to compete more successfully in world markets, American labor must take a more moderate stance. Mr. Alexander goes on to note:

> Organized labor, in turn, will have to be more flexible on wages and be willing to give up rigid work rules that lead to overmanning and inefficiency. The recession may have been a turning point for unions. After rancorous negotiations, workers in both the auto and steel industries agreed to an unprecedented combination of pay cuts, changes in work rules and givebacks of benefits. But wages are still comparatively high. In the U.S., autoworkers at the Big Three companies now average $21.50 an hour in wages and benefits, compared with $12.60 an hour in Japan. Now that the recession is over, the talk in union halls is of catch-up instead of giveback. If executives and labor forget

---

[18]Ian A. Galbraith, "What Automation Really Means," *Management Today,* November 1980, p. 134.
[19]Talpaert, p. 25.
[20]Alexander, p. 70.

the harsh lessons administered by the recession and foreign competition, their companies will continue to weaken.[21]

The strength of unions is likely to diminish in the decades ahead. "For unions, the outlook is somewhat bleak. Their power base is among blue-collar workers, but the growth is in white-collar work where unions have less appeal. With fewer workers per factory, the power of unions is diluted."[22]

## CONTROL IN THE FUTURE

Control will be greatly facilitated by computers and other electronic equipment. Management Information Systems, already widely used, will provide continuously updated reports on sales, inventories, expenses, investments, and other key data needed for making decisions.

Control over the way people work is liable to undergo major change.

> "**Telecommuting**"—working at home while linked to a central office through electronics—is already creating dispersed offices and greater options. For instance, a Minneapolis computer company has 60 of its employees working at home. *Business Week* recently reported on a California stockbroker who works at home using the telephone and a computer to contact customers, keep track of the market, and place buy-and-sell orders as efficiently as he did from the office he once commuted to. He saves three hours of bumper-to-bumper commuting time each day, and $500 a month on commuting, parking, and meal costs, as well as earning tax write-offs for using his home as an office.[23]

Our economy has already made great strides toward the Age of Information, which facilitates the control function, as the following observation suggests:

> Paradoxically, technology also offers means of controlling employees more closely than ever. The loss ratio in a loan officer's portfolio or the number of calls handled by a phone operation can be monitored constantly and compared with norms. So while the boss may not be around as much, employees will be tied more tightly to performance standards.[24]

## OTHER TRENDS AFFECTING MANAGEMENT

Trends directly impacting on the performance of management functions have been noted in this chapter. But other changes in our socioeconomic structure will also influence how managers will attempt to achieve organizational goals.

- Greater Decentralization—Some observers believe huge organizations, both in government and in the private sector, will be broken down into

---

[21]Alexander, p. 70.
[22]Jeremy Main, "Work Won't Be the Same Again," *Fortune*, January 28, 1982, p. 65.
[23]Plotzke, p. 15.
[24]Main, p. 58.

# MANAGERS IN ACTION

## WILL PROFIT-SEEKING HOSPITALS PLAY A LARGER ROLE IN THE FUTURE?

About 10 percent of personal income in the United States goes to pay for medical expenses, most of which are incurred in hospital care. In 1983, profit-seeking hospitals accounted for 11 percent of all hospitals and some experts predict that this percentage will increase to 20 percent during the 1980s.[1]

Proponents of profit-seeking hospitals argue that they are more efficient, make more effective use of computers and other technology, have access to investor capital (this helps the profit-seeking hospital buy the most modern equipment, which results in fewer days in the hospital per patient served), and benefit from standardization.

Hospital Corporation of America is the largest and fastest growing of the for-profit hospital chains. The company claims that it can build a hospital for 30 to 40 percent less than can a municipality.[2]

Much of the success of Hospital Corporation of America can be traced to a carefully developed control system. "H.C.A. expects its administrators . . . to perform and perform well. Every month hospitals are sized up according to a battery of yardsticks: More hours per adjusted patient day, bad debt expense, occupancy. The company expects its administrators to shoot for a 5 percent net profit margin."[3]

H.C.A. also has discount supply contracts with 473 suppliers covering everything from desks to drugs.

Profit-seeking hospitals are frequently criticized because they provide little care for indigent and uninsured patients. Further, such hospitals show little commitment to educating physicians or doing research.

Despite such criticisms, it is likely that more private enterprise hospitals will emerge in the future.

[1] N. R. Kleinfield, "Operating For Profit at Hospital Corporation," *New York Times*, Section 3, May 29, 1983, p. 1. © 1983 by The New York Times Company. Reprinted by permission.

[2] Ibid., p. 22.
[3] Ibid., p. 22.

### QUESTIONS

1. When profit-seeking hospitals refuse medical care to someone who cannot afford to pay, the person is normally referred to a nonprofit community hospital. In your opinion, are profit-seeking hospitals working in the best interests of the public?
2. In the future, is it likely that in the interests of efficiency and productivity, more traditionally nonprofit services such as police protection, sanitation, and education will be provided by profit-seeking groups? Why or why not?

smaller, more manageable units. Decision making will occur closer to the activity being managed. In government, this means shifting responsibility to the states and cities. In the private sector, this translates into more decision making by branch and division managers.

• Demand for Protection in International Trade—Most economists have maintained for centuries that free trade—no tariffs or other artificial restrictions on international trade—benefits all nations. But during periods of economic recession, attitudes of labor and many managers change from support of worldwide unrestricted competition to demands for trade protection to protect American jobs and profits. As one observer explains:

> ... The automatic response of many businessmen and workers when threatened by foreign competition is to demand protection: quotas, tariffs, subsidies, "voluntary" trade agreements, anything to preserve the status quo. In times of recession and high unemployment, the clamor becomes virtually irresistible. As a result, the world is suffering its worst outbreak of protectionism since the 1930s. The U.S. has moved to reduce imports of cars, motorcycles, steel, textiles and a host of other products. ... The list goes on and on.[25]

- More Emphasis on **Quality of Work Life**—More attention will be expected of managers to make work more enjoyable. Managers are beginning to learn that people are more productive if they enjoy their work. This trend will be reinforced because many of the routine, boring jobs will be eliminated and the new jobs will be more challenging.

  However, there is some skepticism about how challenging many jobs in the future will be (see Table 21–1). Looking into the future, one observer notes:

> ... The unskilled or semi-skilled won't have the most interesting or best-paid jobs. But with the growth of the service economy, neither will they be scrapped in the jungle. For the others, the pluses seem to outnumber the minuses. Dehumanizing some of the new tasks may seem, but how human was the work of clerks counting and sorting cancelled checks all day, of welders putting car parts together, of secretaries taking dictation and typing, of managers trying and failing all day long to get a colleague on the phone? These and other deadening, irritating tasks are being taken over by robots and computers. People prepared for the new jobs will find their work freed of the curse of dull repetition, leaving them more time to be creative. In the long run, greater efficiency is the only way to increase jobs and prosperity.[26]

- An Older Work Force—In only 20 years the baby boom children of the 1950s will be approaching middle age. The relatively low birthrates of the last 25 years will reduce the number of young workers as a large percentage of the work force. Because of problems with the Social Security system, better health care, more interesting jobs, and changes in the mandatory retirement age, many people will work beyond the normal retirement age of 60 to 65.
- Other Trends—A number of other trends, separately and in combination, will affect managing in the future. These include slow population growth, smaller households, a major growth in the Hispanic and Oriental popu-

[25]Alexander, p. 66.
[26]Main, p. 65.

lations, greater opportunities for women and minority groups, more business and population expansion in the Sun Belt, less regulation of competitive practices, and more regulation relating to worker safety and the environment.

This chapter's analysis of how managing will change to accommodate contemporary trends did not consider possible "acts of man," such as a major change in the nation's political system; a severe, prolonged worldwide economic depression 1930-style; or nuclear war. Nor was consideration given to possible "acts of God," such as major earthquakes, droughts, floods, and other climatic changes and uncontrollable epidemics.

Events such as these are possible. But defense against them, if any, rests mainly with governments, not individual organizations.

Managers, generally, in the decades ahead will be optimistic, forward-looking, and searching for ways to make life better. As we move into the future, more managers may come to believe society is on the threshold of a golden age.

**SUMMARY**

- Managing in the future will still involve the performance of five interrelated functions: planning, organizing, staffing, directing, and controlling. But the way in which these functions are performed will be modified significantly.
- The society of tomorrow may be described as the Age of Information. The increasing use of computers, satellites, and television will make it easier for management to transmit, process, and use data.
- Less use of staff managers is probable in the future.
- Due to easier and faster transmission of data from operating levels to high echelons of management, the importance of middle managers is likely to decline.
- Retraining managers and operative employees will receive much emphasis in the years ahead. Both private enterprise and government will be involved in retraining activities.
- Many of the new jobs in the future, such as unskilled service work, will lack challenge. However, some jobs in high technology will be very challenging.
- Many managers will seek advanced education, but the conventional MBA may decline in value.
- Working conditions will be less structured in the future. Personnel will have more freedom to set working hours and methodology for performing their jobs.
- Autocratic management will shift to participative management in most enterprises.
- Communication will be faster and easier because of office automation and computers.
- Labor unions are likely to decline in importance in the decades ahead because of the projected decline in mass-production industries and because unions are less popular among highly skilled workers.
- Because of computers and electronic equipment, control will be more accurate in the future.
- The future is liable to bring greater decentralization, demands for protection in international trade, more emphasis on quality of work life, and an older labor force.

Age of Information
high technology
employee retraining

flexlife work
telecommuting
Quality of Work Life

1. Some futurists argue that more changes will affect management in the next twenty years than occurred in the past eighty years. Do you agree? Why or why not?
2. What is meant by the "Age of Information"? How will it affect managing?
3. Why is it likely that there will be less dependency on staff managers in the future?
4. It is predicted that the importance of middle management will decline in the decades ahead. Why?
5. Why will retraining workers become an ever-increasing problem in the years ahead?
6. What changes are anticipated in the kinds of jobs that will be available in the next decade?
7. Do you agree with the views of some observers that the conventional MBA will decline in value? Why or why not?
8. What are examples of less-structured working conditions that may come about? Do you think they will have a negative or positive effect on productivity? Why or why not?
9. Many observers predict much more emphasis on participative management in the future. Why is participative management likely to become more popular?
10. Communicating will be faster and easier in the years ahead. How will this affect managing?
11. Why is the future of organized labor not promising?
12. How will technology simplify the control function?
13. Why will the demand by American labor and some businesses for more protection in international trade be likely to continue? Do you feel trade protection in the long run is good or bad? Why?

**1. Should the Fast-Grow Fertilizer Company teach its foreign employees English?**

The Fast-Grow Fertilizer Company operates in South Florida. Eighty percent of the 360-member work force speaks Spanish and knows almost no English.

The president of the company, Mr. Waterman, meets with Alice Adeleman to discuss whether management should provide instruction in reading and speaking English to the workers who know only Spanish.

Waterman: What do you think about my idea for teaching how to read and write English to our employees of Spanish descent?

Adeleman: I've given it a lot of thought and I've got to say I'm opposed to it for this reason. For one thing, the community colleges in the area offer such instruction now at very low costs. Any employee who really wants to learn English can — and at public expense, not ours.

**557**

Waterman: But as we continue to computerize and automate, it will be essential for more rank-and-file employees to use the English language.

Adeleman: That's not really a good reason for teaching employees to use our language. All of the supervisors are bilingual.

Waterman: That's true. But I'm hoping as we move into the future, we can cut back substantially on our supervisory staff. As we do that, we'll expect employees to communicate directly to upper management. The savings in having fewer supervisors should be considerable.

Adeleman: But as we use more technology, isn't it likely we'll cut way back on the number of operative employees? Besides, I'm afraid as soon as some of our employees learn the English language they'll quit and find higher-paying jobs.

Waterman: Well, we don't have to make a decision immediately. Let's continue to evaluate the idea.

Do you think Waterman's idea is sound? Why or why not?

What other arguments can you advance to support Waterman's viewpoints? Adeleman's?

### 2. Should the Shea Printing Company adopt the management practice of quality circles?

The Shea Printing Company specializes in printing newspapers for fourteen suburban communities in northern Ohio. The company employs fifty people. Recently, Delinor Nalley, vice-president of the company, attended a one-day seminar called "How to Use Quality Circles." The following discussion takes place between Nalley and Shea, the president.

Nalley: I'm excited about quality circles. More and more companies are using them to increase efficiency in everything from production to marketing to finance. I think we should use quality circles in our business.

Shea: But we have only fifty employees. You and I know most of them personally, and we've always encouraged open communication. If anybody comes up with an idea, we listen to it. After all, we own this business, and we're eager to do anything that will make us more money.

Nalley: But the concept behind quality circles is that people within each circle have a defined mission — increase productivity through ideas.

Shea: The idea of quality circles may be okay for large companies, but I think we're too small for the concept to work. I think most of our employees would feel self-conscious discussing ideas with people, most of whom they know on and off the job.

Is the Shea Printing Company too small for quality circles to work? Explain.

What alternatives to quality circles could Shea management use to generate business-improvement ideas?

### 3. Is participative management a good idea for all companies?

Max Adams joined the Infant Wear Apparel Company six months ago. The company, a 75-year-old family business, employs about 200 production workers. Adams, three years out of college where he majored in management, is discussing an idea with Morris Abrams, president and general manager and a substantial stockholder in the business.

Adams: Based on my observations, we give virtually no opportunity to our employees to participate in the management process. We do all the planning for them — when to work and how to perform their jobs. We never ask for their suggestions. I think we should at least experiment with participative management. My professors at the university stressed it, and about everything I read says it's the wave of the future.

Abrams: They were talking about participative management when I went to college fifteen years ago. Granted, it may have some applications in technologically based firms, marketing-oriented firms where ideas are important, and in other non-production-based companies. But our work is carefully engineered. To be sure we're operating efficiently, I retain a team of consultants once a year to make a methods study.

Adams: But it might improve morale if employees had some say in what affects them.

Abrams: As far as I'm concerned, morale is fine. As you know better than I, we have almost no turnover here at Infant Wear. Jobs in this community are hard to come by. Besides, I don't believe our employees really want to participate in managing. They seem content with imposed work standards and rules.

Is it true that participative management works better in some kinds of enterprises than in others? Explain.

If you were Adams, would you pursue your goal of participative management any further? Why or why not?

## FOR ADDITIONAL CONCEPTS AND IDEAS

Alexander, Charles P. "The New Economy." *Time*, May 30, 1983, pp. 62–68.

Higgens, Richard B. "Creating a Climate Conducive to Planning." *Long Range Planning,* Vol. 14 (February 1981), pp. 49–54.

Liebling, Barry A. "Riding the Organizational Pendulum . . . Is It Time to (De) Centralize?" *Management Review*, September 1981, pp. 14–20.

Main, Jeremy. "Work Won't Be The Same Again." *Fortune*, January 28, 1982, pp. 59–65.

Mashburn, James I. and Vaught, Bobby C. "Two Heads Are Better Than One: The Case for Dual Leadership." *Management Review,* December 1980, pp. 53–56.

Naisbitt, John. *Megatrends.* New York: Warner, 1982.

"A New Era for Management." *Business Week (Special Report)*, April 25, 1983, pp. 50–86.

Plotzke, George T. "New Technology Creates the Office of the Future." *Management Review*, February 1982, pp. 8–15.

"Quality of Work Life: Catching on." *Business Week*, September 21, 1981, 72–80.

Talpaert, Roger. "Looking Into the Future: Management in the Twenty-First Century." *Management Review*, March 1981, pp. 21–25.

Willatt, Norris. "The Flexlife Future." *Management Today,* June 1980, pp. 80–84.

Wissema, J. G. "The Modern Prophets—How Can They Help Us?" *Long-Range Planning,* Vol. 15, No. 4 (August 1982), pp. 126–134.

# APPENDIX

# CAREERS IN MANAGEMENT

Selecting a career — choosing the kind of work that you want to do — is important for several reasons. Chances are that the majority of your waking hours are spent working. Since work is a dominant aspect of living, it makes sense to select a career that you enjoy.

Second, people tend to be happier and more productive when performing an activity that they enjoy. Selecting the wrong career can result in job dissatisfaction, mediocre achievement, and limited financial gain.

Finally, a career should be selected carefully because the preparation for it often requires much time and effort. While changing employers may be a simple process, changing careers can be very time-consuming and costly.

This appendix contains four sections designed to help you plan your career.

1. Identification of the careers projected as most promising for the 1980s and 1990s
2. Instruction in how to use a targeted résumé
3. Information on how to prepare for a job interview
4. Detailed information about administrative and managerial occupations in accounting, banking, buying, personnel management, purchasing, and underwriting

Table A-1 lists twenty-seven middle-management positions that are expected to be above average in the number of people employed and the salaries paid in the 1980s and 1990s. The salary data provided is based on the earnings of the top one third of the managers in each position.

The top twelve careers of today, which are expected to grow in importance in the future, are indicated in the table with an asterisk.

## USE OF A TARGETED RÉSUMÉ

Tom Jackson, author of *The Perfect Résumé,* believes that a targeted résumé is the most effective type for use in today's job market. A targeted résumé focuses on a specific job target or position. For example, instead of describing the job you want as a "position in advertising," the targeted résumé would be much more specific and might state your job goal as "media planner in a food products company."

According to Mr. Jackson, a targeted résumé has the following arrangement and features:

* "The job target is specific to attract the attention of the person responsible for that activity.
* The résumé has an opening section headed Capabilities—statements illustrating work you can do, related to your target, even if it is work you have not done. This is a major advantage of the targeted résumé, which permits you to stress your qualifications and not rely on historical information."[1] In order to highlight appropriate skills and experience in a targeted résumé, you need to research and understand your specific job target.
* "The Capabilities section is followed by Accomplishments or Achievements, which details work activities you have done in terms related to the job market.
* It uses a small section at the bottom of the page for your work Experience and Education. Because emphasis is directed towards a specific job target and its requirements, education and experience tend to be in the area of background information rather than leading edge statements."[2]

Figure A–1 shows an example of a targeted résumé. Below the figure are the common complaints personnel placement specialists make about résumés they receive.

---

[1]Quoted from the 1983 Spring Edition of *Business Week's Guide to Careers,* © 1983 by McGraw-Hill, Inc.
[2]Ibid.

Like any other type of résumé, the targeted résumé should be accompanied by a cover letter. Your cover letter should include brief paragraphs stating the position you are seeking, your qualifications for the position, your reason for wanting the job, and a request for an opportunity to discuss your qualifications.

## TABLE A-1

**12 Top Careers: Salary Ranges for Selected Middle-Management Positions in Medium- and Large-Size Companies, 1982**

| Technical | Range for top third of managers |
|---|---|
| *R&D executive | $60,000–79,000 |
| *Corporate construction director | $60,000–77,000 |
| Chief industrial engineer | $50,000–63,000 |
| **Finance** | |
| *Security investments manager | $50,000–76,000 |
| *General accounting (report to controller) | $45,000–68,000 |
| *Tax compliance manager | $50,000–66,000 |
| Financial planning officer (report to controller) | $50,000–62,000 |
| Bank manager (at least $10 million deposits) | $46,000–61,000 |
| Chief internal auditor | $40,000–53,000 |
| **Sales** | |
| *National account manager | $50,000–69,000 |
| Brand manager (sales over $5 million) | $30,000–63,000 |
| International sales | $45,000–59,000 |
| Sales promotion | $40,000–56,000 |
| **Personnel** | |
| *Management training specialist/dept. head | $50,000–76,000 |
| *Personnel/human resources manager | $50,000–68,000 |
| *Labor relations executive | $45,000–68,000 |
| Employee training specialist/dept. head | $35,000–47,000 |
| **Planning** | |
| *Corporate strategic planner | $50,000–70,000 |
| Corporate economist | $50,000–61,000 |
| **Manufacturing** | |
| *Plant manager | $40,000–69,000 |
| Quality assurance & reliability | $35,000–60,000 |
| **Other** | |
| *Management Information Systems specialist/data proc. | $45,000–77,000 |
| Federal relations executive | $50,000–64,000 |
| Corp. insurance/risk manager | $45,000–63,000 |
| Contract administrator | $40,000–54,000 |
| Purchasing manager | $35,000–53,000 |
| Media manager | $30,000–53,000 |

*The top dozen career slots for current middle managers of above-average abilities in medium and large-size companies.

Source: Ross, Steve, "12 Top Careers," *Business Week's Guide to Careers,* Spring Edition 1983, p. 9.

**The Targeted Résumé**

```
                        DANIEL M. KARLOFF
                        390 BERKELEY DRIVE
                       SYRACUSE, N.Y.  13210
                          (315)555-8711


    EDUCATION:  B.A. Syracuse University    1982    Urban Studies


    JOB TARGET:  RESEARCH ASSISTANT WITH AN URBAN AND REGIONAL
                 PLANNING FIRM

    CAPABILITIES:

       *  Write complete and detailed research reports.
       *  Edit written materials for content and grammar.
       *  Work long hours without physical stress or annoyance.
       *  Communicate effectively with librarians and others
          required to support research work.
       *  Read and take useful notes on detailed and complex materials.
       *  Type reports, memos, and letters in draft form.
       *  Receive and carry out complicated instructions and tasks.
       *  Sketch and draw charts and other visual materials required
          to supplement explanatory text.

    ACHIEVEMENTS:

       *  Edited college political magazine and wrote articles on
          social issues.
       *  Successfully researched background material for textbook
          on urban economics written by Professor Alfred Hinderman.
       *  Won Senior Prize for essay on crime in urban ghettos.
       *  Ran successful dormitory newspaper business.
       *  Maintained A- average throughout college career.

    WORK HISTORY:

    1982 - Present          Syracuse University Dormitory Council
                              *  Newspaper Business Manager
                              *  Newspaper Deliverer

    1981 - Present          Professor Alfred Hinderman
                              *  Research Assistant

    1979 - 1980             Syracuse Democratic Committee
                              *  Campaign Worker

    1977 - 1978             Karloff Construction
                              *  Laborer
```

**Common Complaints about Résumés**
* Too long. Contains much useless information
* Disorganized. Information scattered, hard to follow
* Poorly typed and printed. Hard to read, unprofessional
* Not enough information, only dates, titles, addresses
* Overwritten. Long paragraphs, sentences saying little
* Not results oriented. Lists duties, not accomplishments
* Contains irrelevant material such as height, weight, health, sex
* Misspellings and typographical errors, poor grammar
* Overdone. Fancy typesetting, binders
* Misdirected. No reason for candidate applying. Cover letter would help

Source: Reprinted from the 1983 Spring Edition of *Business Week's Guide to Careers*, by special
permission, © 1983 by McGraw-Hill, Inc.

# HOW TO PREPARE FOR A JOB INTERVIEW

Your chances for getting a specific job are improved when you possess knowledge about the company you are considering.

**Know the Company Doing the Interview**

Your College Placement Office may have a general description of the company you are interested in and a listing of its job openings. In addition, the placement office may be able to direct you to former graduates who joined this organization and are willing to share their impressions of the company with you. There are many sources of information in addition to the college placement office.

*Company Annual Reports* —These can be obtained directly from the company and are generally provided free of charge. If the organization is large, a brokerage firm should be able to supply the company's most recent annual report. Many college and public libraries also have copies of annual reports available.

*Other Publication Sources* —Most newspapers have a financial section, which features news about local, national, and even international businesses. Some newspapers and magazines, such as *The Wall Street Journal, Fortune, Forbes,* and *Business Week,* specialize in covering business and financial news. The reference section of most libraries usually includes copies of *Standard & Poor's Register of Corporations, Directors, and Executives* or *Moody's Manual.* These books are standard references that contain extensive information about many companies.

*Employees* —This is an excellent source, but finding representative employees who will give their views is difficult if the company is located some distance away.

**Be Prepared for Typical Interview Questions**

The purpose of the interview is for the employer and prospective employee to learn about each other. The employer wants to determine if you are the right person for the job. The prospective employee wants to make a good impression, as well as making a determination as to whether or not this is the right job and company to work for.

Remember that the interview is not a one-sided affair. It is being conducted for the benefit of both parties. It does not need to be an intimidating experience if you remember that you are not there just to be questioned by a potential employer. You are there to find out answers to questions you might have about the job and the company.

Being prepared for an interview will help you to feel at ease. Below are fifteen questions frequently asked by employers during an interview. Read the questions and formulate your answers. A successful interview is the result of proper preparation.

1. What are your long- and short-range goals and objectives? When and why did you establish these goals, and how are you preparing yourself to achieve them?

2. What specific goals, other than those related to your occupation, have you established for yourself in the next ten years?
3. What are the most important rewards you expect in your business career?
4. How would you describe yourself?
5. How do you think a boss or friend who knows you well would describe you?
6. Why should I hire you?
7. What qualifications do you have that you think will make you successful in business?
8. What do you think it takes to be successful in a company like ours?
9. In what ways do you think you can make a contribution to our company?
10. What qualities should a successful manager possess?
11. Describe the relationship that should exist between a supervisor and subordinates.
12. Why did you decide to seek a position with this company?
13. What do you know about our company?
14. What major problem have you encountered and how did you deal with it?
15. What have you learned from your mistakes?

As part of the preparation for a job interview, it helps to know what qualities an interviewer may be evaluating. Most interviewers will try to determine whether or not a job candidate:

Understand How
You Will Be
Evaluated
in the Interview

* Makes a good first impression
* Exhibits poise and confidence
* Shows an ability to communicate effectively
* Appears mentally alert
* Displays either a positive or negative attitude
* Seems mature
* Possesses knowledge of the company
* Expresses real interest in the job
* Comprehends what the job entails
* Has relevant work experience or achievements
* Possesses the appropriate educational background
* Participates in extracurricular activities
* Possesses leadership abilities or potential
* Has the ability to get along well with others

## ADMINISTRATIVE AND MANAGERIAL OCCUPATIONS

Managers and administrators achieve organizational objectives by planning and directing the activities of others. In a very small enterprise, the owner may also be the manager. However, as a business or other organization grows and becomes more complex, more people are needed to oversee the operations of the work force. Large corporations or government agencies may employ hundreds of managers, organized into a hierarchy of administrative positions.

Top-level managers or executives are primarily concerned with policy making, planning, and overall coordination. Top-level managers include school superintendents, police and fire chiefs, bank presidents, governors, mayors, hospital administrators, chief executive officers of corporations, department store managers, and government agency directors. They direct the activities of the organization through departmental or mid-level managers.

Middle managers may handle a particular area, such as personnel, accounting, sales, finance, or marketing. Or they may supervise the production process at a factory or industrial plant. Middle managers are the people who keep things running smoothly. They organize activities at the operating level and provide direct supervision.

Middle managers work with the assistance of support personnel who plan, organize, analyze, and monitor activities. Support personnel include accountants, loan officers, employment interviewers, purchasing agents and buyers, credit managers, membership directors, promotion agents, and inspectors of all kinds. Jobs such as these require technical expertise or a thorough understanding of a particular procedure or operation.

Managers and administrators are employed in virtually every type of industrial plant, commercial enterprise, and government agency. Large numbers are employed in finance, insurance, real estate, construction, public administration, health, education, transportation, and public utilities. Because of the wide range of establishments employing managers, job duties vary greatly.

As the nature of the work varies, so does the level of education required. Some managers and administrators, including school principals and hospital administrators, need at least a master's degree. Positions such as these require the specialized knowledge and skills obtained through years of formal education. Other positions, including production supervisor, retail buyer, construction manager, and maintenance superintendent, may not require a college degree. People in these jobs often have worked their way up in the organization. Their main qualification is a thorough knowledge of the operating procedures of the workplace. However, most managerial and administrative positions require a college education. In some occupations—such as accounting and medical professions—continuing education is important for maintaining job performance standards or for achieving career advancement.

Despite the differences in formal education and training, successful managers are likely to have certain characteristics in common. Because they work with people, managers need to be able to get along with others and to possess the ability to motivate and influence them. Managers should be able to inspire confidence and respect in their employees.

When they make plans and set goals for their enterprise, managers work with ideas. They need organizational skills, good judgment, and decision-making ability. Successful managers have mastered the art of getting all the facts, coming to a decision, and communicating it effectively. They need a strong sense of initiative to be able to work without close supervision.

For some administrative positions, analytical, evaluative, and promotional skills are essential. Accountants, financial analysts, and others provide the technical expertise upon which management decisions are based. Good judgment and the ability to relate to others are important for people in these occupations.

Earnings for managers and administrators vary widely. They depend on the size and nature of the particular establishment in which the manager is employed. Earnings also vary with the level of managerial or administrative responsibility. Management trainees may start working at salaries that are not much higher than those of the people they supervise. Earnings increase as managers gain experience, prove their ability to handle the job, and take on additional responsibility.

Employment opportunities will be better in some industries than in others. Little employment growth is foreseen in educational institutions during the 1980s, therefore most job openings for school administrators will result from replacement needs. By contrast, projected expansion in the health industry will generate many new managerial and administrative-support positions in hospitals, clinics, nursing homes, insurance companies, pharmaceutical and medical supply firms, and other health-related organizations. Employment growth should also be strong in wholesale and retail trade and in manufacturing.

Both the number and proportion of self-employed managers and administrators are expected to decline during the 1980s, as large enterprises and chain operations increasingly dominate business activity.

### Nature of the Work

Managers must have up-to-date financial information to make important decisions. Accountants and auditors prepare and analyze financial reports that furnish this kind of information.

Three major fields are public, management, and government accounting. Public accountants have their own businesses or work for accounting firms. Management accountants, also called industrial or private accountants, handle the financial records of their company. Government accountants and auditors examine the records of government agencies and audit private businesses and individuals whose dealings are subject to governmental regulations.

Accountants often concentrate on one phase of accounting. For example, many public accountants specialize in auditing—examining a client's financial records and reports and attesting that they are in conformity with standards of preparation and reporting. Others specialize in tax matters, such as preparing income tax forms and advising clients of the tax advantages and disadvantages of certain business decisions. Still others specialize in management consulting and offer advice on a variety of matters. They might develop or revise an accounting system to serve the needs of clients more effectively or give advice about various types of computers or electronic data processing systems.

### Employment

About 900,000 people worked as accountants and auditors in 1980, including more than 200,000 Certified Public Accountants (CPA), 20,000 licensed public accountants, and about 10,000 Certified Internal Auditors (CIA).

Most accountants do management accounting. Many others are engaged in public accounting as proprietors, partners, or employees of independent accounting firms. Other accountants work for federal, state, and local government agencies, and some teach in colleges and universities. Opportunities are plentiful for part-time work, particularly in smaller firms.

Accountants and auditors are found in all business, industrial, and government organizations. Most, however, work in large urban areas where many public accounting firms and central offices of large businesses are concentrated.

### Job Outlook

Employment is expected to grow faster than the average for all occupations through the 1980s, due to increasing pressure on businesses and government agencies to improve budgeting and accounting procedures. Because the occupation is large, many job openings should result from the need to replace workers who leave the occupation, retire, or die.

Demand for skilled accountants and auditors will rise as managers increasingly rely on accounting information to make business decisions. For example, plant expansion, mergers, or foreign investments may depend upon the financial condition of the firm, tax implications of the proposed action, and other considerations. On a smaller scale, small businesses are expected to rely more and more on the expertise of public accountants in planning their operations. Legislation regarding pension reform, tax reform, financial disclosure, and other matters should create many jobs for accountants and auditors. In addition, increases in investment and lending also should spur demand for accountants and auditors.

### Sources of Additional Information

Information about careers in accounting and about aptitude tests administered in high schools, colleges, and public accounting may be obtained from:

American Institute of Certified Public Accountants
1211 Avenue of the Americas
New York, NY 10036

Information on specialized fields of accounting and auditing is available from:

National Association of Accountants
919 Third Avenue
New York, NY 10022

National Society of Public Accountants
   and Accreditation Council for Accountancy
1010 North Fairfax Street
Alexandria, VA 22314

Institute of Internal Auditors
249 Maitland Avenue
Altamonte Springs, FL 32701

## Nature of the Work

Practically every bank has a president who directs operations, one or more vice-presidents who act as general managers or who are in charge of bank departments such as trust or credit, and a comptroller or cashier who is an executive officer generally responsible for all bank property. Large banks also may have treasurers and other senior officers, as well as junior officers, to supervise the various sections within different departments. Banks employed over 400,000 officers and managers in 1980.

Bank officers make decisions within a framework of policy set by the board of directors and existing laws and regulations. They must have a broad knowledge of business activities to relate to the operations of their department. For example, loan officers evaluate the credit and collateral of individuals and businesses applying for a loan. Similarly, trust officers must understand each account before they invest funds to support families, send young people to college, or pay retirement pensions. In addition to supervising financial services, officers advise individuals and businesses and participate in community projects.

Because banks offer many services, a wide choice of careers is available to workers who specialize.

Loan officers may handle installment, commercial, real estate or agricultural loans. To evaluate loan applications properly, officers need to be familiar with economics, production, distribution, merchandising, and commercial law. Also, they need to know business operations and be able to analyze an industry's financial statements.

Bank officers in trust management require knowledge of financial planning for investment research and estate and trust administration.

Operations officers plan, coordinate, and control the workflow; update systems; and strive for administrative efficiency. Careers in bank operations include electronic data processing manager and other positions involving internal and customer services.

## Employment

Employment opportunities in banking will be more challenging in the future as technology increasingly is used to perform routine work. Historically, banks were local institutions serving people living in a small geographical area. This is changing as the trend toward statewide and interstate banking continues. As a result, a person joining a bank may serve in a number of physical locations during his or her career.

Because of deregulation of laws governing banking, numerous other organizations, such as stock brokerage houses, now provide similar services. People desiring a career in banking, therefore, may find highly similar work in "nonbank" firms. However, most employment opportunities in banking are with private banks, since our banking system is owned by investors. Some employment is also available through the federally managed bank, the Federal Reserve System.

## Job Outlook

Through the 1980s, employment of bank officers is expected to increase faster than the average for all occupations. Rising costs due to expanding banking services and the increasing dependence on computers will require more officers to provide sound management and effective quality control. Greater international trade and investment will stimulate international and domestic banking activities, thus increasing the need for bank officers and managers. Adding to this increase in demand due to growth will be the need to replace experienced officers who die, retire, or leave their jobs for other reasons.

Because of the increasing number of qualified applicants, competition for bank managerial positions is expected to stiffen. Once employed, managers and officers are likely to work year-round, even during periods of slow economic activity, because cyclical swings in the economy seem to have little immediate effect on banking activites.

### Sources of Additional Information

General information about banking occupations, training opportunities, and the banking industry itself is available from:

American Bankers Association
Bank Personnel Division
1120 Connecticut Avenue, N.W.
Washington, DC  20036

National Association of Bank Women, Inc.
National Office
500 North Michigan Avenue
Chicago, IL  60611

National Bankers Association
449 South Capitol Street, S.W.
Suite 520
Washington, DC  20003

For information about career opportunities as a bank examiner, contact:

Federal Deposit Insurance Corporation
Director of Personnel
550 17th Street, N.W.
Washington, DC  20429

Federal Savings and Loan Insurance Corporation
Officer of the General Counsel
1700 G Street, N.W.
Washington, DC  20552

For information on careers with the Federal Reserve System contact the personnel department of the Federal Reserve Bank serving a particular geographic area or:

571

*Administrative
and
Managerial
Occupations*

Buyers

Board of Governors
The Federal Reserve System
Personnel Department
Washington, DC 20551

**Nature of the Work**

The job of a retail buyer often brings to mind the glamour of high fashion; indeed, many fashion buyers do lead exciting, fast-paced lives. Not every buyer, however, travels abroad or deals in fashion. All merchandise sold in a retail store—garden furniture, automobile tires, toys, aluminum pots, and canned soups—appears there on the decision of a buyer. Buyers seek goods that will satisfy their stores' customers and will sell at a profit. The kind and variety of goods purchased depends on the store. A buyer for a small clothing store may purchase all of the merchandise carried, from sportswear to formal wear. Buyers in larger retail businesses often handle only one or two lines of goods. Some, known as *foreign buyers,* only handle the purchase of merchandise from outside of the United States.

In order to purchase the best merchandise for their stores, buyers must be familiar with the manufacturers and distributors who have the merchandise they need. They also must keep informed about changes in existing products and the development of new ones. To do this, buyers attend fashion and trade shows and visit manufacturers' showrooms. They usually order goods during these buying trips, and also when wholesale and manufacturers' sales workers call on them to display their merchandise.

Buyers must be able to assess the resale value of goods after a brief inspection and make a purchase decision quickly. They try to select merchandise that will sell quickly at well above the original cost. Since most buyers work within a fixed budget, they must plan their purchases to keep needed items always in stock but also allow for special purchases when a "good buy" presents itself.

Buyers frequently work more than a forty-hour week because of special sales, conferences, and travel. The amount of traveling varies with the type of merchandise and the location of suppliers, but most spend four or five days a month on the road.

**Employment**

In 1980, approximately 150,000 buyers worked for retail firms. Although buyers work in all parts of the country, most are in major metropolitan areas where retail stores are concentrated.

**Job Outlook**

Employment of buyers is expected to grow about as fast as the average for all occupations through the 1980s as the retail trade industry, where buyers work, expands in response to a growing population and higher personal incomes. Besides jobs that will be created by increased demand for buyers, many job openings will arise each year from the need to replace workers who transfer to other occupations, retire, or die.

Competition for buying jobs is expected to be keen because merchandising attracts many college graduates. Prospects are likely to be best for qualified applicants who enjoy the competitive, existing nature of retailing.

### Sources of Additional Information

General information about a career in retailing is available from:

National Retail Merchants Association
100 West 31st Street
New York, NY 10001

Information on schools that teach retailing is available from:

U.S. Department of Education
Division of Vocational/Technical Education
Washington, DC 20202

National Association of Trade and Technical Schools
2021 K Street, N.W.
Washington, DC 20006

## Credit Managers

### Nature of the Work

Over the years, buying on credit has become a customary way of doing business. Consumers use credit to pay for houses, cars, appliances, and travel, as well as day-to-day retail purchases. Most business purchases, such as raw materials used in manufacturing and merchandise to be sold in retail stores, also are on credit.

For most forms of credit, a credit manager has final authority to accept or reject a credit application. In extending credit to a business (commercial credit), the credit manager or an assistant analyzes detailed financial reports submitted by the applicant, interviews a representative of the company about its management, and reviews credit agency reports to determine the firm's record in repaying debts. The manager also checks at banks where the company has deposits or previously was granted credit. In extending credit to individuals (consumer credit), detailed financial reports usually are not available. The credit manager must rely more on personal interviews and credit bureau and bank reports to provide information about applicants.

Particularly in large organizations, executive-level credit managers work with other top managers to formulate a credit policy. They establish financial standards to be met by applicants, and thereby determine the amount of risk that their company will accept when offering its products or services for sale on credit. Managers must cooperate with the sales department to develop a credit policy liberal enough to allow the company's sales to increase, yet strict enough to deny credit to customers whose ability to repay their debts is questionable. Many credit managers establish office procedures and supervise workers, such as application clerks, collection workers, bookkeepers, computer operators, and secretaries, who gather information, analyze facts, and perform general office duties in a credit department.

In small companies that handle a limited number of accounts, credit managers may do much of the work themselves. They may interview applicants, analyze information gained in the interview, and make the final approval. They frequently contact customers who are unable to or refuse to pay their debts. If these attempts at collection fail, credit managers may refer the account to a collection agency or assign an attorney to take legal action.

### Employment

An estimated 55,000 persons worked as credit managers in 1980. About half were employed in wholesale and retail trade; most others worked for manufacturing firms and financial institutions.

Although credit is granted throughout the United States, most credit managers work in urban areas where many financial and business establishments are located.

### Job Outlook

Employment of credit managers is expected to grow more slowly than the average for all occupations through the 1980s. Nevertheless, many jobs will become available each year due to the need to replace persons who leave the occupation.

Anticipated increases in business and consumer purchases are expected to result in a greater use of credit in the future. However, several factors are expected to continue to limit growth in employment of credit managers. The use of computers for storing, retrieving, and processing information has enabled credit managers to evaluate applications for credit more efficiently. The use of telecommunications networks has enabled retail outlets to centralize credit operations. Also, businesses will continue to reduce or eliminate their credit departments and will rely on their customers use of bank credit cards. These bank operations also maintain more efficient centralized operations.

### Sources of Additional Information

Information about a career in consumer credit may be obtained from:

National Retail Merchants Association
100 West 31st Street
New York, NY  10001

For information about training programs available in commercial credit, write:

National Association of Credit Management
475 Park Avenue, South
New York, NY  10016

### Nature of the Work

Medical and health care is provided by organizations that vary from large teaching hospitals to storefront clinics. It is the job of the health services administrator to provide effective management for these facilities under the general supervision of a board of directors or other governing body.

Administrators direct the various functions and activities that make a health organization run smoothly. They have overall responsibility for management decisions of many kinds: budget preparation; establishing rates for health services; directing the hiring and training of personnel; and directing and coordinating the activities of the medical, nursing, physical plant, and other operating departments. They must also plan and negotiate for expansion of facilities and services to keep pace with community requirements. They may handle these matters alone if the organization is small, or, more commonly, direct a staff of assistant administrators. Even where assistant administrators direct daily operations of various departments, the chief executive keeps informed through formal and informal meetings with assistants, medical staff, and others.

Many health administrators also help carry out fund-raising drives and promote public participation in health programs. This phase of the administrator's job often includes speaking before civic groups, arranging publicity, and coordinating the activities of the organization with those of government or community agencies.

### Employment

About 220,000 persons worked in some phase of health administration in 1980. Most administrators work in patient-care facilities, including hospitals, nursing homes, rehabilitation centers, home health agencies, and health maintanence organizations. Hospitals employ about half of all administrators; some of these work for the federal government in the Veterans Administration, Public Health Service, and Armed Forces hospitals and clinics.

Some health administrators work for state and local health departments. Others work for voluntary health agencies that support medical research into the causes and treatment of particular diseases or impairments. These agencies also conduct professional and public education and community service programs. Still other health administrators are employed by consulting firms that provide management services for a fee.

### Job Outlook

The number of graduate programs in health administration has increased rapidly in recent years; in addition, administrative specialists with graduate degrees in other fields are entering the profession. Consequently, competition for jobs has intensified, particularly in hospital administration. This situation is expected to continue, and it may become difficult for persons with less than a graduate education to obtain administrative jobs in hospitals. In nursing homes and other long-term care facilities, where a graduate degree in health administration is not ordinarily a requirement, job opportunities will be good for individuals with a business or management background.

Employment of health services administrators is expected to grow faster than the average for all occupations through the 1980s as the health industry expands and health services management becomes more complex. Not all areas of health care will experience identical rates of growth, however. Population migration has caused the closing of some hospitals where population is declining and the opening of hospitals in areas of population growth—notably in the South and

West. Overall, however, hospital administration may not contribute heavily to employment opportunities for health administrators in the coming years. Although hospitals have been growing in size and increasing the scope and sophistication of their services, the number of hospitals is decreasing. Demand for administrators will be stimulated, however, by the formation of group medical practices and health maintenance organizations. Administrators also will be needed in nursing and convalescent homes to handle the increasing amount of administrative work expected as these facilities expand. Job openings also will result from the need to replace personnel who transfer to another field, retire, or die.

### Sources of Additional Information

Information about health administration and the academic programs in this field offered by universities, colleges, and community colleges is available from:

American College of Hospital Administration
840 North Lake Shore Drive
Chicago, IL 60611

Association of University Programs in Health Administration
One Dupont Circle, N.W.
Washington, DC 20036

National Health Council
Health Careers Program
70 West 40th Street
New York, NY 10019

American College of Nursing Home Administrators
4650 East-West Highway
Washington, DC 20014

### Nature of the Work

Protecting the public from health and safety hazards, prohibiting unfair trade and employment practices, controlling immigration, and raising revenue are responsibilities of the government. Health and regulatory inspectors enforce the laws and regulations that govern these responsibilities.

The duties, titles, and responsibilities of federal, state, and local health and regulatory inspectors vary widely. Some types of inspectors work only for the federal government, while others also are employed by state and local governments.

Health and regulatory inspectors work with engineers, chemists, microbiologists, and health workers to insure compliance with public health and safety regulations governing food, drugs, cosmetics, and other consumer products. They also administer regulations that govern the quarantine of persons and products entering the United States from foreign countries. The major types of health inspectors are: consumer safety, food, agricultural quarantine, and envi-

Government Health
and Regulatory
Inspectors

ronmental health inspectors. In addition, some inspectors work in a field closely related to food inspection — agricultural commodity grading.

### Employment

About 112,000 persons worked as health and regulatory inspectors in 1980. Employment was nearly evenly divided among the three levels of government — federal, state, and local. The largest single employer of consumer safety inspectors is the U.S. Food and Drug Administration, but the majority work for state governments. Most food inspectors and agricultural commodity graders in processing plants are employed by the U.S. Department of Agriculture. Agricultural quarantine inspectors work for the U.S. Public Health Service or the U.S. Department of Agriculture. Most environmental health inspectors work for state and local governments.

Most federal regulatory inspectors work in regional and district offices throughout the United States. Air safety inspectors work for the Federal Aviation Administration; wage-hour compliance officers, for the Department of Labor; and alcohol, tobacco, and firearms inspectors, for the Treasury Department. Occupational safety and health inspectors and mine inspectors also work for the Department of Labor, as well as many state governments. Like agricultural quarantine inspectors, immigration and customs inspectors work at U.S. airports, seaports, and border crossing points, and at foreign airports and seaports. Immigration inspectors are employed by the Department of Justice. Customs inspectors work for the Treasury Department.

### Job Outlook

Employment of health and regulatory inspectors as a group is expected to increase more slowly than the average for all occupations through the 1980s. Employment growth is expected to be constrained by slow growth in government regulatory programs and in government spending. Most job openings will be to replace those who transfer to other occupations, retire, or die.

Because health and regulatory inspectors are government workers, their employment is seldom affected by general economic fluctuations. Most inspectors work in programs which enjoy wide public support. As a result, they are less likely to lose their jobs than many other workers when government programs are cut.

### Sources of Additional Information

Information on federal government jobs is available from local offices of the state employment service, area offices of the U.S. Office of Personnel Management, and Federal Job Information Centers in large cities throughout the country. For information on a career as a specific type of inspector, the federal department or agency that employs them may be contacted directly.

Information about state and local government jobs is available from state civil service commissions, usually located in each state capital, or from local government offices.

**Personnel and
Labor Relations
Specialists**

### Nature of the Work

Attracting the best available employees and matching them to the jobs they can do best is important for the success of any organization. But many enterprises have become too large to permit close contact between management and employees. Instead, personnel and labor relations specialists provide this link — assisting management to make effective use of employees' skills, and helping employees to find satisfaction in their jobs and working conditions. Although some jobs in this field require only limited contact with people outside the office, most involve frequent contact. Dealing with people is usually an essential part of the job.

Personnel specialists and labor relations specialists concentrate on different aspects of employer–employee relations. Personnel specialists interview, select, and recommend applicants to fill job openings. They keep informed of rules and regulations pertaining to affirmative action and equal employment opportunity and oversee the implementation of policies governing hiring and advancement. They handle wage and salary administration, training and career development, and employee benefits. "Labor relations" means union-management relations, and people who specialize in this field, for the most part, work in unionized establishments. They help company officials prepare for collective bargaining sessions, they participate in contract negotiations, and they handle daily labor relations matters.

In a small organization, personnel work consists mostly of interviewing and hiring, and one person can handle it all. By contrast, the professional staff of a large personnel department may include recruiters, interviewers, job analysts, benefits specialists, training specialists, and labor relations specialists. Personnel clerks and assistants handle routine tasks such as issuing forms, maintaining files, compiling statistics, and answering inquiries.

Personnel work often begins with the recruiter, who maintains contacts within the community and may travel extensively — usually to college campuses — in the search for promising job applicants. Recruiters talk to applicants, and refer and recommend those who appear qualified to fill vacancies. They may administer preemployment tests and check references. These workers need to be thoroughly familiar with the organization and its personnel policies, for they must be prepared to discuss wages, working conditions, and promotional opportunities with prospective and newly hired employees. They also need to keep informed about equal employment opportunity (EEO) and affirmative action guidelines.

EEO representatives or affirmative action coordinators handle this complex and sensitive area in large organizations. They maintain contact with women and minority employees, and investigate and resolve EEO grievances. They also examine corporate practices for possible violations, and compile and submit EEO statistical reports.

Job analysts, sometimes called compensation analysts, do very exacting work. They collect and examine detailed information about job duties in order to prepare job descriptions. These descriptions or "position classifications" explain the duties, training, and skills each job requires. Whenever a large organization introduces a new job or reviews existing ones, it calls upon the expert knowledge of the job analyst. Accurate information about job duties also is required when an organization considers changes in its pay system.

Establishing and maintaining a firm's pay system is the principal job of the compensation manager. With the assistance of staff specialists, compensation managers devise ways to ensure that pay rates within the firm are fair and equitable. They may conduct surveys from time to time to see how their pay rates compare with others. Being certain that the firm's pay system complies with laws and regulations is another part of the job, one that requires knowledge of compensation structures and labor law.

Human resource development is emerging as a major specialization within personnel administration. Training specialists are responsible for a broad range of employee education and training activities. They work with adults in a variety of business and industrial settings, as well as in local, state, and federal government agencies. Trainers conduct orientation sessions for new employees and arrange on-the-job training for them. They develop in-house programs as needs are identified. They may, for example, instruct experienced workers in the impact of new procedures or the operation of new equipment, or they may teach management skills to new supervisors. In addition to designing, developing, and conducting programs, these specialists assess employee training needs, maintain records of company training activities, and monitor and evaluate the effectiveness of various kinds of training. Helping employees prepare for future responsibilities is an increasingly important part of the job. Sometimes, this means setting up an individualized training plan, which provides a timetable for strengthening existing job-related skills and acquiring new ones. Career development may involve employer-financed study outside the company as well as job rotation to different parts of the firm. The training function within a company and the role and responsibilities of training specialists vary greatly, depending on the size of the firm and organizational goals and objectives.

Employee-welfare managers handle the employer's benefits program, notably its insurance and pension plans. Expertise in designing and administering benefits programs is increasingly important in the personnel field, in part because of the enactment of the Employee Retirement Income Security Act (ERISA). ERISA reporting requirements are an important responsibility for personnel departments in large firms.

The scope of employee benefits has grown considerably, and many firms offer their employees such benefits as dental insurance, accidental death and disability insurance, auto insurance, home owners' insurance, stock options, profit sharing and thrift/savings plans in addition to conventional health insurance and pension coverage. Benefits analysts and benefits administrators handle these programs. They also are responsible for developing and coordinating services as diverse as van-pooling, child care, lunchrooms and company cafeterias, newsletters, annual physical exams, recreation and physical fitness, and counseling. Personal and financial counseling for employees approaching retirement age is becoming a more important part of the job.

Labor relations specialists advise management on all aspects of union-management relations. When a collective bargaining agreement is up for negotiation, they provide background information for management's negotiating position, a job that requires familiarity with sources of economic and wage data as well as extensive knowledge of labor law and collective bargaining trends. Actual negotiation of the agreement is conducted at the top level, with the director of labor relations or another top-ranking official serving as the employer's representative, but members of the company's labor relations staff play an important role throughout the negotiations.

Much of the work of the labor relations staff concerns interpretation and administration of the contract, the grievance procedures in particular. Labor relations specialists might work with the union on seniority rights under the layoff procedure set forth in the contract, for example, or meet with the union steward about a grievance. Doing the job well means staying abreast of current developments in labor law, including arbitration decisions, and maintaining continuing liaison with union officials.

Personnel specialists in government agencies generally do the same kind of work as those in large business firms. There are some differences, however. Public personnel specialists deal with employees whose jobs are subject to civil service regulations. Because civil service jobs are strictly classified as to entry requirements, duties, and pay, much of the emphasis in public personnel work is on job analysis. Training and career development are growing in importance in the public sector—so much so that an entire "industry" of educational and training consultants helps provide staff training for public agencies. Labor relations in the public personnel field have changed as union strength among government workers has grown. This has created a need for more and better trained workers to handle negotiations, grievances, and arbitration cases on behalf of federal, state, and local government agencies.

### Employment

In 1980, about 178,000 people worked as personnel and labor relations specialists. Two out of three worked in private industry, where they were employed by businesses of every description. Personnel and labor relations specialists work for firms that engage in manufacturing; construction; trade; transportation and communications; finance, insurance, and real estate; and services. Some work for labor unions. Others are employed by, or run, management consulting firms that specialize in such areas as compensation, pension planning, and staff development.

Approximately 55,000 personnel and labor relations specialists worked for federal, state, and local governments in 1980. They handled recruitment, interviewing, job classification, training, and related matters for the nation's 15 million public employees: police officers, firefighters, sanitation workers, teachers, hospital workers, and many others.

Labor unions employed about 12,000 of these workers in 1980. An elected union official generally handles labor relations matters at the company level. At national and international union headquarters, however, the research and education staff usually includes specialists with professional training in industrial and labor relations, economics, or law.

Some personnel and labor relations specialists teach college or university courses in personnel administration, industrial relations, and related subjects.

### Job Outlook

The number of personnel and labor relations specialists is expected to grow about as fast as the average for all occupations through the 1980s. Most of this growth will occur in the private sector as employers, aware of the potential benefits, try to provide effective employee relations programs for an expanding work force.

Within public personnel administration, opportunities probably will be best in state and local governments. At the federal level, most job openings will result from replacement needs. In addition to new jobs created by heightened demand for these workers, many openings will occur every year as personnel and labor relations specialists change occupations, retire, or die.

Legislation setting standards for employment practices in the areas of occupational safety and health, equal employment opportunity, and pensions has greatly increased record keeping and reporting requirements as well as legal requirements, thus stimulating demand for personnel and labor relations workers. Continued growth is foreseen as employers review and evaluate programs in these areas.

Every year, billions of dollars are spent on employee training in the public and private sectors, and the amount is expected to increase in the decade ahead. Greater emphasis on productivity is expected to stimulate greater investment in job-specific, employer-sponsored training that aims to improve performance by sharpening employees' skills and heightening their motivation. Continued expansion in the area of human resource development will contribute to the projected increase in the number of personnel and labor relations specialists during the 1980s.

### Sources of Additional Information

For general information on careers in personnel and industrial relations, write to:

American Society for Personnel Administration
30 Park Drive
Berea, OH 44017

For information about the field of employee training and human resource development, contact:

American Society for Training and Development
600 Maryland Avenue, S.W., Suite 305
Washington, DC 20024

A brochure describing a career in labor-management relations as a field examiner is available from:

Director of Personnel, National Labor Relations Board
1717 Pennsylvania Avenue, N.W.
Washington, DC 20570

## Purchasing Agents

### Nature of the Work

If an organization does not have the right materials, supplies, or equipment when they are needed, its entire production process or work flow could be interrupted or halted. Purchasing agents see to it that this does not happen. Purchasing agents, also called industrial buyers, obtain goods and services of the quality required at the lowest possible cost, and see that adequate materials and supplies always are available. Agents in industry and the government, depending on the nature of the operation, may buy machinery, raw materials, parts and components, furniture, business machines, vehicles, office supplies, and services.

Purchasing agents buy supplies when the stock on hand reaches a pre-determined reorder point, when a department in the organization requisitions items it needs, or when market conditions are especially favorable. Because agents often can purchase from many sources, their main job is selecting the supplier who offers the best value.

Purchasing agents use a variety of means to choose suppliers. They compare listings in catalogs, directories, and trade journals. They meet with salespersons to discuss items to be purchased and examine samples, and attend demonstrations of equipment. Frequently, agents invite suppliers to bid on large orders, and then select the lowest bidder among those who meet requirements for quality and delivery date.

Sometimes purchasing agents negotiate for custom-made products. To meet specifications, agents must thoroughly understand the products and their uses. In some cases, such as computer equipment, this means agents must have considerable technical knowledge. After placing an order, the purchasing agent checks periodically to insure prompt delivery.

Purchasing agents develop a good business relationship with suppliers in order to get cost savings, favorable payment terms, and quick delivery on emergency orders or help in obtaining scarce materials. Agents also work closely with other employees in their own organization. For example, they may discuss design of custom-made products with company engineers, defects in purchased goods with quality control technicians, or shipment problems with workers in the shipping department.

### Employment

About 172,000 persons worked as purchasing agents in 1980. Over half worked in manufacturing industries. Large numbers also were employed by government agencies, construction companies, hospitals, and schools.

About half of all purchasing agents work in organizations that have fewer than five employees in the purchasing department. Many large business firms and government agencies, however, have much larger purchasing departments; some employ as many as one hundred specialized purchasing agents.

### Job Outlook

Employment of purchasing agents is expected to increase about as fast as the average for all occupations through the 1980s. Many job openings will occur as employed purchasing agents transfer to other work, retire, or die.

Demand for purchasing agents is expected to rise as the volume of goods and services produced increases and as their importance in reducing costs is increasingly recognized. Large industrial organizations will expand purchasing departments to handle the growing complexity of manufacturing processes. Many opportunities also should arise as service organizations such as hospitals and schools also recognize the importance of professional purchasers in reducing costs.

Persons who have a master's degree in business administration, a bachelor's degree in engineering, science, or business administration, and whose college program included some courses in purchasing should have the best opportunities. Graduates of two-year programs in purchasing should continue to find good opportunities, especially in small firms.

### Sources of Additional Information

Further information about a career in purchasing is available from:

National Association of Purchasing Management, Inc.
11 Park Place
New York, NY 10007

National Institute of Governmental Purchasing
1735 Jefferson Davis Highway, Suite 101
Arlington, VA 22202

## Underwriters

### Nature of the Work

Insurance companies assume billions of dollars in risks each year by transferring the risk of loss from their policyholders to themselves. Underwriters appraise and select the risks their company will insure.

Underwriters decide whether their companies will accept risks after analyzing information in insurance applications, reports from loss control consultants, medical reports, and actuarial studies (reports that describe the probability of insured loss). Their companies may lose business to competitors if they appraise risks too conservatively or may have to pay more claims if their underwriting actions are too liberal.

When deciding that an applicant is an acceptable risk, an underwriter may outline the terms of the contract, including the amount of the premium. Underwriters frequently correspond with policyholders, agents, and managers about policy cancellations or other requests for information. In addition, they sometimes accompany salespeople on appointments with prospective customers.

Most underwriters specialize in one of three major categories of insurance: life, property and liability, or health. They further specialize in group or individual policies. The property and liability underwriter specializes by type of risk insured, such as fire, automobile, marine, or workers' compensation. In cases where casualty companies insure in a single "package" policy, covering various types of risks, however, the underwriter must be familiar with different lines of insurance. Some underwriters, called commercial account underwriters, handle business insurance exclusively. They often evaluate a firm's entire operation in appraising its insurance application.

### Employment

About 76,000 persons worked as insurance underwriters in 1980. Over three fourths were property and liability underwriters in regional or home offices; most life insurance underwriters were in home offices in a few large cities, such as New York, San Francisco, Chicago, Dallas, Philadelphia, and Hartford.

## Job Outlook

Employment of underwriters is expected to rise about as fast as the average for all occupations through the 1980s as insurance sales continue to expand. Each year many jobs will become available as the need for underwriters grows and as those who die, retire, or transfer to other work are replaced.

Several factors underlie the expected growth in the volume of insurance and the resulting need for underwriters. Over the next decade, many more workers will enter the 25 to 54 age group. People in this age group have the greatest need for life and health insurance and protection for homes, automobiles, and other valuables. A growing demand for insurance coverage for working women is also expected. Growing security consciousness should also contribute to demand for more insurance protection. New or expanding businesses will need protection for new plants and equipment, insurance for workers' compensation, product liability, and mandatory insurance against long-term gradual environmental damage caused by hazardous waste. Competition among insurance companies and changes in regulations affecting investment profits also are expected to increase the need for underwriters.

Since insurance is usually regarded as a necessity regardless of economic conditions, underwriters are unlikely to be laid off during a recession.

## Sources of Additional Information

General information about a career as an insurance underwriter is available from the home offices of many life insurance and property and liability insurance companies. Information about career opportunities as an underwriter also may be obtained from:

American Council of Life Insurance
1850 K Street, N.W.
Washington, D.C. 20006

Insurance Information Institute
110 William Street
New York, NY 10038

Alliance of American Insurers
20 N. Wacker Drive
Chicago, IL 60606

# GLOSSARY/INDEX

centralized activities, 269
decentralization of, 268
Congress, use of committees, 295
Constraints:
 as considerations in decision making, 166
 on corrective action, 512–13
**Consultative leader** A leader who delegates
 responsibility extensively, seeks the opinions of
 subordinates, and uses reward more than
 punishment as a motivator. 433
Contingencies, principle of, 43
**Contingency** An event that occurs without intent and
 that is considered possible but not probable. 68
 plans, 68, 90
 strategies for, 114–115
 unforseen conditions, *91*
**Contingency or situational theory of leadership**
 Leadership theory, developed by Fred Fiedler, that
 proposes that a leader's success is based not only on
 personality traits but also on situational factors (kind
 of organization, nature of the task, and so on). 436
**Control** An inherent function in managing, and one
 needed in organizations to make sure that plans are
 carried out and desired results are achieved; control
 entails setting standards for work performed,
 measuring performance against the standards, and
 taking corrective action as needed. 35, 487
**Control devices** Methods used to determine if work is
 being performed according to plan. 231
 span of control and, 231–232
Controllable variables, 143
Controlling, 35–36, 487–515
 break-even analysis, 524–25
 in the future, 553
 Gantt chart, 525, 527–30
 interrelationship with other functions, 37
 management information systems, 532–37
 network analysis, 530–32
 principles of, 44–45
 of staff activities, 496
 step 1 in (setting standards), 490–498, 500–501
 step 2 in (measuring performance), 501–508
 step 3 in (taking corrective action), 508–13
 steps in process, 487–88, *489*
 techniques for, 517–41
 use of audits, 523–24
 use of budgets, 518–23
**Cooperation** Joint effort, not motivated by purely
 selfish interests, to achieve a common goal. 198
 coordination and, 198–200
 external, 289
 illegal forms, 289

589

*Glossary/Index*

 internal, 289
 management's interest in, 289
 versus competition, 288–89
**Coordinate** To organize activities so that the desired
 result is achieved in the most efficient manner. 194
Coordination, 194–96, 198–200
 committees facilitation of, 293
 functional departmentalization and, 207–208
 goal attainment and, 194–96
 of goals, 93–94
 guidelines for, 196, 198–200
 in managing, 14
 of plans to support objectives and strategies, *116*
 of procedures and objectives, 125
 product departmentalization and, 215
Corporations:
 as an artificial person, 296
 board of directors, 296–300
 charter provisions, 297
 corporate officers' appointments, 298, 300
**Corrective action** Action taken to amend, remedy,
 rectify, or in some other way make right what is
 wrong. 36, 488
 constraints and, 512–13, *513*
 in controlling process, 508–13
 diagnosis of problems, 511, *512*
 guidelines for taking, 511–12
 judgmental, *511*
 prescribed, 509, *510*
 principle of, 45
Cost standards, 49
**Cost-benefit analysis** Decision-making technique by
 which the cost of each alternative is estimated in
 terms of human, capital, and material resources and
 then weighed against the expected benefits. 167
Costello, John, 478n
Costs:
 fixed, 519, *521*
 variable, 519
**CPM (Critical Path Method)** A form of network
 analysis used to determine time requirements for
 projects with which managers have had experience;
 only one time estimate is made for each facet of the
 project. 532
Creativity, specialization and, 197
Credit, strategy of obtaining, 111

## H

Human relations, Mayo and, 15
*Human Side of Enterprise* (McGregor), 19
**Hygiene job factors (maintenance factors)**
   Necessary job factors before an individual can be
   motivated, such as acceptable salary and working
   conditions, job security, company policy, supervision,
   and interpersonal relationships. 407

I

Iacocca, Lee, 377, 447
**Image** A mental conception or impression. 471
Image building, and communications, 471–78
**Immaturity-maturity theory** Leadership theory,
   developed by Chris Argyris, that proposes that
   employees tend to place personal needs ahead of the
   organization's welfare, therefore personnel should be
   provided with a climate in which they can
   mature. 435
Implementation, MBO program, 98
Improper conduct of employee, 119
**Inbreeding** A problem associated with promotion
   from within in which an enterprise may tend to
   stagnate if all managers share the same
   organizational experience. 323
**Incentive compensation** Some form of financial
   reward directly related to results achieved. 356
Incentives, use of budgets as, 523
Income, as a strategic control point, 502
**Incremental budgeting** Traditional budgeting
   practice that requires justification of new
   expenditures only. 520
Independence of action, as motivation, 415
In-depth investigations, manager selection and, 327
**Indirect horizontal communication** Communication
   that occurs between people at different
   organizational levels in different departments. 455
**Individual bonus** Bonus that is given only to certain
   people who have performed in an outstanding
   manner. 357
Industrial psychology, 15
Inflation, expenditure forecasting and, 137
**Informal evaluation** A subjective method of
   evaluation based solely on observation of a
   manager's performance. 375
   advantages and disadvantages, 387
   explanation of, 385–87
   use of, 386
**Informal groups** Groups created by the group

members themselves. 281
   amusement, 292
   as communications channel, 456
   fear and, 291–92
   management and, 292
   transmission of information and, 291
Informal observation, 506
**Informal orientation** An overview of an organization
   given by peers to a new employee. 345
Information:
   committees and, 293
   goal-setting and, 94
**Inherent objectives** Objectives that may not be
   explicitly stated but that guide — or should
   guide — the organization's planning process. 81
   explanation of, 81–85
   production of gains, 82–85
   survival, 81–82
**In-house training** Training programs developed by an
   outside firm but presented exclusively to managers
   who work in a specific organization. 352
Initiative, Fayol's principle, 43
*Integrating the Individual and the Organization*
   (Argyris), 17
Integrity, managers, 317
Intelligence tests, 327
Interdependency, specialization and, 193
Interdisciplinary approach, of operations research, 143
Interest tests, 327
**Interlocking directorships** The practice of individuals
   who serve simultaneously on the boards of
   companies that are in competition with each
   other. 297
Internal approaches to manager development, 344–51
   assistant-to positions, 350–51
   coaching, 348, *349*
   geographic rotation, 347–48
   job rotation by department, 347
   level-by-level development, 346
   organization development, 350
   orientations, 345
   service on committees, 352
   temporary appointments, 351
**Internal audit** Audit conducted by an organization's
   own personnel to examine financial reports to
   determine if they accurately and honestly reflect the

**Norms** Behavioral standards that group members are expected to meet. 283

Norris, William C., 67

O

Objectives:
  basic considerations, *87*
  coordination and, 197–98
  derivative, 85–86
  fundamental questions, 86–90
  guidelines for setting of, 92–94
  inherent, 81–85
  primary, 85–86
  verification of, 90, 92
Observation:
  formal, 506–507
  informal, 506
  personal, 504
  scheduled versus surprise, 507
Occupational Safety and Health Act, The (OSHA), 64
O'Donnell, Cyril, 384, 384n
Oldham, Greg, 421
Operating budget, 518
Operating procedures, committees, 303, *305*
**Operations managers** Managers that utilize the potential developed by strategic management through the efficient conversion of inputs on a day-to-day, routine basis. 107
**Operations research (OR)** A scientific approach to forecasting that uses mathematical models to predict which course of action from among the available alternatives will produce the best result. 142
  applications of, 146
  characteristics of, 143
  examples of, 145–46
  explanation and use of, 142, 145–56
  steps in process, 143, 144
Operative skills, managers and, 30–31
Opportunities, goal-setting and, 87–88
Opportunity for advancement, as motivator, 416
Order, 43
**Organization** A group of people who work together to achieve common goals. 3
  activity designation, 242, *243*
  categories of objectives, 17
  cooperation in, 198–200
  delegation of authority, 260–79
  dynamics of, 267
  finance function, 206–207
  inherent objectives, 81–85
  leader versus followers importance, 262

  line and staff, 240–45
  marketing function, 206
  matrix organization, 216–19
  multiple bases for departmentalization, 219
  primary and derivative objectives, 85–86
  process departmentalization, 215–16
  production function, 206
  project organization, 216
  pure line form, 239
  task force departmentalization, 219
**Organization chart** Visual device that shows reporting relationships among people and departments. 207
**Organization development (OD)** Form of manager development that attempts to modify managers' attitudes, motives, and viewpoints toward themselves and toward the organization. 350
Organizational charters, constraints imposed by, 50
Organizational design, Weber's guidelines, 15
Organizational goals, management by objectives and, 95
Organizational image, 471–78
  affecting factors, 471–75
  public relations and, 476–78
  responsibility of management, 475–76
Organizational loyalty, loyal behaviors, 318
**Organize** To arrange or form into a coherent whole. 34, 183
**Organizing** To arrange or constitute into a coherent unity in which each part relates to each other part. 34
  committees, 292–306
  coordination, 194–96, 198–200
  delegation of authority, 260–79
  departmentalization, 204–21
  examples of violation and adherence to principles of, *189*
  in the future, 545–47
  group dynamics, 281–92
  interrelationship with other functions, 37
  line and staff authority, 238–56
  overview of, 183–200
  principles of, 44, 187–88
  process of, *185*
  span of control, 222–34
  specialization, 188–94
  steps involved, 34
**Orientation** Process of introducing new employees to the organization and to their specific jobs. 345

**Vertical integration** Performance of a business at different levels in the same industry. 110
Vertical loading, 422
Voluntary termination, 373
Vorstand, 446
Vroom, Victor, 410

# W

*Wealth of Nations, The* (Smith), 190
Weber, Max, 15
Weihrich, Heinz, 98–99, 99n
Weir, Tamara, 333n
Wetzler, Robert, 22
Willatt, Norris, 549
Wissema, J. G., 544n
Woman:
    as managers, 331–33
    success in management, 335
    in work force, 65
Work, 55
    division-of-work principle, 188
    motivation and, 412
    span of control and, 230–31
*Work and the Nature of Man* (Herzberg), 18

Work environment, business responsibility for, 64–65
Work ethic, decline in, 55
**Working capital** Capital used to conduct day-to-day operations. 150
Working conditions, as motivators, 417
Worldwide interdependency, forecasting and, 149–50
Writing, business school graduates and, 316
Written policy, 122–23
Written procedures, 125

# Z

Zager, Robert, 415
Zaleznik, Abraham, 430, 430n
**Zero-base budgeting (ZBB)** A budgeting method that requires every dollar of proposed expenditures to be justified for each budget period. 520
Zimmerer, Thomas W., 263–64, 263n, 277, 277n